Be a teacher

ROBERT THOMAS DIXON

Be a teacher

A History of the Ontario English Catholic Teachers' Association 1944-1994

Published by the Ontario English Catholic Teachers' Association
65 St. Clair Avenue East, Toronto, Ontario M4T 2Y8

Manufactured and printed in Canada

Formatted at OECTA
65 St. Clair Avenue East
Toronto, Ontario

Dixon, Robert Thomas, 1935-

ISBN 0-9698131-0-4

Design: Daphne Hart
Cover art: Agnes Aru

CONTENTS

FOREWORD

In 1944 the Catholic separate schools of Ontario were scattered throughout the Province and staffed, primarily, by religious orders of women, brothers and priests. Catholic schools struggled to survive due to lack of financial resources. This book gives a view of the fifty years of struggle and development, progress and success of the Ontario English Catholic Teachers' Association.

The history of OECTA is a tribute to the women and men who provided Catholic education in small rural areas, in larger urban centres and did it with excellence in an attempt to live up to the mandate provided in the Constitution Act of 1867 which permitted the Province of Ontario to have a second separate school system.

Our history is also a tribute to the parents, my own included, who saw the necessity of giving their children the opportunity to live out the foresight founded in the women and men who developed and delivered the constitutional rights to Roman Catholic parents and ratepayers who founded our Province and who believed in the opportunity and the freedom to ensure that their children were provided a Catholic education in a Catholic school system.

The fifty year history of the Ontario English Catholic Teachers' Association is an opportunity for us to reflect with pride on the work of those who have come before us. The torch is now being handed to the Catholic teachers of today and tomorrow to continue the progress and to keep the vision of what it is to be a Catholic teacher teaching in a Catholic school system in the Province of Ontario.

The Provincial Executive resolved that a history of our Association should be written at the time of the 50th Anniversary. The author, Robert Dixon, was chosen because of his commitment to Catholic education. Bob is a Catholic parent. He has been a Catholic teacher and continues to work on a part-time basis as a Catholic teacher in the separate school system. He has had the opportunity of working as a Supervisory Officer, Director of Education and to lead, through his writing and his example, in the development of Catholic school system in the Province.

We are aware that we live in a world of change. We are also aware that certain things should not change. It is up to us, as we read these pages and re-live the history of fifty years, to be challenged by the question - Do we want Catholic education to survive in our Catholic schools in the Province of Ontario?

It is with great pride that I acknowledge that it is great to "Be a Teacher."

James J. Carey
General Secretary

PREFACE AND ACKNOWLEDGMENTS

In early 1991 James Carey, general secretary, Ontario English Catholic Teachers' Association (OECTA), discussed with me the executive's wishes that a fifty-year history of the Association be written. We agreed that the finished product should be both a commemorative celebration and academic contribution to the history of education in Ontario in general and of Catholic education and the Association in particular. We recognized that there would be a certain tension between these two aims. For example, the previous general secretary, Rev. Fr. Frank Kavanagh, a qualified historian, had decided that he had been too close to federation events over the last thirty years to render an objective account. To a degree I had the same problem, having been a district president of OECTA and having worked closely with the Association both as a separate school supervisory officer and as a researcher on a number of separate school issues. Nevertheless, James Carey felt that I was sufficiently an outsider to take on this task.

The reader should be aware that I have been a strong supporter of separate schools and OECTA and have written briefs and affidavits on topics like the Catholic high school issue, the corporation tax problem, and the Tomen et al. Ontario Teachers' Federation (OTF) case. With this book I have attempted to be as objective as possible and to place the Association's history in the total Ontario educational environment.

Special thanks go to James Carey and the OECTA Executive for their confidence, encouragement, and financial support, to the OECTA past presidents and executive secretaries who donated time and expertise in interviews, and to, again, James Carey, and Dr. Harry Smaller, author of a history of early teachers' unions in Ontario, public high school teacher, and lecturer at the Ontario Institute for Studies in Education (OISE), and Fr. Kavanagh, past president and general secretary of OECTA, Suzann Jones, all of whom read the entire manuscript, served as readers, editors, resource persons, and contributors of objectivity. In addition a number of people read parts of the manuscript covering their time at OECTA: Ed Alexander, Pat O'Neill, Ab Dukacz, Mike Haugh, Terry Mangan, Claire Ross, Peter Murphy, Neil Doherty, and Doug Knott. Thank you.

CHAPTER ONE

THE ORIGINS OF THE ONTARIO TEACHERS' FEDERATION AND ITS AFFILIATES

Why not secure some of the advantages labour was gaining from united and organized effort?[1]

Background. Egerton Ryerson, chief superintendent of education for the province, having seen "Teachers' Institutes" in Europe, implemented them in Canada West in 1850 and planned them to reach untrained teachers, who were the majority then, and to promote professional improvement. His hope was for them to purge from the rank of teaching "every inebriate, every blasphemer, every ignorant idler",[2] an interesting aim in light of the current question of how much control OTF should have over certification and de-certification of teachers.

These Teachers' Institutes evolved collectively into the Ontario Teachers' Association of Canada West in 1861 with forty-two units by 1877 and fifty-nine in 1880.[3] They also were under tight government control.

J. M. Paton, in his *The Role of Teachers' Organizations in Canadian Education*, calls this period the "Go-to-Meeting with their Betters" stage.[4] These centrally controlled organizations, concerned solely with teacher certification, curriculum and professional development, were "very effective in deflecting or preventing classroom teachers from forming their own strong protective organizations".[5] Worse still, they were resented and, before official compulsion began, poorly attended.

However, it would be simplistic to regard Paton's label as the whole picture. These government-directed teachers' organizations did provide some impetus for teachers to express their thoughts in a unified manner and teachers began to submit papers on matters of professional self-interest: salaries based on experience, improvement of salaries in general, dismissal of staff for replacement by lower-paid teachers, tenure, teacher/trustee relations, teacher certification, compulsory attendance of pupils, larger units of administration, and better education for girls. They also prepared papers on why teachers should receive copies of the high school inspector's report on the school and staff, on government grants, and on inspectors' powers.[6] The victories for the teachers were few; at a time when printers were earning $1664 a year, stenographers $1200, charwomen $321, street sweepers $421, and stockyard labourers $546, female common school teachers received between $187 and $324.[7] But the Ontario Educational Association (OEA) managed to get the government to replace the inadequate 1853 plan for "worn-out common school teachers"[8] with the *Teachers' and Inspectors' Superannuation Act* of 1917.[9]

By the turn of the century two conflicting trends had established themselves in Ontario: first, department-controlled teacher associations; and second, voluntary self-initiated local teachers' associations.[10]

Western Canadian Teacher Federations. By the turn of the century there were a number of provincial teachers' associations in Quebec, Prince Edward Island, Newfoundland, Nova Scotia, and New Brunswick. Also, resembling OEA in their control by government officials, the Saskatchewan Educational Association (1890), the Alberta Education Association (before 1914), and the Manitoba Educational Association (1909) came into existence.[11] However, according to Paton, these groups were still in the first "Go-to-Meeting" stage of operation.

Between 1914 and 1920 eight new, independent, province-wide teachers' organizations appeared permanently on the scene, as examples of Paton's "Stage Two, 1914-1935: The Struggle for Corporate Unity and Self-Determination"[12] and as precedent-setting models for the post-World War II OTF and its five affiliates. They were formed in the west and Ontario, including the Federation of Women Teachers' Associations of Ontario (FWTAO) (1918)[13], the Ontario Secondary School Teachers' Federation (OSSTF)[14], and the Ontario Public School Men Teachers' Federation (OPSMTF) (1920)[15]. Finally, the Canadian Teachers' Federation (CTF) was formed as a result of the executive of the Manitoba Teachers' Federation inviting the teachers' organizations in Alberta, British Columbia, and Saskatchewan to confer with them on common problems.[16]

The objectives, discussion, conflict, and legislation that surfaced in the first two decades of the teachers' associations in western Canada were similar to those a little later in Ontario. Precedents emerged, and some Ontario teachers noted them through CTF, through their own provincial associations, and through the press.[17] Three crucial questions for the federations were the following. What aims and objectives should be part of the federation's constitution? How can the federation achieve 100 per cent membership? Should the federation be an assembly of professionals, union members, or professional union members (the latter an oxymoron then and perhaps still in the minds of some teachers and citizens)?

As early as 1924 at the annual general meeting of the Saskatchewan Teachers' Alliance, a resolution was passed calling for government legislation for compulsory membership of all teachers in the association.[18] But it was the Great Depression which "was the hammer which had pounded Saskatchewan teachers and their organizations into a new unity."[19] Nine successive years of drought and crop failure had resulted in teacher salaries being in arrears and sometimes never being paid and in underbidding for positions by teachers. In this volatile situation the Saskatchewan Rural Teachers' Association in 1933 specified as an aim statutory membership, amalgamated with the Saskatchewan Teachers' Alliance to form the Saskatchewan Teachers' Federation (STF) and, as that body, approached the Minister of Education, Mr. Justice Willard Estey (later one of the Supreme Court of Canada judges in the Ontario Constitutional Reference regarding the extension of the separate school system). He promised a bill if voluntary membership reached 70 per cent. Within two years this target was achieved, and the *Saskatchewan Federation Act* of 1935 was passed with little opposition. This Act making membership in the STF a condition of employment with a school board was the first of its kind in the English-speaking world.[20]

Alberta soon followed with its own statute. In 1932 the Alberta Teachers' Alliance (ATA), in its declaration of principles, stated that non-membership of a teacher was unethical, there being no standard of morality apart from the group (emphasis added), and that it was the duty of members to instruct persons seeking entrance to the profession in the ethical code. In the 1935 election the Social Credit Party came to power. Premier William Aberhart, previously a Calgary school principal, with several teachers in his cabinet and on the back benches, passed the *Teaching Profession Act* of 1935 which provided for automatic membership and enabled ATA to discipline members for unprofessional conduct.[21] With the important exceptions of teacher training and certification the Alberta teachers now had status and some powers similar to those people employed in architecture, law, medicine, nursing, and pharmacy.

Following Alberta and Saskatchewan's example, other provincial legislatures passed teaching profession statutes: New Brunswick and Manitoba (1942), Ontario (1944), Prince Edward Island and the Protestant teachers of Quebec (1945), British Columbia (1947), Newfoundland and Nova Scotia (1951), and the French and English Roman Catholic teachers of Quebec (1960).[22] Permanent, very positive results accrued for teachers.

First of all, obviously, membership and, therefore, revenue from fees rose. Dr. Lazerte of the University of Alberta saw an immediate change in teacher attitude:

> ... there was a feeling that the public had now given concrete evidence of its long-professed high regard for the work of the teacher....Teachers seemed lifted to a higher plane, and the teachers' organization, freed from the time-consuming business of soliciting memberships, turned with renewed vigour to more professional phases of its work.[23]

L.G. Hall sees a cause-effect link between Alberta's Teaching Profession Act and Board of Reference legislation.[24] It is safe to say that such legislation moved the federations from Paton's "Stage Two" to "Stage Three: 1935-1955: The Struggle for Recognition and Participation."[25]

One issue that was not resolved as clearly as mandatory membership during this period was that of whether to regard the teachers' association as a grouping of professionals or of union members. To a degree the tension between these two concepts still exists. Before a look at how this conflict affected actions in western Canada, some definitions are in order.

Paton defines the professional as follows; s/he

1. has specialized knowledge;
2. uses specialized skills and techniques;
3. serves society and people;
4. has a corporate voice.[26]

He applies this definition to the teacher.

A. Kratzmann in his doctoral dissertation adds two more criteria:

5. The professional person achieves authority over, and is guaranteed respect from his/her clientele by their confidence in his/her expertness in such knowledge and in his/her technical competence.

6. The professional performs his/her service for a clientele for an established fee or salary.[27]

Harry Charlesworth, who was general secretary of the British Columbia Teachers' Federation, defines profession as follows. It has:

1. high qualifications for entrance;
2. a long period of efficient training in up-to-date institutions;
3. ample provision for post-professional training;
4. a professional attitude on the part of members;
5. observance by members of a strict code of ethics;
6. absence of deadening control by too-rigid inspection, rules, and regulations;
7. freedom of initiative and research;
8. control of the profession by the profession;
9. respect for the profession by the public.[28]

Paton also describes teachers' organizations with professional characteristics.

> Teachers' organizations...may be defined as those which have been established by the teachers themselves (a) to serve their professional and personal interests effectively, and (b) to serve equally effectively the public interest, by safeguarding standards of professional competence and of ethical behaviour.[29]

A union, also called a labour union or trade union, is an alliance or association of workers organized to improve working conditions and advance mutual interests.[30]

From the perspective of an Ontario educator I agree that all of the attributes of a profession and professional listed above would be desirable to the teacher and either have been achieved or are being sought. But many teachers now would regard themselves also as union members as well as being professionals. The early decades of this century regarded this combination of concepts as controversial.

An examination of the name changes in teachers' associations makes the point. The proposed constitution of the ATA envisaged a federation of "local unions", but the designation was changed to "local alliances".[31] The Saskatchewan Union of Teachers took its name from the National Union of Teachers of England and Wales. Later, the name was changed to the Saskatchewan Teachers' Alliance "when it becomes apparent that the term 'union' does not appeal to many teachers."[32] On the other hand, the designation the Manitoba Teachers' Society was chosen to parallel that of the Manitoba Law Society.[33] Eventually, all the teachers' associations in Canada, with the exception of the Nova Scotia Teachers' Union, either changed or avoided from the start the term "union" in their official names.

It is not difficult to speculate why the affiliation and the term "union" were dropped, since residual negative feelings about union association still exist in Ontario to this day. S. G. B. Robinson, an OSSTF member, associated the term with the Russian Revolution of 1917, with the strikes in the steel mills and coal fields of the United States in the earlier part of the century, and with the Winnipeg General Strike of 1919.[34]

Paton in his history of Canadian teachers' federations reveals his close professional association with the CTF when he writes:

> Our critics sometimes [say]...we are like trade unions...This view...ignores the work of the organized teachers in the field of ethics and discipline, and their concern for their clients, the pupils in school, and in everything they advocate and do to improve the curriculum and the achieve equality of educational opportunity.[35]
>
> The constitutions and by-laws of the western Canadian teacher federations, the significant achievement of teaching profession acts, the use of the teacher strike, and the discussions about the concepts of "union" and "professional association", all received close attention (sometimes demonstrated with congratulations and even emulation, sometimes with animosity) [36] from OTF and its predecessors.

The Forerunners of OTF in Ontario. As mentioned above, FWTAO, OPSMTF, and OSSTF came into existence near the end of World War I at about the same time as the western teachers' associations, when the high cost of living was exacerbating the long-time low status and salaries of the teacher.[37] The trustees had already been organized since 1887 and had become so dominant in OEA that the teachers in this association, with whom the trustees had affiliated in 1886, felt that "the tail was wagging the dog."[38]

Why did three different federations come into existence? After all, the three had many similar aims, constitutions, and activities: elevating the teacher's professional status, raising her/his financial position, developing professional norms and etiquette, fostering cooperation and united effort, and developing public interest in education and the teacher.[39] All three federations successfully negotiated or provided uniform contracts, group insurance, sick benefit funds, benevolent funds, drama and oratory events, vocational education and guidance programs, educational research scholarships, conferences, improved school grants and taxes, mutual loans, a minimum salary, superannuation legislation, and an education week.[40] At times they met together formally on matters of common interest, for example, to discuss contract and tenure difficulties and to approach the Minister of Education for a legislated appeal procedure for dismissed teachers, which eventually became a Board of Reference statute.[41]

Many of the leaders in each association had a similar attitude on the question of the professional association versus the union. Teachers by the very nature of their work, transmitting society's values, probably were reflecting the public's fear and suspicion of the early unions. Striving for acceptance and approval of their new federations, some were reluctant to be identified as labour union members. The educational environment was not friendly to such a label.

Thus, as in the western provinces, the federations stressed professional association over the union concept. OSSTF did study the question and there was widespread internal membership debate about unionization.

Similarly, FWTAO avoided the union label. One of its predecessors, the Women Teachers' Association of Toronto, "abhorred the very mention of labour affiliation and had promised sincerely that they would never go to the extreme of striking."[42] FWTAO did not endorse CTF's call for cooperation with organized labour; such a move would have been considered too radical.[43]

In short, although there were many assembly debates and motions on the question of union membership, none of the three federations passed motions at provincial meetings to become unions or to be affiliated with labour unions.[44] On the contrary, as Harry Smaller explained, they emphasized the technical and ethical standards of a profession and sought to regulate their members as professionals, a practice not performed by unions.[45]

Given that these three federations had similar aims, concerns, and activities, as well as identical attitudes to the union question, the question remains why did the teachers of Ontario not follow the western model of one provincial teachers' association?

A simple answer would be that the numbers of teachers in Ontario permitted the formation of the three federations between 1918 and 1920. FWTAO had a potential of 12 000 members, OPSMTF of 1 669, and OSSTF of 2 276 (not counting the continuation school teachers, who were spread throughout rural Ontario and difficult to recruit).[46]

Part of the answer may lie in the situation that led to the break-up of the Ontario Teachers' Alliance. This association, formed in 1908, had membership for the most part only in urban areas, but at least purported to represent all teachers. However, about ten years later, aware of its weakness, its members, many also in OEA, made formal what had been the reality: the Ontario Teachers' Alliance was taken over by OEA which, when formed in 1892, had organized itself into the subdivisions of trustees, elementary teachers, and secondary teachers. In 1920 one teachers' group within OEA was proposed, but the teachers felt that the trustees were dominating OEA and that two collective voices for the teachers were, therefore, better than one.[47] Consequently, the structure of OEA and the failure of the Ontario Teachers' Alliance pointed to the elementary/secondary split. Probably, also, the perception of trustee control of OEA prodded the teachers into forming their own independent federations.

Perhaps, too, the formation of three different federations may have been a matter of certain strong-minded people providing crucial influence. For example, eight women, convinced that the all-male executive of the Toronto Teachers' Association were ignoring the views and needs of women teachers, formed in 1885 a separate organization, the Women Teachers' Association.[48] The belief on the part of leaders of the elementary-school female teachers, elementary-school male teachers, and secondary-school teachers that each group had its own special interests seemed to carry the day.

The women teachers in Toronto had an agenda that would stimulate unity of effort: equal pay for equal work, elimination of inferior salaries for teachers of the lower grades which were usually taught by women, the break-up of the male monopoly of administrative positions in public elementary schools, and the elimination of lower salaries for women public school teachers. These women teachers, aware of the recent enfranchisement victory and of their success at forming local women teachers' associations, used the occasion of the 1918 OEA annual conference to meet and discuss the idea of a provincial federation. Under the leadership of the Women Teachers' Guild of London, FWTAO came into existence at that time.[49]

The idea of the men public school teachers joining with this movement for a common association seems impossible to envision. The public school men teachers, determined to protect their economic privileges, established their own organization at the 1920 OEA annual convention.[50]

The secondary school teachers did not get involved with either of these movements. A group of them from Toronto, Hamilton, and western Ontario had met during the 1916 Christmas holidays and founded OSSTF. Once their association came into existence, over 90 per cent of the eligible teachers joined, a marked contrast to the 30 to 40 per cent of the potential membership in FWTAO and OPSMTF; amalgamation, they felt, would only weaken their influence.[51]

Time would only reinforce the "academic snobbery"[52] of OSSTF and FWTAO's concern for women teachers' rights. The multi-affiliate structure was the wave of the future. Meanwhile, what was happening with the Franco-Ontarian and English Catholic teachers?

Franco-Ontarian teachers not only were a small number of the total provincial teaching force, but they also were quite beleaguered. There was no legislation recognizing the existence of French-language schools until the late 1960s. Where Franco-Ontarian pupils were gathered together in a separate, and occasionally in a public school, it was only either with the voluntary cooperation of the board, usually urban, or due to most or all of the pupils being French in a rural school section.[53]

Perhaps some of the Franco-Ontarian teachers in the elementary public and separate schools belonged to FWTAO or OPSMTF, but it was not until 1936 that the St. John Baptist Society of Ottawa called together Franco-Ontarian teachers for the purpose of organizing. They would remain linked also to l'Association d'éducation française, but this new Association de l'enseignement bilingue de l'Ontario would feel freer to pursue salary objectives for its university, Normal School, and elementary school teachers. In 1939 a constitution was developed. At the first annual meeting in 1940 the association endorsed its aims, among which were to improve the financial status of its members, to secure the best results in the teaching of English and French, to increase the number of French-language courses and schools, and, in general, to solve educational problems.[54] The future affiliate l'Association des enseignants franco-ontariens (AEFO) was born.

This left the English Catholic teachers in Ontario's Roman Catholic separate schools and private high schools. Some of the latter may have belonged to OSSTF. Some single women in the elementary schools did join FWTAO because of the insurance group benefits,[55] but the majority belonged to no association. Why had the English Catholic teachers not formed a provincial federation of their own between 1916 and 1944?

A cursory knowledge of the history of separate schools in Ontario provides the most likely answer. The absence of any government grants or municipal taxes for classes beyond grade ten and the almost total lack of corporation tax revenues meant a number of serious problems, among them low teacher salaries. It was a question of survival for separate schools. Many retired teachers explained that it had seemed pointless to organize when the trustees had insufficient funds to improve salaries anyway. It is difficult to speculate when this attitude would have changed, because in 1944 the provincial government required all teachers to be in OTF.

Another factor was the large proportion of sisters and brothers employed by separate school boards, especially urban ones. In a very real sense these teachers already belonged to an association - a Roman Catholic teaching order; indeed, some of these orders already had annual renewal sessions, in a sense, professional development days of their own. This left a small number of lay teachers to form a federation if they so desired.

Although the idea of integrating the English Catholic teachers into the existing federations was briefly considered in 1944, there were three countervailing structures suggesting a separate federation. First of all, the very existence of constitutionally-protected separate schools in a dual-school system in Ontario would be a parallel to teachers' associations divided on religious grounds. Secondly, even though Alberta and Saskatchewan had one teachers' association for both public and separate school teachers, Quebec had the Provincial Association of Protestant Teachers and the Provincial Association of Catholic Teachers, a structure mirroring section 93 of the *British North America Act* (BNA Act). Finally, the already existing division along elementary/secondary and female/male lines provided a certain logic to a French/English and public/separate division.

The Ontario Teachers' Council (OTC). Having the advantages from setting up their own associations, the three federations soon saw additional benefits from working together on some matters. By 1923 they were holding informal joint consultations on contract problems.[56] By 1931 they concluded that they had made little progress on getting legislation for boards of reference, a standard teachers' contract, improved superannuation, or a higher minimum salary, because they were not speaking to the government as one voice and thus they suggested forming OTC.[57] In May 1935, FWTAO, OPSMTF, and OSSTF founded OTC as a kind of umbrella organization to deal with the government on common concerns. If this was the dominant motive, it worked: bills establishing boards of reference and amending superannuation quickly followed OTC submissions.[58] However, the catalyst to immediate formation of OTC was a "practical", "mundane", and "uninspired" one: the paying of the $1000 annual fee to CTF as one association, OTC, instead of $3000 as three federations.[59]

Mandatory Membership and Professionalism.

The Teaching Profession Act. As early as 1928 FWTAO approached Premier Ferguson for mandatory membership of teachers in an association.[60] Mandatory membership would empower the federation to insist on professional standards of behaviour for all teachers and would heighten status, power, and revenues. Although OSSTF consistently had over 90 per cent of high school teachers in its federation (a statistic that explains why OSSTF was not initially enthusiastic about the idea of automatic membership[61]), in 1942 OPSMTF had enlisted only about 65 per cent of its potential members, FWTAO about 45 per cent, and AEFO about 35 per cent.[62]

Once the legislation was passed in Alberta and Saskatchewan, the topic assumed a high profile in Ontario's educational circles. The Department of Education became interested and in the fall of 1936 distributed a circular to all public school inspectors asking for information on Teachers' Institutes. Public school inspectors were supportive. Votes taken in FWTAO, OPSMTF, and OSSTF revealed over 70 per cent of their members were in favour of mandatory membership and legislated professionalism. FWTAO's annual general meeting (AGM) of 1935 formally approved such legislation, and OTC planned a campaign for a 1937 bill.

FWTAO had strong motivation for supporting such a bill. It had difficulty raising its 45 per cent figure because of the low salaries, inaccessibility, and mobility of single rural teachers subject to the vagaries of trustees and to the prospect of marriage; the Association did not have the resources to deal with these obstacles to a higher membership.[63]

With the election of George Drew's Conservative government in 1943, the timing was propitious. He and, particularly, his provincial director of education and ex-dean of the Ontario College of Education, Dr. J. G. Althouse, were favourable to the idea of a professional statute for teachers. Their positive attitude was doubtless reinforced by the concern of Drew and the Tories about teachers' moving to the left of the political spectrum. Impending teacher unionization was a distinct possibility. In any case, Drew seemed to have his own beliefs which determined the matter. In the December 1943 issue of the *Educational Courier,* Drew wrote, "It will be the aim of the present Ministry in Ontario to place the work of the teacher on an ever higher plane and to advance the interests of the teacher from every point of view."[64]

The fact that Drew as Premier had also taken the post of Minister of Education both indicated the high importance he assigned to the education portfolio and caused events to move forward smoothly and quickly. In October 1943, Agnes Meek of FWTAO, Arthur McAdam of OPSMTF, and Norman McLeod of OSSTF discussed with Drew a bill they had drafted. The latter teachers then met seventeen times with Dr. Althouse between Christmas and Easter. Althouse, who had Drew's fullest confidence, was very supportive. He was convinced that the proposed legislation would attract intelligent people to the profession and would give teachers status.

The bill passed through the legislature with remarkable speed, little discussion, and no dissent. The teachers of Ontario had their *Ontario Teachers' Federation Act,* an historical achievement (see Appendix A).

The teachers had become professionals in the eyes of the law with at least sufficient status to prescribe and enforce ethical behaviour and to communicate directly through OTF with the government of Ontario and Ministry of Education officials. Breakaway unions had become impossible and compulsory membership gave OTF and each affiliate unity and power. It became possible to work systematically for adequate minimum salaries and other contract benefits and to provide activities for the professional growth of the teachers. A new era in teaching began.

NOTES

1. S. G. B. Robinson, *Do Not Erase* (Toronto: The Ontario Secondary School Teachers' Federation, 1971), 114.
2. Harry John Smaller, "Teachers' Protective Associations, Professionalism and the 'State' in Nineteenth Century Ontario" (Ph.D. diss., University of Toronto, 1988), 84.
3. J. G. Althouse, "The Ontario Teacher. An Historical Account of Progress, 1800-1910," (D. Paed. diss., University of Toronto, 1929), 60-61, 63, 129.
4. J. M. Paton, *The Role of Teachers' Organizations in Canadian Education*, 2.
5. Smaller, "Teachers' Protective Associations," 163.
6. Althouse, "The Ontario Teacher," 63; John H. Hardy, "Teachers' Organizations in Ontario," (D. Paed.diss., University of Toronto, 1938), 12; R. A. Hopkins, *The Long March* (Toronto: Baxter Publishing, 1969), 35; Smaller, "Teachers' Protective Associations," 146.
7. Doris French, *High Button Bootstraps* (Toronto: Ryerson Press, 1968), 20-21; Hardy, "Teachers' Organizations," 44.
8. Robinson, *Do Not Erase*, 114.
9. W. G. Fleming, *Ontario's Educative Society / VII, Educational contributions of associations* (Toronto: University of Toronto Press, 1972), 56; Hopkins, The Long March, 36.
10. Smaller, "Teachers' Protective Associations," chapter 5.
11. Paton, *Teachers' Organizations*, 34.
12. Ibid.
13. French, *High Button Bootstraps*, 3.
14. Robinson, *Do Not Erase*, 12.
15. Robert M. Stamp, T*he Schools of Ontario 1876-1976*, Toronto: University of Toronto Press, 1982, 102.
16. J. W. Chafe, *Chalk, Sweat ,and Cheers. A history of the Manitoba Teacher's Society commemorating its fiftieth anniversity, 1919-1969*, Canada: The Hunter Rose Co., 1969, 39.
17. Saskatchewan Teachers' Federation, Argos 1983 (Saskatchewan Modern Press, 1983), 17; Hardy, "Teachers' Organizations," 143, 155; Robinson, *Do Not Erase*, 318.
18. Argos, 7.
19. Ibid., 11.
20. Ibid., 12; Paton, Teachers' Organizations, 45-47.
21. Ibid., 127-129.
22. Paton, *Teachers' Organizations*, 56.
23. Quoted in Chafe, *Chalk, Sweat, and Cheers*, 121.
24. L. G. Hall, "A Historical Study of Salary Payments and the Emergence of Scheduling in Alberta, " (Ed. D. diss., University of Toronto, 1967), 103.
25. Paton, *Teachers' Organizations*, 34.
26. Ibid., 19-20.
27. A. Kratzmann, "The Alberta Teachers' Association: A Documentary

Analysis of the Dynamics of a Professional Association" (Ph.D. diss., University of Chicago, 1963), 18.

28. Chafe, *Chalk, Sweat, and Tears*, 64.

29. Paton, *Teachers' Organizations*, 22.

30. Funk and Wagnall's Standard College Dictionary, Canadian ed., 5.V., "union" and "labour union".

31. John W. Chalmers, *Teachers of the Foothills Province. The Story of the Alberta Teachers' Association* (Toronto: University of Toronto Press, 1968), 18-19.

32. Argos, 5.

33. Chafe, *Chalk, Sweat, and Tears*, 123.

34. Ibid., 15-16.

35. Paton, *Teachers' Organizations*, 22.

36. Smaller, "Teachers' Protective Associations," 278 ff.

37. Stamp, *Schools of Ontario*, 101.

38. Hardy, "Teachers' Organizations," 26,119; Hopkins, *The Long March*, 24.

39. Ibid., 47; French, High Button Bootstraps, 45-46; Robinson, *Do Not Erase*, 22.

40. Hardy, "Teachers' Organizations," 154; French, *High Button Bootstraps*, 65.

41. Hopkins, *The Long March*, 70; Robinson, Do Not Erase, 33.

42. Wendy E. Bryans, "Virtuous Women at Half the Price: The Feminization of the Teaching Force and Early Women Teacher Organizations in Ontario" (M.A. thesis, University of Toronto, 1974), 66.

43. French, *High Button Bootstraps*, 31, 33, 50, 59-60.

44. Stamp, *Schools of Ontario*, 147.

45. Smaller, "Teacher's Protective Associations," 5, 9.

46. French, *High Button Bootstraps*, 53; Hopkins, The Long March, 50; Robinson, *Do Not Erase*, 32.

47. Hardy, "Teachers' Organizations," 17, 26, 30; Hopkins, *The Long March*, 45; Fleming, contributions of associations, 56.

48. Bryans, "Early Women Teacher Organizations," 42.

49. Ibid., 43, 82; French, *High Button Bootstraps*, 32.

50. Stamp, *Schools of Ontario*, 102.

51. Hardy, "Teachers' Organizations," 86; French, *High Button Bootstraps*, 105; Hopkins, *The Long March*, 50, 101, 120, 173; Robinson, *Do Not Erase*, 27

52. Stamp, *Schools of Ontario*, 147.

53. A number of studies have examined the controversial Franco-Ontarian educational history. Some helpful ones are the following: Marilyn J. Barber, "The Ontario Bilingual Schools Issue, 1910-1916," *Canadian Historical Review* (September, 1966), 227-248; Roland R. Bériault, *Report of the Committee on French Language Schools in Ontario* (Toronto: Queen's Printer, 1968); Robert Choquette, *Language and Religion. A History of English-French Conflict in Ontario* (Ottawa: University of Ottawa Press, 1975); Robert T. Dixon, "The Ontario Separate School System and Section 93 of the British North America Act" (Ed.D. diss., University of Toronto, 1976); Margaret Prang, "Clerics,

Politicians, and the Bilingual Schools Issue in Ontario, 1910-1917," *The Canadian Historical Review* (1960), 281-307; Franklin A. Walker, *Catholic Education and Politics in Ontario* (Toronto: The Federation of Catholic Education Associations of Ontario, 1964); David Welch, "The Social Construction of Franco-Ontarian Interests Towards French-Language Schooling, 19th Century to 1980's" (Ph.D. diss., University of Toronto, 1988).

54. Jacques Schrybert, "Affidavit," Tomen et al. v. F.W.T.A.O. et al 70 O.R.(d) 48 (O.C.R., 1987) ; A.E.F.O., *Historique de l'Association des Enseignants franco-ontariens*, 1951.

55. Raymond Bergin, founding member of the O.E.C.T.A., interview, North York, 6 June 1991.

56. Robinson, *Do Not Erase*, 33.

57. Ibid., 289-290; Hardy, "Teachers' Organizations," 143.

58. Ibid., 143-144.

59. Fleming, *Contributions of Associations*, 44; Hopkins, The Long March, 109.

60. French, *High Button Bootstraps*, 66.

61. Derrick M. Topley, "The Professional Policies of the Ontario Secondary School Teachers' Federation, 1919-1966" (Ed.D. diss., University of Toronto, 1969), 107.

62. Fleming, *Contributions of Associations*, 81; Stamp, *Schools of Ontario*, 180.

63. French, *High Button Bootstraps*, 53, 105.

64. French, *High Button Bootstraps*, 53, 105.

CHAPTER TWO

The Birth of OECTA

I recall the summons from His Excellency Bishop Kidd of London requesting me to proceed to Ottawa to discuss the advisability of an Organization of English Catholic Teachers.[1]

The Ottawa English Catholic Teachers' Association.[2] Although OECTA was the last affiliate to be formed, separate school teachers in a few Ontario cities had formed informal associations. For example, in 1932 a diocesan priest, Fr. Martin Mooney, needed help to run a sports league for the elementary pupils in Ottawa's separate schools and turned to the male teachers of the board. Raymond Bergin, later the third provincial president of OECTA, and five or six other teachers (the total male complement) met with him in St. Malachy separate school where they formed the Ottawa Catholic Men Teachers' Athletic Association.

From this quite limited start evolved a broader organization. Dr. Frank McDonald, appointed in 1927 separate school inspector for Port Arthur, had been transferred in 1930 to Ottawa and arrived with a number of stimulating ideas. One of them was that an Ottawa Catholic teachers' association should be formed. An impressive educational leader in the eyes of his contemporaries, he would in 1951 receive the Papal Decoration "Pro ecclesia et Pontifico". This forward-thinking professional used to call all his Ottawa teachers together for professional development once a month in the early afternoon (much to the delight of the students); therefore, one could conclude that such an inspector's association would serve his purposes sufficiently. But as a product of separate schools, both as student in London and teacher at Cathedral

High in Hamilton, he realized that the salaries of teachers employed by separate school boards with their tiny corporate assessment were resulting in small salaries, savings, and pensions; he was particularly concerned about unmarried female teachers who eventually would have to exist on an insufficient pension, sometimes with no other means of support. For example, the salary of Dr. C.C. Goldring as director of the Toronto Board of Education was about $25 000 annually; his pension was $1 200 a year, the maximum possible then. A teachers' association "would give some clout with their board."[3] Also, Dr. McDonald believed that such an association would further the cause of Catholic education.

Finally, Dr. McDonald felt that teachers needed activity outside of the classroom to broaden them socially and professionally. Thus, he called a few of his teachers, among them Cecilia Rowan, a principal and later the first provincial Secretary of OECTA, to a meeting at the Carnegie Library where an executive was chosen. A majority of the approximately forty English lay teachers of the Ottawa Separate School Board quickly joined.

Although there were no restrictions on the relatively large number of sisters of the religious Orders joining the new association, none did join: the rules of the Order did not permit their members to be out in the evening. Furthermore, in the opinion of one member, Raymond Bergin, the teaching sisters did not have the same financial or social needs as the lay teachers, since the Order looked after them.

This new teachers' association engaged in a wide variety of professional and recreational activities: monthly grade meetings for the pooling of resources in children's literature and for the sharing of ideas in classroom practice; conventions in American cities where, for example, in Syracuse, schools were visited; a drama club which put on a play annually; a bridge club; a bowling league; dances; regular banquets; and a yearly picnic. On rare occasions, a committee of the association with the French teachers would meet with the school board to discuss salaries.

It was visionary on the part of Dr. McDonald to bring about such an organization, especially during the Great Depression. On the other hand, the Ottawa teachers' association could not be compared to those existing in the rest of Canada or in Ontario. It did not have a constitution, did not articulate any over-arching aim or purposes, did not include the teachers in religious Orders or in private Catholic high schools, and did not spend much time on or achieve any success in improving salaries or working conditions. The latter point is revealing when one considers that the salary of Raymond Bergin began at $750 a year as a teacher and was $1000 as a full-time teaching principal; by 1940 he was still only making $1500. Obviously, the Ottawa Catholic teachers' association was at Paton's first stage of development. Typical of this first stage, it was a priest in the first instance and an inspector in the second instance who provided the initial impetus and leadership to form a Catholic teachers' association. However, almost all the lay teachers did join.

By 1942 the ideas of mandatory membership of teachers in a provincial organization and of legislated professionalism were very much in the air in Ontario. In addition, the English Catholic teachers had watched their French-language fellow employees of separate school boards form a provincial association a few years before. Therefore, it is not surprising that Dr. McDonald and the Ottawa teachers moved to the next step with their organization: the formation of "The Ottawa Catholic Teachers' Association" with a constitution and a membership open to all the lay and clerical teachers in the separate schools, the Catholic teachers in the private schools, the Catholic professors and instructors in Catholic colleges and universities, and the separate school inspector. Among the ten Articles were the following aims:

1. To promote the principles of Catholic education
(a) by the study of education problems;
(b) by appropriate action in solving these problems;
(c) by encouraging the spirit of cooperation and mutual helpfulness.
2. To promote the interests of the teacher
(a) by serving as a medium of united action in matters of equity and justice;
(b) by improving the financial standing of the members.

The standing committees were Research, Resolution, Service, and Programme. The annual fee was one dollar.[4]

Significantly, a sister, Rev. Mother St. George, became the first president. With the shift from an association which concentrated on social and recreational activities to one which included the good of the separate school, its teachers, and its pupils, Dr. McDonald was able to convince the members of the religious teaching orders that it was their responsibility to join their fellow lay teachers. The Ottawa Catholic Teachers' Association's emphasis on the welfare and professionalism of the teacher and on the nurturing of Catholic education provided a model closely followed in the constitution of OECTA.

Dr. McDonald's ambition lay beyond Ottawa. He acted as a catalyst for the formation of a Catholic teachers' provincial organization. To this end he engaged the support of other separate school inspectors, urging them to lead in the establishment of local Catholic teachers' units.[5] There had existed up to that time only two other such organizations in Ontario. In the 1920s and 1930s, leaders like Marion Tyrrell, Mary Babcock, and Rose Cassin, who were later to serve on the OECTA executive, were negotiating with the Toronto Separate School Board on behalf of all its teachers, lay and religious, in a Toronto Separate School Teachers' Association, as well as running social events, raising money for charitable organizations, helping hospitalized teachers, and from 1939 knitting sweaters for the soldiers.[6] Also, in the 1940s a number of the single women teachers with this board had formed a unit of FWTAO in order to have certain medical and life insurance benefits.[7] About 1941 a Windsor Catholic teachers' association under the leadership of Eva Deshaw, Margaret Lynch and Alicia Martin had also succeeded in getting recognized by the Windsor Separate School Board for salary negotiating purposes and had negotiated a medical plan good for that particular period.[8] The timing was propitious for Dr. McDonald's aim of spreading such organizations throughout Ontario under the umbrella of a provincial Catholic association. After all, the separate school trustees had founded the Ontario Separate School Trustees' Association (OSSTA) in 1930 and the English Catholic Education Association of Ontario (ECEAO) was being formed at the same time as Dr. McDonald was making his efforts.[9] Consequently, when George Drew was elected premier in 1943, Catholic educators were ready to respond to his proposed legislation for a provincial teachers' federation.

The Founding of OECTA. It is not surprising that Dr. McDonald and the Ottawa teachers were the first to act on the rumours about an impending teaching profession act from the new government. They chose Fr. Lawrence K. Poupore to represent the interests of Catholic teachers and to bring back information from the Toronto meetings. Once Drew made it clear that he wanted all the teachers covered by the proposed statute, Poupore became the key man for the English Catholic side.[10] He was most qualified for this task. Born in Quebec and raised in an Irish Catholic milieu, he had a university degree, a teaching certificate earned at the Ontario College of Education (OCE), and a seminary degree. As a member of the English Oblates of Mary Immaculate (OMI), Poupore at various times in his career had been at St. Patrick's College, Ottawa, as well as being a high school teacher, university lecturer, principal, and rector. This "down-to-earth" priest with a heavy Irish accent was well known throughout the province. For example, at the 1941 annual conference of OEA he had been the keynote speaker on "The Catholic Philosophy of Education".[11] In addition to these assets, the Ottawa Catholic teachers appreciated the fact that their representative could travel to all these Toronto meetings at the half-fare rate offered by the railways to clerics and stay free of charge with the Basilians at St. Michael's College.

Poupore soon advised the Ottawa Catholic Teachers' Association that the government, OTF, and AEFO were moving fast. Dr. McDonald advised Cecilia Rowan to write all the Bishops to inform them of events transpiring, to enlist their support for a provincial Catholic teachers' organization, and to request that each diocese send representatives to an organizational meeting to be held at the Notre Dame Convent Library in Ottawa on February 18 and 19, 1944. Invitations also went to separate school inspectors and to Fr. Vincent Priester, executive director of ECEAO.

One notes from the start the special close relationship between what was to become OECTA and the Catholic Bishops and clergy. FWTAO, OPSMTF, and OSSTF deal with the provincial government, the school boards, parents, and the public. So does OECTA, but in addition it has an important relationship with the Catholic hierarchy. It would have been out of the question for the Ottawa teachers to proceed without seeking the support, even the authorization, of the Bishops. According to Roman Catholic Canon Law, "A Catholic school is understood to be one which is under the control of the competent ecclesiastical authority" (i.e., the Bishop). Furthermore, "The formation and education in the Catholic religion provided in any school...is subject to the authority of the Church" and "The diocesan Bishop has the right to watch over and inspect the Catholic schools situated in his territory....He has also the right to issue directives concerning the general regulation of Catholic schools."[12] In Ontario the Bishops and their priests had always taken these duties seriously, subsidizing separate schools with diocesan and parish funds, staffing them with sisters, brothers, and priests who worked for extremely low wages, and providing priests who acted as chairmen, trustees, and secretaries on separate school boards for no honoraria.

Therefore, the separate school teachers not only had an obligation to work in partnership with the Church, but also could expect support in forming a provincial teachers' organization. As far back as 1891 Pope Leo XIII in his encyclical Rerum Novarum stated "the moral right of workers to organize into unions" and Pope Puis XI more recently in 1931, in his encyclical Quadragesimo Anno, stipulated that "workers [were] to participate with management in decision-making."[13]

ECEAO, which had on its governing council the Catholic hierarchy and the clergy, at its inaugural meeting of April 1943, had given further support to the idea of organized teachers by stating that "provision was made ... that teachers would be given representation."[14] A year later, at its May 1944 meeting the minutes stated that "the teachers might be representable by representatives of their own choice if they had a provincial-wide organization."[15]

On the other hand, the Catholic teachers had to be careful not to let their appreciation of ECEAO's support complicate their moves toward a provincial teachers' organization. ECEAO's governing council contained membership from the Bishops, the priests, the private Catholic high schools, the separate school trustees, and the parents. Its intention was to become the official voice of Ontario's Catholic educational community. It was at least possible that in such an organization the Catholic teachers could become a mere appendage in a situation similar to that of the teachers in the OEA of the early part of the century. In addition, joining at that time could confuse or diffuse the efforts of the Ottawa teachers to form a provincial teachers' association. It was the opinion of Bergin that the foundation of ECEAO hastened the work of the Ottawa Catholic teachers to organize provincially. Until this task was completed, they did not approach ECEAO.

Asking the Catholic Bishops for assistance in organizing the Ottawa meeting bore fruitful results. Fr. Priester advised Fr. Poupore of their support for the formation of a provincial organization and informed him that "Archbishop McGuigan thought it proper that you should ask all of the Bishops of Ontario to lend their name as patrons of the proposed Association."[16] OSSTF, in Bergin's opinion, particularly helpful to the Catholic teachers in their efforts to become part of the contemplated statute, was aware of the importance of the hierarchy's endorsement; consequently, it sent two Catholic members of the Association, Miss Aileen Noonan of Windsor, a past president, and Mr. J. W. Morriss, editor of OSSTF's magazine, along with Miss Mary Mallon, past president of the Toronto district, to present to the Archbishop the details of the proposed professional act, drawn up by OTC.[17]

As a result of all this, seven of the eleven dioceses sent representatives to the Ottawa meeting,[18] among them Miss Margaret Lynch of Windsor, the first provincial president of OECTA, who recalled, in a record she wrote of the first few years of the Association, "the summons from His Excellency Bishop Kidd of London requesting me to proceed to Ottawa to discuss the advisability of an Organization of English Catholic Teachers."[19] (The word "summons" is illuminating.) The dioceses represented and the names were recorded in the minutes: Alexandria (Rev. Sr. Francesca, Holy Cross), Belleville (Rev. Sr. Mary Hilda, House of Providence), Cornwall (Miss Kathleen MacDonald), Kingston (C.P. Matthews, Kingston school inspector), London (Bro. Stanislaus, Margaret Lynch), Ottawa (Cecilia Rowan, president, Ottawa Catholic Teachers' Association, Rev. Fr. Poupore, Sr. Maureen, Dr. McDonald), Pembroke (Frank McElligott, Mattawa), Peterborough (Rev. Sr. Lucretia, S.J.), and Toronto (Rev. Sr. Mary Therese, I.B.V.M.). Fr. Priester also attended from ECEAO.

This list merits a few comments. The delegates appointed in the dioceses of Sault Ste. Marie and Hearst were unable to attend. This was perhaps due to distance and expense; apparently it was not due to disinterest; Bergin recalls that the Sudbury delegation to the first Toronto meeting a few months later was quite forward in its urging to organize an English Catholic teachers' association as a separate affiliate of the proposed OTF. Secondly, the great number of sisters relative to the total number of delegates at the Ottawa meeting is evidence not only of their large number on the separate school staffs, particularly urban, throughout the province working for sacrificial salaries, but also of their commitment to a professional organization of teachers. At the Toronto April 1944 convention, they, with the priests and brothers, constituted over half of the approximately 600 delegates. (Bergin remarked that the Royal York Hotel had never seen so many religious habits within its establishment.) Thirdly, since many of those present were from Ottawa and since Miss Rowan and Fr. Poupore had done much of the preparatory work, there was a conscious attempt, according to Bergin, to avoid any appearance of an Ottawa takeover; this was apparent in the temporary executive elected. Finally, there were no Catholic lay teachers from Toronto at the Ottawa meeting. Most of them were women and belonged to FWTAO because of medical, life insurance, and professional benefits; they were understandably hesitant about giving these up for an organization that did not yet exist (although later most became either regular or associate members of OECTA).

At the meeting Dr. McDonald spoke of his purpose to form a provincial association as a historical event. The issues to be considered had already been aired the previous fall. As a result of the letters and discussions of Dr. J. Bennett of Toronto and other separate school inspectors, Mary Prunty, President, and Wilma Lecour, Secretary of the Toronto Separate School Teachers' Association (a unit of FWTAO), had sent a letter to all of the separate school teachers of Ontario exploring the pros and cons of joining with one of the existing federations or organizing a provincial separate school teachers' association as a fourth unit in the proposed OTF. A ballot attached to the letter requested the teachers to indicate either of the two choices.

Their letter listed three advantages for Catholic teachers to join one of the three existing public school teachers' federations. First, they could participate in all the professional and personal benefits. Second, where they were a small number in certain parts of the province, they would be involved in a single organization for public and separate school teachers, rather than feeling isolated in their own small group. Third, where they already had an organization, it could be a local association of the appropriate public school teachers' federation. The two disadvantages were stated as not having as strong a separate school representation on OTF's board of governors and possibly encountering "personal antagonism from some narrow-minded individuals which would have to be worn down."

There were two pros and three cons outlined for forming OECTA. The English separate school teachers would be another unit in OTF and they could concentrate on their own particular problems. On the other hand, the relatively small number of separate school teachers in Ontario would bring in low revenues which would hamper activities; therefore, the Association would be unable to provide as many services as the public school organization. Also, because the separate school rural teachers were often geographically scattered, they would have difficulty forming local units.[20]

The results of this ballot must have been favourable for the establishment of a separate English Catholic teachers' association, since Lynch's record of the events on February 18 and 19 in Ottawa indicate no controversy. Bishop Kidd supported the concept of a special association for both the sisters and the lay teachers of the separate schools, but thought that isolated separate school teachers, with the consent of the

Catholic association, might belong to one of the other federations.[21] Inspector Matthews questioned whether it was possible to be in the new Catholic association and still remain a member of an existing federation.[22] The solution developed was regular and associate membership, the latter for those wishing to stay in a public school affiliate and for those not possessing a teaching certificate.[23]

In any case, "after discussing the matter for a whole day and after all the difficulties had been considered, the delegates agreed unanimously that one Ontario English Catholic Teachers' Association should be formed."[24] "It was moved by Frank McElligott and seconded by Sr. Maureen that Ontario English Catholic Teachers' Association be the name of the organization;" this passed. "It was moved by Bro. Stanislaus and seconded by Miss Lynch that the meeting go on record to support any resources undertaken to improve the financial status of the Catholic Teachers, Religious and Lay, in the Prov. of Ontario;" this passed.[25] The purposes of the association to be brought to an Easter convention in Toronto for ratification were the following:

> To propagate Catholic ideals and principles,
> To raise the status of the Catholic teachers, and
> To ensure proper remuneration as a means to an end.
> The association also will be a medium through which teachers of the separate schools can receive help in their work.

A provisional Council was elected to prepare for the Easter meeting, to draft a constitution, and to meet with OTC and the government. It consisted of Margaret Lynch, president, Rev. Sr. M. Therese, first-vice president, Frank McElligott, second vice-president, Rev. Sr. Lucretia, third vice-president, Cecilia Rowan, secretary treasurer, and four councillors: Rev. Fr. Poupore, Rev. Bro. Stanislaus, Rev. Sr. Mary Hilda, and Kathleen MacDonald.[26]

They had much to do in a short period of time. With the assistance of Aileen Noonan and Norman McLeod of OSSTF, Lynch's sister, Emily, who was a Windsor lawyer, and Rev. Fr. Garvey, CSB, the executive prepared a draft constitution. Noonan, in a letter summarizing the topics covered at a meeting with the executive, made the distinction between a Catholic education association consisting of teachers in separate schools, private schools, and colleges and an association of Catholic teachers in tax-supported elementary schools (i.e., up to the end of grade eight or, in a few cases, of grade ten) functioning as a fourth unit of OTF. She also rejected the proposal, under active consideration, that this fourth unit be comprised of both English and French Catholic teachers, since the English "did not want to be dominated by the French group" and AEFO "had asserted its claim to be a fifth unit" (as Poupore had already learned directly from Roger St. Denis at the organizational meetings). Noonan provided the OSSTF's constitution as an example and drew attention to the federation's division into districts, in turn subdivided in some cases into locals.[27]

Meanwhile, certain confusions had arisen with some of the religious orders over the distinction among ECEAO, the proposed OECTA, and possible local English Catholic teachers' associations. In one example, Miss Noonan and another OSSTF official met with the Loretto Order and listened to concerns about, among other topics, the dangers of Communism infecting teacher associations, the fear of Toronto's lay separate school teachers that the sisters would dominate OECTA, the possible superiority of diocesan Catholic teachers' organizations, and the constitution already being developed by one of the sisters for a Toronto Catholic teachers' association.[28] Through Fr. Priester, the Bishops, and much discussion, these problems were cleared up.

On March 11, Lynch attended a meeting in Toronto, to which Dr. Althouse of the Department of Education had invited her, in order to consider with the various groups involved the Teaching Profession Act proposed by OTC.[29] Here it was agreed that, because the separate school teachers would only add up to one-eighth of the total membership and because AEFO had only 1300 members, each of these two affiliates would have only five members on OTF's board of governors, while each of the other three would have ten.[30]

A number of letters then had to go to all the separate school teachers of Ontario. First, Lynch advised them to indicate on a form sent by FWTAO that they supported the concept and wording of the proposed Teaching Profession Act and the intent to have a provincial separate school teachers' association as part of OTF.[31] Next, details of the formation of OECTA in Ottawa and of its first convention to be held on April 11 and 12 at the Royal York Hotel had to be sent to all the teachers. They were urged to help form local teacher organizations before the Easter Convention. Finally, correspondence was necessary to encourage areas of the province to organize and to send delegates to the convention.[32] In all this, Cecilia Rowan, the unpaid Secretary, operated efficiently and unstintingly from her apartment in Ottawa, somehow with no financial resources keeping in touch with the president in Windsor. Bergin remembers her as an organized workhorse, a woman of about sixty who "ran a tight ship". She was to continue as Secretary for another five years.

The First AGM. The industry and organization of Lynch and Rowan contributed significantly to the large number of delegates, over 600, who attended the first Annual General Meeting (AGM) of OECTA in 1944. Bishop Kidd had asked the school boards to aid their teachers in attending. Ten preparatory meetings were held throughout Ontario. London's Bro. Stanislaus, for instance, assured Lynch that there would be twenty delegates sent from that city alone, whose transportation costs had all been guaranteed by Fr. Feeney, the chairman of the board. Bro. Stanislaus had also contacted the separate school inspector, Mr. Walsh, to arrange for teachers outside London to attend. He planned to write to each Superior of all the convents in the inspectorate to ask for at least one delegate.[33] The Bishop-inspector-provisional executive - trustee-teacher network worked well throughout Ontario, judging by the attendance. Presumably, each of these groups saw advantages in a successful OECTA.

This first convention was covered by the *Catholic Register*: It reported that President Henderson of ECEAO, with which OECTA had done some joint sessions, felt that OECTA was "in the interests of teachers, trustees, and ratepayers, and Catholic education generally." Dr. McDonald delivered a keynote address in which he stated that OECTA's "purpose would be truly professional and not simply economic;...the standards of Catholic teachers had to be raised through the teachers themselves and it couldn't be done by the individual only, but would need organization."[34]

The following business was conducted at this first convention. A constitution was adopted (see Appendix A.). The provisional Executive was ratified with the position of treasurer added with Mary Prunty elected. Cecilia Rowan was appointed Secretary. The Board of Directors was to be the Executive plus the district presidents. Standing committees were established and chairpersons appointed: research (Rev. C.J. Crusoe, S.J., Kingston), resolutions (Rev. B.W. Harrigan, Hamilton), service (Joseph Doyle, Toronto), programme (Mary Corrigan, Toronto), finance (Sr. Maureen, Pembroke), publicity (Bro. Arnold, Toronto), lay teachers (R.J. Bergin, Ottawa), constitution and bylaws (Rev. L.K. Poupore, OMI, Ottawa), and religious teachers (Rev. Fr. Guinan, CSB, Windsor).

Fr. Harrigan, Joseph Doyle and Mother Marie Therese formed another committee to work on expansion. Nineteen districts were created, with their boundaries determined: Ottawa (#1), Cornwall (#2), Kingston (#3), Belleville (#4), Toronto (#5), Niagara (#6), Hamilton (#7), Guelph (#8), Kitchener (#9), Walkerton (#10), London (#11), Windsor (#12), Fort William - Port Arthur (#13), Sault Ste. Marie (#14), Sudbury (#15), Kirkland Lake - Timmins (#16), North Bay (#17), Peterborough (#18), and Pembroke (#19). It was decided that local organizations would be established within these districts as conditions demanded. OECTA was truly provincial. The five representatives to OTF's Board of Governors were appointed: Margaret Lynch, Rev. Fr. Poupore, Joseph Doyle, Rev. Fr. Harrigan, and Miss Alicia Martin (Windsor). The annual fee was fixed at two dollars for regular members and one dollar for associate members. Most importantly, the objects of OECTA were determined:

> To promote the principles of Catholic education by the study of educational problems;
> To work for the advancement of understanding among parents, teachers, and students;
> To work for the moral, intellectual, religious, and professional perfection of all the members;
> To improve the status of the teaching profession in Ontario;
> To secure for teachers a larger voice in educational affairs.[35]

These objects resemble those of its predecessor, the Ottawa Catholic Teachers' Association and, with the integration of the Catholic element, those of the professional teachers' association developed in Canada up to that time.

The *Teaching Profession Act* passed in April, 1944 did not contain OECTA because it had not been incorporated. Letters patent were obtained and the provincial body incorporated in the following September. The historic signing for the letters patent took place in the notary's drugstore, Roger's, close by St. Patrick's College, on June 20, with the signers being Raymond Bergin, Fr. Poupore, and Cecilia Rowan and the witness being Agnes O'Hearne, an Ottawa separate school teacher.[36]

All of this took place with a minimum of controversy. The idea of a trade union stigma attaching itself to OECTA did not come up anywhere in OECTA records. The concern in the minds of Catholic leaders regarding the survival of a Catholic Association was assuaged by the

Bishops who not only gave their support to OECTA, but who also encouraged the participation of the teaching priests, sisters, and brothers. The idea that the public school teachers would unite under one umbrella and isolate the separate school teachers was groundless from the start. A worry that OSSTA would be hostile to the birth of OECTA was also without foundation; instead, this association assisted OECTA in its initial organization, perhaps because Drew had insisted that all teachers be in OTF, perhaps because Aileen Noonan and other members of OSSTF were Roman Catholics, or perhaps because OSSTF was aware that a counterforce to the Catholic trustees' association was necessary. The concern that the superiors of the Orders would lose some authority over their members never became an issue. Lynch and Rowan dealt directly with Bro. Arnold, the superior of the De La Salle Christian Brothers, and by all evidence laid his fears to rest.

The new OECTA had many tasks ahead if it wished to realize its aims. But its fast smooth beginning portended well for the prospects of a strong united association.

NOTES

1. A history of the OECTA from 1944 to 1947, in Margaret Lynch's handwriting, undated, OECTAA.
2. I am indebted to Raymond Bergin for much of the material in this section. Interviews, Willowdale, 29 May and 6 June 1991.
3. Sheila Coo, *The First Forty Years. OECTA 1944 - 1984* (Toronto: The Ontario English Catholic Teachers' Association), 1984, 19.
4. "Tentative Constitution," 1942, OECTAA.
5. J.T. Anderson, B.A., Separate School Inspector, Renfrew to Dr. F.J. McDonald, Separate School Inspector, Ottawa, 25 Sept. 1943; John M. Bennett, M.A., Ph. D., Inspector of Separate Schools, Toronto, 24 Sept. 1943, OECTAA.
6. Marion Tyrrell's personal effects, residence of Mrs. Joan Graham, Mississauga.
7. Mary Babcock, interview, Toronto, 22 Feb. 1993; Mary Prunty, President, Wilma Lecour, Secretary, Toronto Separate School Teachers' Association to Fellow Teachers of the Separate Schools in Ontario, Oct. 1943, OECTAA.
8. Ruth Willis, interview, Windsor, 22 Feb. 1993.
9. Franklin A. Walker, *Catholic Education and Politics in Ontario*, vol. III (Toronto: Catholic Education Foundation of Ontario, 1986), 2-5.
10. Coo, *Forty Years*, 19-20.
11. *Canadian School Journal* (May 1941), 158, 162.
12. Can. 803, 804, 806, *The Code of Canon Law* (London: Collins Liturgical Publications, 1983).
13. Joseph Gremillion, *The Gospel of Peace and Justice, Catholic Social Teaching since*

Pope John (New York: Orbis Books, 1976), 11.
14. Summary of the Minutes and Proceedings of the Inaugural Meeting of the English Catholic Education Association, 27 Apr. 1943, OECTAA.
15. Minutes of the Meeting of the Governing Council of the English Catholic Education Association, 24 May 1943. See also ibid., 12 Feb. 1944 where, "It was moved ... that the Governing Council of the English Catholic Education Association go on record as being in agreement with the Catholic Teachers' Association of Ontario....It was agreed by all present that if a Catholic Teachers' Association be formed for the Province, all teachers, lay and religious, must be a part of the Association and that the constitution drawn up by such a group be acceptable to the hierarchy of Ontario."
16. (Rev.) V. Priester, Executive Director and Secretary, ECEAO to Rev. L. K. Poupore, OMI, St. Patrick's College, Ottawa, 24 Jan. 1944, OECTAA.
17. S.H. Henry, Secretary, OSSTF to Rt. Rev. J.V. Harris, D.P., Toronto, 3 Feb. 1944 and reply, 9 Feb. 1944, OECTAA.
18. Description of the Ottawa meeting, in Margaret Lynch's handwriting, 21 Feb. 1944, OECTAA.
19. OECTA, from 1944 to 1947.
20. Prunty, and Lecour, to Fellow Teachers.
21. John T. Kidd, Bishop of London to Most Rev. James C. McGuigan, D.D., Archbishop of Toronto, 7 Nov. 1943, A.A.T.
22. Ottawa meeting.
23. Coo, *Forty Years*, 20-21.
24. To Dear Catholic Teacher, inviting her/him to the 1944 Easter Convention in Toronto, unsigned, undated, OECTAA.
25. Ottawa meeting, *Catholic Register*, 26 Feb. 1944, 3.
26. Ibid.
27. Fragment, probably to Margaret Lynch or another member of the provisional executive of the OECTA from Aileen Noonan, undated, but after the Ottawa Feb. meeting and before the Easter Convention; see also Aileen to Margaret, 16 March 1944, File 0011, 1944, OECTAA.
28. Aileen to Margaret, 16 March 1944.
29. To Miss Lynch, President of the OECTA from (Rev.) V. Priester, Executive Director and Secretary, ECEAO, with a handwritten note on it that Dr. Althouse would send an invitational telegram, 9 Mar. 1944, OECTAA.
30. OECTA, 1944 to 1947.
31. Memo sent to Teachers from Margaret Lynch, copy, undated, 1944,OECTAA.
32. To Dear Catholic Teacher, unsigned, probably from A.C. Rowan, secretary, OECTA, undated, between 19 Feb. and 11 April 1944, OECTAA.
33. To Miss M. Lynch from Brother Stanislaus, 23 Mar. 1944, OECTAA.
34. *Catholic Register*, 22 Apr. 1944, 10.
35. Coo, *Forty Years*, 22-23; memorandum on the organization of the OECTA, 1945, OECTAA; OECTA, 1944 to 1947.
36. Memorandum; Coo, *Forty Years*, 24.

CHAPTER THREE

THE ONTARIO SEPARATE SCHOOL ENVIRONMENT

The minority in both Upper and Lower Canada will be obliged to throw themselves on the justice and generosity of the majority.... But I feel sure that the Protestant majority of Upper Canada will say that if they are strong they can afford to be just.[1]

In 1944 OECTA, along with the Ontario Bishops, ECEAO, and OSSTA, became an organization which, while protecting and advancing the rights of its members, would contribute greatly to the preservation and expansion of the Roman Catholic separate school system in Ontario. To understand fully the meaning of this statement one must know the history, traditions, strengths, and problems that had evolved from the start of separate schools in 1841 to 1944. What was the place of the separate school in Catholic and state education? What part did the Catholic teacher play? How had the Bishops, priests, and religious teaching orders kept separate schools in existence? How had politics, court cases and the *BNA* Act affected separate schools? What was the financial history? What rights and privileges did separate schools have and lack in 1944?[2]

The Role of the Separate School in Catholic and State Education. Canon Law stipulates that the Bishop is responsible for the Catholic education of his people and for the religious education in the Catholic school. Near the middle of the nineteenth century, the Baltimore Council (from which emerged the long-standing Catholic school textbook The Baltimore Catechism) ruled that Catholic education in schools was "indispensably necessary". In the same period, Pope Pius IX in his Syllabus of Errors listed as two grievous errors the beliefs that popular schools open to all should be free from all ecclesiastical authority and that the system of teaching primarily secular subjects to the exclusion of the Catholic faith may be approved by Catholics.[3] At a general meeting of Catholics in Toronto in 1852, the following resolution was passed:

> That, as Catholics, we cannot sanction any system of education for the youth of our community, but one which will at all times secure the full need of religious instruction under a legitimate ecclesiastical authority.[4]

Therefore, when the first separate school clause appeared in the legislation in 1841 enabling "any number of the Inhabitants of any Township or Parish professing a religious faith different from that of the majority of the Inhabitants of such Township or Parish" to dissent from the common school arrangements, elect trustees and establish and maintain their own common school(s),[5] the Bishops with the support of the Catholic press, priests, Catholic politicians, and separate school trustee, urged the formation and maintenance of Roman Catholic separate schools. Such schools would be partners with the home and the Church in the education of the child.[6]

In such schools it would not be a matter of merely a daily period of religious instruction. Along with such periods there would be Mass, the Eucharist, Confession, liturgical activities, and the integration of the secular and religious curriculum. The Catholic newspapers of pre-Confederation times often wrote on the latter point, because it highlighted the distinction between a religious instruction class divorced from the rest of the day in a common school and a religious education programme permeating the catechism period and the rest of the school day.

The Catholic Teacher. Central to all this was the careful selection by separate school trustees of Catholic teachers with pastoral references. Thus, in 1853 Bishop Charbonnel wrote in a circular to his clergy and faithful:

> ...You [parents] will elect school trustees who being your representatives in your most sacred of your duties, will choose the teachers of your children....You see...that the fate of your schools will depend on the choice of the trustees and of the teachers.[7]

In accordance with the teaching of the Church and in light of the virtues stipulated in the 1850 regulation, the teacher was to inculcate

> by example and precept...the principles of piety, justice, and a sacred regard to truth, love of their country, humanity and universal benevolence, sobriety, industry, chastity, moderation, and temperance, and those other virtues, which are the ornament of society and on which a free constitution of government is founded.[8]

Given the essential role of the teacher acting "in loco parentis", it follows that the Catholic leadership of Canada West wanted the control of teacher training and selection. In 1843, the previously wide-open arrangement for establishing a separate school was narrowed in two ways. First, it was given only to Roman Catholics, and to Protestants taken as a group without differentiation among Protestant denominations. Second, the right for Roman Catholics to separate schools arose only where the teacher in the local common schools was a Protestant and vice versa. This formulation of the right to separate schools demonstrates the perceived importance of the faith of the teacher.[9]

The link between the right of Roman Catholics to establish separate schools and the faith of the teacher in the common school persisted until 1855, when the *Taché Act* was passed conferring permanence of existence on Roman Catholic separate school boards.[10] Henceforth it did not matter if any, some, or all of the staff at the coterminous public school were Catholic; the separate school would continue to exist.(Interestingly, the right to Protestant separate school boards still depends on the religion of the teacher being Catholic in the public school.)[11] The *Taché Act* also gave separate school trustees "the special power of qualifying their teachers".[12] In negotiations leading up to the *Scott Act* of 1863, the final statute, constitutionally guaranteed by the *BNA Act* of 1867, the Catholic spokesmen reluctantly gave up this power in return for separate school equality with common school boards. However, the trustees did keep autonomy in the freedom to hire their own teachers certified by the Council of Public Instruction.[13] As well, just before Confederation, the Bishops of Canada and D'Arcy McGee did try to gain the right of "the establishment of a Catholic Normal School" as existed in Lower Canada.[14]

The Catholic School and Teacher after Confederation. The mission of the separate school, the role of the Catholic teacher, and the concern for a complementary curriculum remained unchanged in the minds, publications, and actions of the Vatican, the Ontario Bishops, the separate school trustees, the priests, teachers, and parents. This remains a universal position among Catholics. Ever since the development of State systems of education in France, Great Britain, Australia, Ireland, the United States, and Canada, the belief has been that the Catholic faith should be provided in Catholic schools where religion permeates the curriculum, that moral principles should be taught with a religious basis, that the parent has the right to choose the type of school, and that the State should not discriminate between public and Catholic public or private schools.[15]

Just two years after the formation of OECTA, the Hope Commission began its study of the Ontario school system for Premier Drew. In its final version, the Roman Catholic Minority Report had this to say about the beliefs just listed:

> This has been the universal attitude of the Catholic Church and, as we have seen, Catholics of Upper Canada felt no differently on this point than Catholics anywhere else. The hierarchy has not kept this stand a secret, and if there has been any misunderstanding it must be attributed to Canadian educationalists who have disregarded the Catholic position, or who hoped (in vain) to absorb Catholic schools completely within the common system by dividing the laity from the clergy.[16]

Ryerson and Separate Schools. This vision and practice of education encountered, however, serious opposition from the Chief Superintendent of Education for Canada West (later Ontario), Dr. Egerton Ryerson. His philosophy of education was so forcefully stated, his accompanying practices and legislation so energetically urged and carried out, his administration and leadership so meticulous, his time in office so long (1844-1876), and his influence, for all these reasons, so powerful that the public and separate school system to this day exists and has beliefs surrounding it that can be traced directly to him.[17]

A Comparison of Ryerson's and the Catholic Position on Education. Proponents of both the common and separate school agreed that education should be concerned with the formation of the whole person and that education should be Christian. Ryerson wrote:

> Now, education thus practical, includes religion and morality; secondly, the development to a certain extent of all our facilities; thirdly, an acquaintance with several branches of elementary knowledge...I feel it necessary to...assert the absolute necessity of making Christianity the basis and the cement of the structure of public education.(emphasis in the original)[18]

Since, Ryerson reasoned, there was a common basis of Christianity, the home and the church were to supply themselves what they considered to be the missing elements. "The common day school and its teachers ought not to be burdened with duties which belonged to the pastor, the parent, and the church."[19] Therefore, he argued, separate schools were unnecessary, divisive, inferior, and undermining to the common school system. Conversely, for the believer in separate schools the common school was "godless" and "the ruin of our Catholic minority".[20] To teach only that about which all Christian denominations could agree, they felt, would have left very little to be taught; such a reduced version of Christianity would perforce leave out much of what Catholics believe to be essential to their faith and would prevent the living of their faith in the sacraments and the liturgy during the school day.[21]

The two positions were argued forcefully in the published debates of Ryerson and Charbonnel. With such colourful, some would say intemperate, language as "mongrel interpretations" of religion in common schools[22] and the "ignorance" and "state of vassalage and degradation" of the child in the separate school[23] coming from two prominent leaders, it is not surprising that the separate school issue entered the political fray (there to stay, resurfacing during many elections right up to the present time). Ryerson would have infinitely preferred one State-supported, universal, non-denominational common school system. Charbonnel desired State-supported Catholic schools free from Ryerson or any other official and administered by the Church.[24] The compromise, through many struggles between the two views held conscientiously throughout the history of education in Ontario, resulted in two branches and aims of the public school system, public and separate, both under the governance of the Minister of Education and both with considerable trustee and teacher autonomy in the execution of those aims.

Legislative History of Separate Schools to Confederation. To reach this compromise, unique at that time to North America, required over twenty years of editorials, parliamentary debates, memorials from Bishops and municipal councils, school board petitions, and court cases. For the purposes of examining constitutional guarantees for separate schools and because of the emphasis on the phrase "in law" in section 93(1) of the *BNA Act*, it is the educational legislation that matters the most.

The new legislature of Canada East and Canada West turned its attention to education almost immediately. To replace the permissive legislation, the *Day Act* made the provision of common schools mandatory. Each township was to be divided into school sections small enough to contain a school within walking distance for the children resident in the section; a schoolhouse was to be erected; common school commissioners in each township (in the next statute trustees for each school section) were to be elected to manage and raise money for the schools, hire teachers, and regulate courses; in the cities and towns the governor could appoint a board of examiners to administer the common schools; a permanent fund for common schools (CSF) was created to be distributed by the provincial legislature. Section 44 granted for the first time the right to establish a separate school. It was an almost totally non-restrictive clause. Any number of inhabitants resident anywhere in the township and professing any religious faith different from that of the majority of the township's inhabitants could "dissent" from the proceedings of the common school commissioners and establish a common school of their own, which was entitled to its proportional share of the CSF and township assessment monies raised for common school purposes.[25]

In 1843 the legislature must have feared too much of an increase in the number of denominational schools in the townships, for the *Hincks Act* narrowed and carefully delineated the provisions for forming a separate school. Firstly, the privilege of separation was limited to Roman Catholics or Protestants; secondly, the teacher of the common school had to be of the other faith from the potential applicants for a separate school. Thus began the "protection from insult" idea that Ryerson was to preach as a temporary safety valve. Catholics, he argued, had no need of a separate school if the common school had a Catholic on its staff. Thirdly, there had to be at least ten resident householders within the city, town, or rural school section before a separate school board could be established. Considering the size of a school section, this meant that in many cases a separate school could not be formed. The Act also created the office of Chief Superintendent of Common Schools, paving the way for Ryerson after Robert Murray's brief time in the position. Separate schools continued to share in the CSF, soon to be based on pupil attendance.[26]

In 1847 boards of trustees were created for cities and towns and given the duty "to determine the number, sites, and description of schools...and whether such school or schools shall be denominational or mixed."[27] (Ryerson felt it would be unfeasible to extend this power to rural trustees.[28])

When Charbonnel arrived in 1850 as Bishop of the Toronto diocese, he found many of these separate school clauses objectionable, especially the government of separate schools by a Chief Superintendent, Dr. Ryerson. On the other hand, Ryerson, maintaining the position that Catholics would soon understand both that they did not require "protection from insult" in his common schools and that their separate schools were inferior, held that separate school supporters had no access to taxes raised for common school purposes and, to add insult to injury, had to continue to pay common school taxes to support an institution generally considered to be important for the good of the State.[29] (Presumably, this latter policy would reinforce the feeling of inferiority.) Charbonnel turned his attention to removing each of the restraints on the free operation of separate schools.

First, he took the Toronto common school board to court for not permitting him a second separate school on the grounds that Toronto was just one school section. He lost, but Ryerson and the legislature then corrected this perceived injustice in 1851 by legislating An Act to define and restore certain rights to parties therein mentioned. It stipulated that, upon application from twelve resident Catholics to an urban board for a separate school, they "shall be entitled to have a Separate School in each Ward, or in two or more Wards united."[30]

Next Charbonnel oversaw the action of the Belleville separate school trustees wherein they sued their common school counterparts for receiving and spending what the separate school trustees thought was too great a share of the CSF. The judgment found that the separate school boards were entitled to their share of the CSF equal to the amount raised locally for teachers' salaries plus the local taxes collected from separate school supporters for other purposes. It supported Ryerson's contention that "a Roman Catholic ratepayer is primarily by law a supporter of the public or common school system."[31] An Act supplementary to the Common School Act for Upper Canada exempted separate school supporters from common school rates, provided they paid for the support of their own schools an amount at least equal to the common school rate.[32] Ryerson's prevention of separate school boards operating "on the cheap" was a small price to pay in return for financial access to grants and taxes and for freedom from a kind of double taxation.

But there still remained the teacher clause, one that, in the opinion of J. Harold Putman, a biographer of Ryerson, "would likely have shown Ryerson to be correct" in his assumption that separate schools would eventually vanish.[33] Common school trustees, with Ryerson's encouragement, were hiring Catholic teachers in order to prevent the establishment of a separate school in the coterminous school section or to force its closing.[34] It was at this point that Ryerson's "protection from insult" and Charbonnel's total integration of religious and secular education clashed. For what good was a Catholic teacher in a common school where s/he could not implement the Catholic view of education? Within two years Ryerson had to accept the permanence of separate schools. Taché, a French Catholic member, in 1855 successfully shepherded a bill through the legislature that for the first time gave Roman Catholic separate school supporters a statute of their own: it withdrew the teacher clause, reduced the number of school section resident householders required to form a separate school board from twelve to five, maintained the financial rights already gained, gave the separate school trustees all the power of common school trustees, and gave them the power of qualifying separate school teachers.[35]

In 1863 the last separate school act prior to Confederation was passed. The *Scott Act* made a number of improvements to the *Taché Act*, the most significant being the removal of the requirement for a separate school supporter to declare his/her intent annually and the expansion of the rural separate school board boundaries from those of the coterminous common school section to a three-mile radius from the schoolhouse, a geographical increase of three to five times. All the other advantages of the *Taché Act* were maintained.[36]

As Confederation approached, the Canadian Catholic Bishops sought further improvements. In 1866, in a brief they requested that any rights and privileges granted to the Protestant minority in Canada East with respect to education be guaranteed to the Catholic minority in Canada West. Being more specific, in the same year they submitted a draft Act to Restore to Roman Catholics in Upper Canada certain Rights in respect to Separate Schools, and to extend to the Roman Catholic Minority in Upper Canada similar and Equal Privileges with those granted by the Legislature to the Protestant Minority of Lower Canada, which, among other things stated that there would be separate school access to corporation taxes and a Catholic government-supported Normal School.[37] Robert Bell, the legislative member for Russell, introduced a bill in 1866 that granted the important wishes of the Bishops, but the government, faced with opposition to the bill and anxious to get on with the business of Confederation, decided on no new separate school legislation.[38] Richard Scott, the sponsor of the *Scott Act*, in 1912 wrote that, "At Confederation it was assumed by those who drafted the educational clauses in the *BNA Act*, that the rights of the minority in Quebec and Ontario were sufficiently guaranteed."[39]

The *Scott Act* of 1863 and the *Common School Act* of 1859 (to which the Scott Act refers for powers of trustees and other matters) were now guaranteed by section 93 of the *BNA Act* of 1867, which stated that:

> (1) Nothing in any such [provincial] Law should prejudicially affect any Right or Privilege with respect to Denominational Schools which any Class of Persons have by Law in the Province at the Union.[40]

As far as any new privileges after Confederation of a kind requested by the Bishops, the political environment would be far different. Instead of about half of the members of the government being French Catholic, in the Ontario legislature there would be at first almost no Catholics holding a seat and the first premier, Sandfield Macdonald, a Catholic, had not seen the necessity of separate schools in his riding. Separate school supporters would have to hope that Attorney General John A. Macdonald's words in the legislature in 1866 would be prophetic:

> ...the minority in both Upper and Lower Canada will be obliged to throw themselves on the justice and generosity of the majority....I feel,however, that their confidence in that justice will not be unfounded....I feel sure that the Protestant majority of Upper Canada will say that if they are strong they can afford to be just.[41]

Two Post-Confederation Separate School Problems. The "final settlement" of the *Scott Act*, as Ryerson often described it, turned out to be far from the last step in settling the rights and privileges of separate schools. For the next 130 years there would continue to be vexatious serious problems for separate school boards, most of which were based on how advanced a programme the board has jurisdiction over and how the boards could obtain access to corporation tax revenues, a financial source of ever-growing importance.

The Catholic High School Question. Prior to 1867 the only statutory terms for types of schools were common, grammar, and separate. In regulations, reporting forms, and annual reports such designations as fifth classes (which later were called grades nine and ten), central schools with a "High School, or highest department of the Common School"[42], higher education, and college were used. But the statutory term "high school" did not come into existence until 1871, four years after Confederation, a timing that, because of the pre-Confederation guarantee of section 93(1) of the *BNA Act*, would cause two historic court cases and several decades of difficulties for separate school boards. In 1871, Ryerson, dissatisfied with the grammar school as well as with the overlapping and duplication of common and grammar schools,[43] had the legislature enact *An Act to Improve the Common and Grammar Schools of the Province of Ontario*. It eliminated these two types of schools and established public schools, up to the end of what was later called grade ten and high schools and collegiate institutes from grade nine to thirteen.[44] It was not for almost forty years that this legislation became an issue for separate school boards.

One can only speculate why matters did not come to a head sooner. Between Confederation and the early part of the twentieth century the Bishops did complain about separate school taxpayers having to pay high school taxes and did ask for Catholic high schools with grants and taxes, but not forcefully or with any regularity.[45] Perhaps their concerns about financing elementary separate schools were overriding. Also, society's interest in high schools was quite low in the last century: only about 2 per cent of the separate school population was in a fifth class and Vicar General Rooney, chairman of the Toronto separate school board in the 1880s, wondered whether a high school education for the average son of a farmer or labourer might not be dangerously raising the child's expectations for life.[46] In any case, separate schools were offering fifth and sixth classes throughout Ontario and private Catholic high schools were operating in the cities.[47] No less an authority than Ryerson himself seemed to remove the fears that separate school boards might be unable to conduct classes beyond grade ten. In 1872 he instructed high school inspectors to have nothing to do in the operation of the Act of 1871 with the *Separate Schools Act*.[48]

Furthermore, during an economic slowdown in Ontario, which prevented the expansion of high school building, public and separate school boards were actually encouraged to offer fifth and sixth classes. Under *An Act to Improve the Laws Respecting Public Schools* in 1899 a separate school board could establish a "continuation class" (provided that the coterminous public school board had not already done so) and receive special grants for the students in its fifth and sixth classes. A number of separate school boards did so,[49] and this action was what eventually resulted in the first court case over the separate school board's right to establish and maintain Catholic high schools with grants and taxes. Once the economy recovered, the government returned to its policy of expanding high schools and began to discourage the inferior continuation classes. Three restrictive acts were passed: the first in 1908 subdivided continuation classes into fifth classes and continuation schools, the second in 1909 stipulated that a "Continuation School shall not be established or maintained in a High School District," and the third in 1913 changed the definition of a continuation school from a "public school" to a "high school" and mandated that no continuation school could be established without the Minister's approval.[50]

As a result of this legislation, the Deputy Minister of Education, Dr. A.H.U. Colquhoun, in 1915 advised separate school boards operating beyond the fifth class that they could not use taxes for such a purpose, that they could not do work beyond that level, and that students would not be admitted from a separate school to the lower- and middle-school examinations for entrance to the Normal School or to the Matriculation Examination.[51]

The Catholic Bishops, press, and trustees, under the leadership of Archbishop Neil McNeil of Toronto and the Catholic Education Committee, objected and over the next few years submitted briefs asking for the removal of the three restrictive statutes and for the establishment of grant- and tax-supported Catholic high schools. Finally, after negotiations with two previous provincial governments, Premier E.C. Drury decided that the Bishops' intention to go to court was a good idea to settle the issue and that the action should receive government financial backing. In 1923 Premier Howard Ferguson's Minister of Education, R.H. Grant, announced that the government would pay for a court decision on the method of paying grants to separate schools.[52] The case began.

The Board of Trustees of the Roman Catholic Separate Schools for the School Section No. 2 in the Township of Tiny and Others v. The King began in the Supreme Court of Ontario on December 24, 1925, ran through January 11 to 20, with the judgment delivered May 13, 1926. T.F. Battle, a Toronto lawyer and later a Catholic priest, and I.F. Hellmuth, a prominent Protestant Toronto lawyer, took the following position: that separate school supporters are exempted from tax support of common schools, and high schools are a type of common school; that separate school boards have the right to establish and maintain courses of study and grades carried on in high schools and that the provincial government has no right to limit or confine the common school grades or courses of study offered by any Roman Catholic separate school board; therefore, the Act of 1871, as well as subsequent high school Acts and continuation school legislation, were ultra vires (beyond legal power) of the Ontario legislature because of the *Scott Act* and section 93 of the *BNA Act*.

They put forth the following arguments to support this position on high schools. Firstly, there was no limit or regulation regarding what could be taught in the common or separate school; the Council of Public Instruction's power to regulate separate schools did not mean the authority to curtail the separate school programme. Secondly, the specificity of the *Common School Act* of 1859 authorizing the Council of Public Instruction to determine the textbooks to be used in the common schools suggested that no larger power, such as deciding the extent of the common school grades, was envisioned. Thirdly, the right of a separate school board to educate children from age five to twenty-one could not be cut down, yet education fitting for over age ten or twelve had been refused. Fourthly, the Judicial Committee of the Privy Council in a 1917 Ottawa Separate School Board court case upheld the right of trustees to management of their schools; furthermore, the 1859 *Common Schools Act* empowered separate school trustees in urban areas to determine the kind and description of schools to be established and maintained. Fifthly, the *Taché Act* established the separate school as a unique institution, on a basis of its own with an independent existence, and, therefore, not subject to the Council's restrictive government. Sixthly, the Act of 1871 abolished grammar schools and divided common schools into two divisions, public (elementary) and high (secondary); the common schools had been the only educational structures available to all students and supported by assessment, whereas grammar schools were élitist, not attended by girls, supported with tuition, and, in general, not part of the province's educational system. Seventhly, some common school boards before Confederation were setting up high schools. Finally, the continuation school was merely a kind of common school.

The two lawyers for the government, W.N. Tilley and McGregor Young, responded as follows. The Council of Public Instruction could determine, limit, or expand the courses of study and grades in a common school and a separate school was a common school. They cited the 1917 Privy Council Mackell case to support the concept that the right to establish and maintain a separate school was a regulated matter.

Secondly, the fact that some pupils in common schools were doing advanced work indicated a practice, not a legal right; a normal "give and take" in the early years was understandable. Thirdly, grammar schools were to be between the common schools and universities. Fourthly, the power that an urban separate school board had was to determine the kind of school, for example, a girls',boys', or infants' school. Lastly, the city common school boards operating high schools were examples of voluntary practice and not evidence of rights.

The Hon. Mr. Justice Rose agreed with all the government's arguments. In so doing he concentrated on the statutes, those which the Roman Catholic separate school supporters had "by law" and allowed other evidence only as revealing of the statutes. Therefore, in his judgment, separate school trustees had to obey the Council's (then Department of Education's) regulations fixing the point beyond which a common school education could not proceed and separate school supporters had to pay public high school taxes.

Battle sent a Notice of Appeal. The Supreme Court of Ontario, Appellate Division, heard the appeal from October 25 to 29 and the five judges delivered their decisions on December 23, 1926. All five, Mulock C.J.O., Magee J.A., Ferguson J.A., Hodgins J.A., and Grant J., agreed with Rose's reasoning and judgment and dismissed the appeal. The Court also ordered that Peterborough be added as a party suppliant in order to have the judgment cover all separate school boards in Ontario.

Battle appealed again. The appeal was heard by six judges in the Supreme Court of Canada from April 20 to 25 and the judgments delivered on October 10, 1927. Judges Duff, Newcombe, and Lamont concurred with Rose's judgment. The three Roman Catholic judges, Chief Justice Anglin, Judge Rinfret, and Judge Mignault, allowed the appeal. Generally, they agreed with Battle and Hellmuth's arguments. Because of this three/three tie, the original judgment was upheld.

The necessary steps were taken to bring the case to the Lords of the Judicial Committee of the Privy Council in Great Britain. It began on February 21, 1928 and lasted until March 8; Viscount Haldane delivered the final judgment on the "Tiny Township Case" on June 12, 1928. He too agreed with Rose's judgment and dismissed the appeal. He stated that abridgement by regulation of the separate school to elementary education was not abolition and that the Council's power to grade was essential and not inconsistent with separate school rights.[53] A historian of legal, civil, and human rights, D.A. Schmeiser, in 1964 wrote that the judgment presented difficulties: "How far can the legislature regulate grading without producing total abolition?"[54]

Although a number of judges, including Haldane, reminded the Courts that an appeal for "administrative fairness" to the Governor-General-in-Council existed under section 93(3), the separate school trustees took no steps towards such an appeal. The *Catholic Register* thought the time was wrong. Senator Belcourt wrote to Archbishop McNeil in 1928 that nothing was to be hoped for from the Federal Government regarding Catholic high schools, but that there was more to be gained, with difficulty, from the Premier of Ontario.[55] Perhaps there was a fear that a 93(3) appeal was a dangerous political procedure and that it could result in a final no. From 1928 to the birth of OECTA separate school leaders

> have preferred quietly to urge upon provincial authorities a claim based partly on the theory that Roman Catholic young people should receive a Catholic education at all levels of instruction.[56]

In any case, the Great Depression was at hand. Separate school boards found it too expensive to offer even the constitutionally guaranteed grades nine and ten courses. The corporation tax problem needed immediate attention if separate school boards were to offer satisfactory programmes as in the public schools.

The Corporation School Tax Issue. With the development of industrialization a new entity appeared on the scene and became part of the *Assessment Act*: the corporation. How was one to determine who were the separate school shareholders in the corporation? The *Common School Act* of 1859, *Scott Act* of 1863, and *Assessment Act* of 1865 were of no help. A separate school supporter was an individual residential, business, or "personal" property owner. Although this situation was to cause more and more inequity as corporations, partnerships, and public utilities grew through the decades, even in the years leading up to Confederation, when corporations were relatively small in number, a problem was seen. During the Confederation Debates of 1865 the Hon. John Rose raised the issue: "with reference to Taxes on the property in incorporated companies...there ought to be some more equitable way of appropriating the Taxes, on such property."[57] Bell's 1866 bill proposed a method of distributing corporation taxes according to school attendance, but did not receive final reading.

Although in Quebec in 1869 Premier Chauveau saw legislation enacted which divided taxes paid by corporations between the two classes of schools based on their pupil enrolment, Ontario did not follow Quebec's lead. In a government debate in 1879, a Catholic member, O'Sullivan, urged a similar bill, but to no avail.[58] In 1886, the Liberal government of Oliver Mowat passed legislation which provided that a company "may" direct a portion of its taxes on real property to the separate school board pursuant to a resolution of the board of directors. The portion had to "bear the same ratio and proportion to the whole property of the company assessable within the said municipality, as the amount or proportion of the shares or stock of such company, so far as the same are paid,or partly paid up, and are held and possessed by persons who are Roman Catholics, bears to the whole amount of such paid or partly paid up shares or stock of the company."[59] This legislation did almost nothing for separate school boards because of its permissive nature and, more importantly, because of the impossibility in most cases of determining the exact number of shares held by Roman Catholics.[60]

In 1909, a Catholic Conservative M.P.P., T.W. McGarry, introduced a bill that would provide that all public utility taxes be distributed according to the number of public and separate school supporters, but Premier Whitney announced that the government would consider no amendments to the Separate School Act in that session.[61] However,in 1913,his government did amend the legislation of shares owned by Catholics, provided that the estimate was at or below the actual proportion.[62] This caused no significant improvement.[63]

Meanwhile, the Bishops in Pastoral Letters, letters to the editors of newspapers and members of parliament,and at annual meetings, raised the issue. Archbishop McEvay of Toronto asked Whitney, "Why should Catholics pay their share of taxes to a bonused industry, and have all the school taxes of such industry go to the rich public school? Such a thing is unjust on the face of it."[64] Archbishop Spratt of Kingston in a pastoral letter wrote that a Catholic owning corporation shares was "forced to be a public-school supporter" and that this was resulting in many separate schools "dying of starvation".[65]

With the advent of the Great Depression separate school funding became a grave matter. An organization named the Catholic Taxpayers' Association was formed in 1931 after Martin Quinn unsuccessfully tried to get a board of directors to assign the taxes on a block of stock he owned to the Toronto Separate School Board. The Bishops worked closely with him and the Association in order to educate Catholics and the general public about the injustice of the corporation tax legislation and to lobby the government for appropriate amendments. Archbishop McNeil coordinated these efforts in Sunday Church services throughout the province and with the government of Premier Henry; they asked for an amendment of the *Assessment Act.* A year later, when no action had been initiated by the Henry government, Quinn sent the 1933 brief to Mitchell Hepburn, M.P.P. and leader of the Liberal party. He became premier in 1934 and introduced an amendment to the *Assessment Act* in 1936.[66]

However, the amendment was flawed. It limited the direction of corporate taxes to Roman Catholics and separate school supporters who themselves filed notice with the company and therefore excluded all non-property holders such as wives, sisters, children, roomers, estate executors, corporate shareholders, and all non-residents of Ontario. Furthermore, there were no sanctions to force corporations to attempt to ascertain their number of separate school supporters. A court case resulted over the issue.[67]

Passions were raised. Catholic leaders told Hepburn that a repeal would be judicious, since amendments would be "bitterly divisive within caucus, cabinet, and the country." Henry introduced a bill to repeal the 1936 legislation, "detailed the financial chaos...and argued that any further support for Catholic schools would destroy Ontario's magnificent public school system." Hepburn reluctantly supported the appeal on March 25, 1937, but promised the Catholics that the Liberals would" give justice and equity to all people, regardless of race or religion."[68]

It was back to square one with the wording of the 1913 Act. Archbishop McNeil, ailing and disappointed over both the loss of the Tiny Township Case and the repeal of the amendment, now hoped for better results from another court case.

In 1937, the board of directors of the Ford Motor Company decided to direct 18 per cent of its municipal taxes to the Windsor Separate School Board. It assumed that, based on the population census, this figure would be a fair estimate of its Roman Catholic shareholders, even though it could not determine the actual percentage. The Windsor Board of Education, standing to lose tax revenues, appealed to the Court of Revision. The court ruled that all the company's taxes had to go to the public school board since the 18 per cent estimate was not convincing. On appeal, Judge Mahon of the County Court of Essex made the same decision. The Supreme Court of Ontario allowed the appeal "on the grounds that the statute ought,if possible, to be interpreted and applied so as to effectuate its manifest intention, viz. to provide for an equitable apportionment." The Windsor Board of Education then appealed to the Supreme Court of Canada where a majority in 1941 dismissed the appeal. On appeal to the Privy Council the judgment reversed the decision of the Supreme Court of Canada.[69]

One can appreciate the difficulties in directing corporation taxes to a separate school board when one notes that three courts judged the 18 per cent estimate insufficiently supported and two courts found the estimate reasonable. Separate school boards now faced a financial crisis as corporation tax revenues became a greater part of public school boards' budgets and, consequently, as their mill rates yielded higher sums than those of separate school boards. A number of studies from the Bishops and separate school boards illustrated the problem. For example,in a 1909 report found in the Toronto archdiocesan archives, it was calculated that, if the pupil population of the public and separate school boards in Toronto were compared, the latter's assessment, equitably speaking, should have been 14.562 per cent instead of the actual 7.168 per cent. Part of the reason for this was the $11 532 733 assessment of eight public utilities going totally to the public schools.[70] By 1918 there were twelve public utilities with an assessment of $40 579 977.[71] Another memorandum in the same archives stated that the separate school boards in Hamilton, Oshawa, and Weston had a deficit in 1922 because "the *Assessment Act* unduly restricts the property assessable for the support of Separate Schools."[72] In 1931 Archbishop McNeil published a pamphlet on the problem. In it he reported that the lack of corporate tax revenues had resulted in eight separate school boards with a tax rate higher than the coterminous public school board.[73] In sum, as Martin Quinn wrote, the assessment of stock companies in London was $946 350 in 1886 and $ 22 072 277 in 1930; public schools were becoming wealthier and separate schools poorer.[74]

In operational terms what did all this mean for separate school boards in the 1930s and 1940s? Most of the urban separate school boards, when compared with their public school counterparts, had higher mill rates, lower revenues, and greater numbers of teachers unqualified or with lower qualifications. Programmes were more limited, especially in the areas of kindergarten, manual training, home economics, or special education. Instructional supplies were a problem as pupils had to purchase their own textbooks; school buildings lacked general purpose rooms and libraries; sometimes playgrounds were small or entirely lacking. I recall attending as a child a Toronto separate school that was just a slightly modified home. Bergin talks about the same period when he was teaching in Ottawa, where some schools were storefronts with one toilet and where the "blackboards" were made from black construction paper.[75] For a number of boards survival was completely owing to the large numbers of teaching sisters, in particular, and priests and brothers as well.

This,then, was the world of separate schools into which OECTA was born. It was a world rich in human resources, Catholic tradition and practice, and dedication, but wounded by financial hardship, by a programme truncated by the courts at the end of grade ten, by the necessity of tuition and narrow programmes in Catholic high schools, and by a consciousness of injustice. Many challenges awaited Margaret Lynch, the first president of OECTA.

NOTES

1. *The Globe*, 8 Aug. 1866.
2. Much of the material in this chapter has been drawn from two other works by me: Robert T. Dixon, "The Ontario Separate School System and Section 93 of The British North America Act "(Ed.D. diss., University of Toronto, 1976); Robert T. Dixon, *The Role of the Teacher in Catholic Education in Canada West and Ontario from 1841 to the Present* (Toronto: OSSTA, 1994).
3. Pope Puis IX, "The Syllabus of Errors," *A Free Church in a Free State? The Catholic Church, Italy, Germany, France, 1864-1914*, ed. Ernst Helmreich (Boston: Heath & Co.,1964), 1-7.
4. *Toronto Mirror*, 21 May 1852. See also Circular Letter to the Clergy and Faithful of the Diocese of Toronto from Bishop Charbonnel, 9 July 1853, Charbonnel Papers, AAT; Circular to the Clergy in Reference to Catholic Schools, Bishop A. Pinsoneault, Bishop of Sandwich, 4 July 1861, Pinsoneault Papers, DAL, "The Trustees of the Catholic Schools of Toronto to Bishop Charbonnel," *True Witness*, 11 June 1858; the Speech of Thomas D'Arcy McGee to the Legislature, *True Witness*, 2 July 1858; *Canadian Freeman*, 8 May 1862; *Toronto Mirror*, 31 Dec. 1852; *True Witness*, 5 March 1858; Nicolson, "The Catholic Church," 136.
5. *An Act to make further provision for the establishment and maintenance of Common Schools throughout the Province*, 4 & 5 Vict. c. 18.
6. Murray W. Nicolson, "Irish Catholic Education in Victorian Toronto: An Ethnic Response to Urban Conformity," *Social History*, XVII (1984), 287-306; Susan E. Houston and Alison Prentice, *Schooling and Scholars in Nineteenth-Century Ontario* (Toronto: University of Toronto Press, 1988), 278.

7. Circular Letter to the Clergy and Faithful of the Diocese of Toronto from Bishop Charbonnel, 9 July 1853, Charbonnel Papers, AAT.
8. J. George Hodgins, *Documentary History of Education in Upper Canada from the passing of the Constitutional Act of 1791 to the Close of Dr. Ryerson's Administration of the Education Department in 1876*, Vol. IX (1850-51), 198.
9. *An Act for the establishment and maintenance of Common Schools in Upper Canada* (1843), 7 Vict. c. 29, s.LV.
10. *An Act to Amend the Law relating to separate schools in Upper Canada* (1855), 18 Vict. c.131. (The Taché Act.)
11. *The Education Act*, s.237(3).
12. Circular of His Lordship the Bishop of Toronto on the *Separate School Act of 1855*. See also the Toronto Mirror, 7 Dec. 1855.
13. Dixon, *Role of the Teacher*, 49-50.
14. Dixon, *Ontario Separate School System*, 39-43.
15. Ibid., 12-14.
16. "Minority Report" in Mr. Justice John Andrew Hope, *Report of the Royal Commission on Education in Ontario* (Toronto, 1950), 881-83.
17. There have been a number of books written on Ryerson, some of them approaching hagiography. Among the best are the following: C.B. Sissons, *Egerton Ryerson, His Life and Letters*, Vol. II (Toronto: Clarke Irwin & Co. Ltd., 1947; Goldwin S. French, "Egerton Ryerson and the Methodist Model for Upper Canada," in Neil McDonald and Al Chaiton, eds., *Egerton Ryerson and His Times (Toronto: Macmillan of Canada, 1978), 45-58; Albert F. Fiorino*, "The Moral Foundation of Egerton Ryerson's Idea of Education" in McDonald and Chaiton, ibid., 59-80; Laurence J. Rainey, "Educational Missionary: The Christian Faith and Educational Philosophy of Egerton Ryerson" (M.A. thesis, University of Toronto, 1987); Bruce Curtis, *Building the Educational State*, (London, Ontario: The Althouse Press, 1988), 97-132; Houston and Prentice, *Schooling*, 97-156.
18. Ryerson, *Report* (1846), 147, 151.
19. Ryerson, "Question of Religious Instruction, in Connection with Our System of Public Instruction" in Report (1857), 24.
20. Bishop Charbonnel to Rome, 26 May 1851, Charbonnel Papers, AAT.
21. Houston and Prentice, *Schooling*, 294.
22. Charbonnel to Ryerson, 24 March 1852, *Copies of Correspondence.*
23. Ryerson to Charbonnel, 12 May 1852, ibid.
24. Charbonnel to Ryerson, 24 March 1852, ibid.
25. S.P.C., 4 & 5 Vict. c. 18.
26. *An Act for the establishment and maintenance of Common Schools in Upper Canada* (1843) 7 Vict. c. 29; Dixon, "Separate School System," 19, 217-19.
27. *An Act for amending the Common Schools Act of Upper Canada* (1847), 10 & 11, c. 19.
28. Ryerson to the Hon. W. H. Draper, 12 April 1847, in Sissons, Ryerson, 136.

29. Dixon, "Separate School System," 220-25.
30. Ibid., 221-22; S.P.C., 14 & 15 Vict. c. 111.
31. *The Trustees of the Roman Catholic School of Belleville v. the School Trustees of the Town of Belleville* (1853), 10 U.C.Q.B., 469.
32. S.P.C., 16 Vict. c. 185.
33. J. Harold Putman, *Egerton Ryerson and Education in Upper Canada* (Toronto: William Briggs, 1912), 192.
34. John S. Moir, *Church and State in Canada West: Three Studies in the Relation of Denominationalism and Nationalism, 1841-1867* (Toronto: University of Toronto Press, 1959), 156.
35. *An Act to amend the laws relating to Separate Schools in Upper Canada* (1855), 18 Vict. c. 131.
36. *An Act to restore to Roman Catholics in Upper Canada certain rights in respect to Separate Schools* (1863), 26 Vict. c. 5.
37. Hodgins, *Documentary History*, vol. XIX, 211-12.
38. Dixon, "Separate School System," 39-42.
39. Richard Scott to the Hon. Robt Allan Pyne, Minister of Education, 17 Sept. 1912, Scott Papers, vol. 3, P.A.C.
40. *An Act for the Union of Canada, Nova Scotia, and New Brunswick, and the Governments thereof, and for Purposes connected therewith* (1867), 30 & 31 Vict. ch. 1, s.93(1).
41. *Globe*, 8 Aug. 1866.
42. *Journal of Education* (1849), 67. See also Ryerson, *Annual Report* (1850), 18-19, 187; ibid. (1852), 132, 137; ibid. (1855), 190, 281-82.
43. Dixon, "Affidavit," 24-26, taken from Appeal Case Vol.7, pp.1225-1265, IN THE MATTER of a reference to the Court of Appeal pursuant to section 19 of the Courts of Justice Act, 1984, Statutes of Ontario, 1984, Chapter 11, by Order-in-Council O.C. 1774/85 respecting Bill 30, an Act to Amend the Education Act to provide full funding for Roman Catholic separate high schools.
44. S.O. (1871), 34 Vict. c. 33.
45. Franklin Walker, *Catholic Education and Politics in Ontario*, Vol. II (Toronto: Federation of Catholic Education Associations of Ontario, 1976), 9-12.
46. Dixon, *Separate School System*, 51, 53.
47. Dixon, "Affidavit," 14-22.
48. Dixon, *Separate School System*, 89.
49. Ibid., 55-56.
50. *An Act Respecting Separate Schools, Fifth Classes and Continuation Schools* (1908), 8 Edw. VII, c. 68; *An Act Respecting Continuation Schools* (1909), 9 Edw. VII, c. 90; *An Act respecting Continuation Schools* (1913), 3-4 Geo. V, c. 72.
51. Dixon, *Separate School System*, 65.
52. Ibid., 59-77.
53. Ibid., 79-129.
54. D. A. Schmeiser, *Civil Liberties in Canada* (Toronto: Oxford University

Press, 1964), 145.
55. Dixon, *Separate School System*, 129-33.
56. C.B. Sissons, *Church and State in Canadian Education* (Toronto: Ryerson Press, 1959), 100.
57. "Speech Delivered by the Honourable John Rose, in the House of Assembly, During the 'Confederation Debates' at Quebec in 1865," AAT.
58. Walker, *Catholic Education*, Vol. II, 93.
59. *An Act Respecting Separate Schools* (1886), 49 Vict. c. 46.
60. Walker, *Catholic Education*, Vol. II, 162.
61. Ibid., 224-25.
62. *An Act Respecting Separate Schools* (1913), 3 & 4 Geo. V, c. 71.
63. Ontario English Catholic Teachers' Association, Submission to the Select Committee on Education, "The Financing of Ontario's Elementary and Secondary Schools," 22 Sept. 1989, OECTAA.
64. Archbishop McEvay to Premier Whitney, 14 May 1909, McEvay Papers, AAT.
65. "Pastoral Letter of the Most Rev. M.J. Spratt, D.D., Archbishop of Kingston on Catholic Separate Schools and Public Taxation under the Civil Law," 7 Oct. 1921, AAT. See also Archbishop Gauthier of Kingston to Archbishop McEvay of Toronto, 24 Oct. 1908, McEvay Papers, AAT; Archbishop McEvay to Mr. Kelly, 22 Feb. 1909, ibid.; Minutes of the Regular Annual Meeting of the Bishops of Ontario, 11 Oct. 1917, AAT; ibid., 13 May 1919, AAT; Archbishop McNeil of Toronto," Pastoral Letter to the Clergy and Laity of Ontario," 6 June 1931, AAT.
66. Walker, *Catholic Education*, Vol. II, 355-476.
67. John T. Saywell, *"Just call me Mitch." The Life of Mitchell F. Hepburn* (Toronto: University of Toronto Press, 1991), 296-97.
68. Ibid., 298-300.
69. Norman Bethune and R.T. Dixon, "Survival ...? 1867-1949. A Documentary History of Separate Schools in Ontario," *Teachers' Guide* (Toronto: Ontario English Catholic Teachers' Association, 1974), 71.
70. "Assessment of City," 1909, AAT.
71. "Informal Memoranda Concerning the Workings of the Separate Schools Act and the Assessment Act, in the City of Toronto," about 1918, AAT.
72. "Memorandum," about 1922, AAT.
73. *The Archbishop of Toronto, The School Question of Ontario,* 1931, AAT.
74. Mr. Quinn's Open Letter to Company, 9 July 1931, AAT.
75. Bergin, interviews.

[illegible] 1964), 135.

55. Dixon, [illegible] School [illegible] 1 [illegible]

56. [illegible] Stevens, [illegible] Canadian [illegible] Toronto: Ryerson Press, 1957), 100.

57. "Speech Delivered by the [illegible] Legislative Assembly [illegible]" [illegible] AA.

58. Walker, Catholic Education, Vol. II, [illegible]

59. [illegible] Separate School [illegible]

60. Walker, Catholic Education, Vol. II, [illegible]

61. Ibid., 294-2[illegible]

62. [illegible]

63. [illegible]

[illegible]

[illegible]

[illegible]

[illegible]

[illegible]

[illegible]

[illegible]

[illegible]

[illegible]

[illegible]

66. [illegible]

67. [illegible]

[illegible]

68. Ibid., [illegible]

69. [illegible]

[illegible]

[illegible]

70. "Memorandum [illegible]"

71. [illegible] the [illegible] Act and the Assessment Act, [illegible] City of Toronto [illegible]

72. "Memorandum [illegible]"

73. [illegible] Ontario [illegible] AA.

74. [illegible] Letter [illegible]

75. [illegible] interview [illegible]

CHAPTER FOUR

THE BASICS: UNITY, ETHICS, SALARIES, SECURITY, PENSIONS 1944–1951

Rural teachers must do janitor services, build fires, and break roads. She must be willing to sacrifice her salary because of enforced holidays. And worst of all, she has to await the pleasure of the School Board to receive her salary.[1]

Association Activities. The presidents and their executives in OECTA had no shortage of important activities with which to occupy themselves. They had to get involved immediately with ongoing matters with OTF and the pre-existing affiliates. Then there were activities common to all the teacher associations. In addition, OECTA would always need to be fully engaged in business of particular interest to separate schools and their teachers.

OECTA worked with OTF on such matters as school building specifications, amendments to Board of Reference and superannuation legislation, dental services for schools, measures to counteract juvenile delinquency, teacher certification, and minimum salary legislation. Also, the Ontario Department of Education agreed to consult regularly with OTF on providing Canadian textbooks, dealing with resolutions from public bodies and in accordance with the Regulation Made Under The Teaching Profession Act, and deciding if a teacher's certificate should be suspended or removed.[2] OECTA also supported OPSMTF in its striving for accumulative sick leave plans, larger units of administration and better Department of Education grants to school boards for the purpose of higher salaries for teachers and lower local school taxes.[3] Although in 1945, 919 public school sections had been amalgamated into 149 township school areas,[4] there were still thousands of small rural public and separate school boards in Ontario. This meant that many children attended a one- or two-room elementary school run by three or five trustees with very limited tax or human resources, as compared to the large graded schools with special facilities in the urban and township school areas. In the latter part of the provinces there was a different problem. With the post-World War II baby boom, the growth of the cities, the growing acceptance of the concept of equality of education opportunity and of the importance of education, the increase in compulsory attendance to age sixteen, the building of schools in the expanding township school areas and high school districts, the building of additions for kindergartens, general purpose rooms and libraries, and the expansion of programmes to include programmes in special education and music, the Ontario taxpayer found her/his educational share of the residential and farm mill rate rising. In 1938 the Committee on the Costs of Education had called on the province to take on a greater proportion of local school costs and, indeed, Premier Drew had, in his election campaign, promised to assume 50 per cent of the costs of education,[5] a dramatic increase. OECTA saw the importance of this for better programmes for pupils and living wages for teachers; it supported OPSMTF and through OTF intended to hold the government to its promise.

OECTA also engaged in activities similar to those of the other affiliates. The minutes of committees, the AGM, and the Board of Directors all refer to the release of news bulletins, the first publication of the *OECTA News*, representation on various provincial educational bodies, the composing of a teacher pledge, the establishment of scholarships for teachers and students, the striking of a committee to develop recommendations in aid of ineffective teachers, and research and reports on a number of educational topics.[6] From today's perspective the times were innocent, evidenced by the desire of the directors to have crime radio programmes banned.[7] Still around was the issue of the "problem of teacher portrayals in the movies and the cartoons in comic books, newspapers and magazines,...a vexing one. These ridiculous, sensational pictures...tend to lower the prestige of the teacher."[8] More significant and somewhat ahead of those hierarchical times was the AGM's recommendation that the separate school inspector share her/his evaluation with the teacher.[9] For another twenty years inspectors would continue to rank teachers numerically, from "1" (unsatisfactory) to "4" (excellent), and to keep these rankings confidential except for another inspector seeking a reference.

Regular meetings were scheduled with Cardinal Archbishop McGuigan of Toronto and the bishops on teacher salaries, particularly those of the religious teachers, on textbooks in religion and reading and on the religious education curriculum; with ECEAO on teacher formation, briefs to the government on separate school financing and legislation, a brief to the Hope Commission, and other matters important to the Catholic community; through OTF, with CTF on matters of interest for all Canadian teachers like education week, rural consolidation of school boards, minimum salaries, equal salaries for men and women, and equality of education for all children; also through OTF, with the world teachers' federation formed in the summer of 1946 in Endicott, New York; and with OSSTA on teacher contracts and salaries, government grants, legislation for separate schools, and a host of other items arising from the teacher/trustee relationship.[10] The trustees had a period of adjustment to become accustomed to sharing power with the new teachers' association. For example, OSSTA feared that principals, as part of the Association, would not be able to report on teachers.[11] Also, the Toronto Separate School Board was unwilling to allow OECTA meetings two or three times a year at 2:30 p.m. because "too much time would be lost from school."[12] Time and meetings, meetings, meetings would establish OECTA's presence and importance.

Finally and importantly for OECTA's aims, there were the activities centring on the special interests of the separate schools and their teachers. Among these were the design of an official prayer to begin all OECTA meetings, reports on Catholic education in general, the development of a detailed course of study for all elementary grades in religious education (proposed in 1948, ready in 1950!), in-service on Papal teaching, and the development of a short course in religious education for teachers.[13]

One long-standing problem was quickly solved. The Department of Education's Normal Schools, located in Hamilton, London, North Bay, Ottawa, Peterborough, Stratford, and Toronto, sent their student teachers to practise teach in elementary schools for several weeks, in one-week postings usually, in a different classroom each time. The master from the Normal School, with the "critic" teacher, the regular classroom one, assessed the student teacher's performance. It was the custom to have all the Normal School's student teachers, including the Roman Catholic ones, practise teach in the public schools despite the fact that there were separate schools in all the Normal School locations. One can only speculate why. Perhaps the Department felt that the separate schools were not really a part of the public school system. Perhaps the Normal Schools regarded themselves as a type of public school more comfortable working closely with their counterparts. Perhaps there was a reluctance to intrude on the separate school programme with its daily religion lesson. In any case, some separate school teachers expressed their wish to be critic teachers and pointed out the need for potential separate school teachers to do some practise teaching in separate schools. OECTA met with the OSSTA to deal jointly with the Department about the problem. At the same time the AGM passed the following motion:

> whereas:
> separate school teachers have the same qualifications as public school teachers,
> there are no separate school critic teachers,
> separate school teachers wish to work with Normal Schools,
> separate schools are staffed by Normal School graduates,
> Roman Catholic students are not hired as public school teachers in cities where Normal Schools are,
> separate school inspectors and principals cannot see prospective teachers,
> bilingual students practise teach in bilingual schools,
> be it resolved that the Ontario Teachers' Federation press for action.

Dr. Althouse at the Ministry of Education stalled at first, but Catholic student teachers soon began spending some of their practise teaching weeks in separate schools.[14]

All of these activities described above were important and time-consuming, but the survival priorities of the newly established OECTA would seem to have been the areas of its structure, the unity and ethics of its total membership, and decent salaries and job protection for its members throughout the province. The Association also had to pay considerable attention to grants for separate school boards and separate school rights, Board of Reference and superannuation legislation, possible dramatic changes to separate schools because of the provincial Hope Commission and the Department of Education's Porter Plan, Catholic Parent-Teacher associations, and teacher education. Examination of OECTA's work in these areas substantiates what W. G. Fleming, historian of Ontario education, has written. OTF and its five affiliates

> were all concerned with the protection and welfare of their members, giving continuous attention to salaries, job security, superannuation...They made an extremely important contribution to education through the upgrading of their own membership;...they exerted steady pressure on

educational officials and legislators to improve their own status and to ensure that schools were operated under the best possible conditions.[15]

Structure. Although the first AGM had moved that there be nineteen districts, there remained the task of assisting these centres in forming executives and educating and securing separate school teachers for OECTA membership. As Sheila Coo, author of the forty-year history of the Association, explained:

> The main burden of this administrative task fell to Cecilia Rowan, the Ottawa school teacher whose vision and hard work had helped the organizational efforts of Ottawa lay teachers during the 1930s. The task of organizing 19 districts by mail was not an easy one. Lack of adequate finances allowed only $300 for the Secretary's honorarium, and $200 was added to this the following year for secretarial help. Still, she persevered, working at night in her living room, with an old filing cabinet and battered typewriter;...after the first AGM, she wrote: "I have been terribly busy since our Toronto meeting, getting out material and keeping correspondence answered. So many are stirring now, re organization. Sudbury and Kitchener are organizing on Saturday, Kingston planning their district convention, Guelph organizing, Fr. Harrigan busy with locals around Hamilton. Still no news from Cornwall and Alexandria. I have sent out about 600 constitutions and membership tickets so we are really moving. It is wonderful to think what has been accomplished."[16]

Margaret Lynch and Fr. Priester, executive director of ECEAO, of which OECTA was now a constituent member, travelled the province to assist in organizing districts. Fr. Priester was encouraged by the response. In one letter, hastily written in Toronto, he stated, "I had to leave for the Sault. The meetings up North were very successful. I feel we will have a very successful Catholic Teachers' Federation in the province."[17]

In December 1944, Fr. Harrigan's organization committee reported that another district had been added, Barrie-Orillia, and that in each district an executive had been elected. In 1945 there were forty-five locals within the districts. In 1946 Kirkland Lake and Timmins were divided into two districts, and in 1950 Brant-Paris's application for district status was approved.[18]

The provincial committee structure, to a degree, mirrored OTF's. The committees by 1949 were legislative, budget (formerly finance), relations and discipline (formerly service), teacher training and certification, resolutions, publicity, programme, religious teachers, lay teachers, superannuation, federal aid, parent-teacher, and secondary schools.[19] One of the committee chairpersons established a precedent. Sr. Maureen (Nora Dolan), Grey Sisters of the Immaculate Conception (G.S.I.C.), was the first sister to be chair of any provincial committee - the finance one. A Catholic high school teacher in Pembroke and Ottawa, a separate school principal, a strong believer in social justice, and a supporter of the initiatives of Fr. Poupore and inspector McDonald, she (and presumably both her bishop and her superior) saw no problem with leaving her convent to attend regular meetings in Toronto. She would stay at the convent of the Sisters of St. Joseph.[20] Perhaps her valuable contributions and exemplary witness assisted Cardinal Archbishop McGuigan in deciding in 1949 that religious teachers could attend evening parent-teacher meetings and could serve on executive positions of OECTA.[21] Sr. Maureen and the Cardinal paved the way for Mother Lenore.

The provincial Board of Directors consisted of the district presidents, the chairpersons of the provincial committees, and the provincial Executive. The Executive was comprised of the president, past president, first vice-president, and one member chosen by the new Board of Directors. In 1949 the Board of Directors realized that a part-time Secretary receiving a small honorarium was not adequate for a growing Association offering a multitude of services. It advertised for and interviewed candidates for the position of full-time Secretary with a salary equal to OECTA's recommended maximum for a separate school teacher. It immediately reconsidered the salary and raised it to $2400 annually with four increments of $150 to a maximum of $3000. The Secretary was given a vote on the Executive. Cecilia Rowan resigned and Marion A. Tyrrell, Toronto separate school teacher and chair of the relations and discipline committee was hired on May 14, 1949.[22]

The AGM welcomed as many voting delegates as each district wished to send. The Board of Directors and Executive were expected to attend. Here the new Executive was elected; new and amended policies and positions were discussed and put to the vote; annual reports of the president, of the members on OTF, Department of Education committees and other bodies, and of the chairpersons of OECTA's provincial committees were received and discussed. The Board of Directors, meeting two or three times a year and on an as-needed basis, prepared positions for the AGM's consideration and received questions, reports, and issues for discussion and decision from the Executive as well as monitoring its work. The Executive with the Secretariat served as the day-to-day proactive and reactive implementers of the Association's policies, aims, and constitution.

Office space at first was in Cecilia Rowan's home. In 1947 two rooms were rented in Federation House on Prince Arthur Avenue. in Yorkville.[23]

All of this was to serve the members who grew from 1570 compulsory, 150 voluntary, and 300 associate in 1945 to 2285 compulsory, 86 voluntary, and 197 associate in 1950.[24]

Unity. As with any association or union, it was not enough to collect fees from and serve the members. There had to be a code of behaviour and a unity of outlook and aims in the minds of the members in order to achieve improvement in the lot of separate schools and their teachers. This was not an easy task for a new association consisting of new and experienced teachers, teachers in isolated and populated areas, and teachers belonging to the various unofficial special interest sub-groups: lay, religious,and married and unmarried men and women.

Understandably, considerable attention was paid to the interests and contributions of the religious teachers and their effect on the aims of OECTA. In fact, as already noted, there were two separate provincial committees, one for lay teachers and one for religious teachers. After all, in 1945 there were 1141 sisters, 113 brothers, and 24 priests teaching in Catholic schools in Ontario; they constituted about half of the teaching force of the province's separate schools.[25] In 1949 this total had risen to 1728 religious teachers out of 2568 compulsory, voluntary and associate members paying fees to OECTA.[26] Since they taught for salaries considerably lower than those of their lay teacher counterparts (who were in turn paid much lower than their public school peers), they greatly assisted separate school boards, which were deprived of high school grants and taxes beyond grade ten and of corporation tax revenues, to stay financially afloat.

OECTA minutes reveal an appreciation and sensitivity of this contribution toward the survival of separate schools, while also raising particular problems with the lay teachers of the Association and with OTF. On the one hand, trustees and teachers knew that religious teachers did not pay income taxes, sacrificed certain material goods because of their vocation in separate schools, and had lower living expenses because of purchasing and spending as a group. Furthermore, there was Cardinal Archbishop McGuigan's important belief that:

> as religious teachers we must never lose sight of the fact that there will be a time when charity will demand that we give our services to the Church without any monetary recompense. Our demands should be very moderate as far as religious are concerned; not to express any more interest than is absolutely necessary in regards to finance— so that at no time will the public be able to say that our religious have not a vow of poverty and that they have an equal interest in finances with the lay teachers.[27]

On the other hand, the lay teachers felt that the low religious salaries, sometimes zero in the case of a high school teacher,[28] were holding down everyone's salaries and that the religious were drawing out of the superannuation fund more than they were paying into it. Raymond Bergin, as the lay teachers' representative, outlined their position in a 1944 letter to Miss Lynch:

> (1) It is a matter for the Religious to come to an agreement among themselves.
> (2) If their demand and their reason for such is legitimate we, the Lay Teachers will be agreeable.
> (3) Lay teachers THROUGH AN ACT OF THE LEGISLATURE SHOULD BE PROTECTED AGAINST BEING REPLACED BY RELIGIOUS. We should have air-tight means of preventing school boards from replacing Lay with Religious for economic or other reasons....[29]

Miss Prunty proposed an interesting solution to the problem: 50 per cent of the positions in Catholic schools would be given to lay teachers.[30] As the proportion of lay and religious teachers dramatically shifted in favour of the former in the 1950s and 1960s, this would have presented some dilemmas.

A related matter was OTF's seeking of the support of all the affiliates for a provincial minimum salary and a schedule with government grants and legislation to make them possible. Should the religious be included? The French religious wanted the same salary as the French lay teachers; the English religious agreed with Cardinal Archbishop McGuigan.[31] The issue was potentially divisive for OECTA and required delicate treatment. One of Miss Rowan's letters to Miss Lynch reveal how vexatious the issues were to her:

> I started to write last evening. Then went to the phone and called Fr. Poupore and as my mind was so muddled I tore up the letter....All the Religious seem so opposed to asking the same as Lay. They seem to feel

> that as soon as they ask for the same salary as Lay then their vows of Charity and Poverty are thrown in the discard. Fr. Poupore felt this way all along but we are trying to work in harmony with the A.E.F.[sic] and they were keen for equalization. Now Margaret all our Lay teachers feel that it will be [to] our advantage if the Religious ask for less. Sr. Maureen and Father feel that the Lay Catholics will be given the same as the others if the Gov. hasn't to meet too great an expense in adjusting the religious. I have heard so many angles that my poor brain is a bit addled. Miss Prunty said something to the effect that if the profession is made so attractive for the religious then communities will turn out more teachers and shove out the Lay. The AEF seems to feel if the salaries are not equalized then religious will be engaged because they are cheaper - the one antipodal of the other.[32]

As early as 1944 Frank McElligott on the Executive called for the "striking reform" of religious teachers receiving a salary equal to lay teachers.[33] But in 1945 the religious teachers committee pointed out how such a practice would place many separate school boards in financial jeopardy. Fathers Guinan and Poupore stated that every consideration was being given to the position of the lay teachers, but that definite arrangements regarding religious teachers could not be reached without the consent of the Bishops. The Executive resolved that lay teachers' salaries were to be equal to those of public school teachers and that religious teachers were to receive a "substantial raise", provided that increased government grants materialized in amounts sufficient to prevent any additional burdens on the taxpayer stemming from these two recommendations. A sub-committee of five religious teachers was struck to meet with the Bishops.[34] Because sufficient grants were not forthcoming to enable separate school boards to pay salaries at the proposed OTF level, OECTA was unable to unite with OTF on the matter of a minimum salary for all teachers and the issue continued to percolate. Fr. Harrigan expressed his belief in the principle of equal salaries for all teachers, but immediately acknowledged that religious teachers should not lose their certificates for accepting a lower salary.[35]

In 1947, the Executive minutes reported a compromise: the lay teachers were to press for a minimum salary of $1500, the religious for $800 to $1000.[36] In 1948 the Board of Directors decided to retain the same salary schedule as before, because the OTF recommended $1800 minimum for religious and lay teachers would be impossible for separate school boards.[37] Finally, in 1950 a solution was reached that lasted for over fifteen years. An AGM resolution, approved by the Bishops, was passed stating that religious teachers were to be paid two-thirds of the lay teachers salary.[38] Therefore, OECTA could now push for higher salaries and separate school boards would still benefit financially from the employment of religious teachers.

A related contentious issue was that of the teacher's contract. OECTA, as well as the other affiliates, insisted that school boards offer the teacher the protection of an individual contract worded according to the Department of Education recommended format. But the religious orders traditionally had notified the separate school boards during the summer of how many religious teachers they were allocating and what schools and grades they would staff. The agreement was somewhat one-way - a letter to the board - and did not involve the signing of any contracts. After all, the Orders were offering a religious and charitable service. OECTA first raised the problem at the 1947 AGM. The religious teachers committee was opposed to individual contracts for the religious, but recommended that the Orders inform school boards by June 1 how many staff members they would be sending and by no later than August 15 the names of the staff. Raymond Bergin asked the committee where OECTA would stand if the Hope Commission recommended individual contracts for religious teachers.[39] Indeed, it did so in 1950.[40] The practice, however, was not changed during these early years of OECTA.

The custom of having a religious teacher as principal wherever possible had been a long-standing one. Such a person could offer excellent leadership in delivering a total curriculum integrated with a Christian values system. This had two side effects. First, OTF in 1951 sent a resolution to each of the affiliates for their endorsement of a five-year teaching experience and special course requirement to become a principal. OECTA defeated the resolution with the following rationale: the present method was good enough (that is, selecting from qualified teachers); it would be burdensome for potential principals to require them to take a Departmental course when they were already working on a B.A.; too many teachers would take the qualifying course and, therefore, there would be a surplus of paper-qualified principals (an argument that often recurred when the idea of offering a course for potential school inspectors came up); and religious teachers were often principals in a school for one or two years, then moved to another school - a course requirement would cause hardship for these people.[41]

Second, the lay teachers, particularly the male ones, felt that promotion in separate schools was often closed to them. The male teachers knew that it was often difficult to get even a regular teaching position with a separate school board, because trustees believed that potential or actual husbands and fathers required salaries higher than the board wished to or could pay. President Perdue put it succinctly: "the male teacher as a Catholic teacher in Ontario is looked upon as an expensive luxury."[42] To aspire to a principalship in such an environment seemed unreasonable. And to conceive of a lay principal with religious teachers on the staff was akin to imagining something unnatural for a separate school board.

In 1945, Raymond Bergin, as chairman of the lay teachers committee, was wondering what topic the committee should address for the upcoming annual meeting. Fr. Poupore wanted religious order members to, as Fr. Guinan of the religious teachers committee put it, "make a greater effort to understand the problems of the lay teacher."[43] Fr. Poupore suggested and Bergin agreed that the topic of religious teachers working for lay principals would be appropriate.[44] The discussion of the report at the AGM resulted in several pages of minutes conveying strongly felt convictions articulated by Bergin and Brother Arnold of the Christian Brothers. They focussed on the section of the lay teachers' report entitled "Security", which dealt with the matter Fr. Poupore had suggested. Brother Arnold took issue with the report for four reasons. First, he objected to the fact that the Bishops had seen the report before the AGM delegates. Second, he took offence to references in the report to religious teachers' being hired because they were "cheaper". Third, he took particular umbrage over the continuous references to sisters without the brothers once being mentioned. Fourth, he pointed out that it was contrary to the constitution of most religious orders for a member to teach for a lay principal. Late in the afternoon the meeting was adjourned without the committee's report being accepted. The next day the report was adopted with the "Security" section left out.

The passage of time and the gradual slow increase in the appointment of lay principals took care of the problem. In 1945, wherever an Order of sisters was teaching for a separate school board, it was often the accepted practice that at least two sisters would be assigned by the Order to certain schools and that one of the sisters at each of those schools would be the principal. Thus in many towns and cities the majority of the board's principals were sisters. But by 1955 the sisters were unable to keep up with the expansion of the separate schools; by 1965 the expansion as well as a decline in the number of religious vocations resulted in the vast majority of the separate school principals being laymen. (This would give rise in the 1980s to another issue.)

Another small issue that had to be resolved was whether or not the religious teachers would be able to break the routines of their community life and serve on OECTA executives. After all, not only were they helping the separate school system immensely with their witness and their low wages, but also they, as the majority of the Association's members, were in a strong position to forward the Association's aims. The Executive had the Secretary write the religious communities asking if their members could serve on the provincial offices. In her 1949 report to the Board of Directors Miss Tyrrell summarized eight replies, four against and four in support of their sisters assuming such positions. The sticking point for the Orders was the lack of time the sisters had. Three Sisters of St. Joseph communities felt that since the religious teachers constituted most of the membership they should be willing to share the responsibilities.[45] Changing times would solve this problem.

The lay female teachers in OECTA also had, they believed, particular needs and problems that were potentially divisive to the unity of the Association. For example, in the matter of salaries, the London separate school board was not atypical with its salary provisions. It had four categories of teachers, each paid less than the categories above it: at the top were male teachers (a very small proportion of the staff), then, in descending order, single female teachers, married female teachers (who were not given permanent contracts), and religious teachers. It took several years for the married women teachers to bring their problems on a unified basis to OECTA. But the single female teachers of Toronto demanded and got special treatment from the Association on the membership questions right at the start of OTF.

Section 10 (j) of the *Teaching Profession Act* stated that the OTF's Board of Governors, subject to the approval of the Lieutenant-Governor in Council, could make regulations "providing for the establishment of branches of the Federation". OTF, by regulation, did establish five affiliates and moved toward linking compulsory membership in an affiliate to the type of school in which the teacher was working. The Catholic female teachers of the Toronto Separate School Board objected to this intention of OTF's and at the meetings in Ottawa and Toronto to establish OECTA explained their position. Being independent but low-paid, female teachers in Toronto's separate schools believed that they needed the protection, help, and benefits, particularly group medical and life insurance ones, that FWTAO offered. Enough of them joined FWTAO to form their own unit of the federation, the

Toronto Separate Lay Women Teachers' Association. An appreciable number of their members felt they would be risking giving up the benefits of belonging to FWTAO if they switched to the new OECTA. Therefore, OTF and OECTA left it optional for these teachers to be in either association. However, OTF soon began to submit annually to the affiliates the resolution that compulsory membership be dependent on the school in which the teacher taught. OECTA for the first five years did not approve of the resolution, probably because of its commitment to the Toronto teachers.[46] In 1950 the issue came to a head.

Fr. Priester had stated in 1944 that "many Catholic teachers are leaving the Women's Federation to become regular members of the English Catholic Teachers' Federation."[47] But six years later many had still not followed the example of Marion Tyrrell and others. In February 1950, the OECTA Executive decided it was time to support the OTF resolution and its minutes recorded that Cecilia Rowan would be preparing and presenting a brief to the Toronto Separate Lay Women Teachers' Association on why all Roman Catholics should belong to OECTA. However, that April the Board of Directors approved that, since the Toronto Catholic FWTAO members would most unwillingly become OECTA members, the OTF resolution should be tabled for at least a year.[48] This decision was not taken lightly at the AGM. Brother Cornelius, referring to the motion to support the OTF resolution, stated that "I would not like to see it sit there idle just like that. I would recommend that the Executive give particularly Toronto District some direction in an attempt to educate the members of our district who are opposed to that motion."[49] Patrick Perdue worded the same thought more strongly:

> I would like, as one special wish, to see all Catholic teachers in the Province members of our organization. There is no idea of compulsion in that; it is only a very sincere wish on my part that everybody become an active member. It is rather embarrassing to our organization to think we are not good enough for even our own Catholic teachers.[50]

In the early 1950s OECTA approved the resolution that the Board of Governors had passed in 1947. With similar wording it became an OTF by-law:

(a) That the fees and membership of teachers in Public, Separate and Secondary Schools go to that Federation to which the teachers of that school belong in virtue of their positions, namely:

Public School Men ....O.P.S.M.T.F.

Public School Women..F.W.T.A.O.
Secondary & Continuation School Teachers............O.S.S.T.F.
Separate School Teachers.......................................O.E.C.T.A.
Teachers in public or separate schools where with the permission of the Minister, French is a language of instruction......A.E.F.O.

(b) That any request to change from one affiliated body to another by a member of the Federation be referred to the Executive of OTF who, in conjunction with the Executives of the affiliate concerned, will have the power to change the affiliate of the member, for reason. (It is understood that this is without prejudice to any existing rules for associate membership.)[51]

It was only human nature that the special interests of the lay, religious, male, and female teachers would from time to time cause some tension, especially given the material conditions of separate schools and society's attitudes to working women in those days. But the early years of OECTA showed that the total membership's respect for the aims of the Association and for each other would likely bring about continued consensus-building and conflict resolution. OECTA's concern for and encouragement of ethical behaviour would aid in maintaining unity.

Ethics. Befitting a professional organization, OTF, with input from the five affiliates, developed a Code of Ethics, which the *OECTA News*, for the education of its recipients, printed. It covered proper teacher behaviour and relations with school boards, other teachers, administrators, pupils, parents, the federation, and the community. The same article also reminded teachers that the *Regulation Made Under The Teaching Profession Act* empowered OTF to recommend to the Minister of Education suspension or cancellation of a teacher's certificate.[52] To educate, watch over, and, if necessary, discipline its members, OECTA had set up a Relations and Discipline Committee. (Of course, this committee also existed to assist the teacher when trustees, administrators, parents, or students treated her/him unjustly or unfairly.)

The chair of the Relations and Discipline Committee for a number of the early years was Marion Tyrrell. Her reports reveal the no-nonsense, take-charge attitude of a teacher with high expectations for her charges. They also show that the vast majority of OECTA's members lived up to her standards. The most common matters with which she dealt were teachers bargaining as individuals and teachers illegally breaking a contract. Both of these actions had serious repercussions. The first demonstrated a lack of awareness about the need for group unity in salary matters and the negative consequences of underbidding. The second undercut the Association's efforts to ensure that all school boards gave all their teachers the security of a contract. In 1946 and 1949 the Board of Directors discussed the necessity of taking disciplinary action with teachers who did not observe the conditions of her/his contract and the unethical behaviour of a teacher bargaining on her/hisown behalf.[53] The AGM in 1948 and 1950 heard from Miss Tyrrell that teachers risked having their certificates suspended if they did not sign a contract,[54] that the incidents of teachers' breaking contracts were increasing, and that it was unethical for an individual teacher or part of a staff to negotiate with a board without approval of the entire staff.[55] Thus, it is not surprising that in 1947, acting on a report of the Relations and Discipline Committee, OTF asked the Minister to suspend the certificates of two teachers for breach of contract.[56]

However, although relations and discipline cases must have taken up considerable time and effort on the part of the committee, they were very few in number. In 1951 the committee reported that there were only seventeen problems in total for that year. These included unfair dismissals, resignations at a time not mutually agreed upon, unsatisfactory salary deductions, unreasonable change of position, dismissal at other than the legal date, and breach of contract. The latter were referred to OTF and then the Minister for suspension of certificate.[57]

The Relations and Discipline Committee also reported on some "precariously near cases" of a teacher criticizing a colleague without putting the criticism in writing and showing it to her/him first, giving the recipient a forty-eight-hour opportunity to reply to it before it went to anyone else.[58] There were no formal unethical actions in the record in this area in these first seven years of OECTA.

There was, understandably, some controversy over the part of the OTF Code of Ethics which states that it is unprofessional for a teacher to accept a salary under the approved provincial schedule. Fr. Harrigan at the 1947 AGM asked what the Association would do if a member did accept such a salary.[59] A resolution to the 1948 AGM that teachers get permission from OECTA to accept a salary less than the recommended minimum was rejected. The members realized that some separate school boards could not afford the provincially recommended salary scale and that, in any case, there were no sanctions available.[60]

Smaller recalled conversations with teachers who were confused by this "double" message.

Although there were few cases of unethical conduct by teachers, Marion Tyrrell had little tolerance for these teachers. She told the Board of Directors that no affiliate had a satisfactory method for dealing with teachers who bargained individually. She explained that OSSTF either ostracized them, cited them in its magazine, or expelled them.[61] It is hard to imagine such threatening actions as not being deterrents, but for Miss Tyrrell they were not punitive enough.

According to Miss Lynch in a memorandum written after the period of the 1940s and 1950s, "Individual bargaining has become a thing of the past."[62] On this topic of ethics, Marion Tyrrell, for her efforts, deserves the last word. In a report to the Board of Directors she wrote that "OECTA has a well-behaved group of members."[63]

Salary Negotiating. A top, if not the top, priority for OECTA was to help its members obtain a living wage. The situation in 1944 was not good. A statutory minimum of $500 a year had been passed at the height of the Depression[64] to force school boards to pay something, but neither OTC nor OTF had been able to get new minimum-salary legislation passed. With the improved economy of the war years the average salary of an Ontario teacher in 1940 was $1130,[65] no great sum, and matters had not improved since. The Minister's Report for 1944 listed the following average annual salaries for elementary school teachers:

		City	Town	Rural
Separate	M.	$1131	$1132	$1236*
School	F.	845	885	1017*
Public	M.	2294	1797	1148
School	F.	1443	1082	970 [66]

Comparative annual salaries for 1945 were also illuminating for teacher negotiators:

Plasterers	$2425
Bricklayers	2121
Brewery bottlers	1590

Truck drivers	1373
Elementary school teachers	1209 [67]

One could sympathize with the necessity of paying well the people who built houses, provided alcoholic refreshment, and transported goods, but one would probably have expected society to put at least an equal value on the people who educated children. Exacerbating this condition of low salaries was post war inflation. According to Statistics Canada, between 1945 and 1950 the cost of living rose 37 per cent.

Another problem was the gap between male and female teachers' salaries. Also, although the large number of female religious, most of whom earned only $600 a year, pulled down the separate school average, the difference between public and separate school salaries was still unconscionably large.

* Salaries were lower in the urban separate schools because of the higher number of lower-paid religious teachers.

To complicate this situation of very low salaries for OECTA was the expectation that religious teachers should accept this $600 salary and lay teachers should work for less than their public school counterparts in order to assist the separate school boards with their frugal revenues.

The traditional practices and mind-sets of trustees and teachers when it came to negotiating salaries also presented OTF and its affiliates with serious problems. Bryan Downie in his analysis of collective bargaining in Ontario described various stages. By the 1940s the only positive characteristic for teachers was that school boards had been negotiating with representative groups of teachers. However, such negotiations were informal and strictly voluntary on the part of the board. The trustees could refuse to recognize a teachers' bargaining committee or could withdraw from negotiations unilaterally. At first they limited discussion to salaries and only with time did they allow exploration of topics like insurance plans and leave policies. These "salary agreements" often were not recorded in writing; gradually, school board motions or jointly signed memoranda came into practice. In the absence of any legislation on teachers' collective bargaining, except for a uniform compulsory contract that FWTAO, OPMSTF, OSSTF, and the Trustees' and Ratepayers' Association agreed on in 1928 and saw legislated in 1931,[68] the teachers had no right to bargain, the legality of a strike was "up in the air", and dates for notice to bargain, expiration of a contract, etc., were "murky". OTC had reached a "gentleman's agreement" with the Ontario School Trustees' Council (OSTC) that negotiations at the local level would be between the school board and the local affiliate, that there would be set procedures and timing for the negotiating process, and that, if necessary, representatives from the provincial associations could be asked by the local negotiators to come to a "conference meeting" for "joint mediation". This early version of a provincial "takeover" often entailed, in the case of the Executive and the Salary Negotiating Committee of OECTA, people like Patrick Perdue leaving home on a Friday night after teaching all week to negotiate through the weekend with a group of trustees in some faraway town.[69] Downie cites Donald Noone's three stages of transition from low teacher power to power equality relative to that of the trustees and labels the 1940s as the lowest stage marked by trustees' excluding teachers from decision making and using delay tactics, and by teachers' behaving with passivity, deference, and gratitude for any salary increase.[70]

On the other hand, there was room for some optimism. Firstly, the Catholic teachers were now organized provincially; the OSSTA did recognize OECTA at the provincial and local level. Secondly, the *Saskatchewan Teachers' Salary Negotiation Act*, which would make collective bargaining for salaries and allowances mandatory, was to be passed before the end of the decade. Thirdly, although the general unemployment and the surplus of teachers during the Depression and the wage controls during the war had kept teachers' salaries low, pupil enrolments were beginning to rise and teachers suddenly were in short supply.[71] Finally, Premier Drew was now increasing the government grants for education, the Hope Commission was studying a minimum salary schedule for teachers, which they would later recommend[72], and, as W. G. Fleming, Ontarian educational historian, wrote, "there was general agreement both inside and outside the teaching profession that salaries were much too low."[73]

How did OECTA manage salary matters in this environment? The mechanism was the key. The first AGM established a finance committee (soon renamed the budget committee). Among its tasks it set guidelines for each negotiating unit to follow, required these bargainers to get authorization from it before accepting a board offer inferior to the guidelines,[74] provided data and comparative salaries, and served as negotiators at the local level when the process was in danger of breaking down. The first chair of this committee was Sr. Maureen. Whether this was a deliberate tactic or not, the choice was fortuitous. Mrs. James

Harrington, chairperson of the Special Committee of Rural Teachers wrote in the Association's magazine that, "Many of our rural teachers are forced to live under conditions that are disgraceful."[75] Her comment may not have carried a great deal of weight but a sister, when addressing the bishops or bargaining with trustees, well represented by priests, could say such things and focussed attention. Like some accountant offering indisputable numbers, Sr. Maureen even broke down the annual living expenses of a religious teacher to two decimal places ($717.50) to prove that a salary of $600 was inadequate.[76]

Once Marion Tyrrell was hired as full-time Secretary, she worked closely with the finance committee. Together they would annually advise teachers to accept or reject a board offer and occasionally would censure teachers for unprofessional approaches to the board.[77] With ideas from OTF and the other affiliates, they developed strategies and arguments.

An immediate task was to develop a recommended salary schedule. OTF had already done so with the novelty of "increments" for experience: the recommended salaries for elementary school teachers ranged from $1800 to $2700 with increments of $100.[78] FWTAO had introduced this idea and in 1950 the Hope Commission would endorse it.[79] However, as discussed above, this schedule was too high for separate school boards and too big a leap from existing separate school salaries. The Drew government proposed minimum-salary legislation to OTF and, aware of the problem this would create for separate school boards, intended to leave them out of the legislation. OTF asked Miss Lynch's position and applied some pressure. Mr. McLeod began calling members of the OECTA executive and Miss Noonan contacted Miss Lynch to urge consent to their being left out of the legislation.

> When Miss Noonan called me she asked me if I had made up my mind and referred to the future of our Fed. Did we want to take the responsibility for not having the Min. set for four thousand Secondary Trs. and 13,000 Elem. Trs.? The Dept. could not see its way clear to include Lay Trs. of S. Schools.[80]

Miss Lynch responded to her first major challenge with logic and firmness. After consulting with Mr. Bergin, who was indignant about the telephone call he had received, she told Miss Noonan that OECTA "could not consent to an inequality.... If I hadn't, we would have closed the doors forever on any future opportunities and relegated ourselves to the position of second class citizens."[81] The Minister discarded the idea (without considering solving the real problem, the relative poverty of separate school boards) and, in any case, felt free to postpone any further such initiatives until the Hope Commission would complete its four-year study.[82] (This excuse did not apply when the Minister of Education in a few years would reorganize the school system without waiting for the Hope Report. The Minister's inaction in retrospect was arguably positive for the teaching profession. A legislated minimum salary schedule could have led to provincial salary negotiating as in some other parts of Canada. A move to ask the government to pay the total costs of salaries, contemplated by the AGM in 1946, would have been more dangerous still for the same reason.[83])

Therefore, OECTA, with about 75 per cent of its members receiving salaries well below the OTF schedule, developed its own salary scale. Sr. Maureen recommended minimums of $800 for religious teachers, $1200 for lay teachers, $2000 for high school teachers, with six $100 increments given every two years over twelve years. In addition, teachers with a B.A. would receive an extra $100, and with a special education certificate $50. Principals of schools with more than one classroom would be paid $150 per classroom.[84] To support the concept, OECTA and other affiliates cited Great Britain's wide use of the Burkham scale.[85] Even with this lower schedule OECTA, recognizing conditions especially with some rural separate school boards, gave the negotiators flexibility by specifying that it was not unethical for a teacher to accept a salary less than the recommended one.[86]

As a second priority, negotiators were encouraged to go after group medical and life insurance plans, with the board paying a share of the premiums, and cumulative sick leave plans.[87] Trustees opposed these by arguing that they did not belong with discussions about "salary agreements". Further down the list, but still coming up in some negotiations, were the requests for one day a month during which the principal would be released from teaching, twelve monthly salary payments instead of ten (an idea boards eventually accepted when they calculated that they saved bank interest), and an allowance for the accumulation of one year or more toward a B.A. The latter idea engendered much discussion centring on whether or not university work produced a better teacher and on how classroom work could suffer if the teacher spent too much time on her/his studies while taking night courses. The 1949 AGM approved the concept only in principle after Patrick Perdue urged that OECTA "sidetrack this for the moment".[88] As for "working conditions", this appeared to be a forbidden topic for trustees, although in 1950 OECTA did discuss with OSSTA the topic of lunchroom supervision.[89]

Besides the matter of salaries and benefits there was the issue of the teacher's contract. It was one thing to enforce signing and observing contracts on the membership; it was another matter to get boards to observe the details of the contract, particularly with regard to termination and pay dates. The Department of Education was unwilling to enforce such details,[90] so OECTA had to educate its membership and the trustees.

With all of these contractual and salary matters, careful judgment was required. On the one hand, higher salaries meant higher mill rates, often higher than the local public school ones. This in turn could mean separate school supporters, especially those with businesses or without children, switching their taxes to public school support. And for separate schools this in turn could result in reduced salaries or higher pupil loading or fewer teachers for fewer children. On the other hand, the salaries were much too low and there was a growing awareness that teachers, compared to Catholic parents and taxpayers, were carrying an inordinate part of the burden. The strategy was to attack the problem carefully on two fronts: negotiate with separate school boards for higher salaries even where this meant some financial difficulties for the trustees; and approach the Minister of Education persistently with regard to the unfair and inadequate grant structure[91] and the difficulties boards were having. Over time this plan worked.

OECTA believed the arguments for improving teachers' salaries and securing benefits were sufficiently strong to warrant educating the Ontario Bishops, the trustees, and the public. Formal meetings were held with OSSTA, ECEAO, and the Bishops. A public relations campaign was conducted in Toronto to educate taxpayers on the need to pay higher school taxes to maintain a good teaching staff. In the Ottawa district, OECTA even managed to get taxpayer assistance in getting out the message.[92]

The arguments used with these groups were not difficult to find. The Papal encyclicals explored the concept of the just wage and OECTA compared it to the "deplorable states of teachers".[93] Secondly, negotiators pointed to the cost of living rising "alarmingly". (One would need a new adverb for the 1970s and 1980s.) Thirdly, OECTA explained to trustees that low salaries were causing good teachers to quit the profession, leaving the schools with a greater proportion of student teachers possessing lower academic qualifications.[94] In a brief to all the Archbishops and Bishops of Ontario, the Association reiterated most of these arguments and made a few other points. Firstly, low salaries were causing teacher shortages and the reduction of entrance requirements to Normal School. Secondly, unsatisfactory salaries were forcing teachers to supplement their income by working after school hours and during holidays. "This means that they go to school tired out, with frayed nerves, worrying because of lack of funds." Thirdly, the prestige of the profession as a whole was falling. Fourthly, separate schools, because of the low salaries, had a reputation inferior to that of public schools, with the result that a number of Catholics were sending their children to public schools. Fifthly, the low wages were producing inadequate pensions and a poor standard of living.[95]

One effective strategy for improving salaries developed as it became necessary for boards to compete for teachers: OECTA suggested that boards advertise their salary scale along with the teacher openings.[96] This became standard procedure before very long.

In the event that none of this worked and local negotiations slowed to a crawl or broke down, OECTA on occasion used the pink-listing weapon.[97] This particular sanction entailed OECTA's advising all its members that a school board was "in dispute" with its teachers and that no member should accept a position with this board until further notification. Such action would result in no affiliate support in any possible future problems of a teacher who accepted a position with a pink-listed board. Another sanction, which was used on its own as well as in conjunction with pink-listing, involved the local bargainers collecting written resignations from all or most of the teachers and threatening the board with mass resignation. As teacher shortages developed, this became useful and less risky than actually resigning.

Between 1944 and 1951 there was considerable progress, even though, in the minds of OECTA, much remained to be done. The budget committee reported in 1949 that 400 teachers were making $1100 to $1599, 500 up to $1999, 80 above $2000, 20 below $1100, and most religious teachers receiving $800.[98] In 1950, 50 per cent of the separate school teachers were making $2250 or more.[99] The Hamilton Separate School Board had a medical plan for which it paid 50 per cent. The separate school boards in Kingston, Kitchener, and Ottawa were studying the pros and cons of cumulative sick leave plans.[100]

OECTA was optimistic enough to discuss with OSSTA in 1950 the desirability of all boards' providing such plans as well as accident insurance.[101] The Association even attempted to discuss working conditions with the Department of Education and OSSTA. The 1951 AGM moved that lunchroom supervision be on the OTF Trustee-Teacher Conference agenda. The 1947 AGM decided to ask the Department for a definition of "class" since some school boards were doubling up when a teacher was absent and no substitute teacher was available; the following year it resolved to ask the Department to limit the PTR, but Dr. Althouse replied that it was impossible to do so because of a teacher shortage.[102]

With progress on a united front, OECTA began looking at the issue of equal pay for equal work and equal qualifications. In 1946 CTF and OTF endorsed this position, but OECTA cautiously took the matter under study by setting up a special committee. By 1946 Margaret Lynch was able to express her pleasure that it was then possible for the Association to believe in and support the principle.[103] Action awaited the next decade, but, as Cecilia Reynolds described, the way had been paved.

> Assisted by increased membership and funds, the federations were better able to apply pressure for salary improvement and for the use of credentials rather than personal characteristics in hiring practices. In response to these pressures, the Toronto Board began relying more heavily on "objective" qualifications in order to screen candidates for teaching jobs. This shift was important because it paved the way for teachers' later arguments for equitable treatment regardless of such characteristics as ethnicity, race, or sex. Also, women were able to insist that salaries be based on qualifications and experience and that men should not automatically receive a higher teaching salary.[104]

Protection. Equal in importance to a living wage for the teacher was protection from capricious or unjust dismissal, a not uncommon occurrence.[105] The relations and discipline committee strongly advised the OECTA membership to accept a teaching position only when a contract was offered. The standard form had been developed by the Department of Education in 1943,[106] only the year before the federation's inception; therefore, the practice of using individual written contracts was not yet universal. The Executive cited a Court of Appeal judgment deciding that a teacher without a contract was entitled to not more than three months' salary when dismissed without notice; this was to emphasize the relations and discipline committee's advice.[107] In 1947 the contract situation improved for teachers. If the board did not terminate the teacher by December 1 or June 1, then the contract remained in force. The teacher, in turn, had to observe these dates if s/he intended to resign.[108]

The second protection against arbitrary dismissal was the Board of Reference. This appeal procedure had been legislated after many years of trustee opposition. One educational historian considered the statute possibly "the most important landmark in legislation for the improvement of the status of the teacher since the passing of the *Superannuation Act* in 1917."[109] As early as 1923 the three federations then in existence approached the Minister to establish Boards of Reference and continued to press for the legislation for fifteen years.[110] In 1936 the Minister of Education at the OEA annual convention was still able to say he was "not in favour of any such innovation,"[111] even though such legislation existed in western Canada. Finally, in 1938, "*An Act respecting Disputes between Teachers and Boards*" was passed.[112]

This statute established the framework of the present legislation. A teacher or board could apply to the Minister if it was felt that dismissal by the board or resignation by the teacher was done in an unsatisfactory manner. The request for a Board of Reference had to be sent to the Minister within ten days. The Minister then could grant it, after receiving security for costs from the appealer. The board and the teacher were each then to name a representative to the board, and the Minister appointed a judge to chair it. The school board was not to replace the teacher with a contract until the time for applying for a Board of Reference elapsed or until ten days after the Minister received the Board of Reference's report.

The Act laid down important precedents, but left a few questions. What was the Minister to do with the report? Did the school board or the teacher have to comply with the Board of Reference's decision? What choice did the Board of Reference have if it found the dismissal improper? Amendments to this statute in 1943 improved the law in some ways, but gave unsatisfactory answers to the teachers for two of these questions. The amendments gave the teacher or board twenty days instead of ten to ask for a Board of Reference, required every dismissal or termination to be in writing with reasons furnished, and stipulated no grants for the school board and possible suspension of the teacher's certificate if either of the two parties did not comply with the Minister's directions after the Board of Reference's decision. On the other hand, one amendment stated that the Minister, upon receiving a request for a Board of Reference, could direct the teacher's contract with the school board to continue for up to a year, and another provided that, where the Board of Reference recommended continuance of the contract for up to a year, the Minister was to so direct the board.[113] These one-year clauses spawned references in OECTA minutes to the necessity of improving this legislation. Perhaps the clause was designed to provide either a "cooling-off" period for relations between the board and the teacher to improve or time for the teacher to secure a position with another board. Obviously, this was not a sufficient redress for unjust dismissal.

The *Teachers' Board of Reference Act* of 1946 did not address the problem. It merely changed the request period to fifteen days, specified more precisely that the teacher could not sign another contract until the Board of Reference procedure was finished, stated that the Board of Reference was to be held "in camera", presumably to protect the teacher's name (a practice that was to cause problems about thirty years later), and stipulated that where the applicant did not supply her/his representative to the board, the reference was not to proceed, but, where the other party did not do so, the judge was to name the secondd representative.[114]

In 1949 *An Act to amend the Teachers' Board of Reference Act,* 1946 removed the one-year clauses.[115] This meant that the teacher was either reinstated with her/his permanent contract or the teacher's dismissal was upheld.

As a result of this legislation the Secretary and relations and discipline committee of OECTA were to take on the serious responsibilities of advising a teacher whether or not to ask for a Board of Reference, supplying a representative to the Board of Reference, and paying for a lawyer for the teacher, if it felt the teacher should have a Board of Reference. Although there were no Boards of Reference referred to in the minutes between 1944 and 1951, in 1950 there was a special Executive meeting about two teachers who had been allegedly unsatisfactorily dismissed; Executive members were sent to investigate the matter.[196] Miss Tyrrell was quite clear about the importance of contracts and Boards of Reference. "In no case should a teacher resign if he becomes involved in a dispute with the Board, Inspector, or Principal before seeking help or advice from his Federation."[117]

One problem remained until the 1980s. In 1950 OECTA's legislation committee approved of the probationary contract for beginning teachers with less than three years' experience (for two years), or for teachers with more than two years' experience but new to the board (for one year), even though such teachers could not ask for a Board of Reference and school boards did not have to furnish reasons for terminations of probationary contracts. Fr. Poupore's reasoning was as follows: "If every probationary teacher could call for a Board of Reference, the Board would be almost compelled to keep a probationary teacher on the staff. In other words, there would be no sense in having a probationary teacher at all."[118] (Eventually there would be legal problems with this clause in the statute.)

OTF sought additional protection for the teachers by lobbying for arbitration legislation. Matters advanced in 1949 as far as a draft statute which provided for the right of OTF to demand arbitration from a school board for a teacher who was in disagreement with her/his employer over salary matters. However, the bill never came to the legislature before the end of the session and it was not resurrected in the following year.

Pensions. Hand in hand with the concern for a living wage and job security went the need to provide for old age, the retirement years. As the salaries rose, so would the pensions for teachers, provided the calculations were adequate.

The original plan was more welfare than pension. In 1853 the government established a fund for "worn-out common school teachers" which by 1860 was paying an average pension of $26.54 a year. Society's attitude that males needed pensions whereas females, apparently maintained by fathers, husbands, or children, did not require them was reflected in the 1871 stipulation that it was compulsory for male public school teachers to contribute to the pension plan, but voluntary for their female counterparts.[119] Similar divisive male/female pension attitudes would persist until fairly recent times, thereby contributing both to the lack of unity at first in the OECTA membership, discussed earlier, and to OTF's inability in the beginning to present a united front when requesting improvements in the pension plan from the government. Although the Ontario Teachers' Alliance, which consisted of male and female teachers, had successfully urged the 1917 *Teachers' Superannuation Act* on the government, Doris French, the FWTAO historian, wrote that young female teachers were not particularly interested in the new legislation since they had no intention of staying in teaching long enough to qualify for a pension, and elderly female teachers felt a pension for one of their own was charity. Thus, it was only

OPSMTF that pushed for improvements in the legislation for many years.[120] Other examples of differentiated treatment of male and female teachers existed in the pension plan during the early years of OECTA: females could apply for a pension at age sixty-two, males had to wait until the age sixty-five (the "weaker sex" phenomenon?); the widow, not the widower, received 50 per cent of her spouse's pension. Not surprisingly, the female members of OECTA at first approved of provision for dependents of deceased teachers only if the additional costs to the pension plan would be borne by the government and by those teachers desiring these new clauses, and disapproved of the age of retirement for male teachers being lowered to age sixty-two until equal pay for equal work was the norm.[121]

All of this perhaps slowed progress on superannuation legislation, and progress was necessary. As Miss Lynch put it, focussing on pension benefits meant "the difference between rocking on our own front porch or on the veranda of the old age home."[122] However, improvements did take place between 1944 and 1951.[123]

A typical pension in 1944 for a separate school teacher was $600 x 60 per cent or $360 a year. OECTA and the other affiliates through OTF decided to seek the following improvements:

- eligibility for a type A pension at age sixty with thirty-five years' experience or forty years' experience regardless of age;
- eligibility for a reduced pension (B) at age sixty with more than twenty-five years' and less than thirty-five years' experience;
- a disability pension with at least fifteen years in the plan;
- an increase from 60 per cent to 70 per cent for the maximum percentage of the average salary (e.g., 35 x 2 per cen t);
- a pension for widows or dependants up to age eighteen of a deceased pensioned teacher;
- an average salary based on the last ten years of teaching;
- a minimum pension of $730 a year and a maximum of $1800; and
- a 5 per cent contribution from the government and the teacher.[124]

The amended *Teachers' Superannuation Act* of 1949 responded favourably to these requests with some variations: (1) in order to retire teachers had to be age sixty-two with thirty-five years of teaching or forty years regardless of age, unless disabled; (2) a disabled teacher who could work outside the profession was to receive 25 per cent less than one who could not work at all; (3) the average salary was to be based on the last fifteen years of teaching; (4) the government would contribute 4 per cent to the fund, the teachers 6 per cent. (5) The resulting pensions ranged from $600 to $3000.If the calculations resulted in less than $600, the minimum pension was $600.[125]

OECTA had some other aims unique to its special interests. It wanted special help for teachers receiving very low pensions, a group with a large number of retired separate school teachers. Secondly, because separate schools were limited to grade ten, OECTA had some members teaching part-time or full-time in private Catholic high schools; it wanted them to be eligible for membership in the pension plan. Thirdly, it wanted a member on the Superannuation Commission. It did not make an issue of mandatory retirement at age sixty-five, but it disapproved of the idea.[126] The Association succeeded in 1949 with its three aims. However, it had to rotate a member on the Commission with AEFO. OECTA's first commissioner was Miss Eva Deshaw, the first president of the Windsor district and "a woman of action"[127].

Department of Education Grants. Higher salaries and an improved pension plan required adequate funding. Premier Drew had promised to implement the Committee on the Costs of Education's recommendation to have the government pay a higher share of educational costs. He pledged 50 per cent, but Leslie Frost, the provincial treasurer, appalled at the costs of such a promise, in 1944 changed the funding plan to 50 per cent of "approved costs" (that is,. the school board with grants and taxes could spend up to $115 per pupil; above that, it had to rely totally on taxes). Furthermore, the government based its grants on 50 per cent of the educational expenditures of 1943; William Dunlop, the Minister of Education, explained that the Department could not be tied to the possible extravagant expenditures of trustees. Thus, in Roger Graham's words in his biography of Frost, the government managed an "inglorious escape".[128]

Although under this new grant structure poorer boards received higher grants than wealthier ones and all boards got greater government support, the separate school boards' share of the total provincial grants actually fell to 14 per cent despite comprising 19 per cent of the student population.[129] This was due to the fact that the approved costs grants were based on the previous year's expenditures. Because the separate school boards had no access to corporation taxes, they paid smaller salaries and, therefore, received fewer grants. This problem was compounded by the fact that the grants were also based on the previous year's enrolment, invariably smaller than the current year's. Also, the government did nothing to deal with the growing non-viability of the small rural board. A public school board could form a township school area and build a large central school; a separate school board had to keep its one- or two-room school operational because of the three-mile pupil attendance limit.

OECTA aired these problems at a number of its meetings. For example, Renfrew district in 1945 asked for grants based on present pupil attendance. In 1948 a resolution was passed at the AGM to request that the Department give temporary grants to boards with financial difficulties, and the Board of Directors expressed concern about the corporation tax problem.[130] As far as formal papers to the government, OECTA at this point in its history did not submit its own briefs. For matters of general education finance, it submitted papers to OTF and relied on the latter to approach the government. For separate school funding it knew that OSSTA regularly dealt with the Department and, furthermore, agreed with Fr. Priester that the united Catholic voice of his association, on which OECTA had representation, was the more effective means for influencing the government. The Association also followed this line of thinking with regard to briefs to the Hope Commission.

Meanwhile, OECTA continued to debate with the Bishops, OSSTA and school boards for the minimum scale, while anticipating that the Department would raise grants to help meet higher salaries. Miss Lynch optimistically felt that "in the long run they [the trustees] were rather glad, because it [The Teaching Profession Act] did bring more grants from the government."[131]

The Hope Commission. In 1946 the Drew government established a Royal Commission on Education to examine the aims of public education in Ontario. It was chaired by the Honourable Mr. Justice John Andrew Hope and its members represented the public, separate and bilingual school community; they were educators, trustees and community leaders. It met and received briefs for four years and submitted its report in 1950 to Premier Frost.

For the Hope Commission, OTF and its affiliates decided on the general topics they wished to consider; then each affiliate prepared a paper under those headings; OTF finally incorporated all the papers into one brief,[132] submitted to the Commission in March 1946. Any recommendations disapproved by any affiliate had been eliminated.

This thirty-page brief made a number of significant recommendations, many of which were eventually implemented and some of which OECTA is still urging.

Rural education received extensive coverage. OTF recommended mandatory township school areas, free transportation of pupils residing over three miles from school (or over two miles if under age ten), special education in centralized rural schools, itinerant teachers for special subjects, and (a signal failure) agricultural education to encourage children to stay on the farm. All schools were to offer more guidance, segregated sex education, immunization, school lunches where necessary, and a physical training programme with gymnasia, playing fields, rinks, and, where possible, swimming pools. All this necessitated improved buildings and much better government financing of the building of schools and additions. The schools were to be designed to encourage community use of them.

OTF recommended the elimination of the academic/vocational distinction in the student's programme, examining the grade organization, study of the drop-out problem among high I.Q. pupils, and design of promotion policies for "slow learners" in order to prevent pupil frustration on the one hand and "satisfaction with credits not honestly earned" on the other, four topics thatstill await solution.

The brief contained a detailed section on pupil absenteeism worthy of examination today, and recommended that compulsory attendance be expanded from the period of age eight to fourteen to the period of age six to sixteen, with no work permits.

To improve the quality of teaching, OTF had a number of recommendations. The OTF salary scale was submitted. Primary classes were to be limited to twenty-five pupils and all other grades to thirty, with no class ever having more than thirty-five. A cumulative sick-leave plan was to be universal and pensions were to be improved. Teachers were to be compensated with released time for noon-hour and playground supervision and boards were to hire additional staff for expanded extra-curricular programmes.

Another lengthy section deserving attention still was on the inspection of teachers. Inspectors were to discontinue the grading of teacher performance by a number or letter, were to emphasize helping the teacher who needed it, were to have fewer teachers to facilitate this role, were to make available their evaluations to the teacher, and were to have a new title "less intimidating".

Teacher education needed to be improved, according to OTF.

The one-year course was to be extended. Entrance requirements were to be a minimum of grade thirteen education, and the program was to offer a partial B.A. or B.Ed., eventually a full B.Ed.[133]

As for recommendations specific to separate schools for the Royal Commission, ECEAO advised OECTA to work with it on a brief and to make no separate comment on the Hope Report when it was released.[134] ECEAO submitted a brief in December 1945 and a supplementary one in January 1946. It stressed three topics: the higher school taxes and less revenue per child that separate school supporters suffered, the problem of non-access to corporation and public utility taxes, and the right of separate school boards to offer high school education with grants and taxes.[135]

The Hope Report endorsed a number of the OTF recommendations, among them, a minimum salary. Unfortunately for these ideas, however, the Report was politically impossible to implement in its major parts. After four years the Commissioners were still unable to present a united position. There was a majority and three minority reports split along Protestant/Catholic/Franco-Ontarian lines. A major sticking point was the majority's desire to confine public and separate schools to the period from kindergarten to grade six, while having high schools offering grades seven to ten and junior colleges grades eleven to thirteen. Another was the limitation of separate and bilingual school rights to the 1863 *Scott Act* for the former, and the 1912 Regulation 17 for the latter. Regulation 17 restricted the use of the French language to grades one and two. Faced with these positions, the separate school minority report denied the 1863 "final settlement" concept and demanded a fair share of grants and taxes for separate high schools.[136]

Premier Frost reacted with dismay to the majority report:

> Certainly a matter as controversial as the Separate School issue going back a hundred years in our history is something upon which we can get nothing but a statement of differences from a Commission of this sort...The great difficulty with this Report is that in many respects it lacks any real relationship to reality.[137]

Cardinal Archbishop McGuigan declared the Report would cause consternation and astonishment among Catholics.[138] If the government accepted the tri-level organization and allowed separate schools to operate two of the levels, it would irk the Protestants; if it confined separate schools to grade six, it would offend the Catholics. In the words of

Robert Stamp, Ontario educational historian, "the Hope Commissioners flew directly in the face of the historical realities of Ontario; their tri-level organization would have reopened the explosive separate school issue."[139] Frost shelved the Report.

The Report also quickly became history because Dana Porter, the Minister of Education, in November 1949 did not wait for what was to be a conservative report, but issued his progressive "Porter Plan", a replay of the progressive education movement in Ontario's first two decades of the century and a prelude to the Hall-Dennis years of the 1960s and 1970s. Porter replaced the thirteen grades with four divisions: primary, junior, intermediate, and senior. This structure, he believed, would eliminate lock-step promotions and failures and encourage flexibility of programming for pupils. Although the 1950 AGM regretted that OTF first heard about the Porter Plan through the press, it did endorse its flexibility, abolition of the provincial entrance examination, and the ideal of a 30:1 PTR.[140] There was no mention of the Hope Report in OECTA minutes. After reading the following excerpts, the delegates probably wished to bury it in silence. These excerpts did reveal, however, the work OECTA had in front of it:

> We are compelled to conclude that those who elect to become supporters of separate schools must also voluntarily elect to assume a greater financial burden than would be the case if they had remained public school supporters. This is the price to be paid for the privilege of enjoying denominational schools.[141]
>
> The present financial difficulties arise, in our opinion, mainly because Roman Catholic separate school authorities are attempting to provide educational facilities in grades higher than grade VIII.[142]
>
> [Separate school grants should be based on] the lower of salary paid or the cost of maintenance of such teacher to the religious order or community.[143]

The majority would, if the Commissioners were in the happy position of recommending the organization of an educational system for Ontario unfettered by the past, vigorously oppose permissive authority for the establishment of denominational schools of any description as part of the system.[144]

Catholic Parent-Teacher Associations. In 1947-48 OECTA decided its major project for those years would be the propagation of Catholic Parent-Teacher Associations. Bishop Cody had given a talk advocating such associations as the "missing link" in the education of the child. Together the teacher and parent, in close communication, would reinforce each other's efforts for the good of the child.[145] Fr. Harrigan as past president took on the campaign and within one year there were about 100 functioning units. The movement spread like wildfire. By 1951 there were 7000 members and thirty-six units under a Federation of Catholic Parent-Teacher Associations (CPTA). OECTA enlisted the support of the Bishops and separate school inspectors and contributed the first Spiritual Director for the provincial association in the person of Fr. Harrigan, who left OECTA to assume the position. The Board of Directors urged the teachers not to use the CPTAs just for money-making schemes, although they were helpful in supplying school supplies. The CPTA's early emphases were on improving communications and fighting horror and crime comic books.[146] Far beyond these aims, the potential of CPTAs for fostering the education of the child and for strengthening the partnership of the Church, the home, and the school was realized by OECTA and the separate school community.

Teacher Education. Finally, OECTA and OPSMTF through OTF made recommendations to the Minister on a topic that had grown in importance with the "baby boom." Low salaries and expanding enrolments resulted in a teacher shortage. This, in turn, caused the Department to grant more letters of permission (LP), and to keep standards of admission to Normal School low (grade twelve leading to two years of Normal School or five grade thirteen subjects leading to a one-year course at a Normal School). Admission to university, in contrast, demanded nine grade thirteen subjects. The Department also maintained a short training period for teachers, about nine months. The Department openly admitted that it felt it had to ignore the advice of OTF.

The AGM, citing the figure of 1015 LPs in 1947, supported the OTF stand against LP's ad suggested that school boards should not receive an LP to hire an unqualified teacher who had taught for three years.[147] As for admission criteria, OECTA supported OPSMTF's recommendation that the candidate should have nine grade thirteen subjects. It also endorsed the men teachers' position that the teacher preparation programme should be a three-year faculty of education course.

OECTA added to this that religion and philosophy were to be subjects of study in each of the three years.[148] These ideas proved worthy of implementation, but not until a much later time.

OTF also wanted some powers regarding teaching certification. The AGM supported the OTF concept of screening Normal School applicants with a board of examiners which would include Federation representation and the recurring idea of teacher licensing by OTF.[149] The former became practice, the latter a non-starter, despite the success of other professions in this regard.

One interesting idea was broached, but to my knowledge was only used in a modified way by the Etobicoke Board of Education. OTF suggested a "master teacher's certificate" to be awarded by the Federation. The rationale articulated at the AGM was that the existing certificate did not distinguish between "the successful and less successful" teacher.[150] (Imagine a parent accepting that her/his child is going to be taught by an identified "less successful" teacher.) On the other hand, the AGM opposed the idea of merit pay, recommended by the Hope Report. It wondered who would evaluate the teacher and what would be reliable and valid criteria, questions one could ask about the master teacher's certificate.[151]

Biographies of the Presidents and Secretaries.

Miss Margaret Lynch (1899-1985). It may be difficult for the reader to avoid labelling some of these early biographies as hagiography or at least thinking that I am following the stricture to speak well of the dead. However, talking with people who decades later still feel privileged to have been touched by these teachers does make for a respectful frame of mind. Just reading Margaret Lynch's diaries, written in the round-hand, slant script from the grade seven Department of Education course of studies, reveals a humble, persevering, dedicated personality:

> I am grateful to T.C.A. [Trans Canada Airlines] for the progress in travel when I think of those long train rides to many centres, explaining Ontario Teacher's Federation, OECTA and the Board of Governors.
> Our finances in the beginning were meagre, and sometimes we had to use our own funds. However, we did not mind as the response was wonderful.[152]

Miss Lynch's dedication is all the more admirable when one considers that her teacher's salary was just $1250 a year.

John Fauteux, also a provincial president of OECTA, told of receiving in Windsor the Margaret Lynch Award for Excellence in Teaching and of being curious about the woman in whose honour his award was named. He found her in the Tecumseh Nursing Home and was so impressed with her humanity that he visited her regularly until her death. She still spoke fondly of her days as president and expressed the hope that was realized later that OTF would initiate counselling and guidance for teachers about to retire.[153]

Miss Lynch was born and educated in Campbellford, the oldest child of Daniel Lynch, a lawyer, and Emma McKenna, an artist. She had two brothers, Francis, who died in childhood, and Charles. Her sister, Emily, a polio victim, despite her sex and disability and with the psychological support of Margaret, would become a lawyer and draw up OECTA's first constitution. Miss Lynch attended the only elementary school in Campbellford, a public one, attained a middle-school diploma at the town's high school, then took courses at the Laura A. Miller School of Dramatic Arts.

In 1922 she decided to discover whether teaching was attractive for her and was hired on a letter of permission at St. Basil, Brantford and in the following year at St. Patrick, Guelph. In 1924-25 she got qualified at the Peterborough Normal School for a second-class certificate and then came to Windsor where she would spend the rest of her career. She taught at St. Alphonsus, Walkerville, and at a number of Windsor separate schools: St. Angela, the Bungalows on Parent Ave., St. Clare, St. Joseph, St. Rosaire, Holy Rosary, Sacred Heart, and St. Genevieve. During this time she upgraded her teaching certificate to a first-class one and was a leader in the Windsor Separate School Teachers' Association. From 1960 to her retirement in 1967 she held the position of principal at St. Charles for the Windsor Separate School Board, the first lay woman to receive such an appointment with this board.[154]

As interim, then first president of OECTA, she travelled all over the province to speak at organizational meetings and worked indefatigably at the birth and growth of the Association. The Sisters of St. Joseph would meet her trains and provide her with accommodation in their convents.[155] The Secretary of the Association, Cecilia Rowan, lived and worked out of her home in Ottawa, the other end of the province. They both expended enormous energy communicating by mail and train, sometimes at their own expense. Self-effacing, she would joke that it was easier for a single woman to take the time to move about the province and that her major preoccupation was trying to predict who would buy the new hat for the Easter Convention, she or Marion Tyrrell, chair of the relations and discipline committee.

When reminiscing about her years on the provincial executive, she would say that what she did she did for friendship. She served as the first president in 1944, past president in 1945, and counsellor as late as 1961. During that time, she stressed the Catholicity of OECTA and provided an example of piety, intelligence, capability, pleasantness, and composure. Although John Fauteux recalled that she never talked about money in his presence and was against the concept of a teachers' strike, she had been part of Fr. Garvey's group at Assumption College where they studied the encyclicals on the workers' right to organize. Fr. Garvey remembered her as a woman large of heart and mind.[156]

OECTA could not have had a better person to introduce the Association to the separate school teachers throughout Ontario. In a letter to her about her work aiding the organization of the districts, Rev. Vincent Priester, executive director and secretary of the English Catholic Education Association, wrote, "God will be good to you; you have had heavy trials. If I can be of any assistance to you, I assure you I will be very glad to do anything I can to help the cause."[157] Others shared Father Priester's high regard for Margaret Lynch. In 1953 Queen Elizabeth II awarded her a Coronation medal for outstanding service to her community. In 1964 OTF named her a charter member and a fellow. In 1968 OECTA, to observe its Silver Jubilee, inaugurated the Margaret Lynch Fellowship for the study of catechetics and in 1969 she received a life membership in OECTA. The Windsor separate school teachers had the last word. In establishing the Margaret Lynch Award for Excellence, they stipulated that this was to be the only such award in Windsor; no other teacher was to have her/his name attached to such an award.[158]

Very Reverend Bernard W. Harrigan (1905-1979). The second president of OECTA is interesting in his own right, but is also an example of the Ontario Bishops' method of supporting the Association by encouraging the use of their priests. He was among the contingent of the Hamilton diocese at the founding meeting of the Association and, although already busy with two positions, curate and principal, accepted the dual role of president of OECTA and OTF from 1945 to 1947.

Born in Hamilton, he attended St. Thomas separate school and Cathedral Boys' High School. His father, a commercial traveller, earned a modest income; therefore, higher education was a problem. His older sister, Mary, a secretary, helped him financially as he progressed toward a B.A. in philosophy at St. Michael's College, Toronto. He then attended St. Augustine Seminary, Toronto and was ordained in 1930. At this point he became part of a plan to assist with the continued existence of the Catholic high schools in Hamilton just a few years after the separate school trustees had lost the Tiny Township Case. Bishop J.T.McNally had initiated and Bishop J.T.Ryan was to continue the scheme whereby every priest with a B.A. would attend immediately after ordination the two-summer course at the Ontario College of Education (OCE), Toronto, leading to a high school assistance's certificate (HSA). These priests would then be assigned by the bishop to a parish as a curate and to a Catholic high school as a teacher. High school staffing costs were thus kept to a minimum, and the pastoral presence in the school was assured. Through the Depression, the War, and even after Premier Davis said no to extension in 1971, the Bishop of Hamilton supported with staff and money high schools in Brantford, Guelph, Hamilton, Kitchener, and Walkerton.

Fr. Harrigan, later a Monsignor, attended OCE in 1930 and 1931 and taught chemistry at Cathedral Boys' from 1931. In 1937 he became principal until 1946, when he became a pastor and, according to the plan, left teaching.[159]

As president of the two teachers' associations he was a forceful, yet well-liked and affable spokesperson for Catholic education and the teaching profession. His staff and students regarded him as a bright and fun-loving person, but also as a strong disciplinarian. More than once when he assembled the entire student body to "discuss" discipline and infractions, the proverbial pin could be heard hitting the floor. Yet he still had enough energy to leave a full-time job in the late afternoon and go to another full-time one in his parish church. He brought these organizational and energetic abilities to his office at OECTA, where delegates recall his firm hand at chairing a meeting. His resignation to run his own parish was accepted with regret by the Executive. In 1964 the profession honoured him with an OTF fellowship.

Contemplating all the tasks he carried out simultaneously, one appreciates a humorous comment from his sister who helped him when he could not get a summer job as a student, "He never worked a day in his life." It is likely Fr. Harrigan would have appreciated the joke: he was so known for his Irish wit and storytelling that Bishop Ryan when preparing a speech would call him on the telephone for a story or two.[160]

Raymond J. Bergin (1909-). The third president of OECTA came from another sub-group of the Association: the married men. His career paralleled that of many other Catholic male teachers in Ontario's separate schools. An examination of his background revealed much about both the man and separate school boards often so limited in financial resources that they avoided hiring male teachers who, in accordance with society's expectations then, might get married, become breadwinners, and require a living wage. Thus, Raymond Bergin, as married male teacher, represented a small minority of OECTA's membership.

He was born on a farm in eastern Ontario. Because his family lived outside of the three-mile boundary limit of any separate school board, Raymond attended S.S. # 9, Nepean for about a year. When his father had to sell the farm, the family moved to Ottawa for eight years, where Raymond passed his grade eight entrance examinations at St. Malachy school. They returned to a farm, and Raymond attended two institutions which provided a high school education in rural Ontario: a fifth class (grades nine and ten) in Nepean and the Manotick continuation school for grades eleven and twelve. Since family funds were in short supply, since Normal School was free, and since he had done well at school, a teaching career beckoned. After the school year 1929-30 at the Ottawa Normal School, he taught three years for the Ottawa Separate School Board. In accordance with a 1927 Regulation, all first- or second-class teachers were required to take a second year at Normal School after a minimum of three or a maximum of five years of teaching. Bergin went back after the minimum time. Although this must have been an inconvenience, to say the least, he spoke of this time positively: he had an excellent master in language arts, received special certification in manual training and agriculture, and gained a credit in English and in history from Queen's University. Furthermore, he now feels that after one year of Normal School, many teachers at first hardly knew the front from the back cover of a textbook. After this year he returned to the Ottawa board, after another few years married Evelyn Wilson, and began working on his B.A. at night and summer school. At a time when elementary school boards paid small salaries and made no distinction among teachers with or without a degree, this investment of tuition and several years of work required energy, dedication, and perseverance. One could always look forward to teaching in a public high school where the salary was much higher.

Meanwhile, Raymond Bergin made ends meet. His family was growing; he and Evelyn would have six children, all of whom would go into teaching: Michael, David, Richard, Paul, MaryRae, and

Margaret. To supplement his teacher's salary he worked in the summers as a Canadian Pacific Railway platform inspector, as a leader at a boys' camp, and as a worker at a brewery. His teaching must have been good because in the mid-thirties he secured a rare position for a layman with a separate school board: a principalship first at St. Margaret Mary, then at St. Malachy, his old alma mater. It was in this role that he became involved with the Ottawa Catholic Teachers' Association, serving for one year as its president, became one of the signers of OECTA incorporation papers, and served as provincial president. During his term as president he was hired as a mathematics teacher by the Ottawa Collegiate Board and, since he could no longer be a regular member of OECTA, offered his resignation. However, the Executive asked him to complete his term of office and he did so.

After his time as president, Raymond Bergin continued to take on challenges. He taught high school for eleven years after attending OCE for one summer to get his HSA. He then successfully wrote the examination for an elementary school inspector's certificate and was appointed to Cornwall #2 in 1958 as a separate school inspector for the Ministry. In 1965, he became an inspector with the Metropolitan Separate School Board (MSSB) under new provincial legislation that permitted this board to hire its own supervisory officer staff. (In 1969, all the county and district public and separate school boards were required to do likewise.) A few years later he became deputy director of education for B.E. Nelligan, the chief executive officer of MSSB. He retired from this position in 1973 after forty-three years in education.[161] In 1983 OTF recognized him as a fellow.

Reverend Brother Thaddeus (Joseph Hurley) (1909-1987). Still another sub-group of OECTA was represented with the next president, a member of the Christian Brothers of de la Salle. They operated a number of boys' elementary and secondary schools in Ontario, providing the Catholic witness of their Order at small cost to the separate school boards.

Brother Thaddeus came from rural Ontario Irish stock. His grandfather Hurley from Cork had been discharged from an Irish regiment over a dispute concerning the lack of Sunday Mass for the Catholic soldiers; nevertheless, he received a land grant for Australia or Upper Canada and decided on one near Penetanguishene. Provided he cleared the land within ten years, he would assume ownership. Here Joseph was born, son of John Hurley, a carpenter and sculptor, and Elizabeth

Warne, originally an immigrant from England, then a housekeeper in Toronto. Joseph, along with a sister and brother, was raised by his mother, his father having died when Joseph was a baby. He attended the public school in Penetanguishene, a unique community where the separate school was Protestant while the public school was staffed totally by Catholics.

Joseph took up his religious vocation early. He was a regular altar boy at the 5:30 a.m. daily Mass at the church a mile and a half from his home. The parish priest recommended him to the Brothers, and immediately after grade eight Joseph decided to "go and try" the Aurora Juniorate, saying to his mother, "I'll be back in two weeks," if he became homesick. He stayed in the Order for sixty-two years, loving the life of the brothers until he died. As a true teacher he demonstrated his respect for learning by acquiring a high school education, an elementary school teacher's certificate from the Toronto Normal School in 1929, a specialist certificate in art in 1932 and in music in 1946, a B.A. from the University of Toronto in 1941 after years of summer school, and an M.A. in religion in 1965, all while teaching full-time.

His teaching career included elementary school teaching, principalship of St. Paul in Toronto, and high school teaching of English, Latin, art, and music in Aurora, London, Ottawa, and Toronto. After his year as president of OECTA, he was reassigned from De La Salle high school, London to the Provincial Headquarters of the Christian Brothers as vocational director of the Canadian English Language Province of the Order. Thus, he was unable to continue on the Executive of OECTA.

His fellow brothers recalled Brother Thaddeus's liveliness and dedication as a teacher, his "gift of the gab", and wide interests. Even after his retirement at the end of over forty years in teaching, he studied French and singing and continued to paint scenes from nature. His literary and artistic ability, the *OECTA News* reported, left a strong influence on his students.[162]

Dorothea McDonell (1914-1972). Daughter of Edward McDonell and Susan MacNamara, she was born in Ottawa and educated in the separate school system and at the Rideau Street Convent High School in Ottawa. The family experienced adversity in the death at an early age of two of Dorothea's older sisters, Kathleen and Clare; another sister, Helen, lived a normal lifespan with Dorothea. After attending Ottawa Normal School in 1932-33 for a second-class certificate, she began teaching for the Ottawa Separate School Board. For thirty-nine years she worked for this board at St. Agatha (now Our Lady of Perpetual Help), Dante Academy (now St. Anthony), and the Catholic Lyceum (now St. Patrick). In 1941 she acquired a first-class certificate and in 1948 became a music supervisor, continuing in this position until 1971. After another year as a music consultant she retired. During this time she initiated instrumental music in the senior separate schools. A fellow teacher, Margaret Macdonald, remembers her as outgoing and well-liked; she had never known anyone who could snap a class to attention as fast or teach so much music in so little time. After her years on OECTA's executive and as OTF president (1951-52), Dorothea served in difficult times on the provincial salary negotiating committee. Fr. Conway, another member of the committee and later a provincial president, recalled their journeying to Belleville, Kingston, Cornwall, and other places where local negotiating had run into difficulties. There they would perform a "bad-guy, good-guy" routine with the trustees. Miss McDonell would be the pleasant one reaching the agreement after Fr. Conway "softened them up". In recognition of such work she was made an OTF fellow in 1964 and received a Canadian Centennial Medal in 1967. One month prior to her death the Ottawa unit executive approved her nomination for life membership in OECTA. St. Thomas More, in Robert Bolt's *A Man for All Seasons*, advises Richard Rich to be a teacher because his audience would be his students, their parents, and God, adding "Not a bad audience, that." We leave Dorothea McDonell to her audience.[163]

Patrick Ambrose Perdue (1903-1983). Like Raymond Bergin, Patrick Perdue's career as a Catholic teacher was typically arduous, requiring a love for teaching. He was born the youngest of ten children in Ennismore township near Peterborough. His parents, Thomas Perdue and Kathryn Garvey, sent him to a one-room public school and a continuation school. He began teaching immediately after his junior matriculation in a pioneer settlement, Snake Creek, near Mattawa. One year later, having saved some money, he went to Peterborough Normal School. However, upon graduating in 1922, he was unable to secure a teaching position in Ontario and so went to a one-room school in Delph, forty-five miles west of Edmonton. This was a separate school in Archbishop Cody's territory with sixty-nine Ukrainian pupils, most of whom were beginning to learn English and who were somewhat crowded in the standard forty desks and chairs. Despite or perhaps because of winter temperatures that sometimes hovered at fifty degrees below zero and despite his onerous pupil/teacher ratio, his school won the Strathcona Shield for the best physical education programme in the inspectorate. After this experience with all the elementary school grades and curriculum, he returned to Ontario in 1927 and again did not find a teaching position. He took a job at Massey-Harris-Ferguson in Toronto, but because of the Depression was laid off a year or two later. Finally, in 1930 his teaching career in Ontario began in earnest. He was hired by the Wolfe Island Separate School Board, met and married Margaret, the daughter of a Great Lakes captain, and had four children while living and working on the island.

His salary, family responsibilities, and lack of any salary incentive eliminated any notion of working toward a Bachelor of Arts degree. As it was, he had to supplement his $500 annual salary by selling life insurance and by keeping a cow and a market garden on his fairly large lot. In the winters he and his brother-in-law would go out on the St. Lawrence River in a skiff and saw blocks of ice, which they would store for selling in the summer. In addition, he would return for part of the summer to help on the 150-acre farm of his now elderly parents. After fifteen years of teaching on this island which was equipped with neither doctor nor dentist, Patrick Perdue accepted a grade eight teaching position at St. Patrick with the Niagara Falls Separate School Board. Here he became involved with OECTA. Shortly thereafter, he moved to Scollard Hall high school, North Bay and taught with the Resurrectionist Order. There he became district president of the Association and served on the provincial salary negotiating committee. His daughter, Florence Lafontaine, a separate school teacher, remembered those years of family outings in the car to places around North Bay where he would negotiate teacher salaries with the parish priest who often was either secretary or chairman of the board.

In 1948 the Resurrectionists transferred him to St. Jerome high school in Kitchener, where he continued to teach English, history, physical education, and science. Later he acquired a guidance specialist certificate and was appointed guidance head; in this position he called upon his many years of teaching in an individualized fashion. In 1949 he became provincial vice-president of OECTA and a year later the president. From 1950 to 1954 he was on the OTF board of governors. His major concerns were decent salaries for teachers and the opportunity for married men in separate schools to be principals; therefore, in addition to being president, he acted as a provincial chief negotiator.He remained at St. Jerome as guidance head until his retirement in 1970, having taught for forty-two years. Retirement at an earlier time would have meant some financial hardship. He had lost a number of years where he was not eligible to pay into the superannuation fund, had sent all four of his children to Catholic high schools where tuition was involved, and needed to raise his average salary based then on hislast ten years of teaching. His students remembered him as a lively storyteller, an excellent disciplinarian and listener, and a strong believer in Catholic education.

After retirement he was appointed as a Senior Citizens Advisor with the Kitchener Recreation Commission and kept this position until 1980 when he was seventy-six. In 1982, the year before his death, he became a fellow of OTF.[164]

It is not taking away from the many accomplishments of Marion Tyrrell, the second General Secretary of OECTA, to speculate how the history of Patrick Perdue and OECTA would have been different if he had been appointed to this position instead. Fr. Harrigan, after interviewing Miss Tyrrell, Patrick Perdue, and some others for General Secretary, mentioned to B.E. Nelligan, chairman of the publicity committee of OECTA and one of his staff members at Cathedral High, that the Association would have had to pay a married man too high a salary.[165] Separate school salaries were low and, consequently, Association fees were low; the budget was tight.

Cecilia Agnes Rowan (1889-1976). Miss Rowan was the first Secretary of OECTA, unpaid at first and then receiving a modest stipend, doing the Association's work in her home after school and on weekends.

Her father, John Rowan, emigrated as a child from County Mayo during the Irish Famine to Fitzroy Harbour where his father took up farming. He married Sarah Stanton; they raised two sons and seven daughters on a fifty-acre farm; Cecilia was the youngest. She was educated in a one-room public school, in S.S.# 12, Fitzroy on property donated from the largesse of her father's fifty acres. After high school and teacher training at the Renfrew Model School she began teaching with a third-class certificate in her childhood school. After two and a half years of teaching she went to the Ottawa Normal School in 1911-12 for a second-class certificate, then went on to the Ontario Agricultural College in Kemptville from April to June 1912. (Teachers with special qualifications for the teaching of agriculture received a small allowance from the provincial government.) For the next few years she continued to teach in a one-room school, first back in Fitzroy Harbour, then in S.S.#7, Augusta, near Prescott and S.S.#23, Edwardsburg, South Mountain in the Brockville area. She then went with her sister Elizabeth, also a teacher, for a few years to teach in Carmen, Manitoba. When her sister married and moved to the United States in 1920, Cecilia came to the Ottawa Separate School Board. She brought, according to the memories of some of her students, a formidable will, intelligence, and organizational ability to St. Brigid and the Catholic Lyceum. In 1927 she became principal of St. Mary, in 1940 obtained her first-class certificate, and from 1931 until her retirement in 1957 was principal of Canadian Martyrs. Following her retirement she worked for the board part-time for a year and a half assigning substitute teachers. Her grand-niece and grand-nephew remember her as full of self-giving love and an incarnate faith. She taught for forty-five years and after that was still able to say, "I will miss the children."

She brought to the new Association experience from the Ottawa Catholic Teachers' Association, a discerning and witty perspective revealed in her chatty letters in the OECTA archives, and a willingness to donate her time while teaching full-time and running a school. One can only regard with awe the energy and long hours required to do all this and start up, with Margaret Lynch, a provincial teachers' organization, all at the age of fifty-five. She received a well-deserved life membership in OECTA in 1958 and a fellowship in OTF in 1964. OECTA in her honour annually makes available a $7000 Cecilia Rowan Fellowship for religious studies.[166]

Marion Tyrrell (1896-1982). Miss Tyrrell was the second provincial Secretary of the Association and the first full-time one.

Marion was born in Lynn Valley near Port Dover; her parents were William Tyrrell, a tailor, and Annie Kelly, an elementary-school teacher. She was the oldest child with two sisters, Margaret and Kathryn, and a brother, Wilfrid. When her parents separated, her mother returned to teaching in a one-room separate school at LaSalette and moved her four children there.

Marion passed her entrance examinations at a very early age and went to St. Joseph Academy, Lindsay as a boarder, then returned home to finish high school. She took the train daily for about fifty miles to Woodstock Collegiate Institute where she earned her Senior High School Graduation Diploma in 1915. Marion then wrote special Departmental examinations for entrance to the Toronto Faculty of

Education where she received a first-class certificate and HSA in 1916.

In an interview with the Canadian Register Miss Tyrrell recalled that, "It was practically impossible for a Catholic teacher to obtain a position in a high school. But since my mother taught in the only Catholic school in our county, I managed to get a job in a village public school at a salary of $550" from the Penetanguishene Public School Board. The next year she moved to S.S.# 7, South Walsingham, Norfolk County for a much improved salary of $800. Miss Tyrrell commented to the reporter that at the end of the school year, instead of packing her bags for Europe, she and her students needed to earn extra money. In one case she supervised a group of pupils picking strawberries for the local jam factory. She said, "The earnings were one cent per quart basket and all the berries we could eat."

In 1923 she obtained a position with the Toronto Separate School Board for $1200. She was assigned to St. Francis Boys' as a supply teacher in kindergarten. In her portable, there were about 150, "yes, 150", children. "It seemed that in every corner of the room there was a pile of kids." Accepting this challenge did not help her salary which dropped in the following year to $1080. Until moving to OECTA in 1949, she spent her time teaching at two other schools, Holy Family and St. Rita. During this time she acquired physical education specialist and supervisor's certificates, a music supervisor's certificate, a first aid certificate, and a diploma in shorthand and typing. She never stopped: in 1959 she took the OTF principals' course and in 1960 the Christopher Leadership Course.

Meanwhile, her sister Kathryn had died, leaving a three-year-old daughter, Joan. Joan's father, Harry O'Grady, the organist at Shea's Theatre, Toronto, worked nights and felt unable to care for his daughter. Marion and Margaret made a home for their niece and "lived and died" for her. Anyone who experienced Miss Tyrrell's straight-laced, sometimes imperious, and formidably intelligent manner would have appreciated this anecdote from her sister-in-law, Helen Tyrrell: Joan after a few years asked her Aunt Marion if she could refer to her as her mother. "Certainly," replied Miss Tyrrell. On occasion, when Joan's friends would visit, she would introduce her guardians in the following way: "This is my Aunt Margaret and my mother, Miss Tyrrell."

In the 1920s she helped organize and became president of the Toronto and Suburban Separate Schools Lay Teachers' Association. In 1943 and 1944 Marion Tyrrell was one of the leaders helping to form OECTA and to persuade the Toronto separate school teachers to switch from FWTAO to the new Association. She served on the Relations and Discipline Committee and in 1949 applied for the new permanent position of Secretary.

Her letter of application in May 1949 highlighted the following facts and accomplishments. During the war she worked for five summers for the Wartime Prices and Trade Board, and organized and supervised the first Catholic Women's group to staff the Toronto Red Cross workrooms knitting, sewing, typing, and packing supplies and food, and the St.Michael's Club, a Catholic hostel for soldiers. She practised her high sense of apostolic action in a number of other community and parish activities: executive officer on the St. Joseph's College Alumnae and on her parish council, director of the Toronto Catholic Children's Aid Society, liaison officer for the Toronto Red Cross Society, and member of the Toronto Exhibition Committee. Her association experience included being an executive member of the Toronto and Suburban Separate Schools Lay Teachers' Association for eleven years, where she helped to get an accumulative sick leave plan with the Toronto Separate School Board and was a regular delegate to the FWTAO meetings, where she became interested in superannuation.

There is one experience she did not mention in her letter. As one of the pupils at St.Rita and a next-door neighbour to Miss Tyrrell, I can remember her explaining one of the reasons that prompted her to apply for the position of Secretary. One of her grade six pupils who had dropped out returned to show Miss Tyrrell his first pay cheque, which was larger than hers. Miss Tyrrell brought considerable experience, enthusiasm, and conviction to the position.[167]

At the 1951 AGM Miss Tyrrell succinctly described OECTA's activities from 1944 to 1951. Perhaps, to make her point, she unduly de-emphasized the Association's work in professional matters.

> Much of our energies have been expended on contracts, superannuation benefits, and salary negotiations...but equal vigour must be directed to our first objective - to promote the principles of Catholic Education by the study of educational problems.[168]

NOTES

1. AGM, 8-9 Apr.1947, Vol.1, 1944-1949, OECTAA.
2. AGM, 3-4 April 1945; 29-31 March 1948; 10-13 April 1950.
3. Hopkins, *The Long March*, 122.
4. Stamp, *Schools of Ontario*, 187.
5. Ibid., 184-187.
6. *OECTA News* (March 1948), 5-9, 32; Board of Directors, 28 December 1950.
7. Ibid., 29 December 1949.
8. AGM, 26-29 March 1951.
9. Ibid.
10. Ibid., 3-4 April 1945; 8-9 April 1947; Board of Directors, 28 December 1950.
11. AGM, 10-13 April 1950.
12. *OECTA News* (June 1949), 24.
13. AGM, 29-31 March 1948, 10-13 April 1950; Board of Directors, 29 December 1948, 28 December 1950; *OECTA News* (June 1946), 1,3.
14. AGM, 23-24 April 1946; 10-13 April 1950; Board of Directors, 28 December 1950.
15. Fleming, *Contributions of Associations*, 38.
16. Coo, *Forty Years*, 26-27.
17. Rev. V. Priester, Executive Director and Secretary, English Catholic Education Association of Ontario, to M. Lynch, 20 June 1944, OECTAA.
18. OECTA, 1944 to 1947; *OECTA News* (March 1946), 3; Executive, 4 February 1950.
19. OECTA, 1944 to 1947; AGM, 19-21 April 1949; Board of Directors, 19, 22 April 1949; Executive, 18 October 1947.
20. Sr. Anna Clare Berrigan, G.S.I.C., interview, Toronto, 31 March 1992.
21. Board of Directors, 29 December 1949.
22. Board of Directors, 2 April 1945; 19, 22 April, 1949; 29 December 1949; OECTA, 1944 to 1947.
23. Board of Directors, 13 April 1944; Executive, 22 February 1947.
24. AGM, 3-4 April 1945; 23-24 April 1946; *OECTA News* (June 1946), 2; OECTA, 1944 to 1947; Board of Directors, 28 December 1950.
25. Walker, *Catholic Education*, vol. III, 26.
26. Fleming, *Administrative Structure*, 165; Board of Directors, 28 December 1950.
27. B. W. Harrigan, President-O.E.C.T.A. to Miss Lynch, 1 June 1946, file 0041, 1946, OECTAA.
28. Rev. Fr. J. H. Conway, O.M.I., interview, Ottawa, 8 May 1992.
29. R. J. Bergin to Miss Lynch, 5 Nov. 1944, file 0020, 1944, OECTAA.
30. L. K. Poupore, O.M.I. , to Miss Margaret Lynch, 2 Nov. 1944, file 0020, 1944, OECTAA.
31. Sister Maureen to Miss Lynch, 30 October 1944, file 0020, 1944, OECTAA.
32. Cecilia to Margaret, undated, file 0024, 1944-1945, OECTAA.
33. AGM, 18-19 February 1944.
34. Executive, 18 November 1945.
35. AGM, 19-21 April 1949.
36. Board of Directors, 29 December 1946; Executive, 18 October 1947.

37. Board of Directors, 29 December 1948.
38. AGM, 10-13 April 1950.
39. Ibid., 8-9 April 1947.
40. Hope, *Commission on Education*, 510.
41. AGM, 26-29 March 1951.
42. Ibid., 29-31 March 1948.
43. *OECTA News* (June 1946), 3.
44. Bergin, interview.
45.To Madam President, Members of the Board of Directors, unsigned, 29 December 1949, file 0051, 1949, OECTAA..
46. AGM, 8-9 April 1947.
47. Priester to Lynch, 20 June 1944.
48. Executive, 4 February 1950; Board of Directors, 10, 13 April 1950.
49. AGM, 10-13 April 1950.
50. Ibid.
51. Board of Governors, Easter, 1947, File 0033, 1945-1949, OECTAA.
52. *OECTA News* (June 1947), 26-28.
53. Board of Directors, 29 December 1946, 29 December 1949.
54. The intent of this statement must have been the unethical behaviour of a teacher who, by not signing a contract, feels free to observe or not observe parts of the board's expectations. The legislation surrounding individual contracts and collective agreements has been interpreted to mean that both a teacher who has agreed verbally with a board to accept a position and a teacher who was on a probationary contract and is teaching without a contract are deemed to have permanent contracts.
55. AGM, 29-31 March 1948; 10-13 April 1950.
56. *OECTA News* (December 1947), 14.
57. AGM, 26-29 March 1951
58. Ibid., 10-13 April 1950.
59. Ibid., 8-9 April 1947.
60. Ibid., 29-31 March 1948.
61. Board of Directors, 10, 13 April 1950.
62. Lynch, "Memorandum."
63. Board of Directors, 29 December 1948.
64. French, *High Button Bootstraps*, 21
65. Ibid.
66. *Report of the Minister of Education of the Province of Ontario for the Year* 1944, 117.
67. French, *High Button Bootstraps*, 21.
68. Ibid., 65.
69. Allen Perdue, interview.
70. Bryan M. Downie, *Collective Bargaining and Conflict Resolution in Education. The Evolution of Public Policy in Ontario* (Kingston: Queen's University Press, 1978), 6-7, 10-14.
71. W. G. Fleming, *Ontario's Educative Society/*I. The expansion of the educational system (Toronto: University of Toronto Press, 1971), 275.

72. Hope, *Commission on Education*, 626.
73. W. G. Fleming, *Ontario's Educative Society/III.* Schools, pupils and teachers (Toronto: University of Toronto Press, 1971), 461.
74. . Executive, February 1951.
75. *OECTA News* (June 1946), 6.
76. Ibid. (March 1946), 6; (June 1947), 13
77. A typical year was 1951 when the committee through the executive advised the teachers in Sault Ste. Marie to accept the board offer and those in North Bay to reject it, then censured the Merritton teachers for individual bargaining. It also sent the secretary to Humberstone to assist the local negotiators. Executive, 17 March 1951.
78. Board of Directors, 19, 22 April 1949.
79. French, *High Button Bootstraps*, 137; Hope, *Commission on Education*, 626.
80. Margaret Lynch letter fragment, undated, file 0011, OECTAA.
81. Ibid.
82. Stamp, *Schools of Ontario*, 198; Bergin, interview; *OECTA News* (March 1946),1.
83. AGM, 23-24 April 1946; Sheila Coo, "Margaret Lynch: OECTA's first president," *CT Reporter*, 17-18.
84. Board of Directors, 29 December 1946.
85. Bergin, interview.
86. Board of Directors, 29 December 1948.
87. Executive, 11-12 July 1945; Board of Directors, 19, 22 April 1949; 28 December 1950.
88. AGM, 29-31 March 1948; 10-13 April 1950.89. Ibid.; Board of Directors, 28 December 1950.
90. AGM, 29-31 March 1948.
91. Bergin, interview.
92. *OECTA News* (June 1947), 13; (December 1947), 9; Executive, 1 October 1949.
93. *OECTA News* (June 1947), 13; AGM, 8-9 April 1947.
94. Ibid.
95. The Ontario English Catholic Teachers' Association to the Archbishops and Bishops of Ontario, 12 October 1949, File 0064, 1949-1950, OECTAA.
96. AGM, 8-9 April 1947.
97. Downie, *Collective Bargaining*, 10. Green, gray, and black listing had also been used, but pink became the common popular colour of paper.
98. *OECTA News* (October 1949), 4.
99. Fleming, *The Educational System*, 276.
100. OECTA News (June 1946), 16, 18, 21; Executive,11-12 July 1945.
101. Board of Directors, 28 December 1950.
102. AGM, 8-9 April 1947; 10-13 April 1950; Board of Directors, 28 December 1950.
103. AGM, 3-4 April 1945; 19-21 April 1949; Board of Directors, 29 December 1946.
104. Cecilia Reynolds, "Hegemony and Hierarchy; Becoming a Teacher in Toronto, 1930-1980," Historical Studies in Education (Spring 1990), 109.
105. Robinson, *Do Not Erase*, 188.
106. Ibid., 188.

107. Executive, 7 February 1948.
108. French, *High Button Bootstraps*, 137.
109. Hardy, *Teachers' Organizations*, 170.
110. Ibid.; Hopkins, *The Long March*, 70.
111. Quoted in Smaller, "Teachers' Protective Associations," 277.
112. (1938) I Geo. VI, c. 42.
113. "The School Law Amendment Act," (1943) 7 Geo. VI, c. 26.
114. (1946) 10 Geo. VI, c. 97.
115. "The School Law Amendment Act, " (1943) 7 Geo. VI, c. 26.
116. Executive, 10 April 1950.
117. Board of Directors, 28 December 1945.
118. AGM, 10-13 April 1950; 26-29 March 1951..
119. Fleming, *Schools, Pupils, Teachers*, 482.
120. French, *High Button Bootstraps*, 39-40; Hopkins, *The Long March*, 157.
121. *OECTA News* (December 1945), 5; (March 1946), 7; (March 1948), 18; "Report of the O.E.C.T.A. Superannuation Committee," 18 Jan. 1948, file 0060, 1948, OECTAA.
122. Coo, "Margaret Lynch," 18.
123. The elements of the pension plan as of 1940 were as follows. The government contributed 2 1/2% of the teachers' salaries to the fund and the teachers 3 1/2%. A Commission with teacher- and Minister-appointed representation approved pension claims and made recommendations to the Minister. The pension calculations were based on the teacher's age, sixty-two or sixty-five, as mentioned earlier, experience of forty years, and her/his salary averaged over all her/his years of teaching multiplied by 1/60. If the teacher had taught thirty years, s/he could apply for a B pension with a deduction of 4% for each year of service less than forty and for each year of age less than sixty-two. The calculation could not exceed 60% of the teacher's salary in her/his last year of teaching, could not fall below $500 annually, and could not exceed $1500 annually. A teacher was eligible for a disability pension after fifteen years of teaching. There was no dependents' clause, but upon the teacher's death her/his "personal representatives" received what had been contributed to the fund over the teacher's career minus what s/he had already received while on a pension. Two more requirements were not mentioned in the legislation: teacher staying power and an ability to adjust to a very small income.
124. *OECTA News* (December 1945), 5; (June 1946), 2; (March 1948), 18-20.
125. Ibid. (October 1949), 16-17; AGM, 19-21 April 1949; *The Teachers' Superannuation Act* (1950) 14 Geo. VI, c. 384.
126. *OECTA News* (March1948), 18-20.
127. Ibid. (March 1950), 29.
128. Fleming, The Administrative Structure, 165; Roger Graham, Old Man Ontario. Leslie M. Frost (Toronto: University of Toronto Press, 1990), 246; Stamp, *Schools of Ontario*, 185.
129. Ibid.
130. AGM, 29-31 March 1948; Board of Directors, 29 December 1948; *OECTA News* (December 1945), 3.
131. Coo, *Forty Years*, 25.
132. Margaret Lynch to the Windsor local of the OECTA, undated, file 0035, OEC-

TAA.; Board of Directors, 28 December 1945; OECTA News (March 1946), 5.

133. "A Brief Presented to the Royal Commission on Education by the Ontario Teachers' Federation," March 1946, file 0035, OECTAA.

134. Board of Directors, 28 December 1950; *OECTA News* (March 1947),7.

135. Walker, *Catholic Education*, Vol. III, 26-27.

136. Hope, *Report*, 57, 506, 779-894.

137. Quoted in Graham, *Frost*, 183-84.

138. Ibid.

139. Stamp, *Schools of Ontario*, 189.

140. AGM, 10-13 April 1950.

141. Hope, *Commission on Education*, 527-28.

142. Ibid., 509.

143. Ibid., 511.

144. Ibid., 502.

145. Executive, 10 April 1947; A.C. Rowan to Rt. Rev. Msgr. George L. Cassidy, D.P., V.F., Hamilton, 1 November 1947.

146. AGM, 19-21 April 1949; 10-13 April 1950; 26-29 March 1951; A.C. Rowan to all inspectors, 14 February 1948; Board of Directors, 29 December 1949.

147. AGM, 8-9 April 1947; 10-13 April 1950; OECTA *News* (March 1948), 25-26.

148. AGM, 10-13 April 1950.

149. Ibid., 29-31 March 1948; 10-13 April 1950; *OECTA News* (March 1948), 25-26.

150. Ibid.

151. AGM, 26-29 March 1951.

152. "Memorandum," Margaret Lynch, undated (after 1960), OECTAA, 2-3.

153. John Fauteux, interview, Toronto, 13 June 1991.

154. Staff records, Windsor Roman Catholic Separate School Board; Rev. Fr. C. Hickson, interview, Campbellford, 7 May 1993.

155. Coo, *Forty Years*, 27.

156. Rev. Fr. E. Garvey, C.S.B., interview, Toronto, 15 May 1992.

157. Rev. V. Priester, executive director and secretary, the English Catholic Education Association to Margaret Lynch, 20 June 1944, OECTAA.

158. Coo, "Margaret Lynch." Executive, 16-17 August 1968.

159. Diocesan records, Hamilton Archives.

160. B.E. Nelligan, interview, Toronto, 29 Jan. 1992.

161. Bergin, interview.

162. Christian Brothers' Archives, Toronto; OECTA *News* (Oct. 1950), Vol. 5, #5; Gladys Switzer, interview, Toronto, 24 June 1992.

163. Conway, interview; Margaret Macdonald, interview, Ottawa, 28 April 1993; Ottawa personnel records; *Review* (June 1973), 32-33.

164. Mrs. Florence Lafontaine, interview, Scarborough, 23 April 1992; Allen Perdue, interview, Merrittown, 7 May 1993; *Reporter* (December 1982), 36.

165. Nelligan, interview.

166. Ottawa Separate School Board personnel records; *Ottawa Journal*, 10 Dec. 1957; Michael McBane, grand-nephew, interview, Ottawa, 10 May 1993; Miss Edna

Montague, executrix, interview, Ottawa, 15 May 1993; Gervase O'Reilly, nephew, interview, Quyon, Quebec, 15 May 1993.

167. *The Canadian Register*, 13 June 1970, 28; Mrs. Helen Tyrrell, interview, Toronto, 7 April 1993; Mrs. Joan Graham, interview, Mississauga, 7 April 1993; Miss Tyrrell's personal effects, Mississauga.

168. Ibid.

CHAPTER FIVE

IMPROVEMENT: SALARIES AND PROFESSIONAL DEVELOPMENT 1951-1961

Our OECTA is composed of a somewhat heterogeneous membership - men and women, lay and religious. At one time it seemed as though different circumstances and needs might create tensions, but that time has safely passed and our Association is a brilliant example of unity and diversity.[1]

Background to the fifties. The most significant event of the decade affecting the educational system of Ontario was the "baby boom". Between 1951 and 1956 there was a 45 per cent increase in the number of six-year-olds in Ontario. This resulted in a 39.7 per cent rise in the province's total school enrolment. Between 1956 and 1961 there was another 33.8 per cent jump. To put it in another way, there were 612 000 elementary school pupils in 1950 and 1 126 000 in 1960. This worked out to an increase of about 50 000 elementary school pupils every year throughout the fifties.[2] The higher birth rate and immigration were having a dramatic effect on the educational budgets of the Department of Education and school boards, on teacher training and recruitment, and, consequently, on teacher salaries. In 1951 elementary schools received $97 140 188 from provincial grants, taxes, and other sources; $47 963 199 of this went for instructional salaries and supplies. In 1961 the corresponding figures were $278 961 629 and $147 339 604. These figures did not include funding for the building of schools and additions. Between 1951 and 1961 there were 5054 elementary schools erected at an estimated cost of $514 446 000.[3] OECTA during this period was a part of these statistics and issues. Each year the general secretary, Marion Tyrrell, reported a rise in the number of the Association's regular members. In 1952 the number was 2339 separate schools, in 1961 it was 6270.[4]

Interviews with OECTA provincial presidents and the minutes of AGMs and meetings of the Executive and Board of Directors revealed that Association activities continued to involve unity and ethics issues, superannuation and boards of Reference legislation, the Association structure and fees, the development of a Catholic curriculum, and relationships with the CPTA, the Ontario Bishops, OSSTA, and the new (1950) Ontario School Trustees' Council (OSTC), a federation of seven trustee associations, including OSSTA, OTF and its affiliates, separate school inspectors, and the Department of Education.[5]

However, OECTA's major concerns throughout the 1950s were the pre- and post-service professional development of the Catholic teacher, salary negotiating, and the implementation of the practice of equal pay for equal work. Four of the six presidents cited teacher certification and professional development as a priority; all of them regarded salary negotiations as a consuming activity; four of them specifically identified the equal pay for equal work issue as a top one for social justice and OECTA.

Salary negotiations. By 1951 OECTA had worked out a provincial policy for salary negotiating with the separate school boards. First of all, all teachers were to enter into collective bargaining; conversely, no teacher was to approach or allow her/himself to be approached by a school board for the purpose of individual bargaining. The teachers' official agent was to be the Local Negotiating Committee; no teacher was to sign a contract without its approval. When the Local Negotiating Committee arrived at a tentative settlement with the school board, it sought approval of the agreement from the District Negotiating Committee, then from the Executive. The appropriate committees were to make the Normal School students aware of these policies, so that they would check with OECTA before signing a contract with a separate school board. Finally, local negotiators were urged to begin discussing salaries with the board before it struck its budget.[6]

Of course, much of this required educating and obtaining the cooperation of the trustees and teachers. This was the task of OECTA's Executive, the Secretariat, the Board of Directors, the delegates to the AGM, and the district and local executives. The teacher was made aware that individual bargaining was unethical and would result in no future support from OECTA in possible problems with her/his school board, inspector, or principal. As for the trustees, OECTA continued with strategies it had developed in the 1940s and designed others. One structural issue made the procedure somewhat more complex with certain school boards. Elementary separate school teachers belonged to two affiliates, AEFO and OECTA, wherever the board was operating schools with both English and French pupils. This meant that in places like North Bay or Ottawa both affiliates were attempting to negotiate with the board. Two procedures were practised. Where there were just a few AEFO teachers, they could allow OECTA to negotiate on their behalf. More commonly, both affiliates would bargain jointly with the board. By 1956 some problems had arisen. What if one affiliate wished to negotiate and the other did not? What if one set of salary demands were higher or significantly different from those of the other affiliate? Separate negotiations could be risky for the affiliate with very few members at the local level. This was a solution, however, which, the OECTA Board of Directors decided, should be used only if the District Negotiating Committee requested it as a result of a threatened breakdown of negotiations.[7] In order to reduce the possibility of such an event, joint meetings of the two provincial executives began taking place for the purpose of discussing salary issues. In 1954 they worked out a common salary schedule for the members to use in bargaining with their school boards; it involved AEFO's compromising over the item of salaries for the religious teachers. (See below.) In 1956 they arrived at a policy for dealing with local bargaining units who could not agree on a package of demands to the school board. The two provincial executives would, in such a case, meet to decide whether or not the two local affiliates should meet together or separately.[8]

It was now time to examine the OECTA salary schedule developed in 1946. Inflation had made it out-of-date. A new schedule with a higher minimum and maximum was presented for approval at the 1954 AGM. A mild skirmish erupted when B.E. Nelligan from District #7 moved that the schedule be labelled "elementary" so that Catholic high school teachers, then receiving more than the minimum and maximum in Hamilton, could continue to expect a higher income than their elementary school counterparts. Fr. Siegfried argued that this motion would have a disunifying effect on OECTA's salary negotiations and that, in any case, only the Hamilton Separate School Board was employing grade nine and ten teachers. These arguments, together with the government's policy of giving only elementary school grants to separate school boards operating these two grades, sufficed to cause the motion to be defeated with only one supporting vote.[9]

A second debate took place over the allowance of twelve years of outside teaching experience (at the rate of half an increment per year). Some delegates to the AGM argued that such a clause in the salary schedule would encourage teacher mobility and, consequently, would cause hardship for small rural separate school boards trying to keep staff. The clause stayed. It would take the 1969 county and district school board legislation to resolve this problem. OECTA had its new salary schedule ranging from $2200 to $4600 with $200 increments.[10]

Inflation continued and in 1958 the AGM considered increases in the salary schedule. Fr. Siegfried, however, reminded the delegates that OECTA had promised OSSTA that it would not attempt to change the schedule for five years: there were still two years to go. Father felt it would be immoral to make changes without consulting the trustees' association first.[11] Meanwhile, modifications to the schedule were discussed. In 1959 the idea of rewarding the teachers with salary increases as they advanced towards a B.A. was introduced. Category 2 would have teachers with five university courses, category 3 with ten, and category 4 with a full B.A.. Staff in school lunchrooms discussed whether a teacher with a university education actually became a better teacher or whether s/he neglected classroom preparation and became too erudite to communicate effectively with her/his pupils. The AGM approved of encouraging higher education for teachers in accordance with OECTA's decade-old concern over low admission standards to Normal Schools. In 1960, with the five-year agreement now void, OECTA revised its salary schedule. There were now eight levels culminating in a master's degree in arts or education.[12]

It was one thing to develop these salary schedules; it was another to successfully negotiate at the local level salary agreements that progressed toward the recommended provincial scale. Both the trustees and the teachers had strategies to deal with these efforts.

Separate school boards on occasion would still attempt to bargain with the individual teacher. For example, the Grimsby Separate School Board as late as 1956 tried to ignore the OECTA schedule and to negotiate with individual teachers. The Executive felt it necessary to advise the board that teachers would be disciplined if they negotiated individually.[13] Other boards would not advertise any salaries in the newspaper and then feel free to ask the prospective employee what salary s/he expected. Miss Tyrrell in the *News* warned the members not to apply to such boards; [14] and to eliminate such practices she and the rest of the Executive sought and secured an agreement from OSSTA to urge all its member boards to advertise salary schedules.[15]

Some boards simply did not have a salary negotiating committee and were reluctant to meet with the teachers' negotiating committee. Thus, OECTA recommended the formation of Teacher-Trustee Committees to discuss common concerns (which included salaries); by 1953 eleven districts had them.[16] Another oft-repeated technique was the silent treatment from the trustees. The Penetanguishene trustees, for example, replied in the following manner to the teacher negotiators requesting a meeting: "Your letter will be dealt with in due course."[17] The Orillia Separate School Board, actually meeting with OECTA bargainers, just silently stared at them.[18] Sometimes, the board would have only the business administrator negotiate with the teachers; in other boards the separate school inspector would be present with the trustees at the negotiating sessions and in some cases would draw up a salary proposal for everyone's approval. To counteract such practices OECTA advised its members and OSSTA that negotiations would take place only with trustees and without the presence of business administrators or inspectors.[19]

Throughout the decade the idea of a legislated provincial salary schedule kept resurfacing. The teaching profession had escaped such a situation at least partially because of OECTA's conviction that Premier Drew's contemplated schedule was too rich for the blood of separate school boards. But the idea arose again in 1951. The teacher shortage strengthened their bargaining position; a provincial salary schedule would counteract this strength and save the trustees time and, probably, money spent in negotiating. OECTA announced its opposition to a statutory schedule, but OSSTA continued to push for such uniformity.[20] In 1959 John Wintermeyer, Liberal leader of Ontario's parliamentary Opposition, embraced the idea. The Executive met with him and presented the following arguments against a provincial salary schedule. It would:

- erode the local autonomy of the school board;
- cause local trustee apathy;
- cause lower salaries for teachers; and
- give too much power to the government which might decide who could teach and where.[21]

The idea was held at bay, but some boards did bond together to develop area scales to hold down salaries.[22]

Another trustee strategy, particularly vexatious for experienced teachers, was to raise the board's minimum salary without doing the same with the maximum. This would attract first-year teachers in a market where school boards had to compete vigorously and would result in a smaller board budget for salaries. To OECTA this had the effect of rewarding inexperience and punishing experience and additional qualifications. Separate school boards in North Bay, Oshawa, Sarnia, and other communities were implementing such settlements. In some cases, the Executive discovered, new teachers were making higher salaries than experienced ones with the same board. Exacerbating the problem, as far as OECTA was concerned, was board recognition for salary purposes of two years for teachers who had not completed their training. This situation occurred with those students who would attend Normal School for two summers and teach for the two intervening years before returning to the School to complete their training in the regular school year.[23]

OECTA was not helpless in the face of these trustee devices. As in the early 1950s, there was a growing teacher shortage. Also, OECTA leaders like Sr. Lenore, Fr. Siegfried, and Fr. Conway had the convictions and the stature to educate trustees in the Catholic Church's teachings on social justice and the just wage.[24] If trustees were adamant in offering unsatisfactory salaries, there were still the tools of mass resignation and pink-listing. For example, the Kirkland Lake separate school teachers considered mass resignation in 1953, and the Orillia teachers gave written resignations to the Provincial Negotiating Committee to hold until the board came up with a satisfactory offer. OECTA pink-listed Sudbury in 1951 and Penetanguishene and RCSS #1, McKim in 1956. All these sanctions ended successfully for the teachers.[25] Although the threat was not translated into action in the 1950s, one contemplated sanction was mass resignation at Christmas. OSTC, in negotiations with OTF over the deadline date for mid-year resignations, agreed to December 31 provided the affiliates would discourage the tactic's use in future. The future would show that the teachers would not give up such a useful device and, indeed, would resort to this measure, even though in 1960 OECTA did send to OTF a motion that "we agree to discourage mass resignations of teachers at Christmas."[26]

But these methods were for extreme situations. Even the Association's own members needed time to accept such sanctions as part of their arsenal of weapons. Some teachers, usually in the rural areas, were in 1952, according to Miss Tyrrell, "too timid" and "most reluctant" to seek salary increases.[27] Some groups were hesitant to organize themselves into a negotiating committee. As the Board of Directors put it in 1951, "Drastic sanctions may not be taken at present against teachers who do not cooperate. It will take two or three years to educate our members in the justice of salary negotiations."[28] The OECTA leaders, living in such a reality and confronted with trustees like those on the Port Arthur board whose "general attitude was one of self-righteousness, self-opinion and in general...closed minds,"[29] began to develop as many strategies as possible to fortify the resolution of its members and negotiators.

One argument which may have influenced some sympathetic trustees was, in Mother Lenore's thinking, the following: if teachers worried about their financial security, they would not be able to concentrate on their own professional growth and the development of their pupils.[30] Another way to appeal to well-intentioned trustees was publicly to commend school boards which gave their teachers the recommended basic salary schedule, as OECTA did with the Toronto and Waterloo separate school boards.[31] Marion Tyrrell also paid attention to bolstering the confidence and expertise of local teacher negotiators. She urged them to believe in themselves, to present a unified front, to expect the trustees to negotiate annually, to deliver their demands in a polished professional manner, and to aim for completion of negotiations by Easter.[32] In the absence of any statute or regulation on salary negotiating, Miss McDonell, as chair of the provincial Budget Committee, suggested guidelines to the Board of Directors:

> there should be a signed agreement between teachers and the Board upon completion of negotiations....Personally I feel that the offer made by a Board and accepted by the teachers would involve a letter somewhere along the way, which to one would be an agreement, or if minutes of a Trustee-Teacher Committee Meeting contained approval by the teachers of a Board offer, then this too could be considered as a salary agreement.[33]

The tentative nature of her words revealed the difficulties teacher negotiators were having even in the area of deciding whether or not they had an agreement and what exactly was in it. The Executive unsuccessfully tried to insert something in the Labour Code on salary negotiations between school boards and teachers.[34] In such an environment it was necessary for the Executive and Directors to insist on unity and to provide directives where necessary. For example, the Executive "allowed" the Sturgeon Falls teachers to accept less than the accepted basic schedule, but advised them to press for higher salaries in the following year. Again, in Sault Ste. Marie, although the teachers as a body had decided in 1953 not to engage in negotiations, three male teachers pressed for them. The Executive directed them to set up immediately a salary negotiating committee. Most importantly, OECTA notified all its negotiators that salary schedules constructed differently and in contradiction to the Association's philosophy (for example, those with married men's allowances) would result in no assistance from the Toronto office if difficulties developed with the school board.[35]

Of course, the Executive and the Secretary were willing to provide assistance wherever local negotiators were making little progress or the risk of breakdown was imminent. Miss Tyrrell would respond to telephone calls requesting advice and would talk with and write trustees when necessary. Members of the Executive and the Educational Finance Committee (renamed Salary Negotiating Committee in 1960) along with the Secretary would, on request (and where negotiations were at an impasse), travel to the community and take over the bargaining. Considering that, with the exception of Marion Tyrrell, and from 1959 Mary Babcock, all of these people were working full-time as teachers or principals, the energy invested in such time-consuming assistance throughout the decade obviously exacted a heavy price on their daily lives. Marion Tyrrell reported to the Executive that she assisted by telephone and mail or in person forty-one boards in 1951, forty-four in 1952, thirty-eight in 1960, and thirty-five in 1961. Over a ten-year period OECTA sent negotiators to over forty boards.[36] Fathers Conway and Siegfried and Margaret Drago emphasized in interviews that their collective expenditure of considerable energy was a cause utterly just.

Sometimes the separate school board did not understand the grant regulations sufficiently to get more money to pay the teachers; in such cases Fr. Siegfried recalled assisting the trustees. At other times the board would plead lack of funds because of low grants; Fr. Conway would examine the books and decide if the board could afford to meet the teachers' salary requests, and on occasion, he recalled, he had to agree that it could not.[37] It could not be said that OECTA did not try to be reasonable. On the other side of the pay spectrum, however, there was an instance where the board in Sault Ste. Marie paid its teachers higher salaries in order to have an argument for higher grants from the provincial government.[38]

The result of all this was that between 1949 and 1953 the average salary of a separate school teacher rose from $1301.41 to $1825.70 and by 1961 had risen to $3729.00. This was still about 15 per cent below the public school salaries, but corporate assessment made the difference.[39]

Allowances, benefits, working conditions. Salary negotiations between trustees and teachers mostly involved discussions about the minima, maxima, and number and dollar amount of the increments in the schedule. Certainly, the school boards did their best to confine the negotiating to this, interpreting almost any other topic as a trespass on the sacred ground of management rights. However, much of the time they felt forced to make an exception in order to secure men teachers, who were a scarce commodity; they gave allowances for men responsible for the extracurricular physical education and for men who were married. (I once received two allowances from the Harrow Public School Board.) However, any other benefit was simply not considered.

When the teachers were successful in establishing with the board a Teacher-Trustee committee, it was difficult for the trustees to prevent the teachers from discussing matters of concern to their profession. Furthermore, the Executive was now meeting on a regular basis with OSSTA. At a 1956 meeting they had the following topics on their agenda: trustees insisting on a March resignation date, maternity-leave problems, sexual discrimination, breach of contract, unreasonable teacher transfers, cumulative sick leave, individual bargaining, raising minima but not maxima, requiring women teachers to retire at a younger age than men teachers, and extra-curricular allowances.[40] Thus, local teacher negotiators would not have to deal with a board with a tabula rasa on the subject of benefits; the Board of Directors recommended that Teacher-Trustee committees examine a host of topics related to working conditions and benefits: board regulations, dismissal time on the last school day before the Christmas, Easter, and summer holidays, the school day, the question of principals reporting on teachers, school safety, school collections for charities, noon-hour and recess yard duty, instructional supplies, curriculum planning time, timetabling for special subjects, care of property and premises, extra-curricular activities, the teacher shortage, teacher qualifications, pupil attendance, government grants, group insurance, sick-leave plans, abuse of the twenty-day clause for teacher illness, and the status of married women teachers.[41]

OECTA did make progress in a few of these areas. It recommended that principals with six or more classrooms receive full-time release from classroom teaching in order to supervise, administer the school, and improve educational standards; separate school boards began increasing release time from as little as nothing or half a day a week. The Board of Directors suggested long-service awards; some boards founded twenty-five-year clubs or variations thereof and gave their senior teachers a special annual allowance.[42]

Sick leave was important to the teachers. For decades school boards had in their salary agreements the provision that a teacher could be absent for twenty school days because of illness without losing any salary. The minutes show only one board, the MSSB in 1955, trying to change the provision so that the teacher had two days a month instead; this would mean a loss of income if the teacher were sick for three or more days in the month. It was unsuccessful and the normal practice, fortunately for teachers, became embedded.[43] However, teachers also ran the risk of protracted illness and consequent loss of income. Thus, district and unit negotiators actively bargained for cumulative sick-leave plans. In 1957 the Legislative Committee recommended that provincial legislation make such plans compulsory. The trustees were apparently aware of the insecurity inherent in the combination of mere living wages and a limit to the days one could be sick with income, because by 1960 about 40 per cent of the separate school boards had plans allowing the teachers to accumulate unused sick-leave days to a limit of 200. However, there was one caution sent out to teachers: some boards were giving money annually to the teachers at a 50 per cent rate in return for the unused days being eliminated for accumulation purposes. This practice, OECTA pointed out, defeated the purpose of the plan and discriminated against teachers with extended sickness.[44]

As far as working conditions, the minutes showed no progress, at least in salary agreements. In 1957 the question of noon-hour supervision received considerable attention. District 17, North Bay brought the following motion to the AGM:

> Whereas there is nothing in school law to warrant teacher supervision between twelve noon and one twenty-five p.m.;
> Whereas the number of pupils remaining for the noon-hour period is becoming increasingly larger;
> Whereas some parents seem to be shirking their noon-hour responsibilities toward their children and placing an extra burden upon the teachers;
> Whereas there is a lack of uniformity throughout the province concerning the manner in which the noon-hour supervision is carried on,

> The members of district 17, OECTA are resolved that the matter should be brought to the attention of the Department of Education and after a satisfactory solution is evolved, be incorporated as school law.[45]

Two related motions were also debated at the same AGM. The final resolution was that legislation clarify the right of each teacher to a period at noon "free from supervisory duties unless special arrangements are made with the teacher, with or without remuneration."[46] Miss Tyrrell in her monthly column, "From the Secretary's Desk," suggested three choices to solve the problem: pay the supervising teacher more money, give the supervising teacher compensatory release time at another time in the school day, or designate the extra duties as part of her/his job because of her/his position.[47] OTF favoured the second alternative; the third was left vague. The records showed no progress made on this matter. Marion Tyrrell explained that it was impossible to get legislation because of the one- and two-room rural schools and because of crowded urban schools where the lunch hours were staggered.

Contracts and Boards of Reference. Just as important as the salary for the teacher was the protection of an individual contract. The records showed that almost all separate school boards in general honoured contracts and followed proper procedure with them. A few boards behaved improperly, however, possibly because of poor knowledge of the legalities, possibly because the desire to replace a teacher overstepped respect for procedure. In these situations, when the teachers called OECTA, the Relations and Discipline Committee or Executive gave help. Matters improved when a new standard contract was issued by the Department of Education in permanent and probationary forms. The teachers had the security of an individual contract, while the school boards without giving reasons were able to terminate probationary contract teachers after one year if they had three or more years' experience with other boards or after one or two years if they had less than three years' teaching experience. But, even if the teacher did not have a contract signed by her/himself and the board, s/he possessed a contract in law. In addition, even if the teacher should have been on a probationary contract, the absence of such a contract meant s/he also possessed a permanent contract.[48] OECTA and OTF now began seeking changes so that the board would be required to give reason for dismissal in the same way for both permanent and probationary staff.[49] It would take about twenty years to achieve this.

Meanwhile, there were the special situations to handle. The Executive, Board of Directors, and AGMs' minutes displayed a certain fear of the power of trustees and inspectors with regard to their positions and contracts. For example, Patrick Perdue deemed it necessary to urge trustees not to "penalize" teachers who negotiated with them. Marion Tyrrell had to write the Sarnia Separate School Board because it was forbidding principals to negotiate. The teachers of the Kingston Separate School Board were "afraid" to form a negotiating committee since they had encountered in the past their trustees encouraging individual bargaining, "belittling" the negotiators, and threatening to get rid of the experienced teachers; the Relations and Discipline Committee had to help these twenty-five teachers. A few separate school inspectors were interpreting the clause in the legislation on termination of teacher contracts "with the consent of the Minister" as empowering them as representatives of the Minister to do exactly that; OTF clarified this matter with the Ministry.[50] As teachers gained experience and confidence and as trustees grew familiar with the rights and responsibilities of teachers and OECTA, intimidation was replaced by more sophisticated power games between two relatively equal groups.

Other incidents which flouted contracts and agreements were rare in terms of the existence of over 700 separate school boards,[51] but they were time-consuming. The Sudbury Separate School Board in April 1953 demanded "assurances" from its staff that any teachers not needed by the board in September could be dismissed. The Alexandria Separate School Board was paying "paper salaries" to the Holy Cross Sisters in order to be eligible for grants on these salaries without any actual expenditures. The Fort Frances Separate School Board had offered by telegram a position to a teacher, then mailed a contract with a salary lower than the one accepted.[52] The Executive straightened out all three of these problems to the benefit of the teachers.

One allegedly disciplinary measure used by the Chatham Separate School Board was legally within the board's powers and, therefore, only open to discussion if the board agreed. This was transferring teachers to schools less convenient to their places of residence. Even though the Executive stated that these Chatham transfers were to the "four corners" of the community, the hardship would have been minor, but the device became more common and inconvenient for teachers as the geography of school boards became larger.[53]

Of course, the ultimate disciplinary measure was dismissal of teachers on permanent contracts; those dismissed could then apply to the Minister for a Board of Reference. This legislation had been clarified so that the Minister, in the case of teachers who were successful with their appeal from dismissal, was to direct the school board to continue the teacher's contract.[54] The minutes recorded that during the 1950s only four Board of Reference procedures involved members of OECTA; but they were firsts for the Association. During this period OECTA reserved the right to decide, after an investigation, whether or not to support the dismissed teacher with a lawyer and a member on the Board of Reference. In 1956 the Executive concluded that a particular teacher had not been given assistance or constructive criticism before the dismissal and so it hired a lawyer and began preparations for Fr. Siegfried to serve on the Board; however, the Minister did not grant the Board of Reference.[55] Again, in 1961, when two teachers were dismissed after an inspector's negative report and asked for a Board of Reference, the Executive asked Miss Tyrrell and Miss Babcock to look into the matter: "If the investigation indicated that the teachers concerned were incompetent, OECTA will not support them in their Boards of Reference if granted."[56] In 1957 a teacher in Collingwood was dismissed, in OECTA's opinion, "without cause" and applied for a Board of Reference. The Relations and Discipline Committee met with the school board while the Minister was deciding whether to grant the Board of Reference. As a result of the meeting, the school board withdrew its dismissal.[57] Finally, in 1961 OECTA won a precedent-setting case. The London Separate School Board by legislation had been enlarged geographically. Mrs. Irene Brine, a principal of a rural separate school previously outside of London now found herself an employee of the London board. As such, she was asked to sign a probationary contract; she refused, expecting either a permanent contract or her old one as still in force. The London board terminated her. She won her case. Miss Tyrrell felt this was important for any future amalgamations.[58]

In summary, when OECTA supported the teachers, they won their cases. One could argue that the number of cases were small, but they were important. One could also argue, and later OECTA would do so, that there was some prejudging going on here. But teachers could console themselves that they could not be unjustifiably dismissed without OECTA support and their day before a tribunal.

Short of dismissal there were a number of potential school board actions which a teacher might wish to dispute or appeal, for example, demotion of a principal, assignment of extra-curricular activities causing insufficient time for lunch, or an above-average length in the school day. There was no formal mechanism to resolve disputes over such matters. In the early fifties, however, the Brantford Board of Education and OSSTF took a leaf from the labour union's book and entered into voluntary arbitration. OSTC, thinking the procedure a good one to resolve grievances of trustees or teachers, asked the Department of Education to get arbitration legislation based on the power of either party to call for it, on a three-member panel with one member from the trustees and one from the teachers, and on a binding judgment. OECTA agreed arbitration was a good idea provided that it was a voluntary procedure and that it was used only as a last resort. In 1953 OSTC and OTF met to consider the details of such a procedure. Again, at OSTC request, the affiliates in 1955 discussed the topic.[59] Nothing came of all this activity, but perhaps the way was paved for collective agreement legislation of the 1970s.

Superannuation. Although, as outlined in the last chapter, pensions had increased, there was room for considerable improvement; and, although salary negotiations brought better salaries, there were still impediments preventing these salaries from directly increasing pensions to the necessary degree. Margaret Drago's remark, "Many people gave their life's blood for education only to be virtually abandoned in their old age,"[60] still had application in the 1950s.

OECTA and AEFO had to rotate one member on the Superannuation Commission until 1959, at which time they both had representation.[61] However, all the affiliates were united in their plans for improving *The Teachers' Superannuation Act*.

The most urgent items during these years of inflation and rising teachers' salaries were the raising of the minimum and maximum pension and an improvement in the method of calculating the pension. In 1951 the Executive decided to ask OTF to press for an increase in the minimum pension from $600 to $700 annually and for the removal of the ceiling of $3000 for a maximum pension. Miss McDonell's report in the same year stated OTF would do so.[62] In 1953 the government complied, because (according to W. G. Fleming) pressure was applied by OTF.[63]

The mathematics involved in using the teacher's last fifteen years of teaching resulted in a large gap between her/his last salary before retiring and the annual pension. Miss McDonell, perhaps in a Christmas mood, dreamed about pensions based on the best three consecutive years in her December 1951 report to the Board of Directors.[64] To this day the government has regarded such a provision as too expensive. More realistically, the AGM in 1953 requested OTF to seek a decrease from fifteen to seven years, or at least a gradual reduction for the calculation. In 1954 the goal was partially achieved: the government reduced the years to the last ten.[65]

However, the teachers did not stop seeking further improvements. In 1955 the Board of Directors set its sights on using the best earning years instead of the last ones for the calculation; in 1958 OTF even promised not to make any further requests about pensions to the government if the best-seven-year calculation were granted.[66]

Two other priorities that received considerable discussion in the minutes were the admission of teachers in private Catholic high schools to the pension plan and provisions for children of a teacher where both parents were deceased. Catholic high school teachers were in one of two situations regarding their relationship to superannuation. Either they worked partially for a separate school board operating grades nine and ten (a minority of them in the early 1950s) and partially for a private school offering grades eleven, twelve, and thirteen, or they worked full-time for a Catholic school where all grades of the high school were private. In the first case they could only pay into the pension fund and get credit for their time teaching grades nine and ten; in the second case they could not pay into the fund at all. This was of major concern to OECTA. At first, the government discouraged any exploration of the problem; it was felt that including private school teachers in the plan would be too expensive for the government and, on the other hand, the non-Catholic private school teachers had decided that it would be too costly for them to pay the teachers' and the government's share of the fund.[67]

Undeterred, in 1956 OECTA and AEFO held formal discussions on the problem with the Commissioners. Roadblocks were thrown up. Many religious teachers in high schools received no salaries; the Commissioners felt an "unscrupulous school" could report salaries and apply for pensions for its teachers. Teachers in private schools did not have to be qualified; some were not; the government was not willing to consider letting such staff into the plan. The Department of Education wanted 100 per cent of qualified teachers, including the religious, committing themselves to be in the plan before it would even seriously discuss the matter; some private school teachers were not willing to do so, perhaps because they were too close to retirement or were not staying in the profession. Finally, it was understood that the government would not contribute its 4 per cent share of the 10 per cent of the teacher's salary contributed to the fund annually. In the face of this, the Executive decided to poll the private school teachers on their willingness to carry all the costs and on the mandatory membership issue.[68] A majority was interested in belonging to the pension plan. Negotiations continued between OECTA and the Commissioners and between the Commissioners and the government and a solution was eventually reached. In 1957 an amendment to *The Teachers' Superannuation Act* provided that a private school could be "designated". This meant that private school teachers in such a school could join the plan and even purchase past time with the private school, but they did not have to join. If they did, they paid 6 per cent from their salaries into the fund; the government's other 4 per cent came either from the teacher's private school employer or, again, from the teacher. Most of the Catholic high schools became designated, sixteen of them immediately, and most of their teachers joined the fund.[69]

The problem of benefits for children of a deceased teacher who had been on pension where the widow was also dead was solved in 1960. The dependant's allowance being paid to the widow devolved upon her death or remarriage on any dependant children until the youngest child reached the age of eighteen. The same arrangement was applied in the case of a widower, but only if he was permanently handicapped.[70] The rationale of the Commissioners for not treating married women teachers the same as married men teachers was typical of the times:

> While the wife is considered the legal dependant of the husband, the opposite is not true, except where the husband is completely handicapped. Also, at the present time, by the Superannuation Act, the wife of a married man teacher is assumed to be the married teacher's dependant, but the husband of a married woman teacher is not assumed to be her dependant, unless it has been approved by the Commission.[71]

To fund the plan the affiliates felt that the government should be an equal partner. In 1951 OECTA urged OTF to seek government matching of the teacher's contribution of 6 per cent; in 1957 the government did raise its contribution to the fund from 4 per cent to 6 per cent.[72]

To protect the integrity of the superannuation plan OECTA moved to correct two potentially awkward situations. Some teachers on disability pensions were seeking to teach part time. They were advised that they would lose their pensions if they returned to work.[73] More seriously, religious teachers traditionally had not signed a teacher's contract, nor resigned from a teacher's position, even when retiring. The Superior of the Order or other person in the community administering the teachers would advise the school board each year which religious teachers would be assigned there. OECTA advised them of the necessity of formally resigning in order to apply for a pension.[74]

An interesting footnote to all this is the fact that some OECTA members felt that because of the teacher shortage there should be inducements for teachers not to retire. Among the suggestions was changing the legislation to permit retired teachers drawing a pension to teach more than the statutory maximum of twenty days per year,[75] an idea that was implemented over thirty years later.

Unity and Ethics. It is a truism of the labour movement that in unity there is strength. Salary negotiating and contract matters required unity in OECTA. A major method for achieving a desirable commonality of behaviour on the part of its members was reliance on the professionalism and ethics of the teacher. For example, OECTA expected teachers to give reasonable notice when resigning, to get married and go on honeymoons during holidays, and to accept employment outside of teaching only for work which "does not affect his professional status or his performance adversely."[76] (This latter policy would have required some judgment on the part of those enforcing it. When salaries were low, it was common to see teachers delivering beer or working at the Canadian National Exhibition in the summer.) Most importantly, teachers were to behave with pupils in an exemplary fashion. Mary Flynn gently chastized her peers about the use of certain disciplinary measures, "Children are human beings made to the image and likeness of God. Some of the disciplinary methods used might encourage children to learn the subjects of the curriculum but I'm afraid they'll also induce them to hate the teacher and hate the school."[77]

In case any member of the Association fell seriously short of the standards of professionalism, there was the OTF Code of Ethics. Furthermore, the Code by 1955 had been incorporated into the *Regulation Made Under The Teaching Profession Act.* Its clauses included the following:

> Where a member
> (a) breaks a contract or fails to carry out a verbal agreement to enter into a

contract with a board of trustees, or
(b) makes an adverse report on another member to a board of trustees or a member thereof, a director of education, a superintendent of schools, or another member, without first furnishing him with a copy of the report and giving him an opportunity of replying thereto, it shall be deemed unprofessional conduct.[78]

A variation of the second clause had been under constant attack by the trustees who complained that their principals would never submit reports to them on unsatisfactory teacher performance. It was agreed that school boards would now get reports and the teachers, in accordance with the legislation, would get copies.[79]

To deal with members suspected of unprofessional conduct OECTA approved of an OTF Relations and Discipline procedure. The membership for the first hearing consisted of two representatives from each affiliate. Prior to the hearing a representative from the affiliate that made the investigation was to submit a written report. The member under investigation attended her/his hearing with a "friend" from OTF. After the hearing a report was to be submitted to the OTF executive which heard any appeal from the member. Finally, the OTF Board of Governors decided if a recommendation of suspension of the teacher's certificate should go to the Minister of Education.[80]

Just a handful of cases were referred to OTF during the decade, but, when necessary, OECTA disciplined its members for unethical behaviour. For example, the Executive convened a special meeting to deal with the dismissal of two Toronto Separate School Board teachers after it had received negative reports on their teaching from the two principals. Unethically, the principals had not notified the teachers in any way that they had submitted reports on them. As a result of Executive action, the two teachers were rehired and the principals asked to appear before the Executive. To prevent any such unethical behaviour, the Executive then wrote the Superiors of the religious Orders in the province explaining the requirement that a copy of an adverse report was to be given to the teacher as soon as possible and within three days.[81] On another occasion OECTA recommended to OTF that it send a reprimand to a teacher for signing contracts with two school boards simultaneously, and once it recommended suspension of a teacher's certificate because of the latter's court conviction for passing N.S.F. cheques.[82]

By the same token, OECTA expected ethical treatment of its professionals by OSSTA. To illustrate, OECTA assisted three teachers who had been treated unjustly by school boards: one teacher had legally given her notice of resignation at the end of November and then did not receive her December salary; the second had been threatened with loss of position for unwillingness to attend a PTA meeting; the third had resigned her teaching position just before eligibility for a full pension, because the board had imposed duties outside the classroom which she was physically unable to carry out.[83]

OECTA's Relations and Discipline Committee was kept busy upholding ethical practices on the part of teachers and trustees. For example, in the school year 1951-52, it handled twenty teacher-board situations; in 1958 and 1959 such cases involved unfair dismissals, an application for a position not vacated, salaries unpaid by a delinquent board "for some length of time", salary adjustments, contracts, a violation of the policy regarding an adverse report on a teacher, termination of a contract where the board was overstaffed, breach of contract, salaries incongruent with the schedule, requests for leave of absence for marriage during the school term, and termination without warning of an experienced teacher for inefficiency.[84]

These were all exceptional and rare cases. What about the unity of the OECTA members on the whole? As outlined in the last chapter, professionalism, good will, and negotiating skills were necessary and in evidence to maintain and strengthen unity with a membership of lay and religious, male and female, and single and married teachers. In addition, there was the larger unity in the interests of the education of the child, the unity with the affiliates and the trustees. Each of these sub-groups had special interests that surfaced in the 1950s and which could have been a force for disunity.

Sr. Mary Lenore's words in the quotation opening this chapter were possibly overly optimistic. Certainly, there was unity and diversity, but there was also some tension during the decade. To alleviate it and to ensure representation of the Association's interest groups, the salary negotiations procedure recommended that the local negotiating committee should have membership from the religious and lay, men and women, and married and single teachers.[85] Patrick Perdue in 1953 explained that unwritten policy dictated representation from each of the following groups on the executive: priests, sisters, brothers, laymen, laywomen. He noted that this arrangement had gone askew and asked that the Legislative Committee look into the matter. The following year there was considerable debate on the issue. A resolution was passed which stated that the Nominating Committee should put forth the names of those deemed best for the position without any restriction. The following interchange took place before the vote:

> Fr. Mattice: We did not like to feel the slightest bit of political action entering into this Association, and we all felt we would refuse to act if our hands were tied in any way whatsoever....You just ask a man, Will he stand? I think usually he has to phone and ask his wife, and I am satisfied if he is a diocesan priest he will have to consult his bishop. About the only dictators are the married men, because there is no one above them that they have to ask.
> Mr. Perdue: I would like to say Fr. Mattice is certainly not married, or he would not make a statement like that.[86]

In fact, except for the married women, a representative from each group did become president in the 1950s.

As far as special interests were concerned, one potential threat to unity came from the trustees: the issue of merit pay. OSSTA saw it as a way of rewarding and encouraging outstanding teacher performance. Sr. Lenore pointed out OTF's opposition to the idea, explaining that some trustees may be sincere in recommending merit pay while others may be just trying to save money by increasing the salaries of only a few teachers. She recommended instead that school boards reward exceptional performance with promotions, conference trips, special awards, and other public recognitions. The Board of Directors opposed even the withholding of increments for teachers with unsatisfactory evaluations because this was the "thin edge of the wedge" toward merit pay.[87]

In 1957 the *OECTA News* printed an article ("Merit Rating as Seen by a Trustee") which gave eight arguments against the scheme. John Long wrote that:

- it was impossible to administer fairly;
- it fostered charges of favoritism and "apple-polishing";
- it developed suspicion, rivalry, jealousy, and resentment among staff;
- it complicated advertising;
- teachers opposed it;
- parents would want to know who received the merit pay and would vie for those teachers for their children;
- it had failed elsewhere; and,
- in any case, unless the trustees paid the teacher four times her/his regular salary, the merit would not be rewarded adequately.

The OSTC and OTF's joint report on merit pay could not express a consensus and therefore recommended merit recognition through other methods.[88] This issue died.

Another restive topic was the salaries of the large numbers of religious teachers. Since they constituted 59 per cent of the staff of separate school boards in 1950 and 30 per cent in 1960 and since they "earned" somewhere between nothing and $500 a year without being "on any semblance of a schedule", trustees understandably preferred to hire them over lay teachers.[89] Furthermore, they were esteemeed as providing an invaluable religious presence in the schools. Thus, lay teachers felt vulnerable and insecure; if a religious teacher was available for a lay teacher's position, the school board would often wish to hire that person. Apart from all this, there was also OTF's policy of equal pay for equal work, which OECTA endorsed.

In 1954 the Directors compromised, deciding to seek approval from the religious Orders and the separate school boards for placement of the religious teachers on the OECTA salary schedule at a two-thirds rate. This, they argued, would alleviate the lay teacher's fear of replacement and pay lip service to the policies of equality. OECTA wrote all the religious Order superiors, who, in turn, expressed their concern about the charitable role of the religious teacher and about the inability of separate school boards to pay them more because of inadequate revenues from grants and taxes. They consulted with the Bishops and, as a result, agreed in principle to the two-thirds idea. In 1956 OECTA adopted a policy of equal pay for equal work with the important compromise, "except where such policy would restrict the charity of the religious teachers."[90] Over time separate school boards began to place their religious teachers on a salary schedule and to pay them at the two-thirds rate.

But AEFO was not satisfied with this policy. It wanted the religious teachers in the affiliate to receive parity of wage with the lay teacher. Since sometimes the same school board employed religious teachers from both affiliates, the disagreement had to be solved. At a joint meeting of AEFO and OECTA in 1957, the Franco-Ontarian association asked its English counterparts to reconsider their two-thirds policy. Sr. Lenore reminded AEFO that the Bishops had agreed to this policy. Jean-Marc Tessier, president, "wondered how far the religious teachers were bound to the Bishops in the matter of salary." Sr. Lenore replied that the Bishops originally had requested the sisters not to ask for increased salaries and expressed her opinion of the "grave danger of the Hierarchy setting a flat rate for the Sisters" and her fear of the two-thirds agreement being jeopardized. AEFO still felt the Bishops would not object to equality of salaries for the religious teachers. The Association was correct in the case of some of the Franco-Ontarian bishops in northern Ontario. They felt that religious teachers' salaries on a par with those of lay teachers would provide money to assist in the financing of Franco-Ontarian private Catholic high schools. A few English Catholic bishops felt the same way with regard to the high schools in their dioceses. The two affiliates agreed to survey their religious communities.

The AEFO survey reported that their religious Orders favoured an 80 per cent salary rate and negotiations with the Bishops. OECTA reported that five Bishops felt that even the two-thirds rate was too much and repeated its fear that the salaries would be set by the Bishops if the matter were reopened. The result of this second joint meeting of the two affiliates was another compromise - the words "at least" were added to the two-thirds clause in OECTA policy. AEFO did not give up. In 1961 the topic was discussed again at a joint meeting. Miss Babcock ended the discussion for the time being by pointing out that equal pay for lay and religious teachers would in fact be higher pay for the religious since "they are not subject to income tax and have other financial concessions such as reduced train fares." Further, she warned that boards would insist on individual contracts for religious teachers if they demanded equal pay.[91]

Separate school boards also saved money by appointing religious teachers as principals with no additional remuneration. This practice was so common that Frank Macdonald, the separate school inspector for the Barrie-Orillia area, asked to meet with Fr. Conway, the OECTA president, to discuss the habit of assigning young, inexperienced, low-qualified sisters as principals. Not only was this bad for the schools, but also, in Fr. Conway's opinion, a divisive bone of contention for lay teachers aspiring to be principals. Besides the financial savings for school boards, there were other reasons for this practice. Often the parish priest wanted a religious principal because of her witness as a sister and also because he could easily get rid of those principals who turned out to be unsatisfactory. The superiors of the Orders told Fr. Conway that they felt pressured by the priests, who, even when they were not trustees or secretaries of the board, were powerfully influential. Some of the sisters did not want the job in the first place, but were living the vow of obedience. To complicate matters further, Mr. Macdonald stated that he and other separate school inspectors felt they could not write a bad report on a religious principal because the Order made up such an important part of the school board's staff.

Fr. Conway regarded this issue as crucial for the health of the schools and the unity of the Association. Sometimes lay principals' positions were jeopardized. Fr. Conway reported to the Executive about a call he received from the Mother General of a teaching Order. She had been approached for a sister to take over a school where a lay teacher had been principal and was requesting support in resisting the pressure from the board and parish priest so that she would not be spreading her sisters too thinly. Father went with the problem to Archbishop Pocock of Toronto. The Archbishop agreed with Fr. Conway, describing how in Saskatoon, where he had served as a priest, the sisters were working for lay principals and, in his opinion, did a better job as teachers and counsellors in a non-authoritative role.[92] Matters improved: sisters began working under lay principals and their appointment as religious principals took place only after discussions among the sister in question, the inspector, the board, and the Superior.

Another fractious topic was that of married men's allowances. Unarguably, Ontario society's attitude and the proportion of male wage earners mirrored the widespread conviction that both potential and actual married men as breadwinners merited a higher income. Although the shortage of male workers during World War II and the postwar baby boom necessitated the entry of more and more females into the world of work, the favouring of the male employee was still systemic, even in the province's public elementary schools where females comprised the large majority of teachers. Here the school boards appointed males almost exclusively to administrative positions.[93]

The separate school boards also regarded male teachers more highly. For example, the Toronto Separate School Board had five salary schedules, which were, from highest to lowest salaries, those for married men, single men, single women, religious men, and religious women teachers. Married women teachers did not have a schedule. The London Separate School Board and other urban boards had a similar arrangement.[94]

The position of OECTA was clear: it had a policy of "Equal Pay for Equal Work". But it countenanced or "tolerated" exceptions to the policy while salaries were so low in separate schools. Trustees too knew that the salaries made it difficult to support a family; some boards hired single males, then either terminated them or encouraged them to leave after the probationary period because they could not offer a potential married man a secure future. Other boards simply did not hire men. A number of separate school boards, however, tried to attract male teachers with a married men's allowance of about $400, a 10 per cent or more bonus. Fr. Garvey of the Executive agreed with all of this. In his opinion, because separate school boards could not afford to hire married men, they should acquire a B.A. and work in public high schools, where they could get a position because Catholic and non-Catholic students attended these schools.[95] B.E. Nelligan, Hamilton district president and a single teacher at the time, also argued in favour of married men's allowances, because he knew of married men teachers with children who had to supplement their income by working nights, weekends, and holidays outside of teaching.[96]

However, this contradiction to the equality policy caused a number of hot debates at AGMs between 1956 and 1961. Discrimination and other pejorative labels were attached to the allowance. The Board of Directors felt that some school boards were using the allowance in order to give a salary increase to a small minority of the staff rather than to all the teachers. Miss Tyrrell's attitude was conveyed in a remark made during negotiations with the Peterborough Separate School Board: she wondered why married men were getting paid more for what were essentially extra curricular activities. As late as 1961, Miss Babcock had a special meeting with the Fort William Separate School Board over the issue.[97] Both the practice and its contribution to divisiveness within OECTA remained throughout this period; after 1962, when parity with public school boards became possible, married men's allowances would come under greater attack and eventually disappear.

A third group in OECTA with needs unique from the rest of the Association's members were the married women teachers. As their numbers and contribution to separate schools and to OECTA grew, so did the trustees' and the Association's awareness of the married woman teacher's need for justice and equality.

The place of the married woman teacher was not, to put it mildly, an enviable one in the first half of the twentieth century and earlier. Both public and separate school boards mirrored many businesses by hiring them only when no other teachers were available and treating them less favourably than their fellow male teachers and even single female teachers. For example, in 1921 the Toronto Board of Education struck a policy regarding its married women teachers. Dismayed by the presence of a principal and his wife on the full-time regular staff list, the board eliminated the possibility of the repetition of such an occurrence. The policy required the resignation of all married female teachers; all such teachers automatically ceased to have a contract with the board on the date of their marriage. Those whose husbands were "able to maintain them" were to resign; presumably, this last point left a loophole for women with handicapped, disabled, or unemployed husbands. As a result of this policy some teachers kept their marriage a secret, wearing their wedding rings around their necks. During the war years, the shortage of male teachers necessitated exceptions to the policy, but in 1946 eighty-eight teachers on temporary appointments were forced to resign and make room for male teachers and single female teachers. The rationale of the trustees was simple. A woman's place is in the home; furthermore, there would be no incentive for young girls (emphasis added) to become teachers if they had to compete.[98]

Although this kind of policy or practice existed with a number of school boards, FWTAO at first did not object on behalf of its married members. Doris French quoted two members in her book: "No married woman - except in exceptional circumstances - should be teaching now that there are single girls out of a position;" and "No one can do two jobs well. A married woman is responsible to her family." French commented that her Association "accepted married women reluctantly, sharing the view of most boards that teaching and marriage do not mix. The teacher shortage during the 1950s pressed more and more married women into service but prejudice against them lingered."[99]

Because of the Second World War and the baby boom afterward, school boards began hiring more and more married women teachers on the regular staff. The Canada census reported only 3 per cent of female teachers as married, but in 1951 calculated 28 per cent. The Hope Commission in 1950 wrote that "if married women teachers were to leave the profession, and if Letters of Permission were no longer issued, in many sections of the province at least half the teaching positions in elementary schools would immediately fall vacant."[100] In 1946, as a result of their larger presence on staff, the Toronto Board of Education rescinded its policy on married female teachers. Cecilia Reynolds, Brock University assistant professor and writer on women in education, listed the reasons for the board's change of attitude: the teacher shortage; the training, experience, ability, and education of these women; the appeal to social justice and human rights; appreciation of their work during the war; and grounds of personal liberty.[101] But it was not until the early sixties that the practice of giving married women teachers inferior salaries and temporary contracts ceased.[102]

Ontario's separate school boards treated the married woman teacher no better than public boards. Views and policies discussed above seemed to be sanctioned by the Roman Catholic Church. Pope Pius XI's encyclical on Christian Marriage spoke in language that took for granted the model of the husband as the wage-earner and the wife as mother and homemaker: "In the State such economic and social methods should be adopted as will enable every head of a family to earn as much as, according to his station in life, is necessary for himself, his wife, and for the rearing of his children."[103] The Church upheld the Virgin Mary as the model mother and wife; the Gospel accounts of Martha and Mary reinforced the vocation of spouse and mother as self-fulfilling. Marian piety upheld the virtues of women as passivity, dependence and self-abnegation.[104] Elizabeth Moltmann-Wendel, quoted in a Catholic publication, expressed this with a sad bit of poetry:

> Women...seemed very independent but...fell silent as soon as they were with their husbands...Sometimes they disclosed...what profession they had once wanted to enter...Yet if one encountered them the next day, they had fallen back into anonymity and were once again devoted functionaries of married and family life.[105]

Thus, the Toronto Separate School Board, among others, had a similar policy to that of its public school counterpart. Once a female teacher got married she lost her permanent contract, went off the salary schedule, and, if rehired, became part of the "Emergency Married Women Teachers" list, and was given a temporary position at a salary about 20 to 25 per cent below the minimum for a regular teacher. Appeals to the board asking to be moved from the emergency to the regular staff list came in the 1940s from married women teachers who described their husbands as being unemployed, going overseas to war, or ill; the board, however, did not grant exceptions.[106]

OECTA began grappling with the situation shortly after coming into existence. Teaching positions had been scarce; single female and married male teachers seemed to need the jobs more than women with salary-earning husbands; religious teachers were providing a special witness and subsidizing separate school budgets. It is not surprising that, given all the conditions discussed in the previous pages, the Association would take some time before applying clearly and in a united way its equal-pay-for-equal-work policy to the married women teachers.

In 1946 the *News* reported the results of a survey of answers to the question, "Do you think a person's state in life should interfere with her professional standing?" Most districts answered no; only two replied that a married woman should not be employed if a single "girl" were available. In 1949 the Executive asked the Legislative Committee to look into the legality of dismissing married women teachers. Its answer was that the school board had a right to lay down certain regulations regarding the dismissal of a teacher and that the only way to test the legality of such a dismissal would be to make it a test case by asking for a Board of Reference.[107] (This would not happen until 1960.)

Meanwhile, the Lay Teachers' Committee was also looking at the topic of married women teachers. The members found it a "vexing" one, and, in its report to the AGM, reiterated the conviction that school boards should not hire as a new teacher a married woman when a suitable, qualified, and capable single teacher was available. However, the Committee did state that when a "girl" on staff married during the summer, she should be kept on staff in September and be paid according to her experience.[108]

The fifties would see OECTA enforce this right and others on behalf of its married women members, but the consensus would be reached gradually. On the one hand there was the attitude revealed in the following opinion in the Executive minutes of 1951: a three-year teacher-training course would

> cut off excellent young women teachers who ordinarily give good teaching service for approximately five years; these young women ... would naturally expect to become Canadian wives and mothers and ... later might wish to return to the profession in times of teacher shortage; (emphasis added)

and in the following anonymous letter to Miss Tyrrell filed in the archival correspondence: "God has commissioned me to tell your Federation that you are commanded to get rid of all married women in the Roman Catholic Schools."[109] On the other hand, Fr. Conway clearly remembered forty years later that as president and as salary negotiator he had as a major objective securing satisfactory wages and contracts for married women. He recalled being asked by a Walkerton Separate School Board trustee, "Should married women be making as much as you are demanding?", to which he replied, "Women have rights too."[110]

In 1951 the Lay Teachers' Committee submitted another report similar to the last one, but this time added the thought that consideration should be given to widowed and married teachers "definitely in need".[111] In 1952 the same committee, chaired by a married woman, Mrs. Marigold, sent the following three recommendations to the districts for study:

> That school boards should make every effort possible to be absolutely certain that vacancies cannot be filled with a qualified single teacher before hiring a married woman. That single teachers or widows should be given first consideration, then, if necessary, married women who are definitely in need of work for livelihood should be called upon to fill any vacancies.
> That a widow with small children should have the same right to teach as a single woman, providing the children are being well looked after and under supervision at all times.
> That married women actively engaged in teaching should be required to take on the full responsibility within the classroom and outside school hours in work pertaining to school matters.[112]

Such a policy would seem to have required some kind of means test, as well as close supervision of the professional and personal life of apparently less than ideal teachers. In any case, the Board of Directors rejected the policy, commenting that the supervision of children at home was beyond OECTA's jurisdiction and that the efficiency of the teacher should be the determinant of the teacher's professionalism, not her marital status. They referred to the next joint meeting of OECTA and OSSTA executives only the recommendation that married women teachers teaching consecutive years should receive the same increase in salary as single female teachers. The Executive then asked Fr. Siegfried to discuss this position with Bishop Berry of Peterborough.[113]

But in 1953 OECTA and other affiliates approved a policy brought forward by FWTAO that removed all discrimination from the OTF's view on married women teachers' salaries and contracts. They were to be employed by school boards on the same basis as single women; marriage was not to be considered as grounds for termination of contract; adequate maternity leave was to be granted; and married women returning to teaching after five or more years were to take a refresher course. The last point OECTA did not regard as discrimination because this was its position regarding any teacher away from the classroom for this period of time. However, this part of the policy would not seem to encourage having a child.[114]

OECTA was now united on the issue, but the task remained to educate its members, particularly its negotiators, and the trustees on the new policy. The teacher shortage would help. In the same year as the policy was approved, OTF met with OSTC to discuss the need for married women teachers because of what the trustees were calling a "national crisis" related to teacher supply. OSTC understood the new policy and how it would help in teacher recruitment, but were unwilling to dictate to public and separate school boards which were still demanding resignations from teachers who got married and placing married teachers on yearly contracts.[115]

It was at this point, 1954, that the married women teachers' issue assumed crisis proportions for the Executive: about sixty married women teachers of the MSSB advised their employers that they were going on strike within a few days unless their salaries and contracts improved.

This event merits close examination for a number of reasons: it reveals the powerlessness of teachers who do not act with the unified support of their federation; it shows the willingness of separate school trustees in the 1950s to use appeals to higher authorities (like the Roman Catholic Church) in order to close off negotiations; it suggests the Executive's total disapproval of strike action, a disapprobation so strong that it would outweigh considerations of policy and sympathy for the married women teachers of Toronto; it illustrates the attitude of the Toronto press to the idea of a teacher strike and to working married women teachers.

Emotions ran so high that it is important to isolate the unvarnished facts from the opinions expressed at the time and now, forty years later. In October 1953, there was a meeting of the Negotiating Committee of District 5, Toronto, which included one married teacher, Mrs. Mary Nevins. Among other matters the Committee expressed its support of the married women's concern over the board's long-standing practice of discrimination. In November the Committee met with the board's Teacher Relations Committee and felt that something might be done for the married women. On January 7, 1954 the Committee had Mrs. Nevins take the board's offer to her group. The salaries were to be raised to $1800 a year, compared to $2400 for the single female teachers; no other improvements were offered.[116]

On Thursday, January 14, thirty-six members of the Toronto Catholic Married Teachers' Association met at Rosary Hall to consider their response to the board. Claiming in a press interview that they could "get better salaries as store clerks," they voted unanimously with four abstainers to notify the board that they would not report for work on Tuesday, January 19 unless they were paid according to their experience. Monsignor H. J. Callahan, chairman of the board, stated to the papers that, "I think if people have a grievance, they have a perfect right to strike." Joseph Whelan, president of district 5 and chief negotiator, pointed out that nothing could be done for the married women teachers while they had no contracts.[117]

Saturday's *Toronto Daily Star* contained another statement from Msgr. Callahan and Mr. Whelan. The chairman explained that the board had recently changed its policy and begun hiring married women because of the teacher shortage. Mr. Whelan said negotiations were not closed and the teachers were "mixed up and acted hastily."[118]

By now the Executive felt it necessary to issue a Press Release:

> The OECTA deplores the threat of strike action by the married women teachers of the Separate Schools in Toronto and will give no support in such a procedure. Strike action is a violation of the Code of Ethics of the Ontario English Catholic Teachers' Association and of the Ontario Teachers Federation. The married women teachers of the Toronto separate schools have not approached the Provincial Executive in their salary dispute.[119]

The Executive also sent on Friday, the following night, this letter to sixty-seven married teachers:

> This will advise you that if the strike threat is carried out, the OECTA provincial executive will immediately take disciplinary action recommending to the Department of Education the suspension of your teaching certificates. A letter has gone to your district president clarifying our position in this issue.[120]

Marion Tyrrell commented to the Star that these letters were not to threaten but to advise and assist the teachers. Mrs. Mary O'Brien, the chair of the married teachers' association, responded that she failed "to see how we can be accused of breaking contracts which do not exist."[121] Of course, OECTA would regard an oral agreement or a board motion as ethically binding.

The Toronto papers were divided on the strike threat. The *Star's* editorial of January 18 was vaguely sympathetic, citing studies showing that married women's salaries were often needed for the support of the family. On the other hand, the *Globe and Mail's* editorial the next day labelled the strike action as unprofessional and improper, "forsaking the pupils,...using the children...[and] intimidation."[122]

The war of words continued in the press. On January 18, the day before the scheduled strike, the executive of the married women teachers' association expressed its dissatisfaction with the "ineffectual" bargaining by their Negotiating Committee. Joseph Whelan complained that the MSSB had not been given time to deal with the married women teachers' demands and that "we cannot reopen negotiations...if the married women insist on telling us how to run things."[123]

The night before the strike Mrs. Anne Wright and Mrs. Jacqueline Matte were asked to appear before an in camera session of the board to present the married women teachers' case. Msgr. Callahan advised them that, "A strike against the board is a strike against God." The combination of remarks like this and the Executive's night letter had caused support for the strike to dissipate over the weekend. Married women were telephoning the executive to express their fear of losing their certificates, their need for the salary, their accessibility to their schools, and their never-absent reluctance to see their pupils suffer. Thus, between the end of their meeting with the board and about 3 a.m., Mr. Whelan and the married women teachers agreed that the Negotiating Committee would continue bargaining on their behalf and that the strike would be "postponed". The teachers were telephoned; about a dozen who had not been reached showed up at Rosary Hall according to the original plan; they were sent by taxi at board expense to their schools. On January 20 forty-eight of the married women met again at the Hall and formally voted to continue negotiating.[124]

The crisis was over and the married women teachers ended up with almost nothing. On January 26 the Secretary of District 5 requested that negotiations be reopened. In March the board decided that, in view of the "generous increase" in salary to the married teachers and because of the "unsettled situation financially" of the new MSSB (legislation had just amalgamated the Toronto Separate School Board and surrounding separate school boards), there would be no further salary increase. However, the board would give contracts to the married teachers (still just annually) and would change its policy so that any female teacher who married during the school year would stay on the regular teacher's contract and salary until the end of June.[125]

It remained for the Executive to try to pick up the pieces, eliminate any possibility of strike action, and help the local negotiators to implement OECTA's policy regarding married women teachers. In March it met with Mr. Whelan and his committee. Mr. Whelan believed that the threatened strike and newspaper publicity had antagonized the school board to such an extent that it now felt giving in to any of the demands would encourage future unsatisfactory behaviour by the married teachers. Patrick Perdue expressed his disappointment that the local negotiators had allowed the morale of the married women to deteriorate and pointed out that this kind of disunity causes underbidding by teachers and lower salaries for everyone. After polling the married teachers, he recommended that any further negotiations be put off until the fall in order not to jeopardize improving the situation in the following year.[126] It was 1957 before the board finally admitted that, "sooner or later, the Board must consider their qualifications in the light of the single female teacher" and 1959 before it rescinded its policy on married women teachers and paid them the same salaries as the single female teachers.[127]

Two of the participants in this event, interviewed in 1993, still felt a sense of outrage over the way they were treated.

Mrs. Mary Nevins recalled Msgr. Callahan telephoning her at home to ask her if, as one of his parishioners, she was going on strike. She replied that she would do what the group decided was right. The chairman of the board then lectured her in an "arrogant" fashion on how she should be ashamed of herself.[128]

Mrs. Anne Wright remembered how no one seemed to support them. Some of their parents asked them if they had become communists. Even Whelan told them that the board would not change its policy and that they knew what they were getting into when they married; they had not been forced to marry. When he finally made a promise to represent them adequately, they called off the strike. All they had been looking for was agreement that they were suffering injustices. The whole experience was so devastating for Mrs. O'Brien, one of the leaders, that she became seriously ill, and left teaching. On the other hand, Marion Tyrrell, when interviewed on this matter in 1979, did not remember any details about the events.[129]

It is difficult to comment on all of this without appearing to write revisionist history. Perhaps the night letters represented overreaction, but the Executive was on the record as not supporting strikes in western Canada and was working hard to present an image of the professional teacher to trustees, parents, and society. Take away the issue of the strike and the actions of OECTA demonstrated a relatively quick growth and change in attitude regarding the place of married women teachers in separate schools. The Association, after the striking of the OTF policy, began forcefully to protect the interests of its married women members. In the files of OECTA was a copy of a letter dated 1955, from the Director of the Fair Employment Practices Branch to the assistant secretary of FWTAO, explaining that "*The Female Employees Fair Remuneration Act* lists no categories of exceptions. Therefore, no other interpretation is possible than that the Act does apply to women teachers."[130] This legislation, along with the Board of Reference statute, would provide OECTA with the moral and legal weapons to begin convincing school boards to abolish discriminatory practices with staff. It took awhile before recourse to Boards of Reference was used, perhaps because teacher contracts were not universal in this decade and perhaps because the initial tactic was the education of trustees.

At any rate married women teachers began receiving effective help from OECTA. In 1956 the Mattawa Separate School Board sent a memorandum to its staff stating that married women did not belong to the teaching personnel and that contracts for them would be for one year at a time. Miss Tyrrell responded by advising these teachers that they were in law on "continuing contracts" and could be dismissed only with written reasons related to the statutory duties of a teacher. In 1957, at a joint meeting of AEFO and OECTA, the French teachers announced that they had arrived at an agreement with l'Association française des conseils scolaires de l'Ontario wherein married women were to be engaged on the same basis as single women. OECTA stated the MSSB was one of only a few boards still discriminating on the basis of salary. In 1960 the president of District 11, London told the Board of Directors that the London Separate School Board was keeping its married teachers on probationary contracts, paying lower salaries, and not informing them until July if they would be rehired. Miss Tyrrell explained the regulations regarding probationary contracts and promised assistance for them if asked. She felt that some married teachers, on account of tradition, were still accepting term contracts and lower salaries; in her opinion much work was necessary to eliminate such practices. In 1961 the practice appeared to be stamped out. The Oshawa Separate School Board sent a letter to its married women teachers stating that they would be re-engaged for one year only. The Executive determined that this procedure was illegal since all the letters were addressed "Dear Madam" as opposed to a specific person, and so advised the board; subsequently, the teachers received the regular permanent contracts. In the same year Miss Sonia Harlow, who was on a permanent contract with the London Separate Board, was notified that in view of her impending summer marriage her contract would be terminated. The lawyer for OECTA advised that, unless her contract specified that she would be terminated upon marriage, the board could not carry out its intentions. Finally, an important legal precedent was set. Mrs. Conrad Grenier, on a permanent contract with the Cochrane Separate School Board, was asked for her resignation because of her marriage. She asked for and received a Board of Reference. OECTA hired a lawyer for her and the school board withdrew its request.[131] This appeared to settle the matter for any similar actions of school boards in the future.

By the 1960s OECTA, with its married men and women, single lay men and women, and religious members, was able to proceed on a united front. But an interesting footnote to the married women question appeared in the minutes of the Special Committee to select an Assistant Secretary for OECTA. Two married women applicants were rejected without an interview; no reason was in the minutes.[132]

OECTA, while developing a unity of purpose, also had to work at a wider solidarity with the other affiliates of OTF. As described below, positive activities of OTF took place with the Ministry in such areas as teacher education and certification. A serious problem, however, flared up in the area of salary negotiations. In 1952 OPSMTF brought in a "Single Salary Scale" and moved that it be OTF policy. AEFO regarded it with favour, since its members were the lowest-paid teachers in the smallest affiliate. OSSTF was so concerned about the risk that such a scale might cause secondary school teachers' salaries to drop that, after heated discussion, they left the meeting. OECTA members of OTF knew that separate school boards could not afford the OPSMTF scale at that time and wished to work toward somewhat lower objectives. In a recollection ten years later, Dorothea McDonell expressed the opinion that this issue caused OTF to come "close to disintegration". However, further discussion concluded with the conviction that a salary schedule developed for all the affiliates as a single entity would risk salaries reflecting the lowest common denominator. OTF decided to vacate the salary field, leaving the affiliates autonomous in the area of salary negotiating and of salary schedules.[133] The policy has held to the present.

Professional Development. Fr. Conway recollected in an interview that the low salaries of the 1940s and 1950s were an obstacle to the fostering of a professional spirit among OECTA members.[134] Despite or perhaps because of this obstacle, the Directors and Executive expended considerable effort "to work for the moral, intellectual, religious, and professional perfection of all the members" in accordance with the Association's Constitution.

The speeches and actions of Sr. Lenore, Fr. Siegfried, and Margaret Drago demonstrated a major concern with the fact that many young lay teachers without any background in religious education were coming into an expanding number of separate schools. Part of the fall-out from the *Tiny Township judgment* was that only a small minority of separate school graduates went on to private Catholic high schools. Tuition, space, accessibility, and entrance examinations kept the majority of Catholic students out. Furthermore, because of higher taxes for separate schools, an insufficient number of school buildings, a feeling that separate schools lacked adequate resources, and other negative attitudes about these schools, the Hope Commission estimated in 1950 that "probably less than two-thirds of the children of Roman Catholic parents are enroled in separate schools."[135] Thus, many of the new separate school lay teachers had a secondary school education in the secular subjects and only an elementary school or no education in religion, the subject that was supposed to permeate the total curriculum and life of the child.

The Executive decided to attack the problem first at the only root available to it - the Normal School. In 1953 it met with Cardinal McGuigan of the Archdiocese of Toronto to discuss among other topics the training for teaching of religion being offered at the Normal Schools (about to be named Teachers' Colleges). All at the meeting agreed that the short weekly optional period given by a local priest was inadequate. The Cardinal suggested that specially qualified teachers instead of priests be used for this purpose and that separate school boards hire supervisors to guide young teachers in the delivery of religious education. Sr. Lenore referred to a summer course being offered in Kingston that issued certificates in religious education; the school board was requiring this certificate when engaging new teachers.[136] The Lay Teachers Committee was asked to investigate these ideas to determine the best way to reach lay teachers not educated in Catholic schools. In addition, the Executive discussed the problem with Fr. Priester of ECEAO and through him with the province's bishops.[139]

For the next year Margaret Drago made the matter her personal top priority. To the Directors and the AGM she aired the following problems:

- separate school boards' staffs had as many lay as religious teachers due to the expansion;
- they were hiring teachers educated solely in public schools;
- inspectors were not evaluating the teaching of religious education;
- promotions did not depend on the ability to teach religion;
- and the religious education lessons at the Teachers' Colleges were negligible in the one-year programme and non-existent in the two-summer-school programme preliminary to the one-year course.

She and Fr. Siegfried recommended to the Bishops a chaplain for each Teachers' College, a religious education and methodology course with an examination, a special diploma in religion, hiring preference for those possessing the diploma, and the appointment by school boards of religious education supervisors.[138] Here was the genesis; all of this and more would eventually happen. Meanwhile, OECTA would have to obtain a coordinated effort from the Department of Education, its separate school inspectors, the Teachers' Colleges, the Bishops, OSSTA, and its separate school boards. Some of these players would not be too enthusiastic.

The inspectors came on board immediately. The Executive sent a letter to them asking them to inspect religion, to have principals assist the new teachers in planning religious education lessons, and to recommend to school boards that they require on teacher application forms information on what school the applicant had attended and what professional preparation for teaching religious education s/he possessed. Dr. McDonald was requested to interest the Archbishop of Ottawa in seeking better religious education training at the Ottawa Teachers' College. The separate school inspector for the Niagara Falls area, Alex Kuska, began to push for a course in religious education for student and practising teachers; he wanted the course to lead to a certificate and an annual increase of $50 for the salaries.[139]

In the absence of any religious education courses for the student teachers in the two summers prior to their year at the Teachers' Colleges and given that they started teaching at the end of the first summer, OECTA decided to fill the gap itself. In 1955 the Association struck a committee to prepare a four-afternoon course for the summer-school student teachers; it began that summer and continued annually until the Department abolished the summer-course route to obtaining an elementary school teacher's certificate. Some cooperation was acquired from the Department of Education. F. S. Rivers, the Superintendent of Professional Training for the province, agreed to ask the Teachers' College principals to announce the four-afternoon summer course; he felt unable, however, to countenance an increase from twenty to thirty periods of religious education in the regular one-year or two-year course; instead, he suggested that OECTA might consider religious education for the student courses after four p.m.[140] That one never got out of the gate.

By 1959 the Teachers' Colleges were issuing religious education certificates and OECTA was convinced that the separate school community was ready to expect that student and practising teachers take an in-service course in religious education and methodology. It began talks with OSSTA.[141]

OECTA was also anxious about maintaining and improving standards of admission to the teaching profession during this time of teacher shortage. The period of the teacher supply and training problem, described by historian Robert Stamp as a time of gravest crisis, resulted in the debasing of the teacher's certificate.[142] In 1953 W. J. Dunlop, the Minister of Education, responded in six ways to provide elementary school teachers:

- he reduced the number of grade thirteen subjects required for admission to the one-year course at Normal School;
- he permitted graduates of grade twelve to attend a two-year course at Normal School, also leading to a first-class certificate;
- he gave these junior matriculation graduates the option of taking a summer course at the Normal School in order to begin teaching immediately after in September; the candidate would return to the Normal School for a second summer, teach a second year, and then attend the Normal School for a full year for the first-class certificate; this third alternative was called the completing course;
- he eliminated the requirement for teachers qualified outside of Ontario and Canada that they write Departmental examinations after teaching for a year on a "letter of standing" in order to get a regular Ontario teacher's certificate;
- he abolished the imperative that teachers take in-service courses to convert their interim certificates to permanent ones after two years of teaching;

- finally, he changed the name "Normal School" to "Teachers' College" in order to raise the status of the institution.[143]

Even though the academic demands of a full grade thirteen programme were now gone, Dunlop was reluctant to admit a teacher shortage; Stamp wrote that he would not even admit that standards had been lowered. It was probably not surprising to OTF and OECTA that they would have very little success in getting standards raised or even in having consultations with him. Dunlop described objections to the summer programmes, for example, as "part and parcel of a campaign to transfer to the Federation, from the Minister, the power and responsibility of determining who shall teach in the Province."[144]

Nevertheless, OECTA and other affiliates did achieve some small success and, of course, prepared the way for the seventies when the standards for admission to the elementary school teacher-training course would be dramatically raised.

OTF initially responded to Dunlop's changes by agreeing "very reluctantly" to the grade twelve admissions plans as a temporary measure only for an emergency.[145] Then, with the affiliates, it developed a policy that there be two kinds of teachers' certificates: a Type A, which would mean grade thirteen plus three years of university, and a Type B, which would be awarded for eight grade thirteen credits; any lower training would lead only to a provisional certificate.[146] In addition, OTF wanted the Department to grade certificates according to the teacher's academic background. This request, at least, the Board of Directors was able to report at the 1955 AGM, resulted in a compromise; the Department would write on the back of the certificate what education the holder of the certificate had.[147]

By the late 1950s even the supply of grade twelve graduates was insufficient to meet staffing needs. OECTA expressed its concern about the number of teachers on "letters of permission" (that is, unqualified) and asked that the Department demand at least 60 per cent in grade twelve results. A joint OTF-OSTC report on "The Teacher Supply Situation in Ontario" concluded that summer courses were here to stay and recommended that candidates be tested for at least grade eight competence in reading, arithmetic, and spelling and that completing-course candidates in the first summer do some practise teaching in the classroom (emphasis added). Also, OECTA felt it necessary to defeat a motion that there be refresher courses for those out of teaching for five years.[148]

In 1960 OECTA was gratified to hear the new Minister of

Education John Robarts announce that grade twelve admission to the Teachers' Colleges would be abolished. It would be another five years before this was possible.[149]

On this topic of teacher training there was one issue where OECTA disagreed with OSSTF. Once elementary school teachers acquired a B.A., they could attend a one-summer course at OCE in order to acquire a HSA. OSSTF took the position that this route should be abolished to maintain high standards. OECTA replied that its members had already attended a Teachers' College for one year; to require a second full year would be an unnecessary hardship. The one-summer course remained.[150]

Finally, on the subject of teacher certification and professionalism, a topic surfaced that was and still is of importance to all teachers' associations throughout Canada: the "licensing" of teachers by OTF. The Board of Directors of OECTA drew parallels with the *Registered Nurses Act* of 1951 which stipulated that the Board of Directors of the Registered Nurses Association of Ontario was to decide on standards of admission to schools of nursing, the setting of examinations to be required for registration of nurses, the courses of study in nursing schools, and the renewing or cancellation of certificates of registration.[151] Only with regard to the last point has OECTA through OTF had any say and then only in an advisory capacity. Some teachers and other members of the public would argue that until OTF has these powers it is not representing a true profession.

As far as teacher evaluation was concerned, the separate school inspectors working exclusively for the Department of Education (only urban boards of education had the power in law to hire their own directors of education and superintendents) and OTF had no input. Inspectors would visit the classroom, evaluate the teacher on a one-to-four rating, then put the evaluation in a file confidential even from the teacher. A motion from the Board of Directors was designed to improve this reductionist procedure.

> Whereas there are evidences of some teachers...suffering nervous reaction which is detrimental to good teaching and against the best interests of the children [and which is] due to negative criticisms on the part of some Elementary School Inspectors
>
> and
>
> Whereas it would seem that there is a lack of uniformity throughout the province in the methods of issuing Inspectoral reports,
>
> Be It Therefore Resolved that the OTF be asked to approach the

> Department of Education with a view to having developed a uniform "Report of Inspection" to be issued confidentially to teachers and wherein the Inspectors shall be encouraged to follow any negative criticisms with constructive help.[152]

It would be about two decades before evaluation files came open for teachers to examine. Meanwhile, OECTA dealt with inspectors directly on behalf of its members. For example, it met with W. J. Bulger, separate school inspector, to discuss his practice of recommending only young teachers to school boards and its feeling that weak teachers were not being assisted sufficiently before dismissal. OTF, in response to a similar problem, urged that inefficient teachers be told within three to five years of possible dismissal instead of stalling for ten to fifteen years when it would be more difficult for them to change careers. As a result of such Federation actions, G. A. Pearson, Superintendent of Elementary Education, issued a two-year procedure for inspectors dealing with older, inefficient teachers.[153]

One proposed solution to the problem of peremptory inspections by outside occasional visitors was the shifting of part of this responsibility to the principal. OTF suggested that the regulation be changed so that elementary school principals would have the same powers as their secondary school peers; that is, they would have the power and duty to evaluate teachers. This was premature for separate schools because, as Brother Cornelius pointed out, principals were usually teaching full-time and were, therefore, unable to report on deficiencies.[154] Eventually, this shift would take place in the separate schools as it had happened in the high and public schools.

A Catholic Curriculum. One OECTA aim was to improve teacher education; a complementary task was to provide a curriculum suitable for and helpful to the Catholic teacher in a separate school. Sr. Lenore devoted a number of years on the Association's executive to working at this occupation. She was convinced that "teachers had been too passive in former years in taking dictation in many matters - for instance, accepting a Course of Studies as a 'fait accompli'"[155] and she set out to develop a Catholic curriculum permeating all the secular subjects, a "true integration in education, the physical, intellectual, emotional, and spiritual." In her first year as president of OECTA she called a planning meeting at the Martyrs' Shrine, Midland;[156] the mechanism developed there was the Catholic Curriculum Development Conference (CCDC), an event which first took place at the Royal York Hotel, Toronto, in December 1952 and which became an annual occurrence. Each year a keynote speaker concentrated on one subject in the curriculum to show how religious education could be integrated with it. The position of all the speakers throughout the 1950s can be expressed in the words of Reverend John M. Beahen, D.C.L., the 1954 speaker:

> The child who sees religion relegated to twenty minutes in a class cannot but grow up to be the man who, at best, gives it a half hour on Sunday mornings.... We must realize that the truth of God is not circumscribed by the limits of the catechism class, but that all truth falls within His domain and to teach it as if it did not is something of a sacrilege....One day...you will be given to see that you have been fashioning the sons of men into the children of God. You will see that, for others, you have bridged two worlds to bring your charges to eternity....The day that you decided to become a teacher you yourself put one foot in Heaven.[157]

By 1957 the CCDC had considered philosophy, psychology, English literature, social studies, science, music, and art from the perspective of the separate school curriculum, and had received congratulations from the Ontario bishops as well as the encouragement and presence of Cardinal McGuigan.[158] One guest speaker conveyed confidence in the teacher to strive, for example, in science "to arouse in the students a feeling of wonder, awe, reverence, and humility for the vastness and complexity of the universe...and a feeling of thankfulness for its multitudinous variety of God-given gifts;"[159] another speaker urged them to teach the social doctrine of the Roman Catholic Church in the social sciences and literature, wherever the student encounters human relationships with their effects, both good and bad.[160]

At the same time OECTA gave careful attention to the textbooks used in separate schools. It established a special sub-committee to review a new Catholic reader in 1951 and another one in 1956 to evaluate the religious education textbooks being used in the Catholic high schools throughout Ontario. In 1959 the Executive reassured Veronica Houlahan, an Ottawa teacher, that her worry about the imminent removal by the Department of Education of a Catholic series of readers was being addressed. Also in the 1950s a committee worked on a revision to the decades-old Baltimore Catechism and developed religion course outlines for the elementary schools.[161]

OECTA also kept a careful eye on Circular 14 which listed the textbooks approved by the Department of Education in the public and separate schools. For example, the Board of Directors sought authorization of a primary division reader by a Fr. John A. O'Brien and the Executive struck a committee to prepare a supplement of sacred music for a Circular 14 text, High Roads of Song. In 1955 OECTA considered preparing a list of religious texts for inclusion on the permissive list of Circular 14, but decided not to act on this plan for fear that the Department might feel it had authority in the area of religious education in the separate schools.[162] (The "hands-off" attitude of the Minister, deemed desirable here, was a problem with some separate school inspectors who stayed away from visiting teachers during religious education lessons, an absence which, as discussed above, OECTA regarded as undesirable.)

The Association applied its talents, in addition, to special curriculum topics to assist its members. Position papers and detailed written aids were developed on the gifted child, on how to teach English as a Second Language, on the use of filmstrips, together with a list of titles geared to certain age groups and subjects, and on salacious literature.[163]

The idea of a Catholic Institute of Child Study discussed by the Executive and Cardinal McGuigan in 1951 would have to await the genesis of the Institute for Catholic Education.[164]

To highlight the professional development and curriculum activities of OECTA, Sr. Margaret, S.S.N.D., supervisor of art for the Kitchener Separate School Board, designed a coat of arms. It consists of a trillium as the floral emblem of Ontario, a torch representing knowledge and teaching, an open book for a symbol of imparting knowledge, and the cross signifying the Catholic religion. The inscription, "Euntes Ergo Docete" (going, therefore, teach) is, in Sister's explanation,

> an apostolic challenge to every teacher to teach and instruct the students unto justice and the fullness of Christ in their minds by a knowledge of their duties to God, neighbour and self, and in their hearts by the practice of virtue in the service of God and neighbour.[165]

Protection of Separate School Rights. The 1950s were marked, in Roger Graham's words, by "an undercurrent of demand" by separate school leaders for kindergarten to grade thirteen, and for corporation taxes.[166] OECTA was part of these activities because most of the problems it encountered regarding separate schools were directly connected to the high school and finance issues.

OECTA minutes did show some residual fretting about the 1950 Hope Commission Report, especially its recommendation for junior high schools. Once the South Peel, East York, and North York Boards of Education opened up these intermediate schools, the Association saw them as another reinforcement of the separate school ceiling of grade ten. Franklin Walker, separate school historian, wrote that the ECEAO even promised Catholic silence for burying the Report; for how long and on what topics it was not specified, but the climate was nervous.[167] Ultimately, however, OECTA's apprehension was unwarranted: the Hope Report quietly died. When *OECTA News* mentioned it in an article, J. C. Walsh, a high-placed Catholic official with the Department of Education, wrote to Miss Tyrrell:

> It is not deemed politic to resurrect that Report. Let sleeping dogs lie. The present Ontario Government has contributed discreetly but effectively towards relegating the Hope Report to the Limbo of lost causes.... Anyway, the idea of a 6-4-3 school organization seems to have lost much of its vogue.[168]

Nevertheless, OECTA remained cautious when it came to Catholic high school topics. It had been a tradition for public high schools to hold final examinations early in June, then dismiss the students for the summer holidays; presumably, this was to allow time for the teachers to mark the examinations. The Catholic high school principals considered asking the Department of Education for permission to follow the same practices, but OECTA's Secondary Schools Committee decided against this idea for fear that the separate school boards would lose some grants for their grades nine and ten, or that the boards' right to offer these grades would come under scrutiny. For the same reasons and despite the *Tiny Township* judgment recognizing grades nine and ten as part of a separate school, the Committee decided not to question the Department's custom of allowing only public high school students to attend make-up courses at the OCE summer school and only prospective public high school teachers to enrol in the emergency two-summer OCE course leading to a HSA. In this climate of apprehension it was, of course, deemed "unwise" to seek any government aid for private Catholic high schools.[169]

On the other hand, Fr. Conway's Secondary Schools Committee did act to protect Catholic high school rights such as they were. Fr. Priester of the ECEAO was urging separate school boards to take advantage of their right to operate grades nine and ten and, despite the sacrifice involved in receiving only elementary school grants for doing so, the Committee encouraged such action. The Committee also submitted a brief to the Department asking for a waiver or reduction of the fee for the annual inspection of private Catholic high schools.[170] OECTA, as well, did not hesitate to disagree with OTF affiliates when it was a question of separate school rights. When OSSTF brought a motion to OTF that teachers of grades nine and ten should be required to attend OCE and get a HSA, Patrick Perdue pointed out that such a requirement would work against separate school interests. The elementary school teacher's certificate qualified one to teach in the primary, junior, and intermediate divisions. The AGM decided to approve the motion if it applied only to public high school teachers. In a second topic of controversy in OTF, OECTA decided to stay quiet while FWTAO and OPSMTF argued with OSSTF over such issues as salary and affiliate membership in junior high schools. Sr. Lenore and Fr. Conway publicly expressed doubts over how well students in grades seven-to-nine schools would be prepared for grades ten to thirteen, but privately, their real concern was the risk of separate school boards being prevented from operating beyond grade six.[171]

A more difficult question for OECTA and its Catholic high school principals was who should be admitted to the student body. With the absence of grants and taxes for the senior division and the inadequate revenues from these sources for the intermediate Catholic division on the one hand and the Catholic school's mission to educate all the Catholic children on the other hand, a dilemma presented itself. Tuition and very limited classroom space would shut out a large number of students. At a 1958 meeting of the province's Catholic high school principals, the decision was made to admit only those students who could meet relatively high academic standards and who could afford the tuition. The risk of elitism was weighed against the strategy of educating students who, in the future as leaders, might bring about changes in government policies and funding for Catholic high schools.[172]

The other problem for separate schools, the lack of corporation tax revenues, also received the Association's attention. It was exacerbated in the 1950s by the baby boom, the increase in immigration, urban growth, the drop in the proportion of religious teachers, and the "vexatious" problem of the many small rural school sections (this last difficulty was compounded by the separate school board's three-mile limit).[173] As the decade advanced, the funding shortage was having more pervasive effects on separate schools: a lack of adequate or sufficient school buildings, a dearth of special facilities for kindergartens, libraries, and gymnasia, crowded classrooms and high pupil/teacher ratios, costs to pupils for some of the instructional supplies, salaries lower than those in the public schools, fewer qualified teachers than those in the public schools, a mill rate higher than that of the coterminous public school board, and, particularly in Toronto, large numbers of Roman Catholic *public* school supporters.[174] The financial problem was not only a matter of protection of separate school rights, but also of the Association's self-interest.

OECTA strategy was to work with the ECEAO so that the entire Catholic community would lobby the government.[175] Thus, meetings with AEFO and OSSTA took place to prepare background papers for the ECEAO on such topics as the need for better grants for rural separate school boards, better funding for all separate schools, the harmful effect of in an expanding enrolment basing grants on the previous year's expenditures, and the need for an amendment in legislation so that separate school boards could somehow, in spite of the three-mile-limit clause, consolidate inefficient one- and two-room separate schools. In 1959 ECEAO decided the best group to present the final brief to Premier Frost would be the OSSTA politicians talking to politicians.[176]

It is difficult to determine how much influence this work had on the government since, traditionally, the latter usually designed any improvement in school financing in such a way that public and separate school boards would get the same benefits. Things did improve, though not enough. In 1958 two concepts were introduced into the grant structure: equalized assessment and a growth needs factor. The first innovation meant that the Minister of Education could now determine the relative wealth of each board and increase grants tied to need. There would now be fifteen categories of school boards with different grant rates. The second concept addressed the problem of the burgeoning population in Metropolitan Toronto and other centres. These two initiatives benefited separate school boards enough to prompt the Grand Orange Lodges of Ontario and the Public School Trustees' Association of Ontario to object to higher grants for separate schools translating into lower ones for public schools.[177]

OECTA also worked at the local level on the financial problems of separate school boards. Fr. Siegfried sometimes had to assist small separate school boards to understand the grants sufficiently to take full advantage of them. For example, OECTA advised the Sarnia Separate School Board to obtain a subsidy from the Church parishes so that it could pay higher salaries, claim higher grants, and then partially refund the parish. When the Spanish Separate School Board and RCSS #1, Shedden were unable to pay their teachers for two months, Miss Tyrrell convinced the Department in the first place to arrange a loan for the board and in the second place to advance the grants.[178] And, of course, OECTA supported the CPTAs that often donated instructional supplies and library materials.[179] By dint of such efforts, crises were averted, but the financial situation for the separate schools of Ontario remained serious.

Administration of OECTA. Some housekeeping and refinements took place as the Association moved through its first decade. Attention was paid to the Executive, AGM, types of membership, districts, committees, and budget.

The Executive was required to include at least one former past president with time served on the OTF executive who was to be one of two counsellors. Candidates for president or first vice-president were required to have served at least one year on the Executive. Candidates for second vice-president needed only experience at the district level for two years. The Executive was further expanded with the new office of assistant secretary created in 1959 to help the secretary treasurer (previously secretary).[150]

Miss Mary Babcock (1907-) was selected from twenty-seven applicants to assist Marion Tyrrell, who reluctantly gave up her place as editor of the *OECTA News* and welcomed assistance in the areas of relations, discipline, and salary negotiations, to name a few. The Special Committee selected Miss Babcock because of her teaching experience, her work with an OECTA forerunner, the Toronto Catholic Teachers' Association, her organizational and managerial skills, and her public-speaking ability.

The daughter of James Babcock, a locomotive engineer, and Anastasia Healy, a public school teacher, Mary had four brothers, Peter, Joseph, Vincent, and Gerald, and two sisters, Margaret and Agnes. She was educated at St. Francis de Sales separate school and Smith Falls Collegiate Institute. After receiving her secondary school graduation diploma, she attended North Bay Normal School. With the tight job market she still did not have a teaching position in August 1926, but at that time her uncle, chairman of the Thessalon public school board, offered her the place of a teacher who had just resigned at a salary of $1000, almost double what she expected. After five and a half years there, Mary Babcock got a teaching position with the Toronto Separate School Board. Because Holy Rosary separate school was about half a block outside Toronto city limits and because Miss Babcock now had her music supervisor's certificate, she received an extra $50 a year from the Department of Education. She earned it by having a school choir and rhythm band and teaching music on rotary. She left teaching in the 1930s to become an insurance saleswoman and one year later was promoted in her company to unit supervisor. She went on to be the first female branch manager in Canada. Later she was a training assistant at her company's home office and a chartered life underwriter. Outside of work she was involved in a number of community activities: president of her parish's Catholic Women's League, president of the Pro Aliis Club and the Soroptimist International of Toronto, director of the Life Underwriters Association of Toronto, president of the Elizabeth Fry Society, and regional director of the Services Objectives Committee for Eastern Canada Soroptomist International.

She would eventually replace Marion Tyrrell upon her retirement. The selection committee appointed her after expressing in the minutes that no suitable male was available for the post. One can be thankful that at least they had the sense to consider Mary Babcock above any less qualified male. [176]

The next task was to spell out the duties of the AGM: to determine membership fees, approve the OECTA salary schedule, receive the annual financial statement from the Budget Committee, amend the Constitution and by-laws, determine general policy, elect the president, three vice-presidents, treasurer, and two executive counsellors, elect the member to the Superannuation Commission, and discuss such matters and business transactions as may be brought before it.[177]

District boundaries were changed. In 1952 Kirkland Lake and Timmins became two separate districts. In 1954 the new district of Sarnia was created.[178]

As OECTA expanded its activities, new standing committees were created under the headings of Salary Negotiating, Secondary School, Mental Health, Audio-Visual, Catholic Curriculum Development, and Professional Development. The Educational Research and Policies Committee was renamed Educational Studies. In view of the developing unity of all OECTA's members, the Lay and Religious Committees were abolished.

In one incident the chair of the Religious Committee wrote to the province's Bishops and Superiors of Orders to elicit their reactions to the Association's proposed revision of the salary schedule. This unilateral action served to clarify the modus operandi of provincial committees. In theory, they were to take action solely on the advice of the Executive, Board of Directors, or AGM. Similarly, district resolutions were not to be implemented until they came through these bodies.[179]

Descriptions of the various types of membership in OECTA were redeveloped. The term regular was changed to statutory. Associate members were statutory members of another affiliate. The Executive could sponsor a person for honorary membership: the candidate was to have been a statutory member for ten years, ineligible to be such any longer, and an outstanding contributor to education. Teachers in private Catholic high schools could be voluntary members; separate school inspectors were ruled out because they had their own association and made confidential reports on teachers for the Department of Education. Finally, there was the life membership to honour retired teachers who had given distinguished service to OECTA. The choice was in the hands of the Board of Directors.[180] The first two life members were the aforementioned Cecilia Rowan and Fr. L.K. Poupore, O.M.I.

The *News* of June 1958 printed a biography of Fr. Poupore to note the event. He was born in Chichester, Quebec, son of Mr. and Mrs. Thomas Poupore, a pioneer family of Pontiac County. He attended the Universities of Ottawa and Maynooth, Ireland. After his ordination he joined the Ottawa St. Patrick's College staff where he served ten years as principal. He then spent a total of nine years as a professor of economics and Rector of the College. He headed the Institute of Social Action, was chaplain of the Ottawa Newman Club, and in 1956 Provincial of the English-speaking Oblate Fathers. His most noteworthy contribution to OECTA was, as a member of the Ottawa Catholic Teachers' Association, his negotiations with the government in the formation of OECTA in 1944. He then served on the new Association's Legislative Committee. His commitment to the concept of a Catholic teachers' organization was of the highest order.[181]

Finally, the most time-consuming task sometimes at AGMs was the setting of membership fees. In addition to the inevitable debate over how much increase to set in inflationary years, OECTA had to submit the new fee to the Minister of Education for approval. Fr. Siegfried, in an unsuccessful attempt to simplify the procedure and cut down on future debates, tried to convince the AGM to tie the fee to the teacher's salary. This plan would have seen fees go up as a percentage of rising salaries. Father felt that this scheme would eliminate annual debates and approvals, keep up with inflation and derive higher fees from those most able to pay. Years later in an interview, he was still regretted this failure.[182] However, his success was in the establishment of a reserve fund initially set at one dollar per member. It was to be used for grants or loans to teachers experiencing dire need, unforeseen illness, or catastrophe and for students at Teachers' College unable to continue the programme for lack of money.[183] Later, it became indispensable as a fund to assist teachers on strike, for the preparation of unanticipated briefs, and for expenses related to emergency political action.

Biographies of the Presidents.

Sr. Mary Lenore Carter, S.P., (1897-1990).[184] It is noteworthy that the first seven presidents of OECTA were three religious and four lay teachers, three female and four male teachers. With the exception of the married women teachers (who had to wait until 1970), the subgroups of the Association had been represented in the top position. The other two male-female affiliates, OSSTF and AEFO, did not have as good a record in this matter. Mother Lenore added another distinction: she was the first sister to be president of OECTA and of OTF.

Irene Carter, born in Montreal, was raised in a devout Irish Catholic household there. Her father, Tom, was an active member of Hibernian societies and, in the words of his son, G. Emmett Cardinal Carter, Archbishop emeritus of Toronto, he was a "union man", perhaps instilling in his daughter Irene an appreciation of the value of teachers' associations.[185] Her mother, Mary Agnes Kerr, originally from New York, later Quebec City, was the traditional devout Irish Catholic wife and mother. They had three girls and five boys, two of whom became sisters (Irene, a Sister of Providence, and Maery, a member of the Religious of the Sacred Heart of Jesus), and two of whom became princes of the Church (Alexander, bishop of the Sault Ste. Marie diocese, and Emmett, bishop of the London diocese, archbishop of the archdiocese of Toronto, and a member of the College of Cardinals).

Tom was not initially supportive of Irene's decision to enter the Sisters of Providence in Kingston,[186] possibly because of her youth, but she prevailed and served the Order from 1916 until her death in 1990. She attended Ottawa Normal School in 1920 and immediately began teaching. Her assignments were St. Francis, Smiths Falls, Maryvale Abbey, Glen Nevis, St. Joseph, Lancaster, St. Margaret, Glen Nevis, and St. John, Kingston (1935-38). During this time she worked on her B.A. in the summers, graduating from Queen's University in 1937. She then attended OCE in 1940 and acquired a HSA. Next she embarked on both a secondary school teaching career and an M.A. in English at Ottawa University (1947). Her teaching experience embraced most of the grades in elementary and secondary school; her brother, the Cardinal, said she taught everything, with the possible exception of high school mathematics and science. Her assignments included teaching at the Glen Nevis convent separate school (famous for operating high school classes with grants and taxes before and during the Tiny Township controversy), and being principal of St. Michael's high school in Belleville from 1938 to 1959, when she retired from teaching.

In 1951 she became president of OECTA. She had already been active in the Association since its inception, had served as district president in Belleville for two years, and had been the first chair of the provincial OECTA Adult Education Committee. She would continue to serve on the provincial executive for ten years and be president of OTF and a director of CTF.[187] Her dedication was revealed in her own words in a 1981 interview.

> At the time I was principal of St. Michael's High School in Belleville and I recall that for many years I left the school at 2 p.m. on Friday afternoons in order to catch the train for Toronto. OECTA executive members held their meetings at Federation House on Prince Arthur Street [sic] after working from nine in the morning until nine at night. We had a break for supper when we walked from the old house to a restaurant on Bloor St. where you could get a pretty good meal for about $3.50. By Sunday noon I was back on the train for Belleville. I did this for a number of years, about fifteen in all, I believe, both for OECTA and OTF, when we were laying the foundation for the federation.[188]

In the same interview she explained her considerable interest in and her ten-year involvement on the OECTA executive: "I wanted to try and make people more aware of the existence of Catholic schools, what was separate and important about them, so that they had the correct understanding of what Catholic schools stood for." Her dream, which was realized, was to establish an annual Catholic Curriculum Development Conference (CCDC) under OECTA auspices, an idea she got from Washington Catholic University and the National Catholic Education Association. "I had a plan in my head to devise and develop a truly Catholic curriculum of education, one permeated throughout by Christian values." She soon became a provincial leader in the movement to revamp religious education methodology. "Just memorizing things didn't convey the spirit of religion. I think you needed something more gripping. Just memorizing Butler's Catechism without understanding too well just what the meaning was certainly wasn't my idea of teaching."[189]

Fr. Conway, later a provincial president, recalled Sr. Lenore at AGMs conducting the business with the intelligence and dispatch of a chief executive officer of a large corporation; there was no question of who was in charge. Her niece described her as a combination of mildness, sweetness, and strength, the iron hand in a velvet glove.[190]

Two professors at St. Jerome's College wrote of Sr. Lenore as follows. She "served in a leadership capacity, often in an unprecedented way, on the executive of the Ontario English Catholic Teachers' Association and the Ontario Teachers' Federation."[191] This charismatic leader with an Irish sense of humour had the respect of all the affiliates and of her Order. She was made a Fellow of the Canadian College of Teachers in 1964 and a life member of OECTA in 1966, served as mother general of the Sisters of Providence from 1965 to 1971 and as superior at St. Michael's Convent in Belleville from 1971 to 1977, and received a Coronation Medal from Queen Elizabeth in recognition of her contribution to education. Probably equally touching for her was the spontaneous bursting into song of the entire body at the 1953 AGM when she retired as president: "For She's a Jolly Good Fellow".[192]

Margaret Drago (1906-). In 1953, for the third time in the first ten years of OECTA, at the AGM OECTA elected a lay woman as president. Margaret had already been president in Niagara Falls, had served on the first Relations and Discipline Committee, and had been asked to replace Lorraine Ganter as a counsellor on the executive.

Margaret Drago was another product of an era when single women lay teachers made small salaries and often stayed in the same school for decades. With a class size of about fifty pupils, an income of about $1000 a year, and a $50 raise as rare as the sighting of a new planet in the skies, such teachers derived their satisfaction from their vocation and did not consider mobility.

Margaret's sense of responsibility developed at an early age. The daughter of Louis Drago, a passenger agent for the New York Central Railroad, and of Annie, an organist and active member for the Church, she lost her father at age twelve. At that time her oldest brother,

Clarence, was advised to leave the seminary to help his mother raise Margaret and her other children, Eleanor, Louis, and Isabelle. Each child got work as soon as possible and helped with the household expenses. Margaret followed this pattern. Although born in Toronto, she lived from an early age right across the street from St. Patrick, Niagara Falls. Having earned her junior matriculation from the Loretto high school by the age of sixteen, in 1922 she went to Hamilton Normal School and returned to teach at St. Patrick.

On more than one occasion she affirmed that she had always wanted to be a teacher and always loved the work. Teaching from age eighteen to sixty-six certainly demonstrated that. Through the Depression, World War II, the baby boom, the equitable funding of elementary separate schools in 1962, and the advent of county boards, she taught several generations of primary pupils at St. Patrick, as well as helping out in other classrooms with music and entering her pupils in city-wide choral singing contests. Her mother, sister Eleanor, and OECTA members of AGMs and Executive meetings enjoyed her humorous anecdotes garnered from the daily life she spent with the children. Since she lived at home across from the school, she was able to devote many hours beyond the contract requirements to her teaching. Typically, she made a joke of this, telling how she promised her doctor, who said she needed more exercise, that she would walk to school.

When her school board began offering kindergarten in 1949, Margaret initiated this programme at St. Patrick and for many years introduced her pupils to school. Late in her career she took on a new challenge. Once a category system of salaries finally came into existence, Miss Drago was able to assemble certificates in music, kindergarten-primary methods, and elementary and intermediate special education that she had acquired between 1926 and 1962, and, together with a 1969 course for the specialist's certificate in special education, moved to standard two of the elementary school teacher's certificate. She then began as a teacher diagnostician for the new Welland County RCSS Board. In 1971 she was sixty-five years old, the mandatory retirement age for teachers, but she asked to continue for another year in her new position; the Board was happy to grant the extension, then gave her a retirement farewell presentation in 1972. Even after this she stayed active, becoming president of the Superannuated Teachers of Ontario (STO) in 1981 and serving on the Greater Niagara General Social Planning Council.

Her commitment to Catholic education went beyond St. Patrick. During the years of severely straitened financial circumstances for separate schools, Miss Drago worked after hours checking assessment records at city hall, then visiting the families of Roman Catholic public school supporters to explain how they could change their residential taxes and receive a separate school education for their children. She was also music director at St. Ann's Church.

To the office of president of OECTA she brought the concerns discussed in the previous chapter: security of tenure, superannuation benefits, salaries, and curriculum development. But her major thrust would be addressing the problem of delivering a high-level religious education programme in separate schools often staffed by young, inexperienced teachers. Here she made a significant difference. Her fellow Executive members remember her for this and for her great sense of humour and ability to be the life of any party. She was such a great storyteller that Mary Babcock remembered one meeting when all present sat glumly through her comical anecdotes in an attempted practical joke on her; it backfired, however, since they were unable to keep straight faces.[193]

Her exemplary career brought her signal recognitions: a life membership in OECTA in 1966, an OTF Fellowship award in 1964, and a Coronation Medal from Queen Elizabeth.[194]

Reverend Cornelius ("Corky") Louis Siegfried, C.R., (1916-1989). Described as a "titan" in the teaching profession by the University of Waterloo newspaper,[195] OECTA's second priest-president received an astounding number of signal honours during his career.

Born in Formosa, the son of Bruce County farmers, Anthony Siegfried and Margaret Ditner, he moved at an early age to Walkerton and began his education at Sacred Heart separate school. Along with his six brothers and sisters, Anthony, Willard, Kathleen, Verna, Gertrude, and Rose, he grew up in the snow-belt and cottage country of Ontario. After graduating from St. Mary's high school (now Sacred Heart), he was offered generous assistance to pursue pharmacy, but declined in order to discover if he had a religious vocation. In 1933 he enroled in philosophy at St. Jerome's College, Waterloo and the following year entered the novitiate of the Congregation of the Resurrection. In 1941 he completed a B.A. from the University of Western Ontario and his theology courses at St. Peter's Seminary. That same year he was ordained.

Fr. Siegfried promptly attended OCE in the school year 1942-43 and began teaching science and mathematics at St. Jerome. After he spent three years of teaching and some time on acquiring an M.A. in physics from the University of Michigan, the Order appointed him president of St. Jerome's College, at age thirty-two the youngest president ever. After serving in this office, he became president of North Bay College. He returned to Waterloo to be president at St. Jerome twice more, 1955 to 1965 and 1972 to 1979, when he resigned because of heart problems. During this time he was greatly influential in obtaining a university charter for St. Jerome's, and he helped draft the federation agreement with the University of Waterloo, as well as supervising a building expansion. Between his second and third term of office as president, Fr. Siegfried was provincial superior of the Resurrectionist Order, making a total of thirty-one continuous years in executive positions.

Even after retirement he continued to help out in the Kitchener-Waterloo parishes and remained active in the Knights of Columbus. He did, however, enjoy some recreation: curling, sailing, and playing bridge. By the time of his death he had accumulated the following recognitions: senior fellow of Renison College, Fellow of OTF (1964), honorary doctor of law from Waterloo University (1966), life membership in OECTA, a centennial medal, the Queen's Silver Jubilee Medal, president emeritus of the University of St. Jerome's, Hamilton diocesan medal of honour, the OSSTA award of merit, and the establishment of the C. L. Siegfried CR Scholarship Fund at the University of St. Jerome's College.[196]

OECTA was fortunate to have Fr. Siegfried in its early years. In 1951 Fr. Garvey resigned from the executive as OTF representative to take up duties with the Basilian Order. Patrick Perdue, the president, had taught with Fr. Siegfried and thought of him immediately as a replacement. Mr. Perdue

> went in to see Fr. Siegfried, who was the principal, to tell him of Fr. Garvey's resignation. His question was: "Who is going to take his place?" My reply was: "You are." It was the first time I ever found him speechless. But he agreed and became an outstanding representative of OECTA.[197]

Father's acceptance was not surprising: he had been in support of OECTA from its inception because of its potential to protect and raise the status of the teacher.

Father, throughout the fifties, worked in the salary negotiating, finance, and executive committees and from 1955 to 1956 as provincial president. His fellow executive members regarded him as a financial wizard, although in 1983 he was still remembering with great regret his failure to change the Association fee from a flat rate to a percentage of the teacher's salary. His positive memories were of working for improved grants for separate schools, equal pay for equal work, uniform teacher certification, the establishment of a reserve fund for the Association, and better salaries. As a priest he made special mention of the decision by religious teachers to present a united front together with the lay teachers in their collective push for more equitable salaries.[198]

In 1975, in an address to the graduates of Sacred Heart high school, Walkerton (his old alma mater), Father said, "No one is isolated in this world, and no one goes to Heaven alone."[199] Judging by his curriculum vitae, Fr. Siegfried worked very hard to bring himself and as many people as possible with him through the gates.

Mary Flynn (1913-). Once again OECTA elected as provincial president a woman, an action not typical of the times.

Mary Flynn, daughter of Bernard Flynn, a Canadian Customs worker, and Catherine Roch, housewife, and sister of Bernard, Frank, and Anne, was born, her family often said, to cause World War I and other wars besides. Such a strong personality chose a suitable profession: teaching. After attending St. Mary's girls' separate school (sex-segregated schools were not rare in urban public and separate schools until recent times) and Cathedral Girls' High School, Hamilton, Mary with her junior matriculation went to Hamilton Normal School in 1931-32. With her second-class certificate she managed to obtain a position as permanent supply teacher, the only person hired that year by the Hamilton Separate School Board.

The Depression was causing both a surplus of teachers and low salaries. Miss Flynn began in 1932 at a salary of $50 for a period of 12.5 days per month, whether she supplied or not. If she worked for more than the guaranteed 12.5 days, she accumulated another $4.00 per day. The following year she became a regular teacher at her old alma mater, St. Mary's girls' separate school, then went to St. Mary's boys' school, then St. Lawrence's "mixed" school. By then she had taught all eight grades. Her first regular teacher's salary, in 1933, was $630 a year, which represented a 10 per cent cut from the staff salaries of the previous year. There were to be two more 10 per cent salary cuts before the Depression was over, reducing the teachers' salaries to about $500. Despite the lack of financial reward for upgrading, Mary Flynn worked on her senior matriculation at night school and got a first-class teaching certificate; over the years she took university and Department of Education courses until she reached Standard 3 of an Elementary School Teacher's Certificate.

Miss Flynn became involved immediately in 1944 in the Hamilton organization of OECTA. In 1950 two male fellow members approached her with the thought that Hamilton should have an OECTA female president since so many members were women. She agreed and was invited to run for the office. Thus, she took on provincial responsibilities, serving on the relations and discipline and relations committee and working up through the three vice-presidents' positions to become president from 1956 to 1958. Unfortunately, for health reasons she had to resign as past president in 1959, but recovered and continued her career with the Hamilton Separate School Board.

While on the provincial executive Mary Flynn regarded the fostering of CPTAs as one of her most important aims. While principal of the new St. Bernard and St. Christopher's, she actively encouraged a PTA. As a result of her work in this area, she received the first Distinguished Service Award in 1956 from the Federation of the CPTA.[200] Miss Flynn in a recent interview expressed her disappointment in the decline of these associations and her hope that they would once again flourish.

After her retirement in 1975, Mary for several years was a volunteer driver for the Catholic Children's Aid Society. She continues to enjoy travelling and spending time with her seventeen nephews and nieces.[201]

Sr. Mary Vincentia, C.S.J. (Helen Collett) (1911-). The largest teaching Order of sisters in Ontario now saw one of their own become provincial president from 1958 to 1960. This Sister of St. Joseph brought to the office great energy and zest as well as a unique background.

Helen was born in Port Hope of Vincent Collett and Mary Doherty. Her father volunteered to serve as a private in the Canadian Army in World War I and was killed in Belgium in 1916. Just before the news arrived, Helen's mother contracted pneumonia and died two weeks after receiving the telegram. Helen, age five, and her brother James, younger by two years, were orphans. Her mother, knowing that Helen's grandfather in England would want to raise her two children as Protestants, had specified in her will that their guardians were to be the Sisters of St. Joseph. Thus, the children went to St. Vincent's orphanage, Peterborough. (Decades later members of the Order would ask when Sister entered; Sister would reply jokingly at age five.)

Soon after the deaths, the grandfather began to seek custody of the children. However, the Lusitania had sunk the year before and the Canadian government urged that its citizens not travel by ship. The sisters, worried about Mr. Collett, sent Helen and James to the home of a childless couple, Mr. and Mrs. Dennis O'Leary, out in the country. The children returned to St. Vincent two years later when Mrs. O'Leary died. Eventually, Mr. Collett accepted that Helen and her brother were better off in Ontario, and they stayed at the orphanage. Sr. Vincentia described this part of her life as a happy Anne of Green Gables existence.

In Peterborough Helen went to St. Mary's girls' separate school. At age eleven she was separated from her brother and moved to St. Joseph's orphanage, Cobourg, where she attended St. Michael's school. In 1925 she passed her grade eight entrance examinations and set her mind on going to the Cobourg collegiate institute with her classmate friends. Bishop (later Archbishop) O'Brien intervened and offered her a choice of several Catholic high schools. Helen became a boarder at St. Joseph's Academy, Lindsay and acquired a senior matriculation in 1930, whereupon she went to Peterborough Normal School, getting a first-class certificate and an elementary art certificate. In a tight job market she got a teaching position at St. Mary's girls' separate school, Lindsay. In 1932 she entered the novitiate of the Sisters of St. Joseph at Mount St. Joseph, Peterborough and was assigned for 1932-33 to grades one and two at St. Peter's boys' school, Peterborough. Here she and another teacher had about ninety pupils in a large basement room, where they practised an early form of team teaching.

In 1933 Helen received the Habit and took the religious name Sr. Mary Vincentia and in 1934 returned to St. Peter's. Transferred to Almonte, near Ottawa, Sister coped with no water, telephone, or indoor toilets. Finally, the separate school board blasted out a basement for washrooms. Meanwhile, Sister turned hardship to advantage by inspiring her pupils to regard as a great privilege the task of bringing in wood from the pile for the stove.

From 1940 to 1947, Sister taught a regular class and music throughout the school at St. Stanislaus, Fort William. Here she had four choirs: one each for the Church, the radio, the school, and funerals. At this point the birth of OECTA occurred. The sisters in Fort William were suspicious that the Catholic teachers would be submerged in a provincial public school organization, but Fathers Poupore and Priester visited them to allay their fears. The Port Arthur-Fort William district was formed.

Sister next taught at Immaculate Conception, Peterborough and St. Peter's boys, in the same city. In 1956 she became principal for the first time at Immaculate Conception. In addition she taught grade eight full-time and served as her own secretary using the "hunt and peck" method of typing. Now she became involved with OECTA because she had her audio-visual certificate. The Department of Education had developed an extensive library of films and Sister, as chair of the Association's Audio-Visual Committee, travelled the province encouraging the use of films and showing teachers how to operate 16 mm film machines. In this capacity she met Nora Hodgins, the secretary of OTF, who asked her about her OECTA experience at the district level. Sister replied that is consisted of "making sandwiches and washing dishes." Miss Hodgins expressed her satisfaction that as a consequence, Sister working at the provincial level would have no bad habits to break. Invited by Sr. Clotilde, who lived in the same convent and who was on the nominating committee, Sr. Vincentia served on the provincial Executive and went on to be president.

After that, Sister, tired from surgery and all these responsibilities, asked to be relieved from her duties as principal at Immaculate Conception. This relief consisted of a transfer to Port Hope, where she opened a new school, St. Anthony, and was the principal. This was a grades seven to ten school, a rarity in those days, supported by a visionary Bishop and school board.

Next, Sister was assigned as principal to Our Lady of Fatima school, Jasper Place, Edmonton. During this period she took library courses and a B.Ed. at the University of Alberta (1970). As the Order moved into contemporary clothing, Sister also took a dressmaking course from the Northern Alberta Institute of Technology. From 1971 to 1974 she was the superior of St. John's Convent, Edmonton. Restless from relative inactivity, she taught half-time at St. Rose in 1973, but after surgery again and upon doctor's orders, retired from teaching.

Asked what she would like to do, Sister asked to be cook, a position she held for the next eighteen years, first in Almonte, then in Cobourg. During this time Sister served on Cobourg's St. Michael's senior citizens' executive as president, on the Ontario Association of Superannuated Women Teachers, Northumberland West, as vice-president, president, and past president, on the Christopher Course as chaplain, on the public library board, on the Cobourg General Hospital auxiliary as a volunteer for chronic-care patients, and in the Cobourg Philharmonic Choir and Symphony Orchestra as a singer. Since 1992 Sister has managed the sewing room at Mount St. Joseph, Peterborough.

This dynamo was recognized as a Fellow of OTF in 1964 and as a life member of the Canadian College of Teachers in 1977.[201]

Reverend J. Harold Conway, O.M.I. (1911-). From 1960 to 1962 a priest who was a major contributor to the advancement of education in Ontario, Canada, and Africa assumed the provincial presidency of OECTA.

"Hank" was born on a farm in East Hawkesbury township, Prescott county in a small Irish Catholic community surrounded by French villages. His father, Thomas Conway, was a farmer and his mother, Laura Hoysted, the daughter of a farmer. Hank had three brothers, Cecil, Kenneth, and Raymond, and three sisters, Ellen, Evelyn, and Rita. Their mother from a very early age had them reading the *Montreal Daily Star*, getting interested in current events, and pursuing an education. Cecil, Ellen, Hank, and Rita would all become teachers, and Cecil would later produce five more teachers among his children. Hank attended a one-room public school (there was no point in forming a separate school board since the teacher and most of the pupils were Catholic), then progressed to a senior matriculation at Vankleek Hill Collegiate Institute. During those five years he was a "basket boarder", that is, a student who roomed with a relative or retired farmer inside the boundaries of a high school board; his parents would give him food for the week, delivering him on Sunday and picking him up on Friday after a two-hour wagon or sleigh ride; higher education was worth the sacrifice.

Since Hank was too young at age sixteen to be admitted to a Normal School and had no money for university, he worked on the family farm for two years, after which he attended the Ottawa Normal School in 1929-30. With his first-class teaching certificate he wrote many public school boards and received only one response; very few boards were hiring and separate school boards usually avoided employing laymen. In the school year 1930-31 J. Harold Conway taught all eight grades for the South Plantagenet public school board. Then he saw an advertisement for a forms I and II (grades nine and ten) teacher at St. Patrick's College High School in Ottawa for $700 a year. He bought a suit at Tip Top Tailors for $25 and was hired for the position. Here he taught all the subjects and was paid by the Ottawa Separate School Board. (A number of separate school boards after the *Tiny Township Case* of 1928 were following lawyer Battle's advice and exercising their right upheld in the Privy Council to operate grades nine and ten.)

Attracted by the life of the Oblates of Mary Immaculate staffing St. Patrick's, he joined the Order in September 1932 and embarked on eight years of full-time study at the Holy Rosary Scholasticate in Orleans: one year novitiate, three years philosophy, and four years theology. He was ordained in 1939 and returned to St. Patrick's to teach the first two forms again. In 1940 he completed his B.A. at the University of Ottawa and attended summer school immediately after to get his HSA certificate.

At this point he first became involved with a teaching organization, becoming chaplain to the Ottawa English Catholic Teachers' Association.

Similar involvements would occupy much of the rest of his life. Once OECTA was established, Fr. Conway, encouraged by Fr. Poupore, served on the Association's provincial negotiating committee for ten years and on the Executive, while also carrying out his duties as principal of St. Patrick from and earning an M.A. in Education (guidance) from Columbia University Teachers' College in New York. His belief, which he did not hesitate to share with his bishop, was that the separate school teachers were donating too much to the Catholic Church by working for such small salaries. His Order urged him to stand up for the rights of weak teachers and of separate schools.

An effective negotiator, Fr. Conway recently recalled travelling to a number of boards where negotiations had broken down and there playing a tough role at the start, then watching his fellow committee members, Veronica Houlahan and Dorothea Macdonell, charm the trustees.

In 1963 he became principal of Catholic Central High School, London. By this time he had been president of OTF, and went on to be president of CTF. In these positions he also served on the Executive and attended the annual meetings of the World Confederation of Organizations of the Teaching Profession (WCOTP). In 1964 he visited ten national teacher organizations in Africa as a goodwill ambassador from OTF and CTF and there set up an exchange whereby Canadian teachers donated their time and energies to help teachers in Africa upgrade their qualifications.

After, Father was superior of the Oblate Scholasticate, then chaplain of Vaudreuil English Catholic High School near Montreal. In 1973 he returned to teaching, religion and English, at St. Pius X high school for the Carleton County RCSS Board. Three years later he retired, but only from teaching. He went to help a former student and assistant, Fr. Peter Sutton, O.M.I., who had become bishop of Labrador. He was parish priest of Our Lady Queen of Peace Church in Happy Valley, Goose Bay, then he returned to Ottawa to be parish priest at Canadian Martyrs Church until 1985, when a severe stroke forced him into a second retirement.

After he partially recovered,

> his love of young people and the teachers of Ontario found him phoning me [Sr. Anna Clare] as principal of St. Patrick's High School to see if he could help out at the school....Since 1986 he has come to school almost every day where he presents to the students a beautiful modelling of one who loves, cares for and respects them....He has welcomed immigrant students and takes a special interest in them.[202]

As late as 1987 and 1988 Fr. Conway acted as an alternate delegate for the Ottawa Unit at the AGM, on one occasion replacing a delegate who was ill, thus becoming at age seventy-seven a voting delegate.[203]

During his decade of very active work with the Executive and provincial committees, Fr. Conway dealt with all the issues described below, but recalled in an interview three of his top priorities: negotiating with separate school boards for satisfactory salaries for women teachers, moving toward equity with public school salaries, and coordinating the Catholic high school staffs throughout the province as integral parts of OECTA. His dream of a Catholic Teachers' College on the model of Strawberry Hill, England has yet to be realized.

His career brought him considerable recognition and four special awards: a Fellow of OTF, a life membership in OECTA, the Order of Canada, and the Ontario Medal for Good Citizenship. His teachers and students who worked with him when he was principal have fond and grateful memories. Strong on student government, encouraging student leadership and always concerned about the future of his students, he would listen at staff marks meetings while some teachers would explain why a student's mark should be kept in the forties. Father, aware of the mitigating strengths in some of the student's other subjects, would say,

"I've heard the debate. Now take your pen and write 51." A number of clergy, chartered accountants, lawyers, and doctors can thank him for such decisions. Father also paid attention to the aesthetic development of the student body by bringing in various performers for student assemblies. But he kept firm control with such strictures as, "No laughing, no talking, no whistling, no cat-calling, no stamping of the feet, no rapping the steel chairs, but enjoy yourselves."[204]

In a curriculum vitae that Father wrote in 1987 he attributed his abiding interest in OECTA and OTF to his father:

> I think I owe my involvement in teachers' organizations to my father who was always involved in every election, municipal, provincial, or federal, not as a candidate but as a canvasser for votes for the best man (no women running then). He never would tolerate the idea of sitting on the fence and not getting involved. As my mother used to say, "We might be better off if you had kept your mouth shut."[205]

As OECTA moved into the next decade, the 1960s, it stepped onto the world stage by joining the World Confederation of Organizations of the Teaching Profession. In 1960 it sent Fr. Conway to its annual convention as a delegate. It also took up new quarters at Federation House, 1260 Bay St., opened by the Minister of Education, John Robarts in the same year.[206]

NOTES

1. Sister Mary Lenore, presidential address, AGM, 6-9 April 1953.
2. Stamp, *Schools of Ontario*, 185, 198; Fleming, *Expansion*, 94; A. K. McDougall, *John P. Robarts: His Life and Government* (Toronto: University of Toronto Press, 1986), 52.
3. *Report of the Minister*, 1951, 39; ibid., 1962, S-5, S-23, S-160.
4. Board of Directors, 14 April 1952; AGM, 4-5 April 1961.
5. *OTF at 20. Recollections of the First Two Decades of the Ontario Teachers' Federation*, Toronto: Ontario Teachers' Federation, 1964.
6. Board of Directors, 29 December 1951.
7. Ibid., 4 April 1961.
8. Joint Meeting of the Executives of the OECTA and AEFO, 16 June 1956.
9. AGM, 21-22 April 1954.
10. Ibid.; Board of Directors, 19 April 1954.
11. Ibid.; AGM, 8-9 April 1958.
12. Ibid., 31 March - 1 April, 1959; Board of Directors, 18 April 1960.
13. Executive, 29 May 1956.
14. News (March 1960), 51.
15. OSSTA-OECTA Executive Meeting, 2 April 1956.
16. Board of Directors, 9 April 1953.
17. Executive, 21 January 1961.
18. Ibid., 6 May 1961.
19. Ibid., 25 August 1960; AGM, 31 March - 1 April 1959.
20. Executive, 29 December 1951; 19 June 1956.
21. Board of Directors, 3 January 1959.
22. AGM, 31 March - 1 April 1959.
23. Ibid., 4-5 April 1961; Executive, 9 February, 13 April, 24 August 1957; 14 February 1959.
24. Conway, interview; Rev. Fr. C. L. Siegfried papers, Archives of St. Jerome's College.
25. Executive, 16 June 1951; 13 June 1953; 15 January, 9 June 1956; 6 May 1961.
26. Ibid., 1 March 1945; 4 June 1960.
27. Board of Directors, 14 April 1952.
28. Ibid., 26 March 1951.
29. Executive, 9 May 1959.
30. Coo, *Forty Years*, 42, 60.
31. Executive, 19 May 1951.
32. Board of Directors, 19 December 1959.
33. Ibid., 27 October 1956.
34. Executive, 10 April 1958.
35. Ibid., 19 May 1951; 25 October 1953; 13 February 1960.
36. A sampling of the minutes of the AGMs between 1950 and 1961 shows that the following separate school boards were involved with provincial negotiating: Barrie, Brampton, Chalk River, Chapleau, Cornwall, Douglas, Douro,

Eganville, Fort Erie, Fort William, Galt, Guelph, Humberston, Kitchener, Korah, McKim, Merritton, Midland, Minnow Lake, Niagara Falls, North Bay, Orillia, Oshawa, Ottawa, Pembroke, Penetanguishene, Port Arthur, Port Credit, Renfrew, Richmond Hill, St. Catharines, St. Thomas, Sault Ste. Marie, Stratford, Sudbury, Thorold, Timmins, Toronto, Walkerton.

37. Board of Directors, 6 January 1962; Executive, 7 April 1962; Conway, interview

38. Board of Directors, 4 April 1961.

39. Ibid., 29 December 1954; *Report*, 1962, S-62.

40. OECTA-OSSTA Executive, 2 April 1956.

41. Ibid., 26 January 1952.

42. Board of Directors, 14 April 1952.

43. Ibid., 11 April 1955

44. Ibid., 7 January 1961.

45. AGM, 23-24 April 1957.

46. Ibid.

47. *Review* (June 1955), 39.

48. AGM, 19-21 March 1969.

49. Board of Directors, 23-24 February 1968; AGM, 20-22 March 1968.

50. Executive, 3 March 1956; 16 January 1960.

51. *Report*, 1962, S-59.

52. Executive, 21 March 1953; 10 April 1958.

53. Ibid., 25 August 1960.

54. Board of Directors, 20 December 1952.

55. Executive, 16 June, 26 August 1956.

56. Ibid., 10 June 1961.

57. Ibid., 5 January 1957.

58. Ibid., 8 July 1961.

59. Ibid.,17 December 1955; 9 February 1957; file 0063, OECTAA; AGM, 7-9 April 1953.

60. Coo, *Forty Years*, 43.

61. AGM, 31 March - 1 April 1959.

62. Board of Directors, 29 December 1951; Executive, 19 May 1951.

63. Fleming, *Schools, pupils and teachers*, 492-93.

64. Board of Directors, 29 December 1951.

65. AGM, 19-22 April 1954.

66. Board of Directors, 11 April 1955; Executive, 13 December 1958.

67. Board of Directors, 19 April 1954.

68. Executive, 11 February 1956.

69. Superannuation file 0096, OECTAA; AGM, 9-10 April 1958.

70. Fleming, Schools, pupils and teachers, 492-93.

71. Board of Directors, 2 April 1958.

72. Ibid., 29 December 1951; News (June 1957), 43.

73. Board of Directors, 30 December 1952.

74. Executive, 31 January 1953.
75. *News* (June 1954), 18; Board of Directors, 5 January 1957.
76. AGM, 8-9 April 1958.
77. Board of Directors, 4 January 1958.
78. *News* (June 1955), 39; file 0097, OECTAA.
79. AGM, 8-9 April 1953.
80. Executive, 9 March 1957.
81. Ibid., 23 February, 10 May, 1952.
82. Ibid., 12 December 1959; 15 September 1961.
83. AGM, 19-20 April 1960.
84. Board of Directors, 14 April 1952; 4 January 1958; 30 March 1959.
85. *News* (October 1954), 31.
86. AGM, 8-9 April 1953; 21-22 April 1954.
87. Ibid., 3-4 April 1956; 24-25 April 1957; Board of Directors, 5 January 1957.
88. *News* (March 1957), 32-34; October 1957, 19.
89. Coo, *Forty Years*, 53; Board of Directors, 19 April 1954.
90. Ibid., 19 April 1954; 2 April 1956; Executive, 19 January 1957.
91. Joint Meeting of the Executives of the OECTA-AEFO, 13 April 1957; 25 August 1958; 23 September 1961; files 0091 and 0119, OECTAA; Walker, Catholic Education, Vol. III, 184.
92. Conway, interview; Executive, 11 February 1961.
93. John Abbott, "Accomplishing 'A Man's Task': Rural Women Teachers, Male Culture, and the School Inspectorate in Turn-of-the-Century Ontario," *Ontario History*, No. 4 (December 1986), 313-30; Judith Arbus, "Grateful to be Working: Women Teachers during the Great Depression," in Frieda Forman et al., eds., *Feminism and Education* (Toronto: Centre for Women's Studies in Education, 1990); Wendy E. Bryans, "Virtuous Women at Half the Price. The Feminization of the Teaching Force and Early Women Teacher Organizations in Ontario" (M.A. thesis, University of Toronto, 1974); Alison Prentice, "Multiple Realities: The History of Women Teachers in Canada," in Forman, *Feminism and Education*; Cecilia Reynolds, "Hegemony and Hierarchy: Becoming a Teacher in Toronto, 1930-1980," *Historical Studies in Education* (Spring, 1990), 95-118; ibid., "Naming the Experience: Women, Men and their Changing Work Lives as Teachers and Principals" (Ph.D. diss., University of Toronto, 1987); Nora Hodgins, retired secretary of the OTF, interview, Toronto, 19 March 1993.
94. Executive, 21 March 1953; Mrs. Irene Brine, interview, Cambridge, 18 April 1992.
95. Board of Directors, 14 April 1952.
96. Nelligan, interview.
97. Coo, *Forty Years*, 54; Executive, 12 May 1956; 10 June 1961; AGM, 19-20 April 1960; Board of Directors, 16 September 1961; Miss Mary Babcock, interview, Toronto, 8 June 1993.

98. Reynolds, "Hegemony and Hierarchy," 100; ibid., "Too Limiting a Liberation: Discourse and Actuality in the Case of Married Women Teachers," 145-168, in Forman, ed., *Feminism and Education*; ibid., interview, Brock University, 9 March 1993.
99. French, *High Button Bootstraps*, 133-34.
100. Reynolds, "Too Limiting a Liberation," 147; Hope, *Report*, 559-60.
101. Reynolds, "Too Limiting a Liberation", 155-61.
102. Stamp, *Schools of Ontario*, 199.
103. *Encyclical Letter of Pope Pius XI on Christian Marriage*, Boston: Daughters of St. Paul, n.d., 62.
104. Padraic O'Hare, "To Each (Her) Due: Women, the Church and Human Rights," Regina Coll, ed., *Women and Religion* (Ramsay, N.J.: Paulist Press, 1982), 18; Regina Coll, "The Specialization of Women into a Patriarchal System," Coll, ed., *Women and Religion*, 12; Louis Bouyer, *Women in the Church* (San Francisco: Ignatius Press, 1913), 59.
105. Quoted in O'Hare, "Women, the Church and Human Rights," 19.
106. Board Minutes, 29 June 1942, MSSB Archives. Cathy Maclean, archivist, attests to a number of other appeals in the minutes, all rejected.
107. *News* (June 1946), 3; Executive, 30 July, 1 October 1949; AGM, 12-13 April 1950.
108. Ibid.; Board of Directors, 29 December 1949.
109. Executive, 28 December 1951; unsigned letter to Marion A. Tyrrell, 22 November 1952, file 0078, OECTAA.
110. Conway, interview.
111. AGM, 28-29 March 1951.
112. Board of Directors, 14 and 17 April 1952; Executive, 17 May 1952.
113. Ibid.
114. Ibid., 13 June 1953.
115. Ibid., 29 December 1953; AGM, 21-22 April 1954.
116. Married Women Teachers file, OECTAA.
117. *Toronto Daily Star*, 15 January 1954.
118. Ibid., 16 January 1954.
119. Married Women Teachers file.
120. Married Women Teachers file.
121. *Star*, 18 January 1954; Miss M. Tyrrell to Mrs. P. E. Burke, 21 January 1954, Married Women Teachers file.
122. Ibid.; *Globe and Mail*, 19 January 1954.
123. *Toronto Telegram*, 19 January 1954.
124. Ibid.; *Globe and Mail*, 21-22 January 1954; Mrs. Anne Wright, interview, Toronto, 22 March 1993.
125. Board Minutes, 26 January, 4 March, 9 March 1954, MSSB Archives.
126. Executive, 20 March 1954; Marion Tyrrell to Joseph Whalen, 13 April 1954, Married Women Teachers file.
127. Relations Committee, 17 December 1957; Board Minutes, 17 December

1957, 20 January 1959, MSSB Archives.
128. Mrs. Mary Nevins, interview, Hastings, 16 March 1993.
129. Wright, interview; Mary-Eileen Carey-Hill and Maureen Teixeira, "The Pathway to Militancy within the Ontario English Catholic Teachers' Association," unpublished paper, April 1979, OECTAA.
130. Louise Fine, Director, Ontario Department of Labour, Office of the Director of Fair Employment Practices Branch to Elizabeth D. Taylor, Assistant Secretary, FWTAO, 19 December 1955, OECTAA.
131. Executive, 11 February 1956; Joint Meeting of the OECTA and AEFO, file 0091, OECTAA; Board of Directors, 18 April 1960; Executive, 6 May, 10 June, 1961; 25 August 1960.
132. Minutes of the Special Committee to select an Assistant Secretary, file 0087, OECTAA.
133. *OTF at 20. Recollections of the First Two Decades of the Ontario Teachers' Federation* (Toronto: OTF, 1964), 19; Nora Hodgins, interview, Toronto, 19 March 1993.
134. Coo, *Forty Years*, 60.
135. Hope, *Report*, 459-60.
136. Board of Directors, 6 April 1953; Executive, 3 April 1954; Annual Meeting of the OECTA Executive with His Eminence James C. Cardinal McGuigan, 21 March 1953.
137. Executive, 9 May, 25 October 1953.
138. Board of Directors, 29 December 1953; AGM, 21-22 April 1954.
139. Executive, 10 May, 13 June 1954.
140. Ibid., 12 February, 14 April, 11 June 1955.
141. Ibid., 3 October 1959; Board of Directors, 30 March 1959.
142. Graham, Frost, 244; Stamp, *Schools of Ontario*, 201; Fleming, *Schools, pupils and teachers*, 431.
143. Ibid., 435; *News* (December 1952), 26.
144. Stamp, *Schools of Ontario*, 198-200.
145. *OTF at 20* 19.
146. *News* (December 1954), 15.
147. Board of Directors, 29 December 1953; AGM, 21-22 April 1954; 13-14 April 1955.
148. Board of Directors, 19 December 1959; *News* (October 1957), 19; AGM, 16-17 April 1952.
149. Ibid., December 1960, 41.
150. Board of Directors, 26 March 1951.
151. Ibid., 9 April 1953.
152. Ibid., 29 March 1951.
153. Executive, 19 January 1957; Board of Directors, 5 January 1957; 17 October 1959.
154. AGM, 8-9 April 1953.
155. Board of Directors, 4 January 1958.

156. Coo, *Forty Years*, 39-40.
157. Reverend John M. Beahen, D.C.L., Ottawa, "Responsibilities of Educators," *News* (December 1954), 4-7.
158. AGM, 3-4 April 1956; Board of Directors, 30 December 1952; file 0088, OECTAA.
159. Sister M. Henrietta, C.S.J., "The Integrating Value of Mathematics and Science," *News* (March 1957), 23.
160. Reverend Robert Meagher, S.J., "Teaching the Social Doctrine of the Church in the Elementary School," *News*, 11.
161. Board of Directors, 29 December 1951; 30 December 1952; 7 January 1956; Executive, 14 February 1959, 11 February 1956.
162. Board of Directors, 29 May 1951; Executive, 12 March 1955; 14 April, 27 August 1955.
163. Board of Directors, 11 April 1955; 22 April 1957.
164. Ibid., 29 December 1951
165. File 0106, OECTAA.
166. Graham, *Frost*, 244.
167. Fleming, *Schools, pupils and teachers*, 48; Walker, *Catholic Education*, Vol. III, 81.
168. File 0076, OECTAA.
169. Board of Directors, 11 April 1955; 18 April 1960; 7 January 1961.
170. Walker, *Catholic Education*, Vol. III, 83-84; Board of Directors, 9 April 1953.
171. AGM, 8-9 April 1953; Executive, 16 January 1960; Board of Directors, 3 April 1961.
172. Board of Directors, 7 April 1958.
173. David M. Cameron, "The Politics of Education in Ontario, with special reference to the Financial Structure" (Ph.D. diss., University of Toronto, 1969), 94-95, 155, 206.
174. Robert T. Dixon and N. L. Bethune, "Teacher's Guide," Completion...? *A Documentary History of Separate Schools in Ontario* (Toronto: OECTA, 1974), 26-27.
175. Minutes of the Bishops of the Ecclesiastic Provinces of Toronto and Kingston, 17 May 1951, AAT.
176. Joint Meeting of the AEFO and OECTA Executives, 3 April 1954; 12 February, 16 April 1955; "Brief to the Prime Minister of Ontario, Leslie M. Frost from the Ontario Separate School Trustees' Association", November 1959, OSSTAA; Joint Meeting of the OSSTA-OECTA Executives, 3 April 1954; Executive, 13 February 1954; 3 March 1956.
177. Cameron, "Financial Structure," 92-97; Walker, *Catholic Education*, Vol. II, 383-86.
178. Coo, *Forty Years*, 54; Executive, 3 March 1956; 10 June 1961; Board of Directors, 3 April 1961.
179. Walker, *Catholic Education*, Vol. III, 87.

180. AGM, 24-25 April 1957; 19-20 April 1960; 3-4 April 1961.
181. Minutes of the Special Committee to select an Assistant Secretary, file 0087, OECTAA; News (October 1959), 37; Babcock, interview.
182. AGM, 3-4 April 1961.
183. Board of Directors, 30 December 1952; Executive, 22 April 1954.
184. AGM, 8-9 April 1958; 31 March-1 April 1959; 19-20 April 1960; Executive, 3-4 April 1954; 14 May 1955.
185. AGM, 3-4 April 1961; 8-9 April 1953; 8-9 April 1958.
186. *News* (June 1958), 25.
187. Coo, *Forty Years*, 55; AGM, 16-17 April 1952.
188. Board of Directors, 17 April 1958; AGM, 21-22 April 1954.
189. I am indebted to Lenore Duggan, Mississauga for most of the material in Sr. Lenore's biography, interviews, 19 and 23 February, 1 March 1993, and to Sister Gail Desarmia, S.P., Kingston, 4 March 1993.
190. G. Emmett Cardinal Carter, Archbishop emeritus of Toronto, interview, Toronto, 18 November 1993.
191. Michael W. Higgins and Douglas R. Letson, *My Father's Business. A Biography of his Eminence G. Emmett Cardinal Carter* (Toronto: Macmillan of Canada, 1990), 9-10.
192. Sr. Marion Farnard, S.P., interview, Kingston, 3 March 1993.
193. Sr. Mary Lenore Carter, interview with Sheila Coo, Kingston, 30 August 1981.
194. Ibid.
195. Conway, interview.
196. Higgins and Letson, *My Father's Business*, 10.
197. AGM, 6-9 April 1953.
198. Babcock, interview.
199. Mrs. Eleanor Levesque, sister of Margaret Drago, interview, Niagara Falls, 19 February 1993; Coo, *Forty Years*, 42-44; Staff records, Welland County RCSS Board; *News and Views*, November 1972.
200. *U W Gazette*, 6 September 1989, 8.
201. Siegfried papers.
202. Coo, *Forty Years*, 37.
203. Ibid., 53-56.
204. Siegfried papers.
205. AGM, 2-4 April 1956.
206. Miss Mary Flynn, interview, Hamilton, 1 March 1993.
207. Sr. Mary Vincentia, C.S.J., interview, Peterborough, 2 March 1993.
208. Sister Anna Clare, principal, St. Patrick's High School, "Nomination of Rev. J. Harold Conway, O.M.I., for the Ontario Medal for Good Citizenship," 15 March 1989, OECTAA.
209. Ibid.
210. Conway, interview; Sister Anna Clare, "Nomination;" Rev. Fr. J. Frank

Kavanagh, O.M.I., interview, Toronto, 1 March 1993; Rev. J. Harold Conway, "Curriculum Vitae," OECTAA.
211. Conway, "Curriculum Vitae."
212. News (June 1960), 34-35; Coo, *Forty Years*, 58.

CHAPTER SIX

EXPANSION OF MEMBERSHIP, CENTRAL STAFF BUDGET, VISION, PROFESSIONAL DEVELOPMENT, AND SALARY NEGOTIATING STRATEGIES 1962-1971

In times such as these we teachers (as leaders) cannot pick the obviously safe issues on which to make pronouncements. I again reiterate that we all cannot go off to Africa to help the lepers, but we surely can show the same love of neighbour right here in our own backyards.[1]

Background to the 1960s. A number of government initiatives and philosophical and religious movements dramatically altered the status, shape, size, curriculum, and staff of the separate schools in the 1960s. By the end of the decade the separate school, often an isolated, financially vulnerable, small operation, became part of a relatively well-funded and well-administered large separate school system with well-qualified staff and much-improved facilities and instructional supplies and with programmes that reflected the thinking of the Hall-Dennis Report and Vatican II.

The Ontario Foundation Plan. The expansion of the school system continued in the 1960s. In the school year 1960-61 there were 36 533 elementary school teachers, in 1965-66 there were 44 967.[2] By 1970 elementary school enrolment rose by 40 per cent and the OECTA membership from 6 897 in 1960 to 15 381, an increase of 123 per cent.[3] The government and public's willingness to support the education of their future citizens also continued in a positive fashion. However, this growth exacerbated the problem of corporation taxes.

OECTA was sympathetic and helpful with this revenue difficulty; its negotiators often accepted lower salaries after examining the school board's balance sheet and would in some communities assist the trustees in contacting Roman Catholic public school supporters to discuss switching their taxes to the separate school board.[4] For strategic purposes the Association did not approach the government about the corporation tax problem, since such an initiative could have been perceived as self-serving and since the topic was logically a trustee matter.

The trustees and the Ontario Catholic bishops both submitted briefs to Premier Robarts in the early 1960s. A joint brief from OSSTA and l'Association des commissions des écoles bilingues de l'Ontario (ACEBO) in July 1961 on behalf of the Hamilton, London, Metropolitan Toronto, Ottawa, Sault Ste. Marie, and Windsor separate school boards outlined the revenue problem, citing higher mill rates, church contributions, and a per pupil income of $179.33 compared with a public school one of $291.83. It stressed the government's policy of equality of educational opportunity and showed trustee concern for teachers by pointing to a "discrepancy in salaries [which] is disturbing," a difference of $2000.[5] The following year the bishops with the help of two separate school inspectors met with Robarts to discuss their brief in which they made the same points. In December 1962 OSSTA and ACEBO submitted a second brief calling for a grant scheme similar to Alberta's foundation plan, one based on need, educational equality, and grants compensating for revenue deficiencies.

Robarts's initial reaction was negative; he expressed the thoughts that schools of choice could not be on an equal footing with public schools and that such compensatory grants were perhaps unconstitutional. However, his government's official response on February 21, 1963 was much more in the tradition of regarding the separate schools as part of the public school system. Robarts announced the Ontario Foundation Tax Plan. It was designed to meet the problems associated with the growth in the school system, the rise in societal expectations of the school, and the poor assessment school boards, many of which were separate and/or isolate. The plan was based on the cost of education for a model school programme, estimated from sample boards. This foundation level mandated a certain mill rate to be divided locally with the balance coming from grants. It included a corporation tax adjustment grant that made board revenue equal to what it would be if it had access to the corporation assessment in the same proportion that it had access to residential and farm assessment.

The results were dramatic. Elementary school grants for separate schools rose quickly and steadily to the point where in 1971 the per pupil revenue for separate schools was 95 per cent of the public school revenue. Edward Brisbois, chairman of the MSSB, was grateful that salaries and school buildings would be improved. Toronto and Ottawa had enormous capital expenditures in the 1960s. Separate school boards built libraries, gymnasia, kindergartens, science, music, and art rooms, and industrial arts/home economics facilities; they also provided larger playgrounds; and with competitive salaries hired teachers who would make a permanent career in the profession; as well, they were able to relieve principals full-time from teaching and employ their own superintendents.[6]

County and District School Boards. With the successful implementation of the Foundation Plan, the Minister of Education could now move to a more efficient delivery of policies, programmes, and funding through larger units of administration. A vexatious problem for many decades was the thousands of public and separate school boards with an unsatisfactory number of one- and two-room schools. In 1961, 3713 of these types of schools were operating. Even after township school area boards became mandatory in 1965, there were still 518 one- and two-room schools in 1968;[7] furthermore, the three-mile limit prevented the formation of township boards administering separate schools. The solution for this and other problems in the schools of Ontario was seen to be the legislated formation of county and district school boards.

At first, both the government and OSSTA wondered if such legislation could apply to the separate school system. However, the judgment of 1962 in the *Vandekerckhove case* had made the plan possible. A combined separate school board had operated two schools since 1944 in the townships of Middleton and West Walsingham. In June 1959 the board closed its school in Middleton and transported the pupils to West Walsingham. Because of the three-mile limit the Middleton township assessment department determined that the parents of these transported pupils were now public school supporters. The appeal moved through the Court of Revision, the Supreme Court of Ontario, the Court of Appeal, and the Supreme Court of Canada with a final judgment in 1962 favourable to the Norfolk County separate school supporters. It was decided that the three-mile limit was "subject to other provisions in the Act" and that, therefore, the separate school board could close a school and move its students to another of its schools in the interests of efficiency. As a result of this judgment the Ontario legislature one year later passed *An Act to Amend the Separate Schools Act* which empowered the school board to use its school or a piece of property it owned or a designated "imaginary" school site to establish the three-mile radius for determination of the separate school board boundaries.[8] Thus, a county or district RCSS board could close one- and two-room schools and could form new three-mile limit "zones" without building a school or designating a school site. The boundaries of the county or district board would be all of the zones in the county or district. (Of course, this still left potential separate school supporters and their children residing in a county or district outside of any separate school zone, a problem that would not be solved for another twenty years.)

In view of the *Vandekerckhove judgment* and the government's rationale for larger units of administration, OSSTA agreed that the contemplated legislation should apply to the separate school system. The Minister of Education, William Davis, announced on March 15, 1968 that county and district boards of education and RCSS boards would come into existence on January 1, 1969. They would provide a larger, more efficient tax base and, in the opinion of the Ministry of Education, continuous pupil progress from kindergarten to grade thirteen, considerable movement toward equality of educational opportunity in urban and rural Ontario, better and new programmes in such areas as special education and kindergarten, and an administrative and teaching staff with higher and variegated qualifications in music, art, and other specialized disciplines.[9]

As with the Foundation Plan, the results of the legislation were instant and dramatic. The number of one- and two-room separate schools, which were 289 in 1961, were down to 113 in 1970. Within a few years after that they would remain for the most part only in isolate boards outside of the district board structure in northern Ontario. Teachers would acquire more mobility and better working conditions. Rural Ontario would have programmes previously available only in cities and towns. On the other hand, there would be a distancing, sometimes an alienation, between the local school supporters and the central board office. CPTAs, which had been in decline, continued to lose their members. Finally, for OECTA there were positives and negatives in dealing with the forty-eight larger, more sophisticated, more united separate school boards.[10]

Teacher Certification. The reforms of the Department of Education in this area changed the profile of the teacher in Ontario, particularly in elementary schools. Although the ongoing expansion in pupil enrolment continued to cause teacher recruitment problems, OECTA and OTF had been gratified to see the grade twelve admission to Teachers'

College eliminated in 1964. The next objective would be a requirement that the entrance standard be a B.A.. This was reached in stages. In February 1962 the Department of Education announced its new certification classification consisting of four standards. A teacher would receive a standard two or three certificate if s/he submitted five or ten credits from Department or university courses and a standard four if s/he had a B.A.; OTF had been urging such a plan. It was "designed to encourage teachers to improve their academic and professional competence through university study and through successful attendance at Departmental summer courses or equivalent Departmental winter courses."[11] Standards were raised again in 1969 when the Minister of Education issued a memorandum specifying that no more than five Departmental courses could count toward standard three. The 1965 and 1968 AGMs had debated the old chestnut of whether university work produced a better teacher and had passed a resolution that ten Departmental courses continue to be the maximum for reaching standard three; OECTA would continue to advocate this position into the late seventies, but OTF each time rejected this in favour of the Department's plan.[12] These measures both assisted OECTA salary negotiators to bargain successfully for at least a four-level grid and also raised the professional and academic standards of the teachers. By 1968 only 59 per cent of the separate school teachers were at standard one compared with over 90 per cent in the fifties.[13] Many of these standard one teachers would soon be at standard two.

Further changes were in the works that would improve still more the status of the teaching profession and place elementary school teachers on an academic par with their secondary school peers. In 1964 the Minister of Education established a Study Committee on the Training of Elementary School Teachers. C. R. MacLeod, a superintendent with the Windsor Board of Education, tabled the Report in February 1966. Among the Committee's recommendations were the requirement of a B.A. and a B.Ed. for all teachers and the transfer of teacher education, pre- and post-service, from the Department of Education to the universities. Both recommendations would be implemented in the early 1970s. The second plan began almost immediately at the Faculty of Education, Lakehead University. All the other Teachers' Colleges would close as negotiations with the universities were completed.[14]

Along with the rising professional and academic education of the teachers came the hiring of many teachers trained in other provinces and overseas, particularly England, Ireland, Scotland, and, to some degree, Australia and New Zealand. These teachers affected OECTA in two ways. Many of them had more extensive academic and/or professional education than the Ontario Department of Education demanded as a minimum for entrance to a Teachers' College; this reinforced the growing status of the teacher. Secondly, most of them came from a teaching environment where there was a greater familiarity with and use of more militant union bargaining methods; this would affect to some degree OECTA's salary negotiating methods and perspectives as these teachers came to AGMs.[15] Their numbers were significant. Between 1960 and 1970 the Department of Education issued 12 520 letters of standing to teachers applying to teach in Ontario.[16]

Finally, the number of unqualified elementary school teachers declined despite the increase in student enrolment throughout the decade. By 1970 only 0.5 per cent of the teachers were unqualified.[17]

The Hall-Dennis Report. Along with raising the academic and professional standing of elementary school teachers, the Minister decided to look at the curriculum. In 1965 by Order-in-Council, William Davis established a Provincial Committee on Aims and Objectives of Education in the Schools of Ontario "to identify the needs of the child....[and] to set forth the aims of education." Twenty-four members from business, the Ministry, the professional and academic world, the trustees' associations, and the teacher federations conducted hearings, studied other school systems in several other countries, conducted research, and held meetings for four years. Sr. Stanislaus, C.S.J., the supervising principal for the Peterborough Separate School Board, represented OECTA on the Committee; however, she suffered a heart attack and died while attending a Committee conference in October 1965. OECTA appointed as her replacement Sr. Alice Marie, C.S.J., the supervising principal of the London Separate School Board.[18]

The Report, submitted to the Minister in 1968, sounded a clarion call for progressive education, kindergarten to grade thirteen, in the schools of Ontario. The reverberations echoed with considerable volume for some years and with effects lasting to the present. W. G. Fleming had this to say in 1972:

> The report brought progressive ideas to the centre of the stage;...[it was] lyrical...an adoring tribute to the nature of the child; a statement of limitless faith in his potentialities if developed in an ideal educational environment under the guidance of inspired teachers;...a powerful condemnation of rigid, inflexible, outmoded, and unproductive activities and practices found in schools.[19]

Stamp described the Report as "the most radical and bold document ever to originate from the bureaucratic labyrinth of the provincial department of education." To the tune of Dewey it called for the elimination of the lock-step system of grades and streams in favour of the continuous progress of the pupil, kindergarten to grade thirteen.[20]

The educational committee and public at large understandably did not greet the Report with 100 per cent endorsement. The split between the traditional and progressive educator had had a long history in Ontario. At the turn of the century the theory and methodology of progressive education, following the ideas and practices of Pestalozzi, Herbart, Froebel, and Dewey, began to appear in the speeches and writings of educational leaders and in the previously traditional school curricula. The gradual shift from a traditional curriculum to the "New Education" was marked by the following emphases:

- from a curriculum of cultural imperatives and societal values to one built on the child's interests and needs;
- from a teacher-centred to a child-centred curriculum;
- from external discipline to self-discipline;
- from a classroom atmosphere of fear to one of love;
- from education as work to learning from play;
- from subject discipline courses of study to relevant current problem-solving accomplished in a multidisciplinary fashion;
- from abstract bookish learning to concrete activity-based learning;
- from impersonal to social and personal learning;
- from memorization and lectures to the discovery approach;
- from competitive and isolated to cooperative learning;
- from intellectual development to development of the whole child;
- from treating the child as one who is either a tabula rasa or a weak vessel with the results of original sin, a child who must be transformed into an adult as quickly as possible, to facilitating an environment where the child lives and learns in accordance with the findings of child psychology and human growth and in harmony with beliefs about the fundamental goodness and innocence of the child.

With the arrival of the Depression and the opposition of traditionalists, the "New Education" movement languished. However, in the mid-1930s a second move to reform the curriculum in favour of an ideal child-centred approach began. The result was the new "Programme of Studies for Grades I to VI" issued by the Department of Education in 1937. V. K. Greer, the chief inspector, described it in part as follows:

> ...a child-centred programme is a better programme than a subject-centred one;... the teacher should, as far as possible, act in the capacity of a guide and director only, and permit the child to develop his own power of initiative and to depend upon his own judgment and abilities.[21]

From 1951 to 1959 William J. Dunlop, a traditionalist, was Minister of Education. He stressed "hard work" and the three Rs and criticized too many fads that encouraged self-expression and daydreaming. The U.S.S.R.'s success in launching the world's first space satellite and Professor Hilda Neatby's *So Little for the Mind* damning the neglect of formal grammar, written composition, history, and literature, the excessive faith in guidance and extra-curricular activities, and the lax promotion standards reinforced Dunlop's position.[22]

The pendulum swung again in 1959 when the progressivist John P. Robarts became Minister of Education. Although Professor Northrop Frye in his *Design for Learning* was deriding progressive education and lauding Jerome Bruner's theories of structured inquiry within subject disciplines, Robarts and his successor, Davis, began implementing progressive education ideas even before the publication of *Living and Learning*. In 1967 six high schools introduced on a pilot basis a non-graded credit system with individual timetables catering to student choices based on their needs and interests. A Department of Education bulletin in the same year discussed individual needs and a non-graded organization in kindergarten to grade six; open areas and small group instruction were recommended.[23]

Like the educational community at large, OECTA found itself divided between progressivists and traditionalists, but caught up in a progressive wave that greatly affected the curriculum, organization, and necessary pedagogical skills in separate schools at the elementary and secondary levels.

Vatican II. The tenets of progressivism were applied also to religious education in the 1960s.

In January 1959, Pope John XXIII, at the age of eighty and after only ninety days in office, announced the convocation of the Catholic Church's Twenty-First Ecumenical Council, the first since Vatican I in

1869-70. After four years of preparation, it opened on October 11, 1962 and continued to December 8, 1965. Its final sixteen documents examined such topics as the Church, liturgy, ecumenism, the religious life, the laity, religious freedom, and education.[24] This so-called caretaker Pope had ushered in what became a cliché: the winds of change blowing open the doors and windows of the Church and its schools. One of its specific results was a fundamental change in the content and methodology in the religious education programme of the separate school.

The new "Come to the Father" series of religious education textbooks embraced an experiential, developmental approach to teaching and learning. Instead of apologetics, which since the Protestant Reformation had stressed the defence of the Faith, the teacher was to use a "kerygmatic" methodology. Instead of relying on the catechism, which had the child memorize answers to questions, sometimes in a lifeless and uncomprehending fashion, the teacher with the priest and parent presented religion as life; Scripture, liturgy, and paraliturgy, witness and apostolic action, and, yes, dogma made up the religious education period and was integrated to a reasonable degree with the subjects across the curriculum and with the child's life. Most importantly, God was to be presented not as an abstract concept or a First Cause and certainly not as a watchdog or accountant, but as a loving Father and Mother, a being whom the child's deepest nature could relate to, understand, and love.[25]

This content and methodology were to be geared to the age and psychology of the child. And since the school ideally was a Christian community and part of the world community, the child was to apply her/his religious formation to loving God and man. Rather than keeping the child away from the world lest s/he be contaminated, the teacher, with principles of guidance and supervision, was to help the child work out her/his salvation in the concrete situation in which God had placed her/him and by contributing to the community.[26] Thus, the world entered the religious education curriculum; topics like pollution, world hunger, poverty, racial discrimination, the plight of the First Nations, and the need for peace were treated in terms of religious faith, social responsibility, and social justice.[27]

All of this demanded teachers with a professional level of up-to-date Catholic theology, ability in the specific methodology of religious education, and the traditional mentoring by precept and example across the entire curriculum in the widest sense of the term. These developments in Catholic education were occurring at the same time as the expertise and personal witness of the teaching sisters shrank to a "drastic" degree.[28] The enrolment in separate schools was growing while many post-Vatican II sisters examined themselves as individuals, sometimes for the first time, and took on other vocations outside the convent and the classroom. As well, Vatican II enhanced the role of the lay person in the Church. As Bishop Carter expressed this concept to OECTA, "the mind of the Bishops is to emancipate the lay people in the field more and more. It was their intention to put into effect the principle of subsidiarity restoring the Bishop to his rightful place and the laity to theirs in the Church."[29]

The laicization of the separate schools placed the large numbers of new, young separate school teachers right at the centre of the new "Come to the Father" series. While Ontario's Catholic newspaper, *The Canadian Register,* wrote numerous articles in the mid-1960s with headlines like "Church Learning Renewal 'Lessons'" and "Doctrinal Renewal Needed But 'Risky'."[30] separate school teachers grew in the consciousness that they too would need to change content and methodology in their religious education programmes and indeed in many of their subject areas.

Salary Negotiating. The constellation of developments described above required committed Catholic teachers with a professional degree of academic and pedagogical education. But the separate school system seemed to be expanding faster than the supply of teachers.[31] OECTA and OSSTA, among other things, would have to assure that salaries were sufficiently improved to attract young men and women into the profession.

At the provincial level the separate school trustees and teachers agreed with this necessity. For example, in 1962, when discussing the OSSTA brief to the government, Francis G. Carter, past president of the Association, stated that "our separate school teachers are not getting anywhere near equality of treatment on the matter of salary when we compare them to their public school brethren."[32] About the same time the Niagara Falls Separate School Board made the point more graphically: "The case history of the married male, separate school teacher having to sell groceries at Loblaws on evenings and Saturdays, in order to support his four children would do more to sway the Cabinet than 100 politely worded resolutions."[33] Furthermore, OECTA continued to be understanding when a board's finances simply did not permit it to meet all the teachers' requests. In 1962 the Executive decided that steps could not be taken against the Midland Separate School Board because of its financial position and in 1968 urged the teachers to reopen negotiations with the Belle River Separate School Board since the Executive felt that the board had offered a fairly good schedule.[34] This type of cooperation also manifested itself in the four-step procedure that a Joint Provincial Teacher-Trustee Committee developed with the involvement of AEFO, FWTAO, OECTA, OPSMTF, and OSTC. Negotiations were to begin between the local affiliate and school board. Next, if necessary, the teachers' association central office people could negotiate with the board. If a resolution still was not reached, the teachers and trustees' central office members would get involved with negotiations. Only if the third step was unsuccessful were the teachers at liberty to contemplate a pink letter against the board. The Teacher-Trustee Committee also agreed upon legal details such as a letter of transmittal, a memorandum of the terms of settlement, and a formal ratification by the teachers and the school board.[35]

Obviously, with 3676 school boards in 1960, 1673 in 1965, and still 1446 in 1968,[36] the diplomacy and sometimes harmony at the provincial level were not always in evidence at the local level. The role of the teacher and trustee as negotiator was perceived by the participant as adversarial and in conflict. No amount of appealing to the Christian charity of the separate school teacher or trustee could remove this perception of role-playing. Thus, the school boards and teachers went on employing the negotiating tactics of the 1940s and 1950s, as well as designing new ones in the 1960s.

The trustees continued to deal with the teacher shortage by raising the minimum salary to attract new teachers while freezing or giving less of an increase to the maximum to offset the budget increase. The temptation to treat unfairly even the teachers whose salaries would affect impending pensions was too much for some boards; after all, teachers on staff, particularly married women, were often not in a position to go to another board because of such unfairness, and, if they did, the board could replace them with a beginning teacher at a lower cost. The Executive and Board of Directors' minutes called attention to situations like the Chapleau Separate School Board's raising second-class-certificate teachers' salaries more than those at the other levels, like the Cochrane-Iroquois Falls Separate School Board's paying to teachers on a letter of permission a higher salary than to some of its qualified teachers and, more commonly, like the Orillia Separate School Board's paying new teachers more than the previously negotiated salary schedule.[37] In 1966 OSSTA approved and forwarded to OSTC a resolution from the Sault Ste. Marie Separate School Board "that the OSSTA strongly exhort all Separate School Boards in the province to maintain a maximum in this Category [1]."[38] As the teacher shortage worsened, this tactic became less effective, but meanwhile Mary Babcock advised negotiators to concentrate on raising the maximum salaries so that the senior teachers would obtain a decent pension, and Fr. Conway asked the trustees not to apply such a practice to teachers within ten years of retirement in order to assist those "who have carried on the fight during the tough days."[39]

Other hangovers from the previous decade persisted in some boards, but finally disappeared almost totally by 1970. These practices were the conducting of bargaining with teachers in the absence of any written agreement and the allowing for just half the teaching experience with other boards; the second device, in the trustees' minds, discouraged staff mobility.[40] The idea that separate school teachers should sacrifice parity of salary with their public school counterparts was still in the public consciousness. *The Canadian Register* in 1961 in its editorial called for such sacrifices. However, in the next month the newspaper quoted from the OSSTA 1961 brief that "the unskilled labourer and the school custodian with Grade 8 standing fare much better" than the separate school teacher.[41] After the Foundation Plan this argument faded, although John Kuchinak occasionally felt impelled to ask during negotiating sessions if the trustees as proprietors of businesses would grant discounts to teacher purchasers who were working for a discounted wage.[42]

New bargaining techniques surfaced. Separate school boards became more unified, sending trustees to the annual OSSTA convention, reading the new quarterly, *The Catholic Trustee*, and acting on positions taken by both OSSTA and OSTC. With the advent of county and district boards it became easier for the trustees to generate a unified stance on a number of issues and attempt to disregard teacher presentations.[43] Thus, the trustee associations called on the government to enact legislation that would provide a provincial salary schedule and would keep principals and vice-principals outside of the teachers' salary negotiating, since, according to trustee thinking, they were the school boards' managers.[44] School boards were advised to confine negotiations strictly to salary matters and not to consider any teacher requests connected to fringe benefits or working conditions. Such matters as time for lunch,

Delegates to OECTA's 1954 CCDC with Fr. CL Siegfried, a member of the OECTA Executive and OTF Board of Governors.

Whether 1954 or 1994, CCDC delegates, have always appreciated the opportunity the conference provides to exchange ideas with colleagues from across the province.

OECTA's first full time Executive Secretary Marion Tyrrell with Inspectors Kinlen, Hodge and Bennett, at the 1955 CCDC.

Doreen Brady, OECTA president with Fr. Vincent Dwyer author of Genesis II a program to foster adult spiritual renewal, keynote speaker at the 1979 CCDC.

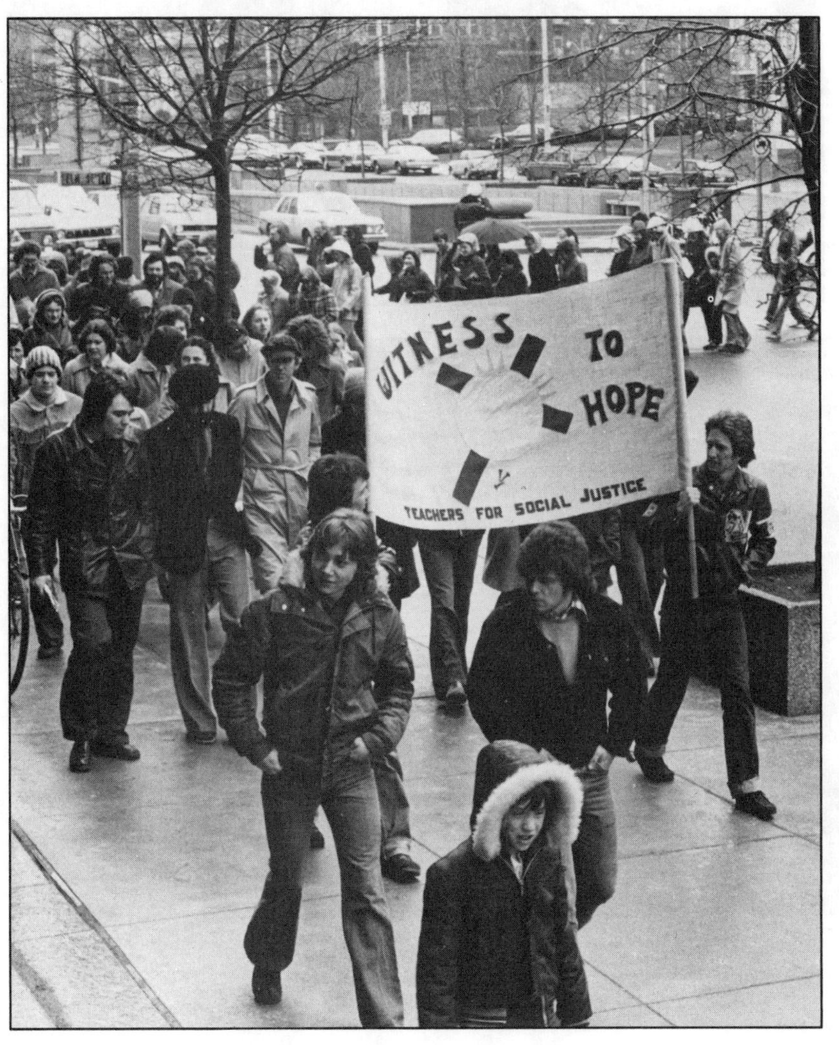

A vigorous Social Justice movement flourished over the years within the membership. Here OECTA members lead a solidarity march on Good Friday, 1980.

Author Fr Henri Nouwen with companions from the L'Arche Community was a CCDC keynote speaker in 1987.

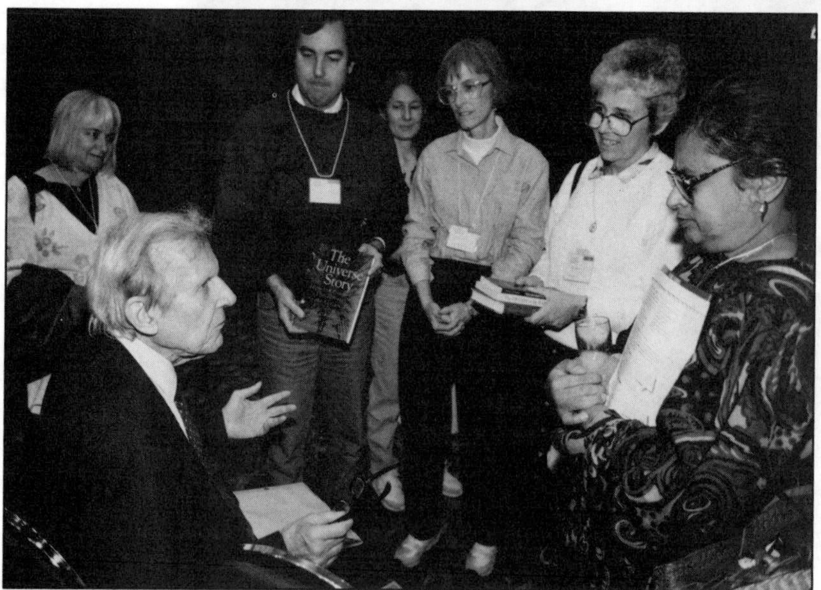

Fr Thomas Berry called upon teachers to work to save the Earth while telling The Universe Story as the 1992 CCDC keynote speaker.

Staff worked around the clock in the heady days of 1973. From left, Neil Doherty, Frank Griffin Executive Secretary.

BELOW: **Teachers marched on Queen's Park in December 1973, to demonstrate their demand for the right to strike.**

Fourteen years after teachers won the right to strike, and after strikes had become a familiar event, teachers in Prescott-Russell pack up their signs. Last minute negotiations had averted a 1988 strike.

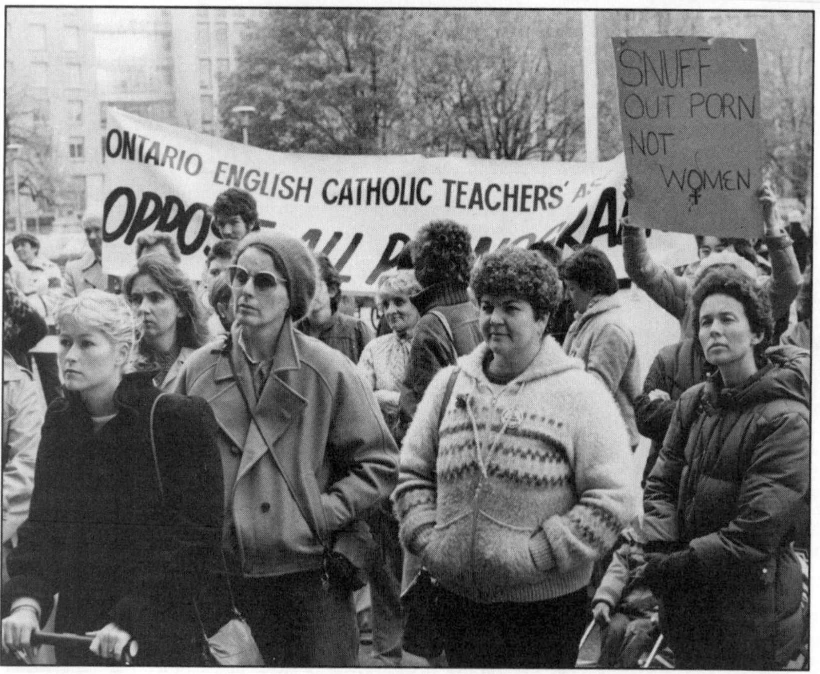

A particularly explicit series of photographs in the March 1984 issue of Penthouse magazine, led OECTA to demand that the issue be banned from Canada. It was.

Provincial treasurer Robert Nixon heard what 25,000 teachers had to say about their pension plan in Copps Colliseum in Hamilton. OECTA's Marie Kennedy kept the crowd under control.

The Ontario government's 1993 Social Contract Act took a legislated bite from teachers salaries and arbitrarily changed their working conditions. OECTA members took part in demonstrations and special events across the province.

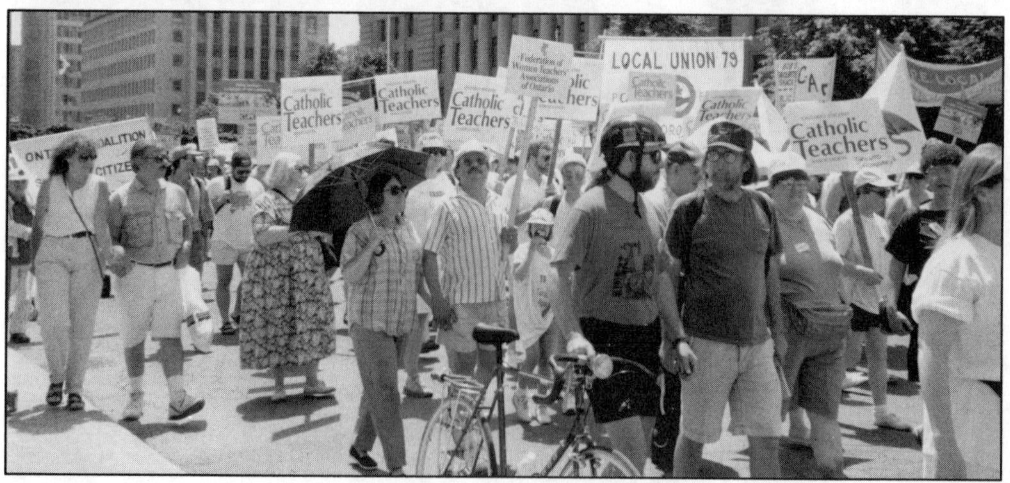

pupil/teacher ratios, or sabbaticals were to be contemplated, if at all, only by the board or, if it had one, by a teacher-trustee committee or its equivalent.[45] Finally, school boards began the habit of releasing the salary settlement as a percentage increase which included the increment for experience, thereby, in the teachers' opinion, endangering the concept of an increment and conveying to the public a higher salary increase.[46]

All four of these positions and practices made the teachers' negotiating task more challenging; in fact, most of them would continually resurface to the present. In addition, there were other school board techniques that were eliminated, but only after time and effort on the part of OECTA and other affiliates. For example, one group of separate school boards tried to establish a zone wherein the salaries would be the same. Another technique was used by the London Separate School Board when it issued a press release on the "ridiculous" demands of its teachers. To avert repetition of this behaviour, OECTA negotiators had to secure agreement that neither side would make any statement to the press until a salary schedule was ratified. More significantly, the Renfrew Separate School Board claimed that the mass resignation of its teachers was illegal; in the absence of any legislation on teacher-board bargaining, this was a troublesome point. Another problem for the teachers was the singular lack of empathy with which OSTC took the position that teachers should not receive their salary when sick unless they had accumulated the days beforehand; instead of being credited with twenty days of sick leave at the start of the school year, the teacher would receive two days at the end of each month.[47] (Sickness would have to be carefully scheduled.)

Not only were unified school boards making negotiating more demanding for OECTA, but the government and some separate school inspectors were increasing the difficulties. The Ministry of Education did not anticipate the costs of implementing the new county and district boards in 1969. Some rural boards had been paying very low wages and had not been maintaining their instructional supplies or capital spending budgets at levels comparable to those of the urban boards. Furthermore, some boards in 1969 overspent just before their demise. Consequently, the Premier, Minister of Education, and Provincial Treasurer in 1969 called a meeting of the chairs and directors of education of all the school boards to discuss budget constraints and the necessity of holding the line on expenditures. Residential taxes had risen 25 to 50 per cent in some areas; the government would soon impose expenditure ceilings.[48]

A rash of budget-cutting broke out. In connection with this an irregular incident involving one separate school inspector took place in the Stratford area. He sent a memorandum to all his boards in 1963 recommending a salary schedule. Miss Babcock immediately contacted the Department of Education which agreed that inspectors should not issue such advice.[49] The inspector got the message.

Coping with these actions on the part of the trustees and others required considerable efforts on the part of Miss Tyrrell, Miss Babcock, and the members of the Salary Negotiating (renamed Salary Policy) Committee. Full-time assistance for them became necessary and, as will be described below, the structure of OECTA was re-examined. Meanwhile, Miss Babcock reported to the Executive that in 1962 she assisted twenty-two local salary negotiating committees, in 1963 fifty-five, and in 1965 thirty-five.[50] Frank Griffin, when he came on staff as Mary Babcock's replacement, initiated a new technique to counter the growing sophistication of the school boards and to spread the workload. With the help of district presidents he chose among the teachers of a given geographical area a resource person with whom to consult for salary negotiators in each of the area's school boards; he then provided these hand-picked teachers with a two-day workshop conducted by a national expert in bargaining.[51] In order to have experienced local negotiators and to protect the "very precarious position" of new teachers whose probationary contracts could be terminated without the board's giving reason, the Board of Directors and the Executive advised that only permanent-contract teachers should be on bargaining committees.[52] They also urged the local negotiators to go after written agreements, a four-category salary schedule paralleling the four teaching certificate standards, and a starting date for negotiations prior to the board's setting its annual budget.[53]

Once the four-category scale was in place with most boards and once the Department began moving toward a B.A. for entrance to a teacher-training institute, OECTA, along with AEFO, FWTAO, and OPSMTF, began advising its members to bargain for a seven-category salary schedule, one that would have three categories beyond a three-year pass B.A. To assist both teachers and school boards in arriving at level definitions, all of the affiliates except OSSTF formed a Certification Committee. Miss Doreen Brady, a future provincial president, and George Saranchuk and John Ware, two high school teachers, met with three members from each of the other three federations almost every second Friday night and all day Saturday for two years,

1969-70, to develop and obtain agreement on the seven levels and their definitions. Out of this work came the Qualifications Evaluation Council of Ontario (QECO), a body supported by the four affiliates which appraises academic and professional qualifications from anywhere in the world and issues a level statement to the teacher.

OSSTF stayed out of this process because it had its own rating system and because it regarded the QECO chart as applicable to generalist applications only and inferior to its own for specialist qualifications. For a number of years OECTA had paid OSSTF to evaluate the qualifications of the teachers in Catholic high schools and continued to do so even after QECO came into existence. George Saranchuk, as OECTA's Certification Officer, would employ OSSTF to evaluate high school teachers' qualifications and QECO for the elementary school teachers. However, once Frank Dillon was hired in 1975 as QECO's administrative coordinator, his OSSTF background allayed any fears about QECO's evaluating of high school teacher qualifications.[54] All of this allowed OECTA to concentrate on moving school boards from a four-level to a seven-level salary schedule.

To achieve this task and other objectives like expanding the scope of negotiations beyond salaries and raising minimum and maximum salaries which would both provide a decent living and would keep up with the growing problem of inflation, OECTA used successful methods from the previous decade. In addition to quoting from the Papal encyclicals "Quadrigessimo Anno" and "Rerum Novarum", the teachers could cite a new encyclical, Pope John XXIII's "Pacem in Terris". Most germane to their salaries were the following excerpts:

> Human beings have the natural right to work. Indissolubly linked with those rights is the right to working conditions in which physical health is not endangered....Women have the right to working conditions in accordance with their requirements and their duties as wives and mothers....Furthermore - and this must be emphasized - there is the right to a working wage, determined according to criterions of justice and therefore sufficient in proportion to the available resources to give the worker and his family a standard of living in keeping with the dignity of the human person.[55]

If the appeal to authority did not work, there was still pink-listing. OECTA used pink letters successfully with the Fort William and Oshawa Separate School Boards in 1962, the Renfrew and Tilbury Separate School Boards in 1968, the Welland Separate School Board in

1969, and the Windsor and Middlesex Separate School Boards in 1970. In Welland the technique was refined; the letter went out before the date set for hiring at the Teachers' Colleges. In Renfrew it was combined with the effective threat of mass resignation.[56] The Oshawa Separate School Board found that pink-listing worked so well for the teachers that it asked OSSTA to "take whatever action is deemed necessary to remove this awesome and abominable practice of pink-listing by the OECTA."[57]

During the 1960s OECTA also rated separate school boards. They were labelled as fair, good, or excellent based on criteria related to the board's attitude to educational improvement, the relations between the board and the staff, and the working conditions. One board objected to this practice so much that it threatened to rate its teachers publicly and in the same fashion.[58] Another public relations tactic was used by the Kingston Separate School Board's teachers when they placed an advertisement in the newspaper to discuss the board's bad faith bargaining.[59] This practice had to cease when OECTA and OSSTA concurred that press releases should either be joint or agreed on by both parties while negotiating was in progress.

OECTA used the carrot as well as the stick on occasion. It would congratulate boards that were paying good salaries and would assist boards to get better grants by raising salaries.[60] However, some boards needed reminding that the additional revenues for separate school boards from the corporation tax adjustment grant were not to be used to lower the mill rate; in other words, they were advised to prioritize teachers' salaries.[61]

Regardless of the negotiating strategies employed, as teacher supply improved greatly and as school boards, particularly the county and district boards, took unified positions, OECTA and other affiliates made little headway on widening the scope of negotiations beyond salaries. Working conditions were anathema to trustee negotiators.[62] One could regard as a rare eccentricity the intention of one board to have its teachers paint the school in the summer if it granted the staff's request to be paid over twelve months instead of ten.[63] But the issue was much more serious for teachers across the province than this anecdote in the minutes suggested.

On the one hand, OECTA's Salary Policy Committee was designing provincial policies on non-salary matters for action by the local negotiators. On the other hand, OSSTA and OSTC were advising all boards to negotiate only salary matters. With growing conflict in a number of centres, OECTA and OSSTA set up a joint committee in 1969 to study "scope of negotiations".[64] All of these thrusts resulted in the following topics raised at bargaining sessions throughout the province and at Executive, Board of Directors, and AGM meetings: sabbatical leave policies, released teaching time for principals, size of school for vice-principals, amount of time allotted to the teacher for lunch, compulsory in-service during the school day, spares for the elementary school teacher, the pupil/teacher ratio, the establishment of grievance committees, and the development of board policies after joint consultation between teachers and trustees. The last three the trustees perceived as unreasonable encroachments on their management rights.[65]

Pressure Points. Clearly, OECTA had to be unified in its outlook in a number of areas if it were to represent its members well in the 1960s and in the future. To maintain solidarity the Association had to resolve three internal questions. Could OECTA foster the interests of the whole while harmonizing them with the concerns of the parts, particularly the religious teachers, the married men, and the married women? Should the Association continue to develop a provincial salary schedule? And, most significantly for the coming decade and for the state of negotiations and the teacher supply in the late 1960s, should OECTA use other new sanctions, the strike and working to rule?

The religious teachers, especially the sisters because of their numbers, had been invaluable to the separate schools for over one hundred years. As OECTA, in an inflammatory environment and after the 1962-63 Foundation Plan, began to negotiate vigorously for improved salaries and fringe benefits, the sisters experienced new problems that deserved consideration. For all practical purposes the sisters served two masters - the school board and the Bishop. Traditionally, the religious Orders would advise the boards during the summer how many of their members were being assigned and to what schools, who would be principals and in what schools. Unofficially, the Orders had been staffing certain schools within the board for decades. The agreement was between an official of the board and of the Order. No contract was involved.

By the 1960s OECTA was encouraging the Orders to have their members sign standard individual contracts and follow the laws and regulations centering around teacher employment. However, tradition was holding sway even after Vatican II fostered a certain amount of individualization in religious life. Thus in 1966 Fr. Conway met with the religious Superiors to discuss the fact that many of the sisters felt like second-class citizens because the boards were still dealing only with their Superiors rather than with them. Fr. Conway realized that it would take awhile to educate everyone for new practices; therefore, at his meetings he reviewed the existing law regarding negotiations and employment and the necessity of notifying school boards as early as possible before May 31 about the transfer of sisters, particularly principals.[66] Of course, even though the Orders cooperated, some of the school boards at first were reluctant to give up the convenient custom of deciding what to pay the religious teachers independently of salary agreements for the lay teachers. For example, in 1967 the Oshawa Separate School Board refused to include the religious teachers' salaries in negotiations. As late as 1970 the Windsor Separate School Board tried to get away with drawing up probationary contracts for the sisters, despite the fact that they had been teaching for the board for a number of years. (Legally, these sisters who had been teaching for the board without contracts were deemed to be in possession of permanent contracts; it would be some time before teachers and boards would fully grasp this nicety.) Despite initial problems, it is likely that by 1970 most religious teachers were on individual contracts, since the AGM passed at that time a motion that all members of religious orders were to sign contracts.[67]

This meant that it was now official that the religious teachers had two superordinates. They were responsible to the diocesan Bishop for carrying out the teaching mission of the Church. Furthermore, in the absence of any government grants or tax revenues for grades eleven, twelve, and thirteen in the Catholic high schools, the Bishops, using parish collections paid the salaries, such as they were, of the staff, many of them religious, in these grades. Understandably, the Bishops took an interest in salary negotiations, since the separate school salary settlements would have an impact on the private school salaries. Bishop Ryan, whose Hamilton diocese had many high schools, flatly stated, after Fr. Conway's letter to all the teaching Orders, that his religious teachers were not to be part of negotiations, adding that "it would be a sorry day when the religious would become subservient to the Laymen." Two years later, in 1969, he was still not permitting the religious teachers to negotiate.[68] Bishop Carter of the London diocese at first felt the same way. When the negotiations with the Windsor Separate School Board became quite stormy in 1966, he informed OECTA's local chief negotiator that he would handle negotiations for the religious as he had in the past; "anyone who made the pretence of negotiating for the sisters was misrepresenting his position." However, in the same year he reconsidered and advised the Superiors that he would no longer be part of the process.[69] The issue did die down provincially, except in the Hamilton diocese.

With the religious teachers on individual contracts, OECTA had to revisit another question previously debated between it and AEFO: the percentage of salary the religious teacher should receive compared to the lay teacher's salary. The same arguments as before were raised. At the 1964 AGM an attempt to raise the figure to 85 per cent resulted in a compromise: religious teachers were to receive not less that 66 2/3 per cent and not more than 85 per cent; otherwise, Fr. Conway feared they would lose their tax exemption status. Lay teachers as prospective employees or candidates for promotion now felt more competitive. At the 1965 AGM the motion passed that the percentage should be 85 per cent. In 1970 new arguments surfaced. Separate school boards could now afford to pay their religious teachers at par; therefore, OECTA held that it should apply its equal-pay-for-equal-work principle to its religious members. The unspoken but well-understood thought was that the higher the salary for the sisters, brothers, and priests, the more money the Bishops would receive to help the private Catholic high schools. At the 1970 AGM the motion passed that religious teachers should receive 100 per cent of the lay teachers' salaries.[70] The other reality behind all these motions was that religious teachers in the province's separate schools had shrunk from 51 per cent of the total separate school staffs in 1950 to 29 per cent in 1962, 20.4 per cent in 1963, 15.4 per cent in 1965, and was still dropping after that year.[71]

The married men in OECTA, a growing number now that it was possible for them to consider a lifetime career in the separate school system, also had special needs. Since in the 1960s OECTA was just beginning to make significant progress in negotiating fringe benefits, there were many separate school boards with no medical plans for their teachers. Most of these boards let the MSSB set the precedent, and it too lacked any such plan. About 1961 a group of married men teachers in the employ of the MSSB, concerned about medical bills, particularly for care of their spouses during pregnancies, and about the cost of private plans, investigated the possibility of a group plan through the Ontario Blue Cross. There were two hurdles. First, at least 75 per cent of the group had to pay for the coverage; but the religious teachers had their own group plan and many of the married women were covered through their husbands' plans. Second, the school board would have to process the deductions from the pay cheques and payments to the carrier; the chairman and business administrator of the MSSB hesitated because this processing would be a cost to the board and because they feared the negotiators or those teachers on the Teacher-Trustee Committee would in the future ask the board to pay a percentage of the costs. The religious orders, after some meetings, generously agreed to become part of the plan; the 75 per cent target was reached. With the encouragement of the OECTA Directors and Executive, the local teachers persuaded the MSSB to start a group medical plan. Other separate school boards gradually followed this lead.[72]

However, as discussed in the previous chapter, sympathy for the custom of paying married men's allowances was evaporating. Salaries were improving after 1962; it was difficult to defend this exception to the principle of equal pay for equal work. And certainly, there was zero tolerance on the part of the Executive for unmarried male teachers receiving an allowance. There was no debate on this topic in the minutes of the AGM, Board of Directors, or Executive and very few references to problems at the school board level. These married men clauses disappeared from salary agreements during the decade. So, for example, the Ottawa Separate School Board in 1962 set an interesting precedent when it stopped paying the $500 married men's allowance if the wife was earning more than $1000 a year. When the Renfrew Separate School Board proposed paying its married and single male teachers a bonus above the schedule, the teachers refused to ratify the agreement; the following year the Executive wrote this board advising that all the teachers should receive a bonus of $600 since two married male teachers were receiving it.[73]

Miss Babcock had the last word on this topic. At the 1962 AGM she reported that:

> It has been a painful experience in some areas to eradicate the practice of including in salary schedules certain clauses which give additional allowances to a favoured few which results in other teachers being paid lower salaries in order to subsidize these extras;...boards use such methods to keep salaries down.[74]

As for the needs of the married women teachers, OECTA had come a long way in its attitude since the time when it indirectly conveyed the message that they should stay home with their children. The minutes made only two references to their contractual status, both in the early 1960s: the Fort William Separate School Board was agreed to put its married female teachers on permanent contracts, and the Executive met with OSSTA to discuss permanent contracts for all the province's married women teachers.[75] Of course, the shortage of teachers affected the viewpoints of teachers and trustees on this subject.

Now that equal pay and equal treatment of this group was the norm, the educational agencies examined their opinions about maternity leave and took action. In the 1964 AGM it was reported that the central office was receiving more complaints about maternity leave than on any other single issue. It would appear that some married women teachers were not scheduling their pregnancy leaves at a time convenient for the trustees and schools. A flexible attitude toward the future, specifically with regard to separate school enrolment and more generally with regard to the propagation of the human race, would not be prevalent for a few years. One Department of Education official had even equated pregnancy with sickness in his interpretation of a section in *The Schools Administration Act*; this would have permitted pregnant teachers when staying home to claim sick days.[76]

However, matters improved at the end of the decade. OTF developed a policy on maternity leave: the leaving date of the pregnant teacher was to be at the discretion of the teacher and principal; the leave was to be a minimum of seven weeks and a maximum of two years; her teaching position was to be guaranteed. This policy applied to a teacher on permanent contract and to a teacher adopting a child. OSSTA immediately agreed to the policy. A year later, in 1970, a new provincial statute reinforced OTF's policy: *The Women's Equal Employment Opportunity Act* specified that the pregnant teacher was to be granted leave of absence for six weeks before and after the birth without loss of benefits or seniority.[77]

Not all boards moved with the times. Sometimes a physician would require the pregnant patient to stay home early in the term because of physical conditions related to the pregnancy (such as varicose veins or severe nausea). In such cases the teacher would naturally claim sick leave, expecting to receive salary for the sick days accumulated. The Sudbury and Welland Separate School Boards took the narrow view that these teachers were not ill; they were pregnant; therefore, they were to receive no salary. In 1969 and 1970 OECTA took both boards to court and won: sick leave was to be allowed during pregnancy if an illness occurred because of the pregnancy.[78] OECTA was protecting the interests of the married women teachers as well as it did so for the rest of its members. As for Miss Tyrrell's lament at the 1962 and 1964 AGM that there were few female lay principals and a paucity of candidates coming forth for these positions,[79] this problem would have to wait another twenty years for action.

Another pressure point challenging the unity of OECTA was disagreement over its provincial salary schedule. In the early years of the Association it had served the useful purpose of providing a standard for the separate school boards to meet. But in a time of inflation and, in some parts of the province, aggressive salary negotiators, its usefulness began to be questioned. The catalysts were the AGM delegates from the Sudbury and Windsor districts. John Rodriguez, Elie Martel, and Bob Fera from the north began in 1965 with a motion that there be a $500 allowance on the salary scale for northern Ontario teachers. This motion was defeated. They next proposed an amendment to establish a northern Ontario salary schedule; however, Fr. Siegfried, unaccustomed to debates on positions developed at the provincial committee and Executive level, summarily ruled the amendment out of order because it was not in the spirit of the main motion to accept the OECTA salary schedule.[80] Disappointed with these defeats, they and other males in the Sudbury district began to complain that the OECTA's membership was predominantly lay female and religious teachers who had insufficient sympathy for the concerns of the male teachers. They even went so far as to investigate the possibility of forming a Catholic men teachers' affiliate like OPSMTF; Karl Bohren and Fr. Conway travelled to Sudbury to explain *The Teaching Profession Act* to them and to point out the small size of their group. The idea for a splinter group soon died, but the intention to eliminate the OECTA salary schedule gathered force.[81]

Due to inflationary pressures, the shortage of teachers, and the additional grants from the Foundation Plan, salaries were increasing annually. Four times between 1960 and 1965 it was necessary to revise upward the salary schedule, on each occasion with a considerable investment of time at the AGM discussing each clause of a multi-category grid with a number of allowances for special situations.[82] Despite this, in 1966 the Windsor Separate School teachers were rejecting a board offer in excess of the OECTA schedule, while the Board of Directors was refusing to pink-list the board because of the Windsor teachers' "unrealistic" demands.[83] This, in turn, raised the question of whether or not pink-listing of the Windsor board would even be possible when the board was meeting the levels of the provincial schedule.[84]

The schedule soon became history. In December 1966 the Salary Policy Committee recommended that the salary table not be prepared for at least one year since there was a great variance of situations throughout the province and since one could not foresee future conditions in the present economy. The following year the Directors voted down the schedule. Finally, in 1968 the AGM suspended the policy of presenting a salary schedule.[85]

The Question of Sanctions. The differences of opinion discussed above were resolved relatively easily without any lasting effects on membership solidarity. However, the issue of expanding sanctions beyond pink-listing and mass resignations to those of work to rule and strikes was and would continue to be vigorously debated among the members of OECTA and other affiliates. The arguments raised for and against the union concept earlier in the century in other parts of Canada would surface again in Ontario over the right to strike. The matter would eventually be resolved with a statute, which to this day is arguably the most important piece of legislation affecting teachers since *The Teaching Profession Act*. The 1960s began the debate culminating in the 1975 statute giving the teaching profession a number of rights, including the right to strike, in the area of collective agreements with school boards.

Bargaining, provincial takeovers, and pink-listing had been effective during the teacher shortage of the 1950s and the early and middle 1960s. The threat of mass resignation, carried out by collecting letters of resignation for the negotiators to hold during the sessions with the trustees, was rarely used and quite effective. But once supply met demand in the late 1960s, all these techniques lost their old power and mass resignation became a risky strategy. It worked well in Windsor in 1969 and 1970 because of the unity of a large number of teachers there; 670 out of 732 teachers submitted resignations on May 26, 1969. In 1970, 640 resigned; the *Canadian Register* headlined, "Nervous Wind: will schools open in the fall for 650 classes?"[86] The MSSB teachers in 1969 considered the same tactic, also because of their large numbers. Their negotiators were going to make it more threatening by submitting the resignations at the end of November, but OECTA could not support this plan because of an agreement between OSTC and OTF to use mass resignation only on the May 31st date.[87] The large numbers of teachers in Windsor and Toronto made recruitment of replacements impossible. But what if the trustees were willing to see the schools closed? OECTA found itself considering the necessity of a reserve fund and voluntary contributions from working teachers, revenues that would quickly be used up with such large boards.

As for the smaller boards, Edwin Alexander, later a member of the central office staff, used the mass resignation threat in New Liskeard in 1967. It was also used with the Renfrew Separate School Board a year later. Alexander's analysis of this type of sanction revealed its shortcomings. Even when used with pink-listing (an absolute necessity to remove the risk of replacement staffing), there were serious problems. There was much work required to ensure a united front, so that no teacher would go back to work unless all the teachers were rehired. And even with pink-listing, the procedure was risky when only a small number of teachers would have to be recruited from inside or outside the province. In 1970 OECTA was sufficiently fearful that the Middlesex County Separate School Board would accept the mass resignations that it began arrangements for a voluntary $79 donation from its members for a reserve fund that would be distributed weekly, $50 for a single teacher, $75 for a married one. In 1971 Alexander in a statement to the *Canadian Register* labelled mass resignations as "employee suicide".[88] Furthermore, the Board of Directors had tabled a motion that described the process as "distasteful and harmful to the students."[89]

If mass resignations were becoming ineffective and any form of strike was unethical according to OTF policy, how was OECTA to counter the increased unity of the school board? Withdrawal of extra-curricular activities and working to rule were approved as retaliatory measures at the 1967 AGM, used as a threat with the Anderton Separate School Board, and put into practice with the St. Catharines Separate School Board. But this type of sanction was practical only in high school; most separate schools were elementary.[90] Teachers could also release frustration by picketing, a new tactic for them, but an old one in the labour unions. The Hastings-Prince Edward County RCSS Board, even after involvement with the Executive and OSSTA, refused to implement recommendations from its Teacher-Trustee Committee; the teachers then picketed the board at a motel breakfast meeting of the latter group.91 But this strategy, encouraged particularly by the new male members from overseas, encountered some disapproval. One member wrote the editor of the *OECTA News and Views* about this incident: "I disagree that this support has to take the form of so low and unbecoming an attempt, so primitive and uncultured, as picketing. Have any protest marches ever solved a problem adequately?"[92]

Two other novel devices were used in Belleville: the AGM voted that each teacher who wished to leave the Hastings-Prince Edward County RCSS Board would received a $1000 subsidy from OECTA; in addition, teachers across the province were encouraged to write letters or send telegrams to the board and OSSTA. If none of these actions produced results, there was always prayer. The AGM passed a motion "that teachers across the province offer special prayers asking God for Divine Help to solve the problem in Hastings-Prince Edward County."[93]

The opinion was strengthening that none of these negotiating measures in and of themselves had enough influence in difficult bargaining situations without the right to strike. The teachers had promised in 1944 not to use the strike weapon in return for the passing of *The Teaching Profession Act*. But twenty-five years had passed and there is nothing final in legislation. The previously unthinkable began to be seriously considered.

The years between 1966 and 1970 were marked by teacher-trustee conflict in some large boards. Picketing occurred in three more places: Toronto, Waterloo, and Windsor. The MSSB negotiators considered a one-day walkout, and the Windsor teachers voted to take strike action.[94] The arguments put forward will be examined in the next chapter as preludes to collective agreement legislation. For purposes of this discussion it is fair to say that, although the Board of Directors was unable to support a strike, the events in Toronto and Windsor acted as stimuli for certain AGM motions. Actually, some OECTA members had always had sympathy for strike action. The 1962 AGM was not held at the traditional location, the Royal York Hotel, because of a strike there.[95]

John Rodriguez and Elie Martel had been expressing solidarity with the parents of their pupils striking against Inco. And although Karl Bohren was finding rumours of strike action or general sick leave "disturbing" at an Executive meeting in March 1966, just a few months later he, John Rodriguez, and Elie Martel were appointed to an OTF committee to study a possible change in the position of teachers regarding compulsory arbitration, the union movement, and all aspects of collective bargaining. Most significantly, a motion moved by two delegates, Frank Griffin and Patrick O'Neill, passed at the 1966 AGM. Its wording was as follows: "Whereas there are no effective retaliatory measures available to the teachers in case of dispute with a board, be it resolved that OECTA formulate a policy for effective retaliatory measures to be employed in such a case." It was referred to the OTF committee along with a second motion that "since *The Teaching Profession Act* limits bargaining rights, the OECTA requests the OTF to press the government to amend *The Labour Relations Act* by deleting S.2 (f) excluding teachers." On the other hand, John Rodriguez would find it necessary in conscience to resign from the OTF committee because of his opposition to the general disapproval of a teacher's right to strike. In addition, the resolution he took from his Sudbury district to the Board of Directors in 1968 which recommended that OECTA establish a reserve fund for living expenses for those who have to "deny their services," was disapproved.[96] But the momentum had started; other affiliates, especially OSSTF, were moving in the same direction. Frank Griffin, in his new position as deputy executive director on the central office staff, expressed the new reality for teachers and trustees in his column "Frank Comments" in the *OECTA Review*.

> Teachers give notice
> That they will no longer go shamefaced and diffident to the bargaining table to collectively beg for that which they honestly believe to be their right.
> That they will no longer accept the grudging 5 or 6 per cent thrown at them after months of acrimonious wrangling during which their motives, their qualifications, their abilities, and their status are called into question.
>
> That they have driven the last nail into the coffin of the stereotype docile genteel spinster-lady-teacher and that she is dead and gone forever.[97]

Ethics, Protection and the Board of Reference. Equally important as salary negotiating for OECTA was protection of its members' contracts and positions. But this was a two-way street. To have the support of their Association, teachers had to meet the standards of the OTF Code of Ethics. Although in terms of the total membership, the number of teachers or trustees not adhering to the legislation or the Code was small, there were still enough incidents to keep the OECTA Relations and Discipline (renamed in 1965 the Counselling and Relations) Committee busy investigating whether each matter could be cleared up internally or whether it had to be referred to OTF. The most common occurrences were breach of contract. To deal with the teacher shortage, school boards would approach the students at the Teachers' Colleges early in their school year and would also recruit large numbers of teachers at the Park Plaza Hotel. Some of the inexperienced teachers, faced with a choice of many school boards interviewing in many rooms, would be quickly signed up on a contract and then have second thoughts. OECTA or OTF would have to judge whether or not to report the teacher for breaking a contract or call on the understanding and tolerance of the board with the contract. By the late 1960s the problem had diminished.

Reports from the Relations and Discipline Committee between 1962 and 1967 revealed the following unethical actions on the part of school boards and teachers: broken contracts, illegal contractual terms, dismissal of lay principals in order to replace them with religious principals, individual bargaining, discrimination regarding married women teachers' contracts and salaries, poor classroom discipline, inefficiency and incompetency, unprofessional conduct, immorality, unreasonable pregnancy leaves, assault on a pupil, charges against the criminal code, and giving alcohol to students. Some of these resulted in suspension of teaching certificates by the Minister of Education.[98] A possible reason for this list of offences being longer than in the 1950s was the greater number of teachers, many of them young and new to the profession.

The Relations and Discipline Committee felt that in general, ethical standards and professionalism prevailed with most of the teachers. But it judged it necessary to make two special comments as part of its reports to the Directors. It urged school boards to report morals charges to OECTA lest other children be at risk. Secondly, it lamented the casualness with which a few teachers would criticize fellow professionals. Miss Tyrrell expressed her concern over a few cases where teachers were alleged to have been inconsiderate in their contacts with fellow teachers. Frequently, the explanation was that it was "just a personality conflict." Miss Tyrrell regarded this as an "overworked expression" and restated her conviction that the only criticism of a teacher which was valid was that "which stems from a desire to improve the educational process and which is directed at issues rather than personalities."[99] At a time when the teachers were attempting to get copies of inspectors' evaluations of them, it was important for teachers to follow the Code of Ethics regarding adverse reports on their fellow professionals.

Historically, the Department of Education's inspectors, after visiting the teacher's classroom, would rank the teacher, in rising order of competence, one to seven on an official card; s/he would file this report and the teacher would not see it. The affiliates had two problems with this procedure: the teacher is not just a number and s/he should be shown the inspector's evaluation. After an OTF meeting with the Minister in 1965, the process was improved somewhat: elementary school teachers who had been rated below average or poor would be informed in writing with reasons; other ratings would be available for perusal on request. The following year the Department announced another modification:[100] inspectors would summarize their opinion of the teacher's ability with a word instead of a number; the adjectives would range from "unsatisfactory" to "excellent." Only those teachers rated unsatisfactory would receive a written statement, since, in the opinion of the Department, to do the same for those teachers categorized as "fair" would be "unduly discouraging" for them and would not contribute to a successful collaboration between the inspector and the teachers for the improvement of instruction. Inspectors would, however, tell each teacher his/her grading and the reasons for it.[101] The AGM was not satisfied and at its 1967 meeting passed a motion that OTF request the Department that the inspector's report be given to the teacher, the Department, the principal, and the school board. This, in the opinion of the AGM, would oblige the inspector to justify and defend a negative report on a teacher.[102] Nothing came of this motion; presumably, OTF saw a dangerous precedent if the trustees, non-professionals, received copies of reports on teachers.

With the formation of county and district boards less than two years away, OECTA would have to develop with the new board superintendents a professional procedure for teacher evaluation. Most teachers after 1969 would no longer be visited by provincial inspectors. Discussions began in 1971 with the Ontario Catholic Superintendents and Inspectors Association (OCSIA).[103]

OECTA also had to educate some principals on teacher evaluation. The time when these administrators taught almost full-time and looked after the budget, building, discipline, and organization for a small allowance had disappeared with most boards by the end of the 1960s. Principals were now to evaluate programme and teachers. The OECTA's Principals' Committee reported in 1968 that 30 per cent of the province's principals of separate schools were required to submit written reports on teachers to their board superintendents, and that many of them saw a conflict between their role of evaluator and of master or principal teacher assisting and encouraging staff. At the same time, the trustees were still pushing for principals to be out of any teachers' association, so that they could be managers for them. In this new set of circumstances, a few principals were trying to avoid confrontations by not giving copies of adverse reports to the teachers in contravention of section 18 of the *Regulation Made Under The Teaching*

Profession Act.[104] Principals became educated about their new role, so that this unethical practice generally vanished, but the trustees' wish to remove principals from OTF and the tension in the principals' two roles remains to the present.

It was crucial for OECTA to straighten out problems associated with teacher evaluation because the documents engendered from the process often became determining pieces of evidence in the case of a Board of Reference. The documents also helped OECTA decide whether or not to support a dismissed teacher in a Board of Reference. Up until the 1970s most of the affiliates did prejudge the merits of such teachers' cases. The philosophy of OECTA on this topic was summed up at the beginning and end of the decade by members of the Executive. Fr. Conway expressed the idea succinctly: "The Federation does not exist to protect teachers regardless of their conduct."[105] Mary Babcock elaborated: "An erroneous idea seems to exist among some of our teachers that the Association is bound to support them, right or wrong. The Association would not long command any respect if it failed to observe the regulations and policies governing the profession."[106]

The Board of Directors reviewed the policy in 1965 and recommended to the AGM that where an investigation showed guilt on the teacher's part, then OECTA would not support the member in a Board of Reference but, where it revealed reasonable doubt, OECTA would provide legal counsel. The AGM referred this recommended policy to the Legislative Committee and decided that meanwhile the Executive Secretary and President were to decide whether or not to support the member.[107] Practice followed this policy throughout the decade. For example, in 1962 the Relations and Discipline Committee reported to the AGM that, "We had made a thorough investigation of the case and since we were unable to get sufficient evidence of efficiency, the Executive, at a special meeting, was reluctant to support her."[108] In 1965, 1970, and 1971 the Executive decided not to support a member applying for a Board of Reference.[109]

With the exception of OPMSTF, the other affiliates also placed preference on upholding professional standards over automatically supporting the dismissed teacher. AEFO's position was identical to OECTA's. OSSTF would support the member when it was confident of winning, in other words, when the teacher was in the right according to the affiliate's investigation. FWTAO believed that every teacher deserved her day in court, but this did not mean that the Federation had to support the teacher in a Board of Reference. Even OPSMTF, which would almost always support the dismissed teacher without prejudging, would make an exception with the likes of sexual abuse or an indictable offence outside of the school.[110]

In the 1970s the attitude of the affiliates changed. Prejudging was ruled out in favour of letting a Board of Reference decide on the justice of the school board's dismissal of the teacher. With this attitude, similar to that of presuming a person innocent until proven guilty, the federations began automatically paying the dismissed teacher's legal fees and providing a member on the Board of Reference. In 1972 OECTA for the last time did not support a member. In my position as director of education, I had been sending copies of evaluations on the teacher for several months to OECTA and asking it to assist the teacher. The assistance was rejected; the teacher was fired. Frank Griffin argued at an Executive meeting that OECTA had no business wasting money on a hopeless case. Pat O'Neill argued for the process; OECTA should not be the judge. Mr. Griffin's view prevailed. But the practice of prejudging was abolished soon thereafter by removing the word "support" of the dismissed teacher from the policy. OECTA could pay the legal costs of a teacher without suggesting approval of possible unprofessionalism.[111]

This same evolution in attitude and practice took place with regard to Catholic separate school teachers marrying outside of the Catholic Church. A principal of a Catholic high school dismissed a teacher who did not marry in a Church ceremony over the summer; OECTA advised him that he could apply for a Board of Reference, but that it would not support him. In 1966, only John Rodriguez was opposed to an Executive decision not to support teachers in this situation. But in 1971 the Executive took the position that it was in no position to pass judgment on any member who was accused of not practising the Catholic faith. The Counselling and Relations Committee in its report to the 1971 AGM summed up this contentious point:

> teachers should not be victimized because they fail to measure up to someone else's arbitrary standard of conduct or because of their human and private failings. However, if the conduct of the teacher gives rise to public scandal and makes nonsense of the philosophy of Catholic education, then...the teacher should not be supported in any consequent dispute with the board.[112]

As discussed previously, a teacher on a probationary contract when dismissed could not request the Minister for a Board of Reference. Furthermore, the school board did not have to give reasons for the contract termination as it did for permanent contract teachers. Recognizing an unfairness here, the 1968 AGM passed a motion that reasons be given for dismissal of a probationary teacher and that OTF approach the Minister to make the necessary legislative amendments. However, the affiliates at an OTF meeting defeated the OECTA motion; they argued that reasons for contract termination would not help the probationary teacher because s/he had no means to challenge the decision. They also felt that it would not be wise to have an unsatisfactory report follow the teacher to her/his new teaching position; no reason was better than such a report.[113] The idea of recourse to the courts was not advanced, nor did the minutes raise the possibility of seeking a change both in the legislation and in the Minister's practice of granting Boards of Reference just to permanent contract teachers.

Superannuation. Protection of the rights, salaries, and working conditions of the teachers included the safeguarding and improvement of their pensions. The three principal changes sought were, first, the lowering of the number of years for the calculating of the pension from ten to seven; second, the reduction for the eligibility for an A pension from forty to thirty-five years at age sixty; and, third, a drop in the minimum number of teaching years to qualify for a pension from twenty-five to fifteen years. The 1960s and 1970s saw these upgradings.[114] The OTF Executive had thought that using the average salary of a teacher's last seven years to calculate the pension would be enough to ask from William Davis, but OPSMTF and OSSTF, bringing up the possibility of an economic recession in future years, argued for the best seven years. In fact, effective January 1, 1966, the Act was amended in favour of the best seven years.[115]

Other improvements were also pursued. For example, there was sexual discrimination in the statutory provision that female pensioned teachers could not also receive the widow's pension from the teacher's pension of her deceased spouse; males could.[116] However, inflation had made the plight of the retired teacher so serious that the Minister decided that there would be no new requests for changes in the pension statute until this critical problem of inflation was solved.[117] In 1967, at age 78, Cecilia Rowan, the first Secretary of OECTA, wrote to the Commission studying the structure of OTF a poignant handwritten letter:

> Since the OTF has declared to the Department its interest and concern regarding retired teachers, we have been given more than just a 'ray' of hope. Saying just a few words on the plight which still exists may I put before you the Salary Schedule under which most of us worked in Ottawa Separate Schools for most of our lives.
> Minimum was 800.
> Teach 10 years and you reach the maximum of 900.
> The Principals drew a little extra. I am not sure just what governed the latter.
> So what chance had we to save? And the salaries had just begun to roll when many of us reached retirement age...Teachers who have given over forty years as mentors of future citizens should not have to worry now with the fear of having to turn to friends and relatives. It would be a cruel fate at the end of a scholastic trail. May we humbly ask your best efforts in getting a flat increase for all.[118]

Various proposals came forth. An amendment made it possible for a retired teacher to teach for twenty days in a school year without any effect on the pension, but this represented only about 10 per cent additional income. One suggestion was that these days be increased to 120; another was that there be a pension adjustment for cost of living every five years.[119] Working teachers received the significant improvement of the best-seven clause, but this did not benefit the retired teachers. OTF called for action to raise the minimum pension and to provide an escalation clause for times of inflation.[120] Finally, a breakthrough occurred in 1967: a retired teacher could teach in a school year up to the point where her/his salary plus the pension equalled the salary of her/his last year of teaching. As for the teacher who wished or had to stay retired, the minimum salary was raised to $2400 (still a pittance). In 1968 a group of retired teachers, after meeting with Nora Hodgins of OTF, organized the Superannuated Teachers of Ontario (STO) to promote and protect the interests of retired educators in the areas of pensions, health care, and insurance. Art McAdam became the first president.[121]

The Professional Development and Religious Education of Teachers. As discussed, the object in the OECTA's Constitution "to represent members in all matters related to collective bargaining" consumed considerable time and effort. Equally, if not more important was another constitutional aim, "to work for the moral, intellectual, religious, and professional growth of its members."[122] As the separate school system expanded with beginning teachers and as Vatican II and the Hall-

Dennis Report called for new professional and personal attitudes, knowledges, and skills, this second object also necessitated great expenditure of resources. OECTA's concentration on professional development progressed along two tracks: Teachers' College and in-service.

In 1962 the Ontario Bishops' Brief to Premier Robarts described the ideal solution for the preparation of separate school teachers as a Catholic Teachers' College, but admitted that the idea was impractical at that time; candidates would continue to attend the nearest Teachers' College, and the general public would label the idea of one Catholic College as segregationist. On the other hand, the established provisions were described by the Bishops as "almost intolerable." Fr. Conway listed three factors deterring effective training in the teaching of religion at Teachers' Colleges: the shortage of time allowed for the task, the voluntary attendance at the religious education sessions, and the Catholic chaplains' lack of pedagogical background. The Bishops asked for more time for the course at the Colleges, as well as credit recognition for the subject. Fr. Raymond Durocher, O.M.I., editor of the *Canadian Register*, concurred in the *Catholic Trustee*; a course that would integrate dynamic biblical and psychological elements into an experiential, developmental religious education approach required all the prestige and recognition the Department of Education could give it.[123]

The Catholic community was divided on the issue of its own Teachers' College. After all, the Franco-Ontarians had two such institutions, one in Ottawa and one in Sturgeon Falls, later Sudbury; Bishop Emmett Carter had taught and headed up a Catholic Teachers' College in Montreal; and Ontario's Catholics since before Confederation had expressed their desire for their own teacher-training facilities. Even after the Bishops' Brief, OSSTA printed in its quarterly journal an article by Rev. John J. O'Flaherty of London expressing the need for Catholic Teachers' Colleges with a compulsory course in catechetics. The Kingston separate school board and other boards in the diocese also advocated them.[124]

But Fr. Conway and the Executive were against the idea at that time for a number of reasons. The separate school leaders were after better grants, access to corporation taxes, and extension of separate schools; requests for Catholic Teachers' Colleges would endanger these other objectives and would cut the separate school community off from the mainstream, rendering it uninfluential as a group of complete separatists. In any case, in Fr. Conway's opinion, the idea was unrealistic because the Catholics did not have a sufficiently expert staff for such institutions. Instead, Fr. Conway argued, it would be a better strategy to have Catholics attend the same secular Teachers' Colleges so that OECTA could claim that its teachers were no different from their public school counterparts in their general preparation for a teacher's certificate and therefore, were entitled to equal treatment for themselves and their pupils from the government. Bishop Carter, chairman of the Bishops' education committee, reluctantly agreed, but wanted to work with OECTA and OSSTA for a set-up at the Teachers' Colleges wherein the Catholic students could study religious education, the Catholic philosophy of education, and some other subjects under Catholic auspices. Premier Robarts settled the argument in favour of a variation of the latter plan when he announced the Foundation Plan headlined in the *Canadian Register* as "New Grant System Announced For Schools, But Robarts Rejects Bid To Include High Schools and Teachers' Colleges." He did however, suggest, religious education credits.[125]

OECTA set to work. In 1965 its brief to the Hall-Dennis Committee, authored by Mother St. Philomena, I.B.V.M., Sr. St. Boniface, C.S.J., Veronica Houlahan, and Virginia Stumpf, urged that there be one period a week of religious education at the Teachers' Colleges and that theology be recognized as a university subject for entrance to the OCE. Sr. St. Boniface, now Sr. Jacqueline O'Brien, recently recalled how necessary changes in teacher training were. For generations Catholics had studied religion in a catechetical "apologetic" manner with a set of memorized formulae with little or no life in them. Now, the teacher was to present the "good news," the Gospel, from God as Father and Mother, from a Person who loves. Sister, instead of moving to the office of provincial president of OECTA, felt impelled to attend the Lumen Vitae institute in Belgium for a year to develop her soul and mind to teach religious education. If such professional and personal development were necessary for Sr. O'Brien, one can appreciate why the *Canadian Register* worried that teachers had little background in the Scripture, liturgy, or the new concept of the Church.[126]

In 1967 OECTA submitted jointly with OSSTA to the government the "Brief on the Training of Teachers for the Teaching of Religious Knowledge". Written by Paul Forestell, a Welland lawyer hired by OSSTA, and edited and presented by Mary Babcock, Fr. F. C. Malone, C.S.B., and Sr. Frances McCann from OECTA, Chris Asseff, Ab Klein, and Fr. Dennis Murphy from OSSTA, and Fr. Durocher on behalf of the Bishops, the Brief, among other things, contained a suggested topic outline for a course in religious education at the Teachers' Colleges.[127] By the end of the 1960s the situation had improved greatly at the Colleges, and separate school boards were developing the habit of asking prospective employees if they had taken the religion course at the College.

To assist its practising teachers and principals to teach the "Come to the Father" curriculum, OECTA moved on several fronts: its central office, the districts and units, the Department of Education, OSSTA and separate school boards, and OCSIA. Even before the publication of the Vatican II documents, the Professional Development Committee in 1962 was planning workshops on the implications of the forthcoming Ecumenical Council and had developed a booklet entitled "Philosophy of Education of School Principals" which indicated that one of the aims of a principal was to ensure that religious instruction prepare the child to learn, love, and live conscientiously her/his Christian heritage.[128] In 1964 the Professional Development Committee made, and the Directors passed, the recommendation that each district and/or unit establish in-service in the teaching of religious education for its members and that the school boards be encouraged to stipulate attendance at the in-service of all teachers with three years, or less experience in separate schools as a condition of employment. By 1966, the Committee was able to report that 60 per cent of the districts were concentrating on the apostolic formation and emerging role of the religion teacher in separate schools. Meanwhile, the annual principals' course, which OECTA had been running since 1959, encompassed such topics as the religious education programme, the principal as Catholic leader, and the apostolate of the principal.[129]

The main thrust of OECTA would become the development of certificate-bearing courses in religious education. Regardless of improvements at the Teachers' Colleges, at best the students there would receive only about thirty hours of instruction in religious education. The emphasis would have to be on in-service. Both the OECTA Brief to the Hall-Dennis Commission and the OECTA-OSSTA Brief to the government on the training of teachers asked for Departmental recognition of religious education as a course in separate schools and as a certificate-bearing course for teachers.[130] In 1967 Mary Babcock and Chris Asseff met with Premier Robarts and William Davis, the Minister of Education, to elicit their response to the OECTA/OSSTA brief and were told that they would receive their answer before the end of the year. When this did not happen, Babcock and Asseff decided to go ahead without Ministry endorsement.[131] In 1968 preparations for such a course began in earnest. Frank Griffin, the new deputy executive director of OECTA, promoted the concept that the course should parallel Department of Education courses for special certificates in subjects like art, music, and physical education, so that status and recognition would accrue.[132] Mary Babcock began the administrative tasks and the development of contacts. Her main partner in the effort was Chris Asseff, executive director of OSSTA and a recent candidate under the Progressive Conservative banner to represent Thunder Bay in the provincial legislature. These two leaders kept the Bishops, the trustees, OECTA, and William Davis on track. Realizing the size and importance of the objectives, OECTA set up a professional development department and hired Claudette Foisy as coordinator in 1969. That same year Mary Babcock invited Sr. Sheila McAuliffe, C.N.D., to prepare the first teachers' course in religious education; the following year she became Miss Foisy's administrative assistant. Claudette Foisy oversaw the administration, Sr. McAuliffe provided the content and pedagogy for the course.[133]

All the stakeholders cooperated. Bishop Carter approved of the course content, and when Sr. Sheila and Claudette Foisy met with him at his London residence, Miss Foisy and the Bishop discovered they had a common interest, a love of dogs. She established immediate rapport with his three large hounds and gained the trust of the Bishop in the matter of the OECTA-OSSTA religious education course. Sr. Mc Auliffe, despite some reservations from some of the committee members that things were moving too fast, had a staff ready to go for the first summer course at D'Arcy McGee separate school, MSSB, in 1969, followed at once by the first winter course at St. Kevin in Welland.[134] Archbishop Pocock advised the OSSTA executive that every school area should have a department of religious education; the county and district separate school boards began hiring religious education coordinators and consultants. OSSTA encouraged boards to give credit recognition for advancement on the salary grid and began making annual contributions of several thousand dollars to match OECTA's subsidy and to keep the tuition low for teachers. OSSTA and OCSIA agreed with OECTA that the course should be necessary both for applying for a teaching position and for obtaining a permanent contract with a separate school board. The latter point put pressure on Sr. McAuliffe and her staff to make the course as excellent and welcoming as possible, since, unfortunately in her mind, some teachers were present under duress. However, the teacher surplus beginning about 1970 contributed to the trustees' resolve to insist on the course, despite the pleas from some teachers that they were working on their B.A. extramurally.[135]

The important task remained: getting the Minister of Education to recognize the courses. Despite the delay here, OECTA began developing Parts II and III of the course so that religious education would correspond to other Departmental courses leading to a primary, intermediate, and specialist's certificate. In 1970 OECTA mounted four winter courses. Contributing to this expansion was the tour of the province by Sr. Sheila and Claudette Foisy. Meeting with school boards, teachers, priests, and Catholic Women's Leagues on the "Chicken Circuit," they claimed they clucked when they spoke. They journeyed in a small car, stopping for the night at old local hotels with doors that had hooks but no locks; prudently, they propped chairs against the doors.[136]

They were able to describe the courses with pride. To ensure excellent staffing OECTA had established fellowships with enough money to live for a school year; successful applicants went to Lumen Vitae in Brussels, the Strasbourg institute, Notre Dame in Indiana, the Catholic University in Washington, and, later, St. Michael's College in Toronto. A network of religious education specialists quickly developed. The course itself offered theology, Scripture studies, pedagogy, and liturgy in an adult learning model. Staff members strove to provide an atmosphere free from fear - one conducive to discussing one's faith life with feelings of trust and safety.[137]

Meanwhile the ad hoc committee on religious education, consisting of John Kuchinak, Bishop Windle of Pembroke, Miss Babcock, Ab Klein, president of OSSTA and Chris Asseff, were meeting with the Department of Education. They had to satisfy three questions. Was there a common curriculum for the 125-hour courses? Was there an evaluation component? Was there a similar introductory course for the Teachers' Colleges? At a meeting with William Davis, Claudette Foisy spoke up. "We've met the Ministry requirements. Why can't it be recognized?" Davis replied, "I don't see why not." Finally, on January 26, 1971 the Department approved of the three OSSTA-OECTA courses in religious education. It would now be possible for a teacher to obtain three credits equal to a university credit or to another Departmental course for advancement to the next standard of a teacher's certificate and/or toward the next salary level. The *Canadian Register* pointed out that this milestone marked the first time in Ontario's history that the Department had given any credit recognition to religious education and found this particularly striking because Departmental courses in the other subjects and divisions were being phased out in anticipation of the takeover by university faculties.[138]

Many separate school boards would request these religious education courses for their communities. Dr. Franklin Walker, historian of Ontario's separate schools, summed up the work as follows: "In the end the religious training of teachers which the teachers' association and the trustees provided would be the main support for the religious orientation of separate schools."[139]

The Separate School Curriculum. OECTA, in accordance with its constitutional aim "to promote the principles of Catholic education" and with its mission to assist its members in the delivery of curriculum, became somewhat more involved with the development of curricula appropriate to separate schools. The annual CCDC continued with such topics as "The School - a Christian Community," "The Catholic School in our Pluralistic Society," and "The Special Role of the Catholic Teacher." The Secondary Schools Committee was pursuing Departmental recognition of religion as a subject of study. Regarding textbooks, the Association promoted the development and use of materials to meet the needs of the Catholic pupil. Thus, at the 1962 and 1963 AGMs it was announced that Ginn publishers were bringing out a music textbook with a special supplement of Catholic hymns and a Catholic series of readers developed by Dorothy Dunn, a separate school inspector, with the assistance of some OECTA teachers.[140]

There existed a certain tension with this curriculum mandate which was similar to that present in the debate over a Catholic Teachers' College. On the one hand, some OECTA leaders wished to avoid the negative connotation surrounding the concept of separation and to stress the similarities between the public and separate schools. With this positive emphasis one could make a case for equality of treatment in funding, kindergarten to grade thirteen, between the two partners in the government's public school system: the separate and public schools. On the other hand, all the OECTA leaders realized that the broad aims of education of the Department of Education and its shift of many years' standing from government-published "courses of study" to "curriculum guidelines" allowed the design of specific teacher objectives and pupil outcomes particular to separate school needs. Indeed, the Hall-Dennis Report and the Department's curriculum policies and guidelines issued after it encouraged the design of curriculum unique to the wants and needs of the teacher's individual students and classroom.

One can see this tension in an Executive decision of the early 1960s: "It was the considered opinion of the OECTA Executive that we should continue to cooperate with the members of the other affiliates in developing a Christian curriculum rather than attempt to set up a curriculum and texts for separate schools only, at this time."[141] (emphasis added) Of course, limited and financial resources applied to other OECTA concerns would have affected this decision. But, with the publication of the Keiller Mackay Report on religious education in the public school in 1966, awareness of the multicultural aspects of the public school was heightened;[142] in the opinion of the Executive any attempt on the part of the Ministry toward "developing a Christian curriculum" would have been offensive to the other religions and beliefs in Ontario's post-World War II society. Consequently, faced with totally secular Ministry curriculum guidelines, in 1969 the Directors passed quite a different motion, compared to the Executive decision earlier in the decade. It was moved that OECTA go on record as encouraging publishers of texts to include Christian approaches to life for use in separate schools since it was not intended that "the Christian environment be restricted to the one religious programme period per day."[143]

The discussions over what constituted a separate school curriculum were intensified by the debate between traditionalists and progressivists over the Hall-Dennis Report and the new curriculum documents emanating from the Department. The dialectic was carried on within OECTA and the Catholic community.

As far back as 1937, when the second wave of progressive education was moving over the Department of Education, Dr. John Bennett, a separate school inspector, went on the attack. Taking exception to the "naturalistic", "socialist", and "secular" elements of progressive education, he labelled the new learning social expedience. He criticized activity-based learning as a methodology inferior to a curriculum consisting of a significant degree of prayer and meditation to arrive at truth. He quoted Dr. Hutchins, president of the University of Chicago, who denigrated progressivism for ignoring the past, for providing "little fake experiences," for reducing education to information, and for basing the curriculum on the "whim of children." Dr. Bennett ended his address at the annual education conference with an advocation to study the Christian character and Christian principles which, he held, do not change with time, environment, or circumstances.[144]

In 1943 and again in 1960 the prominent Catholic philosopher, Jacques Maritain, also attacked what he saw as the pragmatic, child-centred curriculum of Dewey in his book *Education at the Crossroads.* He decried the "cult of the means...without an end" and the curriculum development around the interests of the child without "standards for judging the purposes and values...emerging in the pupil's mind." He called for, instead, an "ultimate end of education [which] concerns the human person in his personal life and spiritual progress, not in his relationship to the social environment." Otherwise, there would be, Maritain feared, a "perpetual experimental reconstruction of the ends of the educator himself."[145]

At two of the AGMs of the 1950s, Rev. E.C. Garvey, C.S.B., Ph.D., professor and chairman of the philosophy department at Assumption College, Windsor and one of the founders of OECTA, and Sr. Lenore attempted to synthesize the positions of the traditional and progressive educator. Dr. Garvey praised the progressives for making teachers focus on central goals, on education rather than mere instruction. At the same time, Catholic educators, accepting progressive pedagogy, had to centre its purpose of education not on the production of Dewey's good citizen but on the formation of the Christian. He blamed extreme one-sided views of traditional and progressive education for the debate and urged an integral position:

> Most of us are neither materialists nor idealists; most of us adhere to value [sic] of the Christian tradition....Neither pragmatic naturalism nor Platonic essentialism are true philosophies;...the integral position recognizes both the natural and supernatural orders....Angelism in education is just as erroneous and incomplete as materialism in education....The pseudo-traditional extreme...is characterized by a one-sided intellectualism which neglects the importance of material and psychological factors. This tradition tended to treat human beings as thinking machines....The development of the imagination and learning through experience...tended to be neglected....Rousseau...stressed the importance of factors neglected by the Cartesians: individual differences, the sense and emotion.[146]

Sr. Mary Lenore in her presidential address agreed on the value of a synthesis. She praised many progressive methods and found "of particular worth" the study of child development and individual differences: "We must freely admit that in the past two centuries our system of education has tended to be overweighted on the side of intellectualism. The 'Progressives' have brought back to our attention many of the things which were in our own tradition." Sr. Lenore announced that the next CCDC would have as its theme child development.[147]

Perhaps these two addresses were too philosophical for busy practising teachers, because the division of opinion within OECTA continued. In 1961 OECTA distributed a "Philosophy of Education for School Principals" which expresses its belief in two progressive ideals. The statement asked the principal to ensure, among other things, that the pupils be accepted at their level and that the ultimate objectives be established "on the fact that the curriculum has been prepared for the child, not the child for the curriculum."[148] Yet in the same year the *News and Views* printed a memorial to arguably the most conservative Minister of Education the century had seen:

> To Dr. Dunlop we are greatly indebted for stemming the tide of 'progressive education,' He took an implacable stand against overemphasis on athletics and fun and the things he called 'frills',...focusing attention on the essentials of education and discouraging the worst features of the 'new-education'.[149]

Fr. Conway's 1962 presidential address told the delegates that, "We all learned our lesson in the days of Progressivism. I might point out that OECTA, AEFO, and OSSTA united in OTF to fight the evils of the Progressive Movement and were successful."[150] The Hall-Dennis years were just around the corner.

OECTA's brief to the Hall-Dennis Commission stayed out of the debate completely; it did not anticipate the third progressive education movement in Ontario; rather, it repeated recommendations for upgrading requirements for entering the teaching profession, establishing a teacher recruitment program, funding school libraries, and recognizing the importance of religious education at Teachers' Colleges, of the five-week OECTA-OSSTA course in catechetics, and of theology courses at university.[151]

But the debate arose again after the publication of the Hall-Dennis Report. Sr. Alice Marie, C.S.J., had represented OECTA on the Commission and signed the final report. Furthermore, most teachers had already begun implementing many of the methodological recommendations of the Commission. But, not surprisingly, a few Catholic leaders attacked the Report. The *OECTA Review* printed a critique by Fr. J. Geary, a Catholic high school principal with the MSSB. He was impressed by the "almost religious reverence" with which the

Commissioners approached the topic of educating children, by its concern for truth and by its regard for the rights of the child who is so powerless in asserting or defending his own rights." But he decried the utopian view implied of the perfectibility of human nature through education:

> The Report seems to celebrate man as the glory, to ignore him as the jest and to deny him as a riddle. Man, according to the whole drift of the Report, is good - period....What does Christian theology have to say in reply to all this? It tells of a human race, deeply wounded by some mysterious catastrophe...a race which must still strive mightily, though now with the aid of God's grace, toward a brighter day of union with a hitherto estranged God.[152]

James Daly, a Catholic history professor at McMaster University, expressed similar praises and criticisms in an article for the *OECTA Review* and in a booklet, *Education or Molasses?*. He commended the Report's emphasis on the non-utilitarian aspects of education, its reminder that children should not be force-fed with knowledge, its solicitude for minorities, its emphasis on integration of children with special learning difficulties, its advocacy of ungraded schools and individual timetables, and its call for better-trained teachers.[153] Certainly, there was enough here to keep Ontario's teachers positively engaged in implementing the Report. But Professor Daly went on with the bad news, maintaining that the Commissioners romanticized youth. Two quotations from *Education or Molasses?* encapsulated his complaints: "A teacher who permits his students to decide what to study, whether to study, and what is relevant, such a teacher is not a democrat but a fool" (quoting Professor Michael Hornyansky); and "The progressivists used to say that we teach the child, not the subject. But surely we teach the subject to the child."[154]

At a practical level these arguments, at least within the Catholic educational community, quickly became rarefied and continued to have this quality for quite some time and for two reasons. First, two new Department of Education policy and curriculum documents, "The Formative Years" and H.S.1, converted the principal philosophical ideas and recommendations into practices to be followed and aims to be pursued in the elementary and secondary schools of Ontario. Second, the separate school leaders saw in their embrace of the Report's concept of continuous progress, kindergarten to grade thirteen, a seemingly irrefutable argument for completion of the separate system to the end of high school with grants and taxing powers.

The Catholic High School Issue. Since the 1928 defeat of separate school aspirations in the *Tiny Township Case*, the question of government funding for Catholic high schools had retreated to the background. The depression, World War II, the lack of corporation tax revenues, immigration, and the baby boom preoccupied the separate school community almost fully. Of course, OECTA, especially influenced by the perennial Fr. Conway, a secondary school principal, represented the interests of its separate school teachers in grades nine and ten and encouraged the teachers of grades eleven, twelve, and thirteen in private Catholic high schools to join the Association. For example, the 1962 AGM discussed the problem that potential Catholic high school teachers could not attend the emergency two-summer course at OCE leading to high school certification unless s/he had proof of September employment in a public secondary school. The following year the Board of Directors sought to have the Department of Education use separate school inspectors, instead of public high school inspectors, to inspect grades nine and ten separate school teachers; indicative of the modest expectations of OECTA regarding high school hopes was Fr. Conway's feeling that it would be impossible to obtain such a change in Departmental policy. Similarly, with the advent of the Robarts Plan, OECTA presented a case for funding of Catholic high schools from the federal technical grants, but in the end was forced to accept the opinion of Dr. S. Rendall, Superintendent of Secondary Education for the Department of Education, that Catholic schools would be unable to offer technical education courses.[155]

On the other hand, OECTA had two successes with high school matters. Under the leadership of Fr. Conway, the Catholic secondary school principals worked with the Bishops to counter any proposal from the Ontario Committee on Taxation to discontinue exemption of private schools from taxes. In 1964 the Secondary Schools Committee was empowered to hire Woods, Gordon & Co. to prepare a brief on the topic. The exemption remained. Secondly, OECTA stirred up enough interest in high schools that Ottawa, Hamilton, Toronto, Niagara Falls, and Windsor began forming high school units within the Association's districts; later these would become districts. Each district president throughout the province was expected to report on the activities for the teachers of grades nine to thirteen; a provincial secondary schools conference was held in 1965.[156] Obviously, it was in the interests of OECTA for its organizational welfare to cater to the needs of Catholic high schools and teachers, but these activities were part of a total separate school community thrust for funding for Catholic high schools that began in and continued throughout the 1960s.

The initial impetus came from the Bishops' 1962 Brief. In addition to asking for corporation tax revenues, it pursued funding for high schools. The expansion of separate elementary schools had put pressure on the limited resources of the Catholic high schools. Most of them were offering only the traditional five-year academic program leading to university. This strategy of long standing involved educating future Catholic leaders who, it was hoped, would deal with the government to solve the funding problem. But there remained the ethical question of admitting only the "brilliant few" to Catholic high schools. There was also the fear that the new public composite high schools of the Robarts Plan would reduce the Catholic academic high schools to an educational backwater.[157]

The Bishops advanced two arguments that would become part of many future briefs, speeches, articles, and legal court presentations. Firstly, the Brief referred to the Canadian Conference on Education of 1958 that called for equality of educational opportunity (a phrase echoed by the Progressive Conservative Party of Ontario in the 1960s). Secondly, it argued that a basic education for the province's children was no longer to the end of grade eight; it embraced all of high school.[158]

As discussed earlier, Robarts responded to the Brief with the Foundation Plan. Now that separate schools were soon to be on a firm financial base with a growing number of well-educated and well-trained lay and religious teachers committed to the system as a lifelong career, one could say that the corporation tax adjustment grant of 1963 "paved the way for Catholic attention to their secondary institutions." Furthermore, diocesan funds, which had been used to supplement separate elementary school budgets, could now be concentrated on assisting with the survival of Catholic high schools.[159]

At first, OECTA and other separate school leaders, with their new-found funding, maintained what they considered a prudent low-key approach in their efforts to obtain government support for Catholic high schools. The *Canadian Register* expressed disappointment in the Foundation Plan's confinement to separate schools to grade ten, but counselled patience. The *Catholic Trustee* printed an article by J. M. McKenna, president of Association of Catholic High School Boards of Ontario (ACHSBO), which repeated the Bishops' definition of a basic education as kindergarten to grade thirteen.[160] OECTA struck a committee to study the Bishops' Brief and required that it be discussed in all of its districts. But Archbishop Philip Pocock of Toronto wanted no further action for the time being. He specifically asked OECTA to regard the high school question as a matter applying to finances and to separate school trustee affairs. He felt that too much pressure on the government might jeopardize the cause. The Executive decided in 1963 to delay any action. OECTA did, however, take steps to stop FWTAO and OPSMTF from condemning the Bishops' Brief through OTF.[161]

By 1965 a few important developments raised optimism and resulted in high-profile activities in OECTA and among other separate school leaders pushing for separate school extension. The Saskatchewan government, which had constitutionally guaranteed separate schools to grade ten since entering Canada in 1905, passed in 1965 *An Act to Amend the Secondary Education Act*. It extended high school rights to separate school boards throughout the province. Previously, separate school supporters operating a secondary school also had to pay taxes for the public high school, if their high school was within a public high school district; the statute eliminated this system of double taxation. Saskatchewan had joined Alberta, the Yukon and the Northwest Territories in funding a separate school system to the end of high school. Ontario's separate school supporters felt this made their case stronger.[162]

Secondly, in January 1965, three years before the publication of the Hall-Dennis Report, Davis announced the reorganization of the Department of Education. He stated:

> At one time...that elementary education was general education and secondary education was something for the few;...more and more parents, and children too, see secondary education as basic.... The effect of this integration will be to strengthen the concept that both elementary and secondary education are part of a continuous process."[163]

Davis reinforced the point made in the Bishops' Brief about a basic education and provided an argument for a continuous-process, separate school continuum, kindergarten to grade thirteen. The members of the Hall-Dennis Commission were to use this concept as the backbone of their Report, and Ed Brisbois, chairman of the MSSB, Progressive Conservative, and member of the Commission, was quick to understand and employ in many speaking engagements and press releases the two principles of a basic education and the continuum to the end of high school.[164] The separate school leaders would make these two concepts the linchpins of their campaign for extension of the separate school system.

On the surface, it would appear that OECTA had little to do with this campaign between 1965 and 1971. Walker described in considerable detail the work of the Bishops, OSSTA, ACHSBO, and the Catholic Education Council, but gave almost no mention of OECTA. In reality, its influence was just as important as that of the other groups in the task of preparing the brief requesting extension that went to the government.

The OECTA's brief to the Hall-Dennis Commission, discussed earlier, said very little, but did state a position on Catholic high schools:

> It is not the purpose of your Commission to deal with the specific problems of secondary school education. However,...we must state for the record that, due to the financial difficulties under which private Catholic secondary schools are operated, it is possible to provide formal religious education for only a minority of the total Catholic Secondary School population of the province.[165]

OECTA did not elaborate for a number of reasons. First, there were members of the Association on the newly created ACHSBO, which would at a 1966 conference and through other presentations push the basic education and continuum arguments.[166] Second, Archbishop Pocock advised OECTA to wait for the Ontario Catholic Education Council brief on extension. The Association felt it would have input through the Council, and, when it discovered it might not, approached Dr. Joseph Fyfe, a member of the Council, financial expert for the OSSTA, and Sudbury Separate School Board trustee. OECTA asked him why OSSTA, ECEAO, and ACEBO had representation on the Council and it did not. Dr. Fyfe gave the not entirely satisfactory answer that the Council had neither a charter nor a constitution, but was only a forum for exchange of ideas between the English and French Catholic education communities. OECTA at least satisfied itself that the Council's contemplated brief merited support; the Executive met with Fr. Durocher, who represented the Bishops and was preparing a draft for the Council. It then formally at an Executive meeting expressed both its disapproval over not being on the Council and its support for its paper.[167]

Once the Hall-Dennis Report was published in 1968, OECTA became much more involved. The Report not only developed the basic education and continuum concepts that had been circulating since 1962, it flatly stated that, "Some arrangements acceptable to all should be found - one which will bring the two tax-supported systems into administrative cooperation,...which will bring to an end a controversy that has burdened the administration of education in Ontario since Confederation."[168]

At the time in 1968, OECTA was speaking for seventy-five English Catholic high schools, six of which offered grades nine and ten only. 90 per cent of these schools had their grades nine and ten under the separate school boards. There were 31 285 students, 90 per cent of whom were in the five-year Arts and Science programme. Not only were they, for the most part, not able to offer the Business and Commerce or Science, Trades, and Technology programmes, they were also admitting, except for eleven schools, only five-year students and, because of limited facilities, turning away 38 per cent of them. Financing came from separate school board revenues for grades nine and ten and parish/diocesan funds for grades eleven, twelve, and thirteen in the private school. Most consequentially, the religious Orders taught for extremely low wages. 782 of the 1729 high school teachers belonged to an Order. About half of the 1729 teachers belonged to OECTA.[169] These teachers represented an important constituency for the Association, and their schools were in trouble; indeed, twelve small Catholic high schools had closed within the previous two years.[170]

OECTA began a number of initiatives. One of its members and a delegate to AGMs, Fr. Patrick Fogarty, C.Sc., principal of Notre Dame High School in Welland, and some other Catholic high school principals with B. E. Nelligan, superintendent of the MSSB, were preparing a brief for ACHSBO to go to the government.[171] The Secondary Schools Committee recommended that all Catholic high school teachers belong to OECTA in order to present a united front. The AGM passed motions that established equality of educational opportunity as a governing principle of the Association, instructed the Board of Directors to design ways of working with OSSTA, CPTA, and ACHSBO to achieve funding for kindergarten to grade thirteen, and added as an object of the Constitution "to promote the completion of the Catholic school system; and equal funding of that system."[172] Also, the Executive and districts were helping considerably with the Provincial Education Programme (PEP Plan). This movement aimed to communicate with and educate Catholic leaders, pastors, diocesan and parochial organizations, provincial organizations, provincial government party leaders, and MPPs on the case for completion of the separate school system. It had been organized by Bishop Ryan of Hamilton and Fr. Fogarty.[173]

Arguably, the most important enterprise of OECTA during this period was the work of the Ottawa high school Unit on a brief. Fr. Fogarty, Ed Brisbois, Fr. Durocher, and the Bishops had all agreed that the argument to the government should not be support for private Catholic schools. Rather, it should be a constitutional, historical, and legal brief presenting the case for completion of the separate school system; it would update the argument with references to the Hall-Dennis continuum and its concept of a basic education that included high school. At this point, OSSTA determined that it should present the brief. On the one hand, as its executive director Chris Asseff pointed out, a presentation to the government developed by Fr. Fogarty and Fr. Matthews for ACHSBO would appear to be a request for financial assistance for the members of that association, that is, for funding for private Catholic high schools. On the other hand, a brief from the trustees would reinforce that the issue was taxation powers and provincial grants for separate schools operating to the end of high school and would be a logical scenario for politicians presenting a brief to politicians. OECTA, along with the other Catholic groups, agreed with this reasoning and struck a committee to prepare a paper for OSSTA.[174]

The committee consisted of Saundra McKay, president of the Ottawa high school Unit, Sr. Joan Lawlor, C.N.D., Sr. Helen Nolan (Evangelista), G.S.I.C., Sr. St. Ann, C.S.J., Fr. J. Frank Kavanagh, O.M.I., all of whom were Ottawa Catholic high school teachers, and Dr. Dalton McGuinty, a professor of English at the University of Ottawa. Dr. McGuinty served as the researcher and writer for the committee.[175] At the 1968 AGM Miss McKay, the delegates from the high school units, and others were concerned that the high school issue had not been discussed on the first day, and Saundra prepared a short speech that night. The next day she addressed the AGM stating that "the issues the teachers have been discussing, while although not insignificant in themselves, dwindle to the point of trivia, when compared with the issue of equality of educational opportunity for 402 000 students in our Catholic public schools."[176] She received a standing ovation and the topic was discussed fully.

Once the committee's brief was finished and approved by the Executive and Directors, OECTA designated Fr. Kavanagh to represent it on the OSSTA committee preparing the final brief. He brought in

OECTA's arguments that emphasized the pedagogical rationale for completing the separate school system. But Fr. Durocher's draft had contained little about this. The other members of the committee, B. E. Nelligan, Ed Brisbois, Joseph Redican, representing the Ontario Catholic Students' Federation, Ab Klein, president of OSSTA, and Dr. N. Mancini, trustee, weighed the two approaches and agreed with OECTA's position, which Ed Brisbois and B. E. Nelligan had also been emphasizing in speeches, that the best strategy was to work from the Hall-Dennis and Department of Education's philosophy based on a kindergarten-to-grade-thirteen continuum. Thus, OECTA's paper became the "backbone" of the OSSTA brief.[177] At the completion of the trustees' brief, Chris Asseff wrote the Executive that "the contribution made by your representative, Rev. J. F. Kavanagh, was simply outstanding."[178]

The brief, appropriately titled Equal Opportunity for Continuous Education in Separate Schools of Ontario, was presented on May 26, 1969 to the Premier and Minister of Education and later that day to the caucus of the NDP and of the Liberal Party. It was the product of six months of meetings; it had not been easy to convince some trustees, particularly Dr. Fyfe, that separate school boards could afford to offer high school programmes even with grants and taxes because of their small assessment base. Furthermore, Premier Robarts would later say that some of his Catholic friends preferred public high schools and others wished their Catholic high schools to remain private, free from close management by trustees and the Department of Education. But OECTA and OSSTA were united on the question.[179]

The brief's statement near its opening summed up the position:

> The purpose of this brief is to obtain for separate public schools of Ontario that equality which is basic to the eduational policy of the province, which is demanded by official promotion of continuous child-centred education, and which is implied in the modern reorganization of the school system. This request seeks the removal of the pedagogical and financial shackles which restrain the separate schools from offering a complete educational service from Kindergarten to grade 12 (13) at the present time.[180]

The separate school community optimistically awaited the government's reply to the Equality brief. It had received one setback the year before when Premier Robarts, in response to the Royal Commission on Bilingualism and Biculturalism criticisms of Franco-Ontarian education, had enacted legislation that guaranteed French-language elementary schools under public or separate school boards and French-language high schools under high school boards, numbers warranting. This divided the separate school block, since the Franco-Ontarian trustees no longer required completion of separate schools as the single possible source of a French-language high school education.[181] On the other hand, since the Premier had provided high schools for the French, he might be equally inclined to do the same for OSSTA.

Countering this setback were a number of affirmations. In 1969 the Bishops issued a statement endorsing the Equality brief. That same year the Liberal caucus supported OSSTA, provided that sharing of facilities took place between the public and separate school boards. Elie Martel, M.P.P. for Sudbury East and ex-delegate at AGMs, and John Rodriguez piloted a similar resolution through the NDP Convention. Also in 1969 the *Toronto Star* came out in favour of completion of separate schools. In 1970 the Ecumenical Institute of Canada, having Anglican, United Church, Baptist, Lutheran, Presbyterian, and Roman Catholic representation, issued a brief supporting extension on constitutional grounds. Here, Fr. Fogarty, as a member of the committee, was influential.[182]

During this time OECTA remained actively involved in the campaign. It developed a pamphlet and distributed 30 000 of them throughout the province. When an estimated 20 000 to 30 000 students attended a rally organized by the Ontario Catholic Students' Federation at Maple Leaf Gardens, Toronto, on October 25, 1970, their separate school and Catholic high school teachers accompanied them.[183] After waiting six months for an answer to the Equality brief, Mary Babcock and Chris Asseff wrote Premier Robarts asking for a response. At a 1969 Executive meeting John Rodriguez wanted the AGM to adjourn and march silently on Queen's Park; the Executive responded, "the time is not right" and the AGM amended the motion to approach ECEAO with the idea. Instead, the students held their rally.[184]

OECTA also assigned staff for a sustained effort in 1971. Kevin Kennedy was to deal with northern Ontario, John Flynn, a superintendent borrowed from the MSSB, with central Ontario, Fr. Kavanagh and Saundra McKay with eastern Ontario, and John Sweeney, director of the Waterloo County RCSS Board, with western Ontario. Working through the directors of education, they held educational meetings with the principals, expecting them to carry the information to their staffs and parents.[185]

With the retirement of Premier Robarts and the choice, under the shadow of an advancing provincial election, of William Davis as P.C. leader, the latter's non-response grew deafening. Robarts, in a letter to Fr. R. Drake Will, had expressed very negative opinions on the issue before his retirement. Extension would add a burden to the taxpayers; other denominations would ask for funding for private schools; extension would fragment the very fine public high school system; the existing structure did not impede continuous progress or the continuum because public school students were shifting to another school after grade eight without problems and because public and separate school boards would cooperate to ensure a smooth transition from a separate elementary school after grade eight or ten to a public high school. He left the door open a crack by saying the matter was still under study, but Fr. Kavanagh reported to the Directors that the Conservatives were confusing masterfully separate schools with private schools.[186]

Finally, on August 31, 1971 Premier Davis gave the government's answer. He expressed his great difficulty in turning down OSSTA's request and gave a number of reasons for the negative response. Historically and constitutionally, separate schools had the right to exist, but since the outset secondary schools were non-denominational. A denominational high school system would "fragment the present system beyond recognition and repair, and do so to the disadvantage of all." Furthermore, moving from the separate to the public school system would not break the continuum, provided the receiving board treated students on an individual basis; in fact, changing school environments could be advantageous for the student. Although the principle of a single secondary school system was the key issue, the costs of funding an extended separate school system would be great, a point that caused "intense and vexatious public controversy" in the past. In addition, if the government were to fund Catholic high schools, it "would be obliged to provide...a further system for Protestant students, another for Jewish students, and possibly still others representing the various denominations of Protestants."[187]

Along with his refusal to extend the Spadina Expressway Premier Davis took his rejection of the Equality brief into an election and won a majority of seats for his Party. There was nothing for OECTA to do for the present but to accept Davis's decision and continue to press for completion of the separate school system. OECTA's president in the September *Reporter* printed an open letter to the Premier replying to his arguments for refusal.

Social Justice and OECTA. The Catholic high school campaign was not the only new enterprise for the Association in the 1960s. Social justice as an idea and as the basis for fresh projects permeated the AGMs.

Social justice has always been an integral part of Christianity, at least in the ideal. The two great Commandments, love of God and love of neighbour as oneself, make the point. OECTA members who had attended Catholic high schools had studied applications of the concept of social justice in the encyclicals of Popes Leo XIII and Pius XI. Leo XIII's "Rerum Novarum" in 1891 insisted on the right to a just wage and to form worker associations. Pius XI reiterated and developed the topic further. His encyclical stated that the primary motivation in the economy had to be the common good rather than profit, and the primary social process had to be cooperation rather than competition. To strive for these goals, Pius XI highlighted the principle of subsidiarity and called for intermediate groups to facilitate harmonious effort between management and labour, employers and employees.[188] OECTA had been citing these sources when justifying its existence and when salary negotiating, but Vatican publications of the 1960s called for Catholics to apply the ideas of Leo XIII and Pius XI not only to themselves but to the wider world. Apostolic action was implied, even stated, in the two encyclicals, but those of Popes John XXIII, Paul VI, and, later, John Paul II seemed to state them more vigorously and to relate them to modern times.

Pope John XXIII in his 1961 encyclical "Mater et Magistra" commemorated "Rerum Novarum" 's seventieth anniversary. In it he held up the Church's social doctrine as a necessary part of its teaching on how people should live. The doctrine included the description of social justice as a concept requiring a degree of equality in the distribution of the world's goods, the upholding of the dignity of the worker and the fostering of labour unions. The encyclical called particular attention to the question of rich and poor nations and the conditions of agricultural workers as contradictions of social justice. He reminded his reader that "I am a farmer" and lamented waste: "To destroy or to squander goods that other people need in order to live is to offend against justice and humanity."[189] His encyclical "Pacem in Terris", written two years later, dwelled again on social justice applied to war and peace and defined unions as the "indispensable" instruments for safeguarding the dignity and freedom of the human person and preserving a sense of responsibility.[190]

The documents of Vatican II, issued between 1963 and 1965, were filled with references to social action, social change, social conditions, social ethics, social education, social order, social problems, social reform, social welfare, social justice, and solidarity. Of particular relevance for OECTA was the "Decree on the Apostolate of the Laity" which was firm and clear:

> The laity must take on the renewal of the temporal order as their own special obligation,...As citizens they must cooperate with other citizens,...Everywhere and in all things they must seek the justice characteristic of God's kingdom,... Outstanding among the works of this type of apostolate is that of Christian social action. This sacred Synod desires to see it extended now to the whole temporal sphere.[191]

The Catholic newspaper, the *Canadian Register*, printed these encyclicals and documents and wrote numerous articles on social justice that chronicled the plight of farm workers in Central South American and other underdeveloped countries, where the poor lived in hovels and received wages barely keeping them from starving. The Catholic seminaries were urged to unite doctrine and social justice, because, in the *Canadian Register's* words, nineteenth-century Roman Catholics had observed the sacraments, but had not considered service for social and economic justice. At a conference of Canadian Catholic Bishops in Halifax in 1961, the call went out: "Schools have [the] duty to communicate social doctrine."[192]

OECTA, in accordance with its Constitutional object "to promote the principles of Catholic education"[193] and as potentially one of the most influential educational arms of the Church in Ontario, became part of the social justice movement and remains so to this day. As Michael Ryan wrote in 1986, discussing Christian social teaching in Canadian society, "the goal of mankind is not a private heaven but a community of love and justice....There is no such thing as being uninvolved or nonpolitical. All our actions have a social meaning."[194]

At the 1962 AGM in his president's address, Fr. Conway pointed the way: "We must face up to our duty to help these [third world] countries."[195] The Association began budgeting monies to work with OTF, CTF, and the World Conference of Teaching Professionals in assisting teachers and pupils in underdeveloped countries. Starting in 1962, OECTA devoted money and staff to Project Overseas and later Project Africa. The minutes annually to 1971 listed a number of activities, mainly in the area of providing two teachers to conduct in-service summer courses in third world countries. In 1964 Fr. Conway visited Ghana, Nigeria, Northern and Southern Rhodesia, Kenya, Nyasaland,

Tanganyika, Uganda, and the Congo to assist these countries in strengthening their teacher organizations and in encouraging the teachers in the mission schools to join the associations of teachers in the government schools. Members of OECTA, sponsored by the provincial budget or by specific districts, conducted teacher in-service in Thailand, Jamaica, the Bahamas, Kenya, and a number of other African countries.[196] When OECTA was twinned with the Trinidad-Tobago Catholic Teachers' Association, it began in 1967 sending teachers to conduct in-service in, for example, the new mathematics and physical education and sending money to help these island teachers take summer courses in Ontario.[197]

In 1966 the Department of Education started to coordinate groups wishing to assist Caribbean schools with furniture and textbooks. OECTA became involved in this program also. After a few years, however, it stopped since it discovered that Ontario's "white" textbooks were not positive aids in the Caribbean. Instead, it developed a "black" catechism for use in the Trinidad-Tobago schools.[198]

In 1971 OSSTA sponsored a seminar on religious education in Nassau. Sr. Sheila McAuliffe and members of OECTA taught the course.[199]

The minutes recorded numerous other financial gifts to underdeveloped countries. For example, $500 for a duplicator was sent to a Rhodesian school, $500 for instructional supplies to the Oblate Vocational School in Comas, Peru, $800 to a Mr. Itek of Nigeria to assist him with university costs in England, a sum of money to a Nigerian Teachers' College, $1337 to a Nigerian teacher-priest for study at the University of Toronto, textbooks, maps, and science materials to a convent school in India, and encyclopedias to Trinidad.[200]

With all of these gifts of human and financial resources the attitude of OECTA, expressed by the Executive, was, "We have an obligation to our Catholic teachers in developing countries. We are favoured and we should be willing to assist our Catholic friends who are in need of financial support."[201] In 1971 the Executive combined the budget for domestic and foreign aid into an educational aid fund as a permanent commitment to third-world countries; 2 per cent of the gross revenues were to be allocated annually.[202]

With the arrival of John Rodriguez on the Executive in the late 1960s, social justice topics assumed a high profile. He began revealing his special interest with a motion at the 1967 AGM that OECTA support the Scarborough Council in its intention to place in a particular neighbourhood, despite residential hostility, a home for children with severe learning disabilities. The motion was defeated on the grounds that it had nothing to do with education.[203] John reorganized his approach and the following year was influential in having the CCDC devoted to "The Catholic Teacher and Social Involvement."[204] The opening quotation for this chapter put his position clearly.

At the 1969 AGM Rodriguez hit his stride with the grape-boycott issue; Cesar Chavez (1927-1993) came to public attention with a strike in Delano, California, where Reagan was governor, against the owners of table-grape farms. On behalf of Spanish-American migrant workers he sought to gain recognition of the United Farm Workers Union (UFW). Facing the opposition of the growers, he launched a grape boycott and solicited support throughout North America. In 1968 Toronto City Council passed a motion in support of the union and the boycott. The *Canadian Register* headlined this news and wrote that "for those with a social conscience, no other course was open. Who could ignore a boycott aimed at helping workers who, as Mayor Denison pointed out, are faced with a life of low wages, unspeakable working and living conditions, and little hope for the future?"[205] Rodriguez obtained material from Chavez, distributed it at the CCDC, and began planning to get an appropriate motion passed at the 1969 AGM.

The motion was that OECTA "support the UFW of Southern California in their struggle for justice in the same manner in which OECTA supports the struggle for justice of all people of the world." His speech in support of the motion was impassioned. An excerpt reveals its spirit:

> I feel the Christianity of the Catholic teacher is used much like a raincoat - it protects him from the elements. It is taken off indoors and put on when he goes outdoors. Similarly, we set up a group of young people to make all the desirable ethical discoveries, but somehow they have no relevance to the teachers' lives outside the classroom....The Christian teacher...must believe that his role as a teacher is the most important social function he can ever perform. The children are looking for examples of men and women in their teachers - not just in the school but also in the community.[206]

He culminated his speech by throwing on the floor and squashing a handful of grapes.

The motion ran into some opposition; delegates argued that supporting a boycott had nothing to do with Ontario education and the business of OECTA; in addition, the motion placed the teachers on one side of a two-sided issue. Behind this debate lay deeper motivating factors. Although John Rodriguez's speaking style and content was dramatic and moving, at the same time it did, according to some delegates, convey the message that they had been remiss in the past regarding their duties to social justice. Some delegates would recall the donations of people, supplies, and money described above; others perhaps simply resented receiving a sermon. The editor of the *OECTA Review*, Paul Wharton, at the end of an article by Rodriguez on the need for OTF to have a political action committee in order to identify issues affecting school and community, felt obliged to write that, "The opinions of the reader on this topic are welcome, as many conservative teachers have indicated disagreement with this viewpoint."[207] Also, a natural resentment likely existed in some delegates because of John Rodriguez's actions and words declaring that he and some of the other male delegates like Elie Martel, Bob Fera and John Kuchinak were the "young Turks" who would change the Association's attitude to the strike issue, open up the methods of elections and of setting agendas, and lead the Association into new apostolic activities. Finally, but not least in importance, some delegates negatively identified Rodriguez's concerns with the NDP.[208]

But John Rodriguez with his motion was on the side of the angels. When Chavez died in 1993, the *National Catholic Reporter* wrote a worshipful obituary, describing how he had worked to prevent farm labourers and their families from living and working as robots, devoid of dignity and decent wages, how he had been committed to gospel-based values, how he had taken directly from the Catholic Church's social teaching documents for the constitution and by-laws of the farm workers union, and how his labour had been deeply rooted in prayer life.[209]

OECTA would continue to be involved with social issues. Fr. Conway in a recent interview said that John Rodriguez was perceived as too extreme to be effective, but that he served a good purpose in rallying the Association to implement the aims of Vatican II.[210]

Structure. Given OECTA's expansion in membership and aims, it was necessary to enlarge and reorganize the central office and the districts. In 1962 Margaret Lynch's report recommended that everything remain the same except for the renaming of locals as units.[211] But after the Foundation Plan of that year and the increasing teacher salaries thereafter, the consequent additional revenues for the Association from better-paid and more numerous members made it possible to provide more services. The rest of the decade saw a number of changes in OECTA.

The consultants' firm of Edward N. Hay Associates was hired to look at the Association's structure and delivered its report in 1970. It identified two result areas, professional development and teacher welfare, the latter including the " vast new area" of working conditions in salary negotiating.[212] As a result of this report the central office was to be reorganized into four departments: teacher welfare, communications, professional development, and administration. Each department was to have a coordinator and, except for administration, would be staffed by an administrative assistant.

The administration department had responsibility for budget control, fees, investments, legislation, computer operation, office management, personnel, records, facilities, and maintenance. The communications department looked after public relations, publications, field service, recruitment, and international activities. The teacher welfare department administered economic welfare, working conditions, certification, superannuation, contracts and tenure, supervisory personnel, transfer review boards, and counselling and relations. The professional department managed teacher education, educational media, educational studies, mental health programmes, the CCDC, Christian development, and in-service programmes. Administering these departments were an executive director (previously executive secretary) and deputy executive director.

A number of new faces appeared on the scene during the expansion and reorganization period after 1965. Marion Tyrrell, after seventeen years as executive secretary, retired in 1966, moving on to help organize STO, becoming its first secretary-treasurer from 1968 to 1973, and to work with the Liberal leader, John Wintermeyer, on the Catholic high school campaign. Mary Babcock replaced her. To fill her previous position Frank Griffin was hired in 1966. He would move on to become Miss Babcock's replacement again when she retired in 1973.

The professional development department followed the Hay model; Claudette Foisy (now Foisy-Moon) was employed as coordinator and Sr. Sheila McAuliffe, C.N.D., as executive assistant. (There was to be a distinction made between executive assistants who possessed a university degree and administrative assistants, but these two titles were soon merged into one.)

Claudette Foisy was born in Chatham. Her father, Firmus Foisy, a banker, and mother, Velina King, a merchandiser, moved the family to Ottawa where Claudette attended St. George's and Immaculata High to the end of grade thirteen. She then entered the Grey Sisters of the Immaculate Conception and spent two years in their Pembroke novitiate. While becoming qualified as a teacher in the Ottawa completing course, Miss Foisy taught English and history at Immaculata High. The Order then assigned her to Holy Family school in Timmins, where she taught for six years. During this time she acquired her B.A. at Ottawa University in summer and correspondence courses. She was promoted to principal at Cathedral separate school in Pembroke and took the principal's course. After two years in that position, she became part of the questioning, self-evaluating ferment of post-Vatican II and left the religious life. The MSSB hired her as vice-principal of St. Jude. After one year she became principal of St. Matthew. A year later she was the successful applicant for the position of professional development coordinator. She had been involved with OECTA since her first year of teaching. She even remembered Dr. McDonald when she was a high school student. Feeling a sense of injustice over the low salaries of separate school teachers, she became district president in Pembroke and then chair of the provincial Professional Development Committee. In this latter position she helped set up the first in-service programs in religious education. After serving as an OECTA coordinator from 1969 to 1974, Claudette Foisy-Moon moved to the position of executive assistant with OTF. Since retirement in 1990 she has been a volunteer at the Art Gallery of Ontario. In 1992 OTF honoured her with a fellowship.[213]

Her executive assistant, Sr. Sheila McAuliffe, was born in Lonsdale, Tyendinaga Township, near Belleville. Her father, Francis McAuliffe, a farmer, and mother, Margaret Ellen Kennedy, had seven younger children: Mary, Anne, Theresa, Norah, James, Helen, and Maureen. Like their mother, all became teachers, except Theresa, who became a nurse. Sheila attended S.S.#29, Tyendinaga's one-room public school built on land donated by her mother's family. From there she went to Desoronto Continuation School for grades nine, ten, and eleven and to Notre Dame High School, Kingston for grades twelve and thirteen. Immediately thereafter, Sheila entered the Congregation of Notre Dame and spent two years at its novitiate in Montreal, becoming fluent in French as a bonus. After attending Toronto Normal School, Mother St. Francis (her pre-Vatican II religious name) taught for sixteen years at

St. Patrick's elementary school, Ottawa, St. Francis Xavier, Brockville, and Cathedral intermediate school, Kingston. Having taught all the grades from one to twelve and the high school subjects of French, geography, history, and religion, Sister became principal of St. Mary, Brockville, then Holy Cross school, Toronto. During these years she had earned a B.A. from the University of Ottawa, mostly through correspondence courses, and high school certification in French, geography, and history. Offered the opportunity to attend the Divine Word Institute in London with sponsorship by the Archdiocese of Kingston, she went instead to Washington University where after seven summers and a year she earned an M.A. in religious education. She spent some time as a religious education diocesan director for the Kingston archdiocese and religious education consultant for the separate school boards. It was in this capacity that she was noticed by Mary Babcock to be a well-qualified, experienced person to set up the first OECTA-OSSTA religious education course. She served as executive assistant in the professional development department throughout the 1970s and 1980s, responsible first for religious education courses and then for all other in-service courses. Since retiring in 1990, Sr. Sheila has been a counsellor and a superior for her Order. Currently, she is designing a preventive program for female high school students who are potential drop-outs. OTF and OECTA have recognized her service by awarding her an OTF fellowship and an OECTA life membership. The OECTA professional development award is named after Sister and she was selected for the Greer Award in 1993.[214]

The teacher welfare department also followed the Hay model, hiring Douglas Knott as coordinator and Edwin Alexander as administrative assistant. Douglas Knott would become deputy general secretary a few years later.

Ed Alexander, son of George Alexander, a machinist and union man, and Mary Broughton, was born in New Liskeard. He began his education at Sacred Heart "mixed" school (that is, where English and French pupils shared the same building), then moved to St. Ann for grade eight in Iroquois Falls. After completing the five-year Arts and Science course at Iroquois Falls High School, he decided on teaching. Since he was the oldest of seven children, Rosemary, Kathleen, Frederick, Helen, Anne, and Stephen, he did not have access to family money. Therefore, he worked for one year at Abitibi Pulp and Paper, then went to North Bay Teachers' College in 1961. He began teaching at St. Francis, New Liskeard. His successful year plus the fact that he was male resulted in his being promoted to principal in his second year. He became an AGM delegate at once, as well as a local negotiator and the secretary-treasurer of the Unit. In 1967 he organized a mass resignation from seven schools in New Liskeard in order to achieve a favourable salary contract. He then moved to St. Ann's mixed school, Iroquois Falls to be "head teacher" for the English section, while the building principal was the principal of the French section. There he felt obliged to protest to the Ministry that the principal was interfering with the English section and moved to the Kirkland Lake District RCSS Board in 1969 as a grade eight teacher. When the promised position of vice-principal or principal did not materialize there, Ed consulted with Frank Griffin about suing the board. Mr. Griffin advised him instead to apply for the administrative assistant's position in teacher welfare. He was successful over a number of applicants. From 1970 to the present Ed Alexander worked in teacher welfare and counselling and as the Metropolitan Toronto staff assistant. During his career he married Thérèse Courchesne, a teacher, and had four daughters, Stéphanie, Mélanie, Natalie, and Emilie. As well, he acquired a B.A. from Laurentian University and an MBA from York University.[215]

The communications department received an administrative assistant, but not a coordinator. Patrick O'Neill was born in County Monaghan and raised in County Armagh. His father, Patrick O'Neill, the proprietor of a public house, and his mother, Roselleen McKenna, had three younger children, Eamonn, Brendan, and Dymphna. Patrick received his elementary education at St. Malachy and secondary at St. Patrick's College, Armagh. He then worked for a year and a half as an unqualified teacher at Holy Rosary high school in Birmingham. Next he got an allowance to attend St. Mary's College of Education, Strawberry Hill, England. After this three-year course, in which he specialized in art and English, Patrick taught for one year at St. Agatha's elementary school in London. Having been turned down for a position at a United Nations school in Nigeria, Patrick, along with so many other teachers from England, Ireland, and Scotland, heard about the recruiting of the MSSB, wrote, and was hired. In 1965 he taught for three days at St. Barbara, then was transferred to St. Richard, where he taught in the open area grades three to eight and set up the library. He arrived in Ontario already interested in Federation matters; he had been involved in student politics and had been helping to plan a one-day strike when he left St. Agatha. He was the OECTA school staff representative in his first year in Ontario, then an AGM delegate in 1966,

1967, and 1968. He ran unsuccessfully for the district executive, but then successfully the following year for treasurer. At the AGMs he was noticed as a well-prepared delegate proposing amendments and resolutions on salary negotiating topics. In 1968 he was nominated for provincial treasurer and won over two competitors; he was re-elected in 1969. Meanwhile, Frank Griffin began to use him in provincial salary negotiating takeovers. Among other duties O'Neill would be the driver while Frank would prepare his strategy. He also began putting on workshops on open-area teaching with Doug Knott. Karl Bohren suggested he apply as administrative assistant to Claudette Foisy. He got the position and, when professional development and communications became two separate divisions, he took on the latter. Seven years later he moved to counselling and relations where he has remained as coordinator. During his time at OECTA he has been blessed with a wife, Vikki Debonis, and three children, Nicole, Katrina, and Patrick. He also obtained a B.A. from York University and an M.Ed. from OISE.[216]

The administration department was set up differently. It consisted of an accountant, Anne Glorioso, and an office manager, Alma Ryan. For many years with a skeleton staff they managed their departments and carried out their duties under Mary Babcock. Anne had aspired to be a teacher, but her education was cut short because of having to help at home; she was happy to be working with teachers at OECTA.

There was also an administrative assistant to Mary Babcock, Mary Ellen Daly (now Carey), who looked after organizing the CCDC and AGM, liaising with the Teachers' Colleges and grade thirteen students, and serving on teams interviewing applicants from outside of Ontario who applied for a letter of standing to teach in Ontario.

Mary Ellen Daly was born in Hamilton, daughter of "Tex" Daly, a salesman, and Marie Dosman, originally a Saskatchewan teacher. She grew up with five sisters and three brothers: Marilyn, Maureen, Michael, Lynne, Christine, Daniel, Kerry, and Colleen. Educated at Our Lady of Mount Carmel in Hastings and at St. Mary's elementary school and St. Mary's High School, Kitchener, Mary Ellen went to Stratford Teachers' College and began teaching in 1960 at St. Leo, Kitchener. One year later she moved to St. Alexander, North Bay. In 1965 she spent a year teaching at St. Frances Cabrini parochial school, Los Angeles, with seventy grade-five pupils in the curfew area, where the tanks rolled by on the anniversary of the Watts riots. The next year Miss Daly joined the St. Jerome staff with the MSSB. Most of her teaching had been in the primary division. In the summer of 1967 she taught mathematics methodology in the Department of Education's primary methods course. She had left teaching in June and, despite an exploratory interview with Mary Babcock, decided to try business. This was not for her and so, spotting an advertisement, she applied and was interviewed in November 1968 for the position of administrative assistant. The committee recommended her. Mary Ellen would serve OECTA until 1991 and is currently administering Options for Life, a service agency for pregnant single women.[217]

Prior to Mary Ellen Daly's arrival, Rose Cassin had been assisting Mary Babcock. Although she only worked at the central office from 1965 to 1968, when she died suddenly, Miss Cassin had made such a great impression on her fellow teachers and had contributed so much to OECTA over many years that the Rose Cassin Memorial Scholarship was inaugurated in 1969. Rose was born in 1904 on a farm near Alliston. Daughter of Patricia and Thomas Cassin, a farmer known locally as the "King of the Potatoes," she was raised after her mother's death by her aunt, Rose Haydon. Her brother, Joseph, became a farmer and her sister, Kathleen, became Sr. Philomena, I.B.V.M. Rose attended the town public and high school. She went to the Toronto Normal School graduating with a second-class certificate, which she converted to a first-class certificate in 1953. She began teaching for the Fort Frances Separate School Board. She came to the Toronto Separate School Board in 1927 and taught at St. Anthony, St. Cecilia, and Our Lady of Sorrows until joining the provincial office staff. During her career she taught mostly grades seven and eight and, using her music certificate, conducted school choirs. Rose Cassin had been one of the original members of the Toronto Separate School Teachers' Association, serving as vice-president. For OECTA she was provincial treasurer and second vice-president. She is remembered as a gentle, considerate person who was always on the go for her pupils and fellow teachers.[218]

Other structural changes were made in the 1960s. The AGM became a three-day session. The Secretariat and the Executive, as advisors to the Board of Directors, counselled themselves on the absolute necessity of being united on issues when at Directors' meetings. A speaker or, in case of her/his absence, a deputy-speaker was appointed to conduct the AGMs starting in 1968. Some meetings had been stormy; agenda items had been rushed or even unfinished. Some presidents, who had been running the meetings, had problems; they tended either to dominate the meetings with remarks or to feel they should say nothing. John Flynn was appointed the first speaker and managed to bring order to the difficult meeting of 1968.

In 1971 the standing committees with their sub-committees or specific tasks in brackets were the following: awards (scholarship, life membership), economic policy (salary negotiating, salary policy, salary research), finance (budget, investment), legislation (policy, organization), nominating, professional development (CCDC), resolutions, supervisory personnel, secondary schools, superannuation, teacher education and standards of certification, relations and counselling, educational aid, and Christian philosophy. Finally, the district-unit structure was replaced by thirty-five units, including five high school units. The teachers in a unit could subdivide into "branch affiliates". The new boundaries reflected as closely as possible the 1969 county and district separate school board boundaries. However, it was impossible then to do this for the high schools. Instead, the five high school units, Hamilton, Niagara, Ottawa, Toronto, and Windsor High would embrace the geographical areas closest to each of them, including the Catholic high schools in northern Ontario. The Niagara High district in 1967 had sent in a resolution to have a separate secondary school teachers' identity within OECTA (an idea that would surface again after the extension of the separate school system), but it was defeated.[219]

There were changes also in the procedures regarding nominations for executive positions. With the influential presence for many years of leaders like Fr. Conway and Fr. Siegfried and with the relatively much smaller numbers of teachers available to take executive positions when they received little or no releae time from their duties back in the school, the Executive was eventually perceived as maternalistic or paternalistic. As membership expanded and a new generation of leaders arrived looking for involvement and democratic processes, nominating procedures came under scrutiny. Originally, the Executive would appoint a Nominating Committee that would bring a slate to the AGM; the delegates would quickly elect the president, vice-presidents, and other members of the Executive. The minutes for a 1963 Board of Directors' meeting showed that matters had become more formalized: the Directors were to name the three districts that would select the representatives for the Nominating Committee. However, Fr. Siegfried stated at the 1962 AGM that additional nominations could be submitted to the chair of the Nominating Committee on forms signed by three delegates from three districts before 10 a.m. of the day when elections would take place.[220] In 1965, for the first time, there was a contest for second vice-president.[221] In 1966 the Nominating Committee deemed it necessary to explain why it had introduced some choice on its slate. "In view of the keen interest shown in submitting nominations, the committee felt that it was advisable and more democratic to submit four names," but only for third vice-president. "For the other offices it was felt that experience on the executive is important, but this does not, of course, eliminate nominations from the floor."[222]

Matters changed quickly from 1966 on. Although Fr. Conway explained to the delegates that it had not been the custom to have the candidates for the Executive make election speeches and that it had been the custom for the first vice-president to move up automatically to president, customs were not always followed. Résumés of candidates were sent to the delegates; three minutes were allowed for candidates or their nominators to speak at the AGM; nominations from the floor did take place, and John Rodriguez defeated a candidate for second vice-president on the Nominating Committee's slate. Finally, the constitution was amended to allow for more flexibility while paying respect to experience. A candidate for president was to have held office on the executive for at least one year; a candidate for first vice-president was to have the same experience or at least two years on a district executive or as chair of a provincial committee.[223] Henceforth, the AGMs would have some election fever.

During this decade of delegate involvement the relationship among the AGM, Executive, and Board of Directors, though not defined in any detail, assumed a certain pattern. The AGM continued to reject, modify, or pass resolutions from the Executive, Board of Directors, and units. (These had increased greatly, especially from the units.) The Executive would then be the administrators and implementers for these resolutions, as well as the leaders and spokespersons for the separate school teachers. The Board of Directors would set the budget, using the fee established at the AGM, and act as advisory board for the Executive. The minutes revealed some concern about the size of the Board of Directors, consisting of the thirty-five unit presidents, but participation and democracy ruled the day. In summary, compared to the 1950s the 1960s saw a power shift from the Executive to the Board of Directors, but the relationships remained somewhat fluid.[224]

The philosophy and make-up of the provincial budget also changed. Two interesting statistics of the period are worth noting: revenues for 1961 were $115 049, and for 1971 were $927 039.[225] Perennially, there would be some debate over whether to raise this money from a flat fee or from a percentage of the teachers' salary. A compromise was reahed in 1967 with a flat amount plus 1/2 per cent of salaries.[226] Loans for attendance at Teachers' College or summer courses were discontinued; there had been too much delinquency and administration. Instead, fellowships were established for teachers doing studies in religious education, and grants on an exceptional basis were available for cases of dire necessity. Finally, an innovation was the establishment of a reserve fund in 1969 in case of expenditures needed to meet such potential expenses in salary negotiations as legal fees, numerous meetings in the case of a provincial takeover or possible mass resignations.[227]

The Ontario Teachers' Federation. OECTA not only examined its own structure, but that of OTF. As well, the question of whether or not OTF should license teachers was revisited. The topic was raised at least three times. In 1965 the Executive recommended that OTF be asked to seek an amendment to the *Teaching Profession Act* so that a "registry" of qualified teachers be established by OTF and so that the teacher's name on the registry be a requisite for teaching in Ontario. In 1967 the AGM passed a motion that OTF press for the power to issue licences to teach in Ontario along with the authority to withdraw a licence from a teacher. That same year a brief to an OTF Commission expressed this thought in a manner reminiscent of presentations in western Canada in earlier decades. It stated that OTF should have the power to licence so that it could:

> maintain a greater control over its members. Licenses would be issued to all teachers at the time of certification and could be withdrawn from those members who failed to comply with the regulations of OTF and of the member's respective affiliation;...we insist that if we are to attain true professional status, OTF must be able to control its members.[228]

No progress occurred with this issue. Ed Alexander, a veteran of over twenty years with the provincial office, speculated that the reason for such lack of progress was threefold: licensing would be costly for OTF; there would be some disagreement over exactly who or what body would make the decision on behalf of OTF to remove the licence of a teacher; the affiliates and the Ministry of Education might feel OTF had too much power if it could issue and take away licences.[229]

Another attempt to change the *Regulation Made Under The Teaching Profession Act* failed. The process under section 19 whereby the Minister of Education asks OTF for an investigation and an opinion concerning whether or not s/he should suspend or remove a teacher's certificate was open to improvement in the AGM's mind. In 1970 it passed a motion that OTF acquire the power to suspend a member without the Minister's consent or action.[230] But certification and decertification remained in her/his hands.

With another OTF matter, though, OECTA was successful. In 1967 OTF established the Ontario Teachers' Federation Commission on the Structure and Function of the Ontario Teachers' Federation. The Federation was over twenty years old; it was time to re-examine it; furthermore, the Hall-Dennis Commission was studying OTF. OECTA took this opportunity to point out that, due to its increased size, it should have ten instead of five members on the OTF Board of Governors. As John Kuchinak put it, "We couldn't understand why OECTA still had only 5 delegates...when our membership had outstripped the public school men's association, who [sic] had 10 representatives."[231] Cecilia Rowan's letter to the OTF Commission put the matter historically:

> OECTA as the toddling infant was very happy and satisfied with the feeling of unity. As I recall in 1944, our membership was fewer than three thousand. It was amazing to learn that the membership now of OECTA stands at 11 000. It would seem, therefore, in keeping with original aims that some changes are in order - this affiliate should have a greater voice on the Board of Governors, thus placing them on equal status.[232]

The OTF saw the logic. *An Act to amend The Teaching Profession Act*, 1969 stipulated ten OECTA members on the Board of Governors: the president, past president, first vice-president, the second vice-president, the secretary-treasurer, and five members elected at the AGM.[233]

Another large question the Commissioners considered was whether or not there should still be an affiliate structure. OPSMTF at its 1967 AGM had voted to support an integrated OTF and then submitted eight reasons for this position to the Commission:

1. the existing structure is obsolete and ineffective; it institutionalizes and entrenches vested interests, thereby hampering real progress; the

historical need of each of the affiliates is outdated in the light of the compelling need of the profession as a whole;
2. an integrated OTF would provide unity and strength in the service of teachers, education and pupils;
3. it would eliminate harmful frictions, wasteful digressions and overlapping efforts;
4. it would eliminate cumbersome, slow processes in which it can take up to two years to form a policy;
5. it would eliminate harmful competitive and partisan aspects;
6. it would eliminate wasteful duplication of services;
7. it would match trustee organizational unity (an inaccurate statement);
8. it would match the Minister's kindergarten-to-grade-thirteen policy and its common training for elementary and secondary school teachers.[234]

The smaller size and revenues of OPSMTF could have had something to do with its position on integration.

All of the other affiliates disagreed with the OPSMTF stand, but it did have an ally in the Hall-Dennis Commission members who also recommended a single teachers' organization, since "these groups have not merged their individual loyalties for the common good of education."[235] It should not be surprising to the reader that AEFO was not interested in being submerged. It recommended keeping the same structure for four reasons:
1. homogeneity within an affiliate promotes unity of action;
2. effectiveness cannot be measured only by speed of decision-making; solidarity and strength are factors;
3. a sense of belonging is stronger in a homogeneous group;
4. the grouping of Ontario French-speaking teachers into a single association has enabled them to remain closer to their ethnic group, to take an interest in its problems, and to cooperate with trustees, and inspectors to try to find solutions for the problems.[236]

OECTA wrote a similar rationale for integration, making the additional points that the affiliate structure provides more opportunity for teacher involvement and protects pluralism. The brief recalled that, "Over the years so great has been the struggle and so costly the sacrifice to preserve the identity of our schools that we are perhaps more conscious of the need to retain our separate affiliation." It also made the important point that each affiliate should have the right to approach the Minister directly on matters specific to the affiliate's interests.[237]

OSSTF agreed with the integration and affiliate direct-access positions, asking only that the OTF and affiliate zones be defined and clarified. FWTAO spoke up for the necessity of an OTF to safeguard the interests of the profession as a whole, to voice teachers' opinions, and to provide leadership with curriculum, methodology, and teacher training, but it also concurred with the affiliate structure, summing up the situation with the remark that the interests of each of the affiliates "are bound to differ and there is still work for the affiliates to do for their membership."[238]

The Commissioners also received a letter from John Rodriguez. In his inimitable anti-authoritarian style and with a perspective that opposed OTF's position on the teacher's right to strike, John wrote, "I firmly believe that the OTF Board of Governors may be compared to the Canadian Senate. It has become a rubber stamp for parochial affiliate thinking, a mouthpiece for the Department of Education rather than the initiator which it should be."[239] In the 1960s John Rodriguez and the American novelist Judith Freeman were at opposite ends of the spectrum. To her, "to question authority meant asking the local bishop for advice."[240]

The Commissioners' report, "A Pattern for Professionalism", 1968, recommended a compromise. The affiliates would be retained in the same structure, but there would be local, regional, and provincial OTF meetings. Nothing came of the second idea, because, as FWTAO put it, it would have been too costly to implement and it presumed a greater involvement than teachers were prepared to have.[241] A short-lived OTF implementation committee looked at "A Pattern for Professionalism". At its first meeting the chair asked each committee member to answer the question, "How many affiliates should there be?" The OPSMTF member said one; OSSTF, one for secondary school teachers and another for elementary school teachers; FWTAO, one for male teachers and another for female teachers; AEFO, one for Franco-Ontarian teachers and another for English-Ontarian teachers; and OECTA, one for separate school teachers and another for public school teachers.[242] "Plus ça change, plus cest la même chose." OTF and its affiliates moved into the next decade affirmed in its structure.

Biographies of the Presidents and Executive Directors.

Patrick O'Leary (1909-85). Another precedent marked this presidency of 1962-63, the first single male lay president.

Patrick was born in Port Lambton, Ontario to farming parents, Albino and Margaret O'Leary. The family, which included Arthur, Christopher (who became a Christian Brother teacher), Andrew, Ignatius, Fred (who died in World War I), Mary, and Celestine, moved to Seaforth. After graduating from St. James there, Patrick went to the Aurora Juniorate where he became Bro. Gilbert of the Christian Brothers in 1926. After completing his scholasticate and novitiate and doing some supply teaching at St. Ann, Montreal, he attended Toronto Normal School. Bro. Gilbert taught at St. Angela, Windsor for twelve years, except for one year as principal at De La Salle elementary school, Windsor. During this time he acquired an industrial arts certificate and began working on his B.A. at Assumption College. Next, for eleven years he taught at St. Mary, Toronto and then received, upon request, his dispensation from the Order. Patrick O'Leary then taught elementary school for the Windsor Separate School Board. Finally, he came to Our Lady of Fatima separate school in Brantford. After a few years the board transferred him to grades nine and ten at St. John's College, a boys' high school, where he taught science until his retirement in 1969.

He was a very private man who kept house with his sister Celestine until his death, loved classical music, smoked a pipe, worked on his B.A. at the University of Western Ontario, and devoted most of his time to his classroom and, in the 1960s, to OECTA and OTF. He served as third vice-president and president of OTF. For his contributions, OTF made him a Fellow and OECTA awarded him a life membership. Mary Babcock remembered him as a thoughtful man effective in his quiet way.[243]

Veronica Houlahan (1904-79). The daughter of George Houlahan and Mary Ann Lynch, Veronica grew up on a farm in Fallowfield near Nepean with four brothers, George, Frank, Joseph, and Austin, and four sisters, Mary, Catherine, Clare, and Lea, the last two of whom also became teachers. In this large Irish family she developed as a lively, active, and friendly girl, popular at the one-room public school near her family's farm. She continued her education at the continuation school in Jockvale, then boarded in Ottawa to finish her high school at Lisgar Collegiate. She proceeded directly to Ottawa Normal School in 1922 and the following year started teaching for the Ottawa Separate School Board.

Here she had a long and rich career. She taught at St. Brigid and Our Lady's Murray Street until 1954, when she was appointed as primary supervisor, the first such position for any separate school board, one she held until her retirement in 1967. In this capacity she set up a board-wide remedial reading programme and the first induction programme for new teachers; she also implemented kindergartens for the board. By this time she had acquired a specialist certificate in primary methods, written two books, Parables and Programme in Phonics, and assisted in the writing of a series of Catholic readers for Ginn and Company.

She brought to the presidency of OECTA in 1963 a strong interest in its welfare and in curriculum matters. She had been an active member in the Ottawa English Catholic Teachers' Association, a close friend of Dr. McDonald's, and the president of district #1 for OECTA. She also served on a number of curriculum committees for the Association and travelled about with Fr. Conway negotiating salaries: "I was usually on the salary negotiations. When the going became real tough I usually inherited the chairmanship."[244] In this capacity she would often win over the trustees with her wit, a useful attribute when OECTA had a limited arsenal of weapons. In addition she found time to institute a programme to introduce OECTA to Teachers' College students.

In 1961 Margaret Drago convinced her to join the provincial executive. (Once the Nominating Committee put one's name on the slate, being elected was a foregone conclusion.) Veronica accepted the nomination out of a professional sense of duty. She admitted that "Truthfully, every weekend that I had to go to Toronto was a sacrifice for me. Checking into a hotel never ceased to be a lonely experience."[245] At the provincial level Miss Houlahan served on the committee that prepared the brief to the Hall-Dennis Commission, on the OTF committee revising the kindergarten-to-grade-six curriculum, and on the OTF Commission examining its structure.[246]

In 1967 Veronica Houlahan retired, since "being the richest girl in the graveyard did not appeal to me." Fr. Conway recalled that she was one of the best teachers in Ottawa for the task of preparing pupils for First Communion. Mrs. Marie Kennedy, a future president of OECTA, regarded her as an exceptional primary teacher. Her nephew, Lorne Lawson, remembered her as his favourite aunt, a family person, a witty card player, and a pious Catholic. After her retirement she continued to attend Mass daily. OECTA was fortunate to have her in the Association and recognized this by making her a life member. She received the identical honour from OTF and was awarded a Canada Medal. OTF also made her a Fellow.[247]

Sr. John of Valencia, C.N.D. (1908-). After Vatican II some religious sisters reverted to their family name, which in Sr. John's case was Frances Mc Cann. However, when president from 1964 to 1965, Sister still used the name she took when she professed.

Her parents, John McCann and Ellen Mary Donaghue, were farmers in Westport raising a large, boisterous family: Josephine, Geraldine, Anne, Claire, Frances, Wilbert, Michael, and John. Frances attended the Westport separate and continuation schools, housed together in the same four-room building. The latter establishment assumed historic importance as one of the separate schools cited in the Tiny Township Case for offering a high school curriculum with provincial grants and local taxes.

Upon graduating from the continuation school in 1926, Frances McCann entered the novitiate of the Congregation of Notre Dame at its mother house in Montreal. After two years there Sr. John of Valencia went to Ottawa Normal School and began teaching at St. Patrick's elementary school in Ottawa. While at this posting she worked off her B.A. extramurally at the University of Ottawa. She then went on to acquire an M.A. in history. The Order next asked her to take the summer course at OCE to obtain a HSA. She then moved into teaching history and English at Notre Dame in Kingston, the Westport Continuation School, her alma mater, and Notre Dame in Toronto. The staffing of people like Sr. John in Catholic high schools enabled these institutions to survive on little or no revenues from the government.

Sr. John and her Order supported both the Ottawa English Catholic Teachers' Association and OECTA, which held monthly meetings at the Notre Dame Convent on Gloucester Street. Sister became president of OECTA district #3 in Kingston. She was both a prefect of studies (a position akin to a vice-principal) and a member of the OECTA Executive. After thirty-six years of teaching, Sister retired in 1976. She then went to Montreal to take courses in English-French translation and in secretarial work at the Order's College. Still active today, Sister is the librarian at the Kingston convent.

Sr. Frances feels that her vocation on the Executive and as a member of the Association has always been "spreading the good news." She remains very interested in OECTA and regards its biggest accomplishment to be its role in the completion of the separate school system with full funding to the end of high school. OTF made her a Fellow.[248]

Karl Bohren (1922-91). Like Raymond Bergin and Patrick Perdue, Karl Bohren started working for a small salary, and after marrying supplemented his income with a second job, working weekends at a beer store, to meet household expenses for his wife and large family; even a principal's salary did not permit him to drop the second job. During the same period he took courses extramurally to improve himself. From these modest beginnings he became president of OECTA (1965-66) and a director of education later in his career.

Karl was born in Binbrook, near Hamilton to Godfrey and Sarah Bohren, immigrants from Switzerland. He was the oldest child with three brothers, Herman, Fred, and Norman, and three sisters, Marion, Cathy, and Lorraine. When the family moved to Toronto, Karl attended Perth Avenue public school and delivered for a florist for a dollar a day. Money was scarce since Karl's father had to stretch his salary as a railroad worker with seven children. Karl would occasionally ask for a nickel for the movies; his father would tell him a nickel would buy a loaf of bread. Thus, as soon as Karl finished his grade twelve at Western Technical School at age seventeen, he joined the army (1939). Two years later he married Eileen Carey and became a Roman Catholic. Upon leaving the army in 1945, he used his veteran's training grant to attend Toronto Normal School.

He commenced teaching at Holy Name separate school in Kirkland Lake, then moved to St. Anthony in Gatchell, near Sudbury. Since he was that scarce and apparently indispensable commodity for administrative purposes, a male teacher, he was promoted to principal the following year and remained in this position until 1968. During this time he and his wife had six children: Robert, Michael, Margaret, Karleen, Mary-Jane, and Thomas. He also acquired a B.A. extramurally from Laurentian University, his M.Ed. from OCE, and his elementary school principal's and inspector's certificates. It was in these years that Karl Bohren was active in OECTA at the local and provincial levels and on the OTF provincial executive.

The latter part of his career was spent as a supervisory officer, first as a superintendent with the North Shore District RCSS Board, then as director of education there until 1977, the year of his retirement. Widowed in 1983, he married Yvonne Elizabeth Shamas, who was a widow and mother of two children. Until his death Karl Bohren stayed active as a Liberal Party worker, and as a trustee for the school board he had administered, while engaging in his hobbies of travelling, playing golf, and reading.

His reputation among the teachers was that of a well-liked, compassionate, and generous Christian. His work was recognized with an OTF fellowship, an OECTA honorary membership, and the Gold Medal of the Diocesan Order of Merit from the Sault Ste. Marie diocese. He often would say, "I have a position to uphold." He did.[249]

Sr. Aloysia, S.S.N.D. (Gertrude Zimmer) (1907-). With Sister's election to the president's office in 1966, four Orders of teaching sisters had now been represented in this position: the Sisters of Providence, the Congregation of St. Joseph, the Congregation of Notre Dame, and now the School Sisters of Notre Dame. These and other Orders of sisters[250] had for decades constituted a large proportion of the province's separate school staff, thereby keeping the schools alive. It was appropriate that four sisters became OECTA presidents in the 1950s and 1960s.

Gertrude was born to a farming family in Formosa, then moved to Mildmay, Ontario. Her father, David Zimmer, a stonemason, and mother, Louise Schill had eleven children: the first five were boys: Alphonse, who died as a baby, Alphonse, named for his older brother, Edwin, Leonard, and David; her mother wept at this point because there was no one to help with the dishes (a skill males have since been encouraged to learn). But five girls followed: Caroline, Anna, who also entered the S.S.N.D. Order, Elizabeth, Clara, and Gertrude. The last, but not least, baby was William, who became a priest.

Gertrude attended Sacred Heart separate school in Mildmay to the end of the fifth class (grades nine and ten) and then finished her grade twelve at St. Anne in Kitchener in a residence for those students intending to become sisters. She went to Hamilton Normal School, taught for one year at St. Joseph, Kitchener, then entered the novitiate in 1928. Sr. Aloysia taught at Holy Family, Hanover and Sacred Heart, Walkerton. She became principal and a full-time teacher of four grades at St. Agatha in RCSS Wilmot #15 1/2, a position at which she persevered for eleven years. Sr. Aloysia was then principal at St. Clement in the town of the same name. The Kitchener Separate School Board recognized her energetic and lively personality and ability by appointing her as supervising principal. The last ten years of her teaching career she spent as principal at St. Mary, Oakville and St. Clement, Preston. In 1973 she retired after forty-six years of teaching, but it was only a technical retirement for pension purposes. Sister would remain an active, dynamic influence in her Order and wider community.

Sr. Aloysia had always improved herself for the benefit of others. Instead of working on a B.A., she acquired certification in agriculture, art, audio-visual methods, guidance, home economics, and manual training. With such a variety of special skills Sister set up, for example, an industrial arts/home economics program in a two-room school at St. Agatha, using the convent space nearby.

While on the provincial executive Sister served on an OTF committee to address the problem of low pensions for teachers, organized annually several principals' conferences and with a committee produced a professional handbook for principals. She regarded the latter as her most worthy contribution; in my opinion, the contents of that handbook are still potentially useful for principals.

Since retiring, Sister has become a valuable resource for Kitchener. She and Sr. Kathleen Kunkel initiated with federal seed money a home support service for the housebound elderly in Kitchener, RAISE (Retirees Assisting in Serving Each Other), now a flourishing organization. She also served on the Community Advisory Committee of the Psychiatric Services of the Kitchener-Waterloo Hospital, on the Waterloo Region Senior Citizens Needs Advisory Committee, and on the St. Anne's Parish Council. Currently, Sister is a member of a senior citizens travel club, follows politics, is an ardent sports fan, and loves to play bridge.

She has received special recognition for her work over the years. The Kitchener Separate School Board named a school after her. OTF made her a Fellow. She was inducted into the Waterloo County Hall of Fame for her outstanding contribution to education. At Kitchener's request, Sister received the Queen's Medal. The Kitchener-Waterloo Sertoma Club presented her with the Service to Mankind plaque for community service. The Rotary Foundation named her a Paul Harris Fellow in appreciation of her furtherance of better understanding and friendly relations among the peoples of the world. The Hon. John Sweeney, Minister of Community and Social Services, presented her with the Community Service Award at the first Provincial Volunteer Awards Night. Two years ago, the organizers of the Kitchener Mayor's Dinner, whose purpose was to raise money for the unemployed and for soup kitchens, asked her to be the official guest in order to attract donors.

It is significant that such an outstanding human being saw as an important part of her vocation serving OECTA as president, and in other roles. In a recent interview with me, Sr. Aloysia left a special wish for the Association's members: "May all who will be serving in the next fifty years and thereafter continue to do as Scripture says in 1 Peter 4: 'Put your gifts in the service of others in the same measure as you receive.' "[251]

Ruth Willis. By the time she assumed office in 1967 as the eighteenth president, there had been nine female presidents. This could be regarded as a positive statistic for the recognition of women in a dual-sex teachers' organization. It should be pointed out, however, that the large majority of OECTA's members were female throughout the 1950s and 1960s, and in the next decade the statistics would turn to a disproportionate number of male presidents.

Ruth was born in Thamesville. Her parents, J. Clair and Georgina Willis, had four other children: Roy, Jack, Marjorie, and Donna. The family moved to Windsor, where her father worked for the bus company and her mother did what most married women did in those days, became a full-time housewife. Ruth attended St. Alphonsus separate school, then St. Mary's Academy to the end of grade thirteen. She acquired a first-class teaching certificate at London Normal School and landed a job at once despite scarce positions.

The Windsor Separate School Board, where she spent her entire career, placed her at Holy Name, St. Alphonsus, St. Clare, and then St. Angela. While teaching, she earned a B.A. from the University of Western Ontario at its Windsor College. In the evening she attended university classes. Miss Willis also completed an M.Ed. from Wayne State University in Detroit. In the summers she taught primary methods at Hamilton Teachers' College. The school board used her abilities by appointing her primary supervisor, then head consultant for coordinated studies. She retired at the end of her fortieth year in teaching, having been awarded an OTF fellowship.

Throughout much of her career Miss Willis was active in OECTA. She was secretary for the Windsor district and then came on the Executive as third vice-president, working up to president. She held office at a time when John Kuchinak and John Rodriguez were also on the Executive. They rather forcefully represented the interests of members looking for change. Miss Willis remembered them as somewhat aggressive at first, but calm good leaders later. Perhaps she had a pacifying effect. During contentious discussions, Ruth would tell a lively story and maintain harmony.

In her retirement Miss Willis follows baseball, basketball, and hockey avidly, travels extensively, plays the horses, and regularly flies to her favourite spot, Las Vegas, "to court Lady Luck," she says.[252]

John Rodriguez (1937-). With this leader's arrival on the Executive, the Association took on a new vision and new objectives. Without abandoning the original aims in OECTA's constitution, John Rodriguez and other members in the Association with similar interests and education attempted to balance the traditional involvements centring around the status and welfare of the teacher, students, and education with a fresh concern for issues in the world outside of the classroom calling for social justice. Rodriguez's term of office (1968-69) began a division of OECTA's aims (and sometimes of its members) that continues to the present. His early life and career explain to some degree his zeal for apostolic action.

John was born in the village of Bartica in Guyana. His parents of Portuguese descent, Clement Rodriguez and Gloria Texeira Da Silva, with John and their other two sons, Peter and Brian (the latter is now a trustee on the Sudbury District RCSS Board), moved to the country's capital, Georgetown, where the father, formerly a law clerk, became a government auditor. John received his elementary education at St. Anthony in Bartica and Sacred Heart in Georgetown and his secondary schooling at St. Stanislaus College, graduating in 1954.

His first employment was at the Royal Bank of Canada where he met his first Canadians. He found them democratic, progressive, and friendly, especially when compared to the British, to whom as a student he used to shout in demonstrations for his country's independence, "Limey, go home." In 1956 he decided to use his British passport to emigrate to what seemed an interesting, snow-covered country, Canada. Arriving in Toronto with a suitcase and fifty dollars, he took the subway to Bloor Street and walked one block east until he saw a room for rent at seven dollars a week. The next day he used more of his diminishing cash to place an advertisement in the newspaper announcing his availability for work. He received fifteen telephone calls and accepted a position across the street from his residence in the accounting department of the Crown Life Insurance Company (where he soon met Mary Babcock). After six months with the firm, John was given an assistant. He taught her her duties so well that she advised him in turn to consider what she was going to pursue, a teaching career.

Fortunately for John Rodriguez, the "completing course" route into teaching was still available. John submitted his grade-twelve-equivalent diploma to the Department of Education, was accepted into the 1957 summer course, and was hired by the Grantham RCSS Board. After the course he embarked on the S. S. Cayuga across to Niagara-on-the-Lake where the trustees met him and introduced him to his first teaching assignment, English and French at St. Alfred Junior High School.

At the end of the two years he had not saved enough from his $2100 salary to meet expenses for his year at Toronto Teachers' College. He contacted Mr. Silcox at the Department, the official who had originally admitted him, who got him a four-to-ten job cleaning the washrooms each night at Eastern High School of Commerce. After a busy year, Mr. Rodriguez returned to the now-amalgamated St. Catharines RCSS Board, where he taught grades two and three at St. John and handled the school's sports programme for $200 extra. The following year, John married Bertilla Bobbato, whom he had met at St. Alfred's Catholic Youth Organization.

His concern for the disadvantaged manifested itself early. At St. John he had in his sports programme some new Canadians whom the principal took off the team until they learned English. John began at no cost operating night classes in his home for these children so that the sister would allow them to play on teams.

While in St. Catharines Mr. Rodriguez started his B.A. at Niagara University, New York and spent one summer polishing his Spanish at the Universidad Nacional de Mexico. In the spring of 1962, while on a visit to his wife's family in Sudbury, he met with the Coniston Separate School Board where there had never been a male teacher since the board started in 1929. He accepted a position with a good salary, accommodation in a company house, moving expenses, and a chance for a principalship. He shortly was appointed principal of the same school, Our Lady of Mercy. (Four years of experience or less in separate schools was often quite sufficient for a male to acquire a principalship in the 1950s and early 1960s.) Mr. Rodriguez took his new responsibilities seriously, acquiring a guidance certificate, finishing his B.A. at Laurentian University and setting up a parent advisory committee that worked with him to establish both an oral French and an instrumental music programinnovations for the separate schools in that area. He convinced the school board to give special salary allowances for certificates in music and art.

Looking for challenges beyond the school, John became interested in municipal and OECTA affairs, while also giving high priority to helping his wife raise a family of five boys: Damian, Brendan, Derek, Declan, and Emlyn. He became concerned for his family and neighbours when he considered the absence in Coniston of a library, park, or dental service; as well, the only physician was moving out. He began attending municipal council meetings, then writing and delivering door-to-door comments on the meetings; they were not complimentary. His school board felt its principal had no business in politics, met, and voted to demote him; the vote was a tie, however, and the motion was therefore lost. Undissuaded, John ran unsuccessfully for mayor, but later successfully for council, breaking the slate of nominations. By this time, at the encouragement of Elie Martel, another separate school principal in the area, he joined the New Democratic Party (NDP).

His interest in OECTA had begun in St. Catharines where he did committee work, and continued in Coniston where he replaced individual bargaining with collective bargaining and a salary schedule, explaining to the trustees that he needed these procedures before he could hire on their behalf at North Bay Teachers' College. In 1967 he became a district president of OECTA, then went on to the Executive, moving up to president.

In 1972 John Rodriguez was elected to the House of Commons. Defeated in 1980, he learned his teaching contract with the Sudbury District RCSS Board had been voided. The policy of having a position for a member of the parliament who might return to teaching had been modified to require annual notification from the sitting member that s/he still was a member and still wished to be considered as on leave from the board. The board stated it had advised Mr. Rodriguez of the change in policy; he replied that he had received no such written notification. Out of a job, John, with the support of OECTA, asked the Minister of Education, Bette Stephenson, for a Board of Reference. Elie Martel, then a member of the provincial legislature, encouraged her to grant it. At the hearing the superintendent of education testified that Mr. Rodriguez was an excellent teacher. Furthermore, the school board could not prove that he had received the letter advising him of the change in policy. All three members of the Board of Reference decided that his contract should be reinstated. After almost six months without income John was back on the payroll. However, the school board waited until the day before Labour Day to notify him of his posting to Immaculate Conception to teach grade seven and eight geography, history, and science. In 1984 and 1988 John Rodriguez won back his old seat in the federal government. He sent the Sudbury District RCSS Board annually the required letter. In 1993 he was caught in the Liberal sweep of the province and is currently reviewing his options. They include returning to teaching, but do not include "walking the malls."

John's sense of justice, his seeming willingness to risk personal comfort, and his placement of honesty and frankness over diplomacy with those with whom he disagrees would be evident at Toronto OECTA meetings. But even Fr. Conway and Mary Babcock, who often challenged his methods and priorities, agreed that he had a positive effect on the Association. In 1972 OTF made him a Fellow.[253]

John Kuchinak (1932-). Like John Rodriguez, the president who followed him in 1969-70 came from a background that fostered kinship with the labour union movement. His father, Alexander Kuchinak, escaped from imprisonment in the revolutionary war in the Ukraine and immigrated to England, Hamilton, Ontario, and finally, Sydney, Nova Scotia where he joined his brother working in the steel plant. His mother, Anna Ostafichuk, was a housemaid and daughter of a Ukrainian immigrant. His parents had four children: Mary, Catherine, Michael, and John.

John grew up in a decidedly multicultural neighbourhood, speaking Ukrainian at home. He attended a Catholic public school and a religiously mixed high school, then went to St. Francis Xavier University, Antigonish. There he encountered the cooperative movement, a determining influence on him. After acquiring a B.A. in philosophy and Latin at the early age of twenty, he spent the next six years in a series of odd jobs before finding his vocation. He decided to try teaching in Ontario. Starting in 1959 he worked for two years with a letter of permission for the Metropolitan Separate School Board at Holy Family school. He then went for a year to OCE to get a HSA in English, history, and Latin and an elementary school teacher's certificate, thus becoming that rare commodity in the early 1960s - a male, qualified separate school teacher with a B.A. besides.

The Board rehired and returned him to Holy Family for three years, then promoted him to principal. (There were no vice-principals in the Toronto separate schools then.) As principal at Nativity school he received an extra $500 plus one half-day a week help from either a teacher or a secretary. With four children, Christopher, Laurie, Anne, and Vicki, John had to supplement his income by doing playground work in the summers.

John Kuchinak served as principal at several schools in Metropolitan Toronto: St. Robert, St. Raphael, St. Jerome, Pope John XXIII, Mount Carmel, and St. Francis Xavier. In the 1970s he took four months off at his own expense to begin an M.A. programme in religious education at St. Michael's College, continued it on a sabbatical year, nd received the degree in 1982.

His roots with the union movement brought him early to OECTA meetings. He had a number of irritants on his mind with which he felt his teachers' union should be dealing: the Etobicoke garbage collectors had a better pension plan than the teachers; the pilot county school board in Peterborough, where John had worked on construction one summer, was producing, in his opinion paternalistic trustees and timid teacher federation members; despite the call from 1962's Vatican II papers for involvement of the laity in the Church, John Kuchinak saw little room for men to progress administratively and financially in Ontario's separate schools. He went to the 1964 AGM as a delegate, met John Rodriguez, Elie Martel, and Robert Fera from the Sudbury district and other delegates, many of them laymen, and proceeded to work with them to "open things up" and get their concerns addressed.

John regarded his most significant accomplishment while on the Executive and provincial committees as helping to develop and obtain the Minister's approval of the OECTA-OSSTA religious education course. He saw one of his tasks as convincing the Executive and Secretariat of the two Associations that they were not moving too fast in mounting the course. He also served on the OTF committee to develop a position on impending salary negotiating legislation. OECTA recognized his contributions with a life membership in 1991 and OTF with a fellowship in 1979. OECTA also used his expertise for fifteen years as a teacher and principal of winter and, most of the time, summer courses in religious education in Belleville, Oshawa, and Toronto. He carried his special interests to the MSSB when he became a founding member of Teachers for Social Justice.

Since retiring in 1989, John spends his time reading, writing, and visiting his two grandchildren.[254]

Marie Kennedy (1926-). The married women teachers of Ontario's separate schools had advanced from a status in the 1950s and earlier that culminated in a threatened strike in Toronto in 1954. Since then their temporary contracts and lower salaries have gradually been replaced by equity in contractual and salary matters relative to the rest of the separate school staff. In 1970 the first married woman teacher became provincial president of OECTA. The Association's policy of equal pay for equal work and the shortage of teachers had produced positive results. (However, to date there has not been a second married woman teacher as president.)

Marie was born in Toronto into a large family. E. J. Neville, an accountant, and his wife and full-time homemaker, Charlotte Bell, had eight children: Edgar, Rita, Marie, Margaret, Charles, Sheila, Donald, and Sharon. Encouraged to become teachers by their parents, all but Rita and Donald took the advice; Edgar went on to become a director of education of the Hastings-Prince Edward County RCSS Board.

Marie went to St. Joseph in Toronto. When the family moved to New Liskeard, she spent two years in grade nine placing a high priority on having a good time. Her father then accepted a position in Ottawa and Marie went to Immaculata High School. Faced with the formidable task of preparing for the Department of Education grade thirteen examinations and still emphasizing her social development, she took advantage of a temporary provision by which a student could be excused from writing the final examinations if s/he helped out with the war effort. Marie decided to work on a relative's farm from May to August, thereby, in her words, "averting disaster."

In 1945 she went to Ottawa Normal School, housed then on the second floor of a public school, since the Normal School building was being used as a war office. The following year she began teaching at St. Patrick's girls' school for the Ottawa Separate School Board. Because of the inspiration of her inspector, Dr. McDonald, and a mentor, Cecilia Rowan, she grew interested in the newly constituted OECTA. "Cheesed off" with a salary of $1000, she expressed her philosophy this way: "A teacher is supposed to be dedicated and poor; I could be even more dedicated if rich." It would be some time, if ever, before she would have the opportunity to be more dedicated in this fashion. In 1948 Marie married Donald G. Kennedy and thus her contract was terminated: "I thought nothing of this, since that was what was done and I didn't intend to return to teaching." Over the next ten years Mrs. Kennedy and her husband had four children: Donna, the 1993 president of the Carleton Unit of OECTA, Christine, now a criminologist, Leslie (also a teacher), and Jennifer (a marketer). Eventually, Marie would have ten grandchildren.

She did some supply teaching during this period, but did not return full-time to the profession until 1962 at Our Lady of Fatima school, Ottawa. Obviously, she was an exceptional teacher, because the next year Miss Dorothy Dunn, the separate school inspector, asked her to be a principal. At first Marie turned down the offer, but then accepted conditionally; conscious that she possessed only a standard one teacher's certificate, she stipulated that she would turn away the promotion if someone more qualified became available. She held the position of principal of St. Louis for twelve years.

Marie's outspoken personality and sense of humour had interesting results for herself and later for OECTA. For example, when Dr. McDonald inspected her as a beginning teacher, she asked him, "Who was the idiot who put grades three and four together for this class?" He replied, "I was." Again, after one year as principal teaching half-time, she advised the school board that both her teaching and principalship were suffering and that she would return to teaching full-time unless this situation were rectified. She became a full-time principal that fall.

In 1974 Mrs. Kennedy accepted the invitation of a superintendent with the Carleton RCSS Board to be a principal there after she had had a disagreement with her superintendent in Ottawa. Once again her abilities outweighed her lack of paper qualifications: the superintendent obtained permission annually from the Ministry of Education to appoint her as principal without a B.A.. She was principal of St. Bernard, Gloucester and of the Bayshore separate school in Nepean until her retirement in 1986. After that she taught adult literacy at the prison and helped to establish a hospice in Merrickville.

When Marie returned to teaching in 1962 she immediately became the Ottawa district OECTA president. Commenting on her total absence of any Ministry of Education or university courses, she explained that she was too busy with her family, principalship, and OECTA; she knew that was a costly decision, but, in her opinion, worth it. She remembered her balancing of the three roles as the best of times.

OECTA benefited from this juggling. In the same year that she was district president she also became provincial treasurer and proceeded to advance to third, then first vice-president, then president. During this time she was grateful to an "incredibly competent" teaching staff and a cooperative school board, who were proud of her accomplishments and released her for days to attend OECTA meetings. She contributed markedly to the development of the religious education courses for teachers, the separate school extension debates, and the discussions about the right to strike. In addition, she represented OECTA on a provincial committee investigating the sharing of facilities between public and separate school boards, did counselling of teachers while on a six-month leave, served for many years on the Relations and

Discipline Committee, and managed the unique feat of holding the office of past president of OTF without ever having been its president.

Strong-willed and highly visible, Marie once led the teachers' march to the Ottawa parliament buildings during a one-day strike. On another occasion, when being kept waiting for a scheduled appointment with William Davis, the Minister of Education, she hurried matters along by stating to his secretary, "If you can prove to me he's busier then I am with four children, a school, and OECTA, I'll wait." Throughout these productive years she kept her sense of humour. She recalled that she and the rest of the Executive would sometimes fight like devils, but then after the meetings would socialize with a few drinks, always being careful to throw the empty liquor bottles into the garbage of the affiliates in order to influence public perception. When her picture appeared in a newspaper in Sydney, Australia, while she was at the World Federation of Teachers convention, the caption read, "Fr. Conway and Sr. Marie Kennedy." Marie quipped that she was nun for a day.

OTF honoured Mrs. Kennedy with a fellowship and OECTA with a life membership.[255]

Mary Babcock. After six years of assisting Marion Tyrrell, Mary Babcock in 1965 became the executive director of OECTA. The title had been changed from secretary-treasurer to give the position more status. Her great success in her previous position, particularly as salary negotiator, quickly narrowed the field to her for Miss Tyrrell's replacement.

Her earlier biography has already been described and the results of her work in this new position have been seen in this chapter. She had a different management style from her predecessor. Miss Tyrrell, in the words of John Rodriguez, acted as if she owned the place. One could argue in her defence that a firm hand was necessary, since she functioned at a time when OECTA was in its infancy, with an Executive of teachers working full-time and with a very small support staff. Mary Babcock assumed the position when the Executive and Board of Directors were expecting to be more involved and when her larger staff and provincial OECTA committees called for a democratic leadership without over-direction. In the opinion of those who worked with her, Miss Babcock, with her business, educational, and Association background, moved with the times and administered well, listening, providing guidance, considering alternatives, facilitating consensus, and making recommendations for the Executive and Directors. Her staff found her loyal, consistent, organized, knowledgeable, and well prepared. She combined a business-like manner with an infectious loud laugh. She would impose rarely but when necessary; instead, she developed her staff by exemplary behaviour.

Claudette Foisy-Moon and Sr. Sheila McAuliffe, members of the central office staff, recalled her formidable salary negotiating skills in provincial takeovers. In Timmins she presented to an all-male, somewhat dazzled board a complete set of figures showing exactly what it could afford; the trustees had to agree that she knew her facts. In Kingston she arrived with an extraordinarily large hat, once again marched the trustees through detailed facts and figures, and quickly reached a settlement: a different personality for changed times.

Since Mary Babcock's retirement in 1973 she has continued her activities with the Soroptimist Club, worked during its existence for the Catholic High School Board in Toronto, helped with Meals on Wheels, and served as a volunteer for the Orthopaedic and Arthritic Hospital. She has received a number of honours: an OECTA honorary membership and life membership, an OTF fellowship, and the Catholic Education Foundation of Ontario (CEFO) Award of Merit. One of the three fellowships for religious studies is named after Mary C. Babcock. At her retirement Archbishop Pocock presented to her on behalf of the Pope the distinguished Papal Medal, Bene Merenti; the Archbishop said, "I have presented very, very few of these in my lifetime. The bishops of Ontario are deeply, deeply grateful for the services Mary has provided to Catholic education."[256]

NOTES

1. J. Rodriguez to Miss Babcock, 22 December 1967; Board of Directors, 23-24 February 1968.
2. Fleming, *Expansion*, 264.
3. Stamp, *Schools of Ontario*, 211; AGM, 24-25 April 1962; 22-24 March 1971.
4. Executive, 9 June 1962.
5. *The Canadian Register*, 8 July 1961, 1; 22 July 1961, 7; Walker, *Catholic Education*, Vol. III, 104.
6. Ibid., 110-21; Dixon, "Separate School System," 189; McDougall, Robarts, 96; OECTA Review (October 1967), 71-72.
7. *Report*, 1962, S-33; 1968, 85.
8. André Vandekerckhove and Yvonne Vandekerckhove, et al. The Municipal Corporation of the Township of Middleton (1962), 31 D.L.R. (2d), 304; *Canadian Register*, 9 December 1961, 2; 30 December 1961, 1; Dixon, "Separate School System," 250-53.
9. Fleming, *Administrative structure*, 125-28; Ontario Legislative Assembly, Debates, 28th leg., 1st sess., 15 March 1968, 833.
10. Fleming, *Expansion of the educational system*, 146; *Canadian Register*, 21 February 1970, 9; Report, 1968, 85; 1971, 129.
11. Ontario Department of Education, "Memorandum re Changes in Certification of Elementary-School Teacher," *Circular* 635, 15 February 1962; Board of Directors, 6 January 1962.
12. Ontario Department of Education, "The Four Standards of an Elementary School Teacher's Certificate," *Circular* 635, 8 September 1969; AGM, 20-21 April 1965; 20-22 March 1968; 19-21 March 1969.
13. Board of Directors, 6 January 1962; AGM, 20-22 March 1968.
14. *Report*, 1965, 21; 1966, 15; Stamp, *Schools of Ontario*, 209.
15. Carey-Hill and Teixeira, "Pathway to Militancy ".
16. *Report*, 1962, 6-7; 1964, 6; 1965, 21; 1966, 17; 1968, 9; 1969, 7; 1970, 10; 1971, 13.
17. *Report*, 1971, 71.
18. Mr. Justice E. M. Hall, et al., *Living and Learning, The Report of the Provincial Committee on Aims and Objectives of Education in the Schools of Ontario*, Toronto: Ontario Department of Education, 1968.
19. Fleming, *Education: Ontario's preoccupation*, Toronto: University of Toronto Press, 1972, 220-21.
20. Stamp, *Schools of Ontario*, 217-18.
21. V. K. Greer, M.A., "Appraisal of the New Programme of Studies, Grades I to VI," *Canadian School Journal* (June 1938), 184-99, 231.
22. Fleming, *Schools, pupils, and teachers*, 18; McDougall, Robarts, 52-53; Stamp, *Schools of Ontario*, 192-94.
23. Fleming, *Ontario's preoccupation*, 204-206, 217-19; McDougall, Robarts, 53; Stamp, *Schools of Ontario*, 205.
24. Lawrence Cardinal Sheehan, Archbishop of Baltimore, "Introduction," in

Walter M. Abbott, S.J., ed., *The Documents of Vatican II*, New York: The America Press, 1966, XV-XIX.
25. Sr. Jacqueline O'Brien, C.S.J., interview, North Bay, 8 June 1993; *Canadian Register*, 23 January 1965, 8; 10 February 1968, 6.
26. Most Rev. Alexander Carter, "Introduction. Education," in *Documents of Vatican II*, 634-36.
27. Walker, *Catholic Education*, Vol. III, 177.
28. Ibid., 121.
29. Executive, 19 August 1963.
30. *Canadian Register*, 20 February 1965, 1; 7 August 1965, 1-2.
31. *Report*, 1962, xi.
32. *The Catholic Trustee* (May 1962), 10.
33. Quoted in Walker, *Catholic Education*, Vol. III, 106.
34. Executive, 7 April 1962; 7-8 June 1968.
35. Board of Directors, 25 February 1967.
36. Downie, *Collective Bargaining*, 26.
37. Executive, 26 May 1965; 13 June 1969; 7 April 1962.
38. *Catholic Trustee* (September 1966), 37.
39. Board of Directors, 10 January 1964; AGM, 24-25 April 1962.
40. Ibid.; Board of Directors, 6 January 1962; AGM, 20-22 May 1968.
41. *Canadian Register*, 21 January 1961, 6; 22 July 1961, 7.
42. Coo, *Forty Years*, 66.
43. Executive, 19-20 April 1968; Board of Directors, 30 May 1970.
44. *Catholic Trustee* (September 1967), 12-13; (November 1968), 28.
45. Executive, 10 May 1969.
46. *OECTA Review* (May 1970), 63-64.
47. AGM, 16-17 April 1963; Board of Directors, 10-11 February 1967; Executive, 16-17 August 1968; Board of Directors, 6 January 1962.
48. McDougall, *Robarts*, 227-28; Board of Directors, 19 September 1969.
49. Executive, 9 March 1963.
50. Ibid., 7 April 1962; 9 March 1963; 13 February 1965.
51. Patrick O'Neill, interview, Toronto, 30 May 1993.
52. Executive, 7-8 April 1967; Board of Directors, 25 February 1967.
53. AGM, 24-25 April 1962; 14-16 April 1966.
54. Executive, 13 September 1969; AGM, 22-24 March 1971; Frank Dillon, interview, Toronto, 17 June 1993; John Ware, interview, Toronto, 17 June 1993.
55. Quoted in *Canadian Register*, 20 April 1963, 6.
56. Board of Directors, 30 May 1970; Executive, 9 April 1965; 7 June 1968; 29 April 1969; 5 June 1970.
57. Executive, 9 April 1965.
58. Executive, 12-13 May 1964; Board of Directors, 8-9 December 1967; *OECTA News and Views*, April 1968.
59. Executive, 1-2 November 1968.

60. Board of Directors, 6 January 1962; 13 February 1965; Executive, 13 February 1965.
61. Ibid., 5 January 1963; Executive, 8 February 1964; 13 February 1965.
62. Executive, 10 May 1969.
63. AGM, 31 March-1 April 1964.
64. Executive, 13 September 1969.
65. AGM, 20-22 March 1968; 19-21 March 1969; 23-25 March 1970; 22-24 March 1971; Board of Directors, 6 January 1962; 15 January 1966; 23-24 February 1968; 31 May 1969; 11-12 December 1970; Executive, 9-10 June 1967.
66. Executive, 10 September, 11 November 1966.
67. Executive, 9-10 June 1967; 5 June 1970; AGM, 23-25 March 1970.
68. Board of Directors, 10-11 February 1967; Executive, 13 June 1969.
69. AGM, 14-16 April 1966; Executive, 14 May 1966.
70. AGM, 31 March-1 April 1964; 26-27 May 1965; 23-25 March 1970.
71. Ibid., 24-25 April 1962; 16-17 April 1963; Walker, *Catholic Education*, Vol. III, 179.
72. John Flynn, interview, Brantford, 30 June 1993; Edwin Alexander, interview, Toronto, 30 June 1993.
73. Executive, 7 April, 9 June 1962.
74. AGM, 24-25 April 1962.
75. Executive, 18 August 1962; 6 April 1963.
76. AGM, 31 March-1 April 1964.
77. Board of Directors, 19 September 1969; 18 September 1970; Executive, 13 September 1969.
78. AGM, 19-21 March 1969; Board of Directors, 12-13 December 1969; Executive, 1 May 1970.
79. AGM, 24-25 April 1962; 31 March-1 April 1964.
80. Ibid., 26-27 May 1965; Rodriguez, interview.
81. Ibid.
82. Board of Directors, 19 April 1965.
83. AGM, 14-16 April 1966; Board of Directors, 28 May 1966.
84. Executive, 2-3 December 1966.
85. Board of Directors, 10-11 December 1966; 25 February 1967; AGM, 20-22 March 1968.
86. Board of Directors, 31 May 1969; *Canadian Register*, 18 July 1970, 17.
87. Board of Directors, 31 May 1969; Knott, interview.
88. *Canadian Register*, 8 May 1971, 19; Board of Directors, 30 May 1970; Executive, 4-5 October 1968; Alexander, Toronto interview, 5 May 1993.
89. Board of Directors, 12-13 December 1969.
90. AGM, 28-31 March 1967; Executive, 24-25 January, 7-8 June 1968; Alexander, interview.
91. Executive, 16 January; 6 March 1970, AGM, 23-25 March 1970.
92. Sister Mary Frances to the editor, *OECTA News and Views*, June 1970.

93. AGM, 23-25 March 1970.
94. Ibid., 14-16 April 1966; Executive, 2 May, 5 June 1970.
95. Ibid., 9-10 February 1962.
96. Executive, 12 March, 14 May, 10 September 1966; 8-9 April 1967; AGM, 14-16 April 1966; Board of Directors, 23-24 February 1968.
97. *OECTA Review* (March 1970), 64.
98. AGM, 31 March-1 April 1964; 20-21 April 1965; Board of Directors, 6 January 1962; 5 January 1963; 8-9 December 1967; Executive, 26 April, 9 June 1962; 13 June 1964.
99. AGM, 24-25 April 1962.
100. Executive, 5 January 1965.
101. AGM, 14-16 April 1966.
102. Ibid., 28-31 March 1967; John Kuchinak, interview, Etobicoke, 9 July 1993.
103. Executive, 5-6 March 1971.
104. Board of Directors, 23-24 February 1968; Executive, 7-8 March 1968; AGM, 20-22 March 1968.
105. Ibid., 24-25 April 1962.
106. Ibid., 19-21 March 1969.
107. Board of Directors, 19 April, 18 September 1965.
108. AGM, 24-25 April 1962.
109. Executive, 5 January 1965; 30 May, 6-7 November 1970; 27-28 May 1971.
110. Jacques Schryburt, AEFO, interview, Ottawa, 11 May 1993; Bill Jones, STO, interview, Toronto, 11 May 1993; Florence Henderson, FWTAO, interview, Sault Ste. Marie, 11 May 1993; Harold Pinkerton, OPSMTF, interview, Toronto, 11 May 1993.
111. O'Neill, interview.
112. Executive, 11 September 1965; 2-3 December 1966; 5-6 February 1971; AGM, 22-24 March 1971.
113. AGM, 20-22 March 1968; 19-21 March 1969.
114. Board of Directors, 5 January 1963; Executive, 15-16 January 1971.
115. Board of Directors, 6 January 1962; AGM, 28-31 March 1967.
116. Board of Directors, 19 September 1969.
117. Executive, 4-5 October 1968.
118. Cecilia Rowan to the OTF Commission, undated, stamped received March 1967, OTF Archives.
119. AGM, 24-25 April 1962; 20-22 March 1968; Executive, 15 October 1966.
120. Board of Directors, 19 September 1969; Sister Aloysia Zimmer, interview, Kitchener, 19 April 1993..
121. Executive, 14 January 1967; Coo, *Forty Years*, 43-44; OTF/FEO, *We the Teachers of Ontario*, Toronto: The Ontario Teachers' Federation, 1992, 44.
122. Ontario English Catholic Teachers' Association Handbook, 1992/93, 3.

123. Walker, *Catholic Education*, Vol. III, 112-14; Board of Directors, 15 April 1963; Catholic Trustee (September 1967), 26-29.
124. Ibid. (November 1962), 8-13; Walker, *Catholic Education*, Vol. III, 174.
125. Executive, 14 September 1962; 19 August 1963; Conway, interview, Ottawa, 23 April 1993; *Canadian Register*, 2 March 1963, 1, 3.
126. O'Brien, interview. *Canadian Register*, 23 January 1965, 1, 6, 8; 22 January 1966, 1, 2.
127. File 0136, 1967, OECTAA; Executive, 14 October 1967.
128. Files 0098 and 0129, 1962, OECTAA.
129. Board of Directors, 12 September 1964; AGM, 24-25 April 1962; 12-14 April 1966.
130. Board of Directors, 15 January 1966; files 0098 and 0129, OECTAA.
131. Babcock, interview, Toronto, June 1993.
132. O'Neill, interview.
133. Executive, 6 March 1970; Claudette Foisy-Moon, interview, Toronto, 25 May 1993; Sr. Sheila McAuliffe, C.N.D., interview, Toronto, 22 May 1993; Chris Asseff, interview, Thornhill, 18 July 1993.
134. Executive, 10 May 1969; file 168, 1969, OECTAA; Foisy-Moon, interview.
135. Walker, *Catholic Education*, Vol. III, 188; Kuchinak, interview, 2 April 1993; McAuliffe, interview; Executive, 5-6 March 1971.
136. Coo, *Forty Years*, 69-71; Executive, 6-7 November 1970.
137. McAuliffe, interview; Foisy-Moon, interview.
138. Ibid.; Board of Directors, 12-13 February 1971; *Canadian Register*, 11 July 1970, 9.
139. Walker, *Catholic Education*, Vol. III, 174.
140. Board of Directors, 19 September 1969; Executive, 8 September 1963; 11 March 1967; 7-8 March 1969; AGM, 24-25 April 1962; 16-17 April 1963.
141. Executive, 19 August 1963.
142. J. Keiller Mackay, *Religious Information and Moral Development*, Toronto: Queen's Printer, 1966.
143. Board of Directors, 21-22 February 1969.
144. Dr. J. M. Bennett, "Character Education," *Canadian School Journal* (June 1938), 202-205.
145. Jacques Maritain, *Education at the Crossroads* (New Haven and London: Yale University Press, 1943), 14, 15, 17.
146. *OECTA News and Views*, (October 1955), 10-13. See also AGM, 14-17 April 1952.
147. Ibid., 6-9 April 1953.
148. File 0129, 1962, OECTAA.
149. *OECTA News and Views* (March 1961), 3.
150. AGM, 24-25 April 1962.
151. Board of Directors, 15 January 1966.
152. Fr. J. Geary, "The Hall-Dennis Original Sin," *OECTA Review* (March

1970), 22-27.
153. Prof. James Daly, McMaster University, "The Crisis in Education Today," *OECTA Review* (May 1970), 24-30.
154. James Daly, *Education or Molasses? A Critical Look at the Hall-Dennis Report* (Hamilton: McMaster University, 1969), 20, 54-55.
155. AGM, 24-25 April 1962; Board of Directors, 5 January 1963; 30 March 1964; Executive, 9-10 February 1962.
156. Ibid., 7 November 1963; 8 February 1964; 5 January, 13 February, 13 March 1965; AGM 31 March-1 April 1964; Board of Directors, 18 September 1965; 31 May 1969.
157. Walker, *Catholic Education*, Vol. III, 281-84.
158. "Brief Presented to the Prime Minister of Ontario and to the Members of the Legislative Assembly by the Catholic Bishops of Ontario," October 1962, AAT.
159. Walker, *Catholic Education*, Vol. III, 121, 279.
160. *Canadian Register*, 2 March 1963, 1, 3; J. McKenna, Q.C., "The School Bag," Catholic Trustee (August 1962), 7-8.
161. Board of Directors, 5 January, 9 February, 15 April 1963.
162. Dixon, "Ontario Separate School System," 308-12, 314-18, 321-23; *Canadian Register*, 30 October 1965, 1.
163. *Catholic Trustee* (March 1965), 11.
164. Mrs. Anne Abbott, daughter of E.J. Brisbois, interview, Toronto, 24 May 1993; E.J. Brisbois, "Comment on Report of Provincial Committee on the Aims and Objectives of Education in Ontario," *Catholic Trustee* (August 1968), 15-16.
165. *Canadian Register*, 22 January 1966, 1-2.
166. Walker, *Catholic Education*, Vol. III, 293; *Canadian Register*, 10 December 1966, 1.
167. Executive, 13 February, 16 October, 11 November 1965.
168. Hall-Dennis, *Living and Learning*, 83, 161.
169. Fr. Carl J. Matthews, S.J., "English Catholic High Schools in Ontario. 1968-69," *OECTA Review* (December 1968), 52-54.
170. AGM, 28-31 March 1967.
171. Nelligan, interview.
172. *Handbook*, 3; AGM, 22-24 March 1968; Executive, 2 December 1967.
173. Ibid.; Walker, *Catholic Education*, Vol. III, 308.
174. Nelligan, interview; Kavanagh, interview, Toronto, 15 June 1993; Saundra McKay (now Glynn), interview, Mississauga, 8 May, 24 July 1993; Asseff, interview; Walker, *Catholic Education*, Vol. III, 293.
175. Executive, 16-17 August, 4-5 October 1968; McKay, interview.
176. *Canadian Register*, 30 March 1968; AGM, 22-24 March 1968; Flynn, interview.
177. Nelligan, interview; Kavanagh, interview; McKay, interview; Executive, 6-7 December 1968.

178. Ibid, 17 August 1969.
179. Board of Directors, 31 May 1969; Nelligan, interview.
180. Ontario Separate School Trustees' Association, *Equal Opportunity for Continuous Education in Separate Schools of Ontario*, Toronto, 1969, 5-7.
181. Stamp, *Schools of Ontario*, 211-13.
182. Board of Directors, 12-13 December 1969; AGM, 23-25 March 1970; *OECTA News and Views* (March 1969); *Canadian Register*, 25 October 1969, 6; Fleming, *Administrative structure*, 165-78; Walker, *Catholic Education*, Vol. III, 343-44.
183. The Gardens hold about 20 000 people and it was full. There were more students in the street. The police estimated the total at 30 000, according to Ned Lynas, an OECTA writer.
184. Ibid., 346; Executive, 7-8 March 1969; 11-12 September 1970; *OECTA News and Views* (November 1970); Board of Directors, 12-13 December 1969; *Canadian Register*, 3 May 1969, 8; AGM, 19-21 March 1969.
185. Executive, 5-6 February 1971; Flynn, interview.
186. Board of Directors, 13-14 February, 30 May 1970.
187. "Excerpts from Premier Davis's Response to *Equal Opportunity for Continuous Education in Separate Schools*," Historical Document H13A, *Completion...?*, Toronto: OECTA, 1975.
188. Leo XIII, encyclical letter "Rerum Novarum": AAS 23 (1890-91); Pius XI, encyclical letter "Quadragesimo Anno": AAS 23 (1931).
189. John XXIII, encyclical letter "Mater et Magistra": AAS 35 (1961); *Canadian Register*, 22 July 1961, 3; 2 August 1961, 1, 11-14.
190. John XXIII, encyclical letter "Pacem in Terris": AAS 55 (1963).
191. "Decree on the Apostolate of the Laity," Abbott, ed., *Documents of Vatican II*, 498.
192. *Canadian Register*, 22 July 1961, 1, 3; 2 August 1961, 1, 11-14; 21 October 1961, 3; 2 November 1962, 3; 20 April 1963, 1, 3; 11 April 1964, 3.
193. *Handbook*, 3.
194. Michael Ryan, *Solidarity, Christian Social Teaching and Canadian Society*, London: The Divine Word International Centre of Religious Education, 1986, 15-16.
195. AGM, 24-25 April 1962.
196. *Canadian Register*, 4 July 1964, 1; 31 May 1969, 1; Executive, 27 March, 14 October 1967; 12-13 January 1968; 2 October 1970; Board of Directors, 13-14 February 1970; O'Neill, interview.
197. Executive, 10-11 June 1967; 7-8 June 1968; 7-8 March 1969; AGM, 28-31 March 1967; *OECTA Review* (December 1967), 34-38.
198. *Catholic Trustee* (November 1968), 34-35; O'Neill, interview.
199. *Catholic Trustee* (March 1971), 13-14.
200. Executive, 14 August, 8 September, 7 November 1963; 26 May 1965; 27 March 1967; 2 October 1970; Board of Directors, 12 September 1964.
201. Executive, 7-8 April 1967.

202. Ibid., 5-6 February 1971; Board of Directors, 13-14 February 1970.
203. John Rodriguez, interviews, Ottawa, 19 April, 28 November 1993.
204. Board of Directors, 23-24 February 1968.
205. *Canadian Register*, 31 August 1968, 8; Coo, *Forty Years*, 65.
206. AGM, 19-21 March 1969.
207. *OECTA Review* (March 1969), 7, 58.
208. McKay, Glynn, interview; Kavanagh, interview; Kuchinak, interview; Rodriguez, interview.
209. *National Catholic Reporter*, 7 May 1993, 5.
210. Board of Directors, 21-22 February 1969; Conway, interview.
211. M. Lynch, "Report of Committee to Survey the District Boundaries," Board of Directors, 23 April 1962.
212. Earl M. Hyman, "Ontario English Catholic Teachers' Association Report on Organization," Toronto: Edward N. Hay Associates of Canada Ltd., March, 1970.
213. Foisy-Moon, interview.
214. McAuliffe, interview.
215. Alexander, interview.
216. O'Neill, interview.
217. Mrs. Mary Ellen Carey, interview, Toronto, 8 June 1993.
218. Mrs. Helen McLaughlin, interview, Toronto, 20 April 1993; Sr. Consolata, I.B.V.M., interview, Toronto, 21 April 1993; *OECTA Review* (June 1965), 19; (October 1968), 20, 41; Board of Directors, 21-22 February 1969.
219. AGM, 31 March-1 April 1964; 29-31 April 1967; Executive, 11 March 1967; 19-20 April, 10 May, 7-8 June 1969, 2 May, 6-7 November 1970; 8 May 1971; Flynn, interview; Board of Directors, 31 May 1969.
220. Ibid., 15 April 1963; AGM, 24-25 April 1962.
221. AGM, 27 May 1965.
222. Ibid., 12-14 April 1966.
223. Ibid.; Executive, 10-11 February 1967; AGM, 20-22 March 1968.
224. Alexander, interview; Board of Directors, 14 September 1968.
225. File 0108, OECTAA.
226. Executive, 19 November 1967.
227. Board of Directors, 23 April 1962; 31 May 1969; Executive, 7 January 1966.
228. Ibid., 11-12 September 1965; AGM, 29-31 April 1967; "Brief Submitted to the Ontario Teachers' Federation Commission on the Structure and Function of The Ontario Teachers' Federation," 23 March 1967, OTFA.
229. Alexander, interview.
230. AGM, 23-25 March 1970.
231. Coo, *Forty Years*, 67.
232. Cecilia Rowan to the OTF Commission.
233. Board of Directors, 19 September 1969.
234. Ontario Public School Men Teachers' Federation, "A Brief," 1 April

1967, OTFA.

235. *Living and Learning*, 140.

236. "Brief of the Association des Enseignants franco-ontariens to the Ontario Teachers' Federation," June 1967, OTFA.

237. "Brief Submitted to the Ontario Teachers' Federation Commission on the Structure and Function of the Ontario Teachers' Federation," 23 March 1967, OTFA.

238. "Brief to the Ontario Teachers' Federation Commission from the Executive of FWTAO" n.d.; "A Brief to the Ontario Teachers' Federation Commission from the Ontario Secondary School Teachers' Federation," December 1966, OTFA.

239. J. Rodriguez to the OTF Commission, 23 March 1967, OTFA.

240. Judith Freeman, "The Day the 60s Died," *The New York Times Book Review*, 18 July 1993, 6.

241. FWTAO, "The Professional Association," n.d., 98, OTFA.

242. O'Neill, interview.

243. Jim O'Leary, interview, Brantford, 1 April 1993; Babcock, interview; Archives, Christian Brothers, O'Connor House, Toronto.

244. OECTA Annual Dinner, 1975, OECTAA.

245. AGM, 31 March-1 April 1964.

246. OECTA Annual Dinner, 1975.

247. Lorne Lawson, interview, Alexandria, 2 April 1993; Ottawa RCSS Board personnel records; Executive, 14 September 1962; Board of Directors, 15 January 1966; OECTA Review (June 1968), 21-22.

248. Sr. Frances McCann, interview, Kingston, 6 April 1993.

249. Mrs. Bohren, interview, Blind River, April 1993; Director-General History, Department of National Defence.

250. Orders of sisters teaching in Ontario were the Institute of the Blessed Virgin Mary, the Grey Sisters of the Immaculate Conception, the Faithful Companions of Jesus, the Felician Sisters, the Ursulines, the Dominican Sisters, the Daughters of Wisdom, the Sisters of the Congregation of St. John the Baptist, the Sisters of Charity, the Sisters of the Holy Name of Jesus and Mary, the Sister Servants of Mary Immaculate, the Sisters of St. Martha, the Holy Cross Sisters, the Congregation of Notre Dame, the Sisters of Providence, and the Sisters of St. Joseph. Orders of priests and brothers were the Irish Christian Brothers, the Christian Brothers of de la Salle, the Brothers of St. Louis, the Marianists, the Resurrectionist Fathers, the Basilian Fathers, the Holy Cross Fathers, the Holy Ghost Fathers, the Jesuits, the Oblate Fathers of Mary Immaculate, and the Order of St. Basil the Great., AAT.

251. Sr. Aloysia Zimmer, interview; Coo, *Forty Years*, 64.

252. Miss Ruth Willis, interview, Windsor, 1 April 1993; Kuchinak, interview.

253. Rodriguez, interviews; Conway, interview; Mary Babcock, interview, 9 June 1993.

254. Kuchinak, interview. OECTA *Reporter* (October 1979), 20.

255. Mrs. Marie Kennedy, interview, Merrickville, Ontario, 13 April 1993.
256. Babcock, interview, 13 June 1993; Foisy-Moon, interview; Douglas Knott, interview, Toronto, 10 May 1993; McAuliffe, interview; Rodriguez, interview; *OECTA News and Views*, April 1973, 1.

CHAPTER SEVEN

OECTA: PROFESSIONAL ASSOCIATION AND/OR UNION? 1965–1975

Every organization has a rationale for existence failing which it ceases to be. Obstacles placed in one's path can be stressful, distasteful or perhaps unnerving. The same obstacles may be walls which block progress but if the walls are viewed as Emerson observed, that "every wall is a door,, the obstacles can strengthen one's resolve and urge one to purposeful action.[1]

Background to the seventies. Simplistically speaking, the 1960s were the boom years, marked by a strong economy, optimism, expanding school systems, positive and growing psychological and financial support for education, higher salaries for the teaching profession, a progressive Hall-Dennis Report, and new educational programmes. The 1970s represented in many ways a mirror image of the vibrant 1960s. They were an age of decline in the economy, the birth rate, and the funding of education.

The Funding of Education. In March 1969 the provincial treasurer, Charles MacNaughton, called for restraint in education spending and hinted at provincial compulsion if the school boards did not comply. In November Bill 228 gave the Minister of Education the authority to fix the amount to which a school board could raise the local levy. A year later William Davis announced the first budget ceilings to take effect in 1971.[2]

But the timing of all this made things difficult for boards. County and district school boards had just come into existence, January 1, 1969, to the tune of high expectations for equality of educational opportunity. Unfortunately, the Ministry of Education did not seem to have anticipated just how far the rural parts of the counties and districts were behind the urban parts with regard to facilities, salary schedules, programmes, and instructional supplies. One- and two-room schools by the hundreds were closed and, consequently, new schools, additions, and renovations put in the budget. Appreciable numbers of teachers received 20, 30, or even 40 per cent increases in salaries to make them consistent with the urban wages; previously, some rural school boards were not recognizing experience or qualifications adequately or at all. The new directors of education and trustees conscientiously and sometimes enthusiastically extended kindergartens, gymnasia, libraries, special education staff, and programmes, and specialized staff in such subjects as music and physical education throughout these new, larger units of administration. In some jurisdictions all this took place in a fiscal situation where the pre-1969 school boards had deficit financed in order to hurriedly finance new facilities and programmes for their schools before they were merged into the new large board. Suddenly, in an economic downturn, made more complex by the phenomenon of "stagflation," parental expectations and school boards' plans had to be adjusted to "recognized ordinary and extraordinary expenditures" set at 110 per cent, then 115 per cent, of the previous year's spending.[3] This ushered in a decade of most school boards' exceeding the ceilings and, consequently, putting 100 per cent of the excess on the taxpayers. This was particularly burdensome for the separate school boards and other boards with limited corporate assessment. In turn, these jumps in the mill rate had a dampening effect on the enthusiasm of the ratepayers for supporting educational expenditures.

Declining Enrolment. Since much of the provincial grant revenues are linked to the average daily enrolment of the students, the decline in births made matters more difficult for those designing the school board's budget. In the words of Mary Labatt in a recent history of the FWTAO, "The early 1960s was a momentous period for women because the birth control pill became available, an event that revolutionized women's lives by giving them a better chance to plan childbearing."[4] In the late 1960s the Canadian Catholic Bishops endorsed the position that Pope Paul VI's statement in his encyclical *Humanae Vitae* that every act of sexual intercourse had to be open to the possibility of life was an ideal; it was to be taken seriously, but applied to one's particular situation and with an informed conscience. By the early 1970s the decline in enrolment in public and separate schools had begun. It would become such a problem for the school system that the Ministry would appoint the Jackson Commission on Declining

Enrolment in 1977. Thomas Wells at that time predicted that in an eight-year period, the secondary school enrolment would shrink by almost one-fifth and that the decline in the elementary school enrolment would be about 212 000.[5] The decline in immigration during the decade eliminated any mediating effect on the drop in the number of pupils.

Results of the Retrenchment. Many of the results from the above could have been predicted. Some of them were the following:

- a demand for cost controls: the federal government legislated into existence wage control guidelines and the Anti-Inflation Board which restricted salary increases for 1975 to 1977;
- after the federal controls came off, a number of provinces, including Ontario, also enacted wage controls; the contracts of the Quebec and British Columbia teachers were opened and their salaries rolled back (a precedent perhaps noted by Premier Rae when he proposed a "social contract" in 1993);
- a drop from 61.5 per cent in 1975 to 58 per cent in 1976 in the level of provincial proportion of the educational expenditures, a trend that would continue until reaching the present level of about 40 per cent;[6]
- an accompanying cry for prioritizing of educational objectives: the Ministry, trustees, and school administrators began using such terms as management by objectives, accountability, and justification; the government moved toward a secondary school core curriculum, initiating in its curriculum policy document *Ontario Schools: Intermediate Senior* (OSIS) compulsory credits;
- a dissatisfaction with education expressed in the media: editorials blamed the school system for high unemployment, strikes, stagflation, pollution, heavy traffic, the shortage and high price of housing, drugs, crime, terrorism, high oil prices, the shortage of technical workers, and overeducated unemployed graduates;
- a decrying of the lack of rigour and discipline in the progressive schools and of the drop-out rate in the high schools; OISE's analysis of the credit system, OSSTF's "At What Cost?", the *Interface* studies of Queen's University Alan King, and other studies pointed to a serious problem with the general level courses and the high school students taking them;

> • the ignoring of the recommendation in Dr. Jackson's Report on Declining Enrolment that one solution for the teacher surplus was to lower the pupil-teacher ratio (PTR);
> • conflict in contract negotiating between teachers and trustees — all of the items above made it more arduous for the teachers to improve their salaries and working conditions; at the same time, the public's
> expectations of their performance were higher because of the individualization of programming preached in the Ministry's curriculum documents, because of the expanding curriculum in social sciences,
> sciences, and health, and because of the integration of the child with learning difficulties into the regular classroom.[7]

Collective Agreements. In 1944 Premier George Drew promised the *Teaching Profession Act*, but one of the conditions was that the teachers never ask for the right to strike. In 1975 *The School Boards and Teachers Collective Negotiations Act* defined the term "strike" and specified under what conditions a strike could take place.[8] What brought about this historic change?

The Background to Bill 100. Bryan M. Downie, in his *Collective Bargaining and Conflict Resolution in Education: the Evolution of Public Policy in Ontario* has chronicled the involvement of OSSTF in the events leading up to Bill 100.[9] The following actions will detail OECTA's contributions to the collective bargaining.

Downie described the environment in which OECTA and other affiliates were negotiating with trustees between 1965 and 1975.
The factors contributing to conflict were the following.

> • A rapidly changing educational system. The Hall-Dennis Report resulted in expectations that classroom teachers use individualized and small-group instruction, pay attention to the needs of special education pupils, use a multi-textbook and audio-visual approach, and organize pupil learning on a continuous-progress basis. Teacher negotiators began to seek a lower pupil-teacher ratio.
> • A social climate conducive to teacher militancy. All authority, including, of course, school boards, was being held up to scrutiny and questioning. In the separate school the questioning of past practices fostered by Vatican II carried over into traditional teacher-trustee

relations. As early as 1961 and 1962 the *Canadian Register* covered in detail the commemoration of the seventieth anniversary of "Rerum Novarum", the Canadian Catholic Bishops' Conference in Halifax (1961), and the Regional Social Life Conference in Windsor (1962). Governments were urged to enact legislation which would "amend regulations that are made with a view to keeping [citizens] weak,"[10] which would compel bargaining conditions of work, and which would provide arbitration, conciliation, and strike procedures. The Bishops even suggested summer courses in social doctrine for teachers and a primary school curriculum that would teach that "strikes may be and usually are justified."[11]

• The larger units of administration. In 1965 township school areas amalgamated public school boards in rural Ontario. In 1969 the local public and separate boards became, with the exception of the isolate boards, part of the new county or district school boards. This had an obvious distancing effect on teacher-trustee relationships, which facilitated aggressive bargaining, misunderstandings and, sometimes, hostility.

• Teacher militancy. The growing presence of a more educated teaching profession advancing up the category system, of young female teachers asserting their right to have a permanent career in teaching regardless of their marital status, of young male teachers seeking a lifetime career in the separate schools and of teachers from England, Ireland and Scotland with a labour background had a large effect on attitudes to negotiating with school boards and to the use of sanctions, especially the strike. Ontario's teachers also were observing teacher strikes in New York in 1968.[12]

This last point had particular application to OECTA. In historical interpretation individuals and the force of movements are often perceived as interacting. In the case of OECTA it is my belief that certain leaders with a commonality of beliefs had a maximum influence on Bill 100 with its right to strike.

OTF until 1973 and OECTA until 1971 supported Policy 14(11) of OTF. It stated:

> That the OTF regards refusal of teachers to carry out the duties defined by the resolutions of the Schools Act during the term of their contracts as strike action on the part of its members and deems such to be:

(a) breach of contract, and
(b) contrary to the professional obligations of a teacher, and, therefore, such strike action on the part of any group of members shall be considered unprofessional conduct and shall be treated in the same way as breach of contract by an individual member.[13]

Serious questioning of this policy in OECTA began long before Bill 100. In 1962 the AGM was not held at the Royal York Hotel, the traditional location, because of a staff strike there.[14] With the arrival of John Rodriguez on the Executive and Board of Directors after the mid-1960s, discussions of the right to strike appeared in the minutes. He, Elie Martel, and Karl Bohren were asked to follow an OTF study committee's deliberation on compulsory arbitration, the union movement, and all aspects of collective bargaining; in the fall of 1966 Bohren was appointed to this committee. Later, when Rodriguez would discover OTF's opposition to the concept of the teacher strike, he would resign from its salary negotiating committee.[15] When striking teachers in Montreal in 1967 asked for support from CTF, it was a matter of some frustration for the OECTA Executive that it could not act against OTF policy and send money.[16]

If teacher militancy is defined as public demonstrations and open debates about working to rule or withdrawing services, then the phenomenon first appeared in the Essex-Windsor area, home of the Chrysler and Ford plants, where a significant proportion of the working population were members of the United Automobile Workers union. The Leamington teacher demonstration was discussed above. Windsor became a focal point for a sanction debate in 1965 and 1966. Tom Taylor, chairman of the Salary Negotiations Committee, and John Macdonald were the principal advocates of more determined forceful negotiating, to such an extent that Sr. Mary Leo wrote Mary Babcock expressing concern about the Windsor negotiators considering a walkout: "We do not feel that this group is complying with OECTA policy....Do we belong to a labour union?"[17] Miss Babcock, aware that the Windsor teachers were asking for salary parity with the lay teachers for the religious teachers and for a salary schedule higher than the OECTA provincial scale, answered carefully, yet with a qualified blessing for the initiative of a walkout: "Regarding the possibility of a 'walkout',...this would not be supported by the Provincial Association unless a very large majority of the teachers supported it and unless the Executive was convinced that the requests of the local committee were reasonable and within the ability of the Board to pay."[18]

By the following year the Board of Directors and the Windsor Unit were on a collision course. Windsor was complaining about lack of central office support and about the Executive's dictating what the district could and could not do; Karl Bohren had found rumours from Windsor of general sick leave and strike action "disturbing"; the Board of Directors asked Tom Taylor and others to attend its meeting to discuss Windsor's contract demands. The debate carried over to the 1966 AGM. Matters were reconciled, but the discussions revealed how attitudes were changing. The real issue was whether or not OECTA would support the Windsor teachers if they went on "strike" (that is, a walkout).

The Windsor teachers had rejected the board's offer and considered four options:

(1) calling in the Association;
(2) mass resignation;
(3) a walkout by using sick days; and
(4) a general walkout.

Their lawyer advised that the school board would not have to rehire all the teachers or give credit for experience over five years with option 2, that it could demand doctors' certificates for option 3, and that option 4 was illegal, against OTF and OECTA policy and risky as far as the teachers' certificates were concerned. The teachers voted 426 to 60 in favour of walking out; there were four abstentions; 95 per cent of the teachers were present. The AGM motion that it was in sympathy with Windsor's intentions passed 109 to 100 and, on a recount, 109 to 103. Fr. Conway's motion that the Association go on record as being opposed to a walkout was tabled. These minutes revealed a membership far from unanimity, but a growing number of delegates in favour of the strike, a number that would continue to increase in the next nine years.

The arguments for and against were mostly a repeat of those put forward in western Canada earlier in the century. George Matys stated that strikes meant unions and the labouring class and that unions were for workers, not for professionals: "We've struggled for professional status; be professional or go down into the labour rank." Taylor regarded work to rule as "deceitful." On the other side, Tim Blackburn and Kaye Garvey quoted Puis XI on social justice, Pius XII on protection of the worker, and John XXIII on the proper wage and the dignity of the worker. By analysing "Rerum Novarum" and "Quadriagesimo

Anno", they posited that a strike was morally justified, if, firstly, there was a just cause stemming from all negotiations' having failed; secondly, there was no violation of a free contract; thirdly, there was a probability of success; and, fourthly, the good achieved would be at least equal to the evil done. Fr. Conway reminded the delegates that OTF would likely oppose compulsory arbitration. Fr. Fogarty summed up the feelings of many of the non-militant delegates:

> This is a decisive moment in our history. The fact that this action has been taken without recourse to a request for assistance to the OECTA executive is regrettable and may lead to serious problems. I would have wished that the Windsor teachers had not voted for a walk-out, but since they have, I think some means should be found to assure them of our support within our present constitution.[19]

The stage was set for consideration of sanctions by other teacher negotiating teams. In 1968 the St. Catharines teachers withdrew their extracurricular activities. In 1969, 670 out of 732 teachers in Windsor resigned on May 26, demanding a 10 per cent increase in staffing in order to provide release time for planning. In 1970 the county and district boards, more organized and unified than ever before, held the line on salary increases and refused to negotiate working conditions. The Teacher Welfare department and the teachers picketed the Hastings-Prince Edward County RCSS Board at a motel breakfast. The Waterloo County RCSS Board's teachers demonstrated at the board office. Provincial takeovers by OECTA became necessary in Windsor, Nipigon-Red Rock, Wellington, Ottawa, and the North Shore.[20]

Again in 1970 the debate over OTF policy on striking surfaced. Douglas Knott, Johanne Stewart, and Bill Currie, negotiators for the MSSB teachers, were getting nowhere trying to win a PTR clause and were considering a one-day walkout. The Executive could not support the idea and referred the issue to an emergency meeting of the Board of Directors. It too had difficulties. Just the year before, it had tabled a motion that asked for compulsory arbitration since strikes and mass resignations were distasteful to teachers and harmful to the pupils.

Because of the importance of this meeting of the Directors, the OTF executive were invited to observe and comment. OTF had not changed its position. Br. Lapointe, its president, urged the MSSB negotiators to weigh the effect of such action on students, the atmosphere in the schools, and public opinion. He asked what would happen if the tactic did not work. Nora Hodgins, the secretary-treasurer, reminded

OECTA that, "We have not the right to strike. OECTA joined OTF in 1944 rather than a labour organization." The legal opinion was repeated that a walkout was a breach of contract.

Bill Currie put the case for the other side succinctly and strongly: "Most of the OECTA and OTF Handbooks appear as if they were written by the trustees;...our teachers voted 89 per cent in favour of your sanctioning this move that many of you feel is unprofessional." The convictions of the largest Unit in OECTA, led by the influential spokespersons Knott, Stewart, and Currie, had a strong impact on the Board of Directors. It felt unable to sanction the walkout, but did pink-list the MSSB, sought mediation-arbitration through OSSTA and, most significantly, asked OTF to rescind its policy on striking.[21]

Meanwhile, negotiations throughout the province with all the affiliates were going so slowly that OTF in August 1970 suggested that it and OSTC reach a short-term agreement on procedures for the following year and investigate jointly possibilities for a long-term solution. OSTC was suggesting a provincial commission.[22] OECTA, becoming more and more aware of the ineffectiveness of pink-listing and mass resignations in a situation where there was an impending teacher surplus and where the trustees were refusing to negotiate "working conditions" (and sometimes to bargain at all), began to see the need for legislation that would give the right to teachers to negotiate and to withdraw services where necessary. It was all very well for OTF to list seventy "teacher rights," which included compassionate leave, a copy for the teacher of a performance evaluation, consultation before transfers or school placements, sabbatical leave, cumulative sick leave, participation in the setting of the board's budget, planning time, in-service during school hours, a reasonable class size, sufficient learning materials, consultation before being assigned to a timetable, and involvement in determining curriculum, programs, and reporting to parents.[23] But how were teacher negotiators to convince trustees to discuss working conditions? The motion at the 1970 AGM "that teachers across the province offer special prayers asking God for Divine Help to solve the problem in Hastings-Prince Edward County"[24] (carried) was reminiscent in Bolt's *A Man for All Seasons* of Sir Thomas More's response to Cardinal Wolsey's dilemma over King Henry VIII's desire to divorce. He said he would pray. Wolsey replied by all means pray, but God helps those who help themselves. In 1971 OECTA began to help itself, as well as, of course, praying.

The Minister of Education beginning in June 1970 felt it necessary to introduce some order into the growing disarray in teacher-board negotiating. Davis did succeed in getting an agreement from OTF and OSTC to use a five-step process from September 1970 to August 1971: local negotiating, provincial associations assisting, conciliator appointed to assist in arriving at a settlement within thirty days, OTF meeting with OSTC with sanctions of pink-listing and mass resignation possible, and finally, where necessary, the appointment of a board of arbitration.[25] However, this process was likely doomed from the start. The trustees had been refusing to negotiate anything except salaries since 1969; actually, the trustees' reasoning on this issue could be considered almost Orwellian: "a matter is not in dispute if one party did not agree to talk about it in the first place."[26] OTF and OSTC were opposed to compulsory arbitration. OTF was adamant about negotiating working conditions. Such stands resulted in work to rule by high school teachers in the boards of education of Carleton, Frontenac, Sault Ste. Marie, Metropolitan Toronto, and Wentworth.[27]

Regarding this so-called agreement as only a short-term solution to the recurring impasses in negotiating, Davis in June announced that he would appoint a committee of one to make a long-term study and recommendations; in November he upped the committee to three members.[28]

By the end of November it was clear to Mary Babcock, Frank Griffin, and the Executive that it would be essential to expand the Teacher Welfare department in order to provide assistance to the units in bargaining and to research sufficiently to make submissions and responses to OTF, OSSTA, and the Ministry of Education. In 1971 OECTA hired Douglas Knott, in 1972 Peter Murphy, then Neil Doherty, and in 1975 Terry Mangan. Frank Griffin had considerable influence over the hiring of all four of them and, therefore, it should be no surprise to learn that these five men, together with Ed Alexander and Pat O'Neill hired previously, had a commonality of outlook that would have a paramount effect on the government's decision to give teachers the right to strike. Downie and Stamp perceived teachers from Great Britain as union members with a history of militancy and as young men who had lived through boom economies in which they wanted to share. Richard Townsend, an OISE professor, shortly after the Bill 100 events, described such teachers in OECTA as strong leaders with a tough, working-class background who were not afraid to fight their boards.[29] Peter Hennessy, in a research study for CTF in 1975, found that, although the great majority of teachers preferred non-militant methods, Catholic teachers scored highest on role deprivation and militancy and, having witnessed a "quiet revolution" in Catholic education and the secularization of the separate schools' administrators and teachers, had grown to expect the same rewards and status as all other teachers.[30] Charles McCaffray, an ex-president of OSSTF and in 1968 on contract with the Ministry, publicly expressed his opinion of militant teachers in such a negative fashion that OECTA felt compelled to respond to him in a letter that "we have many teachers from the British Isles as members;...we have found them in no way unprofessional."[31]

All of those opinions applied to some degree to Frank Griffin and his Teacher Welfare team.

Douglas Knott. The son of two cost accountants, William Knott and Margaret Freill, and brother of Sylvia, Douglas was born in Toronto. The family moved to Ottawa where he attended Corpus Christi school to the end of grade nine and St. Patrick's College for grades ten and eleven. The family then moved to Madoc where Doug went to Madoc High School for grade twelve. His high school experience had not been the smoothest. Doug decided that the Jesuits would instill self-discipline and went to boarding school at Regiopolis High School in Kingston. He then spent six years in the Jesuit Seminary at Guelph. His studies with the Jesuits took place at Loyola in Montreal, St. Mary in Halifax, and Gonzaga in Washington. During this time he was imbued with the principles of social justice for the working class, refugees, and the downtrodden.

In 1959 Doug Knott left the Jesuits and taught for one year on a letter of permission at St. Philip Neri, MSSB, then went to Lakeshore Teachers' College. At this point he married his first wife, a teacher, Martha McKinney; they were to have four children: Kieran, Moira, Kathleen, and Gemma. They moved to Windsor where Douglas taught in a mixed school, St. Jules, and finished his B.A. at the University of Windsor. Doug and his family returned to Toronto in 1963 and he taught at St. Francis Xavier. The next year he became principal of St. Gregory, then of St. Thomas Aquinas, and of D'Arcy McGee open-area school.

In Windsor Ruth Willis got Doug involved in salary negotiating. In Toronto he became a leader in this area, organizing teacher demonstrations, educating his fellow Association members on the need for collective bargaining legislation, and seeking legal opinions on the possibility of a one-day withdrawal of service of the elementary school teachers. As principal of D'Arcy McGee school he argued for formative rather than summative evaluation of teachers and, when compelled to evaluate staff summatively, ranked them all excellent. His superintendent, now Dr. Anthony Barone, director of education for the MSSB, disagreed with Doug's position, arguing that both board policy and fairness to the teachers who were excellent to a degree superior to that of other teachers on the staff required compliance with the practice of summative staff evaluation.

All of this brought Doug to the attention of Griffin and OECTA and in 1971 he was hired as coordinator of Teacher Welfare.

In this position Douglas Knott designed a five-year action plan to educate the teacher negotiators throughout the province on what salaries, working conditions, benefits, and rights they should be seeking. In addition, he would become very involved with speeches, writings, and briefs to the Ministry and various Commissions on collective bargaining legislation and existing collective agreements. He consciously decided not to be just a resource for unit negotiators, but to educate them through various means on what they should be seeking from their school boards.

In 1973 Douglas became deputy executive director (later deputy general secretary) replacing Frank Griffin who moved up to executive director. In this capacity he was a calm, analytical, and intelligent leader. In 1982 he received his M.Ed. from OISE. From 1978 to 1988 Doug was married to Teresa Riordan. In 1989 he retired. Since that time he has been an educational consultant, serving on Boards of Reference and grievance arbitration boards. His most recent work was as a senior sector advisor to the Broader Public Sector Relations Secretariat for the Ontario Government, recommending to the government revisions to *The School Boards and Teachers Collective Negotiations Act*. OTF made him a Fellow and OECTA awarded him with a life membership.[32]

Peter Anthony Murphy. Peter was hired in January 1972 to help meet the greatly expanding needs for assistance in bargaining at the unit level.

He was born in Derry, Northern Ireland. His father, Michael Murphy, was a headmaster, active in the National Association of School Masters, who received a Papal knighthood from Paul VI for his contribution to Catholic education in England. His mother, Winifred Sheridan, was a commercial artist, but died at Peter's birth. His father remarried; Peter's stepmother was Margaret McKeown, a teacher. His brothers, Sean and Stephen, and half-sister, Catherine, all became teachers.

Peter attended elementary school at St. Mary, Newcastle-under-Lynne and at his father's school, Holy Family, Coventry. His secondary school was the Vincentians' Ullathorne Grammar School. After high school Peter worked for one year as a laboratory assistant, then went to St. Mary's Teachers' College, Twickenham, Strawberry Hill, where he qualified to teach chemistry and the junior and intermediate divisions.

In 1967 Peter Murphy accepted by mail his first teaching position from the Terrace Bay Separate School Board. He acquired a grade five class at St. Martin and a wife, Paulette Boudreau, in the community. She had recently returned home from London where she had been dissatisfied with her office job. She planned to take a retraining course and enter the field of handicapped children, but, as she put it, married Peter instead, thereby carrying out her vocation in a similar way. They would have three children: Michele, Lizanne, and Sarah. A year later, Peter moved to North Bay where he taught at St. Alexander, then at St. Joseph, until he moved to the OECTA Toronto office.

With credits for seven academic university courses at Strawberry Hill, Peter completed his B.A. at Laurentian University, then continued to get his M.Ed. from OISE.

At St. Martin Peter took on a demanding OECTA task in his first year of teaching. The vice-principal mentioned in the staffroom that it was time to put together a salary proposal to go to the board. Peter volunteered and presented the package. In North Bay he continued his activity with OECTA affairs, becoming again a salary negotiating committee member, then a member of the Unit executive and the president. While there he also received an educational introduction to the new larger units of administration. When the Nipissing District RCSS Board came into existence on January 1, 1969, the trustees and administrative staff were not fully prepared. It was several weeks before the teachers received their proper salaries. In the interim the board sent out advances, the same amount to everyone. This, of course, caused problems for the experienced, well-qualified teachers, while the kindergarten teachers working half-time were being magnificently overpaid. Peter as vice-president helped organize a public meeting with appropriate refreshments, so that the press could hear about the staff's problems with the new board. Peter was always exasperated by those teachers who would tolerate conditions of general poverty, yet at the same time would consider themselves as professionals.

Some months later, Peter met a Strawberry Hill classmate, Pat O'Neill, at a school reunion, then again at a North Bay OECTA meeting. Pat told him about the additional staff member needed in the Teacher Welfare department. Peter responded to the advertisement and had a successful interview. The OECTA secretary processing the applicants that day said to Peter afterward that she knew he would be hired for the position because he was the only applicant who asked her for an expense form after his interview.

Peter Murphy still does much of his work in Teacher Welfare.[33]

Neil Francis Doherty. The other teacher to be hired in 1971 by OECTA was Neil. He was born in County Donegal, Carndonagh village, Republic of Ireland. His father, John Doherty, was a horse and cattle dealer; his mother, Mary Doherty (same last name before marriage), a homemaker. The family was large: five sisters - Marjorie, Anne, Maureen, Evelyn, and Eithna - and one brother, Edward. Neil went to St. Patrick elementary school and to St. Columbs College in Derry as a boarder twenty miles from home. Money was scarce; Neil worked at a pea-cannery in the summers and, upon completing high school, went to live with his sister, Marjorie, in Manchester and to work as an unqualified teacher of physical education, English, and history at St. Mary, Leigh, Lancashire. Because of a teacher shortage, Neil received a grant to attend the three-year course at Padgate Teachers' College near Warrington, Lancashire; he specialized in physical education and English. He returned to St. Mary's for two years to teach physical education full-time.

Aware of the higher salaries and teacher shortage in Toronto, he came to Canada in the summer of 1968 and was immediately hired by the MSSB and placed at St. Patrick to teach grade eight and physical education half-time on rotary. Noting the salary schedule with its categories, Neil, rated a standard two by the Ministry, began working on his B.A. at once and graduated from York University in 1971. For a short time he was a physical education resource teacher for the MSSB and was hired for the Teacher Welfare department in 1971.

In England Neil Doherty had been interested in his union, the National Association of Schoolmasters, and had negotiated salaries and lunch-duty clauses. In Toronto he very soon became the OECTA staff representative for St. Patrick and, when the Reville Commission called for briefs and presentations, he wrote a brief in early 1971 that the principal and staff signed. It was the only brief from a separate school and was also unique in asking for the right to strike before OTF or OECTA had taken an official position on the idea. He was also a mover of a successful motion at the 1971 AGM to advocate the strike as a legally permissible sanction. Neil would then become a key player in the mass demonstrations at Maple Leaf Gardens over Bills 274 and 275.

Neil remains in Teacher Welfare as a resource person in collective agreement matters for a number of units. In 1981 he married Kaija Ryynanen, a translator and currently a real estate agent; they have a three-year-old son, Sean Daniel.[34]

Terrence Felix Mangan. He was the last addition to Teacher Welfare in 1975. It was now possible for Doug Knott to coordinate efforts, assist in negotiating where necessary, and assign one-third of the units to each of Doherty, Murphy, and Mangan.

Terry was born in a farming family near Renfrew. His father, Felix Mangan, died when Terry was three, and his mother, Catherine Collins, raised him, the oldest, and his brother, Alfred, and two sisters, Mary and Felicia. Terry had an educational experience similar to Jim Carey's and not as common in the 1950s: he attended RCSS #3, Admaston, a one-room school for grades one to ten. There was a bus transporting students to the public high school in Renfrew, but it would not pick up those who wished to attend Bishop Ryan High School. Terry did get to this Christian Brothers' school for grades eleven to thirteen, challenging years for a student with such a limited schooling.

Due to illness in the family Terry stayed on the farm for two years, then went to Ottawa Teachers' College in 1964-65. His first teaching position was in grade three at Pope John XXIII school in Arnprior. He decided he should work near a university if he wanted to improve himself; therefore, he moved to the Ottawa Separate School Board to teach at St. Michael and to become vice-principal at St. Elizabeth. During this time he did realize his plans, getting a B.A. and an M.Ed., both from the University of Ottawa. In Ottawa Terry met and married Joanne Scime, a teacher. They have two children, David and James.

Terry's first formal encounter with OECTA was an invitation from his St. Michael's principal to attend the Unit meeting. He was promptly chosen as the staff representative and went on to serve as Unit treasurer, chief negotiator, and president. He was involved in two mass resignations in Ottawa. For the one-day provincial walkout by all affiliates on December 18, 1973, Terry Mangan helped organize a meeting of the Unit's teachers at the Ottawa Civic Centre from where they marched to the parliament buildings. Before the walkout Terry had a letter sent home to the Ottawa parents of the pupils in which he advised them to keep their children home because there would be no teachers at school the next day. About 97 per cent of the teachers from the Ottawa-Carleton-Renfrew-Cornwall areas did not report to classes. The school board was not amused; it passed a motion to advise Mr. Mangan that if he repeated such an action he would be fired.

Terry felt that he would never become a principal with the Ottawa board and considered options. After discussing with Doug Knott the still further expansion of the Teacher Welfare department, he watched for the advertisement, applied, and was hired in 1975. He worked in Teacher Welfare until 1989 when he competed successfully for the position of deputy general secretary.

Having worked under Bill 100 for almost twenty years, Terry has always believed that strikes are not desirable, but sometimes necessary. In a recent report on the 1993 social contract the president, Claire Ross, described Terry during the negotiations with the government as possessing "those essential qualities of insight, strength of will, reliability, deviousness, and shrewdness together with a rather admirable though perverse larcenous intent toward each and every proposal and proposition of the government." Considering the climate in which this assessment was made, this should be considered a compliment.[35]

The profiles of Alexander, Doherty, Griffin, Knott, Mangan, Murphy, and O'Neill revealed a number of commonalities relevant to the OECTA push for bargaining legislation. First of all, they were, with the exception of Griffin, young males, most of them in their twenties. All were energetic and ambitious, both to represent the special interests of the new growing male membership in 1970 and to leave their mark on the Association for the good of all the teachers. Secondly, four of the group had been educated in Ireland, Scotland, or England; a number of articles pointed out the sympathy for labour and its negotiating methods which such a background would develop. In addition to possessing a predisposition to be more militant than their fellow staff members educated in Ontario, they would find novel the attitude that regarded separate school facilities and staffs as inferior to public schools and deserving of a subordinate level of public funding; a willingness to accept from trustees a smaller salary in order to help their budgets and live out their vocation for the Church would, in the minds of this like-minded group, merely perpetuate the injustices the separate school system suffered at the hands of the government. Knott with his Jesuit training and Alexander with a union father agreed with this position and operated from principles of social justice. Thirdly, all, before coming on staff with OECTA, had confronted school boards directly and/or indirectly. With these six men as resources and leaders and with the direction of certain members of the Executive and Unit presidents, OECTA and its AGM delegates would move to a majority view that the government should provide negotiating and right-to-strike legislation.

The Reville Report. 1971 presented two major tasks for OECTA. The legislated ceilings increased the recognized ordinary expenditures of school boards by 10 per cent (later in the year raised to 15 per cent after board pressure) in a year when the new county and district boards were encountering cost items higher than anyone had anticipated and when teachers were still trying to catch up with inflation. Secondly, the Minister of Education had announced in November a committee of three to inquire into and report on the process of negotiations between teachers and school boards.[36] OECTA would have to prepare a position paper for OTF. OTF then compiled ideas from all the affiliates in its brief to the Commission.

OECTA had no difficulty reaching a decision about the necessity for a statute giving teachers the right to negotiate and about its opposition both to any limitation on what could be negotiated and to compulsory arbitration. What had to be determined was its position on the right to strike. After all, the debates over the actions of Windsor and MSSB teachers had revealed no clear majority on either side of the issue.

The results of a referendum on the right to strike were reported to the 1971 AGM. The school representatives had collected the individual teachers' votes in the province's separate schools. Rigorous controls were missing and the returns represented only 76.6 per cent of the teachers. Nevertheless, the inconclusive figures showed that the membership was still divided, but that there was a greater majority in favour of strike legislation than there had been in 1966 with the vote to support a walkout in Windsor. 6804 had voted in favour and 4642 against right-to-strike legislation for an overall result of 44.23 per cent of the total membership in favour.[37] At the AGM the motion "that OECTA advocate strike as a legally permissible sanction to be employed by teachers" was put to the floor. Doug Knott, regarded as a calm, most influential leader, stated that it was time. James Carey, an executive member, Neil Doherty, and other delegates supported the motion.

According to *OECTA News and Views*, it passed "overwhelmingly."[38] Doherty then went to the OSSTF AGM with this historic vote and conveyed to the provincial vice-president the news. OSSTF also passed a motion supporting the right to strike.

Meanwhile, the *OECTA News and Views* of February 1971 reported that OTF had voted twenty-three to eighteen against including the strike sanction in its brief to the Minister's Committee on Negotiating Procedures. The AEFO, FWTAO, and OPSMTF governors had voiced their opposition to the strike. Doherty, in an interview with the Toronto *Telegram*, attacked OTF for not consulting its total membership before voting, as OECTA had.[39] In a recent history of FWTAO Mary Labatt gave an interesting reason for its vote, one different from the traditional profession-versus-union argument. FWTAO regarded withdrawal of services as a breach of the individual contract that teachers had worked so hard in the 1930s to get.[40] Its position demonstrated a "remembrance of things past" which it would show again in the 1980s and 1990s Tomen Case.

Hennessy wrote that "the Catholic teachers of Ontario have taken to the barricades in advance of their colleagues."[41] This allusion to the French Revolution perhaps discomfited some OECTA members, but the Association would argue for the next year for a change in the OTF stand. Its submission to the Minister's Committee in 1971 was interesting. Although there was no OTF recommendation for strike legislation, there was some tortuous discussion of the concept.

> The denial of the strike to employees creates a desire for the right to strike. Legislative provision for strike leads to the fear that the sanction may be used indiscriminately. Even the most avid opponent of strike will concede that in extreme cases it may be the only remedy. Any denial of the right of employees to use sanctions unless there are overwhelming reasons for doing so, tends toward a creeping form of totalitarianism which denies the employee many of his rights as a citizen.[42]

This quotation with its almost self-contradictory ambiguity showed the governors arguing with themselves toward the right to strike. It should not have been surprising to the teachers that the Committee Report would not recommend strike legislation.

On the other hand, the brief from the staff of St. Patrick, MSSB, was quite clear. It was signed by Neil Doherty, the staff representative, Camilla Kelly, then a Sister of St. Joseph and daughter of a union movie projectionist, and sixteen teachers. It made the following points.

The teacher surplus had made the two parties unequal in power; mass resignation was no longer a bargaining weapon, but an exercise in "brinkmanship pure and simple and leaves teachers at the mercy of school boards." The right to strike was recognized as an "inalienable right of a free people." Without it school boards could reject the teachers' "suggestions" without "fear of reprisal." To compare teachers with doctors, lawyers, and dentists as an argument against the right to strike for teachers was inapplicable because those three groups did not have a common employer. As for the essential-service argument, the Canadian Union of Public Employees had the power to close a school. In expressing its opposition to mandatory arbitration, the brief made a prophetic statement: "Those who think that some kind of final authoritarianism will smother protest are blind."[43] The Maple Leaf Gardens demonstration was only a matter of months away.

The Committee of Inquiry, consisting of Judge R. W. Reville, L. Hemsworth, and S. Onyschuk, a lawyer and businessman, received fifty-seven briefs and seventy-six presentations.[44] They ranged from one end of the spectrum where Nora Hodgins asked the Committee members to "imagine what would happen if one child were killed during a strike," to the middle ground where OSTC approved of the right to strike, but opposed work to rule as a permissible sanction, to the other end of the spectrum represented by St. Patrick's brief.[45] Its report was expected in the new year, but was not released to the public until October 1972. Since OECTA knew details about it before then, the AGM discussed what the Association response to the Report would be. In the opinion of OECTA the Report was counterproductive.

It began with the interesting title *Professional Consultation and the Determination of Compensation for Ontario Teachers,* which suggested a narrow view of what should be negotiable. Its opening was, in Downie's word "naive."[46] "The Committee of Inquiry...took as its basic concept that conflict in teacher-school-board relations should be, and can be, virtually eliminated."[47] Its principal recommendations were the following:

- that the principals can form their own local negotiating entity;
- that the scope of negotiations be limited to salary, and fringe benefits (cumulative sick leave, sabbatical leave, retirement gratuity, compassionate leave, maternity leave, hospital and medical premiums, group insurance premiums, and other leaves);
- that there be binding adjudication by a permanent Adjudication Tribunal.[48]

OTF and OECTA immediately rejected the Report and over 4000 negative letters about it went to the government.[49] Doug Knott criticized it for agreeing with the trustees that it was "administratively essential" for school boards to control totally working conditions of teachers and for stating its "disenchanted" attitude toward unlimited negotiations.[50] Pat O'Neill in an editorial noted the anti-employee tone of the Report which included such phrases as "self-seeking groups of public servants," "unbridled power," and "coercive tactics."[51] Downie later described the Committee members as being unaware that things had changed. The Report "completely misread, misinterpreted or ignored the times and...attempted to institutionalize, if not canonize, existing teacher-board relationships. These in many cases were paternalistic and authoritarian."[52]

It was now time for OTF and other groups to respond to the Minister of Education with their reaction to the Reville Report. There was little, if anything, to endorse. The trustees could call in help, while the role of OTF was considerably diminished in negotiations. The principals were regarded as a management group. The Committee members had "noted, with dismay, the introduction on a considerable scale of the 'work-to-rule' tactic," could "hardly tolerate thoughts of the wasteful expenditure of time and effort...expended by both sides," and, worst of all, as far as many OECTA members were concerned, seized upon the "ambivalent attitude towards being given the right to strike" expressed in the OTF brief. The Committee members concluded that:

> since the paramount feature of professionalism is an over-riding duty of those claiming the status to exercise their special skills and talents in the interests of the public, it is difficult to reconcile this duty with a voluntary mass action which constitutes a total abnegation of that duty.[53]

The climate in which OTF and the affiliates considered how to respond to the Minister was, if anything, more conflict-laden than in 1971. 1970 had ended with 300 teachers picketing the Lincoln County RCSS Board office to seek parity with the public school teachers. One incident could have been right out of a history of a union in the early part of the century. The police picked up Frank Griffin for blocking traffic and drove him to a plaza. He reportedly said, "I've always harboured a secret desire to be allowed to languish in jail for the sake of a good cause."[54] At the Board of Directors' meeting of January 1972, Knott reported that twenty-one separate school boards still had not settled their 1971-72 contracts. He maintained that the principal reason for this was the trustees' inflexible attitude regarding working conditions.

> School trustees have been adamant in their position that decisions regarding philosophy, curriculum, methodology, school construction, and school organization are not decisions which can be negotiated with teachers. This adamant position is maintained with the fervour of crusaders and protectors of the realm....To deny such rights is to entrench the patriarchal system.[55]

Things remained in an unsatisfactory state when it came time to negotiate the 1972-73 contracts. The Teacher Welfare Department began conducting regional workshops to train and organize unit negotiators. At the 1972 AGM Knott stated that "teachers should be...displaying their convictions by demonstrating or having a mob outside the door during...negotiations."[56] In September twenty-seven separate school boards and over 9000 teachers remained without contracts. The Executive held a special meeting in August to plan negotiating strategies. The plan was to meet with OSSTA on the working conditions stand, press for release of the Reville Report, place advertisements in twenty-seven newspapers, and conduct regional meetings to discuss how to use rallies, demonstrations, and sanctions. Demonstrations would take place wherever seventy-five teachers would show up. The results of this planning were public protests in Ottawa, Cornwall, Chatham, Sudbury, Windsor, Richmond Hill, Sault Ste. Marie, London, Hamilton, Brantford, Mississauga, Oshawa, Burlington, and Toronto. The demonstrations involved from 185 to (in Toronto) over 3000 teachers. These teachers were trying to bargain for higher salaries, a reduced PTR, one secretary per school, group life insurance, lunchroom supervisors, and the establishment of a teacher-trustee committee. The Sault Ste. Marie District RCSS Board was so concerned about board/staff relations that it hired a private investigator to protect it from violence and vandalism.[57]

Because of its size the MSSB became a focus of attention again. In July the Board had offered the teachers a salary decrease; the teachers were asking for a 50 per cent increase.[58] By November, they progressed from this ridiculous start to a situation where the teachers decided not to take part in school activities outside the hours of the legal school day, to boycott the Board's professional development day, and to call for mass resignations. They were seeking among other items a grievance procedure and involvement in the development of teacher evaluation processes. At two special Executive meetings the problem was discussed. Once again the legal opinion was that the teachers' intentions were against OTF policy. Sr. Noreen Howley suggested a variation of what the Education Relations Commission (ERC) occasionally uses now: "We might consider having a day of prayer and inviting the trustees."[59] An agreement was reached without a test of OTF policy.

One encouraging note for the Teacher Welfare Department at this time was the Saskatchewan Court of Appeal judgment on November 7 upholding the teachers' right to strike; the teachers had been conducting half-day rotating study sessions.[60] But in Ontario matters continued in a way frustrating to teachers, trustees, parents, and the government. Resignations were collected in eight units; in November they were submitted en masse to the separate school boards of London-Middlesex, Stormont-Dundas-Glengarry, the North Shore, and Essex. The Executive froze money that normally would have gone to the units, and arranged to pay any teachers who would not be working in January and to hire them as officers of the Association to protect their superannuation.[61]

Essex once again became the centre of activity. Three of the boards settled over the Christmas holidays. But in Essex feelings were riding high. On December 11, 375 teachers had demonstrated with their families at a board meeting in the gymnasium of Holy Name School in the town of Essex. During the month picketing of the board office occurred in teacher shifts. When the Essex County RCSS Board teachers did not return to work in January 1973, the Board declared Wednesday a Professional Development Day and the Director of Education, Gerry Dwyer, closed the schools. The Minister of Education did likewise Thursday and Friday and sent in a mediator. Knott then took the opportunity to state publicly that "the closing of schools underlines the need for legislation." Mediation with the help of Thomas Wells and Leo Normandeau was successful by the end of the weekend.[62]

Although, as Downie described, the impasses over conditions of work were concentrated in separate school boards, strife was elsewhere: in the Ottawa, Peterborough, and Scarborough public schools and in the Ottawa and Peterborough high schools, work to rule was used in 1972. In Ottawa teachers held a one-day study session and at another time booked off sick. In January 1973 there were mass resignations of secondary school teachers in Essex, Timmins, and Windsor.[63] Clearly, trustees and teachers were not reaching collective agreements in a satisfactory manner, and legislation was needed. In this atmosphere Thomas Wells began receiving reactions to the Reville Report.

Responses to the Reville Report. There were two more opportunities for the educational organizations to submit briefs to the government: in 1972 as a reaction to the Reville Report and in 1973 as a response to Premier Davis's intention to have collective agreement legislation enacted.

OSTC was in the beginning not enthusiastic about giving teachers the right to strike. (By 1975 it did support the concept.) The trustees, however, did prefer the idea of a strike as opposed to the sanction of work to rule. If legislation were to give teachers the right to strike, then they should not be able to use it during negotiations. They agreed with Reville that principals should be permitted to have their own association, but went further in stating that they as managers should not be in OTF. They also agreed with the Reville Report that negotiations should be limited to salaries and fringe benefits. They disagreed with the Committee and agreed with the teachers that arbitration should be voluntary. Both groups regarded compulsory arbitration as a risky sacrifice of decision-making power. In addition, OSTC argued that teachers should not be allowed to be trustees because of what the school boards perceived as conflict of interest.[64]

OSSTA took a similar position to OSTC with the caveat that teachers should not be permitted to negotiate any denominational matters protected by Section 93 of the *BNA Act*.[65]

OTF's second brief, as its first, did not ask for the right to strike. It did defend its power with the affiliates to be involved with salary negotiating, recommended an unrestricted scope of negotiations, and rejected the exclusion of principals from the Federation and compulsory arbitration. Its rationale on the working-conditions topic was linked to the progressive education movement of the 1960s and 1970s:

> The new methods call for different kinds of teachers. Such teachers have to be imaginative professionals who will not submit to arbitrary and authoritarian organizational structures. If they were willing to accept such structures, they would not likely be the right people for the function.[66]

Since OTF's position on principals and vice-principals has not changed to the present and since Bill 100 did not give them the right to strike, it is worth while quoting extensively its position articulated in its first brief of 1971:

> Any move to view or treat the principal as other than a teacher will ultimately end in his being not a teacher. When the principal becomes something different and distinct from a teacher, his ability to understand the art of teaching will diminish, as will his capacity to analyze its problems and to propose solutions....Any movement to make the principal less a co-worker and more an overseer, we think, would make the teaching process less responsive to the students' development and less able to accommodate their changing needs.[67]

OECTA, because of OTF's position against the right to strike, decided, as did OSSTF,[68] to submit a brief of its own. Fr. Kavanagh reported to the AGM that OTF had rescinded its opposition to mass resignation in November, but this was evidence merely of a struggle toward an affirmative stand on striking. The OECTA brief resembled OTF's with the important exception of recommending that teachers be given the right to strike.[69] Opposition to this position was declining in OECTA. In December 1972, the editor of the *OECTA Review* had written a lead article in which he voiced his disagreement: "In Toronto we invoked every sanction known short of blowing up the board offices....What about the legality or the consequences of the sanctions?...I would like to single one sanction as being useless to our cause and personally repugnant. I refer to work to rule."[70] This editorial prompted a review of the Executive's duty to monitor the content of the *OECTA Review* and a number of letters to the editor taking issue with his opinion.

Besides responding in words to the Reville Report in 1973, OECTA and the other affiliates responded with actions.

Bills 274 and 275. In February 1973, James Carey decided to get a change in policy at a special meeting of OTF. The Federation's practice was to have unanimity before changing policy, an obviously necessary mode of operating since each affiliate had a veto. Consequently, Carey had no certainty of success when he moved that OTF approve of the strike sanction. He knew that AEFO would go along and that OSSTF was on the record at its AGM. But when Lenore Graham of FWTAO seconded the motion, he saw total consensus would be the outcome. OTF's third brief on "Proposed Legislation and Regulations for Negotiating Procedures" would include a recommendation for the right to resign en masse, strike, or act in concert.[71]

Mary Labatt described the sea change FWTAO went through to support Carey's motion. The "anti-employee Reviled Report" put FWTAO into a frame of mind that it had no choice but to support the right to strike: "If the employer was not going to treat them fairly [and] ...if legislation was to be forced on teachers, then withdrawing services was the only power an employee had." At its 1973 AGM FWTAO with "sadness" and difficult acceptance passed the motion that teachers' collective bargaining include full bargaining scope and all other rights enjoyed by any organized employees.[72]

In May 1973, over 5000 Metropolitan Toronto public school teachers marched to Queen's Park to protest ceilings, and the Scarborough Board of Education's high school teachers staged a one-day "sick strike."[73] Also in that month and in April the OECTA Secretariat met with the NDP and Liberal leadership to discuss bargaining legislation.[74] Meanwhile, Knott was writing about "unions and professional organizations" instead of "unions versus professional organizations"; he explained in the *OECTA Review* how in the early development of unions they "emphasized collective bargaining while the professionals concentrated on the theory and practice of their chosen careers. In recent years the unions have renewed their interest in the development of theory and skill within their own crafts, while professionals have found it necessary to adopt the collective bargaining process."[75] By thus breaking down the dichotomy Knott felt he could ensure that the unit negotiators would "really hold the line" in 1973-74 bargaining and in the face of the opposition to strike legislation in the trustees' and government's camp. The OECTA strategy was to include demonstrations, letters to the government, advertisements, rallies, and, where necessary, withdrawal of services. Understatement was not the order of the day when rallying the membership, as exemplified in Knott's statement to the Executive in September that "if [the legislation] followed the suggestions of the trustees, [it] would place teachers under reprehensible and autocratic conditions of employment not known since the Victorian era."[76]

Evidence of the growing OECTA consensus on the strike issue was notable in a quotation in the October *Review* from Mary Babcock: "Teachers provide an essential service, but not an immediate or emergency essential service. Unless it was a protracted type of strike, it would not really affect the children."[77] In another show of unity OECTA sent a telegram of support to striking Detroit teachers.[78]

The end of November 1973 introduced a heightened level of teacher-trustee conflict. Five boards of education received, mainly from about 3000 high school teachers, mass resignations.[79] On the separate school side resignations had been collected from the staffs of fourteen boards; they were submitted to the trustees of Carleton, Chapleau, Essex, Huron-Perth, Nipissing, Ontario, Schreiber-Terrace Bay, Sudbury, Wellington, and Windsor. With another 4720 teachers possibly not back in their classes in January, the situation was becoming intolerable for Thomas Wells and Premier Davis. Mediators from the Ministry, including Wells himself, arrived in some jurisdictions.[80]

At the December 7-8 Executive meeting the rumour was reported that Premier Davis was considering legislation to compel arbitration and to void the resignations. Wells telephoned OTF on December 8 that he was going to table Bill 275 and "as an afterthought," in Knott's words, he told OTF a little about Bill 274. The source of the rumour must have been reliable because on the morning of Monday, December 10, Wells called in the affiliates to tell them about the two Bills. His news would, in Downie's words, instantly politicize and unify the teachers of Ontario, since Bill 274, a complete surprise to the teachers at large, would, by altering the mass resignation date from November 30, 1973 to August 31, 1974, be an abrogation of the fundamental right to resign and a precedent for the government to alter a legal contract retroactively without consent. (Downie's thoughts were prophetic here in terms of the 1993 Social Contract.) Wells's position was that the government never intended to let teachers use mass resignation as a bargaining technique and that none of the teachers really intended to vacate their positions.[81]

Bill 275 was also unsatisfactory to the teachers. It proposed collective bargaining legislation that would have a compulsory arbitration clause and that would not provide the right to strike. It would, at least, widen the scope of negotiations. As soon as Doug Knott heard the details from the president about the meeting with the Minister, he telephoned Neil Doherty from Queen's Park. Doherty rushed to Queen's Park to break the news of Wells's intentions to the opposition. The NDP caucus had a luncheon meeting at which it decided to oppose even the first reading of the Bills, a notable departure from custom. Wells introduced the two Bills at 3:30 p.m., and the Speaker declared a recess. After supper Bill 274 encountered total opposition from the NDP and support from the Liberals.[82]

In the meantime, OECTA central office staff had spent the afternoon telephoning all the schools to organize a demonstration at 6:00 p.m. at Queen's Park. About 1000 mostly separate school teachers showed up during the debate. During the demonstration a fire alarm sounded, and the members left the House. Joe Ryan and Michael O'Connor from Durham then confronted the Minister, who referred to the teachers as a "crowd of hooligans." Clearly, he was upset by what he perceived as unseemly behaviour.

In order to discuss a filibuster strategy Doherty and Kay Sigurjonsson of FWTAO had supper with Stephen Lewis, leader of the NDP, and Jim Foulds, his education critic. When Lewis calculated how long each member could speak, he commented on one of his prominent colleagues Dr. Morton Shulman: "Morty's good for a long time. The only problem is I don't know what the hell he's going to say."[83]

That same evening the Executive had a conference call meeting. The Executive decided that it did not "feel morally bound by this proposed amendment." Bill 274 was, in its opinion, repressive. This decision was made in the face of the Bill's provision for fines of $200 to $500 a day for non-complying individual teachers.[84]

While all this was happening, Peter Murphy was in Terrace Bay-Schreiber dealing with salary negotiating. There, Chris Asseff of OSSTA told him that the mass resignations would not be a problem because Wells was about to solve it with a bill. Murphy knew better.[85]

Early that same week during the filibuster, OSSTF changed its decision to stage an after-school demonstration; instead there would be a one-day provincial walkout scheduled for Tuesday, December 18. Doherty got the idea that it would be more effective if all the affiliates walked out on the same day. On December 13 the Executive in a conference call committed OECTA to such action. The other affiliates did likewise by Saturday, December 15. On Sunday, Wells met with all the groups that had resigned, to try to reach an agreement. In retrospect, Knott said that it was impossible to make a deal in time to avert the walkout because of the distrust on all sides. On Monday the elements of a deal took shape: the Minister would hold off the Bill if the teachers postponed their resignations. There remained the serious problem of arbitrators being held to ceilings. But the Executive in another conference call that day agreed to the postponement and would talk about the ceilings.

During these events Doherty, now chair of the Walkout Committee, got a second idea: assemble publicly as many members as possible from all the affiliates for maximum impact. On Thursday he called Jim Forrester, OSSTF's vice-president, to discuss his idea. Forrester put him in touch with Liz Barkley, the coordinator for OSSTF's Metro walkout; the two agreed that all the affiliates should demonstrate together; a meeting of all the affiliates took place that afternoon and consensus was reached. Neil thought of the Maple Leaf Gardens for such a mass demonstration, investigated the possibility, and made a commitment with its officials. On Friday OECTA sent a letter of confirmation and on Monday, December 17 Neil signed the lease. The agreement stated that "the performance" was to start at 11:00 a.m. and finish not later than 1:30 p.m.; the rental fee was $8500 and the renter agreed to pay police charges and repairs for any damage to the building. It was now possible for the united demonstration to take place.[86]

On December 18 the second reading of Bill 274 took place. It was passed sixty-five to thirty-three; every Liberal and NDP member voted against it. The same day the teachers of Ontario walked out of every school. There were mass demonstrations at the parliament buildings in Ottawa and the City Hall in Windsor. In total 105 000 teachers throughout Ontario walked out of their classrooms. At the Gardens about 30 000 teachers gathered, possibly the largest mass demonstration ever to take place in Canada, perhaps even larger than the Winnipeg General Strike or the Montreal demonstration over the hanging of Riel. Wells was surprised at its size; he was not alone in this emotion; even more astonishing was its size given the extremely short lead time. Talks continued that night among Wells, Ministry officials, and the teachers in an environment where all knew the historic unity and aroused feelings of the province's teachers.[87]

Talks continued on December 19. Another Executive conference call discussed the fact that Peter Gazzola was summoned to the central office since, as a principal, he had participated in the rally. Nothing further happened. But in London-Middlesex, the Director of Education, Ken Regan, required that the principals stay in their schools that day, much to the permanent regret of one of them, James Carey. In Windsor the repercussions were more serious. The Board decided that it would suspend without pay for ten days Ron Riberdy from his principalship. The other principals had gone to their schools, then to City Hall, but Riberdy went directly to the demonstration. OECTA agreed to pay for his lost time.[88]

On December 19 a deal was reached. Wells contacted each of the chairs of the sixteen school boards. Everyone agreed that the resignations would be postponed until January 31 and that the disputes would be submitted to arbitration. Wells agreed to waive the ceilings on ordinary expenditures for the arbitrators and to withdraw the Bills. He did so in the House on Friday, December 21. The *Globe and Mail* commented that Bob Cooney, OECTA President, had "dug in his heels. He was backed by the other affiliate presidents." Stephen Lewis remarked that "the Government's retreat in this area was very intelligent." All the students and teachers returned to class on January 3.[89]

Bill 100. In an historic confrontation the teachers had convinced the government to back down. Possible explanations beyond the size of the teachers' demonstrations and the unity of their walkout and negotiations could have been the minority government of the Progressive Conservatives, the high regard the public had for education and teachers, the lack of an equal force existing among the trustees, or the haste with which Bill 274 was conceived in a crisis-laden climate. In any case, there was still no legislation for collective bargaining, and the government had not agreed to give teachers the right to strike. 1974 would be another year of stressful negotiations.

At the end of January all but three school boards had settled with their teachers. The Wellington County and Windsor RCSS Boards had agreed to submit their unresolved issues to arbitration. Bob Cooney regarded Windsor's decision as historic: "the first time...that virtually a whole contract, including such items as class size and grievance procedures has been sent to arbitration."[90] But the York County Board of Education did not settle. On January 31, 667 out of 822 high school teachers resigned. In the absence of any legislation defining a teacher strike or of making such a strike legal or illegal, what Hennessy called a "twilight zone strike" lasted from February 1 to March 24. After forty-three days a carefully worded statute, *An Act respecting a certain Dispute between the York County Board of Education and certain of its teachers*, legislated the teachers back to work and provided for final binding arbitration. The PTR would be open for arbitration, and the *Arbitration Act* would not apply as an appeal.[91]

An agreement was reached to put all issues to arbitration; 800 out of 825 Windsor separate school teachers walked out for half a day in order to ratify this deal. A sticking point was that their board wanted to submit the arbitrator's decision to the *Arbitration Act*. Knott explained that this Act was never used to settle collective bargaining issues, which were explicitly excluded by the *Labour Relations Act*, by the *Crown Employees Collective Bargaining Act*, and by the *Hospital Labour Disputes Arbitration Act*. The *Arbitration Act* was used more for business disputes. The school board, apparently not understanding the statute, was attempting to appeal from the board of arbitration, chaired by Senator Carl Goldenberg, who had awarded a class-size clause to the teachers.[92] The incident, quickly resolved, illustrated once again the necessity of teacher-trustee bargaining legislation.

Part of the 1974 AGM was frustrating for the teachers who were waiting for such legislation. Cardinal Carter as the guest speaker at the banquet criticized the teachers for causing scandal with their mass resignations and with their relationships with the trustees. He asked that they work to solve the problem. Afterward, up in the President's hospitality suite, a heated interchange took place involving the Cardinal, Dr. Bernard Nolan, the President of OSSTA, and Bob Cooney. Bob took umbrage with the fact that Cardinal Carter had not placed any of the blame on the trustees for the public differences and conflict. Dr. Nolan argued that contemplated legislation would push OECTA into the arms of a secular OTF and would destroy the Catholic educational community. Cooney held that teachers should have the right to strike, that they were capable of exercising this right responsibly and that, if trustees treated teachers fairly, they would have nothing to fear from bargaining legislation.[93] These arguments, with their elements of exaggeration, emotion, and idealism, were an indication of how tiresome the wait for legislation was becoming.

Negotiations for the 1974-75 school year were no better than in the previous two years. A most significant "strike" occurred, once again, in Windsor. The high school teachers went out on November 19 and did not settle until well into January. The Windsor Board of Education after eight weeks asked for an injunction to order the teachers back to work. The Director of Education declared that the Board deemed the teachers' action to be an illegal strike. The chief negotiator replied that there was no law that said they could not strike. Judge Osler of the Ontario Supreme Court ruled that the picketing was peaceful, that there was no statutory violation to support a back-to-work order, and that no person could be forced to do personal service against her/his will. He did tell the Board that it could dismiss the teachers for breach of contract.[94] This was a major victory for Ontario's teachers; it increased the pressure for legislation.

November 30, 1974 was "déjà vu." Mass resignations took place in Carleton, Durham, Elgin, Essex, London-Middlesex, Nipigon-Red Rock, Nipissing, Ottawa, Sudbury, and Wellington, representing 25 per cent of the province's separate school teachers. $500,000 was earmarked in the reserve fund to give these teachers a *per diem* allowance.

The teachers' priorities were a cost-of-living clause, a grievance-arbitration procedure, and a class-size clause. A number of these staffs did not get back to their classrooms until the middle of January or later. As a matter of course, these boards were pink-listed. The Elgin County RCSS Board announced it would hire teachers and a few applied. Leo Normandeau, the President, issued a press release stating that he would report any teachers accepting a position with the Elgin Board to OTF with the recommendation that their certificates be suspended. Thomas Wells telephoned to ask if he was serious; Leo was. The teachers did not begin working for the Board.[95]

The teaching profession waited for legislation throughout 1974 and until July 1975. The Minister of Education said in the spring of 1975 that there would be a Bill after the legislature passed its budget, but he was encountering problems in the Cabinet; the leader of the Liberal Party, Robert Nixon, wanted the teachers to have self-governance, and there was a provincial election on the horizon. Leo Normandeau was convinced that Darcy McKeough, a Cabinet member, was intransigent over the right-to-strike issue and reluctantly agreed to the clause in the Bill only when the compromise was struck involving principal and vice-principal exclusion.[96]

Another problem, according to Griffin's report to the Executive, was Premier Davis's quandary over compulsory or voluntary arbitration. The former brought about closure, but a 1964 Royal Commission Report on compulsory arbitration with hospital staff had concluded that it acted as a deterrent in negotiations, since both sides were reluctant to give ground before reaching the final tribunal. Griffin opined, "Arbitration is, at best, a gamble. I hope none of our negotiators consider it to be a gambol."[97]

Once the Premier and Minister determined to prepare a Bill, consultations took place with the trustee and teacher organizations. Bob Cooney found them quite challenging; only the presidents of OTF and affiliates, not members of the Secretariats, could attend the meetings. This left him at a disadvantage without Griffin and Knott's expertise at his elbow. However, through this period Cooney found Stephen Lewis extremely helpful. His telephone line was always available to Cooney; he gave well-appreciated advice on negotiating with the Premier and the Minister.[98]

The positions of the trustees and teachers remained as described above. OECTA endorsed an OSSTF "Bill of Rights" that listed the rights to bargain collectively without restriction on a range of items, to be free of externally imposed financial limitations, to have a grievance procedure, and to choose final settlement procedures, including strikes and other sanctions. OECTA submitted two briefs, one on the right to strike for principals and vice-principals to the Minister of Education and a detailed one on Bill 100 to the Social Development Committee.[99]

Bill 100 became the *School Boards and Teachers Collective Negotiations Act* on June 18, 1975. As well as offering general comments, Downie's book analysed the statute clause by clause. A brief analysis suffices here.

Section 2 in part states that, "The purpose of this Act is the furthering of harmonious relations between boards and teachers." The number of strikes has never been nearly as high as the mass resignations of 1973, 1974, and 1975; statistics seem to point to the success of the Act's purpose. The government tried to ensure more positive collective bargaining by providing a number of options for the negotiators: fact finding, mediation, voluntary binding arbitration, and final offer selection, as well as, of course, continued negotiating or striking and locking out. It was hoped that these options would reduce the use of a sanction. Compulsory arbitration was avoided because research revealed that it had a stultifying effect in British Columbia. Instead, the public and students' interests were protected from an indefinite impasse by the creation of the ERC with the responsibility to report to the Minister when the length of a strike was putting the students at risk. The government did give teachers the right to strike. Its reasoning was that strikes could not be stopped and did not harm students; the Act mandated a number of steps the negotiators had to go through before a strike vote could be taken. More controversially, from the trustees' point of view, was whether or not the definition of a strike included working to rule; by this sanction the teachers would continue to be paid while on strike (unless the school board locked them out). The government also, to the dismay of the trustees, did not limit negotiations on any term or condition of employment, except for separate school denominational rights. It reasoned that salary and working conditions were closely related, that it would be impossible to limit the scope of negotiations and that, in the last analysis, trustees could refuse to grant a bargaining demand on a working-condition item. (On the other hand, there was a mechanism for the ERC to determine bad-faith bargaining; it could be difficult to avoid such a charge, if a school board refused to negotiate in principle any working conditions.)

OECTA had agreed to and in general was pleased with Bill 100. Before, during, and since its passage, the Association has grappled with the exclusion of the principals and vice-principals from the right to strike. During its progress from bill to statute, OECTA also struggled with the denominational clause. Thirdly, since the enactment of the Act, the trustees and some of OTF and OECTA's members have questioned forcefully whether or not teachers should be trustees. A recurrence of the debate over the right to strike has not taken place, at least directly, since Bill 100, although there has been one indirect debate on the use of the strike sanction when a crisis erupted over the design of an OECTA annual budget.

OSSTA had two vaguely articulated but genuine concerns about Bill 100. The first was that the statute, in the words of OSSTA's research director, Father Raymond Durocher, would result in union-management power struggles in which "Labour lawyers and industrial arbitrators, expert at oiling assembly lines, thus find themselves moving quickly into the world of pupil processing."[100] Adversarial bargaining under Bill 100 would damage the desirable state of collaborative priest-trustee-teacher-parent-student building toward an ideal Catholic community. Unfortunately for those with this aim, the 1940s, 1950s and 1960s had not been a Golden Age of negotiating from which they could draw example and inspiration. The separate school trustees' second concern was that teacher or trustee negotiators might wittingly or unwittingly bargain away a denominational right guaranteed by the *BNA Act*, like, for example, the right to develop and teach religious education programmes or the right to operate grades nine and ten. Leo Normandeau had a number of sessions moving back and forth between Paul Cavalluzzo, the Association's lawyer, and Father Durocher. Although OECTA felt the clause was unnecessary, Section 51(2) of the *School Boards and Teachers Collective Negotiations Act* now states that, "The provisions of this Act shall not be construed as to prejudicially affect the rights and privileges with respect to the employment of teachers enjoyed by Roman Catholic and Protestant separate school boards under *The British North America Act, 1867*.[101]

The Aftermath of Bill 100. A second controversial topic surfacing from time to time was that of the teacher-trustee. It has been the position of the trustees that teachers are in conflict of interest when they are trustees, whether or not they are on the school board for which they teach or on another board. The Minister of Education, Bette Stephenson, felt it was not within her rights to tell the voters they could not elect teachers to boards. OECTA was divided on the issue. A number of its members in the Metropolitan area taught for one separate school board and supported with their residential taxes another. Others taught in a public high school and were separate school trustees. Still others taught for a separate school board and were separate school representatives on a board of education. A few taught exclusively in a private Catholic high school (that is, grades 11-13) and were on a separate school board. In 1978 a study found that 116 teachers were serving on Ontario school boards.[102]

Opposition to this dual role emerged during the heated period of events around the passage of Bill 100. Some teachers found themselves on salary negotiating committees as trustees bargaining with their peers from another affiliate. Emotions rose. OTF in 1978 arrived at a policy that regarded it as unethical for a statutory member to act as a negotiator on behalf of a school board and recommended to the Minister that an Essex Board of Education principal on the Essex County RCSS Board have his principal's qualifications suspended for one year for contravention of Section 18 of the *Regulation Made Under The Teaching Profession Act*. He had made a motion that the Essex County RCSS Board "ignore the Provincial Executive of the Ontario English Catholic Teachers' Association and proceed to hire teachers as required." The Minister complied. Although the principal won his case in an appeal to the court, the issue was visible and controversial enough to cause debates at the Executive, Board of Governors, and AGM levels.[103]

Two more court cases kept the debate going. In 1979 a judge ruled that under the *Municipal Conflict of Interest Act* two Toronto Board of Education trustees, Spencer and Fisher, whose wives were teachers with the Board were in conflict of interest because one was serving on the Finance Committee and the other on the Salary Negotiating Committee.[104] Again, under the same Act in 1982 a ratepayer took William Lozinski, a Windsor Board of Education teacher, to court for not declaring himself in conflict of interest when, as chair of the Windsor RCSS Board, he voted to break the tie for acceptance of the recommendations of the Board's Salary Negotiating Committee. The judgment was that the vote would stand, but that he should not have voted.[105]

In OECTA the debate revolved around two motions: a 1979 AGM one which would have made teacher-trustees ineligible to serve on the Executive and a 1981 Executive one which would have supported an OTF intention to require a teacher to take a leave of absence without pay if s/he were to become a trustee. Both motions were defeated. The AGM motion after lengthy discussion passed by one vote, but did not have the required two-thirds majority. Supporters of the motions, like Michael O'Connor, believed that "A teacher-trustee is either not representing teachers fairly or he is not representing the taxpayer." Other delegates remembered the Board of Directors' statement that a separate school representative's comments during a Brant Board of Education teachers' strike were "a source of embarrassment to his colleagues in OECTA." Opponents of the motions like Peter Gazzola and George Saranchuk labelled such moves as discrimination. They served as trustees because they could improve education for the students, protect separate school interests at the high school level, and be a source of information for OECTA. For example, Gazzola was active in opposition to the Peel Board of Education's stance against the pooling of corporate assessment for the benefit of separate school boards.[106]

Fred Sweeney, as President of OTF, supported the democratic right of teachers to run for trustee and of electors to vote for them: "Teachers are becoming more active politically and they will probably continue to be just to maintain what they have."[107] Joe Rapai, Chair of the Work Group to Examine the Report of the Role of the Trustee, in 1981 raised the issue to a philosophical level and had the last word in the Association since then: "Trustees choose to serve their communities by seeking election to a board of education. It would seem to us then this is a reasonable way for an educator to serve his community. Any implication that teachers have a sinister motive when serving is an insult to the profession."[108]

OECTA and OTF still seek an amendment to Section 64 of Bill 100, which states, in part, "in the event of a strike by the members of a branch affiliate each principal and vice-principal who is a member of the branch affiliate shall remain on duty during the strike or any related lockout." When the Bill was in draft form, OECTA submitted a brief just on Section 64; it contended that principals and vice-principals are not essential during a strike since the school cannot be kept open then (a point the trustees would dispute by their attempts from time to time to keep schools operating with volunteers, paid non-professionals, and administrators), that principals and vice-principals are conduits without real management power, that their duty to develop cooperatively with their staffs a positive place of learning contradicts their obligation under the law to stay in school during a strike, and that their crossing of a picket line is demoralizing. The month before the Bill's passage the principals of the MSSB and Dufferin-Peel Boards voiced their opposition to Section 64, protesting that they were not managers as the trustees maintained, because they were not involved in the establishment of school board policies or budgets.[109]

A year after the enactment of the Act, the OECTA's Task Force: Principals still had not adjusted to the new reality. Mearl Obee, its chair, held at the AGM that Bill 100 made it impossible for the principals to develop cooperative effort with their staffs and to avoid conflict with other Association members. The Executive sought an amendment and asked principals and vice-principals to donate their full salary during a strike, a policy that stayed in force. To assist the principals to function in a strike situation without violating either Federation ethics or school board policy and the law, Terry Mangan issued five recommendations:

- support the strike morally and financially;
- ensure the safety of the school building;
- stick to the facts when discussing the teacher-trustee dispute, the strike, and related matters;
- refer all questions to the Local Economic Advisory Committee spokesperson;
- do not assign teaching duties to volunteers.[110]

Some trustees would quarrel with the last point. However, since 1975 principals and vice-principals have managed to perform satisfactorily and professionally in difficult strike situations. Peter Gazzola in a recent interview expressed his opinion that Section 64 is still a divisive issue between staffs and principals and his disappointment that OTF has not fought more strongly for its repeal. But OECTA in its briefs to two committees reviewing Bill 100 in 1979 and in 1992 did ask that principals and vice-principals be given the right to strike.[111]

Biographies of the Presidents and Executive Director

(Title changed later to General Secretary).

Reverend J. Frank Kavanagh, OMI. (1927-). Following in the tradition of his fellow-Oblate mentors and teachers, Fathers Poupore and Conway, Fr. Kavanagh devoted his talents to OECTA. These Oblates of Mary Immaculate felt that their work for the Catholic teachers' association was one way of living their vocation of service to God and Catholic education. In 1971 Fr. Kavanagh became the second member of his Order to assume the presidency.

Frank was born in Ottawa into a large Irish-Canadian family. His father, Percy James Kavanagh, a Royal Canadian Mounted Policeman, and his mother, Rose Mae Hearty, housewife, ran a boisterous, outgoing, friendly household with eleven children and assorted relatives and friends of their children. Father's brothers were Clement, Patrick, and Desmond; his sisters, Muriel, Mary, Agnita, Priscella, Marcella, Rita, and Theresa. The armed forces and the nursing profession benefited from the Kavanaghs; Father was the only one to choose the priesthood and teaching.

He attended St. Joseph for grades one to nine, a type of school that demonstrated the Catholic community's commitment to providing a separate school education beyond grade eight even in the "dirty thirties." He then went to St. Patrick's College High School to the end of grade thirteen. At this point he entered the Oblate novitiate. There had often been a "black suit" at his parents' dinner table, and the witness of his Oblate teachers at his high school attracted him to the vocation of teacher-priests.

Father was ordained in 1953, and obtained a B.A. from St. Patrick's, University of Ottawa and an M.A. in history from Cambridge University. By attending the summer course at OCE he acquired his HSA and began teaching history at his alma mater. He was director of athletics and recalled with some pride St. Patrick as the only Catholic boys' high school playing against all the public secondary schools and often winning championships. For twenty years Father served at St. Patrick, Ottawa and Catholic Central High School, London in a variety of roles: teacher, head of the history department, vice-principal, and principal (Ottawa and London). He acquired his Secondary School Principal's and Supervisory Officer's certificates.

After serving as president of OECTA and during his year as president of OTF (1972-73), Father received a telephone call from B. E. Nelligan, the superintendent of the MSSB, inviting him to apply for the position of assistant superintendent with responsibility for the Catholic high schools. At that time the MSSB and the Archdiocese were opening up one new high school a year and Mr. Nelligan wanted a person who had a secondary school background and who could work with the Religious Orders in administering most of the high schools. He knew Father's dedication to completion of the separate school system from his committee work with him. Father accepted the call and acted as assistant superintendent, superintendent, and assistant director of education.

At this point the position of executive director of OECTA was advertised. Fr. Kavanagh had been involved with the Association from the start of his teaching. The relationship between St. Patrick's College and the local district was close. Fr. Poupore, as rector of the high school,

Faculty of Arts, and the graduate school of Social Welfare, believed in OECTA (which, as discussed earlier, he helped form) and made available for its members evening university courses for part-time study toward a B.A.. Fr. Kavanagh naturally evolved into the position of committee member and counsellor from 1956 to 1964. He was instrumental in forming the Ottawa High Unit,to provide nine-to-thirteen professional development, liaison with the grades seven and eight teachers, and a kindergarten-to-grade-thirteen unit. Father and the other four Catholic high school principals, Sr. Mary Christine, GSIC, Sr. Norma McCoy, CND, Fr. Bob Bedard, and Fr. Dick Sheehan, CSB acted as counsellors, thereby ensuring involvement of the three teaching staffs.

Next Father moved to provincial committees, the Board of Directors, the Executive, OTF board of governors, CTF, and the position of supervisory officer with the MSSB. With all this experience his candidacy was attractive to OECTA. In April 1981 Father applied for executive director. Six of the twenty-seven applicants were interviewed by the Personnel Committee; two were seriously considered and Father was offered the position. With decision time upon him, he wavered. The MSSB had another high school about to open; Father was responsible for the largest Catholic secondary school portfolio in the province; finally, the challenges involved in assisting the school board, the Archdiocese, and the director of education in keeping the grade nines and tens and the private schools operating were considerable. He decided he could not leave and informed the president, George Saranchuk, of his decision.

The president, along with some other members of the Executive, believed that it was essential to persuade Father to accept the position. Firstly, the selection procedure was, in the Executive's mind, finished. Secondly, George Saranchuk had established as a main objective of his presidency the attainment of separate school completion, and Father's track record was clear in that area. Finally, OECTA had completed a decade of some debate and contention from the events around Bill 100, and the social justice issue; Father could strengthen links to the Catholic supervisory officers, OSSTA, the Catholic Bishops, and the Ministry of Education.

Saranchuk presented the case to Mr. Nelligan, who agreed with his reasoning and assured Fr. Kavanagh that he endorsed OECTA's choice of an executive director. Father accepted the position. Recently, he recalled the reasons why he applied for and took on the new responsibility. He believed he could:

- build bridges with all of the Catholic educational associations;
- work with these associations for completion of the separate school system;
- enhance the image of the teacher;
- continue to build a strong central OECTA voice as opposed to a destructive fragmentation into individual units;
- signal to the Catholic community that professional activities of teachers acting collectively are in harmony with the social teaching of the Church;
- continue the contribution of the Oblates, Fr. Poupore and Fr. Conway;
- work for an all-important agency, the Catholic school, which spreads the Good News that the world is penetrated by God, is in the process of transformation, and is ultimately aiming toward God;
- spread the vision of the Catholic school as an environment where youth learns to cope with its century and to internalize the lessons from the life, death, and resurrection of Jesus Christ.

Fr. Kavanagh was executive director, with the designation changed to general secretary, from 1981 to 1991. Since his retirement he has been working for the Institute of Catholic Education.

The teaching profession has recognized his contributions with special honours. He became an OTF Fellow, received a life membership from OECTA, and the CTF Special Recognition Award for outstanding service to the teaching profession at the inter-provincial, national, and international levels, and was awarded the CEFO Medal of Honour as an exceptional Catholic educator and leader.[102]

James Joseph Carey (1938-). Like most of his predecessors in the office of the presidency, James Carey brought many years of experience at the local and provincial levels of OECTA.

Jim was born to farming parents near Parkhill, Ontario. His father, Joseph Carey, and mother, Rita Glavin, had four other children: Larry, Patricia, Mary-Eileen (who also went into teaching), and Rita Anne. His elementary school education was unique: grades one to twelve at Our Lady of Mount Carmel Continuation School in Mount Carmel. There, long after the Tiny Township Case resulted in the closing of many separate school classes beyond grade eight and almost all classes beyond grade ten, the Ursulines were operating two rooms in a school and one in the adjoining church hall. They were able to do this legally with government grants and local taxes because the school was outside any public high school district boundaries.

In this very special school Jim absorbed a Catholic curriculum and, of necessity, developed independent study habits and strong self-discipline. When he left Our Lady of Mount Carmel in 1955, the Continuation School closed. But doubtless something significant happened there: there were five students that year in grade twelve; now one is a Supreme Court judge, one a high school department head of history, one an executive with the Department of Highways, and one, Jim, the general secretary of OECTA.

Jim's mother steered her son in the direction of Teacher's College. He wanted to be a farmer, but, being the oldest in a large family with limited resources, he realized that he would have to postpone taking up that life. The two summers plus one year of teacher training were available then for grade-twelve graduates wanting relatively immediate employment; however, Jim was too young to be admitted. He had completed his grade twelve by age sixteen. Therefore, he went to Parkhill District High School for grade thirteen. There he faced a rigorous curriculum with formal final examinations and a classroom full of students who had had the benefit of teachers with specialized education in the various disciplines. It was, in Jim's words, a "rough year," but he was successful. He then went into the Toronto Teachers' College completing course and, at the age of seventeen, began teaching forty-five children at Holy Angels school, St. Thomas.

He had answered an advertisement in the *Catholic Register* in the summer of 1956 and his mother drove him to St. Thomas for the interview. Despite his youth he had a successful year teaching pupils just seven or eight years younger than himself, and the school board had him back for the year after his second summer at the College, this time at St. Raphael in St. Thomas. After his completing year at the London Teachers' College, Jim was offered a position by a priest who was a friend of his father. He was starting a four-room separate school in Zurich and wanted Jim to be the principal until he was able to get the Sisters of St. Joseph to take the school. He was nineteen, male, experienced, and, in the priest's estimation, worth the $2800 he would receive as a teaching principal. He had the position for four years when the sisters arrived.

By now Jim had decided against farming in favour of teaching, a profession from which he was gaining satisfaction and enjoyment. He decided to move to a large urban board where there were opportunities, security, and a university to pursue further studies. He accepted a position at Blessed Sacrament school, London. The following year he was promoted to principal by the London Separate School Board. He was principal of St. George (during which period his employer became the London-Middlesex County RCSS Board), of St. John, and of St. Robert. After a year as president of OTF he was made principal of a "twinned" school, Notre Dame-St. Paul. Some boards were taking two small schools and, for administrative purposes, turning them into one school. This was a cost-saving device that OECTA and other elementary affiliates opposed, because it meant that the principal could not be with one school community more than half the time if s/he were to be fair to both communities. Ironically, James Carey was the spokesperson for the principals' association presenting to the London board its brief against twinning. He found the job quite demanding and somewhat frustrating, but he made the best of a less-than-ideal situation. Next he was principal of the detwinned Notre Dame school.

In January 1984 James was the successful applicant for the position of executive assistant of OTF. His responsibilities were in the areas of administration, membership, and relations and discipline, a portfolio requiring intelligence, judgment and sensitivity. He held this position until becoming general secretary of OECTA in 1991, where he serves today.

During his career James acquired his B.A. from the University of Western Ontario, M.Ed. from Wayne State, specialist's certificate in religious education, principal's certificate, and supervisory officer's certificate. More importantly, he married Rosalie Mollard, a teacher, in 1959;they were blessed with five daughters: Valerie Anne, Colleen (who followed her father into teaching), Stephanie, Kristen, and Shannon, all of whom pursued higher education. Rosalie died at a relatively young age, and Jim married Mary Ellen Daly in 1985.

James has devoted most of his professional life to OECTA and OTF. He served on a number of local and provincial committees, was the president of District 5, won election to third vice-president of OECTA, and held every Executive position above that afterward. He then repeated this accomplishment, becoming third vice-president of OTF and moving up through the executive. He served a total of ten years at the provincial level.

His profession, besides placing him in all these high positions, has recognized his contributions in two special ways. The London-Middlesex OECTA Unit gives an annual scholarship in the name of

James Carey to a University of Western Ontario faculty of education student who exhibits the highest standards in practise teaching. Secondly, he was made an OTF Fellow.[103]

Robert Joseph Cooney (1938-). This next president (1973-74) had much in common with James Carey. He too was part of a large family; his father, William Cooney, a General Motors worker, and his mother, Margaret Goyeau, housewife, had six children. Bob's brothers were Dan and Jim, his sisters Sharon, Mary and Patricia. He was born and raised in Tecumseh, attending St. Anthony there and, like Jim Carey, went to a separate school beyond grade eight, St. Ann, which was also a private school in its senior division. After grade eleven Bob entered the Christian Brothers' juniorate in North York where he completed his grade thirteen. Then, again like Jim, he entered the completing course at Toronto Teachers' College and began teaching at St. John's Training School, Uxbridge and St. Mary, Toronto.

Leaving the Christian Brothers in 1960, Bob signed with the St. Catharines' Separate School Board where he taught at St. Denis and Canadian Martyrs. In 1966 he received a promotion from the Newmarket Separate School Board (in 1969 part of the York Region RCSS Board) where he spent the rest of his career. There he was principal of Notre Dame school, Newmarket, then coordinator of religious education. He missed being a principal and in 1972 went to St. Margaret Mary, Woodbridge. However, he continued for some years to be a staff member and often the principal of the OECTA/OSSTA religious education course in York and, occasionally, in Windsor. For the next twenty years, until his retirement in 1992, Bob was principal also of Holy Name school in King City, St. Charles Garnier in Richmond Hill, and St. Elizabeth Seton in Newmarket. During this time he acquired a B.A. and theology certificate from the University of Windsor, the principal's certificate from the Ministry of Education and an M.Ed. from Queen's University. In 1966 he married Judith Ann Hicks, a businesswoman. They had two children, Sharon and Sean, and now have two grandchildren.

In his retirement Bob is currently organizing the correspondence and files for the archives of the York elementary Unit of OECTA.

Bob's involvement in the Association started at the beginning of his teaching. He attended Toronto Teachers' College with John Rodriguez, and they both went to work in St. Catharines. Although Bob was quite shy and blushed easily from John's bantering ways, he allowed John to bring him to a district meeting to protest the OECTA's salary schedule that did not allow for experience gained in the two years before attending Teachers' College for the completing year. Of course, they lost with this issue, but Bob's interest was aroused, and he became recording secretary and a salary negotiator in St. Catharines.

In Newmarket Bob and his fellow teachers saw that the southern populous part of the district was dominating and, in their opinion, ignoring the north. They attended en masse with a slate, and Bob was elected to the presidency. Once on the Board of Directors Bob served on various provincial committees, including the Christian Philosophy Committee, where he was able to use his catechetical background for the professional development of teachers.

Bob's York supporters talked him into running for the provincial third vice-presidency against James Carey, but he lost. Bob felt that he was not really ready for this responsibility yet and that the better man won. The following year he did win the office of third vice-president, then jumped the second vice-presidency to gain the office of first vice-president.

When he became president in 1973, a tumultuous school year was beginning. This would be the year of mass resignations, Bills 274 and 275, the one-day provincial walkout, and the huge demonstrations at Toronto Maple Leaf Gardens and elsewhere. Bob was the first president with full-time release from teaching duties by the decision of a previous AGM. However, his school board asked if he could continue as principal if it provided him with a full-time vice-principal. He agreed, and OECTA paid half the vice-principal's salary. Although the York board was very cooperative when Bob had to be in Toronto, he still had quite a demanding year. Heated debates on a one-to-one basis with such eminent persons as Cardinal Carter, Premier Davis, Minister of Education Thomas Wells, and Dr. Bernard Nolan, president of OSSTA, had not previously been the order of the day for this unassuming, mild principal with an expertise in religious education. He became aggressive and effective in his role as leader of the English Catholic teachers during the struggle for collective bargaining legislation. After a year as past president, when he came to the difficult decision of voting against OECTA support for a contentious Board of Reference, he returned to his more peaceful position of school principal.[104]

Leo Normandeau (1937-). Serving office in 1974-75, Leo is the first president to take a leave of absence from his school board and serve in the office full-time on an OECTA salary.

Leo was born in Windsor, the son of Leon Normandeau, a Chrysler plant worker, and Alice Vachon, homemaker, and the brother of Richard, Jo-Anne, Robert, and Raymond. Since his father was active as a union leader, Leo imbibed the values of the labour movement, meeting people like Walter Reuther in his home.

He attended De La Salle elementary school in Windsor and after grade eight went into the Christian Brothers' juniorate in North York. After grade eleven he tried the novitiate for one year, but decided this vocation was not for him. Leo returned to Windsor and completed his grade twelve at the Basilians' Assumption High School.

Being the oldest of a family with limited financial resources, Leo went immediately to work. For two years he was at Chrysler's and Kresge's. There he met and married in 1958 his first wife, Beverley Tessor, a saleswoman. They would have four children: Brian, Martin, Paul, and Lori. Now he made up his mind that teaching was for him and began on a letter of permission at St. William, a one-room school in McGregor, Essex County, with thirty-six pupils and two outhouses. He stayed there for three years taking the two summers of the completing course. He could not afford to go to London Teachers' College for the completing year, so continued teaching, this time at St. Gerard Majella, Anderton township, and working nights, weekends, and summers at Woolco. When Windsor Teachers' College opened, he completed his teacher training there.

Now fully qualified, Leo Normandeau returned to St. Gerard Majella; halfway through the year the principal got married and left teaching. Since Leo was male with a grade twelve education and three years' experience, it was not necessary for the board to advertise or interview; Leo received the promotion for an additional $400, which, along with his married men's allowance, made quite a difference.

Leo stayed in this position and school for over fifteen years, except for his two years as president. In his opinion this exceptionally long period without a transfer to another school principalship was due to the separate school inspector (from 1969 the director of education) Gerry Dwyer and the school board's somewhat jaundiced view of Leo's militant involvement with OECTA. Finally, the principals' association lobbied the trustees on his behalf and he became principal of St. Peter, Tecumseh.

In 1982 Leo left St. Peter to go into industry. He has been director of educational relations for the Canadian Life and Health Association with a mandate to develop personal finance-management programmes for students in high schools, colleges, and universities. More recently, he has become an education consultant working mainly on federal government contracts as vice-president of Synergetic Consulting Ltd., concerned with environmental issues in education programmes. He is also a resource person and coordinator for Pathfinder Learning System Corp. with its outcome-based computer software and hardware for all the subjects and grades, and the owner of Active Learning Systems, involved presently with early-childhood educational programmes. Leo has recently remarried; she is his major employee, Eileen Brown.

Leo Normandeau's first involvement with OECTA began with one of his early pay slips. He wondered about the deduction and what OECTA was. Once he discovered that there was a District 17 which took in Chatham and Kent, Windsor and Essex, he concluded that the teachers spread throughout over thirty small boards in Essex were benefiting very little from the district of OECTA. He soon contacted Frank Griffin and learned a unit of the district could be formed, wrote all of the separate school teachers in Essex about this idea, organized a successful slate of Essex teachers for the district executive elections, secured approval for the formation of the unit, and became its first president. Later, he was elected to the district presidency.

He took his responsibilities seriously. A teacher negotiator in Leamington asked for advice on how to deal with his board; it was refusing to bargain with the teachers. Leo called all the teachers of all the county's separate school boards to the Knights of Columbus hall in Essex to discuss how to support their fellow teachers in Leamington. This resulted in the first public demonstration of teachers in Ontario. The Superiors of the Orders had told the sisters that this was a questionable activity for them and that they were not to carry placards. Leo arranged for their moral support by using them as babysitters while the parent teachers demonstrated.

Leo Normandeau's business experience proved useful when he got on provincial committees and the Executive. His ability to use the press and the radio helped the Completion Committee to promote OECTA's position during the extension campaign.

Recognizing his contribution to OECTA and the teaching profession in Essex-Windsor and in Ontario, OTF made him a Fellow.[105]

Frank Griffin (1921-1992). This Scot was the first male executive director of OECTA. He served the Association from 1966 to 1981 as a Secretariat member and was executive director from 1973 to 1981. Some of the Secretariat who worked with him claim that this workaholic burnt himself out in the first five years at the provincial office, but one would never know this from looking at his twenty-five-year record, where his presence was always forceful.

Frank was born in Glasgow, the son of Denis Griffin, a gasworks employee, and Margaret Reilly, originally a domestic servant from Ireland. There were three brothers, Harold, Jack, and Jim, and one sister, Margaret. Even at the age of five, long before Ontario's Bill 100, he was a skilled negotiator. He would wait on the pavement for his father to come home from work on Friday, payday, to ask him for a penny for sweets, knowing that his father would not refuse him in such a public place. Two other traits that stayed with him throughout his life surfaced early: he did not suffer fools gladly, but had an advanced level of charity. His niece remembered him as a young teenager bringing a meal of fish and chips to an elderly down-and-out man and as a beginning teacher caring for and assisting boys in his charge who had problems.

Frank attended St. Francis elementary school and then was the only Griffin to go to St. Aloysius College, a private high school operated by the Jesuits. His mother was extremely anxious that her children get a good education and not have to lead the hard life that his parents had. His family perceived him as the "brainy one" and his older sister, a teacher by then, helped with his tuition. When he graduated from St. Aloysius, the headmaster commented on Frank's Leaving Certificate that he was a well-behaved, industrious, and docile student. Not everyone in Ontario would agree with all three of these adjectives.

From 1938 to 1945 Frank worked in an industry deemed critical for the war effort; he was a quality controller and electrician. Later he was conscripted for service in the Middle East as a signalman during the Suez Crisis. Apparently, he lacked sufficient deference to authority, because he was disciplined twice, once for sleeping on the job and once for not taking off his hat before a superior. However, matters improved; when he decided to enter the teaching profession, his programme at the Jordanhill College of Education, Glasgow was shortened on account of his national service. Upon his graduation in 1949, the director of studies wrote that Frank was "very promising."

Frank Griffin started teaching at St. Vincent junior high school in Carnwadric, then at St. Bonaventure Primary School in Glasgow. After school he worked with delinquent boys at St. Francis Boys' Club. St. Bonaventure's headmaster evaluated him as honest, sober, trustworthy, conscientious, efficient, zealous, cheerful, popular, and sympathetic; he received "high commendation by Her Majesty's Inspector of Schools." In 1957, with the maximum but low salary, Frank made up his mind to emigrate to Canada. With the headmaster's list of virtues, he seemingly would have no trouble abiding by a similar list of duties of the teacher in Ontario's legislation.

At age thirty-nine ("the oldest child to leave home," as his mother put it), Frank arrived in Toronto in 1957 with a friend. He got a teaching position in January from the MSSB with no allowance for his seven years of experience; his friend got a job as a driver at a higher wage than Frank's. However, Frank cut expenses by living at the Boys' house of the Children's Aid Society, and supplemented his income by working part time and selling cars. After six months at St. Brigid he returned to Glasgow. A letter from the boys whom he had been helping with their reading and writing convinced him to return. He would never lose contact again with the troubled boys, helping them in the courts and with their lives. Upon his return to Canada he did pursue a well-paid teaching position in Cleveland, but after spending one day looking for accommodation in an area where, unbeknown to him, no white was welcome and receiving an offhand reception at the office of the school board, he telephoned the MSSB and got his old intermediate division job back. When returning across the border after just one day, he was asked what happened; he replied it was raining. He would finally settle down in Toronto.

He would work for ten years for the MSSB, teaching at Holy Name school, St. Ann, and St. John and being principal of Transfiguration and of St. Maria Goretti. Meanwhile, he worked on his B.A. at the University of Toronto. Bernard Farley, his vice-principal, recalled him as a powerful personality. On the first day of school this new principal lined up the entire student body outside and went over a number of rules, ending each rule with a "Do you understand?" and waiting for the chorus of "yes." Every day he toured the inside and outside of the whole school checking for safety and good behaviour. His interest in curriculum was ahead of the times at the MSSB: he organized the school staff so that Farley could teach music and so that one teacher could conduct oral French classes, even though this second subject was not offered by the board. As well, he expected the students to contribute to the community by planting trees in the neighbourhood.

In 1966 he competed with forty-one applicants for the position of assistant secretary of OECTA; nine were short-listed and Frank Griffin got the job.

He brought to the role, in the eyes of his fellow workers in the Secretariat, an almost Calvinist attitude to work, a sometimes brutal frankness, a loyalty even to a fault toward those who worked for him, an analytical mind, a skill in writing, and an avoidance of any self-seeking. His gruff exterior and honesty combined with one-on-one shyness would cause him some problems in human relations. Arguably his most important character trait in the years around Bill 100 was his strong sense of justice, especially in connection with the government's treatment of separate schools and with the salaries and working conditions of separate school teachers. In an interview with Sheila Coo in 1984 he attributed his attitude on union rights and social justice to his childhood in the Clydeside docks area with its labour traditions and to his education from the Jesuits when he studied "Rerum Novarum" and "Quadragesimo Anno." His quotation in *The First Forty Years* is worth repeating: "A person who offers his labour is offering all he has to offer. As such, he must have the right to withdraw that labour — the right to strike."[106]

Despite Frank's reputation as a tough union man, Ab Dukacz remembers his unwavering respect and affection for formal learning: "During the years when I was doing my doctorate, Griff never failed to ask how my studies were going, or to remind me how important it was to the profession to have its members reach the highest academic levels."[107]

During his time as assistant secretary Frank acquired his elementary school principal's and inspector's certificates and his M.Ed. from OISE. In 1973 he applied for the position of executive secretary. The year before, he had been diagnosed with both throat and lung cancer, but after six months of cobalt treatment the cancer went into remission. Although the treatment had taken away much of his energy, the Executive still felt he was the one for the job. In this position he functioned more like Marion Tyrrell than Mary Babcock. He saw himself as the administrator of OECTA, but had difficulty showing what some Executive members expected as sufficient deference toward the elected officials of the Association. He spoke his mind with sincerity and honesty, but sometimes without diplomacy. Thus, when the era of a full-time president and vice-president arrived, the times were difficult for Frank. He took a year's leave of absence in January 1981 and retired the following December.

But no one would question his long dedication to making OECTA the equal of any of the affiliates and to upholding the dignity of the profession of Catholic teacher. OECTA made him a life member in 1982 and OTF a Fellow in 1981.[108] Doug Knott, who worked with him closely for a long period of time, recently wrote the following tribute:

> He may have appeared quick-tempered and authoritarian to some who worked with him. To those who knew him well and to those who listened to his impassioned plea for salaries and benefits and working conditions in separate schools of no less value than those in the public schools, Frank was a crusader.
>
> As an educator Frank was a firm believer in the arts, particularly music and drama. Toward his staff he was demanding, but at the same time kind and understanding.
>
> In negotiations Frank was inventive, determined, and often eloquent. He had a clear sense of his own dignity and of economic justice. He demanded respect for himself and his fellow teachers. He dared to demand a collective agreement for his fellow separate school teachers the equal of the best in the country. Under his initial organization, OECTA's negotiators were as well informed and skilled as any in the country.
>
> Through Frank Griffin's contribution to collective negotiations and to the advancement of the teaching profession, he earned the respect of his colleagues in every teacher organization across Canada.[109]

NOTES

1. Rev. Fr. F. Kavanagh, "Report of the Executive Director," Board of Directors, 11-12 February 1983.
2. Stamp, *Schools of Ontario*, 237-40.
3. Ontario Ministry of Education, "News Release," 72-10; 7 September 1973; H. Ian Macdonald, *Report of the Commission on the Financing of Elementary and Secondary Education in Ontario*, Toronto: Queen's Printer, 1985, 17-18.
4. Mary Labatt, *Always A Journey. A History of the Federation of Women Teachers' Associations of Ontario*, Toronto: FWTAO, 1993, 82.
5. Executive, 1-2 July 1977.
6. Ibid.; 5-6 November 1982; 5-6 January 1978; Coo, *Forty Years*, 92-93; *OECTAReporter* (October 1975), 22.
7. R. T. Dixon, Lecture 16, "History of French, Public, and Separate Schools" in Ontario, Niagara University.
8. R.S.0. 1990, c. S.2, s.1, 63-70.
9. Downie, *Collective Bargaining*, 13-27. See also Stamp, *Schools of Ontario*, 241.
10. *Canadian Register*, 13 May 1961, 3.
11. Ibid., 21 October 1961, 3. See also ibid., 29 September 1962.
12. Downie, *Collective Bargaining*, 21, 25. See also Peter H. Hennessy, *Teacher Militancy. A Comparative Study of Ontario, Quebec and New York Teachers*, Ottawa: Canadian Teachers' Federation, 1975, 10; Mary-Eileen Carey Hill and Maureen Teixeira, "The Pathway to Militancy within the Ontario English Catholic Teachers' Association," unpublished paper, April 1979, OECTAA.
13. Executive, 15-16 January 1971.
14. Ibid., 9-10 February 1962.
15. Ibid., 14 May 1966; Rodriguez, interview.
16. Executive, 10-11 February 1967.
17. Sister Mary Leo, Holy Rosary Convent, Windsor, to Mary Babcock, Assistant Executive Secretary, OECTA, 17 January 1965, OECTAA.
18. Babcock to Sister Mary Leo, 20 January 1965, OECTAA.
19. AGM, 14-16 April 1966; Executive, 12 March 1966.
20. Executive, 24-25 January 1968; 6 March, 5 June, 11-12 September, 4 December 1970; Board of Directors, 31 May 1969.
21. Executive, 2 May 1970; Board of Directors, 12-13 December 1969; 9 May 1970.
22. Downie, *Collective Bargaining*, 31.
23. Executive, 4-5 February 1972.
24. AGM, 23-25 March 1970.
25. Executive, 11-12 September 1970.
26. *OECTA Review* (October 1970), 64; AGM, 19-21 March 1969.
27. Executive, 11-12 September, 6-7 November 1970; Downie, *Collective Bargaining*, 27.
28. Ibid., 5 June, 6-7 November 1970.
29. Coo, *Forty Years*, 82.

30. Hennessy, *Teacher Militancy*, 27, 39, 54.
31. AGM, 20-22 March 1968.
32. Executive, 10-11 December 1971; Knott, interview, 10 May 1993; Dr. Anthony J. Barone, interview, Toronto, 13 October 1993; Douglas Wm. Knott, Senior Sector Advisor, to Jim Carey, General Secretary, OECTA, 14 October 1992, OECTAA.
33. Peter Murphy, interview, Toronto, 14 September 1993; Paulette Murphy, interview, Toronto, 13 October 1993.
34. AGM, 22-24 March 1971; Neil Doherty, interview, Toronto, 7 September 1993.
35. Terry Mangan, interview, Toronto, 16 September 1993; Claire Ross, "President's Report to the Council of Presidents," 3 August 1993, OECTAA.
36. Ontario Public School Trustees' Association, *Newsletter*, November 1970.
37. AGM, 22-24 March 1971.
38. Ibid.; *OECTA News and Views*, February 1971, April 1971; Mangan, interview; James Carey, interview, Toronto, 17 September 1993; Doherty, interview. Perhaps those in favour of the motion were carried away in their enthusiasm when reporting "overwhelming" results. At the 1974 AGM, Griffin's report stated that the 1971 AGM "narrowly adopted strike as sanction. It would have been defeated in 1970." AGM, 18-20 March 1974.
39. *OECTA News and Views*; Doherty, interview.
40. Labatt, *Always a Journey*, 193-94.
41. Hennessy, *Teacher Militancy*, 27.
42. Ontario Teachers' Federation, "A Submission to the Minister's Commission on Negotiating Procedures," 1971, 22.
43. Staff Members of St. Patrick's Separate School, Toronto, "On the Necessity for Reform of the Procedures for Use by Teachers in Negotiations with their Employers and the Inclusion of Strike as a Legitimate Sanction in these Procedures. A Brief Presented to the Special Committee of Inquiry into Negotiation Procedures Concerning Primary and Secondary Schools of Ontario," n.d. (1971), OECTAA.
44. *OECTA News and Views*, October 1971, 8.
45. Ibid., February 1974, 2; Doherty, interview.
46. Downie, *Collective Bargaining*, 32.
47. R.W. Reville, Judge, Chairman, B.S. Onyschuk, L. Hemsworth, *Professional Consultation and the Determination of Compensation for Ontario Teachers. The Report of the Committee of Inquiry*, Toronto: Queen's Printer, June 1972, 1.
48. *OECTA News and Views*, October 1972, 6-7; Reville, *Report*.
49. Downie, *Collective Bargaining*, 32; *OECTA News and Views*, November 1972, 1.
50. *OECTA Review* (December 1972), 42-43.
51. *OECTA News and Views*, November 1972, 1.
52. Downie, *Collective Bargaining*, 32.
53. Reville, *Report*, 12, 24, 26.

54. *OECTA News and Views*, December 1971, 1, 3.
55. Board of Directors, 28-29 January 1972.
56. Coo, *Forty Years*, 78, 83-85; AGM, 20-22 March 1972.
57. Ibid., 2-3 February, 29-30 September 1972; Executive, 2-3 June, 23 August, 14-15 September 1972; *Globe and Mail*, 19 September 1972, 1; *Toronto Star*, 28 September 1972, 29.
58. Executive, 4 July 1972.
59. Ibid.; 2 and 5 November 1972.
60. Ibid., 10-11 November 1972.
61. Board of Directors, 2-3 February 1973; Executive, 15-16 February 1974.
62. Executive, 5-6 January 1973; *Windsor Star*, 6 January 1973; *Toronto Star*, 8 January 1973; Leo Normandeau, interview, Toronto, 5 October 1993; Peter Murphy, interview.
63. Downie, *Collective Bargaining* 27, 39.
64. Executive, 14-15 September 1973; 15-16 February 1974; Teacher Welfare Department, Provincial Bulletin #20, 22 February 1974, OECTAA.
65. Normandeau, interview.
66. Ontario Teachers' Federation, "A Submission to the Minister of Education in response to *The Report of the Committee of Inquiry into Negotiating Procedures, 1972,"* 1972, 9.
67. Ontario Teachers' Federation, "A Submission to the Minister's Committee on Negotiating Procedures," 63.
68. Ontario Secondary School Teachers' Federation, "The OSSTF Response: Professional Consultation and the Determination of Compensation for Ontario Teachers," The Report of the Committee of Inquiry, June 1972, 1973.
69. AGM, 19-21 March 1972.
70. *OECTA Review* (December 1972), 2.
71. . *OECTA News and Views*, February 1973, 1; May 1973, 1; Carey, interview.
72. Labatt, *Always A Journey*, 194-97.
73. *OECTA News and Views*, June 1973, 1.
74. Executive, 6 April, 11-12 May 1973.
75. *OECTA Review* (June 1973), 8.
76. Executive, 14-15 September 1973; Knott, interview.
77. *OECTA Review* (October 1973), 6.
78. Executive, 11-12 October 1973.
79. Hennessy, *Teacher Militancy*, 1.
80. Executive, 30 November 1973; 15-16 February 1974; Peter Murphy, interview
81. Executive, 7-8 December 1973; Knott, interview; Downie, *Collective Bargaining*, 41.
82. Doherty, interview; Labatt, *Always A Journey*, 196-97; Knott, interview; *OECTA News and Views*, December 1973, 2.
83. Doherty, interview.

84. Executive, 10 December 1973.
85. Peter Murphy, interview.
86. Diary in possession of Douglas Knott; Executive, 13 and 17 December, 1973; Doherty, interview; lease, OECTAA.
87. *OECTA News and Views*, January 1974, 2, 6-7; Stamp, *Schools of Ontario*, 243; Knott, diary; *Agenda*, December 1993; Doherty, interview.
88. Executive, 19 December 1973; 15-16 February 1974; Knott, diary; Carey, interview; Daniel Quinlan, Windsor negotiator, interview, Peterborough, 18 October 1983.
89. *Globe and Mail*, 21 December 1973; Knott, diary; Labatt, *Always A Journey*, 198.
90. *OECTA News and Views*, February 1974, 1; Executive, 6 February 1974.
91. Downie, *Collective Bargaining*, 42; Hennessy, *Teacher Militancy*, 2; AGM, 18-20 March 1974.
92. *OECTA News and Views*, March 1974, 1; Knott, interview.
93. Robert Cooney, interview, Markham, 24 September 1993.
94. Hennessy, *Teacher Militancy*, 2-5; Downie, *Collective Bargaining*, 47-48.
95. Peter Murphy, interview; Normandeau, interview; AGM, 17-19 March 1975.
96. Ibid., *OECTA News and Views,* April 1975, 3; Normandeau, interview.
97. Executive, 15-16 February 1974.
98. Cooney, interview.
99. Executive, 7-8 March 1975; "A Brief in Reference to Section 64 of Bill 100, Presented by the OECTA," 18 June 1975, OECTAA; "A Presentation to the Social Development Committee of the Legislature on behalf of the OECTA. Bill 100 An Act Respecting the Negotiations of Collective Agreements between School Boards and Teachers," OECTAA.
100. *Catholic Trustee* (December 1975), 16.
101. Normandeau, interview.
102. *OECTA Reporter* (January 1981), 27.
103. Executive, 30 September-1 October, 1977; 3-4 February, 31 March-1 April 1978; Knott, interview.
104. Re Moll and Fisher, *et al.* (1979), 23 OR (2d) 609 (Div. Ct.).
105. Executive, 4-5 December 1981; Knott, interview.
106. AGM, 17-19 March 1979; Executive, 6-7 November 1981; Board of Directors, 23-24 November 1979; 11-12 February 1983; *OECTA Reporter* (April 1979), 8; Gazzola, interview; George Saranchuk, interview, Hamilton, 27 September 1993.
107. *OECTA Reporter* (December 1982), 38.
108. Executive, 4-5 December 1981.
109. "A Brief in Reference to Section 64 of Bill 100, Presented by the OECTA," 18 June 1975, OECTAA; Executive, 6 June 1975.
110. Executive, 5-6 September, 4 October 1975; 10-11 September 1976; AGM, 10-22 March 1976.

111. Gazzola, interview; "Presentation of the Ontario English Catholic Teachers' Association to the Commission to Review the Collective Negotiations Process between Teachers and School Boards," 20 December 1979, OECTAA; OECTA, "A Response to the Interim Report of the Broader Public Sector-Labour Relations Secretariat Education Sector Project, February 1993.
112. Board of Directors, 12-13, 29 June 1981; Rev. Frank Kavanagh, OMI, interview, Toronto, 23 September 1993; Saranchuk, interview.
113. James Carey, interview. *OECTA Reporter* (May 1978), 21.
114. Robert Cooney, interview.
115. Leo Normandeau, interview; Coo, *Forty Years*, 90.
116. Coo, *Forty Years*, 82.
117. Albert (Ab) Dukacz, interview, Toronto, 8 April 1993.
118. Margaret Park to Robert Dixon, 31 May 1993, OECTAA; Mrs. Margaret Park, niece of Frank Griffin, interview, Glasgow, 11 May 1993; Bernard Farley, interview, North York, 17 May 1993; Knott, 10 May 1993; Alexander, 5 May 1993; O'Neill, 3 June 1993; Mary-Eileen Carey Hill, 10 May 1993; Coo, *Forty Years*, 79-82; Board of Directors, 11 April 1966; Executive, 4-6 December 1980; *OECTA News and Views*, January 1973, 3.
119. Douglas Knott, papers.

CHAPTER EIGHT

THE AFTERMATH OF BILL 100 AND THE SECOND PUSH FOR COMPLETION 1975–1984

My grandfather always told me that the judges in the Tiny Township Case had made a mistake and broke the Confederation agreement on separate and dissentient schools.[1]

Background. Bill 82. The most important government initiative of this period was the funding of special education and the passing of legislation that aimed to bring more children to regular classrooms and to increase the retention rate. In 1975 the United States Congress enacted Public Law 94-142, the *Education of All Handicapped Children Act*. Great Britain had similar legislation that took the position that *all* children, regardless of any emotional, physical, physiological, social, or intellectual disability were entitled to an education, offered as far as possible with their neighbourhood peers. These pieces of legislation, together with the Council for Exceptional Children's 1970 report, *One Million Children*, raised the consciousness of Ontario's educational community, the public, and the provincial legislators. In 1977 Ms. Evelyn Gigantes, the NDP member for Carleton East, introduced a private member's bill, *An Act Respecting Special Education Programmes*, that would mandate education for all children. The situation then in the elementary and secondary schools was as follows: there were about 15 000 children on waiting lists for special education placement in Ontario; many children were receiving no formal reviews of their progress in special education programmes; and high school special education programmes were rare. In December 1978 the Minister of Education, Bette Stephenson, announced that there would shortly be legislation requiring schools to provide appropriate programmes for every child regardless of the exceptionality. In May 1980 she introduced Bill 82 to the House.[2] There would be new challenges for the teachers of Ontario.

Collective Agreement Negotiations, 1975-1984. In 1979 Dr. Bette Stephenson stated that Bill 100 was working "damn well," citing statistics of twenty-eight strikes or lockouts in the three years before the statute came into force and eighteen strikes or lockouts and 900 settlements in the four years since the Act. The following year Dr. B. C. Matthews in his *Report of a Commission to Review the Collective Negotiations Process between Teachers and School Boards* (Matthews Report) wrote that 98 per cent of the province's school board agreements with their teachers were being settled without sanctions and that all the briefs to the Commission agreed that Bill 100 had improved the negotiating process and had reduced conflict.[3]

Operating under Bill 100, OECTA encountered and dealt with a number of issues, some new, some old. Among them were the following: the imposition of overriding federal and provincial legislation, a problem with increments, the opening up of and rolling back the salaries of a collective agreement, the concepts of provincial and single-team bargaining, the proposal that the Association join the Canadian Labour Congress, negotiations on working conditions (particularly regarding class size), redundancy problems in a declining enrolment, parity with public school teachers, negotiating for a just-cause clause in the collective agreement, and difficulties with the Bill's provision of a fact finder.

Federal and Provincial Legislation. Bill 100 no sooner became law than the federal government decided to attack the problem of "stagflation" with wage-control legislation. Prime Minister Pierre Trudeau announced that there would be an Anti-Inflation Board (AIB) that would monitor and approve wage settlements in the public and private sector. This announcement ushered in a ten-year period of federal and provincial controls over teachers' salaries. Consequently, from a researcher's point of view, it is difficult to measure the long-term impact of Bill 100 until the 1985 to 1994 years. The AIB functioned from 1975 to 1978; this meant, in effect, that the teachers had to negotiate twice, once with the school board and afterward with the AIB. A number of settlements were indeed rolled back. OTF fought the federal legislation in the Supreme Court of Canada, but the court ruled that in an emergency provincial legislation (that is, the *School Boards and Teachers Collective Negotiations Act*) can be placed under federal jurisdiction.[4]

With the removal of the AIB controls, a number of provinces and territories, including Ontario, enacted legislation with the intention of continuing to control inflation. In 1982 the Progressive Conservatives introduced in the Ontario legislature *An Act respecting the Restraint of Compensation in the Public Sector of Ontario and Monitoring of Inflationary Conditions in the Economy of the Province.* The title of the Act said it all. The teachers rallied at Queen's Park (about 2500 turned out) and in London, Ottawa, and Windsor; they feared that bargaining rights would not be restored and protested that wages were being controlled but not prices. Unlike the 1973 rallies, perhaps because of their smaller size, these demonstrations did not deter the government. The Act limited salary increases to 9 per cent in the transitional year and to 5 per cent in the control (second) year, removed the right to strike or lock out and created an Inflation Restraint Board with the power to roll back salary increases.[5]

When this legislation phased out in 1984, the Progressive Conservatives then passed *An Act to Provide for the Review of Prices and Compensation in the Public Sector and for an Orderly Transition of the Resumption of Full Collective Bargaining.* There was to be a voluntary 5 per cent guideline for salary increases; this had some clout because the provincial grants to school boards followed the 5 per cent figure. However, the right to strike was restored.[6] Collective bargaining returned to normal, whatever that meant.

Increments. Since the development of salary schedules, the teachers had always regarded the increment not as a raise in salary but as a recognition of experience. Although the Committee on the Costs of Education wrote that the number of years to move from the minimum to the maximum in each category on the salary grid were too numerous,[7] no one questioned the teachers' position. But in 1977 a number of school boards, including the Durham, Essex, and Ottawa separate school boards, lumped the increment into the total package when calculating the percentage increase. This action was one of the important reasons for a two-week strike (the first separate school strike under Bill 100) in Durham in 1977. However, OECTA won a victory on the increment issue with an AIB Appeal Tribunal ruling on the Essex County RCSS Board's collective agreement in 1977.

The Tribunal agreed with Ontario arbitration rulings of a few years earlier.

Each teacher is subject to evaluation.

> He is expected by the Administration, and knows he is expected, to improve professionally through experience by keeping current with developments in pedagogy, by participating in professional development courses and through other professional activities....A teacher who, after several years of experience, was still performing at the level expected of a first-year teacher might well lose his increment on the basis that his service was 'less than satisfactory'.8

Rollbacks. In the first year of the AIB when negotiators were learning the rules of the game, rollbacks were not surprising. But in 1983 a precedent, unfortunate for the teachers, was set when the Windsor Separate School Board staff voluntarily accepted a rollback rather than risk serious staff cuts. The Board was in a deficit position and the two large private Catholic high schools were in financial jeopardy. The trustees affirmed that they would not even be able to approach the 5 per cent allowed under the *Provincial Restraint Act* and the Director of Education, Bill McCrae, was lobbying the teachers to accept a 3 per cent rollback. Matters reached crisis proportions when the school board at a public meeting read the names of ninety-one teachers with seniority in some cases back to 1976, and thirty occasional teachers who would all have to be declared redundant for budget purposes. Only a vote from the teachers to accept a salary cut would avert such Board action. The vote was very close. The Windsor High Unit and some of the Windsor elementary school teachers feared the closing of the high schools and sympathized with the Board's plight. It was supporting expensive grades nine and ten classes and paying high rental and other costs to assist the Board of Governors of the private Grades eleven to thirteen. Other teachers voted against acceptance of the rollback on the grounds that the threatened staff cuts were so draconian that the Board would be unable to operate the schools properly. The end result was acceptance of a 2.9 per cent salary reduction accepted by a 54 per cent percent vote. The school board and the teachers together then had to petition the AIB to be relieved of the obligation of taking the mandatory 5 per cent increase; the AIB granted the request. It was Peter Murphy's opinion that the AIB did not have the authority to make such a decision, but no one challenged it. *The Social Contract* of 1993 would be a second ride on the merry-go-round for the Windsor teachers. As well, the Windsor action and the opening up of the teachers' contracts and rolling back of their salaries in British Columbia and Quebec could have given Ontario's provincial legislators ideas.[9]

Provincial Bargaining. The possibility of the elimination of the *Collective Negotiations Act* in favour of provincial bargaining has existed since 1975. Newfoundland, New Brunswick, the Northwest Territories, Prince Edward Island, Quebec, and the Yukon already have provincial negotiations and Alberta has regional negotiations. In 1978-79 the Teacher Welfare Department listed the reasons why it was convinced that this type of bargaining was not efficacious:

• the procedure dampens teacher-trustee motivation to establish and maintain constructive relationships;

• it functions in a political environment where public opinion could have a disproportionate influence;

• the government can always legislate itself out of a losing round;

• the teachers would be negotiating everything; as the Quebec experience has shown, even other statutory provisions like the school year, the school day, or duties of teachers could be on the table;

• the local parties tend to absolve themselves of responsibilities for salaries and working conditions and to view themselves as powerless;

• it facilitates the movement of trustees into a detailed concentration on curriculum, methodology, and other school matters traditionally under the purview of the professionals.[10]

Single-Team Bargaining. The Teacher Welfare Department was equally anxious to bury this concept also. With this method the teachers and trustees cooperatively examine the total potential revenues and expenditures, then arrive at a collective agreement. It was used with the Bruce-Grey County RCSS Board where the teachers gave up their retirement gratuity clause and was being contemplated in another small board, the Elgin County RCSS Board, when Doug Knott took the hammer to the technique. In a report to the Board of Directors he wrote that "we will be taken to the cleaners," and be accused the OECTA members of collusion with the school board. "It should be avoided...like the plague." That same year, Knott's reaction to an OSSTA suggestion to explore single-team problem-solving had him quoting the Roman poet, Virgil: "Timeo Danaos et dona ferentes." ("Beware of Greeks bearing gifts.") On the trustees' behalf he warned them that this method of negotiating would erode management rights.[11] The issue has not come up again; single-team bargaining seems possible only with very small boards where communications could be intimate. OECTA warned the units against the method.

Affiliation with the Canadian Labour Congress. In 1983, as a protest against all the provincial legislation that had been coming out controlling local negotiations, OECTA joined a number of other unions in a "Public Sector Coalition" and mounted a demonstration. This was the first occasion in which OECTA declared unity with, so to speak, the working class. Consideration had been given to affiliation of OECTA with the Canadian Labour Congress in 1979, but the Executive judged that the Association would be "lost" within a large secular group and thus would have little influence; the Executive also feared loss of political independence because of the Congress's support for the NDP.[12] Knott believed in eventual affiliation: "We'll come to realize that education spending and education goals are tied to the essential fabric of Canada and that we, albeit specialized professionals, have much in common with other employee organizations."[13] The issue would come up again during the 1993 *Social Contract.*

Working Conditions. A number of issues surfaced after Bill 100, and, with the controls on salaries lasting for several years, OECTA negotiators concentrated on the improvement of working conditions. By 1984 the Teacher Welfare Department felt confident enough about progress on this front that it established a five-year plan to accomplish clauses in all of the collective agreements on the following items: sabbaticals, expansion of positions of responsibility, maximum class size, increase in the number of guidance, library, and special education teachers, and a reduction in class size where special education pupils are integrated into the regular classroom.[14] Because of annual Teacher Welfare workshops and the growth and experience of unit negotiators under Bill 100, the number of provincial takeovers was dropping, and more and more collective agreements had working-condition clauses. The Essex County RCSS Board, however, was continuing to operate in 1977 as if Bill 100 had not widened the scope of negotiations. This was part of a pattern in Essex of dysfunctional teacher-trustee relations. Before Bill 100 there had been three mass resignations and almost an illegal strike; after Bill 100 by 1984 there would be four strikes. D. F. Quinlan, currently a superintendent with the Peterborough-Victoria-Northumberland-

Newcastle RCSS Board and formerly a principal in Windsor, described the Essex trustees as people who, if they were marooned on a desert island, would fight with the sand. Thomas Wells used to dream about giving Essex to Detroit. Nevertheless, out of the Essex strike of 1977 came a fact finder's report that strengthened the hands of the teacher negotiators in Essex and elsewhere. Professor Richard McLaren wrote:

> It is untenable for them [the trustees] to continue to operate as they have always operated. To do so would totally annihilate the benefits to the teachers of collective bargaining... The board cannot refuse to negotiate matters involving management rights in the hope of retaining total power and control.[15]

Class Size. The most important working condition to be negotiated was class size. This became a crucial issue as declining enrolment appeared in the 1970s and as integration of children with learning disabilities into regular classrooms occurred in the 1980s. Dr. Jackson in his *Report on Declining Enrolment* recommended that the elimination of large classes become a high priority and that maximum class size not be confused with the PTR, which includes all the administrative support staff. Also, Neil Doherty suggested as a strategy that unit negotiators stress the need for school boards to increase staffing in order to pay more attention to neglected areas of the curriculum like art, drama, and music and in order to eliminate special education waiting lists. Of course, it was not helpful when Dr. Stephenson as Minister speculated in a public address to OSSTA that it may be possible to teach classes of fifty or sixty: "In some situations 500 may be appropriate. I don't know." OTF replied that it did know: large classes, common sense suggested, were an impediment to meeting the Ministry's call for individualization.[16]

Redundancies. Fortunately, the expansion of separate school enrolment in junior and senior kindergarten, special education, and grades nine and ten, staff attrition due to retirements and other reasons, and the growth of the Dufferin-Peel, Durham and York Separate School Boards made the declining enrolment problem manageable. However, there were redundancies in Kenora, Kirkland Lake, Nipissing, Ottawa, Sudbury, and Wellington with which OECTA had to cope.[17]

Clauses on seniority, right of first call back, transfers, reassignments, and maximum class size became the norm. But not at first. In 1976 the Essex and Lincoln County Separate School Boards followed a practice developed during the teacher shortages of the 1960s, hiring Teachers' College student teachers around Christmastime. In the spring they learned they had budget and overstaffing problems. The Essex County RCSS Board terminated the probationary contracts of thirty-five teachers; the Lincoln County RCSS Board did the same for sixty-eight probationary-contract teachers.

Peter Murphy and the Lincoln Unit decided to demonstrate both at a board meeting and at the conference in St. Catharines of the Canadian Catholic Trustees' Association with Wells as the guest speaker. As he arrived in his car, the teachers applauded him, expressing their confidence that he would look into the situation. In response he appointed F. S. Cooper as a Commissioner to prepare a report. *An Inquiry into the dismissal of certain probationary teachers by the Lincoln County and Essex County Separate School Boards* paid attention to the OECTA slogan, "Reinstate the sixty-eight." His report strongly criticized the two boards for actions that "upset far more people than was necessary" and that demonstrated a "lack of foresight" and "expediency." He found the boards remiss for not involving principals and teachers in decisions about recruitment and allocation of staff and for not having a redundancy policy. The report recommended that the teachers be reinstated and that the trustees in future hire only as vacancies occur.[18] The province's trustees and teachers got the message.

Wage Parity with Public School Teachers. Since the increased government grants in 1963 separate school teachers at the elementary level gradually reached near parity. But the Catholic high school problem, as seen in Windsor, still prevented an ideal match with public school salaries in many jurisdictions. Therefore, it was encouraging for OECTA to read an arbitration of D. Beck for the Frontenac-Lennox-Addington County RCSS Board settlement: "I do not believe that the teachers in the separate school system ought to be called upon to subsidize that system through the wages they are paid, for comparable work to that performed by the teachers in the public school system."[19]

Just Cause. The teacher surplus problem and the Lincoln-Essex debacle pointed to the necessity of a just-cause clause in a collective agreement. School boards, it was believed until some judgments in the 1980s, did not have to give a reason for termination of a probationary contract. OECTA in two briefs since Bill 100, to Matthews and to Knott, and in advice given to all the units, argued for inclusion of a just-cause clause in all collective agreements. OECTA owed Essex for a clear statement of the issue made by the fact finder in 1977:

> Just cause is a concept which is universally recognized as a limitation on management rights... This is a fundamental concept found in collective agreements. To deny the teachers the availability of this concept in the collective agreement means they are denied one of the most widely recognized benefits of a collective agreement. It also means the arbitration procedure is unavailable for a discharged, demoted, or suspended teacher to have his case reviewed by an arbitrator. Presumably, the Board would only act justly in any event. Therefore, there is no reason for its exclusion from the collective agreement.[20]

Fact Finding. Bill 100 established the ERC to serve as a source of statistics and data for the Ministry, school boards and teachers; to train and select mediators, fact finders, arbitrators, and selectors; to supervise strike votes; to advise the Lieutenant Governor in Council when a strike has put the students in jeopardy; to assist negotiators to reach an agreement; and to send in a fact finder when negotiations have reached an impasse or when the agreement has expired. The idea was that the fact finder would clarify issues for the negotiators and act as a kind of mediator; furthermore, the mandatory publication of her/his report in the press would act as a moderating influence on the negotiators and would be a valuable document for an arbitrator, selector, or the negotiators.

OECTA agreed with the role of the ERC, but, along with the trustees, doubted the usefulness of a fact finder. Doug Knott explained to the Board of Directors that fact finding simply delayed the whole process; with regard to newspaper coverage, in the cities the fact finder's report usually was not newsworthy; and in the smaller centres most interested people knew the details before the report was published. He would have preferred more emphasis in the Bill on mediation.[21]

The Report of the Matthews Commission, 1980. In the fall of 1979 Bette Stephenson appointed Dr. B. C. Matthews, President of the University of Waterloo, Dr. R. D. Fraser, of the Economics Department of Queen's University, and John Crispo, a University of Toronto labour-management expert, to the Commission to Review the Collective Negotiations Process between Teachers and School Boards. This was perhaps premature because of the interference of the AIB for two of the four years since Bill 100's passage. Possibly, the fact that Dr. Stuart

Smith, the leader of the Ontario Liberal Party, had called for an end to the right to strike or lock out and for mandatory final offer selection influenced her decision.[22]

OSSTA in its submission to the Commission strongly objected to the work-to-rule sanction; it employs "hit and run tactics which the students perceptively label 'poisonous' and is a form of guerrilla warfare." The trustees also recommended a limited scope to what could be negotiated and came out against provincial bargaining in the interests of separate school autonomy.[23]

OECTA recommended tightening the time lines, eliminating the fact finder, heightening the mediator's role, giving principals and vice-principals the right to strike, and including the private Catholic high school teachers in the collective agreement. It commented that the Association had found voluntary binding arbitration and final offer selection good procedures.[24]

In the end the *Matthews Report* did not recommend any major changes to Bill 100, and Bette Stephenson did not act on any of the recommendations. However, some of the comments and suggestions merit attention; almost twenty years have passed without one single significant amendment to the statute while the *Labour Relations Act* has been kept current. The *Report* recommended that:

- time lines be tightened;
- school boards be given the power to lock out teachers after they hold a strike vote - this would balance power between the two groups;
- vice-principals be able to strike;
- summer- and night-school teachers be included in the collective agreement;
- teachers be given the right to run for trustee, but not the right to serve on trustee negotiating committees;
- there be no compulsory arbitration or provincial bargaining; and
- work-to-rule be banned.[25]

With reference to compulsory arbitration, the Commission provided a rationale similar to Knott's arguments against provincial bargaining. Firstly, since arbitrators wish to be rehired, they sometimes make unwarranted compromises. Secondly, since both parties expect splitting of the difference, there is no incentive to compromise at the bargaining table; the arbitrator would further compromise them. Thirdly, the negotiators can abandon ownership over the negotiations and simply wait and blame the arbitrator and/or delay and force arbitration.[26]

In connection with work-to-rule, the Commissioners made a comment that has often been echoed in the press and elsewhere. They labelled this sanction as an "indictment of their purported professionalism":

> Teachers who engage in partial strikes are really only hurting their students....When teachers actually benefit by hurting their students, the Commission questions both their professional ethics and their willingness to bear the costs which most other workers assume when they have a confrontation with their employer.[27]

On the other hand, how can legislation remove the right of a teacher to withhold voluntary services? Exactly what work-to-rule means is still being defined, but the employer cannot in a practical manner force the teacher to volunteer her/his time outside of the school day for the purpose of offering an extra-curricular programme in sports, music, drama, or other activity. Trustees realize this, since no collective agreement mandates extra-curricular activities to be provided by the staff.

The Strike Issue. The record clearly indicated that the teaching profession was not united in 1975 in its push for the right to strike. Even those teachers demanding the right felt that it should be used only as a last resort and with reluctance. A study by Hennessy in 1975 indicated that mass resignation and the strike were generally disapproved by teachers.[28] A few months before the passing of Bill 100 Claire Ross from the Wellington Unit wrote an article for the *OECTA News and Views* that expressed concern about the way the right to strike would be used:

> Acceptance of the right to strike would mean that in the impasse situation the only road to finality is through trial by combat. It would be to give eloquent testimony to the contradictory 'ideal' that in the real crunch reason offers no solution... Professionalism would deteriorate amid a flood of technicalities... All services would be priced, all services would be defined, and, in the exactitude of the definition, correspondingly limited...
> Teachers would inevitably come to adopt the jargon of unionists, and the adversary employer-employee relationship would generally come to define the relationship between trustees and their teachers. Typical employee goals and standards [could] replace typical professional goals and standards.[29]

Douglas Knott, three years later in a report to the Executive, agreed in part: "The advent of true collective bargaining and the emergence of formal group structure and power may well erode the basis for *rational* approaches...in favour of an adversarial approach."[30]

But the history of salary negotiating between OECTA and the separate school trustees in the years 1944 to 1975 does not present an alternative to Bill 100 with its right to strike. No less an authority than Cardinal Carter, on the anniversary of the encyclical "Laborem Exercens" in 1982 put to bed an idealistic appeal to cooperative, non-adversarial bargaining:

> What is clear, however, is that no solution...can be accepted which abrogates the basic rights of workers to bargain collectively and in some circumstances to turn to the strike as a final resort... Any economic plan that involves the denial of the rights of one segment of society affects the quality of life of us all, and can only make us all poorer as a result.[31]

Gloomy predictions have not come true. Between 1977 and 1984 there were only nine separate school strikes, four of them in the same place, Essex.[32] The vast number of collective agreements were ratified without resort to a sanction. Furthermore, many of the original questioners of the wisdom of a legislated right to strike, like Peter Gazzola and Claire Ross, have grown to an acceptance of the practice where necessary.[33]

The Annual Budget. Bill 100 affected the OECTA budget dramatically. Firstly, the Teacher Welfare Department expanded in order to assist unit negotiators with bargaining and preparing briefs for fact finders, mediators, arbitrators, and selectors. Secondly, OECTA had to share with the school boards in the payment of the selectors and arbitrators. Thirdly, the larger units began finding it necessary and desirable to provide release time from teaching duties for the president and chief negotiator. The policy had been developed to allow up to 20 per cent of the monies sent to the units from the OECTA budget for the purpose of releasing the unit president, but the Board of Directors, for example, allowed the Hamilton Unit to exceed the ceiling in 1982. Fourthly, with the growth of grievance clauses, of local political advisory committees, and of teacher- trustee committees, as well as of the membership, more money had to go to the units. Weighting factors were designed for units with exceptional travel costs from a spread-out geography, with a unit office, with increased membership, with a teacher centre, and/or with a president and chief negotiator on release time. Finally, there were new large costs for the hotel, meals and travel expenses of the unit and Secretariat negotiators involved with the Bill 100 procedures. Fees had to be raised. In 1973-74 and 1974-75 there were deficit budgets. In June 1978 the attempt of the Board of Directors to cut enough out of the budget to eliminate a projected deficit failed. All of this was exacerbated by a reserve fund being handled in an unsatisfactory manner; a stockbroker company was both acting as advisor and purchasing the investments, and the two roles were not always compatible. In addition, there was always the possibility of having to provide strike pay to the staff of a large board. The 1980 AGM, as a temporary expedient, passed a motion authorizing the borrowing of up to $10 000 000 to finance strike action. The debate over the setting of an increased fee became an annual rite of spring. It would be the late 1980s before the fee, the budget, and the reserve fund were put on a sound, fully rational basis. By 1982 the expenditures amounted to about $300 000 a month.[34]

Meanwhile, a vexatious special problem appeared. Claire Ross in his article discussed above had predicted that, "The creation and re-supply of war chests would continuously...raise membership dues."[35] Understandably, he and all of the members of the Wellington Unit, as well as a sizable number of other members, were alarmed when, at the 1980 AGM, there was a motion passed to levy a special $200 fee to be used as a strike fund. The motivations for opposing such a large jump in the annual fee were complex. Obviously, there was the sudden, high additional cost itself. There was also the thought that such a large amount of money in a strike fund would encourage the use of this sanction. Finally, and most important to Claire Ross, who later would run for and become provincial treasurer, there was the improper procedure followed in the passing of this special fee. This last point was the one raised in Claire Ross's letter to the Executive. This should not have been a surprise to Pascal LaRouche, the treasurer, because Frank Griffin had advised the Executive of the flaw in the procedure at the time of the original decision.[36]

A letter from C. A. Maiocco, a lawyer engaged by the Wellington Unit, defined two legal problems with the procedure followed at the AGM. Firstly, there was no proper notice to the membership about the increase. Secondly, neither OECTA nor OTF had the authority to impose a strike levy, the term used at the AGM for the special fee increase. An elaboration of his second point appeared as a question to the Minister of Education in the House. In accordance with the *Teaching Profession Act*, the Cabinet approved the fee increase; the total fee would be a tax deduction for each OECTA member: "In this way, the electorate of this province will be forced to directly subsidize the strike which shut down schools, and school boards will be compelled to collect for OECTA money which that organization will use against such school boards in the event of a teachers' strike."[37]

Also, Ross demanded that the Executive as the editorial board print an article in the *OECTA Reporter* that would outline the rationale for his objection to the fee increase. In it he expressed the fear that the "disproportionately large" reserve fund monies identified for strike purposes could result in an increase in strikes, and a selfish, materialistic, militant radicalism among the members.

In August the Executive at a special meeting rescinded the request for a fee increase. A requested Revenue Canada interpretation of the tax implications stated that the annual dues would not be deductible if used for any other purpose not directly related to the ordinary operating expenses of the Association.[38]

A superficial reading of this internal dispute might suggest a replay of the debate over the right to strike. However, Claire Ross's two articles revealed an opposition to the encouragement or overuse of the strike sanction. With the passage of time, he and other membershave grown in the appreciation of both the rarity and suitability in difficult situations of the use of the teacher strike. Currently, as provincial president, he has stated publicly on a number of occasions during and after the *Social Contract* negotiations his readiness to use the weapon of a provincial strike. The real significance of the debate was the end result. Reserve funds would not be identified for any specific purpose except for the obvious one of providing for any future unanticipated or untoward expenses. Secondly, the Executive with Ross as treasurer and David Fernandes as comptroller would develop a rational investment plan, a short- and long-term budget without a deficit, and a large reserve fund. The working out of this plan resulted in a consensus forged between professional and union views and ended the debate over the right to strike as empowering legislation.

The Porter-Podgorski Case. The beginnings of this case began possibly at one of the worst times. In 1974 the Essex County RCSS Board asked the Minister of Education to dismiss Mrs. Susan Porter under Section 11(2) of the *Department of Education Act.*. The wording of this clause is almost identical to the wording in Section 263 of the *Education Act*, RSO 1990, which states:

> Despite the other provisions of this Part and despite anything in the contract between the board and the teacher, where a permanent or probationary teacher is employed by a board and a matter arises that in the opinion of the Minister adversely affects the welfare of the school in which the teacher is employed,
> (a) the board or the teacher may, with the consent of the Minister, give the other party thirty days written notice of termination;...or
> (b) the board may, with the consent of the Minister, give the teacher written notice of immediate termination.

She had married in a civil and not a Catholic ceremony. Under normal circumstances, the Separate School Board through its director of education would have exercised patience, prudence and charity. Perhaps a sacramental marriage would be taking place later after an annulment of the husband's first marriage. If so, then continued employment with possibly a temporary reassignment to a position not in the public eye would be in order. Meanwhile, a pastoral solution could have been sought. But Essex in 1974 was not a normal environment. There had recently been one mass resignation, there would soon be a second, then a third, followed in the future by four strikes. The teachers and the trustees did not have a positive, cooperative relationship to enable them to deal constructively with such a problem as the Porter-Podgorski Case presented. It would take up the time and concern of OECTA, OSSTA, Bishops, and courts, and cause considerable anguish. The case, did, however, result in an important judgment for the future of separate schools.

When the Minister refused to act on the Essex Board's request, explaining that the legislation was not applicable to such a situation, the Board on June 10, 1974 sent Mrs. Porter a letter of dismissal. The letter did not meet the May 31st deadline under the legislation, nor did it give the required reason for dismissal by referring to the duties of a teacher. This was a straightforward contractual matter as far as the Board of Reference was concerned. Mrs. Porter asked the Minister for a Board of Reference, was granted it, and on August 6 won her case. The Board of Reference ruled that the school board's letter of dismissal did not "satisfy the mandatory requirements...so as to terminate the contract."

By this time the Essex Board had become aware of a second teacher on its staff who had married in a civil ceremony. At a Board meeting of August 26, it passed a motion to terminate both Mrs. Porter (for the second time) and Mrs. Patricia Podgorski effective December 31. The letter mailed to each of the teachers the next day stated that her action was a contravention of the statutory duty "to inculcate by precept and example respect for religion." Both teachers asked for a Board of Reference and turned to OECTA for assistance. The Minister granted their requests.

At first OECTA attempted to resolve the matter by discussing with the two teachers and the school board possible solutions. But neither Bob Cooney, Leo Normandeau, OSSTA, the OECTA lawyer, William Markle, nor Bishop Sherlock of the London diocese found the school board amenable to any action other than dismissal of the two teachers.[39]

The difficult question for the Executive now became whether or not to support Porter and Podgorski. If the Executive had always as policy supported dismissed teachers in Boards of Reference, allowing the member her/his day in court, then the Executive could have followed tradition. But that, as discussed earlier, had not been the policy. As recently as at an Executive meeting of June 15-16, 1973, Frank Griffin advised against supporting a dismissed teacher because in his opinion the person was incompetent, in breach of OECTA policy and "not a credit to the separate school system."[40]

William Markle believed that Porter and Podgorski would win their Board of Reference on the grounds that the duty of a teacher was not meant to be narrowly interpreted as respect for the *Catholic* religion and that marrying in a civil ceremony was not disrespectful of religion. During a lengthy debate at the Executive a motion was presented, defeated, amended, and after two committees-of-the-whole sessions, passed. The arguments against support were that the effects of a judgment against the Essex Board would be harmful to the separate schools, that the public and OECTA members would misinterpret OECTA's support as approval of teachers who were no longer practising Catholics in separate schools, and that separate school boards had no other means of dismissal of teachers publicly leaving Catholicism other than citing the failure of the teachers to observe the statutory duty of a teacher to inculcate respect for religion by precept and example. The arguments for support were that there was no clear statement of what a Catholic teacher was, especially since Vatican II, that a court judgment was needed, that it was not the function of OECTA to seek out for a school board a method of dismissing teachers, and that the Association should not prejudge. The final motions, carefully avoiding the word "support," were that "this Association provide legal service" and that Executive members shall be permitted to express their individual opinion on the matter. For the information of OECTA members and the public, the Executive released the following "Official Statement" on October 19:

> The legal service is provided because the Board has chosen to dismiss these two teachers in such a way that the contractual status of all Catholic teachers in the province is threatened. The Executive wishes to go on record as stating that it believes that all teachers within the Catholic school system must subscribe to the philosophy of Catholic education, which philosophy is rooted in the teaching of the Church. The Executive states unequivocally that it makes nonsense of the Catholic school system to place children in the care of those who reject the teachings of the Church. The Executive further maintains that there should be means available to remove teachers from the Catholic school system who more properly should remove themselves. Moreover,...it will be of benefit to both boards and teachers to have...ambiguity removed.[41]

The Essex County RCSS Board likely received some good legal advice because on October 28 it rescinded its motion to dismiss Porter and Podgorski. Instead, the Board decided to argue the case on constitutional grounds. It dismissed them again stating that under Section 93(1) of the *BNA Act* a separate school board was guaranteed the right to dismiss for denominational cause. It would be "prejudicial" if a Board of Reference could interfere with that right. The director of education's letter to Mrs. Porter on November 13 contained the board's motion:

> Whereas a Roman Catholic Separate Board has the right under the British North America Act to select, employ, or dismiss...teachers in accordance with the denominational requirements of such schools and whereas Mrs. Susan Porter, by entering into a civil marriage, has publicly and seriously infringed upon such requirements, therefore, be it resolved that Mrs. Porter be hereby declared disqualified for employment as a teacher by this separate school board...and consequently dismissed.[42]

Mrs. Podgorski received a letter with the same motion applying to her.

The Executive debated the support question again. Mrs. Porter wrote Frank Griffin that, "I do not feel that this Association any more than the School Board should be a judge of my actions nor of the kind of Catholic which I have supposedly professed to be by my actions."[43]

The Executive split six to three on the decision. The majority felt it had to support the contract. OECTA accepted the denominational rights of separate school boards. What the majority of the Executive did not accept was the idea of a school board with a legal power to dismiss for denominational reasons without having to explain the cause and justify the reasons for dismissal. It appeared that the teacher would have no appeal and could be victimized by the unsupported opinion and judgment of the trustees. The split in the Executive was so trying that two of its members, Bob Cooney and George Saranchuk, had to be convinced not to resign. As Griffin put it two years later, OECTA "was caught on the horns of a dilemma. In the interests of the individual contract the Association could not afford to lose, and yet did not want the Board to lose if it meant an open-door policy in Catholic schools." He emphasized that OECTA kept trying to stay out of court.[44]

It was now up to the courts. The Board of Reference on February 24, 1975 adjourned to provide time for the Essex Board to get a constitutional ruling on whether or not the Board of Reference did have jurisdiction. The ruling had not been acquired when the Board reconvened on April 25. The Board of Reference's decision was that it could not deal with the constitutional question; consequently, it ruled that the school board could not dismiss other than under the contract. The Essex Board appealed for a judicial review to the Divisional Court.[45]

On May 4, 1977 a three-member tribunal heard OECTA's argument that the Board had to follow statutory procedures and that a separate school board should not have sole discretion over what causes denominational reasons for termination and avoidance of the Board of Reference process, and heard as well the Essex Board's argument that the *BNA Act* gives the right to separate school boards to terminate for denominational cause and, therefore, that the teacher does not have recourse to a statutory contract or a Board of Reference. The tribunal agreed with the board. OECTA appealed to the Supreme Court of Ontario.[46]

The appeal was heard from September 13 to 29, 1978. One of Markle's arguments was that marriage in a civil ceremony did not constitute a reason for dismissal for denominational cause. This gave Griffin and many members of OECTA a problem of conscience, but the Association had to accept that a legal argument that was best for the client was not necessarily good for OECTA. "Privileges and rights in the case belonged to the clients, not the Association."[47]

The Supreme Court of Ontario Court of Appeal's three judges Jessup, Wilson and Zuker found in favour of the Essex Board:

> I find nothing in the Common School Act which takes away or diminishes the trustees' common law rights as employer;...if a school board can dismiss for cause, then in the case of a denominational school cause must include denominational cause. Serious departures (emphasis added) from denominational standards by a teacher cannot be isolated from his or her teaching duties, since within the denominational school religious instruction, influence, and example form an important part of the educational process;...to subject the right to dismiss for denominational reasons to a review by a Board of Reference would prejudicially affect the right.[48]

OECTA discussed and rejected supporting Porter and Podgorski in asking leave to appeal to the Supreme Court of Canada.[49] The Ontario Court judgment remains the final one.

Aftermath of the Porter-Podgorski Case. The issue of dismissal of the two Essex separate school teachers for denominational cause lasted four years. It had short- and long-term effects.

For a few years, especially while the Porter-Podgorski Case was progressing through the courts, there was a fear on the part of some separate school boards that their recruitment procedures did not pay sufficient attention to a potential staff member's commitment to separate schools and Catholicism.[50] Discussions between OECTA and OSSTA revealed in a few cases, as Griffin explained, "an excessive preoccupation with religion in the area of professional development and...with the personal religious lives of our teachers." (Griffin)[51] An OECTA committee developed a paper on the question, "Catholic Schools. De Magistris," but the Ontario Conference of Catholic Bishops (OCCB) felt it needed more polishing with regard to theological points. The Ontario Directors of Religious Education, Griffin himself and the Canadian Catholic School Trustees' Association each developed sets of hiring guidelines. The last one was typical in its emphasis on the teacher's essential positive contribution to the development of the student, the impact of the teacher's personal lifestyle on the student, and the incompatibility of flagrant acts contrary to Church teaching with the function of the separate school teacher.[52] Common sense eventually reigned. Archbishop Plourde of Ottawa summed up the prevailing view:

> What, then, can be legitimately expected of teachers in a Catholic school? First, we must guard against two extremes: we cannot demand perfection, nor can we let just anyone teach in a Catholic school. Sinners all, none of us is perfect. But, a Christian worthy of the name must not voluntarily resign himself to a life of sin, but must constantly strive to free himself from its enslavement. His lifestyle must not constitute a public contradiction of the Gospel ideal or the Church's teachings. This does not mean teachers are going to have to pass examinations on their orthodoxy or have their private lives invaded....On the other hand,...when a teacher's lifestyle is openly and publicly contrary to these requirements, he compromises a good...which belongs to every citizen who wants Catholic schools to exist. While our dealings with such teachers must always be inspired by the Gospel, they cannot be allowed to give scandal to children and to jeopardize the whole Catholic school system. Respect for an individual's right must yield to the common good.[53]

Doreen Brady, the president, agreed. Expressing the school board's right to have hiring guidelines, she explained that:

> Teachers do not have to be saints, but guidelines are useful.... Anyone who has spent time in a classroom knows that the thirty pairs of eyes see much more than the body in the front of the classroom - they see the person.. All teachers know also that "do as I say, not as I do" never works. What you are is what you teach.[54]

Over the long term, school boards developed interviewing and reference procedures that ascertained whether the Catholic applicant was willing to grow in the Catholic faith and foster the community life in a separate school.

Another long-term effect of the Porter-Podgorski case was narrow but crucial for the separate school system. If a Catholic separate school teacher performs an act or lives in such a way that s/he is either causing public scandal to the students and parents or has left the Catholic Church, such matters could lead to dismissal for denominational cause. Obviously, the implications of the Ontario Supreme Court judgment do not apply to a non-Catholic teacher working in a separate school. Nor do they pertain to Catholic teachers who by the very nature of their humanity are less than perfect in their spiritual and apostolic acts; the Bishops know that separate school trustees and teachers are all pilgrims striving for an ideal and that judgment is combined with forgiveness and charity.

But in the narrow application of the case, the Waterloo Unit, for example, had no difficulty deciding not to support a grievance to arbitration for a teacher who had been dismissed by the Waterloo County RCSS Board for entering into a non-Catholic marriage. The OECTA lawyer, Paul Cavalluzzo, agreed that the Unit was within its rights since it believed that its decision was in the interests of the Unit and all OECTA members. Similarly, OECTA did not support a Carleton RCSS Board teacher dismissed for the same reason because the teacher's "public act [was] essentially not in accord with the teachings of the church."[55]

A third long-term effect was the inclusion in some collective agreements of a wording that removed the application of just cause where the school board's action was for denominational reasons. The Lincoln County RCSS Board was the first to do this in 1979.[56] As the OSSTA lawyer put it, separate school trustees "do not want secular arbitrators reviewing essentially religious questions." On the other hand, the teachers have been determined to ensure a wording that *does* provide for an appeal under a just-cause from a dismissal for denominational reasons; otherwise, there would be no protection from arbitrary or unreasonable dismissal based on faulty judgment. For example, a parallel situation to the Porter-Podgorski case happened again in Essex with an AEFO member, but because of a new just-cause clause she was able to begin an appeal procedure. Currently, most separate school boards' collective agreements have a just-cause clause applying to the denominational clause.[57]

Finally and most importantly, the 1978 AGM approved the following "Statement of the philosophy of Christian education," which elaborated on Archbishop Pocock's definition of a Catholic school as "one in which God, His truth, His life, are integrated into the entire syllabus, curriculum and life of the school." It defined the role of the teacher still set down in the policy handbook:

> Catholic teachers are formally committed to the philosophy of Catholic education, and attempt, to the best of their ability and with the support of the community, to communicate by their very words and actions the value of that philosophy. The only tenable position from which teachers may validly perform their function is one of personal integrity. The Catholic teachers' integrity evolves from their growth in a love relationship and deepening commitment to the person of Christ.[58]

Protection of the Teacher. Bill 100 improved the protection of the teacher from arbitrary and/or unjust actions of an administrator or school board. Up to 1975 with many school boards the teacher could appeal to a Board of Reference the termination of a permanent contract. Since Bill 100 expanded the scope of negotiations, the teacher negotiators began to get grievance to arbitration clauses in the collective agreement. This meant that the teachers could grieve step by step from her/his immediate superior, where applicable, through to the director of education, the board, and, if the issue was still not resolved, to arbitration. More significantly, the teacher could grieve not only dismissal, but matters like demotion, transfer, denials for leave, timetable, the lunch period, and performance evaluation. Furthermore, if the collective agreement included a just-cause clause, the teacher could grieve termination of a probationary contract.

Thus, OECTA had many more cases in kind and quantity to deal with after 1975. The Executive assigned Counselling and Relations to Boards of Reference and Teacher Welfare to grievances. The statistics showed they were busy departments. For example, in 1973 and 1976 there were about twenty staff situations, but in 1980 there were 138. In 1977 the provincial office received about 300 calls for advice and assistance from teachers; over eight of these required a legal opinion and sometimes legal action.[59] The kinds of staff issues included access to board minutes and the teacher's performance evaluation, staff having to record time of arrival and departure, charges of assault on pupils, contract termination, pressure to resign, transfer, sick and maternity leave, salary arrears, wrongful dismissal, pupil injury, criminal charges, teacher qualifications, demotion, pension, Boards of Reference, personal crisis, credit for experience, leave of absence for medical reasons, libel, copyright infringement, sick leave during pregnancy, retirement gratuity, cumulative sick leave, and professional ethics. The last item was the most common. Pat O'Neill reported that the interpersonal relationship difficulties between teachers and teachers, teachers and parents, teachers and principals, and teachers and supervisory officers were taking the most time, and were the most difficult to resolve. In 1982, for example, the central office became involved in fifty-one interpersonal relationship cases.[60]

Principals at times found themselves in difficulties because of their new role. Prior to the 1963 government funding most principals were teaching full-time and had a minimal function in terms of staff evaluations. Funding permitted release time for principals. Such time was necessary as the Ministry regulations gave elementary school principals powers over staff and budget that traditionally only secondary school principals had and as the new large boards of 1969 gave different duties to supervisory officers while the principal assumed some of her/his staff performance review responsibilities. A period of adjustment was necessary. OECTA had to explain or remind some principals that the *Teaching Profession Act Regulation* required that the teacher not just sign the principal's report on her/him, but also receive a copy of the report. In addition, the new, more complex, and detailed collective agreements curbed the principal's power to act unilaterally. On the other hand, OECTA understood that the principal's duty was to administer board policies, some of which were less than popular. During the learning curve, OECTA sometimes had to mediate.[61]

One dismaying phenomenon of the times was the appearance of sexual abuse allegations and a few convictions of teachers and custodial staff. In order to avoid false accusations of its members, OECTA deemed it necessary to discourage male teachers from getting into a situation where they were working with one student, especially in a closed classroom. Teachers were also told to avoid bodily contact with students. This caused some teachers inner conflict when they would see a child who badly needed a supportive or encouraging hug, but feared their action could be misunderstood by a viewer or the child.[62]

As a result of the Porter-Podgorski case the philosophy of "support" for the dismissed teacher in a Board of Reference received scrutiny again. The word "support" was avoided in certain cases. Instead, OECTA would provide "legal assistance and representation." If the Executive decided that the merits of a case also warranted financial assistance for the teacher, then that would be forthcoming also. Such a policy, it was hoped, would enable the Executive to make choices in such situations like two members involved on the opposite side of a grievance, like the Porter-Podgorski case, and like a member desiring to "teach the board a lesson" with punitive action.[63]

Four special problems emerged during the 1970s related to diversified staffing, term appointments, interim certificates, and probationary contracts. The first three were contained without much difficulty. One of the Hall-Dennis recommendations was that, in the interests of an open-area, flexible, child-centred school, there be differentiated staffing. Teacher aides could perform lower-level tasks and provide some special talents. But OECTA had to disapprove when the concept became a method for using the budget of the teacher salaries to bring more adults into the classrooms as assistants. The principal of St. Barnabas was proposing to employ four aides instead of two teachers; OECTA rejected his plan. The idea did not catch on in Ontario; where aides were employed, they, according to OECTA and OTF policy, were not to be part of the PTR in the collective agreement.[64] As for term appointments, Bette Stephenson and a Ministry publication, *Issues and Directions*, ran up the flagpole the idea that any consultant, principal, superintendent, or other teacher outside of the classroom should have the position for no longer than five years, at which time s/he would return to the classroom. Some school boards put this policy in place for consultants and supervisory officers, but OECTA labelled it a "shallow idea" that ignored the energy and time invested to get and hold the position and the new skills learned in the position. This arbitrary number of five did not spread to principals or vice-principals.[65] The third problem about interim teaching certificates disappeared because the Ministry of Education abolished them in 1978. But while they existed there were occasions as in the Kapuskasing RCSS Board in 1971 where the supervisory officers interpreted the regulations to mean that the beginning teacher was to be on an interim certificate for *at least* two years. OECTA aimed for a provincial practice that would ensure proper supervision procedures leading to a processing of the interim certificate into a permanent one after two years in the case of satisfactory teachers.[66]

The probationary contract problem needed the attention of all the Units. The difficulty was that the school board was not giving a reason when terminating a probationary contract; it merely passed a motion to terminate and sent a letter with the motion to the teacher. The law did not seem to require anything further. At first, OECTA sought the right for the teacher to have a disputed dismissal reviewed by some kind of appeal process. After Bill 100 the Association urged the units to negotiate for just-cause clauses in the collective agreements. Two arbitration decisions were helpful in this OECTA thrust. One report concluded that without a just-cause provision, the teacher had no protection against demotion; only the procedure, not the fairness of the board decision, could be questioned. If the parties failed to include any limitation on the employer's right to demote staff or dismiss probationary contract teachers, the arbitrators had no business rectifying that omission. More helpful than this "red flag" to teacher negotiators was the arbitration that decided that a probationary teacher was *not* hired for a fixed term, even though the period of probation was fixed by statute; the school board still had to make a decision; therefore, the teacher was entitled to a performance review.[67] If the collective agreement had a just-cause clause, the review would be evidence. Reinforcing these two arbitration points was a judgment in the Supreme Court of Canada. In *Nicholson* v. *Haldimand-Norfolk Regional Board of Police*, 1979, the judges wrote that the constable with less than the eighteen-month probationary period "should have been told why his services were no longer required and given an opportunity to respond .... Status in office deserves this minimum protection, however brief the period for which the office is held."[68] It only remained for OECTA to continue getting more collective agreements with a just-cause clause and to apply the Nicholson judgment to school boards.

With regard to Boards of Reference, OECTA won a precedent-setting case. In 1981 the Bruce-Grey County RCSS Board terminated the contract of Anne Lallouet, a blind French-as-a-Second-Language teacher. (Ironically, the termination took place during the Year of the Handicapped.) She had her contract reinstated as a result of a Board of Reference. Judge F. G. Carter, the Chairman, and one member, Frank Griffin, concluded that the removal of the presence of another teacher in the classroom while Miss Lallouet was teaching, the frequent and closely-spaced visits of the supervisory staff, and other factors constituted improper, unreasonable, and unfair actions. The importance of this case that OECTA supported was threefold. First, if a school board knowingly and willingly hires a teacher with a disability that requires some adjustment to her/his contractual obligations, then the board should make those modifications. Second, before a school board makes its final decision whether or not to dismiss a teacher on the recommendation of its director of education, it must give the teacher an opportunity to meet with it and to do so without the presence of her/his supervisors in order to hear her/his side of the story. Third, the school boards must take the time necessary to review all the evidence and information pertinent to the issue of dismissal rather than merely accept and make a motion on the basis of the supervisory officers' reports. The last two points called for a change in the traditional practices of school boards dismissing teachers.[69]

As noted, grievances, Boards of Reference, and staff problems increased during the seventies. Reports from Ed Alexander and Pat O'Neill in 1979, 1980, and 1982 point to an "alarming" increase in personal staff crises because of more and more teachers experiencing untoward stress. They could only speculate on the societal, school-related, and personal reasons for such stress, but they had no trouble listing its manifestations: problems with teacher performance, difficulties with interpersonal relations, psychological problems, alcohol and drug addiction, marital stress and breakdowns, financial troubles, and assault charges. Although the vast majority of teachers lived their vocation happily and successfully, the number of teachers with problems and enquiries to the provincial office for advice regarding a career change was increasing. O'Neill and Alexander recommended that school boards afford four-over-five plans, sabbatical and study leaves, fitness workshops, long-term disability plans, and stress management courses. Units were urged to negotiate employee-assistance programmes and given the characteristics of an exemplary one. A number of school boards implemented non-judgmental, educational, supportive programmes that helped and protected the anonymity of the teachers and their families. The Unit developed and took ownership of the programme for the school board.[70]

Professional Development. The early and middle 1970s saw a preponderance of energy, time, and financial and personal resources spent on matters to do with Bill 100 and teacher welfare and there was even a question in Frank Griffin's mind about whether OECTA's was involved in professional development at all. However, in the late 1970s the balance returned. People like Brock Commeford from the Dufferin-Peel Secondary Unit would criticize the low level of spending (12 per cent) for local professional development and remind the members that OECTA was not only a union, but a professional association.[71]

The Professional Development Committee submitted a policy statement approved in 1978:

> Professional development is a life long growth process. The professional teacher in our Catholic schools accepts responsibility for this growth. The teacher developing professionally must maintain a balance of thought to action, study to experience, belief to knowledge, and individuality to community. It is by means of this balance that we can hope to achieve an enriched mind, a maturing spiritual growth, and the maintenance of physical and mental health. The personal acceptance of this obligation will result in benefits to the teacher and the school community.
>
> As all educators are, because of individual differences, at various stages of professional competence, it then becomes our responsibility to share our strengths, accept our limitations, and develop our potential. We do this because we are professionals.[72]

Working from this philosophy OECTA allocated considerable human and financial resources to the Professional Development department. Albert (Ab) Dukacz had been hired for Teacher Welfare in 1981, but, because of his doctorate in the field of professional development, was transferred there by Fr. Kavanagh in 1983.

Albert Dukacz was born in Kirkland Lake and fit the profile of many other members of the OECTA secretariat in that his father, a Polish immigrant, Antoni Dukacz, was a member of the gold miners' union which during the winter strike of 1941-42 was broken by the mine owners. His mother was Victoria Sikorski whom his father as a recent immigrant had met while farming in Saskatchewan. His brothers, Julian, Paul, Stanley, his sisters, Lucy and Jean, and Ab all went to Holy Name separate school and Kirkland Lake Collegiate and Vocational Institute. The family believed strongly in education; Ab went to North Bay Teachers' College and immediately began teaching at St. Francis, New Liskeard. After two years, in accordance with an agreement made when he was hired, Ab Dukacz was promoted to principal of St. Francis. In 1963-64 he took a year off to study at the University of Western Ontario, where he met his future wife, Kathryn Atmore, a nurse. Ab then worked for the London Separate School Board at Catholic Central, teaching grades nine and ten English and mathematics. Albert married Kathryn in the mid-sixties; they would have two children, Stephen and Krysha. He also acquired his B.A..

Ab was promoted to vice-principal of St. Peter. He became the principal of St. Matthew, then St. Patrick. He would spend the rest of his teaching career in London. He graduated from OISE with an M.Ed. During 1975-76 Ab took a second year off to begin his doctorate; his thesis was "The Role of PD Days in the Implementation of Curriculum." When he returned to the Middlesex County RCSS Board he did not get back a principalship; in Ab's opinion, board administrators saw his role in salary negotiations as "disloyal" and decided he ought not continue as principal.

In 1976-77 he taught at St. Thomas More, then for a third year went to study, thereby demonstrating a singular willingness to sacrifice a teacher's salary for his own growth (although he did get two scholarships from OECTA). In 1978 he passed the supervisory officer's written and oral examinations and returned to teach until 1980 at St. Pius X separate school. For four summers he taught the principals' course, once in Nova Scotia, twice at Queen's University, and once in Yellowknife. In 1983 he received his Ed.D. from OISE.

Albert Dukacz's life with OECTA began in London. He attended a general information meeting called by the chief negotiator who publicly stated that he had gone as far as he could go in negotiating with the school board, because he had been made to feel vulnerable, in his opinion, by the board's secretary treasurer; attention had been directed to his mortgage. ("Things didn't change much over the years," recalled Ab in a recent interview. "One of the negotiators who followed me in London-Middlesex was inexplicably asked to provide a pastor's reference.") Ab felt affronted on the chief negotiator's behalf and began developing a militant attitude. He served on various committees, the local executive, and an OTF curriculum committee. Most significantly for his future, he was chief negotiator when in November 1972, 94 per cent of the teachers' resignations were submitted to the board; a settlement was not reached until the second last day of school in December. "We made a conscious decision to act in mid-year," Ab explained, "because we knew it would be easier to hold our membership together over the Christmas break than over the summer." As a result of this action here and in other jurisdictions, the government moved to prevent a repetition between this time and the later passage of Bill 100.

In November 1980, Ab applied for a position with the Teacher Welfare department along with forty-eight other applicants. After the Personnel Committee interviewed thirteen of them, Ab was offered the position. He is now coordinator of the Professional Development department.[73]

OECTA greatly increased its budget for professional activities a few years before Ab came into the department. In 1977 Derry Byrne, Neil Doherty, and Peter Murphy one evening at the Duke of Gloucester pub in Toronto conceived the idea of a Commission of Inquiry into early childhood and primary education and at the AGM budgeted $75 000. FWTAO, OPSMTF, and AEFO also decided to add another $75 000 each. With this $300 000 Laurier Lapierre, a broadcaster, journalist and former professor, and Ada Schermann, a teacher of early childhood education at the University of Toronto's Institute for Child Studies, were hired. Their report, completed in 1982, was called *To Herald a Child.* It made ninety-two recommendations to combat the narrow definition of the basics, eschewed by government and business, as well as the overcrowding of small children in schools. Some of the reforms prompted by the report were the abolition of corporal punishment, additional government grants for school boards with grades one and two limited to about twenty pupils, day-care centres built as part of new high schools, tightened regulations and procedures for discovering and reporting child abuse situations, all-day and junior kindergarten programmes, and procedures for early identification of learning problems.[74] When the Welland County RCSS Board announced its intention in 1983 to eliminate junior kindergarten, the OECTA Unit through the use of a rally, radio spots, and news releases, fought the idea; the Board reconsidered.[75]

The main, large annual conferences OECTA mounted each year were the CCDC, principals', and secondary schools', as well as a collective bargaining forum. In addition, workshops were held for unit executives, consultants, and teachers involved with grievances, political action, and professional development. A host of other workshops, short courses, and seminars took place on an as-needed and response basis. Some of the topics were classroom management and discipline, unit and long-range planning, employee assistance plans, teacher evaluation, communication techniques, special education, designing learning experiences, stress management, interviewing skills, and leadership effectiveness. There were study/travel trips to Great Britain, Athens, and Israel and visits to schools in Durham and Liverpool.[76] Besides all this, the now high-profile Professional Development department had responsibility for the OECTA/OSSTA religious education courses and other short courses concentrating on the personal, spiritual development of the teacher.

As teachers and OECTA grew professionally, they expected that teacher evaluation would be conducted by principals and supervisory officers in a professional manner. This meant for OECTA and OTF that, first of all, coordinators, consultants, and department heads should not be involved in teacher evaluation; their job is to assist teachers and help them deliver and evaluate their curriculum; secondly, there should be a clear distinction between and different procedures for evaluation for improvement of performance (ideally, the most common purpose) and for employment decisions; and, thirdly, staff should be involved in the design of evaluation processes, and such processes should be incorporated into the collective agreement.[77]

In 1972 OECTA developed an evaluation policy. It stated that written evaluations were to be conducted openly, with a copy available to the teacher and that there was to be a conference with the teacher before the final version of the evaluation was written. In 1983 Paul

Glynn conducted a survey among the members on evaluation. It revealed that teachers appreciated clear criteria at the start of the year, with updates as needed, several conferences based on *all* objective data, several classroom visits by the principal, followed by an interview discussion, and a team approach. Teachers were disturbed by evaluation based on one visit per year, lack of clear criteria, one-sided evaluation, evaluation focussing on one facet only, a testing judgmental atmosphere, and a subjective and/or negative modus operandi.[78]

Religious Education. The principal focus of the Professional Development Department was on the formation of the members in religious education. Every year, summer and winter, from 1971 to 1984, there were between five and eleven centres offering the OECTA/OSSTA religious education courses, Parts I, II, and III. By 1982 over 9400 teachers had completed Part I.[79] Where tuition could not cover all expenses, especially in the smaller centres, OECTA and OSSTA would subsidize the courses. The MSSB provided the courses free to its teachers; the rest of the school boards supplied space and equipment.

Fr. Frank Ruetz, C.R. When Sr. Sheila moved into other professional development activities, OECTA in 1976 hired Fr. Ruetz to take over her responsibilities. Father spent his early years on a dairy farm near Walkerton, but his father, Henry Ruetz, and mother, Eleanor Schnurr, could not make enough from it to support the large family: Kathleen, Theresa, Gerard, Jack, Albert, Robert, and Frank. They moved to Kitchener where Henry worked in maintenance for Bell Telephone. Frank attended St. Mary elementary school and St. Jerome high school. He then entered the novitiate of the Congregation of the Resurrection and was ordained a priest in 1958. During this time he acquired a B.A. from the University of Western Ontario and four years of theology.

In 1959 Fr. Frank began teaching English and French at Scollard Hall, North Bay, then attended the two summers in London for his HSA. He taught Latin, then for nine years Latin and religious education as department head at St. Jerome High School. In the summers he went to Loyola University, Chicago where, as he put it, he "scrambled for answers to questions he had never been asked before Vatican II." The University awarded him a Master's in Pastoral Theology. From 1968 to 1970 Father served as chaplain at St. David intermediate school, Waterloo; as the faith person in the school he had to ask himself such questions as what does a Catholic school do and what is a Catholic teacher. To help him answer these questions he asked his Order for some time. For three years he worked on a Ph.D. dissertation on the correlation between the faith development of the student and the faith expression and environment of the staff. Notre Dame University, Indiana conferred on him a Ph.D. He returned to the Waterloo County RCSS Board to be its staff development officer and to run the grade eight residential retreat programme. He brought this extensive academic and professional background to OECTA from 1976 to 1989. Then he was asked by the Resurrectionists to be Director of their Centre for Lifelong Learning; it offers graduate-level courses for people who feel called to be educational lay leaders.[80]

Derry Byrne, the president when Father was employed, encouraged him to let the principals and staffs take care of the OECTA/OSSTA religious education courses once he organized them. This would allow him to provide workshops, seminars, and professional development days in faith development for the teachers and their schools. With the Philosophy of Education Committee and its chairperson, George VanderZanden, he offered four programmes during his time with the Association. "AFFIRM" was an acronym for awareness of others, fullness of life, faith interdependence, responsibility, and mapping the journey. "Genesis 2" was a faith development process to help a staff integrate Gospel values in the school. "Shepherding the Shepherds" was for principals, vice-principals, and supervisory officers. All these numerous workshops concentrated on the quality of life of the teacher, helping teachers to help themselves and to provide a living faith community in the separate schools. In addition, there was the annual CCDC which in 1981 took as its theme faith development.[81]

Fr. Ruetz did have to pay considerable attention to the OECTA/OSSTA religious education courses because of some special questions that arose.

The first problem Father inherited concerned the religious education programme for Catholic students in the pre-service teachers' course in the faculties of education. Some faculties were offering no courses in religious education; others anything from fourteen to twenty-four hours. Considering that some Catholic student teachers had never attended a Catholic high school and, therefore, the instructor had to be concerned about both knowledge and methodology, there was insufficient time in all of the faculties. OECTA and OSSTA began an "intensive" effort to have a forty-hour course at all of them. This would take some time and would not result in complete success. Currently, there is some kind of course everywhere, but there is not consistency of content or number of hours.[82]

In 1976 the Brock University and University of Toronto faculties of education went a different route. They offered the full 120-hour OECTA/OSSTA religious education course to their student teachers. Later, others would do the same. But OTF decided that the university year allowed only enough time to prepare the student for the regular teacher's certificate; acquiring an additional qualification in, for example, physical education or guidance would have to wait until after the pre-service year. OECTA and OSSTA applied this same rationale to religious education and ceased offering the 120-hour course with the faculties. There was some consternation and pressure put on the Associations, but they reaffirmed their position. In 1983 the Ministry solved the problem by eliminating additional qualifications in the pre-service year.[83]

The second problem with the religious education courses, for student and practising teachers, was that there was no province-wide curriculum guideline or course of studies for Catholic high schools. It was difficult for the instructors to prepare the high school teachers as well as they did the elementary school teachers, using the *Come to the Father* series for the latter. In 1980 OECTA engaged Sr. Magdalen O'Rourke, C.N.D., to prepare a course outline for religious education in the high school grades. Her B.A. and B.Ed. from St. Francis Xavier University, Antigonish, M.R.E. from the University of Toronto's St. Michael's College, and experience as a religious education coordinator qualified her for the task. Her course became the start of the development later of more detailed curricula.[84]

The third question was whether or not OECTA should have a policy that the pre-service course in religious education be a prerequisite for employment of a Catholic teacher by a separate school board and that Part I be a prerequisite for a permanent contract. The arguments on both sides of this issue were obvious, but the outcome was not. Between 1971 and 1982 the debate arose a number of times at the Executive, Board of Directors, and AGM levels.[85] Frank Griffin stated the one side in his customary strong style:

> It's quite unforgivable...to even think of debasing our certificates in religious education into passports for promotion or into vouchers for purchase of security of tenure....It would be tragic if what the teachers instituted

> from a high sense of purpose were to turn into a weapon to be used against them.[86]

Those OECTA members who asserted that teachers had training in education in the other subjects they taught and, therefore, should have the same in religious education and religion across the curriculum sought a compromise. At first, they proposed a policy that would label the religious education certificate as "desirable," but the Executive dismissed it with the remark that such a policy would be "tautological. This Association would not be running a course and granting a certificate if it were not a desirable professional qualification for our members."[87] But the Joint Executive of the OECTA/OSSTA in 1980 did accept the premise when it passed the motion that the forty-hour faculty of education course be the "acceptable minimum" and Part I be the "desirable basic qualification."[88]

Finally deciding that OECTA was not the appropriate agency to be designing policies that would restrict the employment of its members, the Joint Executive emphasized an invitational and strongly encouraging philosophy and exhorted directors of education and separate school boards to sponsor the OECTA/OSSTA courses.[89] The whole argument became academic when a number of boards developed policies that required Part I for a permanent contract and Part II for an administrative position.

A very serious matter absorbed the energies of OECTA throughout the decade: potential separate school teachers with a background in theology sometimes could not get into a faculty of education; practising separate school teachers could not get additional qualifications in theology, except for the OECTA/OSSTA courses. The reason for this lay in the regulation *Ontario Teacher's Qualifications*. Schedule A in the regulation listed all the subjects that were "teachable" in the secondary schools. To get into a faculty of education the candidate either had to pick up other courses outside of religious education or avoid such courses and divinity degrees altogether when attending university. The implications for staffing of separate schools were quite negative. In 1977 OECTA asked OTF to request the Ministry to recognize religious education for credit purposes in grades nine and ten. OTF concurred and the Ministry granted the request the following year.[90] Now that religious education had equal status with the other subjects for high school credit purposes, OECTA, working with Ontario Conference of Catholic Bishops (OCCB) and the Ontario Catholic Supervisory

Officers' Association (OCSOA), mounted another bid to have religious education added to Schedule A. They met with the deans, secured the support of OTF, and submitted a brief to the Ministry. H. K. Fisher, the Deputy Minister of Education, expressed the position succinctly. "All the qualifications listed there [in Schedule A] relate directly to curriculum guidelines....There is no guideline for Religious Studies for secondary schools. Accordingly, there can be no related qualification which could be listed in Schedule A."[91] The letter was worded carefully: only separate schools could offer grades nine and ten religious education credits; separate schools could not operate high schools. By dint of semantics the Ministry kept religious education off Schedule A until the fall of 1993. Joe Culliton, chairperson of the Committee to Have Religious Studies Made a Teachable Subject, summed up the problem. Teachers desirous of recognition of an academic background in theology for admission to a faculty, of faculty courses in religious education methodology at the secondary level, of inspection of practise teaching in religion, and of certification in the additional qualification of senior division religious education were out of luck.[92]

Finally, there was the administrative task of staffing all the OECTA/OSSTA courses. OECTA continued to award annually two scholarships and three fellowships for teachers to obtain a leave of absence from their boards and study religion.[93] A complement was built up. Since by canon law the Bishop is responsible ultimately for religious education in the diocese, OCCB set up a committee to approve the principals to be appointed to the OECTA/OSSTA courses and to discuss procedures for evaluating the courses, staffs, and guest speakers. The Auxiliary Bishop of Toronto, Aloysius M. Ambrozic, advised Fr. Ruetz that this advisory committee of Toronto would assist the Bishops with their responsibility. It was OECTA's policy that, if any potential staff member were considered unsuitable, the committee would state in writing the reasons for its opinion and would provide a hearing for the person. S/he could ask OECTA for support in getting reconsideration.[94]

Such monitoring, as well as the participation of Bishops Doyle, McCarthy, and Sherlock as guest speakers in the courses, was perhaps providential when Peter Worthington of the *Toronto Sun* attacked the so-called left-wing slant of the courses. In the July 28, 1983 issue he described the course as one that revolved around "opposing nuclear testing, abolishing the cruise missile, praying for Nicaragua's Sandinista regime, pulling for the revolutionaries in El Salvador, and attacking

American imperialism." The course, in Worthington's opinion, stressed liberation theology and social sin with a radical, Marxist critique.[95]

Kuchinak's reply was printed in the August 30 edition. As principal it was his duty to make candidates aware of problems in society and, particularly, of the Pope's denunciation of nuclear arms proliferation. This did not mean he neglected the five areas of the course: Scripture, ethics, doctrine, catechetics, and sacramental theology.[96] In the following two months Fr. Thomas J. Day, a trustee with the MSSB, and Bishop Ambrozic both defended the course. In a letter to OECTA and OSSTA Fr. Day stated the course's purpose was "to absorb...the gospels, a number of papal encyclicals, and the statements of our Canadian bishops" and praised it for "sound doctrinal theology and scriptural teachings." Further responding to Worthington, he wrote, "Suspiciously, the strongest opponents of the course were not participants. The vast majority of participants were immensely enriched, stimulated, and inspired. The criticisms are compounded hearsay."[97] Bishop Ambrozic in a letter to the president, Kevin Kennedy, referred to the "magnificent service of the OECTA and OSSTA." [98]

Nevertheless, teachers taking the OECTA/OSSTA course were not getting the "oldtime religion." As one participant expressed it, "It was with great difficulty that I had to sever myself from the memorized answers, stencilled formulas, and discover who I am." The candidate explained that there had been nothing else to give teachers "insight into the call of Vatican II" and described the course as "unique adult catechesis" for teachers, many of whom had not been given the opportunity to continue their Catholic education beyond grade eight.[99]

Social Justice. Not only in the religious education courses, but also in a number of other areas, OECTA continued to pursue social justice issues as it had started to do in the previous decade. The Association applied social justice principles to its retired members and female members, then to the pupils with learning disabilities, then to the funding of separate schools, and next to the third world countries.

Superannuation. After years of inflation many retired teachers found their superannuation inadequate as a sole source of income. OECTA and OTF made the solution to this serious problem a high priority. As a temporary expedient the government responded to OTF's descriptions of needy cases by providing an escalation clause in the pension of 4 per cent in 1970 and 2 per cent in 1971. The federations pushed for a permanent, annual escalation based on the cost of living. Effective January 1, 1976, the *Superannuation Adjustment Benefits Act* marked the most significant improvement in pensions since superannuation began; it provided for automatic adjustment of pensions geared to the cost of living index to a maximum of 8 per cent per year; if the cost of living exceeded 8 per cent, the excess would be a future credit applied in a year when it was less than 8 per cent. Pensioned teachers for the first time could maintain the purchasing powers of their pensions.[100]

OECTA and the other affiliates also realized three other notable improvements in teacher pensions. As of 1984 the calculation for the pension would be based on the best five years of teaching. This would protect the pensions of teachers who for one reason or another left higher-paying positions of responsibility to return to the classroom. The calculation also resulted in higher pensions than those based on seven years. Secondly, that same year introduced annualization. Staff members, for example, kindergarten teachers, who had taught only half-time or less than full-time, could count each calendar year toward the number of years required for a pension, instead of just a fraction. Thirdly, in 1971 teachers no longer had to wait until age sixty-two or sixty-five for a full pension. If the teacher's age and experience added up to ninety and the teacher was at least fifty-five years old, then s/he received 2 per cent times the number of years taught up to a maximum of 70 per cent; the second calculation involved the average of her/his best seven, later five, years of salary.[101]

Women's Issues. In 1967 the United Nations passed a declaration on discrimination against women. In 1970 Canada's *Royal Commission on the Status of Women Report* expressed concern about sex-role stereotyping in textbooks, day- and after-school child care, and equal opportunity of the sexes in employment and sports. The same year Ontario's *Women's Equal Employment Opportunity Act* prohibited discrimination in hiring, firing, training, or promoting because of sex or marital status. In 1973 the Ontario government published a Green Paper, "Equal Opportunity for Women: A Plan for Action"; it contained recommendations for education, guidance and counselling and the establishment of the Ontario Advisory Council on the Status of Women; it and a federal counterpart came into existence. At the same time Thomas Wells sent a memorandum to all school boards urging them to provide equal opportunities for women and to base promotions solely on merit. His next memorandum in 1976 stated that progress had been too slow. In 1979 a government report, "Today and Tomorrow" repeated that progress was still slow; the Ministry of Education began including a sex-equity policy in its curriculum guidelines. In 1983 the Ontario Women's Directorate was established to report to the Minister Responsible for Women's Issues; it coordinated a number of programmes, including those concerned with the education of young women in secondary schools. Again in 1983 Judge Rosalie Silverman Abella was appointed Commissioner for the Commission of Inquiry on Equality in Employment. At a 1984 conference, "Focus on Leadership: Affirmative Action in School Boards," organized by FWTAO and supported by all the affiliates, Bette Stephenson announced that she was officially requesting that each school board in Ontario adopt a formal programme of affirmative action for women employees.[102]

OECTA was part of this movement, moving no faster on this social justice issue than the rest of society, but moving. The low point of the 1954 threatened married women's strike was in a different time, even though vestiges of old attitudes survived. Peter Murphy recalled the chair*man* of the Terrace Bay Separate School Board (emphasis added), a woman, telling him as chief negotiator that, "We think this is a very good starting salary for a young woman."[103] Suzann Jones and Liz Dorner remembered reports in the mid-1970s from the variously named committees on women's issues being received by the AGM delegates with quiet tolerance and sometimes a few jokes. Victoria Hannah recalled that at one AGM there was a lengthy debate when her Committee recommended an allowance for child care for married women attending the AGM or OECTA meetings and conferences. One male delegate with injured feelings assured the assembly that he did the shopping for his wife. One married woman reflected the attitude of a number of delegates when she said that she managed to attend OECTA meetings without the kind of help being proposed. A single woman felt compelled to tell the delegates that it was a woman's choice to have children and, therefore, she should not expect special consideration. With 199 female delegates out of 502 one would have thought that there would have been enough male votes which, combined with the female votes, would have passed the motion; not so. Victoria Hannah and some of her supporters surmised that her Committee report was a contributing factor to her defeat when she ran for provincial vice-president.[104]

Attitudes developed over a lifetime did change. Certain statistics were brought to the Association's attention. A 1979 report stated that

68 per cent of the total OECTA membership was female, yet only 45 per cent of the AGM delegates, 35 per cent of the provincial committee members, 30 per cent of the unit presidents, 28 per cent of the Board of Directors, 20 per cent of the OTF Board of Governors, and 9 per cent of the Executive were women. In 1982 the *OECTA Reporter* wrote that the average salary of female teachers in OECTA was 22 per cent below that of their male counterparts.[105]

OECTA, somewhat painstakingly, developed a structure to deal with these problems and to reflect the provincial government's initiatives. In the mid-1970s the Women in Catholic Education Committee was established. It did not have sufficient support to become a standing committee, but after some discussion was allowed to continue for another year in 1976 and again in 1977. In 1978, having been disbanded, the Committee was resurrected. Sr. Sheila, Liz Dorner, and Doreen Brady were the driving forces behind the Committee, but neither its title nor its status reflected the aims of the movement for the equality for women. Doreen Brady at the 1978 resurrection had the Committee become an Executive sub-committee; this meant that the Executive would handpick the members and that the Executive would be on the sub-committee. With this level of support the sub-committee in 1981 evolved into the Equal Opportunity Special Committee.[106]

The aims of these three committees consisted in the main of the following: to counter myths about women as leaders, to eliminate sex stereotyping in textbooks, guidance, and teaching, to promote day care centres, to deal with outmoded expectations of the Church and society with regard to the roles of women as mother, wife, and single woman, to improve interviewing and promotion practices with female applicants, to get decent maternity and adoption leave plans in collective agreements, to examine ways and means of improving the level of involvement of women in OECTA, to inform all members of current trends, issues, and problems regarding sex-role stereotyping and women's studies, to assist in the development of curriculum that promotes women's studies, to ensure that all members have equal promotion opportunities, and to ensure the observance of human rights.[107]

Doreen Brady in a report to the Executive listed attitudes that teachers needed to erase in themselves and other adults conditioned by a sex-stereotyped upbringing. Society (and some women themselves) believed that women must care for their children, that a working mother/wife must carry out all the homemaker duties too, and that their husbands' careers were more important than the wives working on a

B.A. or qualifying themselves for promotion. Some women, Doreen maintained, had subconscious inhibitions against running for office, travelling alone, or "pushing themselves ahead of men."[108]

In 1975 Sr. Jean DeLuca, C.S.J., at the CCDC gave a visionary, forward-looking speech on how society had narrowed the lives of married women:

> Even allowing for full time, pre-school care by the mother, women today need not stay home more than a decade. At the same time, the life expectancy has doubled. Today's woman is asking, 'Must I be expected to spend my life on the fringes of today's world?'...Women have been obliged to live vicariously in their husbands. But to live vicariously in anyone is to make an idol out of that person, to deny one's own integrity.[109]

As awareness rose, OECTA took some actions:

- In 1977 it asked Fr. Kelly Walker to write a brief to the Canadian Conference of Bishops on ministries for women. One of the original recommendations was that women be eligible to receive all seven sacraments; the 1977 AGM rejected it. The final draft submitted, which the Executive endorsed, advocated that lay ministers be welcomed to perform a variety of roles in the Church and that women be equal associates in the roles;[110]
- the OECTA's employment application forms were submitted to the Ontario Human Rights Commission to be appraised;
- the *OECTA Reporter* printed articles on women's issues, including one on battered wives and one on the inequality of women in the Church;
- the Association with the MSSB sponsored an Affirmative Action conference and wrote each unit president, all school board chairs, the Minister of Education, the Women's Directorate, and the NDP and Liberal educational critics recommending that every school board establish affirmative action policies;
- the Equal Opportunity Committee helped units to form their own Equal Opportunity committees; the Council of Presidents encouraged them;
- Doreen Brady got together all the female secretaries for networking and dealing with common concerns; and
- the 1984 OECTA objectives included the encouragement of Equal Opportunity Committees to provide affirmative action programmes.[111]

OECTA regarded with some optimism the future of equal opportunity and affirmative action when it considered that the 1984-85 Executive was 50 per cent female: Susan LaRosa and Eileen Lennon were counsellors, Noella Mulligan treasurer, and Suzann Jones second vice-president.

Bill 82. OECTA's principal and important contribution to Catholic education in the area of special education was its successful fight for the rights of the Catholic parents and children who, to use the legal phrase employed then, were educably mentally retarded (EMR).

The first school for trainable mentally retarded (TMR) children in Canada opened in Kirkland Lake in 1947; others followed, run by the Ontario Association for the Mentally Retarded (OAMR). In 1967 the Report of the Ontario Legislature's Select Committee on youth recommended that these children and 104 schools be under boards of education. Then the children could be considered as high school students for grant purposes. They were deemed too expensive to be educated with elementary school grants. The Ministry of Education's acceptance of this premise eliminated separate school boards from the plan.[112]

In the early 1970s the provincial government released a white paper on de-institutionalizing children where possible and invited responses. Bernard Farley, a superintendent with the MSSB, had a daughter, Mary Ann, with Down's Syndrome, who was about to start school. He wondered why it was necessary and deemed proper to remove her from her peers and send her to a special segregated class in a public school. He developed a paper and contacted his previous principal, Frank Griffin, now at OECTA. Griffin found the paper well written and recommended that it become an OECTA brief. "To Break the Silence" was presented to the Honourable Robert Welch, the Provincial Secretary for Social Development, in 1973. It expressed the belief that development as a total person necessarily included spiritual growth in a God-centred education system and described the desirable threefold human bond with the child, the family, and the Church. The brief recommended that the schools for TMR children include separate schools. The aim would be to provide for Catholic handicapped children increased freedom in life and spirituality, further development of their awareness of their own human value, and further human and spiritual growth for the whole Roman Catholic community "through the inspiration afforded by daily interaction with its handicapped members."[113]

The brief was sent also to the three provincial political leaders, the Bishops, the MPPs, and the separate school boards. The following year Onésime Tremblay, superintendent of the Sudbury District RCSS Board, wrote Thomas Wells requesting on behalf of his board the right to operate classes for TMR children. He pointed out that under a section in the legislation permitting public and separate school boards to purchase facilities and services from each other the Sudbury District Board of Education was buying education for its French-language TMR children from the separate school board. Tremblay then wrote to all the separate school boards asking for their support in pressuring the Minister of Education into amending the legislation to empower them to operate TMR classes.[114]

The responses to OECTA and the Sudbury board from certain quarters were not favourable. Margot Scott, president of the OAMR, responded in July 1973 to the OECTA brief. The old argument of fragmentation was raised: "the best interest of retarded students would be served by having one school system rather than two."[115] In 1974 the Ministry did not allow the agreement between the two Sudbury boards to be renewed.[116] In 1976 at the OTF Board of Governors, FWTAO, OPSMTF, and OSSTF blocked the AEFO-OECTA resolution that OTF press the Minister of Education to amend the legislation to allow separate school boards to operate TMR classes and schools.[117]

OECTA and OSSTA did not let the matter rest. In 1976 OSSTA and l'Association française des conseils scolaires de l'Ontario (AFCSO) submitted "Separate School Education for Trainable Retarded Children" to Thomas Wells. In 1978, OECTA in its brief to the Jackson Commission on Declining Enrolment repeated its 1973 recommendation. In 1979, Elie Martel, MPP and ex-OECTA district president, introduced a private member's bill with the desired amendment. Also, OECTA did not give up on OTF, going to it again in 1977 and in 1979 with the motion OTF defeated in 1976. The vote remained thirty to twenty against any extension of funding or rights to separate schools.[118]

By then Bill 82 was on the horizon, and the focus narrowed to making sure the separate school right to educate TMR pupils was included in the Bill. Given the philosophy of inclusion, mainstreaming, and least restrictive environment in the Bill, this turned out to be not a difficult task for OECTA and other Catholic associations. Although the Association of Large School Boards of Ontario (ALSBO) and OTF were still opposed,OECTA's meetings with sympathetic MPPs and a telegram to Bette Stephenson convinced a government probably already persuaded to give the legislative power to separate school boards to operate classes for TMR children.[119]

OECTA during the time of Bill 82 developed a philosophy, workshops, and curriculum publications for its members. It worked from the following 1979 position:

> Children by virtue of their God-given humanity have the right to an education that develops their potential to the fullest within the least restrictive environment while giving full consideration to their individual needs. Exceptional children, as unique children of God, have the right to be a part of the mainstream of education to the extent to which it is practical and beneficial to each child. This implies providing the best educational milieu in the regular schools for all students regardless of their exceptionalities, but it is not the placement of students into a classroom without consideration of their exceptionalities or without the provision of supplementary aids and services.[120]

The OECTA publication that served as the major support for teachers, schools and boards implementing Bill 82 was the 1982 *Room for All*, developed by Michael McGinnis, chair of the Ad Hoc Exceptional Child Committee, Anne Androvich, Anne Dube, Paul Loosemore, and Robert Scott, with David Murray as their principal writer. This forty-page booklet contained a philosophy and action plan for implementation with regard to in-servicing the teacher, developing curriculum, educating the parent, using the resource withdrawal model, and providing a religious dimension. It recommended a primary division class size of twenty pupils with two integrated pupils and in the junior division twenty-five with three; otherwise, there would be "wholesale dumping."[121] (This would later become a strike issue with the MSSB.)

The second major publication was "That They May Have Life" by Sr. Mary Hamilton, C.N.D. It consisted of a series of lessons in religion for special education pupils, each lesson containing a theme, aim, Scriptural reference, message, response, and paraliturgy. Sister's ideas were incorporated into the OECTA/OSSTA religious education course. Also, OECTA met with the Bishops to discuss how the exceptional child could participate fully in the liturgy of the Church and the desirability of a pastoral ministry for the handicapped in every diocese. Finally, for use in the many special education workshops OECTA conducted, a twenty-minute film documentary was produced to show how the Hamilton-Wentworth RCSS Board mainstreamed severely handicapped children and a media kit was made to accompany *Room for All*.[122]

Corporation Taxes. Once Thomas Wells imposed ceilings on the amount of money eligible for grants that a school board could raise from taxes and spend, inequity returned. The public school board with access to corporation taxes could exceed the ceilings and forego the grants; the separate school board with in most cases a grant rate of 80 per cent and higher, could not, practically speaking, spend over the ceilings. As more and more boards went over the ceilings, separate school boards' per-pupil expenditures dropped below those of the public school boards. The level of government support for education dropped from 60 per cent across Ontario in 1972 to 51.5 per cent in 1979.[123]

The pressure was building for a solution to the inequity of corporation tax revenues for school boards. In 1967 the Ontario Commission on Taxation Report recommended that corporation taxes in each municipality be collected and "pooled" for distribution to the public and separate school board on the basis of pupil enrolment. In 1977 the provincial government announced tax reform; the next year the Commission on the Reform of Property Taxation in Ontario recommended pooling on the basis of the residential assessment of the public and separate school board. Also in 1977 the Mayo Report recommended pooling in the Carleton-Ottawa area. In 1982 James Martin of the Ministry of Education announced his pooling plan.[124]

The opposition to pooling from OSSTF, FWTAO, OPSMTF, and ALSBO was constant. Although one might admit an inequity, one was not anxious to solve the problem by reducing one's own revenues. When the ALSBO 1983 brief to Martin's Advisory Committee on Financing Elementary and Secondary Education stated that pooling was "an unacceptable solution to the problem of unequal assessment," and appealed to the principle of local control of locally generated revenues, the three OTF affiliates agreed.[125] This prompted Kevin Kennedy, the president, to say, "I can only admire the forthright way in which some affiliates go after their own interest and will use any vehicle to do so."[126]

Thus, in 1976 OECTA reinforced the OSSTA-AFCSO brief by submitting its own to the Blair Commission. In the 1980s it tried to influence the outcome by its membership on OTF and on Martin's advisory committee. But the votes were never quite there. OECTA did, however, convince OTF to ask the Ministry for equality of funding in grades nine and ten between public and separate school boards. In 1983 the Association chose as one of its objectives the pursuit of improved funding for separate schools and launched a communications campaign with radio spots on seventy stations drawing attention to the separate school boards' lack of corporate assessment and fair funding.[127]

Project Overseas. OECTA did not confine itself to social justice issues only in the Ontario school system. Responding to the call of the Canadian Bishops in general and, in the case of Project Overseas, to CTF in particular, the Association reached out to the developing countries.

The concept of Project Overseas surfaced in 1961 when the Nigeria Union of Teachers at a conference of the WCOTP asked CTF to send two Canadian teachers to assist the Union in organizing and conducting a training programme for unqualified or under-qualified teachers in Nigeria. Since 1962 CTF has sent over 1200 teachers to developing countries. Project Overseas' aims are to raise the status of the teaching profession, to assist teacher organizations to mount programmes to enhance the status of their members and to pass on the skills to leaders so that they can carry on independently, since the philosophy is "Teachers helping Teachers"; school administrators, specialists in teaching English as a second language, textbook authors, designers of curriculum, and exemplary classroom teachers are in demand.[128]

In 1971 the Educational Aid Committee dedicated itself long-term to Project Overseas. CTF and the host teachers' union have organized the sessions and OECTA has sent two (starting in 1977 three) teachers each summer. From about thirty-five applicants per year, the Committee has selected the teachers and paid their travel and living expenses. Since about 1981 the Association has been sending in the winter two retired teachers or teachers who can get released to Project Overseas II teacher education courses. OECTA has been a participant in Project Overseas in a large number of Third World countries; Belize, Botswana, British Honduras, Ethiopia, Fiji, Gambia, Ghana, Grenada, India, Jamaica, Kenya, Mali, Nepal, Nigeria, St. Lucia, St. Vincent, Sierra Leone, Thailand, Uganda, the Virgin Islands, and Zimbabwe have been some of the hosts.[129]

Two of the Association's members wrote vignettes about their Project Overseas experiences. They had received "helpful hints" from CTF before setting out. They included:

- Remember to begin taking your anti-malaria tablets two weeks prior to your departure;
- Electric razors may be a problem, since they need electric power;
- Cleaning and pressing establishments are limited, often non-existent;
- Pictures of snow, Indians and Eskimos are of major interest;
- Be prepared to adjust to a slower tempo of life and to appointments not kept;
- Be discreet in displaying or discussing your wealth.[130]

Fr. Clare Malone, C.S.B., described his summer in Ethiopia in 1971 teaching basic English to sixty-three teachers from eight provinces. Eileen Lennon wrote Doreen Brady about her summer in Belize in 1978:

> We all went through a couple of days of "culture shock" upon arrival. Open sewers, unpainted buildings on stilts, unpaved, bumpy roads, unreliable plumbing, numerous bugs, and incredible humidity were definitely overwhelming to comfort-oriented Canadians such as ourselves. Schools without running water, no audio-visual equipment, and virtually no supplies certainly called for ingenuity on the part of the teachers....Within a couple of days, I started to see beyond the seemingly shabby surface of Belize City. I began to enjoy the slower pace of life, the lack of sophistication in society and the friendliness of the people....Many [teachers] have not completed high school....They do, however, care about the children they teach and were appreciative of any new ideas and methods the Canadians could give them.[131]

Educational Aid. In addition to Project Overseas, OECTA responded to a large number of other requests. It allocated at first 1 per cent, then 1.5 per cent, then 2 per cent of its annual net revenue to educational aid. This meant that, for example in 1984, after subtracting the OTF, QECO, and WUCT fees and assigning monies for the reserve fund, and special assistance and incentives to the Units, the Educational Aid Committee had a budget of $47 646. It could donate up to $1000 to any cause; amounts in excess were handled by the Executive. Grants went to teacher associations, for example, those in Papua New Guinea, Peru, St. Lucia, Spain, and Thailand. Most commonly, money was sent to schools for textbooks and library books, instructional supplies, facilities and equipment, construction, and lunch programmes. Antigua, the Bahamas, Bangkok, Belize, Dominica, the Dominican Republic, India,

Kenya, Pakistan, Papua New Guinea, Sierra Leone, Tanzania, Thailand, Trinidad, Uganda, and the West Indies all received aid. For a number of years the Association paid the expenses of Trinidad-Tobago teachers to get in-service in Canada. Adult literacy and job training programmes were funded in Brazil, Peru and Santo Domingo. The religious in the Dominican Republic, in Guatemala, Kerala, and Uganda received funding. Neither did OECTA ignore its own fellow citizens: the schools in Moosonee and Wikwemikong, the Canadian Association in Support of the Native Peoples, and the World Association of First Nations were sent money.[132]

Three special projects stand out. In 1979 the Simcoe Unit sponsored a refugee Vietnamese family. In 1981 OECTA gave Josephine Lal Din $10 000 to help her build a school for destitute children. Miss Lal Din had left her town of Sialkot, Pakistan, where she had been teaching, to pursue a lifetime vocation. She wanted to buy property and build and staff a school for orphans and children with unemployed parents. She knew that she would not be able to save enough money there, so she came to Canada. After a year or two of being a domestic and using her Urdu language for the Toronto library board, she had polished her English enough to obtain a teaching position with the MSSB. After fourteen years of teaching she had saved enough money to purchase the property. The OECTA grant of $10 000, as well as continued funding from the Fatima House Trust, a registered charity set up by its secretary-treasurer Liz Dorner, and from the Dufferin-Peel, Metropolitan Toronto, and other Units, enabled her to build the school and hire staff. She started with about sixty students in Sialkot with its 60 000 people and now has over 700 enrolment, about fifty of whom are boarders.[133]

To observe the Year of the Child OECTA decided in 1979 to adopt a school: the Salesian Fathers' Sacred Heart High School in Hatico Mao in the Dominican Republic was chosen and given $10 000 to help build a school addition. The letter of gratitude from Fr. Joaquin Soler to Frank Griffin revealed how much $10 000 meant to him:

> I was surprrised [sic] to see your letter on my desk. I did not what to do. [sic] I was afraid to opon [sic] the letter and see a "NO," yo [sic] our request for help. The hope to receive a big "YES" was stronger. I was right. THANK YOU VERY, VERY MUCH, for your kindness to adopt our school. May God bless you all;...we are most interested in building a "4 CLASSROOMS EXTENSION OF OUR SCHOOL." We need them to have 200 more poor boys....We intend to place a plate with the

> Donor's name in the entrance of the building....Be sure of our dayly [sic] prayers....I am not too good with my English. Please be patient with me.[134]

Teachers for Social Justice. The social justice initiatives of OECTA in the 1960s were inspired and reinforced further in the 1970s and 1980s by the Bishops. In 1975 Pope Paul VI issued his encyclical "Evangelii Nuntiandi" that elaborated on the theme of social justice discussed during the Vatican II years. The Canadian Conference of Catholic Bishops began applying his encyclical in a series of documents: *From Words to Action* (1976), *A Society to be Transformed* (1977), *Witness to Justice* (1979), and *Ethical Reflections on the Economic Crisis* (1983). They censured the economic philosophy that regarded profit as the key motive for progress, competition as a supreme law, and private ownership as an absolute right with no corresponding social obligation. This capitalist outlook, the Bishops wrote, contributed to such social evils as pollution, economic and social disparity, and massive unemployment. Rather than subscribing to the philosophy of the survival of the fittest, all Christians were called to involve themselves in transforming their ways of living and in improving the social and economic structures.[135]

In 1981 the Physicians for Social Responsibility released a distressingly clinical videotape about the medical effects of one-megaton airbursts over cities in the United States. At once the topic of nuclear warfare erupted in all the media. Religious leaders insisted that moral questions were central, since monies for weapons development could have been used instead to help the hungry and the homeless. In 1983 the National Conference of Catholic Bishops issued a lengthy statement against the nuclear arms race.[136]

It was in this environment that the Teachers for Social Justice emerged in 1978. Some of them had been active in the OECTA support of the grape boycott of 1973. Then the Association had planned the boycott with the OSSTF, NDP, Canadian Federation of Labour, Toronto and District Labour Council, and UFW. Bob Cooney in a letter to the members pointed to Chavez's comment, "What a terrible irony it is that the very people who harvest the food we eat do not have enough food for their own children," and described the low-paid working conditions of the farm workers: fourteen hours a day in the hot sun, with primitive and scarce toilet facilities and without adequate drinking water, sprayed with deadly insecticide, and their children deprived of education.[137]

In March, 1978, a few separate school teachers in the Toronto area, in response to the call of the Bishops to become more actively involved in building a new society, began meeting every few weeks in each other's homes to discuss the call and to ask themselves what they were to do. Their action plan included the development of a "Vision Paper" with the expressed goals of building communities of concern in the schools and helping to provide appropriate curriculum and professional development. They made a conscious decision to penetrate OECTA. A number of them, like Ted and Don Schmidt, Martin Storey, Paul Hansen, Paul Smith, Sr. Mary Van Hee, Sr. Mary Jo Leddy, Linda and Michael Arbour, and others had been involved in the OECTA/OSSTA religious education courses and/or on unit and provincial OECTA committees and executives. Their aim now was to support teachers so that they would be witnesses to liberation and attackers of oppression in their lives and classroom curricula.[138]

Paul Glynn and the Executive, for the most part, encouraged the Teachers for Social Justice to write for the *OECTA Reporter*, run a section at the CCDC, and bring motions to the AGM. One of the 1984 OECTA objectives was to increase the members' understanding of social justice issues.

The *OECTA Reporter* printed in four 1982 issues a lengthy provocative statement by Ted Schmidt on the Canadian Bishops' teachings on social justice and the implications for the teacher. For many members it would not have been a comfortable road. A few typical quotations will indicate the prophetic flavour:

> • If one can only see reality from one's own economic vantage point, that one will then create an educational system to serve that world view - and finally, in our case, one will construct a theology which will try to sacralize or legitimate that world.
> • [Our] lifestyles are purchased at the expense of the poor of the world.
> • The Catholic school must begin to become a zone of resistance to the neo-conservative economies;...a world dominated by the economic metaphor which only values those people who can compete, consume, and produce...will be hostile to the gospel.
> • Sin is apathy and no tears. Sin is business as usual in our classrooms.
> • Do we educate the young to manipulate the world or to transform it?

• El Salvador is a place we get our bananas from, says the Grade 6 teacher, and here is South Africa, the home of diamonds and gold, says the Grade 11 teacher.
• Students need to meet teachers...capable of rage over the torture of fellow human beings and the rape of the environment, teachers who still care about the sanctity of life.
• How would Cursillo, Marriage Encounter, Cor, Charismatic Renewal...appear to Third World people?...The human family has a right to be fed before we turn in on ourselves and cultivate our inner gardens.[139]

OECTA became officially involved in a number of contemporary issues. Numerous articles appeared in the *Reporter* on the repressive governments of El Salvador, Guatemala, Chile, Columbia, Argentina, Nicaragua, South Africa, and Uganda.[140] A number of Catholic high school teachers of English, economics, geography, and history began to combine the Ministry of Education curriculum guidelines with Gospel values to construct their courses of study. When Amnesty International reported that teachers were being imprisoned in El Salvador, OECTA sent a letter of protest to President Humberto Romero in 1977. When the Political Advisory Committee reported of that 126 teachers and several hundred students had been murdered over the years by government forces there, the Association sent telegrams of denunciation to President Napoleon Duarte and the Hon. Mark MacGuigan, Minister of External Affairs. The following year it sent a telegram to the Hon. Allen MacEachen to intercede on behalf of the teachers of El Salvador who were being imprisoned and tortured. Don Schmidt brought an El Salvadorean teacher to the 1983 AGM who talked about teachers who simply disappeared.[141] Telegrams went to the South African government urging compassionate treatment of James Mange under sentence of death, to the Polish prime minister to express its support of the Solidarity union, to President Marcos of the Philippines regarding prisoners. The Association wrote Canadian corporations which were developing mines in oppressive regimes like Chile and to banks doing business in South Africa. A booth with pamphlets on corporate responsibility and on Chile was set up at the 1978 AGM. OECTA advised certain companies that it would not be purchasing stocks out of its reserve fund because of their irresponsibility and publicized this action. Regarding the abortion issue, the Association circulated at the 1983 AGM a petition against abortion on demand; the units were asked to invite speakers from Right to Life and Alliance for Life and to press their MPs and MPPs for action on the rights of the unborn. During the 1978 Inco strike the Sudbury Unit raised money from its members to help the families of the workers; Joe Ryan, president of the Durham Unit, sent two dollars from each teacher, and OECTA sent a grant to match the Sudbury Unit's gift.[142]

The CCDC Planning Committee decided to have conferences on social justice for three years in a row. At the first one in 1983,Sidney Lenz, a Chicago anti-war protestor, and Gregory Baum, a liberation theology professor, were speakers. This, among other things, resulted in a conservative reaction from Kevin Kennedy. He lost his motion to the Executive that 1984 present the other side to the nuclear arms debate and, by a close vote, his attempt to defeat a 1984 AGM motion to oppose the expansion of nuclear power. But he did lead the discussion that ended in the defeat of the motion that the Canadian economy be restructured on the basis of Gospel values, of a preferential option for the poor and of the priority of labour over capital; some delegates said they did not know enough about economics. He also led the debate against the motion that OECTA do business only with institutions that make no loans to South Africa. Again, a majority of delegates agreed with Kennedy that there were a number of other countries not mentioned in the motion, yet were equally deserving of censure, even though they were left-wing regimes. Later, he would write an article in the *OECTA Reporter* on the effective deterrence of MAD (that is, mutually assured destruction) and on the pastoral of France's Bishops discussing the choice between annihilation and slavery with regard to the threat of the Soviet Union. Ted Schmidt countered that there was Soviet barbarism, but God's command is to love one's enemy, and nuclear warfare would incinerate populations. Kevin Kennedy's position was that orthodoxy is preferable to modernism and that the OECTA advocates of social justice had no real religious underpinning, but was just a political and social philosophy.[143]

The debate and polarities of a few of the Association's members did not change the fact that the Canadian Conference of Catholic Bishops and the Teachers for Social Justice reinforced the trend begun by OECTA leaders of the previous decade to involve OECTA in social issues beyond the classroom. As Fr. Kavanagh put it, most OECTA members went on with their lives working at integrating both orthodox spiritual exercises and the apostolic actions of social justice that began with the Sermon on the Mount and the Beatitudes. Peter Gazzola felt that most AGM delegates avoided the extremes of the debate and opted for helping the poor.[144]

Structure. In 1972 OECTA had 15 825 statutory members; 1.2 per cent of them had a second-class certificate, 44 per cent a first-class certificate with a grade twelve or thirteen academic education; 20.5 per cent had five university credits and/or Ministry of Education courses, 10 per cent had ten university credits and/or Ministry courses, and 22.5 per cent had a B.A. or more. In 1971 there were seventy English Catholic schools with high school grades; in 1974 there were 27 542 students in grades nine and ten separate school classes. By 1983 the numbers had increased to 102 and 66 797, respectively.[145] In 1981 OECTA was thirty-seven years old, was much larger, and had a different type of membership and student body. It was time to re-examine the Association's structure. An Internal Task Force on Organizational Restructuring was established with Albert Dukacz as chair and Derry Byrne, Romeo Gallant, John Holowaty, Dick Marcella, Pat O'Neill, Harry Polowy, George Saranchuk, Kevin Kennedy, and Tom Taylor as committee members.[146] The Committee approached the task with three problems in mind. The units held elections for president and for Board of Directors; frequently,there would be two people holding these positions; this made communications between the units and the Executive and Board of Directors problematical at times. Secondly, in the words of the Committee,

> much of our time and energy is spent in inter-necine internal dispute about who has the right to exercise what powers;....the Board of Directors perceives itself as having certain powers, but being unable to exercise them...It also sees its recommendations being too often amended or ignored by the Executive.[147]

The Committee brought in an extensive report to the 1982 AGM; it was sent back for further study. The 1983 AGM received the final report and voted on the Committee's recommendations. The following changes were passed as motions:

- two Executive positions were renamed as general secretary and deputy general secretary; the word "secretary" carried traditionally legal powers, and the titles were congruent with the other affiliates and directors of education of school boards;
- the Board of Directors was renamed the Council of Presidents; accordingly, each unit elected only one person to this body;

• the first vice-president was to be full-time; this had been possible since 1981; now it was automatic; furthermore, the presidency had been full-time since 1972; John Fauteux, speaking to the motion told the delegates that as first vice-president he had been away from home for thirty-five school days, forty-five weekend days and, in total, including the summer holidays, about 100 days; Richard Prophet, also in support of the motion, responded that this meant he had been unable to adhere to the tenets of the Church;
• the Executive was renamed the Board of Directors; this change did not stick, and the old title was restored about a year later;
• the OTF table officer was to be elected at the AGM; prior to this change the ten OECTA governors were electing the officer themselves; besides the undemocratic nature of this procedure, the possibility of a tie-vote, that had already occurred once when Fred Sweeney was elected to the position, was always a danger.

The old chestnut, gearing a fee increase automatically to the member's salary increase, went down to defeat after considerable sound and fury. Also, the recommendation that there be only two Standing Committees, Legislation and Budget, was defeated; the delegates believed that the Standing Committees in existence were not only performing valuable functions, but also were increasing membership involvement in Association affairs. Two other motions, perhaps put forward as cost-saving measures during a difficult year, were defeated: the reduction of the refund of fees to the units from 17.5 per cent to 15 per cent and of the AGM delegates from one delegate for every fifty members to a ratio of one to seventy-five; the units were growing in influence.[148]

Between 1971 and 1984 OECTA made some changes to the unit structure. A new Unit, North of Superior, was created in 1975 to match a new district separate school board. The Durham high school teachers who had been part of the Toronto High Unit merged with the Durham Elementary Unit in 1980. Thirdly, in a move to enhance professional development, the Board of Directors asked for annual reports from each unit on its professional development and teacher welfare activities. Finally, and most significantly for the centralization/decentralization balance, the units were permitted in 1982 to allocate up to 50 per cent of their budget for release time for their presidents; in 1984 the ceiling was removed.[149]

Finally, because of the size of the Metropolitan Toronto Unit, OECTA decided that the Unit's argument for a full-time member of the Secretariat had merit.

Lawyer Bill Markle, escorts Anne Lallouet, Ontario's first blind teacher, near the end of a Ministry of Education Board of Reference in 1983 which reinstated her following an unfair dismissal.

Different eras: AGM 1968, 1984 and 1993.

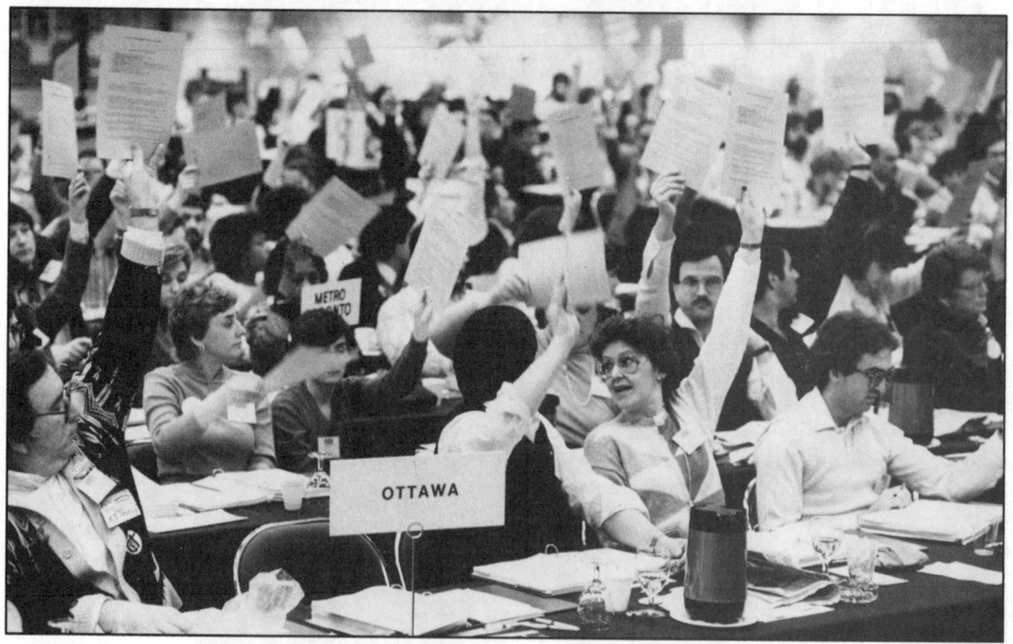

Executive Secretary Frank Griffin with Cardinal Carter at the 1979 Annual General Meeting.

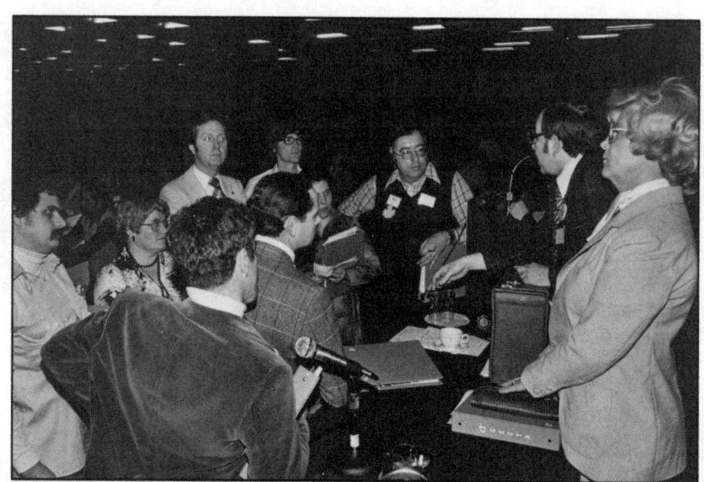

The politics of OECTA, played out by delegates and the provincial executive at the 1979 AGM.

An executive meeting in 1992. Helen Biales president, presides at the end of the table and James Carey General Secretary is seated on her right.

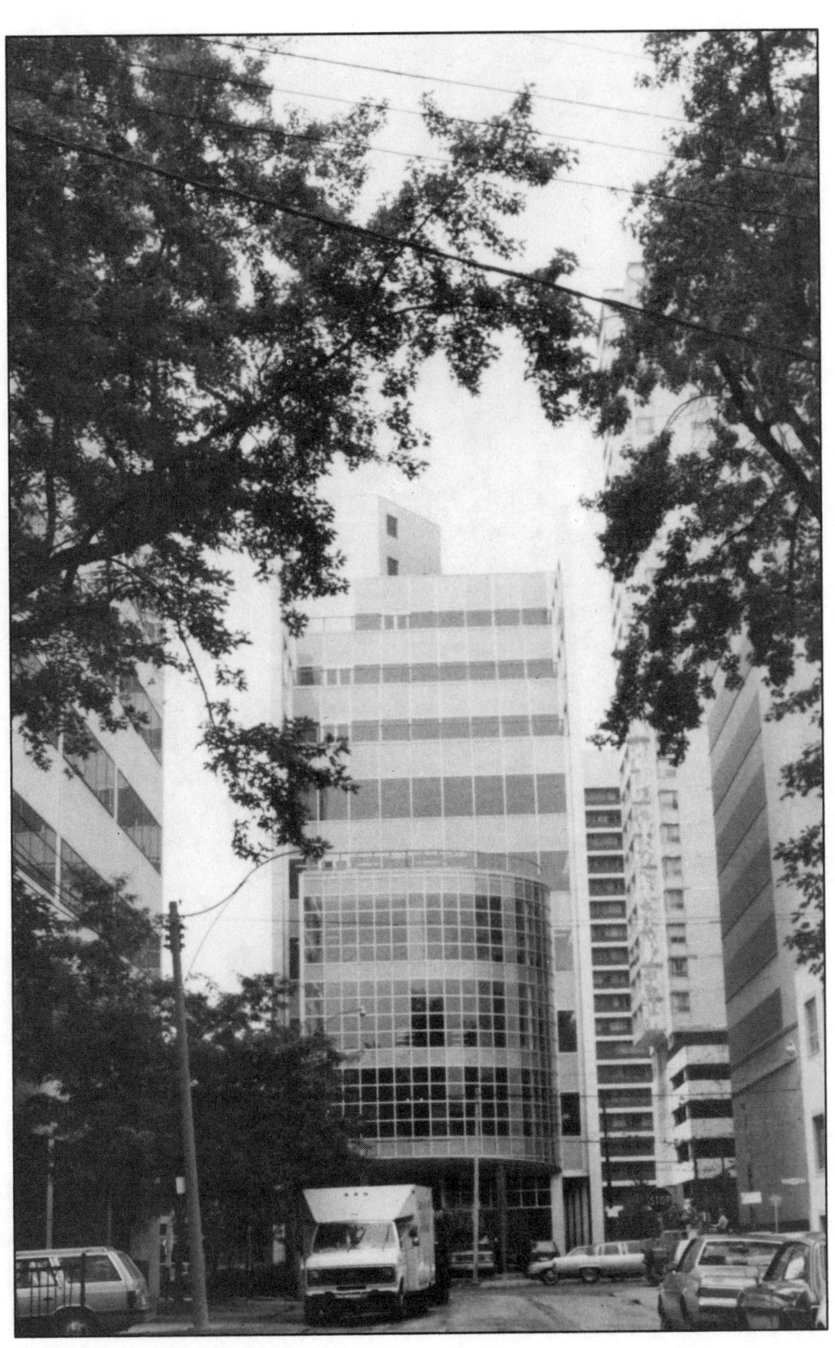

In 1984, OECTA moved from Federation House at 1260 Bay St., to 65 St. Clair Ave. E. occupying the third, fourth and fifth floors in the new building.

For years prior to Full Funding, OECTA members lobbied tirelessly to convince the Ontario government to finance Catholic schools beyond Grade 10. Each year the association sponsored this booth at the CNE.

Premier Willam Davis with reporters and education stakeholders in 1985 after introducing legislation providing for full funding.

Ottawa students Sean May, left, and Rick Chiarelli, executive members of Students for Fair Funding lobbied the Premier to extend funding.

Paul Cavalluzzo describes the Ontario Court of Appeal decision to allow full funding to OECTA's Council of Presidents. The ruling determined that Bill 30 did not contravene the Charter of Rights and Freedoms.

In spite of full funding, Catholic school boards soon found themselves hard pressed to provide facilities for their growing student populations.

Elizabeth Teresa Dorner was hired as a staff assistant in 1975 and assigned to Metro.[150] Her father, George Dorner, had emigrated from Romania in 1928; it took him ten years before he could bring his wife, Elizabeth Pfefferkorn, and four boys, John, Steve, George, and Charles, to Canada. By then he had a farm near Chatham. During the family's first year in Ontario, the twins, Mary and Elizabeth were born.

Liz attended S.S.#17 and 24, Dover and Chatham. Her parents and four other families hired a taxi to bring their children to St. Thomas Aquinas for grades nine and ten under the Wallaceburg Separate School Board and to the Ursulines' Merici two-room high school for grades eleven and twelve. Liz completed her grade thirteen at Wallaceburg District High School. The twins then went to London Teachers' College.

After two years of teaching at St. Mary, London, Elizabeth went full-time for a year to the University of Western Ontario. Next she taught in all three divisions at St. Dominic, Bronte, St. Margaret Mary, Hamilton, St. Michael, London, and St. Sebastian (now St. John Bosco), the MSSB. She was promoted to vice-principal of St. Mary of the Angels, where the Toronto superintendent was so impressed with her language experience programme that she recommended her for principal after one year. She was principal of St. Elizabeth and St. Mark. During this time and shortly thereafter, she acquired a music, guidance, religious education, principal's, and supervisory officer's certificate.

Elizabeth Dorner was president of the Metro Toronto southwest Unit during the mass resignation year. She has served the Secretariat as the Metro staff assistant for eight years, as a counsellor for eight years, and as an administrative assistant for the last three years. She is currently writing her doctoral dissertation for OISE. She continues her avid interest in inland and offshore competitive sailing, having sailed her yacht across the Atlantic in 1985. In 1993 Liz was the navigator for Carlos Costa, the first disabled swimmer and youngest male to swim across Lake Ontario; the Queen's City Yacht Club gave its Community Service Award to Liz for her contribution to Costa's success, which raised $30 000 for Variety Village.[151]

The Secretariat expanded and modified itself somewhat in the 1970s. Its function became one of advising, being a resource, facilitating, informing, and implementing for the Executive and Board of Directors, now Council of Presidents. To carry out these duties it organized itself into four departments: Teacher Welfare, Professional Development, Counselling and Relations, and Administration.

Coordinators and staff assistants were in three of the departments; an office manager and accountant worked in administration. The Teacher Welfare department looked after grievances, contract problems, superannuation, salary negotiating in provincial takeovers and when called to help, and collective agreement seminars. The Professional Development department managed the religious education courses: the CCDC, workshops and short courses, and the booth at the Canadian National Exhibition (CNE). The Counselling and Relations Department dealt with Boards of Reference, personal teacher crises, interpersonal school staff problems, legal matters, and unemployment insurance. The Administration department organized matters for the AGM and Council of Presidents and managed the finances, handbook, committee appointments, and unit administration. Committees were assigned to each department as follows: Educational Aid, Project Overseas, Superannuation, and Teacher Welfare (Teacher Welfare); Professional Development, Secondary Schools, Teacher Catholic Education, CCDC, Chas Workshop, Philosophy of Christian Education, Bill 82, and the new (1983) Principals' Council (Professional Development); Awards, Supervisory Personnel, Equal Opportunity, OTF legislation, OTF work groups, Employee Assistance Programme, and Political Advisory (Counselling and Relations); Finance, Investments, and Legislation (Administration). In addition to these standing committees there were, on an as-needed basis, Executive and adhoc committees.

The Secretariat added two new entities near the end of this period. In 1979 OECTA decided to begin a central library service and to hire a consultant, instead of leaving the task to Mary Ellen Daly in her capacity as administrative assistant. Finally, an OECTA Secretarial Association was formed to negotiate salaries and working conditions.[152]

Looking beyond its own borders, OECTA began to assist STO by paying the first-year membership of a retired OECTA teacher.[153]

The structure of OTF also came under examination again. In 1980 the Ministry of Education in its *Issues and Directions* responded to the Jackson Committee on Declining Enrolment. At the time Dr. Bette Stephenson expressed her belief that teachers had the professional maturity of the other professions and, therefore, should control admission to the profession, certification, professional development, and disciplining of teachers. It looked like an old dream of OTF and its affiliates might come to pass. Responses to the idea were invited. AEFO recommended that all of OTF be in the College of Teachers (Stephenson's coinage), that the College grant teaching licences, evaluate professional and academic qualifications, and discipline teachers. FWTAO agreed; in addition, it specified that the College should determine the requirements for and numbers of teachers, govern admissions to the profession, and control curriculum at the faculties of education. OECTA, OPSMTF, and OSSTF concurred, although Malcolm Buchanan felt that teacher self-government was a ploy to distract teachers from collective bargaining. But an OTF survey showed 82 per cent support for the idea.[154]

Discussions did not advance to fruition. On the one hand, OTF saw the advantages - more status, control of entrance to the profession and, therefore, indirectly of salaries, upgrading of teacher qualifications, influencing curriculum, the Ministry, and the public - but had some questions that needed answers. How would OTF in a symbiotic relationship with the College reconcile goals for education that would sometimes be in conflict with the protection of teachers, especially in the area of adversarial collective bargaining? Does OTF not already have enough influence in the realms of certification rating, discipline and ethics, admissions, and standards for upgrading? Who would pay for carrying out the College's responsibilities?

On the other hand, Bette Stephenson had it firmly fixed in her mind that there should be non-statutory membership in OTF, but statutory membership in the College of Teachers. This, of course, was unsatisfactory to the teachers. Discussions between the Minister and OTF grew so heated that OTF walked out of a meeting and wrote Premier Davis that it had withdrawn from discussions. As Bruce Archer of OTF explained this action, Bette Stephenson was determined to ram her concept into a narrow container and scrape away any unresolved issues. Davis put the idea on ice.[155]

The Catholic High School Issue. Although Bill 100 absorbed much of OECTA's resources in the early and mid-1970s, and Premier Davis's no of 1971 temporarily dampened the will to work for completion of the separate school system, the Association did not abandon the goal and by the late 1970s put most of its energies into a push for extension.

Many of the members had worked hard between Davis's August 31 statement and the fall election to influence the voters and to help bring in MPPs favourable to extension. The Extension Committee and four regional coordinators kept meeting with and sending materials to the unit executives, pastors, and groups of principals. George Saranchuk, the Committee's chair, sent questions to the three party leaders and published their answers in the *OECTA Reporter*. All candidates received a telegram stating, "You can correct this inequity." But Premier Davis swept to a landslide victory, helped, in the pundits' minds, by his refusal to extend separate schools.[156]

One eventual casualty of all this was ECEAO. It had been renamed the Federation of Catholic Education Associations of Ontario (FCEAO) in order to eliminate the E for English and thus, bring in the Franco-Ontarian Catholic education associations. They had been working for their own school system; one FCEAO, it was hoped, could avoid a split and keep a united pressure group. But the campaign for extension had resulted in fault lines. OSSTA felt it should be the body to submit briefs to and lobby with the government, not ACHSBO. OECTA and OSSTA were often at such loggerheads that, as Bob Cooney put it, the merits of an idea were not considered, only the source; ironically, he said, just the members present from the Ontario Catholic Students' Federation were attentive and open to ideas from any source. At the time Cooney wrote a scathing criticism on the tunnel vision of the organizations in FCEAO. In 1981 the Bishops withdrew their support; in 1983 OSSTA did likewise. Despite the efforts of Saranchuk and Gazzola to save it, the Federation disintegrated. However, it was resurrected with a narrower function as the Catholic Education Foundation of Ontario (CEFO). Until completion of the separate school system, it would raise money for and otherwise encourage the survival of Catholic high schools. The Metropolitan Toronto teachers and a few other units wrote into their collective agreements that the money saved from the federal government's reduction in the unemployment insurance premium, where the school board had a cumulative sick leave plan, would go to CEFO. After extension, it would at an annual dinner honour the Catholic educator of the year and the most deserving student in each Catholic high school.[157]

The other casualties were some Catholic high schools. Nineteen of them, in places like Smith Falls and Wallaceburg, were considered too small to keep even the grades nine and ten operating under the separate school boards. Others, like Fort William and Barrie, also took Davis's no as a death knell and closed the grades eleven to thirteen, but did keep their nines and tens running under the separate school board. More seriously, three out of the five Catholic high schools in Ottawa went out of business. Only Immaculata High School of the Grey Nuns, under the principalship of Sr. Anna Clare, remained partly under the Ottawa RCSS Board and partly private. The Carleton RCSS Board, urged by its director Bill Crossan, took over St. Pius X grades nine and ten by means of enabling provincial legislation. The other three, St. Patrick, Notre Dame and St. Joseph, negotiated with the Ottawa Board of Education and managed to keep their students and identity for a couple of years, provided they took in no new students and until the private school students left or graduated.[158]

As for the remaining Catholic high schools, there were administrative problems. The principal had two superiors, the separate school board and the board of governors. The director of education was responsible for the grades nine and ten, yet, when it was a matter of staffing, budgeting, or timetabling, had to administer the school in tandem with the principal and board of governors. This was awkward at best; with inadequate funding the task was daunting. OECTA members had to "donate" spares from their grades nine and ten assignments by teaching in the private school. At F. J. Brennan High School in Windsor three teachers had to go to a Board of Reference after being dismissed from the private school; they won because the Board of Reference ruled they had a permanent contract with the Windsor Separate School Board due to their teaching also in grades nine and ten. Also, despite the financial problems, a few principals wished their schools to remain private and operate with revenues from tuition, thereby controlling the type of student to be admitted.[159]

The Catholic educational community, with the cooperation and often the leadership of OECTA, employed a number of strategies to keep the private Catholic high schools open and even expanding. There were three main sources of income: tuition, Church funds, and monies from the grants and tax revenues the separate school board received for operating grades nine and ten. The first two, tuition and diocesan monies from Church collections, were approaching excessive amounts. For example, a Catholic Education Foundation in Ottawa attempted to run a private high school, St. Thomas More, but in 1977, after only four years, closed it with a debt of $186 000.[160]

Separate school boards and teachers could be very helpful. With leaders like B. E. Nelligan, Patrick Brennan, and John Sweeney as directors of education, the MSSB, Durham, Frontenac, Hastings-Prince Edward, Sault Ste. Marie, Hamilton-Wentworth, Bruce-Grey, Brant, and Waterloo RCSS boards, to name a few, supported the grades nine and ten as much as possible and within the law assisted the private schools. The board often would pay the complete salary of the principal, vice-principal, and guidance and library staff, since they were necessary for the intermediate division and the private school could not afford the salaries. The board provided spares in the collective agreement, some of which were used by the teachers to teach in the private school. Rental was forthcoming for private school facilities like parking, classrooms, gymnasia, libraries, and other space. When the credit system replaced high school grades in 1971, some Catholic high school principals adapted a practice from the public composite high schools: there if a student was taking a technical credit, the school board received a grant for a full-time technical student. Some separate school registers began carrying senior division students taking an intermediate division credit for interest in, remediation or acquisition of, a new skill. (This last funding technique remained available until 1979 when the grant regulations were revised to define a separate school student as a pupil with fewer than ten credits.) All of this was a sacrifice for the teachers and students in both the elementary and secondary schools, since some elementary school revenues for grades one to eight were used to aid the situation in high schools. Nevertheless, OECTA officially encouraged the establishment and expansion of intermediate schools (grades seven to ten) and went after the Ministry for high school grants for grades nine and ten. It managed to convince OTF to ask the government for equitable funding of grades nine and ten in public and separate schools.[161]

In the minds of some advocates of Catholic high schools, there was a risk to implementing grades-seven-to-ten schools. Although they expanded enrolment and made a stronger case politically for extension, the government could find it logical to give intermediate grants and reinforce the boundary between separate schools and private schools. Therefore, some boards like Dufferin-Peel and Halton went mostly with the junior high school model, while others like the MSSB, Windsor, Sault Ste. Marie, Hamilton-Wentworth, and Waterloo integrated grades nine to thirteen under a separate and private board. Regardless of the model, more and more parents in the decade after Davis's refusal chose a Catholic high school for their children. OSSTA in 1973 developed a position paper on the intermediate years that flatly stated that the "separate school board should continue to develop and improve educational systems which offer Catholic education through the crucially formative adolescent period."[162] In 1977 Bill Hillyer, the president of that Association, wrote an article for the trustees asking about grades-seven-to-ten separate schools, "Not Why? But, Why Not?"[163] With this support from the parents, teachers, and trustees, the number of Catholic schools operating beyond grade eight expanded from seventy in 1970 with about 34 000 students to 106 with 70 500 in 1983. The Archdiocese of Toronto opened one private Catholic high school a year for seven years. This was taking place during a decade of declining enrolment in the schools of Ontario.[164]

OECTA encouraged Catholic high school expansion by other methods. In 1974 it loaned $50 000 to the Ottawa Catholic High School Foundation to help keep Immaculata High School open. It investigated how to set up tuition fees as a tax deduction; a number of private Catholic high schools formed charitable organizations for this purpose. It also seriously looked into taking the government to court under section 93(1) of the *BNA Act*, where it would argue that not providing separate school boards grants and the power to tax in order to provide a basic (that is, kindergarten-to-grade-thirteen) education is "prejudicial" to rights guaranteed in 1867. However, Paul Cavalluzzo wrote a list of pros and cons to launching a case that gave the Association pause. The only advantage he perceived, beyond the possibility of winning, was that a court action could publicize the plight of the Catholic high schools due to discriminatory funding. On the other hand, there were a number of difficulties:

- the OECTA case would have to prove that the judges in the *Tiny Township Case* were wrong; agreeing with the 1928 judgment would be an out for the judges;
- the case would be costly;
- a favourable judgment would have large implications for Ontario education; judges prefer to leave such changes to politicians;
- there would be a problem gathering evidence dating back fifty years and more;
- the judges might wonder why the issue had not come before the courts in fifty years;
- the provincial politicians would have a reason to not provide any remedial legislation during the court case; and,
- announcing a court action could hand the Progressive Conservative an election issue similar to the one that helped it in 1971.

No action was taken, but Colm Harty, chair of the Political Advisory Committee, advised further research.[165]

If the court route seemed risky, there was still the political one. Just a year or two after Davis's election victory, John Macdonald from Windsor wrote a letter to the Executive asking if OECTA was going to "sit back and accept" Bill Davis's 1971 decision.[166] This letter prompted a number of actions. A Teacher Catholic Education Committee was established; it and the Political Advisory and Secondary School Committees took on as one of their more important responsibilities helping in a second campaign for completion of the separate school system. Kevin Kennedy, George Saranchuk, and Peter Gazzola on the Executive, Fred Sweeney on the OTF Board of Governors, along with members too numerous to mention, led the campaign with the Secretariat and the Committees. The decision was made to hire a booth at the CNE to promote Catholic Education. Paul Glynn of the Professional Development department was assigned as the Secretariat staff member to work with the Teacher Catholic Education Committee.

Paul Glynn, an only child, was born in Toronto. His father, Thomas Glynn, a printer, and mother, Teresa Marrin, sent him to separate schools in Toronto: Holy Family, St. Cecilia and Blessed Sacrament. He attended St. Michael's High School to grade thirteen and entered the Basilian novitiate. He received his B.A. and his S.T.B. from St. Michael's College, University of Toronto, and was ordained in 1956. During two summers at OCE he got his HSA. After several summers at Laval University, Québec City, he was awarded his M.A. in French. His teaching experience was at St. Michael's High School, history and French, and at St. Joseph's High School, Ottawa, as head of physical education, then of French.

In Ottawa he became an active member of the Ottawa High Unit, serving on the executive and as president. He was also a member of the provincial Secondary School Committee. In 1972 he applied for a position with the Professional Development department and was interviewed by Mary Babcock, Claudette Foisy-Moon, Marie Kennedy, and Don Berlingeri. Claudette wanted an older, more experienced person. Mary Ellen Daly, Pat O'Neill, and Neil Doherty were quite young. Near the end of a very positive interview, Paul Glynn informed the committee that he was being laicized. There was some discussion, and then Mary Babcock ended it with the remark that, "The last five minutes of this meeting have had nothing to do with the rest of it." He was hired.

Paul worked in the Professional Development department for fourteen years, with special responsibilities for the CCDC, the Chas workshops, and the CNE booth. After separate school completion he was transferred to the Counselling and Relations Department. In 1989 Paul retired from OECTA.

Since retirement Paul and his wife Saundra McKay Glynn, whom he married in 1972, have been enjoying life with their two children, Mary Teresa and Caroline. Paul has completed a Master of Religion Education from the Toronto School of Theology. He also works part-time for the Catholic Biblical Association of Canada.[167]

Shortly after his arrival in the Secretariat, Paul Glynn was caught in a ten-year OECTA campaign for funding for Catholic high schools. Dan Kelly, a London principal, got the idea of publicizing separate schools and the logic behind completion by renting a booth at the CNE. Arrangements had to be made quickly; Paul Glynn interrupted a June 1974 Executive meeting and received Leo Normandeau's support. $7000 was allocated. The Booth would run for eleven years, attracting twenty to thirty thousand visitors each fall, according to the number of pamphlets OECTA gave out. Those running it and talking to visitors were all volunteers: members of the Teacher Catholic Education Committee, Executive, Board of Directors, and Paul Glynn, as well as other OECTA members. Some donated fifty or more hours of their summer holidays. Paul estimated that the Booth had only about five seconds to attract people as they walked by; therefore, the emphasis was on colour, sound, motion, and pithy statements like "Schools with a difference." Devices like television where the spectators could view themselves, computers with quizzes on Catholic education and children's art on display drew visitors. At first Lorne Howcroft, Tom Hutchinson, Saundra Glynn, and other managers of the Booth emphasized the continuum argument, then a few years later shifted to the rationale that it was impossible to offer a modern education without full funding to the end of high school. A common theme throughout all the displays was the values promulgated in separate schools. One year the Booth carried petition forms for visitors who wished to express their support for extension. The Booth was also used at some fall fairs throughout the province.[168]

Jim Barry, an English teacher at Brebeuf High School in Toronto, came up with the idea of two cartoon characters, Chas and Chasabelina; he and his students developed cartoons and slides on the history and financing of separate schools and on the basic education and continuum topics. These eventually played a smaller role at the Booth because of the time they required from the moving spectators. But they were valuable in a decade of "Chas" workshops put on throughout Ontario. OECTA leaders realized that there was an educational job to be done with the public and even with the Association's own members, many of whom had not had the opportunity to attend a Catholic high school. Over 800 Chas workshops between 1976 and 1984 were conducted with principals' associations, unit meetings, parishes, Catholic Women's Leagues, parent-teacher meetings, teachers at professional development days, and grade eight and high school students. Chas pamphlets, with the support and encouragement of the Bishops, were distributed at Sunday Masses. In addition to whatever the Ministry decided would be its theme for Education Week, OECTA would add a separate school completion angle and send an outline and bibliography to the units and schools, suggesting that they put on a programme or invite in the Teacher Catholic Education or Secondary Schools Committee.[169]

OECTA had two opportunities during this period to present again the case for extension in briefs: one to the Jackson Commission in 1978 and one to the Secondary Education Review Project (SERP) in 1980. Fred Sweeney reported that SERP received over sixty briefs on the Catholic high school question. These briefs from OECTA units and OSSTA resulted in a SERP recommendation that separate school students in grades nine and ten be considered secondary school students for grant purposes; the Catholic educational community considered this a breakthrough.[170]

Between 1980 and 1984 Kevin Kennedy, George Saranchuk, Peter Gazzola, Fred Sweeney, the new general secretary, Fr. Kavanagh, and other OECTA leaders intensified the campaign for separate schools. The Bill 100 work had died down, there was a minority government, the Franco-Ontarians were getting a positive reception to the idea of governing their own schools, Catholic high school enrolment was marking a new high each year, and the 1977 Mayo Report on municipal government in Ottawa-Carleton had recommended funding for Catholic high schools.[171]

Discussions between Saranchuk and Chris Asseff determined that OECTA would conduct the campaign without OSSTA. The trustees were pursuing corporation tax revenues and felt that a second extension push would jeopardize the chances for an amendment to the *Assessment Act.* Saranchuk expressed his disappointment with the OSSTA position, but supported a completion aim as an AGM objective for each year.[172] The priority was to "press onward in the pursuit of equal funding."[173] The Teacher Catholic Education Committee announced that, "All political parties...need to be constantly reminded that the Catholic community will not let this issue recede."[174] At a 1981 " Chas" convention in Chatham, hosted by the Ursulines, one of the sisters in the audience asked why Catholic high school students were not being encouraged to mount displays at Queen's Park. Saranchuk thought this was a good idea and proposed to the Executive that OECTA finance a plan whereby each of ninety-six Catholic high schools send students for one day to the parliament buildings. The campaign was endorsed. However, not all the high schools were able to send students on the OECTA "Equality Express" buses used for the purpose. Cardinal Carter contacted Saranchuk to ask him, "What's this about demonstrations down at Queen's Park?" The Archdiocese of Toronto and the bishops of the Hamilton and London dioceses did not approve of the plan. In total, about twenty high schools went to Queen's Park between April 21 and May 28, 1981. Each group met with its local politician and stood with placards in front of the parliament buildings while the MPPs were going to and from lunch. Paul Glynn would take pictures that went to the home newspaper. The plan was so successful that Bette Stephenson thought the students were at Queen's Park all the time. The following year the "Equality Express" would go to other centres to present the students' case.[175]

Encouraging events occurred, and Saranchuk believed that the government was changing its attitude. It was reported that the Cabinet was considering aid to private schools; Gazzola immediately explained in the *Canadian Register* the difference between a private school and completion of the separate school system, a distinction lost in the minds of some politicians and members of the public. Bill Mitchell of the Ministry of Education acknowledged that the students' appearances at Queen's Park had caused some Cabinet rethinking.[176] In 1984 the NDP reaffirmed its support for separate school extension in its *Report of the Task Force on Educational Policy*. Again, in that year, meetings between OECTA and the two opposition leaders, Bob Rae and David Peterson, received a favourable response and resulted in an interchange in the House on why Catholic high schools were not being funded.[177]

In 1984 the OECTA campaign stayed in high gear. Jim Cooney, second vice-president, presented a twenty-four-part action plan to the Executive. It involved the media, politicians, pastors, parents, municipal councils, the Knights of Columbus, the Catholic Women's League, and other groups. Each unit was to appoint a "completion coordinator" for implementation of the action plan.[178]

Meanwhile, the Catholic high school students continued to be involved. Rick Chiarelli, a student at St. Pius X high school and a trustee on the Carleton RCSS Board, helped organize and was president of a new organization on the scene: the Ontario Students' Association for Fair Funding. Its aim was to take the provincial government to court under section 93(1) of the *BNA Act*. He got the support of his board; the Archbishop of Ottawa promised $15 000, OECTA $1000 and later (not without some dissension) another $10 000 as needed. Rick visited Cardinal Carter, who said he was with him all the way, but he would have to enlist the support of OCCB, OECTA, and OSSTA. OSSTA decided that they would not become "actively involved."

With this backing, OSAFF engaged Ian Scott and Alain Dubuc to prepare a writ of summons to serve on the Attorney General of Ontario. The Carleton Board agreed to be named in the suit, and a number of other separate school boards agreed to help with resources. However, both the Bishops and OSSTA were less than enthusiastic, and matters did not come to a head. However, Ian Scott, who was to become the Attorney General in the next election and would argue the case for completion under the *BNA Act* for the Ontario government felt that the students had a very strong case for arguing that the lack of grants and tax revenues for Catholic high schools offended section 93(1) of the *BNA Act*.[179]

With all these developments OECTA felt some hope. There was also the realization that both the retired Archbishop Pocock and Cardinal Carter were personal friends of Premier Davis. With constant OECTA public gatherings on the issue, the Queen's Park student demonstrations, the position of the Liberal and NDP parties, and now the impending court case (as well as a court judgment that stated the Franco-Ontarians were entitled constitutionally to governance of French-language schools), the Premier and Cabinet of the Progressive Conservative Party had to be thinking about the Catholic high school question. On the other hand, the Minister of Education Bette Stephenson, remained adamant with her position that the weighted factors for grades nine and ten separate school students (that is, each student counting for a fraction more than one student for grant purposes) were more than adequate and, in any case, these grants were originally designed for continuation schools, a vanishing concept in 1984, in her opinion.[180]

Biographies of the Presidents and General Secretary.

Derry Byrne (1945-). The immediate clue is his name: Derry is the first OECTA president (1975-77) to be part of the large group of teachers from the Republic of Ireland (as well as from Great Britain) who immigrated to Ontario and taught the children of the 1950s and 1960s "baby boom." Unlike the thousands of others who were recruited overseas, Derry did not emigrate in order to teach. Nevertheless, he would become part of that group who would provide a special perspective on the problems of the separate school system and to the debate over the right to strike.

Derry was born in Dublin, the son of John Byrne, a school principal, and Rose Hickey, a homemaker. Like Fr. Kavanagh, he grew up in a large Catholic family, the seventh of ten children: five brothers - Seamus, Sean, Patrick, Kevin, and Brian, and four sisters - Ita, Elizabeth, Roisin, and Maria. Derry attended St. Mary's National School, Rathmines, Dublin for his elementary education and St. Peter's College, Wexford for his secondary education. After graduation, this young man of seventeen, whose father had died years before, decided he had to fend for himself and headed to where his two sisters Ita and Elizabeth were working, Canada. He would live with them and, it was to be hoped, encounter more opportunities than in his mother country.

After about a year of an accountancy course Derry resolved to emulate his father and went in 1963 to Ottawa Teachers' College. He began teaching at St. Gregory for RCSS #12, Nepean. He soon put a high priority on pursuing a B.A. by taking two years off. In 1968 he ran out of money and saw through the year by teaching at a driving school. He heard horror stories about such a job, but found the work accident-free and "lots of fun." He would complete his B.A. from Ottawa University in 1978.

In 1969 Derry Byrne signed with the Carleton RCSS Board and was assigned to Frank Ryan Senior Elementary School in Nepean as chairman of mathematics. Three years later he was promoted to principal of St. Nicholas of Tolentino school, where he stayed until becoming full-time president of OECTA from 1975 to 1977. He returned to the board to be principal of St. Monica, Nepean and in 1980 he moved to the board's central office. Since then he has held the positions of executive administrative assistant, assistant superintendent, superintendent, and deputy director of education. In 1992 he became director of education. During these years as administrator he also took time to get an M.Ed., and then the three courses required to get a B.Ed. in special education; the latter he regarded as necessary after the provincial government's passage of Bill 82.

Derry married Diane Bleau, a French-as-a-Second-Language teacher at St. Puis X High School, Ottawa. Derry and Diane have two children, Aaron and Fiona.

Derry explains his early interest in OECTA to "force of circumstances." Presumably, this means he had a sense of injustice over the status and salary of the separate school teacher in Ontario, because he went right into salary negotiating, then later served as a provincial negotiator and on the Teacher-Trustee Committee. He was on the Executive for eight years and on the OTF Board of Governors for six.

Derry Byrne also served on the Philosophy of Christian Education Committee. He brought to the presidency a strong concern for the Catholicity of the separate school system and for the professional development of the Association's members, a concern all the more crucial at a time when the executive director, Frank Griffin, was questioning whether or not OECTA should confine itself to teacher welfare matters. Fr. Ruetz recalled at his interview for a position with OECTA's Professional Development department Derry's probing questions and comments on the need the Association's teachers have for activities that would contribute to their faith development.

To his term of office as president he also brought a keen analytical mind. Suzann Jones, who worked with him at the local and provincial levels, marvelled that he could shut his eyes for a two-minute rest at a meeting, then open them with a resolution to the discussion in hand. Neil Doherty regarded him as a philosopher and credited him with the idea of a major study on early childhood education that resulted in the publication *To Herald a Child.* For his work in education he has received three recognitions. His staff at the Carleton RCSS Board awarded him a certificate from "the Institute of Chartered Bean Counters"; his fellow-workers believed that his year in training to become a chartered accountant and his time as mathematics chairman had contributed to his success with the school board's budget. More seriously, OTF made him a Fellow and he received the Canadian Achievement Award.[181]

Peter Gazzola (1935-). Peter is a first-generation Canadian, born in Ingersoll. His father Bruno Gazzola immigrated from Italy and eventually settled in an Italian-Canadian community and worked with gypsum lime in Ingersoll. Later he brought over from Italy Lidiuna Albanese to be his wife and to become a mother. They had five children: Angelo, John, Peter, Cecilia, and Anna Marie (who also became a teacher).

Peter's parents were strong believers in the Church and the school. Peter served daily as an altar boy and attended successfully Sacred Heart school and the Ingersoll District Collegiate Institute to the end of grade thirteen. He then attended London Teachers' College and started teaching for RCSS #7, Toronto Township at Queen of Heaven school. After three years there Peter moved to the Oakville Separate School Board to teach at St. James. In 1960 he decided to save some money to go on a trip around the world. He accepted a principalship of St. Basil, White River; although he earned very little extra money for administering this grades-one-to-ten school, he received the higher salaries northern boards were paying and was offered accommodation at the rectory.

A year later he had saved his money and started out with a friend to travel through the United States, Hawaii, Japan, and Hong Kong. Unbeknown to him at the time, part of his journey on shipboard was in the area where the Cuban Missile Crisis was erupting. In the late fall of 1961 Peter Gazzola went to the Hong Kong High Commissioner's office and made enquiries about teaching opportunities in Australia. He was hired by the Ministry of New South Wales and taught at Fort St. Primary School in Sydney until November 1962.

In January 1963 he returned to Ontario to teach for the MSSB at Our Lady of Sorrows school. Next he was promoted to vice-principal of St. Helen and then to principal of St. Veronica. From. 1973 he took on a unique challenge. There had been considerable controversy over a campaign on the part of a few Toronto priests in the Italian-Canadian neighbourhoods to have their parishioners switch their children and their taxes from the public to the separate school board. Many of these Catholic children had been in public schools because in the 1960s there were more pupils than there were spaces in the Toronto separate schools. The priests told the parents that a separate school was more desirable for preparing their children for their first reception of the Holy Eucharist and for their Confirmation. Many children transferred to the separate schools. This caused some space problems, an excess in some public schools and a surplus in others. The politicians got involved and Thomas Wells established a provincial committee to investigate sharing of facilities by public and separate school boards. Over the long term the results were mainly sharing in the areas of transportation, audio-visual departments, and a few other support departments. Marie Kennedy, OECTA's representative on the committee, emphasized that sharing could not be allowed to affect negatively the operation of a Catholic school community with its own staff, curriculum and life. Peter Gazzola became principal of St. Luigi, a school that would rarely be duplicated elsewhere because it shared its grounds and plant with Perth Avenue public school.

From 1973 to 1977 Peter worked closely with the parish priest and the teaching staff to provide the witness, liturgy and paraliturgy, religious instruction, and religion across the curriculum of a separate school. To accomplish this he ensured that St. Luigi had its own gymnasium, library, classrooms, playground, entrances and exits, secretarial and custodial staff, and public address system. When he became provincial president of OECTA in 1977, he did not run for the position for a second year, because he wanted to return to St. Luigi to finish the task he had set himself. The MSSB agreed and he continued as principal there for another four years.

Peter Gazzola then was principal of St. Raymond and after principal of St. Anthony. During his time in Toronto Peter met and married in 1972 a primary division MSSB teacher, Moira McCowie; they have two daughters, Nina and Julie. He acquired his B.A. from Wilfrid Laurier University and his principal's certificate. In the years prior to completion of the separate school system, Peter was a trustee on the Peel Board of Education representing for secondary school purposes the separate school taxpayers; for three years he was vice-chairman of the board. As a trustee Peter felt he picked up much useful information for OECTA and the separate school community striving for an equitable share of corporation tax revenues and for extension of their schools. After Davis completed the separate school system, Peter gained a seat on the Dufferin-Peel RCSS Board.

Peter's interest in OECTA dates all the way back to 1963 when Rose Cassin asked him to run for president of Unit 5, Metropolitan Toronto. She got the votes out, and Peter assumed office. Since then his involvement has continued unabated. He was president again, this time of the Toronto district, acted on the Board of Directors and Executive of OECTA and on the OTF Board of Governors. He was for so many years on so many provincial committees that it would be easier to list the ones on which he was not a member.

Two activities were close to Peter Gazzola's heart. In 1979 he became a councillor for the World Union of Catholic Teachers (WUCT). This organization was constituted in Rome in 1951 to serve Catholic education. It has always had about 300 000 members of between forty and forty-five national teacher organizations affiliated with it. It has held a General Assembly every three, now every four, years. After acting as councillor until 1988, Peter became treasurer and will continue in this capacity until 1995. He has maintained his commitment to the WUCT because, in his opinion, it is important for OECTA to be a presence in a Catholic world organization, to be of assistance to affiliates without OECTA's financial or human resources, and to maintain links with the Catholic teachers' organizations that were behind the Iron Curtain and now are emerging in a national eastern European environment. Peter helped plan the Assembly when Toronto was the host in 1985; OECTA will act again in this capacity in the near future.

The second activity to which Peter devoted much time was being a member of the Teacher Catholic Education Committee. The top priority of this committee was to educate OECTA members, the Catholic community, and the public at large concerning the necessity and justice of completing the separate school system. Although Peter was sometimes the sole elementary school person on the committee, he always had a great sense of injustice over the lack of government support for Catholic high schools. Each year the minutes reported the many hours he logged at the CNE booth operated by OECTA and the various workshops on the extension issue that he helped present throughout the province.

Peter Gazzola's dedication to OECTA can still be witnessed. OTF honoured him with a fellowship.[182]

Doreen Margaret Brady (1935-1982). Doreen was the first full-time female president of OECTA, holding the office for two years, 1978 to 1980.

She was born in Ottawa into a family of three: her father William Brady, a milkman, her mother Pearl Moore, a teacher, and her sister Ruth, older by five years. She began school at St. Francis Xavier, Brockville; when the family moved to their grandfather's farm between Prescott and Brockville, she attended a one-room public school, Haley's in Augusta Township, where her mother taught her from grades four to eight. She then went to Brockville Collegiate Institute where she completed her grade thirteen. Teaching seemed the natural calling for her, since her grandmother, mother, and sister were all teachers; therefore, she got her certificate at Ottawa Teachers' College in 1953-54 and began teaching immediately for the Ottawa Separate School Board.

Doreen taught in Ottawa at St. Joseph's Primary. From 1958 to 1960 she sampled northern Ontario teaching at St. Martin, Terrace Bay. She then went to the London Separate School Board for two years. She had begun her B.A., but wanted to save enough money to take a year's leave to study. She accepted her sister's invitation to join her and her husband John MacReady in Nanaimo, British Columbia where she lived rent-free and taught at Princess Royal public school. Mr. MacReady, a high school teacher, still remembers Doreen returning home upset because she had just been told to fail one of her pupils. He laughed and said that no one fails in grade one. Doreen, who always taught in the primary division, proceeded to lecture him extensively on the importance of love and positive reinforcement for the young child. She made a lifetime impression on her brother-in-law, as she was to do with many others. He regarded her as "the definition of dedication."

During the next school year Doreen completed her B.A. at Ottawa University and returned to the Ottawa board to teach at St. Michael. She became the board's reading consultant, then its integrated studies coordinator. She was promoted to principal of Corpus Christi school in 1974 and, after returning from her presidency in 1980, she was principal of St. Leonard. In these years she continually improved her professional qualifications by acquiring a primary education supervisor's certificate, an M.Ed., an elementary special education certificate, a supervisory officer's certificate, (the only one awarded in 1972 to anyone from Ottawa, despite a number of candidates who had taken the examination), and a religious education specialist's certificate.

Besides improving herself and the lives of her pupils and teachers, Doreen gave her talents to OECTA. She served on Ottawa committees and was president there for three years. Provincially, she was on the original QECO committee. As well, she was on the OTF Board of Governors and president of the Ottawa chapter of the Canadian College of Teachers. She became an OTF Fellow.

Obviously, she brought a wealth of experience to the presidency of OECTA. In addition she added her fine character to the Executive. Victoria Hannah, now on the Secretariat staff, recalled that she was "the conscience of the Executive." George Saranchuk, on the Executive with her, was convinced by her that corporal punishment was improper in a separate school. She looked at the broad perspective, and was interested principally in curriculum, professional development, the Lapierre study on early childhood education, and the advancement of women in the profession. She was and would have continued to be a significant force.

Doreen suffered a heart attack while in Toronto to attend an Executive meeting in December 1981 and a second fatal attack while resting with her mother in Tampa, Florida. She died peacefully with her family present in March 1982. She was unwavering in her faith to the end; the attending priest said that God must have needed a teacher that day.

In 1984 OECTA donated $25 000 to help build a model satellite city to house Calcutta and Bombay street-dwellers; it was planned to provide medical, educational, housing, and employment programmes and was named the Doreen Brady Project.[183] OECTA still honours her regularly in two ways. The provincial Awards Committee, upon application from an OECTA member, may award in any year the $5000 Doreen Brady scholarship for full-time study in primary education. Doreen's mother established an annual scholarship for the most outstanding student at Immaculata High School. The Ottawa Unit of OECTA annually selects an exemplary teacher who has contributed greatly to the Association. The dedication reads: "Doreen's career was spent working with and for the young child. Personally and professionally her philosophy was to nurture each new life God had created. She did this with sincerity and purity of purpose. She did this in an exemplary professional manner."[184]

George Saranchuck (1937-). The work done by the provincial and local executives, the five high school units and the Secondary Schools Committee to encourage membership and participation of the private Catholic high school teachers had positive results. George Saranchuk was the ninth of twenty-nine presidents to come from the secondary sector. Fr. Harrigan, Br. Thaddeus, Patrick Perdue, Mother Mary Lenore, Fr. Siegfried, Fr. Conway, Patrick O'Leary, and Fr. Kavanagh had preceded him.

George was born in Kenora. His father, Eugene Saranchuk, a shoemaker, and his mother, Mary Cormylo, who worked in the store with her husband, believed aggressively in acquiring an education for their two children, George and William. Their belief paid dividends: George became a secondary school vice-principal and William the crown attorney in Fort Frances.

George went to Mount Carmel school and the Kenora-Keewatin District High School. His achievement was high enough to gain him admission to the civil engineering course at the University of Toronto from which he received a B.Sc.. There were few civil engineering positions at the time, so George decided to try teaching; he never regretted this choice. He earned his HSA certificate in mathematics, science and Latin during two summers at OCE. His public high school teaching experience was spent at Western Technical School, Parry Sound High School, where his high school mathematics teacher hired him, and Thorold High School where he was the mathematics assistant head. In 1967 George Saranchuk decided to teach in a Catholic high school. He was the successful applicant for the position of mathematics head at Denis Morris High School in St. Catharines. George had always wanted to teach in a Catholic high school and to send his children to one. He says he would have taken a straight teaching position to work with the visionary Fr. Burns, C.Sc., principal of an expanding school. In 1982 he became vice-principal, remaining with that school until recently. Currently, he is vice-principal of Holy Cross High School. One of the ex-members of the student body, Darlene Cuiffetelli, recalled him as a stimulating mathematics teacher full of concern for his students and a leavening sense of humour.

His belief in Catholic education also led him into a somewhat unusual position. Because he was paid totally by the private Catholic school board at Denis Morris, he was able to run for trustee on the Lincoln County RCSS Board. Rather idealistically, he felt that a teacher on the board would be welcome to improve the education of the students. Some taxpayers must have agreed, because he won the seat for two terms in the 1970s. Then he won a seat on the Lincoln County Board of Education as the separate school representative. There his motives were similar to those of Kevin Kennedy and Peter Gazzola: OECTA would benefit from what he would learn and he perhaps could advance the cause of Catholic high schools.

The same motivation prompted him to become actively involved with OECTA. From 1970 to 1973 he took a leave of absence from the Lincoln board to work full-time at the OECTA provincial office. He was responsible for evaluations of teachers' certificates, first through OSSTF and then by means of QECO, which he helped establish. He also was the Secretariat person on the Secondary Schools Committee and worked with Fr. Kavanagh, Kevin Kennedy, Saundra McKay, and John Flynn on the extension campaign. He could have stayed with the Secretariat, but the family preferred to live in St. Catharines. He had married Colette Poirier, a physiotherapist, in 1961 and they had seven sons: Andrew, John, Peter, James Patrick, Matthew, Thomas, David, and finally, a daughter, Mary Kathleen.

George's commitment to Denis Morris and to OECTA has been constant. He served on numerous unit and provincial OECTA committees and on OTF committees; he was on the Unit executive and president over a five-year period and on the provincial Executive for eleven years. It was fortunate for George that during 1980 to 1982 he was a full-time president because during his term Doreen Brady, the past president, died, Frank Griffin took a one-year leave of absence, and Claire Ross challenged him on the legality of the OECTA fee. Nevertheless, he was able to concentrate the efforts of the Executive, Secretariat, and Board of Directors on the completion issue, a concentration that had historical results.

George Saranchuk was honoured with an OTF fellowship and continues to work for Catholic high school education.[185]

Kevin Kennedy (1927-). The second president to come from Ireland and the third to come from a northern Ontario unit, Kevin brought a perspective somewhat different from those of his predecessors. His brand of Catholicism made him on the one hand wary of the social justice agenda of some of his fellow members and on the other hand united with the membership in its push for collective bargaining legislation, for separate school access to corporate taxation revenues, and for completion of the separate school system. His two-year period as president, 1982-84, saw two of these objectives come close to fruition.

Kevin's road to higher teaching and education was indirect and taxing. He was born in Derryneil, County Down, Northern Ireland and educated to the end of the elementary level in Ballyvarley, then at St. Mary, Chorley, Lancashire. His father, William Kennedy, was a construction worker and his mother, Margaret McKeown, helped on their poultry farm. At age thirteen Kevin was on his own; his mother had died and his father was unable to look after the three children, Kevin, William and Mary. The legal school-leaving age was fourteen; Kevin quit school in the December before his fourteenth birthday. Fortunately, there was plenty of work during the war years and Kevin's uncle provided a place to live in Chorley.

Kevin worked at a number of jobs: in a bakery, driving a truck, and painting. During a large painting job outdoors, in cold weather, Kevin determined that there were more interesting and profitable ways to make a living and began through correspondence courses and self-study to prepare himself to sit for the five examinations leading to university entrance. He succeeded with this course of action while also obtaining his trade papers in painting. His next step was to enter a school for nursing; he completed this training and married a nurse, Edna Turner, in 1953. After a stint again in the building trade, in 1954 he decided on what would be his permanent vocation.

Kevin Kennedy took the Teachers' College courses at Trent Park, Barnet, Herefordshire and then taught in a secondary school in a low-income area in London. His subjects were English, science, physical education, and arts and crafts; Kevin's work experience had provided him with an eclectic variety of skills.

In 1958, as with so many other young teachers in England, Ireland, and Scotland, Canada beckoned. He took a teaching position with the Department of Indian Affairs at Wikwemikong on Manitoulin Island. The attraction for a married man with two children (there would be four: Michael, Moira, Elaine, and Shawn) was the provision of a house on the Ojibway reserve. After two years there, Kevin accepted a transfer to Mobert, northwest of Thunder Bay, where he received an isolation allowance and was principal of a two-room school. He then moved to Whitefish near Sudbury, where he built his own house, and began teaching for the Lively public school board.

In 1964 a priest enlisted Kevin Kennedy's help in forming a separate school board in Naughton, also near Sudbury. They secured the necessary signatures of ten Roman Catholic heads of family resident in the public school section, called a meeting of those interested in forming the board, selected the trustees, chose the school site, and had Our Lady of Fatima school built. The priest became the secretary and, in terms of influence, was the board. Kevin informally negotiated with him for the principalship and his salary. He had yet to become familiar with OECTA salary policies and simply hired his staff at North Bay Teachers' College, deciding on the salaries with the secretary.

However, Kevin was not totally unaware of salary schedules. He had discovered that university courses would raise the standard elementary school teacher's certificate and hence his salary. Consequently, he took a correspondence course from Ottawa University right after arriving in Ontario, then enroled at Laurentian University. He acquired his B.A. there, and his M.Ed. from OISE; he also earned a principal's certificate and a supervisory officer's certificate.

Kevin remained as principal in Naughton for seven years. He took pride in organizing the school on a unit rather than a grade system to facilitate pupil progress without school years being repeated. But when Naughton became part of the Sudbury District RCSS Board in 1969, in the name of consistency the Board closed down the unit system. Kevin moved to the Nipissing District RCSS Board in 1971.

For five years he was principal of a "mixed school" (that is, a building with two separate staffs and student bodies, French and English). On the second floor of St. Anne, Mattawa, Kevin gained experience with a far from desirable situation. (The Jackson Commission study would call the mixed school an agency of assimilation of the French.) Until his retirement in 1986 Kevin Kennedy would be principal of St. Joseph, North Bay, and of Our Lady of Sorrows, Sturgeon Falls.

While working for the Nipissing District RCSS Board, Kevin served two terms of office as separate school representative (that is trustee) on the Nipissing Board of Education. He felt that the representatives were doing nothing to forward the aims of the separate school system, particularly in the matter of completion. He saw no problem with conflict of interest because he would stay out of salary negotiating.

When Kevin Kennedy became principal of Our Lady of Fatima, he began attending OECTA meetings. John Rodriguez got him involved in salary negotiating throughout the district. Going after salaries comparable to those in the public schools, Kevin negotiated with the North Shore and Kapuskasing Separate School Boards: in Sudbury he used the mass-resignation technique, effective because the teacher shortage still existed. During the campaign for extension from 1969 to 1972 Kevin represented OECTA in northern Ontario, holding awareness sessions with the principals of the various separate school boards and writing part of the OECTA 1971 handbook on campaigning for completion. He was chairman of the Completion Committee and, even after Davis's negative response and his large election win, Kevin continued to serve on this Committee, renamed the Teacher Catholic Education Committee.

Kevin won election to second and first vice-president and to president (1982-84). While serving as past president he was advised one day by a journalist to show up at the Ontario legislature because in a few hours Premier Davis was going to make an important announcement. Kevin witnessed the 1985 yes to the separate school system.

He intended to run for a third year as president, but circumstances made this difficult. He had provided leadership and support in the teacher strike against the Nipissing District RCSS Board. One of the fallouts from this was that the new 1980 collective agreement put a limit of sixteen days that a teacher could be out of the school on

OECTA business. When Kevin exceeded the limit, he missed some of the Fridays of the weekend Executive meetings. Relations were further exacerbated when Kevin submitted a grievance for not being guaranteed his principalship upon returning to the board after his term of office. He won this, but the matter arose again when Kevin came to decide whether or not to run for a third term.

After two years as past president Kevin Kennedy in 1986 retired. He spends his time playing duplicate bridge and golf and building and renovating his cottage. He enjoys a life membership with OECTA and is an OTF Fellow.[186]

Fred Sweeney (1942-). Although Fred never had the opportunity to serve as president of OECTA, he was president of OTF in 1982-83 and served on its board of governors, as did James Carey, for about a decade. During the 1970s, therefore, he represented OECTA's views in such crucial matters as Bill 100, grades nine and ten grants for separate schools, the Catholic high school issue, Bill 82, and the corporation tax issue.

Fred Sweeney was born in London and spent his entire career as student, teacher, and principal there. His father, John Sweeney, was a baker; his mother, Muriel Rooney, an accountant clerk at the hospital. He grew up with a brother, Warren, and two sisters, Carol and Cathy. After attending Blessed Sacrament school and Catholic Central High School, Fred went to London Teachers' College. For the next four years he taught at St. Anne and St. Joseph. In 1967 he became a vice-principal of St. Mary, then St. Ann for a total of nine years. During these years Fred earned his B.A. from the University of Western Ontario, his M.Ed. from Wayne State University,a principal's certificate, and a supervisory officer's certificate. He also took the OECTA/OSSTA religious education course and, after Bill 82, special education, parts one and two.

At Teachers' College he met Heather Dyson and married her in 1966. Two children arrived, Jeffrey and Erin. Heather's higher salary with the local public school board for the same qualifications and experiences prompted Fred to become an active participant in OECTA affairs. He served on the Unit executive for four years including a year as president. Provincially, he was on the Finance Committee. After winning election as governor-at-large, he acted on the OTF superannuation and relations and discipline committees, then served as third, second, and first vice-president, president, and past president.

Fred Sweeney was vitally interested in separate school rights. He donated time over the years to the OECTA booth at the CNE. Acting along with other OECTA members on the OTF board of governors as an educator for its awareness of separate school injustices, Fred contributed to progress. Although OTF never did come out in favour of separate school access to corporation taxes or of completion of the separate school system, it did ask the government to make religion a teachable subject in Regulation 269 and did make a brief statement of principle regarding grades nine and ten grants in its annual briefs to the provincial government.

After completing his OTF presidency, Fred returned to London to be principal of St. Anthony, then in 1985 brought his years of experience to the Durham RCSS Board to be superintendent of student services. Since 1988 he has been superintendent of human resources.

OTF made him a Fellow. As a person who gave almost twenty years of service to OECTA and OTF, Fred found it disturbing that at the 1992 AGM there was a little dissension over whether or not ex-presidents should continue to be invited to AGMs if they became supervisory officers. The delegates gave the matter to the Executive to resolve, and it decided that the invitations should continue. The commitment of such people should be clear on the record, Fred Sweeney felt. His record revealed a significant role in the affairs of OECTA.[187]

Reverend J. Frank Kavanagh, OMI. Father's biography has been described above. His style as general secretary was analogous to that of a director of education with a board of trustees. Father acted as a resource for the Executive and as the implementer of the decisions of the AGM, Board of Directors, and Executive. Recently, he summed up his philosophy by which he lived while in the position. He believed that:

- one cannot not teach virtue, but learning leads to doing; conduct is qualifiable as moral/immoral, indifferent/good/bad;
- indifference is the most difficult position to confront: "So then because you are lukewarm, and neither cold nor hot, I will spit you out of my mouth." (Rev. 3:16);
- Catholic education provides the milieu for asking the tough questions about life and death, suicide, abortion, capital punishment, population issues, the conduct of capitalism, and the distribution of wealth;
- education is the Church in action, evangelizing.

With this philosophy he provided leadership and witness to OECTA, while existing with optimism in an Ontario society, where in his opinion, external forces sometimes work contrary to the interests of OECTA, where anti-Catholicism is socially acceptable, where 90 per cent of its citizens know little about separate schools, and where its ethos is inimical (covertly and overtly), sometimes malicious, and most times ignorant with regard to separate schools and Catholic education. Father as priest and general secretary carried this knowledge and his philosophy to meetings after meetings with officials of the government and of many organizations, seizing the opportunity to educate people about the aims of Catholic education and OECTA. He tried to live by Dylan Thomas's words: "Do not go gentle into that good night. Rage, rage against the dying of the light." He worked for OECTA from Davis's no to Davis's yes.[188]

Suddenly, on June 12, 1984, Premier Davis announced to a previously unaware Catholic community that the government was introducing a bill to amend the *Education Act* to provide government grants and taxing powers for separate school boards operating classes above grade ten.

NOTES

1. Ian Scott, ex-Attorney General of Ontario, interview, Toronto, 19 November 1993.
2. Labatt, *Always a Journey*, 184, 246-47; Anne Keeton, "Special Education: A Right or Privilege in Ontario," *Interchange* No. 3 (1978-80), 66-77.
3. Executive, 9-10 November 1979; B. C. Matthews, John Crispo, R. D. Fraser, *The Report of a Commission to Review the Collective Negotiations Process between Teachers and School Boards*, Toronto: Queen's Printer, 1986, 17.
4. Downie, *Collective Bargaining*, 115-37; Labatt, *Always aJ ourney*, 215; Coo, *Forty Years*, 92; *Bulletin*, November 1977, 2.
5. The Education Relations Commission, *Annual Report 1987-88*, Toronto: Queen's Printer, 1989, 11; Executive, 5-6 November 1982; AGM, 19-21 March 1983.
6. Commission, *Report 1987-88*; *Bulletin*, 16 November 1983; 1 March 1984.
7. Executive, 7-8 January 1977.
8. Ibid., 1-2 July 1977.
9. Ibid., 5-6 November 1982; 3-4 June, 2-4 July, 1-2 September 1983; *Windsor Star*, 26 May 1983; Helen Biales, interview, Toronto, 23 June 1983; Peter Murphy, interview.
10. Board of Directors, 16-17 February 1979; Executive, 4-5 July 1978.
11. Board of Directors, 24-25 November 1978; Executive, 2-3 June, 4-5 July, 3-4 November, 1978.

12. Ibid., 2-3 March 1979.
13. Ibid., 2-3 December 1978.
14. Ibid., 1-2 June 1984.
15. Ibid., 2-3 December 1977; D. F. Quinlan, interview; Knott, interview.
16. *Bulletin,* January 1979, 4; Executive, 4 November 1977.
17. Ibid., 5-6 May 1978; 1-2 June 1979.
18. F. S. Cooper, *An Inquiry into the Dismissal of Certain Probationary Teachers by the Lincoln County and Essex County Separate School Boards,* 6 July 1976, OECTAA; Murphy, interview; Executive, 4-5 June 1976.
19. *Bulletin,* May 1978, 2.
20. Executive, 4-5 November 1977.
21. Ibid., 7 July 1976; Board of Directors, 26-27 November 1976; Knott, interview.
22. Executive, 9-10 November 1979.
23. *Catholic Trustee* (March 1981), 23-30.
24. "Presentation of the Ontario English Catholic Teachers' Association to the Commission to Review the Collective Negotiations Process between Teachers and School Boards," 20 December 1979, OECTAA.
25. Matthews, *Report.*
26. Ibid., 22-26.
27. Ibid., 33-34.
28. P. H. Hennessy, "Collective Bargaining and the Professionalization of Ontario Teachers," *Teacher Education* (April 1977), 22-23.
29. Claire M. Ross, "Arbitration. Contract negotiations: where only the strong survive?", *OECTA News and Views,* (April 1975), 16-17, 21.
30. Executive, 2-3 June 1978.
31. Board of Directors, 19-20 November 1982.
32. Peter Murphy's records list the following strikes: 1977 - Durham, Essex; 1978 - Essex; 1980 - Essex, Frontenac, Nipissing, Wellington; 1981 - Essex; 1982 - Carleton.
33. Peter Gazzola, interview, Toronto, 28 September 1993; Claire Ross, interview, Toronto, 15 November 1993.
34. Board of Directors, 26-27 September 1975; 26-27 November 1976; 9-10 June 1978; 11-12 June; 19-20 November 1982; Executive, 9-10 November 1979; 4-5 January 1980; AGM, 15-17 March 1980.
35. Ross, "Contract Negotiations."
36. Executive, 2-3 May 1980; Murphy, interview.
37. Ibid., 4-5 July 1980; 15-17 January 1981.
38. Ibid., 21 August 1980; 2-3 July 1982.
39. Executive, 12-14 September, 18 December 1974; Normandeau, interview; Cooney, interview.
40. Ibid., 15-16 June 1973.
41. Ibid., 18-19 October 1974.
42. Ibid.,27 November, 6-7 December 1974.

43. Ibid., 6-7 December 1974
44. Ibid., 18 December 1974; 25-26 November 1977.
45. *OECTA News and Views* (May 1975), 3, 22; Executive, 19 May, 4-5 July 1975.
46. Ibid., 3-4 June, 1-2 July 1977.
47. Ibid., 2-3 December 1977
48. Ibid., 5-6 October 1978.
49. Ibid., 14 October, 24-25 November 1978.
50. Board of Directors, 4-5 October 1974; Executive, 24-25 May, 18-19 October 1974; 6-7 February 1975; 2 July 1976; 4-5 March, 15-16 April 1977; 31 March-1 April 1978.
51. Ibid., 7-8 January 1977.
52. Executive, 10-11 January 1975; 7-8 May 1976; 4-5 March, 15-16 April, 6-7 May 1977; 2-3 February 1978.
53. *Catholic Trustee* (June 1975), 15-18.
54. *OECTA Reporter* (April 1979), 6
55. Ibid., 6-7 March 1981; *OECTA News and Views* (November 1982), 30.
56. *Catholic Register*, 3 November 1979, 3.
57. Executive, 4-6 June 1981; 8-9 January 1982; Murphy, interview.
58. AGM, 18-20 March 1978.
59. Ibid., 4-5 February 1972; 14-15 September 1973; 2-3 May 1980; AGM, 19-21 March 1977; 15-17 March 1980; Board of Directors, 30-31 January 1976.
60. AGM, 18-20 March 1974, 20-22 March 1976; 19-21 March 1977; 20-22 March 1982; Executive, 4-5 May 1979; Board of Directors, 30-31 January 1976; 25-26 November 1977; 23-24 November 1979.
61. AGM, 19-21 March 1973; Executive, 4 May 1979.
62. Council of Presidents, 3-4 February 1984.
63. Executive, 7-8 January 1979.
64. Ibid., 12-14 September 1974.
65. Ibid., 3-4 October 1980.
66. Ibid., 10 December 1971; 16-17 February 1978; Board of Directors, 28-29 January 1972.
67. Ibid., 1-2 October 1971; Executive, 14-15 July, 5-6 September 1980.
68. Ibid., 7-8 September 1979.
69. *Report in the Matter of a Board of Reference Regarding Anne Lallouet and the Bruce-Grey County Roman Catholic Separate School Board*, 31 October 1983, OECTAA.
70. AGM, 17-19 March 1979; Executive, 6-8 November 1980; 2-3 April, 2-3 July 1982.
71. AGM, 18-20 March 1978; Brock Commeford, interview, Toronto, 17 September 1993.
72. Executive, 2-3 June 1978.
73. Dukacz, interview, Board of Directors, 12-13, 29 June 1981.

74. *OECTA Reporter* (April 1977), 3; *Bulletin* (October 1977), 1-2; Executive, 3-4 December 1982; Labatt, *Always a Journey*, 245.
75. Executive, 4-5 March 1983.
76. AGM, 19-21 March 1983; Board of Directors, 13-14 February 1981; 11-12 February 1983; Executive, 15-17 January, 2-3 July 1981; 8-9 January, 7-8 May 1982; 2-4 July 1983; 6-7 April 1984.
77. Executive, 1-2 December 1972; 15-16 April 1977; 2-3 May 1980; 2-3 April 1982; AGM, 19-21 March 1977.
78. Board of Directors, 28-29 January 1972; 11-12 February 1983.
79. Executive, 2-3 February 1972; 1-2 February, 4-5 October 1974; 26-27 September 1975; 8-9 April 1976; 3-4 June, 9-10 September 1977; 4-5 July 1978; 2-3 July 1979; 2-3 May, 5-6 September 1980; 2-3 October, 6-7 November 1981; 2-3 September, 3-4 December 1982; 4-5 November 1983; AGM, 20-22 March 1982.
80. *OECTA Reporter* (September 1976), 8; Fr. Frank Ruetz, interview, Waterloo, 22 September 1993.
81. Coo, *Forty Years*, 106; Ruetz, interview; Executive, 5-7 February 1981; AGM, 18-20 March 1974.
82. Joint Executive, OECTA/OSSTA, 12 October 1979; Executive, 4-5 May 1979; 4-5 January 1980; Board of Directors, 28-29 September 1972.
83. Executive, 5-6 March 1976; 1-2 February 1980; 4-5 February, 6-7 May 1983; AGM, 20-22 March 1982; 19-21 March 1983.
84. Executive, 1-2 February, 2-3 May 1980.
85. AGM, 20-22 March 1972; 18-20 March 1974; 20-22 March 1976; Board of Directors, 1-2 October 1971; 28-29 January 1972; 19-20 November 1982; Executive, 7-8 May 1976; 12-13 October 1979; 2-3 September 1982.
86. AGM, 18-20 March 1974.
87. Ibid., 7-8 May 1976.
88. Joint Executive, OECTA/OSSTA, 31 March 1980.
89. Board of Directors, 28-29 January 1972; Executive, 12-13 October 1979; Suzann Jones, interview, Toronto, 20 September 1993.
90. Executive, 15-16 April 1977; 3-4 February, 5-6 March 1978.
91. H. K. Fisher, Deputy Minister of Education, to Mr. Jones, OTF, 23 December 1981; Executive, 5-6 February 1982; Board of Directors, 11-12 February 1983; Executive, 4-5 May 1984.
92. Ibid., 5-6 March 1982.
93. AGM, 19-21 March 1973.
94. Executive, 4-5 November, 2-3 December 1983; 6-7 January, 10 February 1984.
95. *Toronto Sun*, 28 July 1983.
96. Ibid., 30 August 1983.
97. Fr. Thomas J. Day to Fr. F. Kavanagh, OECTA and C. Asseff, OSSTA, 28 September 1983, OECTAA.
98. Executive, 4-5 November 1983.

99. *OECTA Reporter* (October 1982), 42-43.
100. Board of Directors, 1-2 February 1974; 26-27 September 1975.
101. Ibid., 28-29 January 1972; *Bulletin*, 1 March 1984.
102. Lise Julien, *Women's Issues in Education in Canada*, Toronto: Council of Ministers of Education, 1987, 22-29; Labatt, *Always a Journey*, 94, 118, 144, 163, 206, 282; Executive, 1-2 September 1983.
103. Murphy, interview.
104. Jones, interview; Victoria Hannah, interview, Toronto, 9 September 1993; Elizabeth Dorner, interview, Toronto, 9 September 1993.
105. Executive, 2-3 February 1979; *Reporter* (February 1982), 25
106. Executive, 7-8 May 1976; 3-4 June 1977; 8-9 September 1978; 5-7 February 1981; Board of Directors, 9-10 June 1978.
107. Executive, 6 June 1975; 8-9 September 1978; 5-7 February 1981.
108. Ibid., 2-3 February 1979.
109. *OECTA Reporter* (December 1975), 22.
110. Ibid. (April 1977), 14; Board of Directors, 25-26 November 1977; Executive, 3-4 February 1987.
111. Council of Presidents, 18-19 November 1983; Executive, 7-8 May 1982; 4-5 March; 30 September-1 October 1983; 4-5 May 1984; *OECTA Reporter* (December 1982), 10; Dorner, interview.
112. Executive, 5-6 September 1980.
113. OECTA, "To Break the Silence. A Presentation to the Honourable Robert Welch, Provincial Secretary for Social Development," 1973, OECTAA; Farley, interview.
114. Executive, 1-2 January 1973; 13-14 September, 18-19 October 1974.
115. Ibid., 14-15 September 1973.
116. *Catholic Trustee* (December 1976), 3.
117. *OECTA Reporter* (May 1976), 6.
118. Board of Directors, 9-19 June 1978; Executive, 15-16 April 1977; 9-10 November 1979; *OECTA Reporter* (December 1979), 24; *Catholic Trustee* (December 1976), 3-16; Fred Sweeney, interview, Oshawa, 5 October 1993.

119. Executive, 30-31 May 1980
120. Ibid., 30-31 March 1979.
121. David Murray, *Room for All. A Report on Special Education*, 1982, OECTAA; Executive, 4-6 January 1981.
122. Board of Directors, 16-17 February 1979; 11-12 February 1983; Executive, 2-3 March 1978; 1-2 June 1979; 14-15 April 1982; Council of Presidents, 18-19 November 1982.
123. Executive, 2-3 July 1979; 30-31 May 1980.
124. L. J. Smith, *Ontario Commission on Taxation Report*, Vol. 2, 1967, 397-98; AGM, 19-21 March 1983; *Catholic Trustee* (December 1977), 12-19; Executive, 1-2 October 1982.
125. Ibid., 4-5 November 1983; Board of Directors, 19-20 November 1982.

126. Executive, 4-5 November 1983.
127. *Catholic Trustee* (December 1976), 17-26; Executive, 5-6 November 1976; 3-4 December 1982; 2-4 July, 2-3 December 1983; 6-7 January 1984.
128. Robert M. Barker, Executive Assistant, CTF, "Dollar for Dollar," 1974, OECTAA; Jim Gillespie, chair, Project Overseas Committee, *STO/ERO Newsletter/Bulletin*, Fall 1993.
129. AGM, 20-22 March 1972; 19-21 March 1973; 10-12 March 1984; Executive, 17-18 January; 15-16 October 1971; 3-4 March,14-15 September 1972; 7-8 December 1973; 21 March, 18 December 1974; 8-9 April 1976; 8-9 September 1978; 2-3 July, 7-8 December 1979; 5-6 September 1980; 4-6 June 1981; 2-3 September 1982; 4-5 February, 4-5 March 1983; Murphy, interview.
130. "CTF Project Overseas 1974. Helpful Hints for Participants," 23 May 1974, OECTAA.
131. *OECTA News and Views*, December 1971, 11-12; Executive, 1-2 December 1978.
132. AGM, 21-23 March 1981; Board of Directors, 12-13, 29 June 1981; Executive, 2-3 June, 10-11 November 1972; 14-15 June; 4-5 July 1974; 12-13 October, 9-10 November 1979; 5-6 December 1980; 8-9 January, 4-5 June, 2-3 July, 2-3 September,1-2 October, 3-4 December 1982; 15 January, 14-15 April, 2-4 July 1983; 6-7 January, 10 February, 6-7 April 1984.
133. Executive, 7-8 December 1979; *Bulletin*, April 1981; Dorner, interview.
134. Executive, 12-13 October 1979.
135. Pope Paul VI, "On Evangelization in the Modern World," Washington, D.C.: United States Catholic Conference Publications Office, 1976; Canadian Conference of Catholic Bishops, Episcopal Committee for Social Affairs, *A Society to be Transformed. A Pastoral Message*, Ottawa, 1977; ibid., *Ethical Reflections on the Economic Crisis*, Ottawa, 1983; Administrative Board, Canadian Conference of Catholic Bishops, *From Words to Action: a Pastoral Message on the Social and Political Responsibility of Christians*, Ottawa, 1976; Episcopal Committee for Social Affairs, Canadian Conference of Catholic Bishops, *Witness to Justice: A Society to be Transformed. Working Instructions*, Ottawa, 1979.
136. Pia Moriarty, "A Freirean Approach to Peacemaking," *Convergence*, Vol. XXII, No. 1, 1989, 25.
137. Executive, 2 November 1973; 19 April, 12-14 September 1974; 1-2 February 1980; 14 January 1982; Knott, personal records; Ted Schmidt, interview, Toronto, 1 November 1993.
138. Executive, 4-5 May, 2 July 1984.
139. Ted Schmidt, "How the Beast of Economics split man from God," *OECTA Reporter* (October 1981), 29-32; ibid., "Silence in our schools belies Christ's radical role in the world," (November 1981), 28-35; ibid., "Piety of the system: is this the faith we pass on?", (December 1981), 26-28; ibid., "Narrow road from narcissism," (January 1982), 20-21.
140. For example, *OECTA Reporter* (February 1977), 44, 46, 50; (April 1977), 28.
141. Executive, 30 September-1 October 1977; 30 April-May 1981; 5-6

November 1982; AGM, 19-21 March 1983.

142. Executive, 7-8 May 1976; 4-5 March, 4-5 November, 2-3 December 1977; 3-4 March, 1-2 December 1978; 28-29 March 1980; 5-6 November 1982; 12 March, 6-7 May 1983; Board of Directors, 16-17 February 1979; *OECTA Reporter* (May 1979), 29.

143. AGM, 10-12 March 1984; Executive, 10 February 1984; *OECTA Reporter* (January 1984), 7; (March/April 1984), 5; Kevin Kennedy, interview, North Bay, March 1982.

144. Gazzola, interview; Kavanagh, interview.

145. AGM, 20-22 March 1972; 10-12 March 1984; *Catholic Trustee* (June 1976), 14-17; *Bulletin*, May 1983.

146. Executive, 6-7 November 1981.

147. AGM, 20-22 March 1982.

148. Ibid.; AGM, 21-23 March 1981; 19-21 March 1983; Jones, interview; Sweeney, interview; Executive, 5-7 February 1981.

149. Board of Directors, 26-27 September 1975; 21-22 November 1980; 18-19 November 1983; Executive, 4-5 June 1982; AGM, 10-12 March 1984.

150. Executive, 31 May-1 June, 8-9 November 1974.

151. Dorner, interview; *Agenda*, November 1993.

152. Council of Presidents, 18-19 November 1983; AGM, 20-22 March 1982; Executive, 5-6 January 1979; 15-17 January 1981.

153. Executive, 5-6 October 1978.

154. Ibid., 6-8 November 1980; 30 April-2 May 1981; 8-9 January 1982; 15 January, 3-4 June 1983; AGM, 21-23 March 1981.

155. Ibid., 2-4 July 1983; AGM, 20-22 March 1982; Bruce Archer, speech, Catholic Community Delivery Organization, Mississauga, 20 November 1993.

156. Executive, 17-18 September 1971; *OECTA News and Views*, (September 71), 1,3; Board of Directors, 1-2 October 1971; Stamp, *Schools of Ontario*, 240.

157. Walker, *Catholic Education*, Vol. III, 370-73; Cooney, interview; Murphy, interview.

158. Walker, *Catholic Education*, Vol. III, 366; Paul Howard, interview, Toronto, 12 October 1993; Board of Directors, 28-29 January 1972; *Catholic Trustee* (June 1976), 14, 17.

159. Executive, 3-4 December 1976; 3-4 June 1977; 31 March-1April 1978; 9-10 November 1979; 2-3 May 1980.

160. Ibid., 9-10 September 1977; 3-4 March 1978.

161. Ibid., 5 May 1970; 2 March 1972; 3-4 February 1978; 5-6 January 1979.

162. *Catholic Trustee* (November 1973), 8-15.

163. Ibid., (May 1977), 1-6.

164. Ibid., (June 1976), 14, 17; *Bulletin*, May 1983; Executive, 1-2 February 1980; Walker, *Catholic Education*, Vol. III, 366.

165. Board of Directors, 24-25 May 1974; Executive, 30 September - 1 October 1977; 6-8, 11 November 1980; 30 April-1 May 1981.

166. Ibid., 2-3 October 1981.

167. Paul Glynn, interview, Mississauga, 27 September 1993.
168. AGM, 18-20 March 1974; Executive, 14-15 June, 12-14 September 1974; 4-5 July, 3-4 October 1980; 2-3 October 1981; 30 September-1 October 1983; Glynn, interview.
169. Board of Directors, 30-31 January 1976; 18-19 February, 10-11 June 1977; 9-10 June 1978; 8-9 June 1979; 12-13, 29 June 1981; Executive, 5-6 May, 3-4 June 1983; 6-7 June 1984; Glynn, interview.
170. Board of Directors, 9-10 June 1978; "Submission to the Secondary Education Review Project of the Ministry of Education by the Ontario English Catholic Teachers' Association," 1 October 1980, OECTAA; Executive, 6-8 November 1980; 4-6 June 1981.
171. *OECTA Reporter* (April 1977), 4; Executive, 3-4 October 1980; Board of Directors, 19-20 November 1982.
172. *Bulletin*, April 1981; Walker, *Catholic Education*, Vol. III, 368-69.
173. Board of Directors, 12-13, 29 June 1981. See also Executive, 3-4 July 1979; 2-3 May 1980; 14-15 April 1983.
174. Ibid., 13-14 February 1981.
175. *Bulletin*, April 1981; Executive, 5-6 December 1980; 4-6 June 1981; 2-3 September 1982; Glynn, interview; Saranchuk, interview.
176. Board of Directors, 20-21 November 1981.
177. Executive, 6-7 January 1984; Council of Presidents, 3-4 February 1984.
178. Board of Directors, 11-12 February 1983; Executive, 4-5 November 1983; 2 March 1984.
179. Executive, 4-5 January, 3-4 December 1982; 4-5 February, 3-4 June, 1-2 September, 30 September-1 October 1983; Council of Presidents, 18 November 1983; 2 March 1984; Walker, *Catholic Education*, Vol. III, 368-69; Kennedy, interview; Ian Scott, interview.
180. AGM, 15-17 March 1980; Executive, 6-7 April 1984.
181. Ibid., 104; Derry Byrne, interview, Nepean, 2 October 1993; Rev. Frank Ruetz, CSSR, interview, Waterloo, 22 September 1992; Suzann Jones, interview, Toronto, 29 September 1993; AGM, 19-21 March 1973; *Ottawa Citizen*, 29 February 1992, G9.
182. Gazzola, interview; Board of Directors, 12-13 June 1981.
183. *OECTA Reporter* (October 1984), 5.
184. AGM, 17-19 May 1975; 10-12 March 1984; Executive, 4-5 December 1981; 2-3 April,7-8 May 1982; *OECTAReporter*, (April 1982), 15; Mr. and Mrs. John MacReady, brother-in-law and sister, interview, Kanata, 22 September 1993; Hannah, interview; Saranchuk, interview; records in the possession of Mrs. Ruth MacReady.
185. AGM, 19-21 March 1977; Saranchuk, interview; Darlene Ciuffetelli, interview, Toronto, 13 August 1993.
186. Coo, *Forty Years*, 116-17; Kevin Kennedy, interview.
187. *OECTA Reporter* (October 1982), 29; Sweeney, interview.
188. Kavanagh, interview.

CHAPTER NINE

DRAMATIC GROWTH AND CHANGE 1984-1994

I would therefore conclude that Roman Catholic separate school supporters had at Confederation a right or privilege, by law, to have their children receive an appropriate education which could include instruction at the secondary school level and that such right or privilege is therefore constitutionally guaranteed under s.93(1) of the Constitution Act, 1867.[1]

Background. Historians are much more comfortable writing about patterns, trends, and significant events in the past. The ferment of ideas and events makes it difficult to distinguish between the important occurrences with long-term implications and the interesting but evanescent happenings. The last decade seems to present this problem to a great degree. One clear pattern is one of change: in public attitudes, the economy, government, educational funding, collective agreements between school boards and teachers, and educational structures, to mention a few with relevance to a history of OECTA.

Between 1984 and 1994 the *Macleans/CTV Poll* has been charting these changes. In 1984 Canadians reported that they were proud, confident, and optimistic; there had been an economic recession, but the problems could be readily addressed. During the decade the poll's respondents shifted dramatically to pessimism about living in an environment of diminished opportunities. This feeling was accompanied by a decline in confidence in, even a cynicism about, public officials. There was and is a sense of losing control when confronted with the unemployment of at least three million Canadians, the huge federal and provincial deficits, the growing epidemic of AIDS, a dangerous dilution of the upper atmosphere's elements protecting humans from the sun's ultraviolet rays, crime, and violence in the schools. The 1992 defeat of the Charlottetown constitutional accord, the 1993 reduction of the federal Progressive Conservative Party to two seats and the rise of the Reform Party and Bloc Quebeçois made some citizens wonder if there would be the political will or the financial and human resources to tackle these problems. All of this affected negatively the willingness and ability of the provincial government and municipal taxpayers to fund education to the degree that advocates for children said they required. The more difficult the economic times, the more children are at risk, either from living in poverty (1.2 million in Canada, estimated) or from experiencing violence in their homes. Concern for children and loss of faith in institutions to help with the concern have grown in the face of 115 Church officials being charged with sexual abuse over the last five years. Pundits remind Canadians that Canada is still one of the best countries to live in the world, but teachers must still help their students cope with problems that seem more numerous and serious than in earlier years.[2]

Accompanying the change in public attitude to institutions and leaders, including those in the educational world, has been a dizzying rotation of Ministers of Education. People like William Davis, Thomas Wells, and Bette Stephenson seemed to have been permanent fixtures; educators could plan in a relatively predictable environment. No longer. Since 1984 there have been four elections, three changes of government, and seven Ministers of Education (now Ministers of Education and Training). Teachers and trustees have had to adjust to the new thrusts of, chronologically, Keith Norton (P.C.), Larry Grossman (P.C.), Sean Conway (Lib.), Chris Ward (Lib.), Marion Boyd (N.D.P.), Tony Silipo (N.D.P.), and David Cooke (N.D.P.).

Each government has taken a look at education, particularly secondary education with its problem of the general-level student dropping out. The Progressive Conservatives established the Secondary Education Review Project in 1980; its report resulted in the Ministry's response in 1982, *The Renewal of Secondary Education in Ontario*; the whole effort culminated in *Ontario Schools Intermediate and Senior Divisions (Grades 7-12/OACs), Program meand Diploma Requirements*, 1984, revised in 1989. The number of credits and compulsory credits were increased, general-level Ministry curriculum guidelines were amplified, and cooperative education, work experience, and linkage programmes were encouraged.[3]

The drop-out problem continued; therefore, David Peterson, the Liberal Premier, asked George Radwanski to look at education in general and the secondary education drop-out problem in particular. His

1987 *Ontario Study of the Relevance of Education, and the Issue of Dropouts* called for the elimination of social promotion in the elementary schools and of ability grouping in the secondary schools, for mastery learning and better reporting to parents, for mentoring and improved guidance for all students, and for teacher education in order to implement these changes. An all-party Select Committee on Education was struck in 1988 to examine Radwanski's recommendations, and to examine, conduct hearings, and report on Ontario's school system. Its "First Report" in December 1988 recommended, among other things, the same homeroom teacher for a number of subjects being taken by a secondary school class, mentoring, unstreamed courses at least until the end of grade nine, school-board power to destream further, and smaller class sizes and teacher in-service in order to implement destreaming and small group/individualized instruction.[4]

Before the government could react to the Select Committee's recommendations, Premier Bob Rae and the NDPs took power. As a socialist government it found the destreaming concept complemented its politics of inclusion. New policies, legislation, and structures emerged on employment and pay equity in relation to women, aboriginals, ethnocultural and racial minorities, and the disabled. Mainstreaming of students in special education programmes and destreaming of basic, general and advanced level students into a "least restrictive environment" presented themselves to the new government as ideologically and pedagogically correct. Tony Silipo announced that grade nine would be destreamed in September 1993. However, some school boards and teachers resisted because the recommendations regarding class size and teacher in-service had not been sufficiently implemented. They have been granted an extension before destreaming.

The second initiative of the Ministry was the publication in 1993 of *The Common Curriculum Grades 1-9.* This document listed the essential and general student outcomes in four core program areas: language, the arts, self and society, mathematics/science/technology. By its very nature it pointed to a multidisciplinary teaching approach with some elements of mastery learning. These were additional challenges for the teacher encountering a destreamed class and using an individualized/small-group methodology for the first time.[5]

Other changes were in the works. David Cooke, the new Minister, stated that the government was examining the governance of education. Perhaps the size and structure of school boards were not the most efficient ways of delivering education to the students. Cooke also announced in 1993 the formation of the Ontario Parent Council that would advise the Ministry on educational matters. In the midst of all these government moves, Cooke announced the establishment of the Royal Commission on Learning, which is to receive briefs, conduct hearings, and issue a report by December 1994. Some educators argued that the Radwanski Report and the many reaction papers to the Ministry documents on restructuring made the Commission's work redundant. Others held that the Commissioners' task was to sort out among all the reports and briefs the priorities for school reform.[6]

Finally, there were changes in the funding of education. After one year in office Premier Rae announced a serious crisis in the government's budget. The deficit had grown to such a size that, in Rae's opinion, the ability of the government to borrow at a decent rate and the quality of the province's social welfare programmes were at risk. Floyd Laughren, the Minister of Treasury and Economics, in February 1991 announced that the transfer payments to school boards would increase by only 7.9 per cent since he was "severely limited" in his options due to the recession. Although Marion Boyd, the Minister of Education "admitted that the government's 7.9 per cent increase ... was disappointing,"[7] it seemed profligate the following year when Laughren announced that grants to school boards would be held to 2 per cent , 1 per cent and 1 per cent over the next three years. The following year he had to revise the transfer payments to increases of 1 per cent , 0 per cent and 0 per cent . Finally, in a precedent-setting move, the Premier announced in the spring of 1993 his "Social Contract" which specified that collective agreements between school boards and teachers would be reopened so that some 5 per cent could be cut from educational expenditures in the years 1993, 1994, and 1995.[8]

To ensure future discussion of more change, in December 1993 the Fair Tax Commission released its report which recommended that the property tax be replaced by a provincial income tax for the funding of education.

Bill 30. The most historic change for separate schools in this century was their funding to the end of high school. There has been considerable speculation regarding why Premier Davis reversed his stand of a decade earlier. Some political analysts thought that the large Catholic vote, particularly in Metropolitan Toronto, influenced him; others felt that, if the Conservatives wished to stay in power, they would have to significantly broaden their base of party support, particularly among ethnic minorities. Ian Scott, the Attorney General in the Peterson government, believed that Davis suspected that the Catholic high school issue could end up in court; OSAFF's writ had been served on the government; the Franco-Ontarians had won the right to govern their schools. Perhaps the Catholic hierarchy would not continue to be patient and quiet.[9] It is my belief that the OECTA campaign with the high school students at Queen's Park and Rick Chiarelli's intention to argue for full funding under the *Charter of Rights and Freedoms* must have had some impact on Davis's thinking. Higgins and Letson in their biography of Cardinal Carter point to the personal friendship and mutual respect between William Davis and Archbishop Philip Pocock and Archbishop Cardinal Carter; the former was a Brampton neighbour and bridge partner. The book argues that "fairness, right reason, and personal friendships" carried the day. In Davis's statement to the House on June 12, 1984 and his extensive interview with the Social Development Committee hearings on Bill 30, he convincingly stated that the children of separate school supporters were constitutionally entitled to a basic education and in the 1980s such an education included high school. In his original statement in 1971 he had expressed his belief in high school students being educated all together in the same public school system as preparation for living in Ontario's society. He likely still believed that in 1984, but, as he said to the Committee, Catholic students would continue to pass his home every day on their way to a school with no funding for grades eleven to the end of high school, a policy difficult to explain or defend to the students.

Davis's announcement encountered predictable opposition. The *Globe and Mail* in its editorial wrote, "Now that he has reversed himself on separate school support, it might be prudent to keep an ear open for the roar of bulldozers and cement mixers at the bottom end of the expressway."[10] (But the *Toronto Star* wrote, "Davis has done the right thing.")[11] The Directors of Education of the province's boards of education expressed dismay: "We simply cannot understand how the development of a competing publicly funded Roman Catholic secondary school system in Ontario will do other than increase costs to legitimize the ancient idea of a separate Protestant Ontario and separate Roman Catholic Ontario." ALSBO was disappointed and called for open access of students and teachers of all religions to separate schools. After the first reading of Bill 30 completing the separate school system, OSSTF at its 1987 AGM passed motions to organize protest actions, including province-wide closure of schools, if any of its members lost jobs due to extension, to support candidates for the provincial legislature who were opposed to Bill 30, and to promote the creation of unified school boards.

The Metropolitan Toronto Board of Education asked for a legal opinion on the constitutionality of Bill 30; the lawyer replied that the *Charter* rendered the Bill unconstitutional.[12]

Meanwhile, there had been a spring election in 1985 ushering in a minority Liberal government. The short reign of Premier Frank Miller after Davis's retirement did not produce the high school legislation. The task fell to Premier David Peterson's government. On July 4, 1985 it introduced Bill 30 into the Legislative Assembly. The Bill's preamble stated that its purpose was to implement full funding for Roman Catholic separate high schools in Ontario and listed reasons for this action:

- separate school guarantees facilitated the creation of a united Canada in 1867;
- Roman Catholic separate schools have become a significant part of the school system in Ontario;
- it has been public policy in Ontario since 1889 to provide for public funds to support education in separate schools to the end of grade ten;
- it is recognized that today a basic education requires a secondary as well as an elementary education;
- it is just and proper and in accordance with the 1867 guarantees to bring the provisions of the law-respecting separate schools into harmony with the provisions of the law respecting public elementary and secondary schools.

Bill 30 permits a separate school board to elect by by-law to perform the duties of a secondary school board with the approval of the Minister. Once the election is made and approved, the separate school board becomes a "Roman Catholic school board" and is entitled to receive secondary school grants and levy taxes. Separate school supporters within the jurisdiction of a Roman Catholic school board are exempt from taxes for the support of public high schools. During the ten years following its election this board must fill positions on its teaching staff by offering employment to teachers on the staff of the coterminous board of education whose services will not be required because of students transferring to the Catholic high school. There were other provisions to the Bill, but those already described would be the ones in dispute in the Courts.[13]

OSSTF, ALSBO, and the Metropolitan Toronto Board of Education began to consider a court challenge. The Liberal government looked at its options. Some of its lawyers were telling it that the Bill was unconstitutional because of the *Charter.* If they were correct, then a case, probably arriving before the Courts in about three years, would take place just at the time of the next provincial election; in Ian Scott's opinion, this would have resulted in the Liberals being thrown out of office as the Conservatives were in the 1985 election over the Catholic high school issue. Furthermore, there would be an unwinding of the legislation disastrous to the educational structure. The Liberals decided to ask for a Constitutional Reference, thereby demonstrating their concern to be constitutionally correct and getting the matter into the Ontario Court of Appeal quickly.[14]

Once the Bill received first reading, Sean Conway, the Minister of Education, announced that it would not advance to second and final reading until the Ontario judges would render their verdict. The government would, however, fund the Catholic high schools, even though they were still technically private. This action caused a court case, but the judgment was that the Minister did have the right to fund the schools by regulation.

In order to coordinate the separate school community in its monitoring of the implementation of Bill 30, in its advice to separate school boards, and in its defence of Bill 30 in the courts, the Completion Office Separate Schools (COSS) was formed. It was supported by OECTA, OSSTA, OCSOA, OCCB, and the Ontario Separate School Business Officials' Association. Tom Reilly, a supervisory officer with the Dufferin-Peel RCSS Board, was seconded to be the executive director. OECTA agreed to pay 45 per cent of the costs of COSS and any legal costs. (The bill would end up being about half a million dollars for OECTA.)[15]

The question submitted by the Ontario government to the Court of Appeal was the following. "Is Bill 30, *An Act to Amend the Education Act* inconsistent with the provisions of the Constitution of Canada including the *Canadian Charter of Rights and Freedoms* and, if so, in what particular or particulars and in what respect?" The following were given leave to present to the Court arguments against the Bill: the Metropolitan Toronto Board of Education, London Board of Education, Peel Board of Education, Waterloo Board of Education,

OSSTF, FWTAO, the Ontario Alliance of Christian Schools, the Ontario Association of Alternative and Independent Schools, the Canadian Jewish Congress, the Canadian Civil Liberties Association, the Coalition for Public Education, the Seventh-Day Adventist Church, the Canadian Holocaust Remembrance Association, the Hindu Federation of Canada, the Humanist Association of Canada, the Loyal Orange Association in Ontario, and eight private citizens. Those presenting for the Bill were the following: the Attorney General for Ontario, OECTA, OSSTA, MSSB, Dufferin-Peel RCSS Board, Renfrew County RCSS Board, Lanark, Leeds & Grenville RCSS Board, Huron-Perth RCSS Board, Kirkland Lake & District RCSS Board, London and Middlesex County RCSS Board, Hamilton-Wentworth RCSS Board, Hastings-Prince Edward County RCSS Board, Carleton RCSS Board, Frontenac, Lennox & Addington RCSS Board, OSAFF and, supporting the Bill in part, L'Association française des Conseils scolaires de l'Ontario. There were thirty-six lawyers involved. The arguments against the constitutionality of Bill 30 centred on the *Canadian Charter of Rights and Freedoms*:;

- Section 15 of the *Charter* indicates equality before the law and equal benefit of the law; Bill 30 should fail since it discriminates against all other religious groups and those of no religion;
- Bill 30 has a religious purpose; therefore, it infringes on the religious freedom of others both by its purpose - to fund one group only - and by its effect - to force other religious groups to pay for their schools;
- Section 93 of the *Constitution Act* can only grant what separate school supporters had by law in 1867;
- the *Tiny* judgment was correct in fact and law;such a weighty decision should not be overturned on the basis of affidavits;
- Section 29 of the *Charter* prohibits anything that will "abrogate or derogate" from separate school rights; this does not apply to legislation passed after the *Charter* came into effect;
- Section 1 of the *Charter* allows a province to escape the provisions of the *Charter* for overriding reasons; Bill 30 does not promote a goal of sufficient value to society in general to justify it as an exception to *Charter* scrutiny.[16]

The arguments in support of Bill 30 stressed the importance of section 93 of the *BNA Act* both as guaranteeing separate school rights and as being free of scrutiny by the *Charter*, the incorrectness of the *Tiny* judgment, and the fact that, in any case, Bill 30 did not offend the *Charter*.

Premier Peterson was intent that Ian Scott as Attorney General of Ontario lead off the case for the government. It was equally symbolic and fitting that Ian Scott, the great-grandson of Richard W. Scott of *Scott Act* fame, appear in court. As a child he had often heard his grandfather, W. L. Scott, an Ottawa lawyer, tell how the *Tiny* judges had erred and the Confederation pact had been broken. He decided that he would like to use the argument that without the agreement to protect Roman Catholic separate school rights in Canada West and Protestant dissentient school rights in Canada East Confederation would not have come about. He ran the argument by Peter Hogg, a constitutional lawyer; he was not enthusiastic about it as a legal argument, but admitted that it had merit as a political argument. Blenus Wright, the Deputy Attorney General, did not want to present the argument. Ian Scott did present it to the Court of Appeal and the Supreme Court of Canada. Both the press in Ontario and the final judgment in the Supreme Court picked up the idea, drawing from the historical record support for such phrases as "the basic compact of Confederation" and "solemn pact."[17]

Scott also developed the point that section 93 explicitly contemplates and authorizes the establishment of separate school systems and that the *Charter* cannot affect this authorization; denominational school legislation should not be undermined by any other part of the Constitution, which includes the *Charter*. He explained that, if the *Charter* did affect Bill 30, then the *Charter* was not time limited and, therefore, would affect all the post-Confederation legislation passed in all the provinces in support of separate or dissentient schools. Clearly, this was not intended by the framers of the *Charter*.

Blenus Wright decided to present the historical case for the error in judgment in the *Tiny case*. Originally, the separate school lawyers, subdividing the arguments, had assigned the historical argument that separate school boards in fact and law were operating schools at the high school level prior to Confederation to the Metropolitan Separate School Board and Dufferin-Peel RCSS Board lawyers, Robert Falby, Hugh M. Kelly, and Peter Lauwers. I, an OECTA member, had been asked to do the historical research and write an affidavit for their use. But Blenus Wright examined the documents in support of the affidavit, made his decision to argue the historical case, and would spend several hours in the Court of Appeal presenting what he described as "massive evidence" that separate school boards prior to Confederation were educating students at what would now be considered a high school level with statutory and regulatory backing and with government grants and municipal taxes. He concluded that the *Tiny* judgment was wrong in fact and law, that separate schools were intended to be equal partners in the school system, and that their rights had been prejudicially affected. Bill 30 was the attempt to restore equality between the two branches of the school system.

Claude Thompson, the lawyer for COSS and OSSTA, argued that the Canadian Constitution recognizes the validity of group as well as individual rights. Regarding *Tiny*, he put forth the fallback position that, even if the *Tiny* judgment was correct, since it allowed contraction of separate schools by regulation, then it must also allow expansion by regulation. (Some of the separate school lawyers were more optimistic about this argument than about the historical one.)

Paul Cavalluzzo, the OECTA lawyer, defended Bill 30 from *Charter* attack. He postulated that the *Charter* demands that those situated similarly be treated equally; but Bill 30 did not offend the equality rights of others since no other group in Ontario was situated similarly with a truncated state school system. He elaborated this point by explaining how Bill 30 had the objective of providing what the Hall-Dennis Commission and the Ministry curriculum guidelines described as continuous education, kindergarten to grade thirteen, to a considerable body of students deprived of such a programme.[18]

The Court of Appeal held the Constitutional Reference for about two weeks in the early fall of 1985 and on February 18, 1986 delivered its judgment. It did not comment on the *Tiny Township* judgment of 1928 since it was from a higher court. It ruled three to two in favour of the constitutionality of Bill 30. Justices Zuber, Tarnopolsky, and Cory upheld Bill 30 because nothing in section 93 of the *BNA Act* of 1867 prohibited Ontario from extending full funding to separate schools unless the legislation could be said to "prejudicially affect any Right or Privilege which any Class of Persons have by Law at the Union." They noted about the *Charter* that it recognizes the importance of group rights over individual rights in some cases and that its section 29 protects separate school rights from any abrogation or derogation of constitutionally guaranteed rights.

The Chief Justice of Ontario Howland and Robins J.A. dissented. They claimed that section 29 protected only rights and privileges that existed at Confederation and that *Tiny* had judged to be only elementary. Therefore, Bill 30 offended section 15 of the *Charter*. The judges did not agree that Bill 30 was "demonstrably justified" under section 1 of the *Charter.*[19]

The Ontario government promptly reopened discussion of Bill 30 and it received third reading on June 23, 1986 and royal assent June 24.

The Supreme Court of Canada heard the appeal from January 29 to February 5, 1987. The Quebec Association of Protestant School Boards, Attorney General for Alberta, and Attorney General of Quebec appeared in defence of Bill 30. Any attack on the Bill was indirectly a possible attack on separate school rights in Alberta and dissentient school rights in Quebec. This Court was able to and did consider the rightness or wrongness of the *Tiny* judgment. Madame Justice Wilson wrote the judgment on behalf of herself and Dickson, C.J., Beetz, Estey, McIntyre, Lamer, La Forest, JJ.; it was released on June 25, 1987. It stated that section 93 of the *BNA Act* demonstrated that its authors intended to permit the provinces to expand denominational rights and privileges beyond their 1867 status. It also concluded that the Privy Council judgment in the *Tiny case* was "unsound," rendered the constitutionalized separate school protection "illusory," and did "wholly undermine this historically important compromise." It was unnecessary to discuss the *Charter.*[20]

There was elation in the separate school community over both the victory and the unanimity of the seven judges on the constitutionality of Bill 30. It had hoped that the Supreme Court would accept the argument that the *Tiny* judgment confirmed only that the Ontario government had the power to contract the separate school system to a degree by regulation and therefore had the same power to expand the system. It seemed almost an unreasonable hope that the judges unanimously would overturn the *Tiny* judgment and define a separate school as both elementary and secondary. OECTA's half a million dollars had been well spent. The OECTA members who had spent enormous time and energy on this critical struggle must have felt a greatdeal of satisfaction; for example, members of the Political Advisory Committee like Colm Harty, Sue LaRosa, Mary Beverage, and others.

Restructuring. As a result of Bill 30 OECTA's statutory membership increased by about 2000 in 1986.[21] This gave rise to discussions by the Secretariat and Executive that the structure, objectives, and activities of OECTA should *visibly* reflect its new secondary school teachers' composition. Some teachers who had been on private Catholic high school staffs were wondering if an Association that had been largely composed of elementary school teachers could properly represent them, especially in negotiating collective agreements. More seriously, OSSTF was wooing Catholic high school teachers in Sault Ste. Marie, Sudbury, and York Region; it took the position that it was the logical federation to represent *all* secondary school teachers. Peter Murphy expressed the problem succinctly: "We have them [high school teachers] as 'bodies' at the moment, but, I suspect, we don't have their hearts and minds."[22]

Other Catholic high school teachers were not considering OSSTF membership; after all, they were aware (and if they were not, the Executive had passed a motion to make them aware) that OSSTF had positions on Bill 30, the pooling of corporate assessment, and the establishment of unified (that is, public/separate) school boards that were hostile to separate school rights.[23] But they were in some units actively considering the formation of high school affiliates, units, or sub-units within OECTA.

OECTA moved in several directions to represent well its new membership. The AGM of 1986 passed an objective to address the issues associated with the increased secondary school component. A motion that a person with secondary school and collective bargaining experience be added to the Teacher Welfare Department was referred to the general secretary. Father Kavanagh in June 1985 replied that OECTA had to respond immediately to the needs of the secondary school members and asked for additional staffing in all the departments of the Secretariat. Two Catholic high school teachers, Bob Denham from Sault Ste. Marie and Sister Evanne Hunter from Toronto, were seconded for a year to work with high school staffs. On their visits throughout the province they listened to concerns of high school staffs and reported back to the Executive. Sister Evanne recommended that OECTA assume a higher profile in dealing with deplorable high school conditions and in convincing school boards to spend some of their new grant money to correct conditions from the private-school days.[24]

Bob Denham's report touched most of the bases:

> After years of making do with inferior facilities and salaries our teachers should have parallel working conditions and facilities to their public school colleagues. The opinion that, "We've taught for less in inferior circumstances because of our faith and now we want justice" is very strong within our secondary members. Often this feeling is compounded by the perception that we didn't mind the sacrifice when Sister or Father ran the school on bingo money and recycled paper, but now they're gone and the Board doesn't understand or appreciate where we're coming from or who

> we are. Often this perception is further coloured by the fact that few of the Board's supervisory personnel have secondary school experience ....In school after school we've heard the opinion that...the elementary teachers who are in the majority in the unit do not understand the needs of our secondary members.[25]

Toronto, Hamilton, and Essex at the 1986 AGM told the delegates that, "If secondary school teachers employed by a separate school board wish to organize themselves into a separate unit within OECTA, they should have the opportunity to do so."[26] But there were pros and cons. Doug Knott felt that, "Short-term goals may be accomplished by splintering, but long-range objectives will be achieved through unity, solidarity, and the power of numbers and dollars."[27] Asked for its opinion, the Teacher Welfare department offered the following: one collective agreement for the unit's elementary and secondary school teachers offers solidarity and, therefore, clout and avoids the risk of one group selling out the other or of the board playing off one against the other. Two collective agreements, on the other hand, matches the situation with boards of education bargaining with OSSTF and OPSTF/FWTAO, respects local autonomy and the wishes in certain units, attacks the working-condition disparities between elementary and secondary school teachers, and leads to two strong groups concentrating on specific limited goals. Neil Doherty urged OECTA to act fast to keep its high school members.[28]

But constitutions usually get amended slowly. In 1984 an Executive sub-committee studied the OECTA by-law which stated that high school units presently existing shall retain their separate unit status until such time as completion of the separate school system is achieved. This seemed to discourage high school units in favour of the kindergarten-to-grade-thirteen philosophy often endorsed in relation to curriculum and the struggle for completion. The sub-committee listed four alternatives: grandparent the existing high school units, extend the high school unit classification to some groups, extend it to all areas where high schools exist, or establish units and sub-units. The 1985 AGM modified the status quo: high school units were to retain their separate unit status until by separate majority votes the two units approved a merger.[29]

Events overtook the debate. OECTA filed notice to negotiate with the Cochrane-Iroquois Falls RCSS Board. AEFO filed to negotiate as two separate agents: elementary and secondary. The Board would meet only with all its employees together. AEFO and OECTA submitted a charge of bad-faith bargaining to the ERC. On July 23, 1986 the Education Relations Commission (ERC) found the school board in violation of Bill 100 and determined that it had to negotiate with OECTA and AEFO branch affiliates as separate entities. On August 1 the ERC found against the board again: AEFO could negotiate as two affiliates, elementary and secondary, because, although the Cochrane-Iroquois Falls RCSS Board was one overarching board, it was an RCSS board for elementary purposes and a "Roman Catholic school board" (Bill 30's terminology) for secondary purposes.[30]

This judgment had two immediate results. Firstly, units like the Hamilton High and Hamilton-Wentworth Elementary, which appeared before the Executive in the month after the judgment to make their case for separate bargaining, could now use the ERC decision as a reinforcing argument. Hamilton-Wentworth was convinced that the right to separate collective bargaining would win back OECTA members who were leaning toward OSSTF. Secondly, the Executive and Council of Presidents experienced some urgency to amend the Constitution. The whole situation was exacerbated temporarily in the month of December when the ERC would not recognize OECTA's secondary affiliates until it received a determination from OTF and suspended its services to them. With consistency OSSTF and OPSTF did not agree that Catholic high school teachers could belong to OECTA. After some lobbying by the York, Dufferin-Peel, Toronto High, and other unit executives, the ERC adjusted to the new reality of Bill 30 and resumed normal services.[31]

Meanwhile, the Executive and Secretariat moved quickly to instruct all units that only a "branch affiliate" could negotiate with a school board under Bill 100 and, consequently, each unit had to be organized as an affiliate with an elected executive and a grievance officer appointed by the unit. In addition, the teachers in the unit had to decide whether they would be in two affiliates, elementary and secondary, or one affiliate. Finally, if there were to be two affiliates, the decision would have to be made whether to bargain with the board jointly or separately. Somewhat nostalgically and with an awareness that two affiliates where there was one would double the costs to OECTA while the revenues remained the same, the Executive advised the units that any wishing to remain together would be "encouraged" to do so and reminded them that branch affiliates existed merely to satisfy the needs of the ERC; however, it added that if any group wished high school status, it could apply to the Council of Presidents.[32]

The die was cast. The end result was five structures: (1) a unit without a high school: one affiliate; (2) a unit with secondary school teachers: two affiliates bargaining jointly; (3) a unit with secondary school teachers: two affiliates bargaining separately; (4) an elementary and secondary unit, in the employ of the same board: two affiliates bargaining separately; (5) an elementary and secondary unit: two affiliates bargaining jointly. There used to be thirty-five units, now there are sixty. Almost every unit president has full- or half-time release, units have an office with a computer and provincially funded conferences, meetings, and business. There is much more money spent out in the units, but there is much greater involvement. Eileen Lennon recalled that the Cochrane-Iroquois Falls judgment caused a mess and the only Executive meeting ever to take place during the Christmas holidays, but it did force Council of President decisions that made many secondary school teachers happy.[33]

There was an interesting postscript to all this. The 1987 AGM heard that the Hamilton-Wentworth RCSS Board was refusing to negotiate with the two affiliates separately and was appealing the ERC's decision in Cochrane-Iroquois Falls. OSSTA, with its understandable preference for seeing boards negotiate with one affiliate instead of two, was interested in Hamilton's move. But in 1988 Mr. Justice James Bonham S. Southey of the Ontario Supreme Court said that the ERC ruling was "eminently reasonable."[34]

The new secondary school membership also changed the Secretariat. There was considerable expansion of staff and efforts to bring into the central office teachers with high school background.

Sister Anna Clare Berrigan was hired in 1989. She was part of a large Ottawa family: her father William Berrigan, a member of the RCMP; her mother Catherine Rooney, a homemaker; her brother Earl; and her sisters Veronica, Anna, and Gertrude. She attended Immaculata High School and after grade thirteen entered the novitiate of the Grey Sisters of the Immaculate Conception and attended Ottawa Teachers' College. For five years she taught at Holy Family and Sacred Heart, Timmins, her last year there as principal. Her first assignment was fifty-two grade one pupils in coal bins converted into a classroom; it was necessary to lift the children out of the windows during a fire drill.

Her next five years were in Whitby, where she started O'Gorman High School. Initially, it consisted of twenty-five students in one room in a church basement. Sister taught all the subjects except science.

While the school board erected a grade nine and ten school, Sister expanded to the secretary's office of an elementary school as a second classroom. Father Leo Austin was the driving force behind the building of a private school addition. By the time the school reached grade thirteen, when Sister was still the full-time teaching principal, there were about 200 students.

After this signal accomplishment, Sister became principal in Ottawa of St. George, Immaculata High School (where she spent thirteen years), St. Mark, and Holy Cross. Twice more she was a key figure in Catholic high school education. When the Ottawa RCSS Board, after Davis's 1971 refusal to extend the separate school board, decided it could not afford so many high schools, Sister's Order agreed to abide by whatever arrangement the principal of St. Joseph's High School, Father Richard Sheehan, could negotiate with the Ottawa Board of Education. But when she attended the meeting as the only representative of her Order and discovered the arrangements were terminal, she announced that Immaculata would stay open as long as it could; the Order supported her decision. Sister is a believer in divine providence; Archbishop Plourde, the alumni, and lotteries helped. The school still flourishes today. Her third contribution to Catholic high schools consisted of rescuing, at the superintendent George Moore's request, St. Patrick's High School, that had deteriorated into a filthy condition with some unsatisfactory student behaviour. She accepted the challenge on three conditions: the trustees were to clean the school, let her staff it, and support her suspensions of students. She was principal there for four years.

She then joined the Counselling and Relations Department from 1989 to 1992. She brought all this administrative and secondary school experience as well as numerous credentials: a B.A. from St. Patrick's College, an M.A. from Ottawa University, a diploma in theology from Regis College, Toronto, and secondary school principal's and supervisory officer's certificates. She had always been contributing her talents to OECTA, serving on the executive in Timmins, Durham, and Ottawa, where she was president; and on numerous provincial committees. Four times she worked for Project Overseas in Thailand, Uganda, and Anguilla. She taught English as a Second Language and administration and was optimistic that their schools would operate more efficiently.

Since retirement Sister has administered a reservation school while the principal was on leave. At Lil-wat-trible she initiated a daycare, breakfast, and "learn to earn" programme. This year she is resting and painting, but will likely becomed involved in volunteer work at the school.[35]

Edward Bogdan Chudak joined the Teacher Welfare Department in 1991. His father, Wladyslaw Chudak, an autoworker, and mother, Anna Presz, sales clerk, were immigrants in 1948 from a refugee camp. They had met in a forced labour camp in Germany. Originally, they came to Ontario by agreeing to work on a domestic servant contract in Toronto, where Ed was born. He has a brother, Henry, and sister, a Dorothy.

Ed attended St. Vincent, as well as St. Casimir for Polish lessons after regular school hours. He then went to St. Michael until grade ten when his mother died. (The labour camp had given her a tubercular condition.) With family resources now limited, Ed completed his high school education at Parkdale Collegiate Institute, where he played football. By means of summer jobs on the CPR work gang, at Ford Motors, and at Brewer's Retail and despite the loss of a year due to an automobile accident, Ed completed his B.A. in history and English at York University in 1975. After graduation he married Carole Perrins, a medical secretary, now operator of a word-processing business in their home. They have two children, Amanda and David. After working for a year at Lever Brothers, Ed went to the University of Toronto's Faculty of Education for a teacher's certificate in history and English.

Jobs were scarce. Ed supply taught. He was fortunate, in his opinion, to get a lengthy stint at Western Technical with a class of grade nine repeaters who had gone through three teachers in a month. On assigned occasional teacher contracts he taught at West Toronto High School, East York Collegiate Institute, and, his first long-term job, Leaside Collegiate Institute. There he got on an OSSTF health and safety committee. In order to supplement his income and widen his qualifications, Ed taught economics at night school, then applied for this additional qualification under the terms of the collective agreement. However, his superintendent rejected Ed's application, stating that night school did not qualify as the necessary teaching experience. Ed grieved and won. Stephen Lewis in his decision wrote, "Justice sometimes comes in instalments."

Ed then decided to look at the York Region RCSS Board. The board was growing and homes were available at a more reasonable price. Despite having difficulty finding the school, Sacred Heart,

Newmarket, amid a sea of portables, Ed got the job. There he became very involved with collective bargaining agreements. His experience with the grievance and his memory of his father's losing their home while on strike had given him strong union convictions. When his school board unilaterally announced that the high school teachers would be receiving only one spare a year instead of one a semester, Ed became a staff representative. When OECTA's negotiating committee brought in a weak contract, Ed, with others, made many calls and the contract was defeated. When a new negotiating committee was formed, Ed was almost left out because of his radical image.

As chief negotiator, Ed took pride in winning contracts that applied both to the separate and private high schools and that had clauses on PTR, planning time, grid compression, and maternity leave. He led the first work-to-rule sanction after Bill 100. He introduced to York the concept of pupil-teacher "contacts" rather than PTR.

Ed was on both the Unit and provincial Executive, winning the second vice-presidency, the latter by one vote, and on the provincial Teacher Welfare Committee. His aim in Teacher Welfare and in negotiating is straightforward: equity of opportunity for children (that is, the same good staffing model for schools with working-class as for those with middle-class children). To anyone who would say OECTA is "just a union," Ed would reply that she/he does not understand what a union is.[36]

Victoria Hannah. Victoria was seconded to the Counselling and Relations Department in 1989 and hired in 1990, helping OECTA, as she waggishly put it, to meet three employment equity quotas: for women, aboriginals, and minor disabled; as well, she had a secondary school background.

Victoria was born in Sudbury. Her father, Edward Hiebert, was a miner who was part of the 1958 strike. Her mother, Doris Solomen, an Ojibway, lost her native status through marriage. Her siblings are Victor, Wayne, and Darryl. Victoria attended St. Patrick in Azilda, Marymount College, Sudbury to grade twelve, and Sudbury High School for grade thirteen. She then took a physical and occupational therapy diploma course at the University of Toronto, married, and returned to Sudbury; a year later she went to North Bay Teachers' College. The rest of her years in the Sudbury area before coming to OECTA would be spent in having and raising two children, Dennis and Erin, acquiring a B.A. from Laurentian, an M.Ed. from OISE, and certificates in guidance specialist, special education, the principalship, and the supervisory officer; and teaching at St. Patrick, Azilda, Our Lady of Fatima, Naughton, St. Thomas and St. David, Sudbury. She was promoted to vice-principal at St. Anne, Hammer and St. Charles High School, Sudbury, and to principal at St. Mark, Markstay.

Her involvement with OECTA began as a staff representative in her second year of teaching: she wanted to learn why she had been assigned to grade one at St. Patrick, why she was not assigned a school closer to her home, and why nothing could be done about the situation. She soon broadened her concerns to those of her fellow OECTA members, serving on the local executive, including as president, on the provincial Political Advisory, Legislative, and Equal Opportunity Committees, and on the Executive.

Victoria has a great sense of humour and an empathy for those with disabilities who, as she does, cope with what they cannot change. OTF has awarded her a fellowship.[37]

Michael Lloyd Haugh. Michael was hired as an executive assistant for the expanding Professional Development Department in 1991.

He was born in Windsor, the son of Lloyd Haugh, a registered industrial accountant, and Marilyn Miracle, an executive secretary of General Motors. His sister, Michelle, is a registered nurse. He was a student at Prince Charles elementary school and Riverside Secondary School. He acquired his B.A. in English at the University of Windsor. Then for Michael it was the toss of a coin between law and teaching; he decided on the latter because of his love of children and physical education. He went to Windsor's Faculty of Education for certification in the primary, junior, and intermediate divisions. Later he acquired his HSA in English. At the same time he married Elizabeth Battle, a nurse, and converted to Catholicism. Her wages plus Michael's part-time job as a security guard at General Motors saw him through his year of teacher training.

Before coming to OECTA Michael spent his entire teaching career with the Essex County RCSS Board. His first year of teaching was at two schools: St. Peter, Sandwich South, in the morning and St. Theresa, Malden, in the afternoon. The next year he was head teacher at St. Peter, Sandwich South. At this point, the principal of St. Anne's High School, Tecumseh, asked for Michael because of his physical education background. He was there for fifteen years: five years as an English and mathematics teacher and librarian, five years as department head in English, and five years as vice-principal. It was his pleasure to work with a staff who delivered quality education in a school with an Ursuline tradition and strong community support. It attracted students from all over the county; enrolment grew from about 450 students to around 1800.

During these years Michael and his wife had three children: Bridget, Megan, and Caitlin. He acquired an M.A. in educational administration from the University of Detroit and did some course work in curriculum at the M.A. level at the University of Windsor. He was also active in OECTA affairs during the tumultuous years of salary negotiating in Essex and the Porter-Podgorski case. Even as a probationary-contract teacher he, as part of the group, submitted his resignation and launched and won a grievance over the director of education's placement of him in QECO category A3 instead of A4. Almost at the start of his teaching he was elected to the Unit vice-presidency, was president twice, and also served as grievance officer and chair of the negotiating committee. Provincially, he was on the Teacher Welfare Committee and on the Executive as counsellor and third, second, and first vice-president. Currently, his Professional Development portfolio includes family life education, religious education, and teacher education.[38]

Jeff Heximer was the first teacher to be hired for the Teacher Welfare Department in response to the new secondary school needs. Although there was some protest from three of the units who asked why an OECTA member was not hired, Jeff's OSSTF experience in negotiating collective agreements along with his other personal and professional attributes was exactly what the Personnel Committee wanted. Out of forty-four applicants, ten of them short-listed, Jeff was the Committee's unanimous choice. He began his duties in August 1985.

Jeff was born in St. Catharines. His father, William Heximer, was vice-president of sales for Oneida Community Plate and his mother, Alma June Froats, a bank teller. His siblings are Susan and Jody. Jeff went to St. Thomas More, Father Hennepin School, and Carmel Senior School in the Niagara Falls area and to Stamford High School. His B.A. from the University of Western Ontario was in economics. After this he travelled for two years through India and nine countries in southern Asia. In 1977 he attended Althouse College for an HSA in economics and mathematics.

The job market was tight. Jeff applied for over sixty positions. Finally, the Unemployment Insurance Commission paid his expenses to go for an interview at Michipicoten High School in Wawa; he was hired to teach business, mathematics, and physical education. In 1980 he became department head of business education. While in Wawa Jeff acquired the equivalent of an honour B.A. in economics, and certificates in law and economics, honour specialist, all from the University of Toronto. In 1984 he went to Korah Collegiate in Sault Ste. Marie.

The OSSTF experience he brought to OECTA included serving as unit treasurer, bargainer during declining enrolment years, division president, and district vice-president and president.

Jeff lives in East York with his wife, Kathy Lampitt (who had been a collective agreement negotiator in London for OECTA), and three children, Julia, Katy, and Amy. Jeff is a strong supporter of mainstreaming and is pleased for Katy, who has special needs, that the MSSB is providing education for her at her neighbourhood school, Canadian Martyrs.[39]

The Snow-Tomen Case. On April 18, 1985, Mrs. Margaret Tomen, vice-principal of an elementary school of the Windsor Board of Education, applied to OTF for statutory membership in OPSTF.[40] (The "M" initial for "Men"was dropped by the association in 1982.) Two weeks after the Ontario legislature passed Bill 30, John Snow, a secondary school teacher with the Sudbury District Roman Catholic Separate School Board, applied to the same body for statutory membership in OSSTF.[41] When the Welland County Roman Catholic Separate School Board began offering grade eleven programmes in the fall of 1986 under the provisions of Bill 30, the Niagara South Board of Education advised Mrs. Patricia Leaming and Mr. Gary Page that, due to declining enrolment from movement of high school students from the public to the separate school board, they had become "designated" teachers and thus would be transferred to the Welland County RCSS Board; they too both immediately applied to OTF for statutory membership in OSSTF.[42]

These four applications constituted challenges to the practice of OTF since 1944 under its by-law 1 and began a process in the Supreme Court of Ontario and with the Ontario Human Rights Commission that has the potential of dramatically modifying the structure of OTF and its five teacher affiliates. With the power given to OTF in the Regulations under *The Teaching Profession Act*, the Federation set up the affiliates,[43] and passed By-law 1 which in its present form requires that all teachers in a French-language school be members of AEFO, all in a

Roman Catholic separate school be in OECTA, all males in a public elementary school be in OPSTF, all females in a public elementary school be in FWTAO, and all in a public high school be in OSSTF.[44] *The School Boards and Teachers Collective Negotiations Act* legislates that school boards negotiate collective agreements only with the appropriate five affiliates.[45] It is the By-law that Tomen, Snow, Leaming, and Page challenged.

All four, having been refused their requests to OTF to be statutory members in an affiliate other than the one stipulated by the By-law, fought this decision in the Supreme Court of Ontario where they argued that such denials were infringements under *The Canadian Charter of Rights and Freedoms* that guarantees, among other rights, freedom of association and freedom from sexual or religious discrimination.

The applicants in the Tomen action were Margaret Tomen and OPSTF; the federation, interested for some time in having itself and FWTAO merged into one affiliate, paid Mrs. Tomen's costs.[46] The respondents were FWTAO and OTF. The applicants in the Snow-Page-Leaming action were John Snow, Patricia Leaming, Gary Page, and OSSTF; the federation, on record for desiring to represent all secondary school teachers in public and separate high schools,[47] paid the court costs for all four applicants. The court admitted AEFO and OSSTA as intervenors because of their special interests in the outcome. Both actions were heard as one case.

The Applicants. The Tomen argument was clear and succinct. OTF's By-law 1 is inconsistent with sections 2 and 15 of the *Charter* that protect freedom of association, provide equality without discrimination and proscribe discrimination based on sex. Tomen said that the By-law forces her to belong to a ghetto, an all-female affiliate, and prevents her from having statutory rather than mere voluntary membership in OPSTF. Furthermore, OTF does not have the corporate powers under *The Corporations Act* to pass By-law 1 since the By-law is contrary to public policy on sexual discrimination and since the By-law is a governmental matter and hence under *Charter* scrutiny.

Tomen explained that court action was made necessary because of the mathematics involved in amending By-law 1 inside OTF. AEFO, FWTAO, and OECTA wish to maintain the status quo; OPSTF and OSSTF wish to amend the By-law. Change has been demonstrated to be impossible for now and the foreseeable future. Tomen's application to OTF for statutory membership in OPSTF was denied.[48]

The affidavits of R. Ross Andrew and David Lennox, past and present general secretaries of OPSTF, offered other arguments in support of Tomen's application. Firstly, Andrew demonstrated female teachers' interest in OPSTF and their leadership in his affiliate; since the first woman teacher was admitted as a voluntary member in 1972, the number of voluntary members from FWTAO by 1986 grew to almost 1600; furthermore, Mary Hill in 1980 and Carole Ann Yuzwa in 1985 served on the OPSTF provincial executive, and from 1984 to 1986 the former was the president of the association. Secondly, in 1982, the Minister of Consumer and Commercial relations allowed the word "Men" to be dropped from the name of the affiliate, clearing the way for membership of both male and female teachers in the federation. Thirdly, since 1952 there have been no salary differentials between members of the two affiliates; in many school boards they engage in joint collective bargaining. Fourthly, OPSTF has been running professional development programmes open to teachers from all the affiliates. Fifthly, Andrew pointed to all the other provinces of Canada that have dual-sex teachers' associations which, he writes, "effectively represent the interests of women teachers." Andrew concluded:

> While there may be historical reasons to support the sex differentiation between the FWTAO and OPSTF, I do not believe that the FWTAO is in any better position today to represent women teachers or to influence public attitudes concerning them than a dual-sex organization would be.[49]

Lennox supplemented Andrew's arguments by citing about 10 000 "occasional" teachers, of whom around 90 per cent are female, who since 1984 are voluntary members of OPSTF. Lennox stated that FWTAO had never shown any interest in representing these teachers. He then quoted at length an Ontario Labour Relations Board decision that supported OPSTF's efforts to represent the occasional teachers working for the Windsor Board of Education. Particularly interesting was this excerpt:

> The respondent cannot point to a single incident or practice in which female members of OPS have faced invidious discrimination because of their gender. Indeed, OPS has taken steps to eliminate sexual discrimination among its ranks and has actually encouraged women to join. That women - although a minority, and only 'voluntary members' - may fully participate in the life of the organization is evidenced by the fact that OPS has a woman president.[50]

Sixteen statutory members of FWTAO who are also voluntary members of OPSTF submitted affidavits to the court. Almost all had served on their local OPSTF executives in a number of boards throughout Ontario. The writer of each affidavit advanced the identically worded argument: the teacher wished to sever her relationship with FWTAO and to become a statutory member of OPSTF: She stated her belief in freedom of choice, in a dual-sex teacher union, in the need for mutual respect between those women teachers who wish to belong to FWTAO and those who do not so wish, in the ability of a mixed union to represent the interests of both men and women, in the absence of any resistance in OPSTF to the advancement of women's rights or the assumption of responsibility by women, in the lack of any greater development of or advantages for women in FWTAO, and in the necessity of learning best how to "compete" by "competing" with men. Tomen and these sixteen teachers argued the case from personal conviction that a single-sex compulsory affiliate is offensive.[51]

Snow, Leaming, and Page attacked By-law 1 from a different perspective. All three had recently become statutory members of OECTA and had applied to OTF to be statutory members of OSSTF. Leaming, a Protestant, and Page, a Baptist minister, believed that their interests would be better represented by OSSTF, an organization both non-denominational and experienced in secondary school matters. Career advancement in a Catholic high school and Catholic school system seemed problematical for Protestants. Page expressed concern about the conflict between his Baptist beliefs and those of the Roman Catholic separate school system. Leaming and Page argued that By-law 1 is contrary to public policy on the basis of religious discrimination. Then, at this point, they followed Tomen's reasoning on the By-law and the *Charter.*

Snow's situation was somewhat different. Prior to the passing of Bill 30, as a staff member of Marymount College, he was under the employ of the Sudbury District RCSS Board for grades nine and ten and of the Board of Governors for the private high school for grade eleven to the end of high school. Thus, he had been a statutory member of OECTA. After Bill 30's enactment, he became a full-time employee of the Board. Consequently, it would seem there would be no dispute about Snow's continuing to be a member of OECTA, especially since he is a Roman Catholic.

However, a problem arose regarding job security. For several years the collective agreement had contained a seniority list of all the Board's elementary and secondary school teachers, developed for eliminating redundant teaching positions. With a declining elementary panel and an expanding secondary panel, elementary school teachers declared redundant could be transferred to the high school. To protect the rights of the high school teachers during the 1985-86 bargaining year, OECTA proposed and the Board accepted the principle of separate elementary- and secondary-level teacher seniority lists. But before the collective agreement was ratified, OECTA changed its mind and refused to agree to such an alteration in the seniority system. This was a very serious decision, because the board had been declaring redundant about eighty elementary school teachers. Thus, Snow felt OECTA was not representing him adequately and applied for, but was denied, statutory membership in OSSTF between July 8, 1986 and February 10, 1987.[52] (Fifteen other high school teachers would apply for OSSTF statutory membership. At a Unit meeting the motion to remain members of OECTA passed by fifty-five to thirty-six. Feelings were riding high.[53])

Meanwhile, in January and February, Snow and a number of other teachers from Marymount College and St. Charles College organized the Sudbury Catholic Secondary School Division of District 31 of OSSTF. One of the principals, Sr. Shirley Anderson, vexed at OSSTF's letters to her school soliciting members, wrote Rod Albert, the Federation's president, that, "It seems ludicrous to me to belong to a federation which spends millions of dollars to put our schools out of existence." Nevertheless, close to 55 per cent of the teachers in the two schools signed OSSTF membership cards. But neither the Board nor the ERC recognized this new unit.[54] After explaining all this in his affidavit, Snow concluded by expressing his lack of confidence in OECTA, especially given the majority of its elementary school members. Like Leaming and Page he argued that OSSTF was more experienced in high school matters and that his freedom of association rights under the *Charter* were lost under the OTF's By-law 1.

James Forster, who has been both a provincial president and assistant general secretary of OSSTF, supported the Leaming-Page-Snow applications and opposed OTF's November 29, 1986 interpretation of By-law 1(2)(b) and (d) when the executive passed a motion ruling that English teachers in Roman Catholic high schools are OECTA members. His affidavit reviewed the historical fact that OSSTF for decades represented all secondary school teachers in publicly supported high schools. Only after 1968, when French-language high schools were legislated into existence, and after Bill 30 extended separate schools to the end of high school, did OSSTA lose by By-law members to AEFO and OECTA, respectively. OSSTF, Forster contended, should continue to represent all English high school teachers. Forster's second argument was that of freedom of choice possessed by teachers in the United States and over sixty other countries. He dealt with the thorny issue that OSSTF was challenging in the courts the constitutionality of Bill 30 by stating that the federation would abide by the court judgment and by predicting that Roman Catholic members of OSSTF would keep off the negotiating table any matters prejudicial to the Catholicity of the separate schools.[55]

These arguments were crucial to both OECTA and OSSTF. If Leaming and Page were successful, then any non-Catholic "designated" teachers (that is, those teachers who under the terms of Bill 30 had been moved from a board of education to a Roman Catholic separate school board)could remain statutory members of OSSTF; perhaps any non-Catholic members of OECTA could switch to OSSTF, FWTAO, or OPSTF. If Snow were successful, then all teachers in Roman Catholic high schools could choose to be members of OSSTF; perhaps the By-law would be revised to have OSSTF represent all English high school teachers in the public and separate school systems. Given the feelings of some of OECTA's high school members, the Association felt somewhat vulnerable. Finally, if Tomen were successful, then the fate of By-law 1 was unpredictable.

The Respondents. Opposing the arguments of Tomen, Snow, Leaming, Page, OPSTF, and OSSTF were FWTAO, OECTA, AEFO, and OSSTA.

FWTAO was the principal respondent to the Tomen factum in terms of the number of arguments it put forth and the time it spent with many affidavits presented by several, mostly female, experts on single-sex teacher unions from around the world. They emphasized that exclusively female teacher organizations contributed significantly to sexual equality, positive discrimination and affirmative action for female teachers, whereas in mixed-sex teacher unions the women teachers were under-represented in positions of leadership, hesitant and less verbal at meetings of the teacher organization, and, in summary, controlled by the male members.

The affidavit of Florence Henderson, an officer of FWTAO for many years, detailed the affiliate's history in order to demonstrate how necessary the FWTAO had been and continues to be for the protection and advancement of the rights of female teachers, and how the Federation faced an educational environment where female teachers were paid less, had less access than males to promotion, and were not permitted to negotiate with school boards for salaries except indirectly through spokesmen. At the same time, men teachers were concerned that women would lower salaries and hurt male career advancement.

Henderson described the attempts to amalgamate FWTAO and OPMSTF. The issue came before FWTAO's provincial meetings twenty-one times between 1961 and 1977, when a moratorium was declared. In order to reinforce its aim of amalgamation, OPSTF in 1972 amended its constitution to admit women teachers to voluntary membership and in 1982 dropped the "Men" from its name. FWTAO challenged as misleading this name change in the courts, but lost the case. Henderson argued that OPSTF's paying of Tomen's legal fees was another attempt over a lengthy period to take over FWTAO. Her affidavit then described the positive activities of FWTAO to meet its objectives: among them, fighting for equal pay for equal work, opposing married men salary allowances, offering leadership courses, and lobbying successfully for unrestricted access to principals' courses. Due to the Federation's efforts, the Ministry of Education announced an affirmative action policy. Finally, the association worked on the elimination of sex stereotyping in textbooks, courses of study, and guidance programmes. Henderson concluded that FWTAO has played a critical role in protecting and advancing the rights of female elementary school teachers, that the Association is needed as long as there is discrimination against women teachers, and that the non-existence of FWTAO would place female teachers at a disadvantage.[56]

The factum of the FWTAO summed up the material in these affidavits to demonstrate the necessity of the affiliate's continued existence under the present OTF structure. It also argued that *The Corporations Act* provides that a corporation without share capital (like OTF) can provide by-laws for different classes of membership, and empowers directors to pass by-laws regulating the qualifications and conditions of membership and providing for the division of its members into groups. Further, the factum finds that By-law 1 of OTF promotes sexual equality called for in the *Charter*, that the By-law follows the *Charter* because it ameliorates a group's status, and that these equality and associative objectives are important enough to override the individual's right to choose.[57]

OECTA also submitted a historical affidavit to demonstrate the importance of By-law 1 for the protection of the rights of separate school teachers and schools. The affidavit documented five arguments - namely, that the OECTA:

- was formed by the English separate school teachers of Ontario to protect and further their interests and those of Catholic education;
- worked closely with the Roman Catholic hierarchy and ECEAO to advance the cause of Catholic education in Ontario's separate schools;
- worked to attain quality of Catholic education in the separate schools;
- protected and advanced separate school rights and privileges;
- played an important role in the completion of the separate school system.

The affidavit concluded with the thought that "one finds it at least questionable that the separate school system would be where it is today, if there had not been an OECTA as a statutory affiliate of the OTF."[58]

OECTA's factum referred to its historical affidavit to point out the unique nature of the Association's membership and its concerns. It reminded the court that OSSTF was an opponent in the Bill 30 case, with a position diametrically opposed to a long-held aim of OECTA to secure grants, taxation powers and statutory recognition of separate schools as encompassing grades eleven, twelve, and thirteen. The factum also analysed the *Charter* to demonstrate that it does not guarantee collective bargaining rights or the right not to associate. As for Leaming and Page's concern about their Protestant status, the factum directed the court's attention to the conscientious objection clause in the *Education Act,* whereby a potential designated public high school teacher could refuse the transfer to a Roman Catholic high school on religious grounds.[59]

OSSTA, as an intervenor in the Snow-Leaming-Page issue, was concerned that it would lose control over its right to negotiate collective agreements only with OECTA, co-religionists with an understanding of and sympathy for the special nature of the separate school system. Thus, its factum concentrated on the constitutional rights of separate school boards and the *School Boards and Teachers Collective Negotiations Act.* This legislation, the factum argued, protects the special relationship between the teachers and trustees in a community of faith, a relationship transcending the customary one between employee and employer and necessitating a commonality of purpose. The factum stipulates that

OSSTA would not have agreed to the collective negotiations statute if it had not been assured of its power to negotiate teachers' collective agreements only with OECTA.[60]

AEFO was also an intervenor. Like FWTAO and OECTA, it submitted affidavits that described the history of the Association in order to show the need for its past and future existence. AEFO attached a history of the 1912 Regulation 17; most of the AEFO affidavits and the factum referred to it. This traumatic legislation prohibited instruction in French beyond grade two in the French-English public and separate schools of Ontario and resulted in fifteen years of strife, students in private schools in Ottawa, the loss of teachers' certificates, and court cases.[61] It is from this low point in the history of Franco-Ontarian education that AEFO marked its struggles.

Jacques Schrybert, general secretary of the AEFO at the time of the writing of his affidavit, reviewed the Association's aims: to seek to obtain equal access to French education for all Franco-Ontarian children without regard to their place of residence in Ontario or the financial status of their municipality, to assist schools in Ontario attended by French-speaking students to produce the best results possible in both the teaching of French and English, to promote better education of Francophones in Ontario by the professional development of its members and studies of problems in education, and to work toward French-speaking students having the opportunity to study in French schools and to be taught all subjects other than English in French, whenever possible. Schrybert gave two examples of AEFO's "luttes": the ten-year campaign for the substitution of four compulsory French, instead of English, credits in OSIS and the battle in the Supreme Court of Ontario for French-language educational management rights, resulting in victory in 1984.[62] His affidavit reminded the court that OPSTF and OSSTF opposed the establishment of French-language boards and sections of boards in the 1984 case and then appealed to the Supreme Court of Canada, although they later abandoned their appeal. His conclusion was that without the compulsory membership in AEFO, its capacity to promote Franco-Ontarian interests would be diminished "irremediably."[63]

Marc Cazabon, assistant general secretary of AEFO at the time, explained in his affidavit that the Association sometimes negotiates jointly with another affiliate for a collective agreement, but when, as has occurred in a number of places, notably in Penetanguishene and Essex, the interests of the two affiliates differ, there are separate negotiations. This has happened, for example, when a school building or additional courses in French are sought by AEFO and the local Franco-Ontarian community.[64]

Hervé Casault was the vice-principal of LaSalle high school in Ottawa and had held various executive positions in AEFO. His affidavit referred to the Franco-Ontarians' fight for a high school of their own in Penetanguishene, and he believed that the $50 000 the Association spent for publicity and lobbying contributed greatly to Bette Stephenson's decision to grant the school despite the small enrolment.[65] Casault also claimed that if AEFO is dismembered, there will be a loss of representation and power for the Franco-Ontarian education system; only AEFO has the historical and financial resources to struggle for French rights.[66]

Finally, Gabrielle Levasseur, secretary of AEFO from 1957 to 1974, wrote in her affidavit that the Association has supplied the teachers with instructional materials that the Ministry of Education was unable to develop. The other four affiliates, being English in a predominantly English environment, do not have such problems. Any change in the structure of OTF that would remove the compulsory membership in AEFO of Franco-Ontarian teachers would be damaging to French aspirations, since such interests would be represented "difficilement" by the English affiliates.[67]

The OTF factum agreed with AEFO, FWTAO, and OECTA that By-law I should continue to exist. The Association presented *Charter* arguments:

- The *Charter* is not applicable to the By-laws in question.
- If the *Charter* **is** applicable, By-law 1 does not offend it, because the By-law's object is to improve conditions of groups or individuals disadvantaged because of sex, religion, or language.
- If the By-law **does** offend the *Charter*, it is a "reasonable limit as can be demonstrably justified" under its section 1.
- If the *Charter* applies to the By-law, then its section 1 saves the By-law.
- If the *Charter* applies, the right of association has not been infringed because of the member's power to have voluntary membership in an affiliate other than the one in which he/she has statutory membership.[68]

The Judgment. Mr. Justice Eugene Ewaschuk in the Supreme Court of Ontario heard the case from June 1 to 5 and 8 to 12, 1987 and released his judgment on September 16, 1987. He ruled that a matter of sexual or religious discrimination must first be pursued under the Human Rights Code before recourse to the court. His judgment was that

> By-law 1 is a private law devised by teachers to regulate their membership in the five affiliates....[It] regulates only membership internal to the OTF and its five affiliates. In no way does By-law I have a public dimension.[69]

OPSTF appealed on behalf of Snow, Leaming, and Page, OSSTF on behalf of Tomen. The Ontario Court of Appeal heard the arguments from May 23 to 26, 1989 and delivered its judgment. Judges Howland, Tarnopolsky, and Catzman upheld Judge Ewaschuk: "Compulsory membership in the various affiliates is not dictated by Ontario government legislation, but by teachers themselves and the response to change the structure rests with teachers." Costs were awarded to OECTA, FWTAO, and OTF. Paul Cavalluzzo commented on the judgment: the challenge attempted to use the *Charter* "to resolve a private dispute. The authors never intended it to be used as a tool in the arsenal of a union in its political wars against another union."[70]

OPSTF and OSSTF asked leave to appeal to the Supreme Court of Canada, but were denied on June 27, 1991. President Coté expressed his delight that "this decision will end this struggle."[71] By this time OECTA had its complement of secondary school representation on the Secretariat (and even a majority on the Executive) and a new unit structure that allowed considerable local autonomy. Jim Cooney in hindsight thought the Sudbury crisis could have been defused if the Executive had listened more to Snow and responded differently. Eileen Lennon felt everything turned out well for the secondary school members in the end.[72]

But this was not the end. Margaret Tomen and Linda Logan-Smith launched a second challenge against By-law 1 by asking for a hearing before the Ontario Human Rights Commission. Their complaint was similar to the previous one: By-law 1 offends the Ontario Human Rights Code by discriminating on the basis of sex and infringing on their right to freedom of association. Dr. Daniel Baum, a professor of law at Osgoode Hall, was appointed as the commissioner to hear the complaint. His hearings lasted for several weeks over a three-year period, terminating June 30, 1992.

Gene Lewis of OPSTF expressed optimism that day:

> Today a new Federation is on the horizon. The long struggle of Margaret Tomen and Linda Logan-Smith came one giant step closer to resolution as the Board of Inquiry on the Ontario Human Rights Commission recessed .... As we wait for Dr. Baum's ruling we can be confident that the archaic rules governing teacher membership in Ontario are about to be declared out of order. Now is the time to prepare to welcome women teachers into OPSTF, the Federation of choice.[73]

These are fighting words for FWTAO, AEFO, and OECTA. They feel they have struggled for women's, Franco-Ontarian, and separate school rights and need the By-law to maintain and improve upon their gains. The By-law, despite attempts to change it, still stands.

Cavalluzzo in 1992 drew some possible scenarios from the impending decision:

> • the decision could affect only the FWTAO portions of By-law 1;
> • the complaint could be denied;
> • the complaint could be upheld with a solution demanded from OTF with a time limit, after which, if necessary, a resolution imposed by Dr. Baum;
> • OTF could modify the By-law to have optional membership or membership by choice, or to provide a grandparent clause with a window of opportunity for choice, or to let new teachers hired by a school board have a choice;
> • if OTF runs out of money due to a possible lack of funding from the affiliates, the Ontario government could intervene and legislate a solution.[74]

It is January, 1994 and Dr. Baum has yet to release his decision. The length of time since the hearings ended suggest that he is writing his report with an awareness that there will be an appeal to the courts and, therefore, judges will scrutinize his reasoning. OECTA may take some comfort in being a dual-sex Association, but Dr. Baum's decision could mean more changes for OECTA.

Women's Issues. It is a matter of some pride for Michael Coté and Eileen Lennon among other members of the Executive that the Secretariat has a staff now that reflects more closely its male and female teachers. Government and school board initiatives, the Tomen Case, OECTA conferences, the media, and a growing awareness of social justice issues have all played their parts in raising awareness of women's issues in promotions, pay equity, daycare,and superannuation. In the recent past the following people have been employed for the Secretariat: Suzann Jones, Victoria Hiebert-Hannah, Pat McKeown, Aleda O'Connor, Carolyn Stevens, Theresa Robertson, Barbara Grizzle, Brenda Carrigan, and Carol Corsetti.[75]

Brenda Catharine Carrigan was hired for Teacher Welfare in 1989. She was born in Long Branch, now merged with Metropolitan Toronto, the child of Dennis Carrigan, a machinist, and Catharine Dale, a legal secretary, and sister of Laura. She attended St. Maria Goretti and St. Lawrence elementary schools, St. Joseph's Morrow Park, St. Michael's College for a B.A. in political science, and Toronto Teachers' College in the first year when the admission requirement was a degree (1973). Brenda's family environment led her both to teaching and a sympathy for union issues. Influencing her childhood were memories of typing union minutes for her father and enduring with the family two strikes at his place of employment.

Brenda taught for the MSSB at St. Gerald and Blessed Trinity. In addition to regular classrooms she taught drama, library and socially and emotionally maladjusted children. To assist her in these tasks she acquired certificates in religious education, library, computers in education, and special education specialist. Brenda became a staff representative in her second year of teaching and served on the executive of the sub-unit and the Unit, including being president of the sub-unit. She is proud to be part of a union (a "laudatory" designation) that has strengthened the separate school system to the point where there is, in her opinion, no longer the risk that numbers of people will switch their taxes and children from what otherwise could have become an inferior system.[76]

Carol Corsetti was hired in 1991 for the expanding Professional Development Department.

Carol was born in Picton, daughter of Charles Harrington, an Army officer, and Grace Hubbs, a nurse, and the sister of Patricia, Charles, and Robert. She lived in Cherry Valley near Picton and attended the local two-room school in Athol township. When she was in grade four her father was posted to Camp Borden, where she completed her elementary school. Her high school years were at Banting Memorial, Alliston, and Prince Edward Collegiate Institute. After grade twelve Carol enroled in the completing course at Toronto Teachers' College. She began teaching at age seventeen in a one-room school with twenty-four pupils in S.S.#5, Darlington near Bowmanville. After the completing course Carol became principal of a two-room school in S.S.#13, Vespra near Barrie. During her three years there she was one of the teachers in Ontario pioneering the use of TV Ontario.

While in Vespra Carol met and married Alfonso Corsetti from Toronto, embracing in a cultural leap the religion and mores of a large extended Italian-Canadian family. She took a year and a half off and gave birth to Celestino, then taught at St. Benedict for the MSSB. After resigning to have her second child, Roberto, Carol returned to teaching at St. James, then St. Dominic, Oakville. There she left teaching for four months to have their third child, Rose.

Carol is an interesting example of how a person can become a teacher and grow dramatically, if the system is flexible with regard to teachers who are mothers and if it provides optional routes for entrance into teaching. Carol says that with the current inflexible university-degree entrance requirement at faculties of education, she would not have been able to become a teacher. But with a high school education and a love for children she has worked successfully in a number of roles: classroom teacher, principal, communications consultant (junior kindergarten to the end of high school with the Halton RCSS Board), Ministry of Education officer with a portfolio that included the Learning Skills Initiative and School Libraries, and curriculum consultant to the three provincial schools for the deaf. In addition to being fulfilled as wife, mother, and teacher, Carol contributed her talents to OECTA. In the Halton Unit she held a number of positions, including member of the negotiating team for ten years, and president and chair of both the Professional Development and Teacher-Trustee Committees. Provincially, she was on the Professional Development Committee and OECTA representative on several Ministry of Education committees. Able to organize her priorities over a period of years Carol also acquired a B.A. from McMaster University and certificates in visual arts, religious education specialist, library, junior education, and special education, Parts I and II.

Currently, Carol's responsibilities, including being acting coordinator, are the CCDC, curriculum issues, and various workshops. She is also helping to enhance the department's focus on publications that will be of practical use to members.[77]

Barbara Grizzle was born in Summerside, Prince Edward Island. Her father, John Halifax Casselman, was in the Canadian Air Force. (His middle name originated from his birth in the harbour on a boat on which his parents had just immigrated from England.) Her mother was Mamie Thompson, a nurse. She has a sister, Diane, and a brother, Ron, who is also a teacher. Barbara attended Summerside School from grades one to six, where her aunt had taught for thirty years. When the family moved to Toronto, Barbara's mother, concerned for the safety and education of her daughter, placed her as a boarder at Mount Mary Academy, Ancaster, run by the Sister Servants of Mary Immaculate, a Ukrainian Order. There Barbara received her high school diploma, learned Ukrainian, and served the Order as a religious for a number of years.

After Toronto Teachers' College Barbara taught at St. Bernadette and Sacred Heart, Kitchener; St. Ann's, Ancaster; Sacred Heart Academy, Yorktown, Saskatchewan; St. Agnes, Ottawa; St. Barbara, St. Peter, and St. Roch, the MSSB; and Father C. W. Sullivan, Brampton. She has taught all the grades in elementary and secondary school and has been a religious education consultant. During that time she married, had a son, Brian, and acquired her B.A. from Wilfrid Laurier University in religion and her M.Ed. from Brock University.

Sister Aloysius convinced her in her first year of teaching to be a staff representative and Barbara went on to various executive and committee positions in the Toronto Elementary and Dufferin-Peel Units. She also chaired the provincial Teacher Welfare Committee. As the first full-time president in Dufferin-Peel, she moved the OECTA office out of the school board's building and helped plan the founding of the high school Unit.

In 1989 she became the first female member of the Teacher Welfare Department. Her initiation was the forty-one day strike in Kirkland Lake. She is now enjoying her work in Counselling and Members Services.[78]

Theresa Robertson began with Counselling and Members Services in September 1992.

She was born in Hamilton, daughter of Jack Robertson, an accountant, and Genevieve Stortz, a teacher, and sister of Patrick. She was educated in St. Catharines at St. Anthony, Denis Morris High School, and the Teachers' College. Before joining the Secretariat, Theresa taught for the Lincoln County RCSS Board at St. Edward in

Jordan and St. Joseph, St. Theresa, Assumption, Michael J. Brennan, Denis Morris, and Canadian Martyrs in St. Catharines. In those schools she had quite a variety of teaching assignments: a grade one, bottom-stream (Theresa considered this streaming an insidious practice), music on rotary, open-area team-teaching, contract-method teaching, resource teaching for the gifted, teaching for activity-based learning, resource teaching in special education, and high school teaching in an independent learning centre. Theresa is a progressive educator.

She also improved her professional and academic qualifications and became active in OECTA. Theresa has a B.A. and an M.Ed. from Brock University and certificates in religious education, Parts I and II, computers in education, and special education, Parts I and II. In the Lincoln Unit Theresa has been a negotiator and chair of the Status of Women and Professional Development Committees, held all the Unit executive positions up to first vice-president, was the grievance officer, and the first ombudsperson. Her clearest memories are of establishing a special teacher-trustee committee in the collective agreement to eliminate the practice of trustees complaining about teachers at open board meetings and of getting a double-digit salary increase ratified at 11:58 p.m. just before the AIB rules kicked in. Provincially, she was chair of the Teacher Welfare Committee.

Presently, Theresa deals with matters of professional ethics, counselling, safe schools, marriage annulments, and dire distress grants. She regularly receives calls for advice and assistance from teachers, principals, and supervisory officers.[79]

Carolyn Anne Stevens was employed in 1989 for the Professional Development Department.

Carolyn was born in Rouyn-Noranda, Quebec. Her father, William Wiltsey, was a prospector and her mother, Marie McGregor, a homemaker. Carolyn has two sisters and two brothers: Sharon, Lynne, Martin, and Peter. She received her elementary education at the mixed Catholic Superior School and secondary at Noranda High School. Anxious to broaden her horizons beyond the Quebec mining community, Carolyn went to North Bay Teachers' College for the two-year course after grade eleven. Before coming to OECTA she always taught in the North Bay area: for the West Ferris RCSS Board at Our Lady of Fatima, for the Widdifield RCSS Board at Pope John XXIII, and for the Nipissing District RCSS Board at St. Alexander, St. Mary, St. Theresa, Corpus Christi, St. Joseph, and St. Rita in North Bay. The

Nipissing Board promoted her to the positions of special education resource teacher, then coordinator.

While in the north Carolyn married, had two children (Kenneth Craig and Allison Rae), and took numerous courses for a B.A. and a B.Ed from Laurentian University, an M.A. in educational administration from the University of Central Michigan, and certificates in special education specialist, primary education specialist, the principalship, and religious education. She still found time to serve OECTA, although she deliberately stayed away from the Unit presidency. She was a staff representative, and on the local executive. She shared her expertise in special education by teaching it at Laurentian University, Nipissing University, and in a teacher in-service programme in Anguilla, the West Indies. Her current responsibility in the Professional Department is all the equity issues. She had originally applied to OECTA looking for an assignment in special education. Luckily for some people in her workshop audiences, equity is special education for their own personal development.[80]

These women, together with the male and female members of the Secretariat, especially in the Teacher Welfare and Professional Development Departments, and of the Executive, took as an important part of their mandate to bring about employment and pay equity for OECTA members and the elimination of sex stereotyping and systemic discrimination in the separate schools and in this administrative structure. Ray Fredette encapsulated the problem when he wrote "The Way for Teacher Welfare, Five-Year Guidelines" in 1984:

> The Catholic teaching field has advanced considerably from the misogynistic days when women teachers were blatantly discriminated against - all in the best interest of education, of course. No longer are female teachers expected as a matter of routine to resign upon marriage or, in later years, upon pregnancy. Their presence, albeit slowly, is becoming noticeable in positions of responsibility; .... greater difficulty is encountered in the inequities which exist through unwritten, unstated biases .... Many creative methods of circumventing the best of legislation can be found, ... although 71.6 per cent of elementary teachers in 1982 were female, just 12.5 per cent were principals.[81]

The decade did witness considerable OECTA effort in the areas of affirmative action and pay equity. The statistics improved dramatically in the area of pay equity. The concerns broadened beyond women's issues to other groups requiring attention on the grounds of social justice: aboriginals, racial minorities, and the disabled. Government legislation and Ministry of Education policies received full cooperation, approval, and assistance from OECTA.

In the fall of 1985 the Ontario government released its *Green Paper on Pay Equity* in the broader public sector, established an Equal Opportunity/Affirmative Action unit in the Ministry of Education, and struck a four-year Affirmative Action Incentive Fund. Bette Stephenson requested that each school board adopt a policy of Affirmative Action for women employees, appoint a senior staff member to implement it, and collect and analyse data.[82] In 1989 a Ministry report showed a lack of progress in Affirmative Action and employment equity. Chris Ward, the Minister of Education, announced that school boards would be required, commencing in September 1990, to establish employment equity policies for women. "From now on employment equity ... will be the rule, not the exception," said Ward. His goal was a 50 per cent staff of female vice-principals, principals and supervisory officers by the year 2000. This was followed by Policy/Programme Memorandum No. 111 in February 1990.[83] Meanwhile, the provincial legislature had passed the *Pay Equity Act*, effective January 1, 1988: salaries are to be based on the value of work regardless of sex, all employers with 100 employees or more are to develop, post, and implement pay equity plans; a Pay Equity Commission and Hearings Tribunal are established.[84] In 1993 the NDP government restructured the Ministry of Education and Training so that one whole section deals with ethnocultural racial, women's, aboriginal, and the handicapped issues.

OECTA paralleled the government's initiatives, with a number of actions:

- the passing of objectives at AGMs on equal opportunity;
- the designation of the Equal Opportunity Committee as standing to demonstrate commitment and recognize the protraction of the struggle;
- an annual "Images" conference (up to 1992) dealing with such topics as empowerment, mentoring, liberation, and aspirations;
- the funding of a research study that revealed the women members' concerns about the lack of mentoring, pensions, workplace daycare, workplace harassment, and stress from managing a home and a classroom;
- the formal decision to devote part of the *OECTA Reporter* to women's issues and to coverage of the "Images" conferences;

- the expansion of the mandate of the Equal Opportunity Committee to include developing action plans for the aboriginals, disabled, and visible minorities;
- the investigation of career directions for female students;
- the subsidizing of dependent care expenses of OECTA members attending provincial OECTA meetings (some units also subsidize for their meetings);
- budgeting for bursaries for OECTA members pursuing their first undergraduate degree (often women);
- the development currently of a brief to the Canadian and Ontario Catholic Bishops regarding OECTA's concern about the alienation felt by Catholic women due to sexist and misogynist theologies, traditions, and policies in the Church community that create barriers to the full and equal participation of women in all the liturgical and para-liturgical rights and roles in the Church;
- the publication of a manual on procedures for developing goals, timetables, accountability, and reviews with regard to Equal Opportunity/Affirmative Action;
- the design of a harassment policy that calls for complaint resolution procedures and, where necessary, disciplinary action to eliminate unsolicited sexual advances, remarks, and behaviour made by a person in a position to grant or deny a benefit.[85]

The most remarkable achievement for elementary school women teachers was in the area of pay equity. FWTAO and OECTA, upon the introduction of pay equity legislation, saw an injustice in categories D, C, and B in the QECO salary grid. In 1973 a B.A. became the requirement for entering a teacher training programme. Since then, the difference in salaries between those below category A1 (the B.A. category) and those at or above A1 grew quite large. Yet the teachers were doing the same basic job when skills, effort, working conditions, and responsibilities were compared. Some school boards and OPSTF and OSSTF argued for the maintenance of *only* academic and professional standards by keeping this salary differential. FWTAO argued against that viewpoint in Pay Equity Tribunal Hearings in Wentworth and Perth County Board of Education. It explained that many women elementary school teachers found the task of working toward a B.A. extramurally while teaching and raising a family either too demanding or too harmful to their pupils and/or family. The educational system was not encouraging them to improve their education and seek promotion.

FWTAO held that those teachers in categories D, C, and B in 1972 should have been grandparented and placed in A1 for salary purposes. The federation drew a comparison with many of the men teachers receiving A1 or higher salaries for having trade experience in place of a B.A.. The Tribunal agreed with this reasoning.[86]

As a result FWTAO negotiated with a consortium of school boards and succeeded in having its members placed in a high percentage of A1. OECTA's Teacher Welfare Department concentrated on each board individually. By 1993 forty-four separate school boards had pay equity plans with nine others outstanding. (Unfortunately, the government as part of its budget slashing has extended the mandatory implementation of pay equity until January 1, 1998.) The plans range from about 85 per cent to 97 per cent of category A1 for the teachers without a B.A.. On average they received a $4465 increase. On International Women's Day, 1991, Coté announced that over 2000 teachers had benefitted from the pay equity plans.[87]

The OECTA Equal Opportunity Handbook deserves the best word on this subject, quoting from the Vatican Council's *Gaudium et Spes*:

> With respect to the fundamental rights of the person, every type of discrimination, whether social or cultural, whether based on sex, race, colour, social condition, language, or religion is to be overcome and eradicated as contrary to God's intent.[88]

Ontario Catholic Occasional Teachers' Association (OCOTA). Another group that would change the structure, size and concerns of OECTA was the occasional teachers. In April 1984 the Executive was faced with a decision where it had to act within a week. The Ontario Public Service Employees' Union had called and advertised a meeting of occasional teachers (that is, those working at casual or long-term teaching positions) to organize them. Word was out that OSSTF was also making overtures in Metropolitan Toronto and other large centres. It is a matter of conjecture whether OECTA would have organized OCOTA without these pressures, but, as Paul Cavalluzzo put it, the exploitation of these teachers, many of them women, by school boards suggests that OECTA would have eventually turned to them in their unequal and weak bargaining power state.[89]

The record shows OECTA moved quickly. It seconded Ray Fredette to organize the occasional teachers. He booked a room at the

Royal York Hotel, sent out advertisements calling a meeting and distributed flyers in front of the Ontario Public Service Employees' Union building. The MSSB occasional teachers were the target. About forty to fifty people showed up for Fredette's meeting; they designed a Constitution, elected an executive, formed an organizing committee, paid a one dollar fee to sign up, and decided on an annual fee of 1.25 per cent of earnings. They became the first "local" of occasional teachers and established an arm's length relationship with OECTA. They immediately saw the advantages of receiving service from all of OECTA's departments, especially Teacher Welfare. They would get certification from the Ontario Labour Relations Board in 1985.

Welland as a medium-sized board was Fredette's next target, then wherever there was unit interest. There was a potential of fifty-four locals, including the isolated separate school boards. The next task was to modify OECTA's Constitution and By-laws to accommodate the new reality. From 1987 to 1990 there were four AGM debates. Controversy revolved around such questions as whether or not they were a professional organization or a union and whether this other class of teacher should be in OECTA. Self-interest swayed some delegates; the fees of the occasional teachers would not cover the services to be rendered by the unit. Once the amendments passed, it was possible for OECTA to ask for status under the *Labour Relations Act*. The argument would be that OCOTA members had the same duties, responsibilities, and privileges and AGM representation rights as OECTA members. The Lambton Unit became the test case because of the support of Patricia Golder, the Unit president, and of Michael Coté. The Lambton OECTA Occasionals got union status from the Ontario Labour Relations Board in June 1989.[90]

It was now desirable and possible to merge all the OCOTA locals with OECTA. Cavalluzzo gave his opinion that it was in OECTA's interest to have influence over the school board's use of casual or temporary teachers and in the interest of OCOTA to have the support of a strong professional organization. Furthermore, OECTA's traditions and philosophy suggest that the Association support vulnerable teachers. Finally, it was *not* in OECTA's interest to have OSSTF represent these teachers in light of the fundamental role of the teacher in the separate school.[91]

However, the 1990 AGM defeated the resolution to merge the OCOTA locals with OECTA because it was worded in such a way that, firstly, union with *any* association was possible and that, secondly, the AGM rather than the Executive should have the power to merge. Opponents of the resolution were not open to amendments. The motion, reworded, was brought back to the 1991 AGM where it passed 300 to 246. The question of a two-thirds majority for a Constitutional change was raised, but no formal objection made. Although some delegates wished to keep OECTA for regular permanent teachers, the AGM raised $10 000 in donations for a long OCOTA strike in Sault Ste. Marie.[92]

The memorandum of agreement for the merger was signed in April 1991 and OECTA applied to the Ontario Labour Relations Board to acquire the right to represent OCOTA. However, total acceptance of the union had still not been endorsed in some units. The Toronto Elementary Unit, concerned about the cost of money and personnel time to represent and serve OCOTA, in 1992 asked for a legal opinion on whether the AGM's merger resolution should have had a two-thirds majority. The Essex Unit sent in a resolution for the 1992 AGM that the merger be terminated and that OCOTA revert to its previous status.[93]

Cavalluzzo sent his opinion to Terry Mangan on January 10, 1992, explaining that the Essex resolution was out of order and legally impossible: OCOTA ceased to exist in law in 1991 and a merger cannot be undone. A second legal opinion was requested on the two-thirds question. It stated that the merger resolution simply expedited a result intended by the Constitutional amendments of 1987 to 1990 and therefore required only a simple majority.[94]

With the controversy over and unity restored, the result in 1994 is twenty-seven locals with about 4800 members. Occasional members now have a legal entity and much-improved status in the eyes of school boards, bargaining rights that have replaced nepotism with a hiring list and that have developed long-term posting rules. They have also been making their own history. They have had OECTA "blue-list" and struck two boards for parity with public school occasional teachers: the Sault Ste. Marie District RCSS Board and the Welland County RCSS Board. As Fredette put it, the occasional teachers have "come from the ether" to a status the equal of that of OECTA members.[95]

Ray Fredette was the person seconded three times in 1984 and 1985 and hired in 1986 to organize and recruit for OCOTA. After its growth the Teacher Welfare Department, including Ray, took over servicing OCOTA.

Ray was born in Sudbury. Both his parents, René Fredette and Avela Brunelle, were teachers, although his father later became a customs officer. Ray has two brothers, Michel and Maurice, and one sister, Hélène. Ray attended two French-language schools, St. Albert and Collège Sacré-Coeur. When the Jesuit high school had to close for lack of government funding, Ray went to the "mixed" Sudbury High School. These types of schools the Jackson Commission labelled assimilation factories, but fortunately, Ray was there only for grades twelve and thirteen. He then went to Laurentian University for one year and one year to L'École Normale in Sudbury.

The MSSB interviewed and hired Ray at the Normal School as a French-as-a-Second-Language (FSL) teacher, but later that year tried to reassign him to a French-language school. This would have made him an AEFO member. Luckily for OECTA, Ray refused the reassignment, explaining that he had already made plans to take the ESL course that summer. Later he would get his ESL specialist certificate, his B.A., and certificates in computers in education, Parts I and II.

Before coming to OECTA Ray taught ESL at St. Gabriel, Our Lady of Lourdes, and Our Lady of Guadalupe. In the Toronto Elementary Unit Ray worked in negotiating every year for nine years. He began during the mass resignation and continued during the Bill 100 and AIB period. In this function he helped create a long-term disability plan and negotiated during the Bill 82 time contracts for the Trainable Mentally Retarded (TMR) teachers switching from the Metropolitan Board of Education to the MSSB (a rehearsal for developing the procedures with the designated teachers of Bill 30). Ray served on all the unit executive positions and was the first full-time unit president in Ontario in 1980. One other first was establishing unit committees in affirmative action and in employment equity. Currently, Ray works with Teacher Welfare. His most recent contribution to OECTA was coordinating the publication of the popular "FSL Resource Manual", which deals with a number of topics for FSL teachers: publishers, resource lists, teacher welfare,and Jeunes écrivaines et écrivains.[96]

Business as Usual. Despite the Snow-Tomen, Bill 30, and Cochrane-Iroquois Falls court cases and the government and OECTA initiatives with affirmative action and employment and pay equity, the Association had its ongoing mandate to serve its members in matters of superannuation, religious education, professional development, counselling, and teacher welfare. As well, OECTA continued to relate to the trustees, supervisory officers, the other affiliates and OTF, and the Ministry/government, and to look beyond the interests of its members and the separate school system to issues of social justice.

Superannuation. This topic assumed a high profile in the late 1980s and early 1990s. Some pundits even believe that the dispute between the Liberal government and the teachers over the pension fund was one of the factors in the defeat of the government by the NDP.

In 1987 OTF began pressing for full and equal participation in the administration of the teachers' pension fund and for investment in more than just Ontario government bonds. In February 1989 Dr. David Slater's study on teachers' and public service pensions was released. It advised (1) immediate steps to protect the superannuation adjustment fund, since it had been running deficits, (2) diversification of investments of the main fund, and (3) a new partnership of teachers and the government as trustees of the Fund: "The way we have dealt with pension matters in the past has been somewhat paternalistic."[97]

Negotiations between OTF and the government were unsuccessful and broke off. The sticking point was the teachers' demand for binding arbitration where the two sides of trustees did not agree. The Treasurer of Ontario, Robert Nixon, found such a concept "inappropriate" and was only concerned about the unfunded liability from the superannuation adjustment fund and the consequent risk of bankruptcy in the future. Sean Conway, the Minister of Education, was blocking the idea of equal partnership. An OTF campaign included the submission of over 60 000 letters to Premier David Peterson, OTF's secondment of Ray Moreau, president of Windsor High Unit and a prominent, diehard Liberal, to lobby on the issue, a rally on April Fools' Day, 1989 of over 25 000 teachers at the Liberal Convention in Hamilton's Copps Coliseum, and a sit-in at Sean Conway's office while the pension bill was being debated in the House.[98]

Bill 66, *An Act to Revise the Teachers' Superannuation Act, 1983 and to Make Certain Amendments to The Teaching Profession Act* received third reading on December 19, 1989. Although it did not provide for binding arbitration, it did establish a Pension Board with five government and three OTF members and a neutral chair; this partially answered OSSTF's complaint that teachers had grown up enough to be trusted with the fund's management. The Bill also merged the regular and superannuation adjustment funds; the government assumed responsibility for the latter fund's liability, and increased the teachers' contribution to 8.9 per cent of their salaries. This calmed Father Kavanagh's fears that OTF could not afford to be on its own with the fund management and without the government guarantee. The fund's investment began to be diversified. In late 1991 Premier Rae's government legislated the *Teacher Pension Plan Statute Law Amendment Act* that provided binding arbitration and a new partner's agreement: four OTF members and four government appointments with a neutral chair.[99]

OTF was successful in getting other improvements in the *Pension Act.* If a teacher is on a four-over-five plan in her/his last five years of teaching, there is no risk of a lower pension as long as the teacher returns to work for the school board for at least one year after the leave. Effective December 31, 1991, the teacher can accumulate 2 per cent credit per year for every year of teaching beyond the previous thirty-five-year maximum. For three years teachers on a pension may teach for up to ninety-five instead of twenty days. Finally, under the *Employment Standards Act* of November 1990, a teacher who has been employed for thirteen weeks is guaranteed up to seventeen weeks pregnancy leave, and another eighteen weeks parental leave. (If there are two parents, each one could take the leave, one after the other.) In addition, the *Pension Act* permits maternity/parental leaves for up to three years. In both these cases the teacher may pay 8.9 per cent into the pension for time credit.[100]

An interesting superannuation event took place related to Catholic high schools. In 1988 the Executive raised the issue of teachers approaching retirement who had taught for Catholic high schools that were closed without ever being "designated" by the Lieutenant-Governor-in-Council under section 119(a) of the *Pension Act.* Bob Scott wanted to see those schools designated after the fact in order that the teachers could now purchase credit for the years they taught in those schools. He was the perfect person to take on the task. He exhaustively researched the names and locations of the schools, twenty-two of them, but, after twenty-seven years of teaching for the MSSB, nine years on OTF's superannuation committee, and nine years as OECTA's superannuation commissioner, he retired. Suzann Jones, with Paul Cavalluzzo, inherited the task of convincing the government to pass the necessary regulation. On July 28, 1991 it did so, stipulating a deadline of December 1991 for buying the credit. It is estimated that several hundred teachers benefited from this.[101]

Suzann Jones was, with George Saranchuk, a key person for OECTA in all these superannuation matters.

Suzann was born in Ottawa, daughter of Emile Le Compte, a civil servant, and Maureen Stapleton, a homemaker, and sister of Paul and Annemarie. She attended St. George, Immaculata, and Fisher Park High School for grade thirteen. After Ottawa Teachers' College she taught at St. Thomas, RCSS #5, Nepean and St. Rita and St. Paul's high school (English, religion, science), Nepean for the Carleton RCSS Board. In her fourth year of teaching she married Edward Charles Chenier Jones. While teaching, Suzann acquired her B.A. and M.Ed. from the University of Ottawa and certificates in intermediate mathematics, primary methods, Part I, family life, religious education specialist, and the principalship.

Her activity with OECTA began in her second year of teaching. She was a staff representative, a negotiator, and a member of the Unit executive, including as president. Provincially, she served on the Professional Development Committee, the Executive sub-committee on pensions, the Executive as third and second vice-president, and with OTF as governor and table officer for two years.

Suzann has been for a number of years OECTA's expert on teacher pensions. During the two statutory changes to superannuation she helped merge the two funds, and negotiated with the government on the issues surrounding the liability and the partnership for management of the fund. In 1990, with an Executive decision, Suzann, as a teacher, sued the Treasurer, Nixon, for lost interest to the fund since the money was not invested for one day; she settled out of court for $400 000, which was added to the fund. In 1990 Ed Alexander reported to the Executive that over thirty calls a day were pension queries and appeals. The Executive decided that a full-time person in Counselling and Member Services was necessary to deal with pension matters. (Ironically, Suzann was unsure of the needs and voted against the motion.) Suzann was hired and began January 31, 1991. She is on the OTF Pension Committee for OECTA, helps conduct pension workshops, and receives numerous telephone calls daily from teachers and supervisory officers. Lately, they have been from teachers, mostly female, who are being pressured to retire to help the school board meet attrition targets under the Social Contract; although they have the ninety factor or are age fifty-five, they often do have only about thirty years' experience. She receives calls regarding pension implications in the case of a will or a marriage break-up and from teachers experiencing stress and needing advice on the number of options available. Her advice is straightforward, factually correct, and leavened with intelligence and a sense of humour. OTF has awarded her a fellowship.[102]

Political Action. Given all of OECTA's involvement with three governments that have been quite proactive in educational matters, the Political Action Committee and the Executive realized that the Secretariat required someone to liaise with the Ministry and the legislature and to advise and keep OECTA informed about government thinking and actions.

Paul Michael Howard was initially seconded in 1985, then hired in 1987 for Teacher Welfare. He was another addition to the secondary school complement of the Secretariat. He moved over to the Professional Development Department with additional responsibilities in political action.

Paul was born in Ottawa, the son of Patrick Howard, a diplomat in the Department of External Affairs, and Kathleen O'Meara, a homemaker and hostess. He went to St. Margaret Mary, St. Joseph, and St. Patrick's High School. As the family moved, he completed his secondary school education at Gonzaga High School, Washington and De la Salle High School, New Orleans. He entered the Oblate novitiate and acquired his B.A. from St. Patrick's College and his S.T.B. and B.Th. at St. Paul's College, Ottawa. After spending two summers at OCE for his HSA in English and history, Paul began a career in teaching which would be quite variegated. He taught history, law, and religious education at St. Patrick, Ottawa, then Catholic Central, London; Church history and philosophy to seminarians at Notre Dame, Dhaka, Bangladesh. After a year of study in leadership and religious formation at St. Louis University and a thirty-day retreat, Paul decided on laicization. After a year working with the ombudsman Arthur Maloney, he signed a contract with the MSSB. After one year at Cardinal Newman High School he was promoted to vice-principal there, then in 1983 as principal of Pope John Paul High School he managed its opening and expansion.

After six years with OECTA during the Bill 30 court case and the hearings of the Select Committee on Education, Paul in 1991 went to OTF as executive assistant for relations and discipline and as assistant to the treasurer. Paul lives in Scarborough with his wife, Jean Enghauser, a high school teacher, and their three children, Andrea, Colleen, and Bernadette.[103]

Gregory John Pollock joined the Secretariat in 1990 as another staff member with a secondary school background. As an executive assistant in the Professional Development Department, Gregory moved into the position of full-time lobbyist in political action after Paul Howard went to OTF.

Greg was born in Toronto in a large family. He has six sisters: Theresa, Susan, Lisa, all three of whom are teachers, Michelle, Maryann, and Denise, and one brother, David. His mother, Helen Cahill, was a teacher aide. His father, a salesman, became a teacher in his late 40s went into teaching. Greg, after attending St. John, Neil McNeil and St. Michael's College (B.Sc.), followed his parents' example and went to the University of Toronto Faculty of Education, where he became qualified in all four divisions. He taught science for the MSSB at Michael Power and Cardinal Newman high schools. After ten years he was hired by the Durham Region RCSS Board as vice-principal of Denis O'Connor High School in Ajax. He as principal opened Monsignor John Pereyma Catholic Secondary School in Oshawa.

While in Toronto Greg was a negotiator for several years and a member of the Toronto High executive, including as president. During this period he helped establish a long-term disability plan and an employee assistance plan. He had the challenging experience of opening Pereyma during a work-to-rule sanction.

Greg has improved his qualifications with an M.Ed. from OISE and the principal's and supervisory officer's certificates. He lives in Scarborough with his wife, Marie Fitzpatrick, who works in advertising, and their three children, Erin, Conor, and Lauren. He is recovering from a turbulent spring and summer as political lobbyist during the Social Contract legislation.[104]

Religious Education. When Father Ruetz went on sabbatical in 1989, **Brian Patrick McGowan** was seconded, later hired, to replace him in the Professional Development Department.

Brian was born in Huddersfield, Yorkshire, England, son of Sylvester McGowan, a warehouseman, and Norah Costello, a homemaker, and brother of Rita, Jane, and Kevin. The family immigrated to Canada when Brian was five. He went to St. Christopher in Mississauga, Clarkson Secondary School, and Lorne Park Secondary School for grade thirteen. At Erindale College, University of Toronto, Brian, motivated by a teacher, concentrated on religious studies for his B.A.. After graduating, he worked as a pub manager for about a year, then went to the University of Toronto's Faculty of Education for his HSA. Because of his academic courses in religious education, Brian was qualified only in history. To fulfil the necessary requirement for teacher training in two subjects taught in high schools, Brian had to select a subject without an academic prerequisite. He chose industrial arts and hoped that he would not lose a limb. He would become part of the struggle with the Ministry to get religion on Schedule A of the regulation on teacher qualifications.

With these qualifications Brian taught what he intended to teach from the start, religious education, first at St. Michael's High School, Toronto, then at Notre Dame High School for Dufferin-Peel RCSS Board. At the same time he was on staff for the OECTA/OSSTA religious education courses. Brian took one year off and finished an M.A. in religious studies at the Centre for Religious Studies at the University of Toronto; his thesis was on technology and ethics.

Since joining the Secretariat, Brian has administered the religious education courses and developed school-based religious education materials. Currently, he is involved with a CD-ROM project, a resource interactive programme called "Exploring the Holy Land", and with a Vision TV series on Catholic education. He is seconded half time as a researcher for Monsignor Denis Murphy, one of the commissioners on the Royal Commission on Learning.

Brian lives in Brampton with his wife, Lyn Bissaillon, a banker, and their two children, Adam and Leigh.[105]

OECTA continued to provide many resources for the religious development of its members and their students:

- The OSSTA/OECTA religious education courses, summer and winter stayed in demand; between nine and thirty-two centres each season offered them. By 1989, 15 847 teachers had completed Part I since its inception, 4 009 Part II, and 2 588 Part III; the courses varied in size from 180 teachers in the Metropolitan Toronto location to as few as twenty in places like Kenora and Timmins. In 1987, for example, OECTA and OSSTA subsidized all the courses with $25 000 each.
- CCDC had its forty-first anniversary in 1993; over 600 teachers attended; Susan LaRosa described it as "what we are all about as Catholic educators. It is the one event that our affiliate offers that other affiliates cannot offer." Ab Dukacz called it "a gathering of Catholic teachers that successfully addresses important issues in the faith lives of our members. It restores and challenges

the Catholic dimension of our members."

• The Philosophy of Education Committee sponsored Visions and Values seminars for leadership training and developed a guide for teachers conducting religious retreats for students; given its popularity the Committee is now developing one for teachers of intermediate/senior students.

• The Committee has also published four parent information sheets on the child's first Eucharist, first reconciliation, praying with the child, and encouraging the teenager to attend Mass; a support document "Seize the Moment" for teaching the Bishops' *This Moment of Promise*; and "Seeing Holy Ground", a grades four, seven, and nine resource booklet on Scripture studies.

• OECTA allocated $5 000 to Vision TV for developing the show, "Seeing Holy Ground", and $50 000 for the development of a thirteen-part Vision TV series on Catholicism.

• OECTA negotiated successfully for recognition of its family life courses by QECO.

• OECTA with OSSTA, OCSOA, OCCB, and OCSBOA sponsored a consortium, the Catholic Community Development Organization, that offers courses leading to the certification of supervisory officers, and one module is on the Catholic perspective.[106]

OECTA continued to press for the addition of religious education on Schedules A and E of the teacher qualifications regulation with the Planning and Implementation Commission, with OTF, in a brief with OCSOA and OSSTA to Chris Ward, and in a brief to Sean Conway. Finally, after a couple of decades, on September 20, 1993 Regulation 559 added religion to both Schedules.[107]

The Teacher Education Committee is presently with the Institute for Catholic Education negotiating with the Faculties of Education to have them offer a pre-service Catholic foundations course with the same status as their other courses (that is, a credit course with library resources, equal timetabling, and tenure-track faculty).[108]

Currently, OECTA is studying the issue of religious education credits in grades eleven and twelve and as an Ontario Academic Credit. On the one hand, such credits are most appropriate for a Catholic high school. On the other hand, the introduction of these courses could have serious implications for the current social sciences staffing.[109]

Finally, the dashed hopes of George Saranchuk, Peter Gazzola, and other members of OECTA when ECEAO went out of existence were revived when the Institute for Catholic Education (ICE) came into existence in 1987. Its mission as an agency of the Ontario Bishops was the support and assistance of all those responsible for anglophone Catholic education in Ontario, the reinforcing of their efforts to define the nature and role of Catholic education and to provide a learning environment that will confirm and nurture the students' Catholic faith. OECTA supports ICE financially annually with an amount of money roughly equivalent to one teacher's salary. In return, it has the satisfaction of cooperating with ICE's mission and of working on common causes with eleven other provincial Catholic education associations, including OSSTA and OECTA. ICE has published for OECTA's teachers curriculum guidelines in secondary school religious education, AIDS education, religious education for special education students, and family life. The first executive director was Monsignor Dennis J. Murphy, who had been among other things, a lecturer in religious studies at Laurentian University and director of the National Office for Religious Education. In 1993 he was succeeded by Sister Joan Cronin, G.S.I.C., who had been principal of eighteen OECTA/OSSTA religious education courses and had served on a number of OECTA unit and provincial committees. With three Masters' degrees and experience in all the roles in separate schools from teacher to superintendent, Sister brought great promise to ICE for the future. Father Kavanagh in his retirement is working part time with ICE. Currently, because of a budget problem, OECTA is not supporting ICE. The matter will likely be reopened because the vote was close, and because many OECTA members do not wish to leave the support and assistance of those providing Catholic education entirely to OSSTA and OCSOA as major influences on ICE policies and practice. There is, however, some gratitude on the part of OECTA for the way in which OSSTA stopped the public school trustees from having the government perform more draconian actions against the collective agreements of the teachers.[110]

The Section 136-la Issue. When Bill 30 had its third reading, a number of amendments were introduced by the NDP and PC MPPs. One of them was section 136, which reads in part:

> For the purpose of maintaining the distinctiveness of separate schools, the Roman Catholic school board may require as a condition of employment

> that teachers hired by the board after the ten school year period ... agree to respect the philosophy and traditions of Roman Catholic separate schools in the performance of their duties.
>
> If it is finally determined by a court that subsection (1) or (2) prejudicially affects a right or privilege with respect to denominational schools guaranteed by the Constitution of Canada, subsections (1) and (2) are repealed.111

The wording of this legislation suggested to the separate schools' lawyers that after year ten of the establishment of the Catholic high school operated by the separate school board, there would be a limitation on the power of separate school trustees in their hiring of teachers. Some saw in the legislation an interpretation that the board could not ensure that the teacher was a practising Catholic, but only that s/he would "respect" the school's philosophy. Separate school boards had always hired non-Catholics, for special needs in areas of the curriculum, or because of the special talents and qualities of the teacher. However, they did not want circumscribing of their latitude in hiring. The reference in the legislation to a possible challenge to the section, unusual in itself, operated as a red flag to the separate school community and it was determined to argue for section 136-l's removal in the Supreme Court of Canada. However, in October 1986 Brian Dickson, C.S.J., stated that, "It is the opinion of this Court that the Appeal should proceed upon the same basis as in the Court of Appeal of Ontario."[112] There the law rests up to the present day.

After the Supreme Court of Canada judgment, COSS began to organize a court case for the removal of section 136-l. Monies were spent for the preparation of a historical affidavit and a factum. However, Eileen Lennon, the president, began to be concerned. To her it did not seem right that OECTA should support a court challenge that could adversely affect some of its members and she also wondered if this were not a management (that is, trustee) matter and what the implications of the Snow-Tomen Case were for OECTA's support of a COSS action. She asked for a legal opinion. Paul Cavalluzzo advised that OECTA had to represent *all* its members. A legal action to remove section 136-l could be interpreted by the judges of the Snow-Leaming-Page issue that OECTA was *not* in a position to represent adequately the interests of Catholic high school teachers who were non-Catholics. Thus, OSSTF could win its case and OECTA would have only elementary school members. Eileen Lennon recommended to the

Executive in November 1989 that OECTA not be involved with the contemplated 1361 case. A letter was sent to the Bishops explaining that, "As non-Catholics hired by boards become OECTA members, the Association cannot take a position that fails to provide fair representation to these members." Michael Coté met with the Sault Ste. Marie RCSS Board to explain the position and state that OECTA would not oppose OSSTA's position.[113]

The Executive decision was a difficult one. Two members could not vote in favour of the motion. Peter Gazzola and Michael Coté had to get involved in a half-hour debate with the Catholic Principals' Council in order to table a motion that would have expressed dissent.[114] Certainly, a review of OECTA's activities described above, of the objectives of various OECTA standing committees and of OECTA's Constitution clearly delineates one of the Association's aims as being the religious formation of the teachers and students in the separate school system. And as recently as 1992 and 1993 the Executive passed motions that would "explore ways by which religious education can be integrated with the core and board-based curriculum" and that would "encourage projects which promote the integrity of Catholic values and teaching into the existing secular curriculum."[115] The fact remains that, Eileen Lennon is convinced she gave the proper advice to the Executive. If the separate school board hires a non-Catholic, then OECTA is bound in conscience and under its Constitution to represent that teacher as it would any other member. Consistent with this position is OECTA's support of the current grievance of the Dufferin-Peel Secondary Unit against the board policy that requires new non-Catholic teachers upon employment to sign a waiver that they will not apply for a promotion and regards current non-Catholic staff as ineligible for a promotion.

Professional development. A number of professional development activities of OECTA are understandably in the area of religious education. However, this department continues to be one of the two result areas the Hay study identified. In the last decade it has expanded to six members in order to serve the new secondary membership and the larger membership from growth in the school system and the inclusion of OCOTA. The pendulum has swung back and forth somewhat from an intensity of activities in the Teacher Welfare Department to an emphasis in teacher professional development. For example, during the days of Bills 274, 275 and 100, Bill 274 received the most attention. It is speculated that for the next few years, when the Social Contract might lessen the time spent on collective bargaining, there may be more emphasis on professional development. The present Executive supports the idea of the Professional Development department publishing resource materials and conducting workshops and short courses on a cost-recovery basis to meet the needs of the membership. There is also the gap to be filled by the 1993 withdrawal of additional-qualifications courses by York University due to the Social Contract. OECTA is examining the possibilities here.[116]

In the last decade the Department has offered numerous seminars, short courses, and conferences. Some of the topics were the following: career exploration, time management, computers in the classroom, the gifted child, thinking skills, creativity, dealing with death, justice and peace, stress, management styles, employment assistance, AFFIRM, personal and classroom planning, early primary education, Visions and Values, 4MAT, junior division novel study, primary language, arts, SMART, discipline, the transition years, ESL, as well as conferences and seminars for principals, coordinators, consultants, unit presidents, and treasurers. The Department's publications have included a primary education handbook, "Side by Side/Learning with the Young Child"; a junior education handbook, "Teachers and Children in the Middle"; a special education handbook, "All Together Now"; a booklet for principals, "When There's Conflict", and one for student teachers, "Welcome Teachers".[117]

The Department's most recent major undertaking has been the development of Family Life Education, Parts I, II, and III, structured like the Religious Education courses for QECO recognition. Part I began for the first time in January 1984 in Metropolitan Toronto, Durham, and York. Part II was piloted in Carleton in the spring of 1993. Part III is nearing completion of the development phase.[118]

The effects on students of all this professional development is incalculable, but no doubt significant. Here is a letter from one pupil who received a Young Writer's Award:

> My name is Emilia Slowikowski. I was born in Poland. I am nine years old. I just had my birthday on April the 6th. I am new Canadian. I just learned to speak English in September. My teacher helped me learn by doing extra reading and writing every day. I love Canada very much. I spend most of my free time drawing and writing stories. I think I like funny stories with endings that make you laugh a lot.... I am very happy about my story winning. You can't begin to believe how excited I feel. I

want to be a paleontologist when I grow up. But now I might think about being an author. Thank you so much.[119]

Counselling and Member Services. This Department has also expanded to five members. Although the percentage of teachers who need to call for help from OECTA is small, the size of OECTA places large demands on the Secretariat. In addition to the usual types of crises discussed in earlier chapters, the Department has found a dramatic increase in the last decade of teachers' personal and financial crises due to family breakdowns, alcoholism in the family, loss of income from the illness or unemployment of the teacher's partner, debt loads because of failed business ventures, and a relatively low income due to being in categories D, C or B or to teaching just half time. Secondly, legal actions regarding injuries and sexual assault allegations have increased. In addition the *Occupational Health and Safety Act* and the problem of asbestos in schools built before 1970 have added to the calls to Counselling and Members Services. [120]

OECTA has responded in a number of ways to the members' needs. Talks are available in the teacher and the law, ethics, stress management, financial planning, career planning, conflict resolution, staff morale, and teacher evaluation. Units have been advised on how to get employee assistance plans and protective clauses on health and safety into the collective agreement. (Unfortunately, under Social Contract pressure, some school boards have dropped their funding of the former plans at a time, arguably, when teachers need this kind of help more than ever.)[121]

Assaults on teachers and students remain a phenomenon. OECTA's 1992 study revealed 158 physical and 133 verbal assaults in the classrooms of the members in the previous year. The Department has developed a manual on procedures with assault incidents; it includes advice on how to involve the medical doctor and police and deal with the assailant.[122]

Heightened awareness of sexual abuse cases has resulted in government initiatives that seriously affect teachers. Patrick O'Neill reported in 1989 that changes to the Criminal Code removed the requirement of the corroboration of the evidence of the young person in sexual assault allegations. He commented that this was a positive change where assault had actually taken place, but put the teacher at risk with any vindictive student not abused or assaulted. In 1992 he reported that local assistant crown attorneys had been directed by the Ministry of the Attorney

General to proceed with charges involving assault on children by parents, teachers, clergy, or any adults, regardless of how insubstantial the case may appear. He cautioned teachers to be aware of the risks of loss of certificate, dismissal, a criminal record, public disgrace, or a prison term. Father Kavanagh recommended minimizing one's risk by avoiding seclusion with a pupil.[123]

The Department also had some advice for school boards, principals, and supervisory officers helping teachers cope with depression, low self-esteem, hypertension, insomnia, suicidal tendencies, and even school phobia. Pressuring these ill teachers into resigning or even accepting their resignations (as happened with ten teachers in 1987) would not be a suitable action for a school board building a Christian community. Instead, OECTA advised administrators in an enlightened fashion to encourage the teacher to see a doctor and recommended to teachers not to resign: "All that is needed is a statement that you are under his/her care.... Illness is not just cause for dismissal."[124]

Accounting, Administration, Communications, Library, and Computer Services. These departments have become sophisticated and important to the needs of the Secretariat and the Association's membership. A complete description of their functions is in Appendix B.

Briefs to the Government/Ministry. The decade has seen numerous briefs written by OECTA. They were requested by the Planning and Implementation Commission, the Select Committee on Education, the Shapiro Commission, the Radwanski Commission, the Fair Tax Commission, to mention a few. They covered such topics as computers across the curriculum, the transition years, the specialization years, technology, teacher education, the early years, the integration of exceptional pupils, and destreaming. The latter two are of particular concern currently to OECTA because of the government's restructuring of education.

Regarding the mainstreaming of exceptional pupils, OECTA had this to say in its 1990 brief: "If boards only decide whether a pupil is (or is not) exceptional and place all students into a regular mainstream, one must question the need for the process at all. If it is expected that the needs of every student can readily be met within the regular classroom setting, we will revert to pre-Bill 82 status." OECTA on behalf of these children called for a maximum size for a classroom with exceptional students integrated into it and for at least one resource teacher in every school.[125]

Related to this topic and the government's policy of inclusion is the topic of destreaming in grade nine. OECTA in two briefs, one in response to the Radwanski Report and one to the Select Committee in Education, supported the idea of destreaming as a solution to the drop-out problem with general level students and as a corrective to an organizational practice with negative pedagogical and social aspects. However, OECTA emphasized that such a reform must be accompanied by a high level of teacher in-service, a maximum class size of twenty-one students, a core curriculum, and a curriculum appropriate to the high-technology/communications environment. Government implementation is proceeding, in OECTA's opinion, without the desirable amount of special planning, funding, inservice, or class-size legislation. Three quotations reveal OECTA's current frustration: "The government sees the consultation process on the restructuring of Ontario education as having consumed too much time." (Ab Dukacz, 1992)[126] "Outrage is being expressed over the belief that the secondary system is being positioned to assume the qualities and attributes of that system which guided the province in the 1950s and 1960's." (Claire Ross, 1992) "The government has embraced a particular ideology that does not necessarily lend itself to easily defined or understood modes of implementation....[We] are severely limited by the rigidity of interpretation and the need to remain faithful to overall philosophical tenets that have little or no relationship to what really does or must happen in the schools." (Claire Ross, 1993).[127]

Social Justice. OECTA continued to fund worthy projects in Africa, Bangladesh, the Philippines, the Caribbean, and Central and South America as extensively as in the previous decade. For example, in 1993 OECTA gave $193 000 in donations. Also, it increased its staff participation in Project Overseas. As part of its fiftieth anniversary celebrations, the Association aimed to collect $275 000 to fund a number of programmes for those displaced by violence in Guatemala. Rigoberta Menchu, the Nobel peace prize laureate, in partnership with the Canadian International Development Agency, was to accept the donation.[128]

The Social Contract. Business Not as Usual. In November 1992, Roy Romanow, premier of Saskatchewan, invited Floyd Laughren to his province to help with the budget process. While there, Laughren grew apprehensive about the possible unwillingness of New York financial institutions to finance Saskatchewan's debt. Ontario faced a potential debt of $14 to 16 billion. In February 1993, W5 did a television show on the severe steps taken by the Labour government in New Zealand to control the deficit: privatization and rollbacks, for example. Laughren and the cabinet became very alarmed. Exacerbating their fears was the perceived threat from the money markets that Ontario's credit rating would be downgraded resulting in higher borrowing rates and a significant increase in the provincial debt. Faced with this outside intimidation, the government moved aggressively to put its house in order by an all-out attack on the broader public services. The idea was floated to try the European social contract method where employees, employers, and the government work cooperatively on industrial strategies, collective agreements, government budgets, and a number of other areas of concern. At the end of March the NDP caucus met in Niagara-on-the-Lake to view a video on how budgets could be cut cooperatively by bringing in all the stakeholders. The invitations went out.

On April 2, 1993 the dance began. OTF decided on a strategy of going to the meeting for information only, not to negotiate. OSSTF wanted to seek a coalition of all the public sector unions. On April 3 in a *Toronto Star* interview Liz Barkley of OSSTF declared war. On April 5 OTF and the affiliates met with Premier Rae and Laughren. The Rae government demanded two billion dollars in savings, a 5 per cent cut, while also desirous of protecting contracts and bargaining. Cooperative problem-solving was the key. He introduced his negotiating team, announced the next meeting would be April 19 and said he would like the whole process wrapped up by the middle of May. The instructions were that the budget cut had to be retroactive to January 1. Each sector was given a target. In education's case it was 500 million dollars a year for three years.

The debate in OECTA and the other affiliates became whether or not to negotiate. The Council of Presidents examined the pros and cons. The arguments for not negotiating with the government were that the negotiating was a dishonest process, and that provincial bargaining was allowed too short a time-line, had an uneven playing field, and put at risk hard-won collective bargaining rights. The pros were that rollbacks and layoffs were being threatened, other affiliates might be there, legislation would take place anyway, absence would be bad public relations, inaction could cause a fee revolt or a charge of neglecting fair representation, OSSTF could bring up the joint-school-board idea as a cost-saving measure, negotiations could effect some savings, and the social contract process could in the future have some benefits. The decision was made to go to the table.

On June 3 the coalition of about forty unions walked out of the negotiations. On July 7, *The Social Contract Act* was passed. It contained clauses that allowed for a lessening of the cuts in government funding if agreement was reached with the government by the new deadline, August 1. Once again the decision had to be taken whether to go back to the table, only this time there was a "fail safe" mechanism in the legislation that would result in much larger cuts. There was no movement in this direction from the other affiliates despite the legislation. Claire Ross, the president, decided with the Executive and Council of Presidents that OECTA would have to seek a sector agreement in order to mitigate losses.

Claire Ross describes the events:

a) Initital Reaction to Social Contract Proposal

The initial response of those to be most directly affected was not overwhelming. Most rejected the idea outright. In essence, the social contract proposal was nothing more than a huge "tax grab" directed to those working in the broader public sector of the province. The Premier was demanding that the representatives of the approximate 950,000 broader public service employees come to the Royal York with their collective agreements in order that the government might take from them what was deemed necessary and appropriate. This, of course, is not the work of employee representatives. The task of such leaders is to defend and promote rights hard won in the difficult crucible of collective bargaining. It was recognized as well that hurried compliance with the Premier's "extraction demands" would only result in further demands for even more draconian reductions in the weeks and months ahead. The stand-off lasted for weeks at the end of which time eight sector tables were formed to conduct what the government characterized as "voluntary discussions" leading to settlement. What the government did not make public were the series of promised "hits" resulting in even greater "injury" should the talks not end in "success." The government refused to make public the total amount of the hits demanded which in the education sector were in the billions of dollars with grid freezes costed into the accounts. On the night of June 3,

1993, as government negotiators were informing the Premier of the "success" of the talks, the Public Services Coalition walked from the Royal York Hotel. Faced with impending disaster, the government moved almost immediately to compel compliance by means of Bill 48, *The Social Contract Act, 1993*. With the passage of this legislation on July 7, 1993, the "playing rules" governing all collective bargaining in the broader public sector effectively changed - at least for the next three years and quite possibly well beyond.

Following the Royal York walkout and immediately after passage of Bill 48, there ensued a period of much doubt and uncertainty. Some unions such as the ONA (nurses) and OPSEU continued to bargain to reduce their losses. Others vowed never to return regardless of the harm or injury to be suffered by such a refusal. In keeping with its direction from the June Council of Presidents, OECTA held to the position that it would return to the bargaining table provided there would be any hope of mitigating losses to our membership. This position was publicly communicated to the media and strongly supported by the Provincial Executive.

b) OECTA Returns to the Sector Bargaining Table

As noted, the passage of Bill 48 ushered in a new era in collective bargaining for public service employees in this province. No longer were public service unions and associations being asked to be a party to voluntary talks. All were being forced to meet the legislated demands of the government. There could be no escape. In this context, a number of important questions must be asked:

c) Why did the broader public services coalition not take more definitive action against the government, that is, call for a provincial strike?

A provincial strike was supported by only a very small minority of the union and association leaders. There appeared to be no real interest in such a strike on the part of the membership as evidenced by the lack of support for organized demonstrations against the social contract across the province. There was also a sense among the union leadership that the situation could be "controlled" and ultimately "finessed." After all, almost all were staunch NDP members whose "party would never let them down in this manner." Most could not believe or accept what was really happening to them under a socialist regime they had worked so hard and loyally to put in place. The Public Services Coalition leadership strongly believed in going the "political route", which meant "cashing in political IOUs" and bringing pressure to bear on MPPs in order to defeat the proposed *Social Contract Act.*

d) Why did OECTA return to the bargaining table?

After July 7, 1993 it was OECTA's position that the legislation which had been passed was significantly different from the Premier's demanded voluntary talks that had failed. This legislation demanded either compliance or disobedience. It had not been possible to generate in any quarters support for a general strike either before or after the passage of Bill 48. Disobedience was realistically out of the question. "Fail safe" provisions of the legislation meant that failure to negotiate a settlement would expose all members to the full force of the extraction demands of the government. This would be absolutely intolerable. It was clear the government's social contract strategy had not wavered from its initial inception. What we were dealing with was a carefully planned assault on fundamental public sector collective bargaining rights that had been completely determined in concept and principle long before the Premier's March announcement. OECTA therefore returned to the bargaining table to:

- Maintain representation rights throughout the life of the social contract.
- Mitigate losses.
- Avoid "fail safe" provisions.
- Gain access to sector table reductions of 20 per cent .
- Attempt to gain access to and use of Teacher Pension Plan gains to reduce total sector target hit.
- Gain access to Job Security Fund in the event of future teacher layoffs.
- Attempt to address and resolve inequities of grid freezes.
- Attempt to clarify and define an "exit strategy."
- Prevent additional losses to employers under the Expenditure Control Plan provisions which under "fail safe" would give them license to achieve.

Prior to making a decision to return to the sector bargaining table, I personally consulted with other teacher leaders across Canada. Bill 48 is not wholly unique to the province of Ontario. Other provincial legislatures have enacted legislation with similar characteristics though not nearly as severe, unfair, or perverse. Unions and professional organizations in Quebec and British Columbia have each felt the sting of their government's attack on fundamental rights and free collective bargaining processes. In discussing these experiences, one common theme was universally articulated: go in and mitigate losses. Do not allow "others" to act under the legislation and complete the process of "doing you in." Save everything that can be saved by whatever means possible. This cannot be done unless you are at the "bargaining table" regardless of your abhorrence for the charade.

e) Particular Difficulties in Reaching Sector Framework Agreement

- Bill 48 had legislatively taken the following: all negotiated grid increases, cost-of-living increases, qualification increases, and experience increments. These amounted in total losses to billions of dollars *none of which were credited as reductions to target.*

- The government demanded further reductions in the amount of some $1.5 billion dollars over the three-year life of the social contract in *additional* compensation reductions.

- The net result of the social contract extractions was to be a *permanent downsizing* in the teacher work force reductions of 4.75 per cent, not counting what might be required to meet the Expenditure Control Plan demands of local boards. The total reduction demanded under the Social Contract was estimated at some 6 000 teaching positions. The further staff reduction to be realized under the Expenditure Control Plan for local boards was guesstimated to be in the order of another 4 000 teaching positions across the province.

- The inability of OTF to unify, coordinate, and be the voice of the teachers of this province was a factor severely limiting the ability of the affiliates to respond in a cooperative and unified way in which the best interests of the teachers would be collectively served. Indeed, the action of three affiliates in totally usurping the spokesperson role of OTF added greatly to the confusion and atmosphere of "everyone for themselves" climate that characterized so much of the time frame April 1 to August, 1993. As July moved rapidly toward August 1, it is no understatement to say that OTF practically disappeared as a player at the sector bargaining table giving rise to the "Chair of the Day" means of affiliate leadership. In this context, OECTA would walk alone in all its critical decisions attempting to mitigate the losses of its membership and find the road of least pain and injury.

f) Settlement of a Sector Framework Agreement

At the last possible moment on Sunday, August 1, teacher leaders reached settlement with the government on a Sector Framework Agreement to determine and govern the extractions legislatively demanded.

The direction to the Provincial Executive by the Council of Presidents had been to "mitigate losses." The direct monetary "hit" to teachers had been reduced from the government's demanded $1.441 billion over three years to $573 million in total. In this respect, losses had been significantly mitigated and the Council direction clearly met.

g) Final Summary: Gains and Losses

Gains

- Maintained member representation rights.
- Prevented transfer of enormous powers to local boards of education under "fail safe."
- Mitigated dollar losses to teachers by some $900 million.
- Won back grid recognition of qualification changes valued at $150 million.
- Gained credit of experience increments in amount of $107 million if experience increments not negotiated.
- Gained access to target reduction of $325 million from Teacher Pension Plan surplus gains.
- Gained access to 20 per cent reduction to target for reaching Sector Framework Agreement.
- Gained access for all members to Job Security Fund in event of future job loss.
- Gained seat at Education Sector Task Force tables.

Losses and Resulting Difficulties

- Destruction of relationship between provincial government, OTF, and its Affiliates.
- Failure to resolve fears and uncertainties of teachers.
- Continuing confusion and conflict over Sector Framework interpretations.

- Deterioration of relationships between local boards and teachers caused by social contract issues.
- Rising anger over deliberate attempts by boards to go beyond reductions demanded by social contract provisions.
- Internal tensions among teachers over increment loss and whether a buyback of increment could or should be attempted.
- Continuing uncertainties surrounding yet-to-be-determined "exit legislation" provisions.
- Loss of collective bargaining rights for three years.
- Salary reductions of approximately 4 per cent per year for three years.
- Permanent PTR increase of 4.75 per cent at the end of social contract period.
- Loss of 6000 teaching positions under *Social Contract Act.*
- Potential further loss of 4000 teaching positions under Expenditure Control Plan for boards.
- Transfer of significant problems to local units, that is,. increment and Sector Framework interpretation difficulties.
- Failure to achieve extraction fairness.
- Failure to resolve injustice of increment freezes.

h) Payment of Extraction Demands

Most teachers are aware of the "options menu" to be used in payment of the extraction demands. In summary, the target must be met by combination of the following "coins":

- Application of Framework Reduction - 20 per cent .
- Use of Teacher Pension Plan monies.
- Possible application of increment credit.
- Use of unpaid leave days.
- Attrition - retirement or underhiring in case of enrolment increase.
- Any other means determined by mutual agreement between parties, that is, board and teachers.

i) Grid Problem

...Teachers just entering the profession stand to lose up to $90 000 each, depending on the legislation drafted to govern "exit" from the Social Contract.... Unless the provincial government recognizes the inequity of this situation and recognizes all years of experience on exit in March 1996, *OECTA will implement provincial sanctions to*

> *address the situation.* From my personal perspective, there can be no retreat from this position... The increment problem is the gravest of matters which in the near future will define our integrity and mettle as "people who genuinely and collectively care for each other."

l) **Final Summary**

The poisons of the Social Contract will take years to work their way through our educational systems. Its full extent and scope are only now beginning to be understood. Particularly hard hit are assessment-poor boards. These boards, regardless of financial situation, pay in the same proportion as boards who are significantly better positioned to absorb and cushion and even deflect such "hits."

The story of OECTA's efforts in response to the June Council motion *"that the Council of Presidents authorize the Provincial Executive to negotiate a provincial plan to mitigate losses under the government's social contract"* has already been told and recognized. These were among the most trying and challenging days ever experienced by OECTA. The decision to return *alone* to the sector bargaining table was possibly the single most difficult decision ever made by an affiliate. As the full story of the social contract unfolds, this one decision will stand as possibly the wisest and most prudent decision ever made by a teacher organization in Ontario. The teachers of this province, whether public or separate, could not afford or long sustain the losses legislatively contemplated under "fail safe". This realization was what finally drove the affiliates collectively in the waning moments of August 1 to reach a settlement with the government to minimize losses and maintain representation rights for all their members....[119]

There was considerable pressure felt by the In-House Steering Committee making the decision to go back to the bargaining table. On the one hand, the president, first vice-president, general secretary, deputy general secretary, and board solicitor had the authority and the flexibility from the Council of Presidents to do whatever they felt necessary to represent the membership. On the other hand, all of the other affiliates had taken the stand that they would not go back to the table. To the Steering Committee the alternative was negotiate to save what it could or be involved in civil disobedience and suffer the full cuts. In my opinion, the Committee really had no choice; neither the teachers nor the system could sustain the full hit of Bill 48.

The units now are working with this new reality. As Tom Reilly, the director of the Dufferin-Peel RCSS Board, put it: "Premier Rae took a marvellous idea, the social contract, and implemented it with the finesse of a dictator." OECTA begins its next fifty years with another challenge. But the history of the Association shows it has successfully met many, some much more serious. James Carey, the general secretary, expressed this thought in 1993:

> Where there is a will to lead and an ability to lead, there will always be the opportunity to lead and provide hope for the membership of OECTA and, for that matter, all those who are so proud of what this Association has done during the past fifty years.[120]

Biographies of the Presidents and General Secretary

Thomas John Fauteux (1950-). John came to the office of the presidency after having been the first full-time provincial vice-president.

John, the son of Louis Henri Fauteux, a farmer, then a worker at Hiram Walker's, and of Elizabeth Taylor, a homemaker, was born in Windsor. As was the case with a number of his presidential predecessors, he was part of a large family: Margaret Ann, Joseph, Mary, Gregory, Martha, Barbara, and Catherine were his siblings. Only John and Martha, in the School Sisters of Notre Dame, went into teaching. John attended high school and the first two years of university in Detroit and in 1968 decided he would like to teach; he attended Windsor Teachers' College, where the staff and students awarded him Teacher of the Year. While there he renewed acquaintanceship with a friend from his Windsor school days, Elizabeth Scharfe, a nursing assistant. They met at St. Theresa's Church youth group, became engaged, and were married the summer after Teachers' College. They have two children: Erin and Melissa.

John began teaching for the Windsor Separate School Board, first at St. Jules, then at J. A. Rooney, an open-concept school; he became the first male kindergarten teacher in Windsor. The board promoted him to the position of resource teacher at Parents' Place at the central office; he assisted teachers with relating to the community and to parents, and with training parents and primary teachers to work together in educating the children. An example of his work was his response to a staff when it was unable to get parents to come to school meetings. John helped the teachers organize a grandparents' night and would not tell the parents who telephoned what was going to happen. The grandparents had the time and interest; the parents became motivated and attendance at school meetings improved. For this kind of creativity, the Windsor Unit presented him with the Margaret Lynch Award for Excellence in Teaching.

John next went to the Executive for three years, after which he was assistant to the director of education and associate director at the Dufferin-Peel RCSS Board, where he worked on accommodation and communication matters. After this year, he was president of OTF for a year. Currently, he is senior coordinator of government and public affairs at the MSSB. During his career he has acquired a B.A. from the University of Windsor and an M.Ed. in special education from OISE. OTF made him a Fellow.

His involvement with OECTA began in his second year of teaching: he went to a general meeting to find out what OECTA was all about. At the meeting mass resignation was being discussed. John expressed his discomfort with the idea. Frank Griffin replied that, if he did not like the decisions that were being made, then he should get involved. He did: he served on virtually every committee and on the executive, including as president of the Unit.

John Fauteux was fortunate to be provincial president from 1984 to 1986 after Premier Davis's historic announcement and during the court challenge to completion. He found this period the most exciting of his life. His ties to the Liberal Party were likely helpful during the Peterson years. John, in addition to carrying out his responsibilities at the MSSB, is engaged in his special interest, philanthropy. He helped establish the Metropolitan Toronto Catholic Education Foundation, that funds co-operative daycare, breakfast programmes and supplying glasses for refugees, and the Redwood Shelter for victims of violence in the home.[121]

James Cooney (1938-). During his term of office, 1986-1988, James received the Supreme Court of Canada judgment declaring the constitutionality of Bill 30's completion of the separate school system and saw another court case begin, challenging the structure of OTF.

Jim belongs to that large contingent of the MSSB staff, the immigrants from Ireland. The son of Patrick Cooney, a farmer, and Bridget Cooney, a homemaker, he was born in Broadford, County Clare, Ireland. He has four brothers: Michael, Edward, Patrick and Denis and one sister, Margaret. He attended Broadford National School and then became a boarder at the Presentation Brothers, St. Mary's College, Cork, an all-boys' secondary school. While there he entered the novitiate and went on to St. Mary's College, Strawberry Hill, a Teachers' College operated by the Vincentian Order. After this three-year programme Jim taught at St. Vincent, a reform school in Dartford, England. After five years of teaching he left the Brothers and for two years explored the possibility of becoming a priest. He immigrated to Canada and enroled at St. Augustine's Seminary, Toronto.

Jim finally decided lay teaching was his vocation and in 1970 signed on with the MSSB. He taught at Transfiguration, St. Jerome, St. Francis de Sales, and St. Blaise. During this time he acquired his certificates in special education specialist, religious education, Parts I and II, the principalship, and library; and two degrees, a B.A. and M.ED. from York University. After serving three years on the Executive as first vice-president and president, Jim returned to teaching at Our Lady of Sorrows and in 1989 was promoted to vice-principal at Nativity. He presently holds this position at Our Lady of Victory and has been short-listed for principal.

Jim became interested in OECTA during Doug Knott's salary negotiating with MSSB. He was unhappy with the three-year collective agreement with the Board and became a school representative. He went on to be a sub-unit president and pursued his special interests in long-term disability protection for teachers, a new concept, and in how to improve professional development days. As an OTF governor, member of the Board of Directors, and then second vice-president, Jim became greatly involved with the Catholic high school issue. Premier Davis's no to completion in 1971 aroused his interest to the point where he worked for the Liberal Party in the election of that year and read my thesis on the case for separate school completion. In the 1970s Jim became a member of the Political Advisory Committee and encouraged the attendance of OECTA members at political conventions. During the second OECTA campaign for extension Jim prepared a detailed twenty-part plan of action for the Units communicating to the public the Catholic high school issue.

With his customary eye for organizational detail, Jim prepared two press releases in 1987: and one if the Supreme Court of Canada declared Bill 30 unconstitutional, one if it declared it constitutional. He was overjoyed to use the latter. Eileen Lennon, who followed Jim into the president's office, found him to be a well-prepared executive, a man of high integrity, and a great mentor. OTF made him a Fellow in 1988.

Jim is married to Gabriele Sembaj, a teacher; they have two children, Denise and Colin.[122]

Eileen Lennon (1949-). The first female president in a number of years, Eileen had the office from 1988 to 1990. Eileen and her twin, Mary Jane, were born in Stratford to Aloysius Lennon, a farmer, and Julia Dwyer, a teacher. They have two brothers: Michael and Thomas. Eileen is another product of a one-room school house, St. John, RCSS #1, Ellice. Rarer was the fact that her mother taught her for grades one to six. Teaching was in Eileen's blood: four of her aunts are teachers. For grades seven and eight Eileen took the bus to Immaculate Conception, Stratford, where she graduated at the top of the class. She then attended grades nine and ten at St. Joseph, a small intermediate division school, and grades eleven to thirteen at Stratford Central Collegiate Institute. After completing a degree in history at St. Michael's College, Toronto, Eileen took the primary specialist's course at Toronto Teachers' College in 1971-1972.

Eileen has spent her entire teaching career with the Dufferin-Peel RCSS Board in the following schools: St. Christopher, Clarkson, St. Catherine of Siena, Cooksville, and St. Gerard, Mississauga. She has concentrated on kindergarten, the junior division, and special education. Often she coached sports and directed school musicals. Curious to discover how a collective agreement is put together, Eileen in her first year of teaching became a school representative, working on the Economic Advisory Committee. She enjoyed this so much that in the next two years she went on the negotiating team, then became the chief negotiator, the first woman in Dufferin-Peel to do so. She has served on numerous unit committees and was Unit president, again as the first female. At the provincial level, she was a member of the Professional Development and Teacher Welfare Committees and began as counsellor on the Executive, working her way up through all the positions. She was continuously elected as governor or to the Executive from 1981 to 1994.

She remembers in 1988 calling a press conference on assaults on teachers. Her report that assaults were on the rise and her recommendation that school boards should design policies to deal with them resulted in front-page coverage in the *Toronto Star* and boards looking at the problem.

Eileen also was a part of the court cases of the 1980s. When the OTF Board of Governors dealt with Mrs. Margaret Tomen's request to be a statutory member of OPSTF instead of FWTAO, it was necessary to vote on whether or not to change an OTF by-law to permit the request. The vote affirmed the status quo, but Eileen voted for a change. She felt that it was discriminatory that a teacher should have to belong to a federation because of her sex. Eileen later concurred with OECTA's decision to support the OTF by-law in its present form both in the court case and the hearing before the Ontario Human Rights Commission, because this support was also a defence of the existence of OECTA as a separate affiliate with separate school teachers as statutory members. However, she still feels that FWTAO and OPSTF should resolve their differences so that membership does not depend on sex. With regard to the Bill 30 case, Eileen always felt optimistic. Ironically, when the Executive held a conference call to convey the news of Premier Davis's announcement that he was extending the separate school system, Eileen missed it. She guessed that the call was to resolve some routine matter and did not leave what she considered more pressing school business. When Jim Cooney telephoned her that night, she still had not heard the news. She said it was like Christmas in June and thought she should pinch herself.

Eileen is at present an OTF governor and a full-time teacher welfare officer (which includes the position of chief negotiator) in the Dufferin-Peel Elementary Unit. She has been awarded an OTF fellowship and has recently completed her M.Ed. at Niagara University.[123]

Michael Dawson Coté (1946-). Michael brought many years of Executive experience to the presidency (1990-92). With persistence he became third vice-president by a one-vote majority, then in a recount by ten votes; for two years in a row he lost his bid for second and third vice-president, but, using the step-down procedure, won the election as counsellor. He labelled himself the candidate for the small units and the following year became first vice-president. Finally, when he reached the presidency, in his second year in the office he was acclaimed.

Michael was born in Sarnia; his father was Homer Coté, a construction worker and shop steward, and his mother Rita Dawson, a nursing assistant and president of the union. He has one brother, Paul. In addition to active union membership being a family tradition, so was teaching. Michael's sister Lorraine is a teaching assistant and his other two sisters, Christine and Linda are teachers. Mrs. Coté had always wanted to be a teacher and helped Michael regularly with his school work.

Michael went to St. Joseph, Sarnia, where the principal one day would have him on his teaching staff. Discipline was strict: Michael was so terrified of him that, when told to stay off the lawns, would stay on the sidewalk all the way home. (As a teacher working with him, Michael still stayed off the grass.) Michael finished his elementary education in a two-room school in Point Edward, St. Edward the Confessor, where he did his grades seven and eight in one year and received $100 for being the top achiever. He went on to St. Patricia for grades nine and ten, then to the private Catholic high school, St. Patrick.

As a student he earned tuition and spending money as a caddy. At age eighteen he began playing golf competitively, was successful in the Qualifying Round of the Ontario Junior Golf Championship, and was offered a golf scholarship at an American university. Michael remains a golfer to the present day, but his father advised him to go to teachers' college as a fallback position; he would be able to golf in the summer. In 1964 Michael attended Althouse Teachers' College, London. As a teacher he retraced his childhood route, beginning at St. Joseph, then moving on to St. Edward the Confessor with the Point Edward Separate School Board. In his fourth year of teaching the trustees promoted him to principal: his main competitor had a B.A. and, therefore, the board found him expensive; furthermore, the trustees knew Michael. When the school was twinned, Michael lost his principalship, but it was 1969 and he was now working for the new Lambton County RCSS Board; he moved to St. Helen, Sarnia, as vice-principal. Inspired by ideas he received at the CCDC, he started a drop-in centre where one night a week students could get help with homework and engage in extra-curricular activities. Michael was promoted to principal and held that position at St. Joseph, Corunna, the twinned school St. Joseph-Father Gerald LaBelle, Corunna, St. Joseph, St. Helen and currently, St. Peter, Sarnia.

During these years Michael married Barbara Ingraham, a nurse, had two children, Russell and Kimberly Ann, and acquired his B.A. from the University of Western Ontario, as well as certificates in religious education, intermediate education, mathematics, art, physical education, Parts I and II, and the principalship.

He became a staff representative very early in his career, feeling that OECTA negotiators could do better than getting a $100 raise. Michael served for fifteen years on various Unit committees, as chief negotiator and in almost every executive office, including as the president during the walkout over Bills 274 and 275. (Since he was a principal, there was a sensitive discussion with Joseph Pace, the director of education, about whether or not he could leave the school; Michael convinced him that as president he had to go to the teacher rally.)

During his time on the Executive, Michael feels his most significant accomplishment was assisting with the organizing of the occasional teachers and with their integration into OECTA.

In 1988 Michael married his second wife, Elizabeth Tucker Plunkett, then a computer resource person in OECTA's computer department. He has four stepchildren: Ernest, Shelley, Jeffrey, and Jennifer.

For all his years on the Unit and provincial Executive and on the OTF Board of Governors, he received an OTF fellowship.[134]

Helen Jean Biales. Helen, daughter of Czechoslovakian immigrants, Joseph Biales, a farmer, and Mary Murza, a homemaker, was born and raised near Glencoe in Middlesex County. She attended a one-room school, S.S.#12, Mosa and Glencoe District High School. After grade thirteen she went to London Teachers' College and started to teach for the London Separate School Board at St. Robert, then Sacred Heart. After four years she moved to the Riverside Separate School Board at St. Cecile. A year later she took a year off to start her B.A., which she later completed at the University of Windsor. She returned to teaching at the Windsor Separate School Board, where she remains today. There she has been a classroom teacher, teacher librarian, and special education resource teacher. She has been a staff member at Holy Rosary, St. Maria Goretti, St. Alexander, H.B. McManus, St. Clare, and Christ the King. She was promoted to vice-principal at C. G. DeSantis and Notre Dame and to acting principal at St. Francis. In 1993 she became principal of H. J. Lassaline.

In addition to her B.A., Helen has an M.Ed. from Wayne State University and library, special education specialist, religious education specialist, principal's, and supervisory officer's certificates. She was well qualified and experienced, but in Helen's reading of the situation it was not the practice of the Windsor Separate School Board to appoint women as principals. It took five applications over twelve years for the position of vice-principal or principal before Helen received a posting. During this period there were only two female principals with about thirty English elementary schools. Meanwhile, male teachers were being promoted within five years.

Helen has served on almost every position on the Unit executive, including president, and since 1983 has been an OTF governor. One of Helen's most memorable experiences was in November and December 1993, when she was chosen to be part of Project II to go to Botswana. There she taught elementary school teachers methodology in language arts. She has also been counsellor, second and third vice-president, and president (1992-93) on the Executive. She is currently past president. OTF made her a Fellow.[135]

Claire Ross (1940-). Claire was the first president since George Saranchuk to come from a Catholic high school teaching background, an appropriate one in a period when the Ministry of Education was restructuring secondary education.

Claire was born in Peterborough, the son of Thomas Ross, a marble tradesman and worker, and Marie Leahy, a homemaker. His mother was determined to see her children get an education. All did. Claire and his brothers George, Daniel, and John each went into teaching. Claire was yet another graduate of a one-room rural school, but does not have fond memories of S.S. #9, Douro. During his eight years there he observed a turnover of two or three teachers a year. Aware of his weak preparation for high school, he arrived at St. Peter, Peterborough terrified about his prospects. Working very hard, he did well. With few financial resources he worked on the farms for $2 a day and tried for a scholarship to university. However, his grade thirteen teacher of mathematics and science had a nervous breakdown; only three of the forty students passed the requisite nine examinations. Although Claire was one of them, some of his marks were low.

He then tried teaching for a year with a letter of permission at St. Alphonsus, Peterborough. The following year he entered St. Augustine's Seminary and academically stood at the top of the class. After completing a B.A. in philosophy and English at St. Michael's College, he decided on teaching as his vocation and left St. Augustine. He became certified with an HSA after two summers at OCE and taught religion, English, and Latin at Bishop Macdonnel High School in Guelph. Although he had a full day of nine periods with no spares, he did find time to meet and marry Annemarie Gruzleski, an elementary school teacher. In 1967 Claire moved to Delta Collegiate Institute in Hamilton and a year later to Centennial Collegiate Institute in Guelph. Anxious to return to a Catholic school, he applied for a vice-principalship at St. James Senior Separate School (later St. James Junior

High School, now St. James High School) and held the position for twenty years.

After one month at Our Lady of Lourdes in 1988, Claire was asked to rescue a technical education project to be housed in a leased ex-brewery. Eight weeks later he presented an implementation plan to the Wellington County RCSS Board, but he was told there was not enough money and given the rest of the year released from his school to come up with a less expensive plan. He managed to get government approval of the new plan as a pilot project with government funding of $4.1 million. It was necessary then to raise $3 million from private industry. Claire delivered the budget, building and programme design, and the capital equipment. As principal of the new Holy Family Education Centre, he saw it open in February 1990. The Centre offers a programme of high technology across the curriculum with a learning methodology that emphasizes individual and small-group student projects and product evaluation of the student. Every student from grade six to the final year of high school is transported to the school for a period of time. Holy Family also operates as a continuing education night school. For this work Claire received the Northern Telecom National Award for creative technology in programme delivery.

In addition to acquiring his B.Ed. and M.Ed. in moral education from OISE and elementary and secondary school principal's certificates, Claire has taken an active interest in OECTA. At St. James he became involved with the campaign for full funding. In the Wellington Unit he was a staff representative, then negotiator during the December mass resignation and the walk-out for the rally at the Gardens. He also held most positions on the Unit executive, including the presidency. In Claire's opinion, his high visibility in OECTA affairs did not help him in his attempts over many years to become a principal.

At the provincial level Claire has been on the Personnel and Political Advisory Committees and has held the offices of treasurer, second and first vice-president, and, currently, president. He had two major thrusts: solving the problem of the investment portfolio and procedure and the method of designing an annual budget; and, secondly, attempting to have the government restructure education in terms of the 1990s instead of the 1950s. Unfortunately, Premier Rae's Social Contract has temporarily deflected him from concentrating on the second thrust.

During these changing, demanding times Claire spends time with his wife and children, David, Bryan, and Andrea and on his hobbies:

jogging, playing hockey, woodworking, and writing articles with a golden pen. The Wellington Unit has recognized his work with an Award of Merit.[136]

Horst Schweinbenz (1949-). It has been Horst's demanding task to be president of OTF in 1992-1993 during the Social Contract, Tomen's challenge of the membership by-law, and OSSTF's unwillingness to approve funding of the Association to a degree deemed necessary by the other affiliates. OTF continues to live with all three problems.

Horst was born in Heidelberg, West Germany. His father, Otto Schweinbenz, a baker, and his mother, Margaret Hofferberth, a homemaker, immigrated with Horst and his brother Heinz to Canada in 1951. Otto got a job as cook at St. Joseph's Hospital in Hamilton and Margaret worked at a bottle factory. Horst attended St. Patrick. When Horst was in grade five, his mother died after a lengthy illness. His father had met Horst's teacher, Genevieve Wilson, at parent-teacher meetings. Soon Horst's teacher was also his stepmother. Eventually, Horst also gained two half sisters, Geraldine and Genevieve. After completing his elementary education Horst went to Cathedral Boys' High School right across the street from his home. After grade thirteen he tried engineering until Christmas at the University of Windsor, but was not attracted to that profession. He went to work at Stelco, but the union went on strike. With time on his hands, he tried Hamilton Teachers' College and enjoyed it. In 1970 he became a teacher with the Hamilton-Wentworth RCSS Board, where he has remained to the present. He has taught at St. John, St. Emeric, St. Thomas Aquinas, St. Christopher, Holy Family, St. Margaret Mary, St. Cecilia, and Corpus Christi. He is now librarian and kindergarten relief at Our Lady of Lourdes. In 1971 Horst married Carol Marshall, a registered nurse's assistant, now a registered nurse; they have two children, Kristie and Amanda.

Horst attended an OECTA meeting in his first year of teaching; he was unhappy about earning a salary lower than what he had been getting at Stelco. He tried to get on the Economic-Advisory Committee, but was told he could not until he received a permanent contract (OECTA policy throughout the province); he attended meetings anyway as an observer. Locally, he became chair of a number of committees and held almost all the executive positions, including the presidency. He was involved with two mass resignations and, during the Gardens demonstration, had the task of counting the teachers on the bus before and after the rally in order to make sure that nobody got caught in the huge crowd and missed the return ride.

At the provincial level since 1985 Horst has been an OTF governor at large, second and first vice-president, president, and currently, past president. At OTF he has learned the value of CTF. It presents papers to the federal government on national education issues and is able to discuss with the government matters like transfer payments, unemployment insurance, and the tax deductibility of payments to registered pension plans. As for OTF, Horst feels that OECTA benefits from its existence in matters like improving superannuation and teacher education. In Horst's opinion, religious education would not have become a "teachable subject" without OTF's support.

Horst continues on OTF to, as he puts it, wrestle with the fallout from the Social Contract.[137]

James Carey. James's biography has been outlined in the last chapter. In 1991 he was the successful applicant for the position of general secretary. He holds this office during a time of uncertainty. What will be the results of the Social Contract, the Baum hearing on the OTF by-law, and the government's restructuring of education? He is confident that the large number of talented professionals in OECTA will meet new challenges, but his watchword is vigilance in the protection of teacher and separate school rights gained in the last fifty years. As he said to the Council of Presidents, "We must be strong;...as Catholic teachers we must continue to be vigilant."[138]

NOTES

1. Reference re Bill 30, An Act to Amend the Education Act (Ont.), [1987] 1 S.C.R. (Wilson, J. at p.1185).
2. "The Nation's Pulse," *Maclean's,* 3 January 1994, 24; Peter C. Newman, "From Hope to Defiance," ibid., 28-30.
3. Duncan Green, chairman, *Report of the Secondary Education Review Project,* Ontario Ministry of Education, 1981; *The Renewal of Secondary Education in Ontario, Response to the Report of the Secondary Education Review Project,* ibid.; 1982; *Ontario Schools, Intermediate and Senior Divisions,* ibid., 1984, revised 1989.
4. George Radwanski, *Ontario Study of the Relevance of Education, and the Issue of Dropouts,* ibid., 1987; "First Report of the Select Committee on Education," December 1988, OECTAA.
5. Ontario Ministry of Education, *The Common Curriculum Grades 1-9,* 1993.
6. Executive, 16-17 October 1992; 7-8 May, 15-16 October, 3-4 December

1993.
7. *OECTA Reporter* (April 1991), 30.
8. Ibid., 1-2 March 1991; Ross, interview, Toronto, 11 January 1994.
9. Scott, interview.
10. *Globe and Mail*, 14 June 1984.
11. *Toronto Star*, 13 June 1984.
12. Executive, 3-5 July 1984; 3-4 October 1985; 2-3 April 1987.
13. *An Act to Amend the Education Act*, S.O. 1986, C.21.
14. Scott, interview.
15. Executive, 6-7 September 1985; AGM, 7-10 March 1986; *Initiatives*, December 1986.
16. AGM, 13-16 March 1987.
17. Scott, interview.
18. AGM, 13-16 March 1987.
19. *Reference to an Act to Amend the Education Act (1986), 53 O.R. (2d) 513, 529 (C.A.)*; Greg Dickinson, "Toward 'Equal Status' for Catholic Schools in Ontario: The Supreme Court of Canada Examines Constitutional Issues," *Canadian and International Education* (November 1987), 5-23.
20. *Reference* (Wilson J.).
21. AGM, 13-16 March 1987.
22. Executive, 6-7 June 1986.
23. Ibid., 3-4 October 1986.
24. AGM, 7-10 March 1986; Executive, 6-8 June 1985; 7-8 November 1986; 15-17 January 1987.
25. Ibid., 30 June - 3 July 1987.
26. AGM, 7-10 March 1986.
27. Executive, 6-7 June 1986.
28. Ibid., 7-8 November 1986.
29. Ibid., 1-2 November 1984; AGM, 8-11 March 1985.
30. Council of Presidents, 20 September 1986.
31. Executive, 12-13 September 1986; Council of Presidents, 6-7 February 1987.
32. Executive, 30 April-1 May 1987.
33. Coté, interview, Toronto, 4 December 1993; Lennon, interview, Toronto, 13 December 1993; Murphy, interview.
34. AGM, 13-16 March 1987; *Agenda*, January 1989.
35. AGM, 13-16 March 1987; Sister Anna Clare, interview, Vancouver, 7 December 1993.
36. Edward Chudak, interview, Toronto, 12 November 1983.
37. Victoria Hiebert-Hannah, interview, Toronto, 11 November 1993.
38. Michael Haugh, interview, Toronto, 11 November 1993.
39. Jeff Heximer, interview, Toronto, 13 November 1993
40. Letter from Mrs. Margaret Tomen to the President, OTF, April 18, 1985, OTFA.

41. Letter from John Snow to Mr. Guy Matte, President, OTF, July 8, 1986; letter from Margaret Wilson, Secretary Treasurer, OTF, November 7, 1986; letter from John Snow to Mr. Doug McAndless, President, OTF, December 4, 1986; letter from Margaret Wilson to John Snow, February 10, 1987, OTFA.
42. Affidavit of Patricia Leaming, Affidavit of Gary Page, *Tomen et al. v. the FWTAO et al., 70 O.R.(2d) 48 (OCR, 1987).*
43. Regulations under *The Teaching Profession Act*, ROC 147/79, s. 1.
44. The Ontario Teachers' Federation, By-law 1, section 2.
45. *The School Boards and Teachers Collective Negotiations Act*, RSO, 1980, c. 464, s.s. 1 (a) and s. 5.
46. Affidavit of Florence Henderson, *Tomen.*
47. Affidavit of James Forster, *Tomen.*
48. Affidavit of Mrs. Margaret Tomen, *Tomen.*
49. Affidavit of R. Ross Andrew, *Tomen.*
50. Affidavit of David Lennox, *Tomen.*
51. Affidavit of Joyce Fulton, *Tomen.* See also affidavits of Nancy Balkwill, Ottawa Board of Education; Olga Bevington, Essex Board of Education; Brenda Fisher, Waterloo County Board of Education; Penny Hammond, Carleton Board of Education; Janet Marissen, Frontenac County Board of Education; Linda Markle, Lennox and Addington Board of Education; Collette Ohlke, Etobicoke Board of Education; Sandy Ophoven, Hamilton Board of Education; Connie Reynolds, Lambton County Board of Education; Carolyn Rollins, Lambton County Board of Education; Bev Russell, Niagara South Board of Education; Steffi Schwan, Hastings County Board of Education; Sally Siegner, London Board of Education; Martha Tobe, Toronto Board of Education; Carole Anne Yuzwa, Halton Board of Education, ibid.
52. Affidavit of John Snow, *Tomen.*
53. Executive, 7-8 November 1986; 6-7 March 1987.
54. Letter from John Snow, Chief Negotiator to H. Onésime Tremblay, B.A., M.Ed.; Director of Education, Sudbury Roman Catholic School Board, January 28, 1987; ibid. to the Education Relations Commission, January 28, 1987; letter from Onésime Tremblay to John Snow, January 30, 1987; letter from R. H. Field, Chief Executive Officer, Education Relations Commission, February 6, 1987, OECTAA; Executive, 6-7 March, 18-19 September 1987.
55. Affidavit of Forster.
56. Affidavit of Henderson.
57. Factum of the Federation of Women Teachers' Associations of Ontario, *Tomen et al. v. the FWTAO et al.*
58. Affidavit of Robert T. Dixon, *Tomen.*
59. Factum of the Ontario English Catholic Teachers' Association, *Tomen.* In a letter explaining why the OECTA would not support a court challenge to section 136-1a of the *Education Act* (which protects the rights of non-Catholic teachers in separate schools) because it would contradict the association's position in the Snow-Leaming-Page matter, the president, Eileen Lennon,

mentions that the president of Page's OECTA unit is an Anglican and his chief negotiator is Jewish.
60. Factum of the Ontario Separate School Trustees Association, *Tomen.*
61. Michel Begley, "Le Reglement 17. Étude d'une crise."
62. *Education Act of Ontario and Minority Language Education Rights* (1984) 47 O.R.(2d).
63. Affidavit of Jacques Schrybert, *Tomen.*
64. Separate negotiations have taken place with the Roman Catholic Separate School Boards of Carleton, Cochrane-Iroquois Falls, Simcoe, and Sudbury, and the Boards of Education of Hamilton and Essex. Affidavit of Marc Cazabon, *Tomen.*
65. Also a sub-committee report on French-language schools done for the Jackson Committee on Declining Enrolment in 1976 had concluded that "mixed" high schools caused assimilation of the Franco-Ontarian students and recommended that they be closed and replaced by French-language schools regardless of enrolment. Robert T. Dixon and André Lécuyer, *Franco-Ontarian Education: Curriculum, Staff, Organization*, Toronto: Commission on Declining Enrolment, 1978.
66. Affidavit of Hervé Casault, *Tomen.*
67. Affidavit of Gabrielle Levasseur, *Tomen.*
68. Factum of the Ontario Teachers' Federation, *Tomen.*
69. Judgment, *Tomen.*
70. AGM, 10-13 March 1989; Executive, 3-4 November 1989; *OECTA Reporter* (October 1989), 14.
71. Ibid., 7-8 July 1991.
72. Cooney, interview, Toronto, 7 December 1993; Lennon, interview.
73. Executive, 11-12 September, 4-5 December, 1992; 10-11 June 1993; 4-5 December 1992; AGM, 10-13 March 1989; 10-12 March 1990.
74. Executive, 4-5 December 1992.
75. Coté, interview; Lennon, interview.
76. Brenda Carrigan, interview, Toronto, 12 November 1993.
77. Carol Corsetti, interview, Toronto, 12 November 1993.
78. Barbara Grizzle, interview, Toronto, 9 November 1993.
79. Theresa Robertson, interview, Toronto, 12 November 1993.
80. Carolyn Stevens, interview, Toronto, 10 November 1993.
81. R. Fredette, "The Way for Teacher Welfare, Five-Year Guidelines," July 1984, OECTAA.
82. Lise Julien, *Women's Issues in Education in Canada*, Toronto: Council of Ministers of Education, 1987; "The Status of Women and Affirmative Action/Employment Equity" in AGM Minutes, 10-13 March 1989.
83. Ministry of Education "News Release," 30 March 1989.
84. Carrigan, interview.
85. Council of Presidents, 22-23 November 1984; 24-25 January 1986; 20-21 November 1987; AGM, 13-16 March 1987; 10-12 March 1990; Executive, 5-6

December 1986; 12-13 April, 13 October, 5-6 December 1991; 5-6 February 5-6 March 1993; *OECTA Reporter* (December 1985), 10-12; (January/February 1986), 34-35.

86. Executive, 2-3 February 1990; Vida Zalnieriunas, "What? You haven't posted a pay equity plan yet?", *OECTA Reporter* (December 1989), 22-26; Carrigan, interview.

87. Executive, 17 January 1992; 4 February 1993.

88. "OECTA Equal Opportunity Handbook."

89. Council of Presidents, 8-9 June 1984; Executive, 3-5 July 1984.

90. Ibid.; 13 February 1987; 3-4 July 1989; 17 January 1992; Fredette, interview.

91. Executive, 17 January 1992.

92. Ibid.; AGM, 8-10 March 1991.

93. Executive, 12-13 April, 10-11 May 1991; 17 January, 27-28 February, 9 March 1992.

94. Paul Cavalluzzo to Terry Mangan, 10 January 1992, OECTAA; Executive, 17 January, 27-28 February 1992.

95. Fredette, interview. "Blue-listing" is the same process as "pink-listing," but applies only to occasional teachers.

96. Fredette, interview.

97. Executive, 30 June - 3 July 1987; *OECTA Reporter* (October 1989) 10-13.

98. Ibid.; Executive, 2-3 March 1989; *Agenda*, December 1989.

99. Jones, interview; Executive, 5-6 January, 13-14 September 1991.

100. Executive, 17 January 1992; 14 January 1993; Jones, interview.

101. Ibid.; Executive, 3-4 June 1988; 10-11 May,18 August 1991; *OECTA Reporter* (February 1987), 41. The schools were the following: St. Ursula Academy, Windsor; Villa St. Joseph, Cobourg; Sacred Heart High School, Kingston; Maryvale Abbey, Glen Nevis; Sacred Heart Commercial High, London; St. Joseph, St. Catharines; Dublin Continuation School; St. Clare, Windsor; St. John's High School, Woodslee; St. Michael, Douglas; St. Andrew; Killaloe; St. Columba, Pembroke; St. Joseph, Barry's Bay; Bishop Ryan, Renfrew; Loretto Academy, Hamilton; Loretto Academy, Streetsville; St. Mary's Academy, North Bay; St. Mary's College, Brockville; Mount Mary Immaculate Academy, Ancaster; St. James High School, Coglan; (mergers) St. Pius X, Chatham; Notre Dame, Kingston; Notre Dame, Ottawa; St. Pius X, Ottawa; Grey Gables, Welland; St. Joseph High School, Windsor; St. Mary Academy, Windsor; Christian Brothers College, Wexford; Loretto Academy/Notre Dame, Guelph.

102. Jones, interview; AGM, 20-22 March 1982; 10-12 March 1990; Council of Presidents, 8-9 June 1990; Executive, 12-13 October 1990.

103. Paul Howard, interview, Toronto, 23 November 1993; AGM, 11-14 March 1988.

104. Gregory Pollock, interview, Toronto, 15 November 1993.

105. Brian McGowan, interview, Toronto, 16 November 1993.

106. AGM, 11-14 March 1988; Council of Presidents, 3-4 November 1989; Executive, 28 February 1986; 18-19 September 1987; 2-3 February, 14-15 September 1990; 16-17 October, 4-5 December 1992; 5-6 March 1993; *OECTA Reporter* (February 1987), 14.
107. AGM, 10-12 March 1990; Council of Presidents, 14-15 June 1985; 7-8 June 1991; Executive, 1-2 June 1990; 15-16 October 1993.
108. Executive, 17 January 1985; Council of Presidents, 5-6 February 1993.
109. Council of Presidents, 14-15 June 1985; Executive, 6-7 May, 3-4 July 1988.
110. Executive, 12-13 April 1991; 7-8 May, 10-11 September 1993.
111. *Education Act*, 5.136(1).
112. Executive, 7-8 November 1986.
113. Ibid., 2-3 November 1989; 1 November 1990; 1-2 May 1992; Lennon, interview.
114. Coté, interview.
115. Executive, 1-2 May 1992; 7-8 May 1993.
116. *Agenda*, October 1993; Executive, 10-11 September 1993.
117. Council of Presidents, 10-11 June 1988; 3-4 February 1989, 30 November - 1 December 1990; 12-13 June, 6-7 November 1992; Executive, 28 September 1984; 3-4 May 1985; 7-8 November 1986; 30 April -1 May; 5-6 June, 11 December 1987; 16-17 September 1988; 3-4 July 1989; 14-15 September, 1 November 1990; 1-2 February, 7-8 July 1991; 5-6 June 1992; 10-11 September 1993.
118. *Agenda*, October 1993; Executive, 3-4 December 1993.
119. Emilia Slowikowski, St. Margaret, Sarnia (a pupil of Mrs. Cindy Jackson), Executive, 5-6 May 1989.
120. Council of Presidents, 22-23 November 1985; *Agenda*, June 1990.
121. Ibid.
122. Executive, 6-7 May 1988; 16-17 October 1992.
123. Council of Presidents, 3-4 February 1989; Executive, 17 January 1992.
124. Council of Presidents, 5-6 February 1988.
125. "OECTA Response to Consultation Paper on the Integration of Exceptional Pupils," Executive, 19-20 January 1990.
126. Ibid., 27-28 February 1992.
127. Executive, 4-5 December 1992; 14 January 1993.
128. *Agenda*, September, October 1993.
129. "Report of the President to the 1994 AGM," Draft.
130. Council of Presidents, 10-11 June 1993.
131. John Fauteux, interview, North York, 29 November 1993; *OECTA Reporter* (February 1979), 23; (March/April 1984), 17.
132. James Cooney, interview; Eileen Lennon, interview.
133. Ibid.; AGM, 15-17 March 1980.
134. Michael Coté, interview; AGM, 7-10 March 1986.
135. Helen Biales, interview, Toronto, 23 June 1993.

136. Claire Ross, interview, Toronto, 1 December 1993.
137. Horst Schweinbenz, interview, Toronto, 2 November 1993.
138. Council of Presidents, 8-9 February 1991.

CODA

AN INTERVIEW WITH THE PRESIDENT CLAIRE ROSS 1994

The president and myself in January 1994 offer the following thoughts and impressions about the present and future of OECTA.

It is a cliché to say we are in a period of change. But clichés, though unoriginal, are often true. Kathleen Dixon would see many dramatic changes in the Association and in the schools, government, the Church, and society, to mention a few. The last few chapters suggest the pace of change is quickening. Mrs. Dixon would see no slowing down in the immediate future now that society has progressed from the horse to the car and telephone to the jet plane, modem, fax, and computer. In this age of instant communication and high technology, she would see a welcoming adventure for OECTA. Certainly, some things should and will remain the same: OECTA's concern for the protection and growth of its members, for the preservation of the rights of the children and the separate school system, and for the poor, the exploited, and the suffering. OECTA members and its leaders will be called upon to meet these concerns in new and challenging ways. Some that occur to me:

- We must always be defining and redefining our role in the Church, in the priesthood of all believers in order to fulfil our mission "To go and teach all nations in the name of the Father and the Son and the Holy Spirit." Many times the teacher is the major influence on the child for her/his spiritual formation. OECTA, in order to effectively live its vocation, must strive always to have a positive effect on the role of the laity, women in the Church, and the building of community in a society that is much different than a generation ago.
- Baum's judgment, expected shortly, could demand that OECTA and OTF make some fundamental changes in the way in which they function and in their constitutions. The challenge for OECTA would be to continue to effect its mission where its members might have a choice of affiliates, to offer a service, fulfilment, and excellence that would attract a strong complete membership.
- We may quarrel with the way that the Ministry is carrying out the restructuring of education, but the reform of education is a North American phenomenon brought on by the need for new skills in a high-technological society of instant data retrieval and integrated communication systems. OECTA's Professional Development Department will be called upon to lead, to be a catalyst for change in the Ministry and

the classroom, and to assist the teachers with their new challenges.

- OECTA's teachers have reached heights of academic and professional education, income, and working conditions undreamed of by its members in the Association's early years. The talent, genius, flexibility, creativity, and experience of its members make us very optimistic, while also aware of the expectation of the members that its leaders are excellent mentors calling the membership to new heights.
- Often the public have seen only the one side of OECTA, either the side that protects its members through hard bargaining and, where necessary, grievances and sanctions, or the other side that fosters the development of its members, the students, and the separate schools through activities like the religious education courses, CCDC, Young Writers' Awards, and professional development seminars and publications. In our opinion, OECTA always needs to be prominent in both aspects so that its membership, the educational community, and the public fully realize the Association's contributions to the life of the child.

At the close of this book there are two pictures in my mind. One is that of the AGM filling a large room in a modern hotel. The other picture is of Cecilia Rowan, the first general secretary of OECTA, sitting at her desk in her living room after teaching a large grade eight class all day and performing her duties as a principal. She is writing letters to the president and various other OECTA members, an almost daily task. The history of the challenges that OECTA overcame in its history to date and these two contrasting pictures strongly reinforce an optimism in the next fifty years of OECTA.

I give Jim Cooney the last word. In his president's message to the 1988 AGM he said:

> Catholic teachers touch a future that stretches to eternity.

APPENDIX A

CONSTITUTION AND BY-LAWS OF OECTA 1946

CONSTITUTION

1. The name of this Association shall be "THE ONTARIO ENGLISH CATHOLIC TEACHERS' ASSOCIATION".

2. The Association is incorporated by Letters Patent dated September 8, 1944.

3. The objects of the Association shall be: (a) to promote the principles of Catholic Education by the study of educational problems; (b) to work for the advancement of understanding among parents, teachers, and students; (c) to work for the moral, intellectual, religious, and professional perfection of all the members; (d) to improve the status of the teaching profession in Ontario; (e) to secure for teachers a larger voice in education affairs.

4. The Association may be divided into the following groups:

(a) Teachers in Elementary Schools.

(b) Teachers in Intermediate Schools.

(c) Teachers in High Schools, Colleges, and Universities.

(d) Association of Lay Teachers for special purposes.

(e) Association of Religious Teachers for special purposes.

The members of each group may meet separately to discuss problems relevant to their work.

5. Relation of the Association to the Ontario Teachers' Federation.

(a) The Ontario English Catholic Teachers' Association is affiliated with and is one of the five constituent bodies of the Ontario Teachers' Federation.

(b) The Ontario English Catholic Teachers' Association shall have five representatives on the Board of Governors of the Ontario Teachers' Federation. These representatives shall be the Immediate Past President, the president, the First Vice-President, the Secretary, and one other member of the Association, and they shall be elected annually at the Annual Convention.

(c) The Ontario Teachers' Federation will retain a portion of the fee of every Regular Member of this Association, the amount so retained to be determined by the Board of Governors of the Ontario Teachers' Federation.

(d) Teachers' who have written themselves out of the Ontario Teacher's Federation, according to Section 4 of the *Teaching Profession Act*, are not eligible for membership in the Ontario English Catholic Teachers' Association.

(e) Every teacher, as defined in the *Teaching Profession Act*, shall be a member of the Ontario Teachers' Federation through one of the five teachers' organizations affiliated with the Federation, unless he withdrew from membership in the Federation not later than six months after the coming into force of the Act.

(f) The text of the *Teaching Profession Act* and of the Regulations made under

the Act will be found at the end of this constitution.
6. The temporary Head Office of the Ontario English Catholic Teachers' Association shall be in the City of Ottawa, in the County of Carleton, and Province of Ontario, and the Post Office address of the business office is 36 Nepean St., in the said City of Ottawa.

BY-LAWS

Article I

POWERS

The powers of the Association shall be: (1) to direct, manage, supervise, and control the business, property, and funds of the Association; (2) to cooperate with other Teachers' Organizations in improving the standards of education by legislative means and otherwise.

Article II

MEMBERSHIP

SECTION 1. The members of the Association may be classified as (1) Regular Members, (2) Associate Members.

SECTION 2. The following are eligible for Regular Membership

(a) Certificated Catholic Teachers in Separate or Public Schools who are not regular members of any of the other Teachers' Organizations affiliated with O.T.F.

(b) Certificated Catholic Teachers in Private Schools in Ontario who wish to be members of O.T.F.

SECTION 3. The following are eligible for Associate Membership:

(a) Catholic Teachers in Private Schools who are not Regular Members of this Association.

(b) Catholic Teachers in Separate or Public Elementary Schools or in Secondary Schools who are active members of one of the other Teachers' Organizations Affiliated with O.T.F.

SECTION 4. Associate Members shall have all the rights, privileges, and responsibilities of Regular Members except that they may not act as representatives of O.E.C.T.A. on the Board of Governors of O.T.F. due to the requirements of the *Teaching Profession Act.*

SECTION 5. Past Service Membership may be granted to any former member of the Association who has held active membership in the Association for five or more continuous years, provided such member has become ineligible for active membership because of retirement from active professional life. A past member shall have all the rights, privileges and responsibilities of an active member except that he or she may not hold office.

SECTION 6. Past Service Membership shall terminate automatically, if and when a Past Service Member enters active business or professional life or makes a change of residence outside the Province.

SECTION 7. Active Membership shall endure during active professional life, unless forfeited or terminated as hereinafter provided.
SECTION 8. Active Membership shall terminate when a member leaves the teaching profession.
SECTION 9. Any member who by personal or professional conduct violates any of the rules or principles of the Association may be expelled from membership by a two-thirds vote of the Board of Directors at a meeting of the Board, provided that at least ten days written notice of such impending action shall have been given to him or her. Such member, if expelled, may appeal to the Association at its next regular meeting.
SECTION 10. Any Regular Member as described in Section 2(b) above, or any Associate Member failing to pay dues within sixty (60) days from the date they are due, after written notification by the Local Secretary, shall forfeit membership in the Association. Written notification of such forfeiture shall be mailed to the member by the Secretary. Such a member may be reinstated upon payment of all back dues, if otherwise eligible for membership.

Article III
PROVINCIAL ORGANIZATION
SECTION 1. THE PROVINCIAL EXECUTIVE.
(a) The Provincial Executive shall consist of (1) President, (2) Immediate Past President, (3) First Vice-President, (4) Second Vice-President, (5) Third Vice-President, (6) Secretary, and (7) Treasurer.
(b) The President, the First Vice-President, the Second Vice-President, the Third Vice-President, and the Treasurer shall be elected at the Annual Provincial Convention.
(c) Their term of office shall be for one year, and until their successors have been elected and have qualified.
(d) The Secretary shall be chosen by the Board of Directors, and shall be a non-voting member whose term of office shall be coincident with the term of his or her employment.
(e) In the case of a vacancy in the office of the Vice-Presidents or of the Treasurer, such vacancy shall be filled by the Board of Directors.
(f) The members of the Executive shall be known as the Officers of the Ontario English Catholic Teachers' Association.
SECTION 2. THE PROVINCIAL BOARD OF DIRECTORS.
The Provincial Board of Directors of the Ontario English Catholic Teachers' Association shall consist of: (a) the members of the Provincial Executive, (b) District Presidents, and (c) Chairmen of Special and Standing Committees.
SECTION 3. THE ANNUAL PROVINCIAL CONVENTION.
(a) The Annual Provincial Convention of the Ontario English Catholic Teachers' Association shall be held during Easter Week, in the City of Toronto, Ontario, or such other place designated at the previous Annual Convention.
(b) At the Annual Provincial Convention there shall take place the election of

Officers, the appointing of Special and Standing Committees, and the discussion of such matters as may be brought before the Convention. Matters of general policy shall be determined at the Convention.
(c) Those entitled to vote at the Provincial Convention shall be: (1) the members of the Board of Directors, and (2) from each District one delegate for every fifty (50) members or major fraction thereof, provided that each District shall be allowed at least one voting delegate in addition to the District President.
(d) Any member of the Association may attend the Convention and all members are encouraged to do so.

Article IV
DUTIES OF OFFICERS
SECTION 1. PRESIDENT. The duties of the President shall be:
(a) to call meetings of the Provincial Association, of the Provincial Executive, and of the Provincial Board of Directors;
(b) to preside at all the above mentioned meetings;
(c) to determine the personnel of the Special and Standing Committees of the Association;
(d) to act on all committees;
(e) to exercise a general supervision over the interest and welfare of the Association;
(f) to represent the Association officially
SECTION 2. VICE-PRESIDENTS. The duties of the Vice-Presidents shall be:
(a) In the event of a vacancy in the office of President, or of his or her inability to perform his or her duties, the ranking Vice-President shall take over the duties of President.
(b) The First Vice-President shall assist the President by acting for him or her when requested.
(c) The Vice-President shall assist other officers.
SECTION 3. SECRETARY.
(a) The duties of the Secretary shall be:
(1) To record all minutes.
(2) To receive, answer and keep all correspondence.
(3) To keep all records.
(4) To countersign all documents executed by the Association.
(5) To receive all money paid to the Association, and to turn some over to the Treasurer within thirty (30) days, taking receipt therefor.
(6) To have the records open at all times to the inspection of the Board of Directors, the Executive and the President.
(7) To keep accurate records of the membership and to be responsible for the proper distribution of Membership Fees.
(8) To submit to the Ontario Teachers' Federation at the end of June each year a written report of the work of the Association during the year. This report will

be presented at the annual meeting of the Board of Governors of the Ontario Teachers' Federation.
(9) To present a report at the Annual Convention and to the Board of Directors when requested.
(b) The Secretary shall give a bond, in an amount fixed by the Board of Directors, for the faithful performance of his or her duties.
SECTION 4. TREASURER.
(a) The duties of the Treasurer shall be:
(1) To receive from the Secretary all funds paid to the Association and to deposit them at such banking institution as may be designated by the Board of Directors.
(2) To issue receipts for all money received.
(3) To sign all cheques, which must be countersigned by the President or the Secretary, the accounts having been duly authorized by the Board of Directors, or by the Executives, or by the President.
(4) To present a report at the Annual Convention and more often if required by the Board of Directors.
(5) To keep the accounts ready for inspection by the Board of Directors, the Executive, the President, and any auditors named by the Board.
(b) The Treasurer shall give a bond, in an amount fixed by the Board of Directors, for the faithful performance of his or her duties.

Article V.
DUTIES OF PROVINCIAL ORGANIZATIONS
SECTION 1. THE PROVINCIAL EXECUTIVE.
The duties of the Provincial Executive shall be:
(a) To carry out the instructions of the Annual Convention.
(b) To deal with all matters which, in its opinion, required action between Annual Conventions, including the drawing up and sending of resolutions to O.T.F. and other bodies.
(c) To arrange and direct all communications and interviews with O.T.F. and the Department of Education.
(d) To consult with O.T.F., the Department of Education and other bodies concerning legislation which affects the schools, the teachers, and courses of studies.
(e) To keep in touch with the conveners of Special and Standing Committees in order to be informed of the progress of these different committees.
(f) To employ assistants in carrying on the work of the Association.
(g) To appoint a Nominating Committee of seven members two months previous to the Annual Convention.
(h) In conjunction with the Relations and Discipline Committee to investigate all professional matters affecting members of the Association and to take such action as may seem advisable. The Executive shall have the power to terminate the membership of any teacher, but the teacher shall have the right to appeal to

the next Annual Convention.
(i) To pay all legitimate expenses incurred in the conduct of authorized Association business.

SECTION 2. THE PROVINCIAL BOARD OF DIRECTORS

The duties of the Board of Directors shall be:
(a) To fix the salary of the Secretary and the Treasurer, if compensated.
(b) To receive reports of the Provincial Executive and of Conveners of committees.
(c) To give direction and advice to the Executive on any matter requiring attention before the next Annual Convention.
(d) To give assistance and advice in preparing the agenda for the Annual Convention.
(e) At its first meeting after the Annual Convention to advise and assist the new Executive in outlining the program for the ensuing year.
(f) To manage and control the affairs and business of the Association and to make all appropriations of its funds, but it shall have no power to incur any indebtedness or obligations in an amount which shall exceed the probable income of the Association in the fiscal period in which such indebtedness or obligation is incurred.
(g) To hold at least two meetings during each calendar year; the first meeting to be held in the Convention City within twenty-four (24) hours following the Annual Convention; the second meeting to be held in the Convention City within twenty-four (24) hours preceding the first session of the following Annual Convention, written notice of which shall be mailed by the Secretary to every Director at least twenty (20) days in advance thereof.
(h) To meet at other times at the call of the President.
(i) To fill vacancies on the Board of Directors, except in the case of District Presidents.
(j) To fill vacancies on the Provincial Executive.
(k) The Board of Directors may transact business by mail, telegraph or telephone. In such event a copy of the resolution or motion to be voted upon shall be sent to every Director, and the vote shall be in writing. A favourable vote of a majority of the Board of Directors received within seven days after forwarding such resolution or motion shall be necessary to the adoption thereof. Within a reasonable time the Secretary shall report the result of the vote to every Director and shall preserve all the ballots unless ordered by the Board of Directors at its next meeting to destroy same.

Article VI.

DISTRICTS

SECTION 1. CREATION OF DISTRICTS

The Board of Directors shall create Districts and shall have authority to change the boundaries thereof subject to the approval of a majority of the members of the District. Such members must be given ninety (90) days' notice of any proposed change after the District has been established.

SECTION 2. DISTRICT EXECUTIVE

(a) The affairs of every District shall be under the immediate control of a District Executive consisting of (1) President, (2) Immediate Past President, (3) Vice-President, (4) Secretary-Treasurer, and (5) not more than three councillors.

(b) Where there is only one Local Association in a District, the Local Executive shall serve as District Executive also and shall be constituted in accordance with Article VII, Section 2.

SECTION 3. DUTIES OF DISTRICT PRESIDENT

(a) Each District President, under the supervision of the Board of Directors, shall promote the interests of the Association within the District.

(b) The District President shall call District Meetings, preside thereat, and plan the program thereof.

(c) The District President shall supervise the compilation of the District budget, and authorize and approve the District expenses.

(d) The District President shall keep the Provincial President and the Provincial Executive informed of District Meetings.

SECTION 4. DUTIES OF DISTRICT VICE-PRESIDENT

(a) The Vice-President shall perform the duties of the President in his or her absence.

(b) He shall assist the other members of the District Executive.

SECTION 5. DUTIES OF DISTRICT SECRETARY-TREASURER

The duties of the District Secretary-Treasurer shall be:

(a) To keep all minutes and records and to answer all correspondence.

(b) To receive and acknowledge all money from Local Secretary-Treasurers.

(c) To keep accounts of all money received and spent.

(d) To forward to the Secretary of the Provincial Association a record of all members in good standing.

(e) To forward all money received for transmission to the Secretary of the Provincial Association.

(f) To forward to Local Secretary-Treasurers the Locals' share of the fees of Regular Members received from the Provincial Secretary.

(g) To sign all cheques for authorized accounts, such cheques to be countersigned by the District President.

(h) To give a detailed annual report, properly audited.

(i) To send to the Provincial Secretary the names of the district delegates to the Annual Convention.

SECTION 6. DUTIES OF DISTRICT EXECUTIVE

The duties of the District Executive shall be:

(a) To promote the interests of the Association within the District.

(b) To report to the Provincial Executive any case of un-professional conduct alleged against any member of the District.

(c) To receive and consider reports of alleged unfairness on the part of any

School Board within the District, or any professional difficulties between members of a staff, and, if necessary, to work with the Provincial Relations and Discipline Committee to secure a settlement.
(d) To refer to the Secretary of the Provincial Association all questions requiring legal advice.
(e) To determine the number of locals required to carry on the work of the District.
(f) To fill vacancies in the membership of the District Executive.
(g) To choose the delegates to the Annual Convention.
SECTION 7. DISTRICT MEETINGS
(a) The annual District Meeting shall be held as soon as possible after the annual meeting of the Local Associations in the District. These local meetings are to be held as soon as possible after the opening of the school year in September. The District meeting should be held at the end of September or early in October.
(b) At this Annual Meeting the election of the District Executive shall take place. Care should be taken to insure that every local is represented on the District Executive.
(c) In the election of the District Executive it has been found that the most satisfactory method is to appoint a Nominating Committee on which all locals are represented. After the Committee has presented its nominations, additional nominations for each office may be made from the floor of the meeting. This method may seem to give the Nominating Committee too much power, but experience has shown that in the long run no other method is as satisfactory.
(d) At the District Meeting those entitled to vote shall be (1) Local Presidents, and (2) from each local one delegate for every twenty (20) members in the local or fraction thereof.
(e) All the members of the different locals are encouraged to attend the District Meetings, and the District Executive should endeavour to have at least three District Meetings each year, one in each term.

Article VII
LOCAL ASSOCIATION
SECTION 1. A local shall consist of the teachers in one or more schools in a District who are members of the Provincial Association.
SECTION 2. The executive of a Local Association shall consist of (1) President, (2) Immediate Past President, (3) First Vice-President, (4) Second Vice-President, (5) Third Vice-President, (6) Secretary-Treasurer, and (7) not more than three councillors.
SECTION 3. If the Local Association is a small one it may elect only one Vice-President and one or two councillors.
SECTION 4. If the Local Association is a large one, a Recording Secretary, a Corresponding Secretary and a Treasurer may be appointed.
SECTION 5. The Local Executive shall be elected at the Annual Meeting of the Local Association. This meeting shall take place as soon as possible after the

opening of the school year in September.
SECTION 6. The Duties of the Local Executive shall be:
(a) To promote the interests of the Provincial Association within the local.
(b) To make provision for the Annual Meeting of the Local Association and for such other meetings as may be deemed advisable.
(c) To discuss matters of interest to members of the Local Association and to forward to the District Executive such recommendations as may be deemed advisable.
(d) To prepare the annual budget of the Local Association.
SECTION 7. The local Secretary-Treasurer shall collect the fees of all Associate Members and of all Regular Members in private schools, and shall forward same to the Secretary-Treasurer of the District. He or she shall pay all authorized accounts and shall prepare and present a properly audited annual report.
SECTION 8. The delegates to the Annual District Meeting and to the Annual Provincial Convention shall be elected at the last regular meeting of the Local Association prior to the Annual District Meeting and the Annual Provincial Convention respectively. Local Associations may send delegates to the Annual Provincial Convention, it being understood that only District delegates may vote at the Convention.

Article VIII
COMMITTEES
SECTION 1. Upon election to office the President shall appoint, subject to the approval of the Board of Directors, the following standing Committees:
(a) budget
(b) Educational Finance
(c) Educational Research and Policies
(d) Legislation
(e) Publicity and Education Week
(f) Relations and Discipline
(g) Superannuation
(h) Lay Teachers
(i) Religious Teachers
(j) Programme
SECTION 2. The President shall also appoint such special Committees as may from time to time appear necessary.
SECTION 3. DUTIES OF COMMITTEES
(a) BUDGET COMMITTEE. The Budget Committee shall prepare a budget for the ensuing year and submit it to the Board of Directors. It shall devise plans for raising the money necessary to promote the aims and objectives of the Association. The Budget Committee shall, at least once a year immediately preceding the Annual Convention, provide for an audit of the books of the Association and shall report at the Annual Convention. The Provincial

Treasurer shall be ex-officio a member of the Budget Committee.
(b) EDUCATIONAL FINANCE COMMITTEE. The Educational Finance shall study such matters as Teachers' Salaries, Legislative grants to School Boards, and all matters connected with educational finance.
(c) EDUCATIONAL RESEARCH AND POLICIES. The Educational Research and Policies Committee shall study improvements in various educational fields, and in matters having direct or indirect bearing theron. The following matters shall come within the scope of the Committee: Health, curriculum, vocational guidance, adult education, post-war problems, Catholic Literature, co-operation between the home and the school, credit unions, etc. The members of this Committee shall be chairmen of sub-committees each of which shall make itself responsible for an intensive study of one or more of the above-mentioned subjects. The chairmen of the sub-committees are urged to choose as members of their sub-committees teachers who are members of their District in order to encourage and facilitate frequent meetings. The Committee shall work in close co-operation with the Educational Research and Policies Committee of the Ontario Teachers' Federation.
(d) LEGISLATION COMMITTEE. The Legislation Committee shall study and report on all matters that may require Legislative action. It shall be responsible for proposing amendments to the Constitutions. It shall receive recommendations from members of the Provincial Association, and the convener of the Committee shall be responsible for bringing such recommendations to the notice of the President and the Executive so that they may be referred to the Ontario Teachers' Federation.
(e) PUBLICITY AND EDUCATION WEEK. The Publicity and Education Week Committee shall be responsible for informing the public of the ideals, aims, purposes and accomplishments of the Association. It shall co-operate with other Teachers' organizations in organizing the Education Week program each year.
(f) RELATIONS AND DISCIPLINE COMMITTEE. The Relations and Discipline Committee shall deal with matters of relations, unprofessional conduct and discipline referred to it by the Provincial Executive or by a District Executive. Matters which the Relations and Discipline Committee not settle shall be referred to the Relations and Discipline Committee of the Ontario Teachers' Federation. Members of this Committee shall familiarize themselves with any conduct which could be termed unprofessional and shall make a special study of those sections of the Regulations made under the *Teaching Profession Act* of 1944 which refer to unprofessional conduct.
(g) SUPERANNUATION COMMITTEE. The Superannuation Committee shall deal with all matters connected with superannuation, pensions, sick benefits, etc.
(h) LAY TEACHERS' COMMITTEE. The Lay Teachers' Committee shall recommend action upon matters affecting their status and devise and execute plans for the improvement of their legal, economic, political and professional status. In matters that require Legislative action the Committee shall make its recommendations to the Legislation Committee.

(i) RELIGIOUS TEACHERS' COMMITTEE. The Religious Teachers' Committee shall study all matters that affect the legal, political, economic and professional status of Religious Teachers and shall make such recommendations as it deems advisable to the Executive or to the Legislation Committee.
(j) NOMINATING COMMITTEE. The Nominating Committee shall consist of seven members and shall be appointed by the President, with the approval of the Board of Directors, two months before the Annual Convention nominations for the different offices for the ensuing year. No member's name shall be placed on the list of nominations unless the said member has signified his or her intention of accepting office if elected. At the Annual Convention when the Committee presents its report, the President shall afford an opportunity for further nominations to be made. If an election for an office is necessary it shall be held during the Annual Convention and shall be by ballot. Election shall be by majority vote.
(k) PROGRAMME COMMITTEE. The Programme Committee shall be responsible for making the arrangements for the Annual Convention, meetings of the Board of Directors, and for such other meetings as may be called by the President. The Convener of this Committee should reside in or near the Convention City.
SECTION 4. The Conveners of standing Committees shall be members of the corresponding standing Committees of the Ontario Teachers' Federation.
SECTION 5. Whenever possible the members of the different standing Committees shall be members of the same district or of adjoining districts in order that frequent meetings of the Committees may be encouraged and facilitated.
SECTION 6. Whenever possible Conveners of Committees should sent their reports to the Provincial Secretary so that copies may be sent to the Members of the Board of Directors and to delegates previous to the Annual Convention.

Article IX
MEETINGS
SECTION 1. The annual meeting of this Association shall be held during Easter Week in the City of Toronto, Ontario, or such other place designated at the previous annual meeting.
SECTION 2. The regular meetings of the Board of Directors shall be held as prescribed in Article V, SECTION 2 (g).
SECTION 3. Seven members of the Board of Directors shall constitute a quorum.
SECTION 4. Special meetings of the Board of Directors shall be called by the President whenever necessary.
SECTION 5. Meetings of the Executive shall be called by the President from time to time. At such meetings of the executive four members shall constitute a quorum.
SECTION 6. Regular meetings of the Standing committees shall be held whenever the Conveners deem them necessary.

Article X
METHOD OF VOTING
SECTION 1. The business of this Association shall be transacted by viva voce vote except in the case of election of Officers, which shall be by ballot.
SECTION 2. The Board of Directors and the Executive may determine the method of voting at their meetings.

Article XI
FINANCES
SECTION 1. The Fiscal year of this Association shall be from August 1st to July 31st.
SECTION 2. All funds shall be deposited by the Treasurer in some Bank designated by the Board of Directors.
SECTION 3. All Bills shall be paid by cheque signed by the Treasurer and countersigned by the President or Secretary.
SECTION 4. The expenses of the members of the Board of Directors, except the District Presidents, in attending the Annual Convention or the meetings of the Board shall be paid by the Treasurer out of the general funds upon presentation of the proper vouchers.
SECTION 5. The expenses of District Presidents and of official District delegates in attending the Annual Convention and of District Presidents in attending meetings of the Board of Directors shall be pooled. The share per District of the total expenses in attending the Annual Convention shall be the total number of delegates from the District, including the District President, over the total number of delegates from all the Districts, including the District Presidents, multiplied by the total of coach fares. The same method shall be followed in calculating each District President's share of the total expenses incurred in attending a meeting of the Board of Directors.
SECTION 6. Where the actual coach fares paid by the President and official delegates from a District exceed that District's share of the total expenses, the Provincial Treasurer shall pay the difference to the District
SECTION 7. Where the District's share of the total expenses exceeds the actual coach fares paid by the District President and the official delegates from the District, the District shall pay the difference to the Provincial Treasurer.
SECTION 8. The Treasurer, before paying out any amounts to the Districts, shall make certain that the amounts paid to him by the different Districts correspond with the amounts to be paid out to other Districts.
SECTION 9. The expenses of the members of the Executive in attending meetings of the Executive shall be paid by the Treasurer out of the general funds upon presentation of proper vouchers.
SECTION 10. The accounts of the Association shall be audited once a year by a certified accountant or other qualified person.

Article XII
FEES
SECTION 1. The annual membership fee shall be:
(a) For Regular Members in Separate Schools:
Salaries up to $800.......................... $5.00
Salaries from $801 up to $1,099............. $6.00
Salaries from $1,100 up to 1,599............ $7.00
Salaries from $1,600 up to 1,999............ $8.00
Salaries from $2,000 and upwards............ $9.00
(b) For Regular members in private schools......... $3.00
(c) For Associate Members who are active members of other Teachers' Organizations affiliated with O.T.F. $1.00
(d) For all other Associate Members $2.00
SECTION 2. The fees of Regular Members in Separate Schools shall be deducted by the Secretary of the School Board and shall be forwarded to the Secretary of O.T.F. A portion of each fee is deducted by O.T.F. and the remainder will be forwarded to the Secretary of this Association.
SECTION 3. The fees of all Associate Members and of Regular Members in private schools shall be collected by the local Secretary-Treasurer before December 31st each year. The O.T.F. portion of the fees of Regular Members in private schools shall be forwarded by the Provincial Secretary to the Secretary of O.T.F. before March 31st each year.
SECTION 4. The division of each fee shall be sixty per cent (60%) to the Treasurer of the Provincial Association and forty per cent (40%) to the Treasurer of the District Association, it being understood that O.T.F. shall retain a portion of the fees of all Regular Members, and that the above-mentioned division takes place after O.T.F. has retained or received its portion of the fees of all Regular Members, including those in private schools.
SECTION 5. In each District a portion of the fees shall be forwarded to the Local Treasurer, the portion to be decided in each District at the Annual District Conference.
SECTION 6. Provided that such action is approved by a two-thirds vote of the Annual Convention, special assessments may be levied.

Article XIII
AMENDMENTS
SECTION 1. The Constitution may be amended by a nine-tenths vote of the delegates present at the Annual Provincial Convention and qualified to vote thereat provided that notice of such proposed amendment shall have been sent to each member at least ten (10) days before the Convention.
SECTION 2. The by-laws may be amended
(a) by a two-thirds vote of the delegates present at the Annual Provincial Convention and qualified to vote therat provided that notice of such proposed amendment shall have been sent to each member at least ten (10) days before the Convention;

(b) by unanimous vote of the delegates present at the Annual Provincial Convention and qualified to vote thereat, previous notice not having been given.

The rules of Canadian Parliamentary procedure shall govern the proceedings of this Association subject to the special rules which have been or may be adopted.

APPENDIX B

The OECTA Units and Service Departments

Units

Atikokan
Brant
Brock Secondary
Bruce-Grey
Carleton
Dryden,Sioux Lookout
Dufferin-Peel Elementary
Dufferin-Peel Secondary
Durham
Durham Secondary
Elgin
Essex
Essex Secondary
Fort Frances, Rainy River
Frontenac, Lennox & Addington
Geraldton, Longlac
Haldimand-Norfolk
Halton Elementary
Halton Secondary
Hamilton Secondary
Hamilton-Wentworth
Hastings-Prince Edward
Hornepayne-Michipicoten
Huron-Perth Elementary
Huron-Perth Secondary
Kenora
Kent
Lambton Elementary
Lambton Secondary
Lanark, Leeds & Grenville
Lincoln
London-Middlesex
Metro Toronto Elementary
Moosonee
Niagara Secondary
Nipissing
North Shore
North of Superior
Ottawa
Oxford
Peterborough, Victoria,
Northumberland, Newcastle
Red Lake
Renfrew
St.Michael's C.S.A.
Sault Ste. Marie
Simcoe
Stormont, Dundas & Glengarry
Sudbury Elementary
Sudbury Secondary
Thunder Bay Elementary
Thunder Bay Secondary
Timiskaming
Timmins
Toronto Secondary
Waterloo
Welland
Wellington
Windsor Elementary
Windsor Secondary
York

Central Office

Library. Established to serve the information needs of the provincial executive and provincial office, the OECTA library provides information and research support in the wide range of educational, religious, and political issues with which the Association is concerned. The Association's collection of some 150 periodicals and 3500 books and documents provides a core source of information that is supplemented by the use of a number of libraries and information sources in Toronto. The library provides assistance to unit presidents in many areas such as grievances, collective negotiations, and professional development, especially in those areas where resources are not available locally.

Susan Williams directs the library and OECTA's library research programme. After graduating from Trent University (B.A., history), Susan worked at the Unemployment Insurance Commission and at Trent as an admissions officer, then went to the University of Toronto Faculty of Education. She taught all grades for the Scarborough Board of Education at Knob Hill Junior, Tecumseh Senior, and Agnes McPhail public schools. Susan then specialized, acquiring an M.Ed. at OISE (history and philosophy) and an M.L.S. at the University of Toronto. Thus, she is well qualified to provide research and library services for the Association.

Communications. This department's history goes back to the beginning of OECTA. There has always been a periodical for educational and news articles, first called the OECTA Review, now the Reporter. Supplementing these magazines were newspapers, the OECTA News and Views, now Agenda. In addition, the Teacher Welfare department puts out a TW Bulletin.. There have been a number of editors: first, Marion Tyrrell, then Mary Babcock, performing the task along with all their other duties; then two MSSB principals in succession, Gerry Levert and Paul Wharton. Eventually, OECTA hired and assigned a person full-time for the job: Pat O'Neill, then Cy Jamison.

Currently, Aleda O'Connor is the director of the Communications Department, and Patricia McKeown is her assistant.

Aleda O'Connor came to OECTA with 10 years' experience in communications that included working as a reporter with the Kingston Whig Standard, news editor of the Picton Gazette, and as a contributor to a number of regional weekly papers and radio stations. She was a public relations consultant for a number of community organizations, producer for community television, and co-founder of a Prince Edward County community magazine, before freelancing as a writer and editor in Toronto.

Aleda joined OECTA as a part-time communications assistant to Cy Jamison in 1981. She became acting communications director in 1984 when Jamison took a sabbatical, assuming the position permanently the following year. One of her first major projects on behalf of OECTA was the public relations campaign following William Davis's 1984 announcement of full funding for separate schools. During her time as director, the Reporter has received awards for excellence in editing, writing and design from the Educational Press Association of America. She also coordinated the selection of the new Catholic Teachers wordmark and blue and white visual identity programme.

Patricia McKeown replaced Vida Zalnieriunas as Aleda's assistant.

Prior to joining OECTA's Communications Department, Pat served with the CBC in the Ottawa Parliamentary Press Gallery, broadcasting in English and French to the United States, Europe, Africa, and the Caribbean. She then became a producer with the CBC shows, "As It Happens" and "Gabereau".

The Communications Department is responsible for all aspects of the implementation of the communications and public relations programme of the Association, providing research, writing and editorial support, design, format, and print consultation services; media relations and crisis communication; and guidance for a wide range of special public relations projects both print and broadcast. This department provides a wide range of communication services to the provincial office, and the executive, and advice to the unit presidents — everything from advocacy advertising in response to the Social Contract and strikes, to editorial services for briefs, scripts for videos, and management of the Association's visual identity programme.

The communications staff, with the support of a graphic designer and a format artist, writes, edits, and produces the Association's monthly news tabloid, Agenda and OECTA's magazine the Reporter as well as Communications, a newsletter sent to unit communication officers, Occasional Teacher, a newsletter sent to occasional teachers, and numerous other special Association handbooks, brochures, print and other media projects.

Computer Systems/Services. The Computing Services Department manages the computer resources of the Association. Computers are used in all aspects of OECTA's business. One of the most vital areas is administrative finance, where the budgeting, general ledger and purchasing are done on computer.

A database with information on each OECTA full-time, part-time, and occasional member is maintained and updated by Computing Services in cooperation with other departments. Membership data include Religious Education course-completion credits, maintained for the Ministry of Education and Training. Statistical and database programmes are used to support OECTA's collective bargaining activities.

Computing technology is being used more and more by OECTA for distribution and sharing of information. A computerized bulletin board system is used almost daily by the provincial office to distribute information to OECTA units. Also, an electronic mail system is used by the Units and staff for correspondence, either one to one or one to many.

In 1988 the provincial office set up a programme of financial assistance for regional unit offices to help them buy personal computers for office use. By 1992 all offices had computers and subsequently, the role of computers in the day-to-day business of the organization increased.

At the provincial office a powerful mini-computer serves as hub to personal computers used by support staff for office automation. This also is the bridge to the computers at unit offices, where they are accessed via modem. It supports all administrative finance, membership, and collective bargaining systems. A staff of three, with the help of computer science and cooperative students, keep things running.

Jack Pledger has managed the department since 1991. Jack's initial involvement with OECTA was on a contract basis, where he worked with Rebus consultants to improve OECTA computerized systems to support collective bargaining. Jack has over twenty years' experience in the computer field. He has worked with the Ministry of Colleges and Universities, where he held the position of Information Technology Coordinator and with OISE for eight years as Computing Services Administrator. Jack is assisted by a programmer analyst and a computer systems assistant.

It has been little more than a decade since OECTA acquired its first computer, and now it would be hard to imagine the organization functioning without computers.

Accounting. This Department headed by David Fernandes, comptroller, assisted by senior bookkeeper Kay McBride and four others, records income and expenses, issues payments as approved by fund managers and banking, administers strike cheques, tracks the budget as approved by the Council of Presidents, and informs the Executive of any overexpenditures.

David Fernandes was born in Karachi, Pakistan, the son of Joseph Fernandes, a manager for Pan American Airways and Blanske Faliero, a homemaker, and brother of Raymond, Ramona, Rebecca, Raulina, and Rollanda. He was educated at St. Philomena elementary school, St. Paul's High School, and St. Patrick's College in its business department. After arriving in Canada as a landed immigrant, David went to St. Michael's College School, Toronto, for grades twelve and thirteen, then to Ryerson Polytechnical Institute for business, accounting, and finance. As an accountant he spent seven years in industry, then five years with the Catholic Charities of the Archdiocese of Toronto. He was interviewed and was short-listed for his present position of comptroller by the OECTA auditor.

David has administered a number of changes in the Accounting Department. Working with the treasurers Noella Mulligan, Claire Ross, and Jim Smith and with the Finance and Ad Hoc Budget Committees, he has expanded the Department to five bookkeepers, set up a computerized system, changed the method of investing the reserve fund, helped move the budget from a deficit to a balanced budget, and implemented the change from line to block budgeting.

David is in his fourth year in a CMA programme.

Administration - Human Resources. The Administration Department is a dynamic and busy department. Proactive in its ongoing and extensive research into the most economic and efficient methodology and technology. With an operating budget of 3/4 of a million dollars, Administration has the responsibility of hiring, training, supervising members of the thirty support staff; providing every aspect of human resource management; and monitoring provincial and federal legislation related to employment, equity and collective bargaining. The department maintains close contact with all departments regarding staffing and the coordination of conferences and business meetings. Recommendations are submitted for the most suitable facilities for AGM, COP, large conferences, small workshops, and summer workshops. Administration also has the responsibility for office maintenance, inventory control, and the monitoring and processing of all purchase requisitions and purchase orders.

Davina Moore, office manager and Susan Weaver, assistant office manager oversee all administrative operations.

APPENDIX C

OECTA Executives, Awards of Merit, Life and Honorary Memberships 1944–1994

Provincial Executives

1944	
Miss Margaret Lynch	President
1945	
Mother Marie Therese	First Vice-President
Mr. Frank J. McElligott	Second Vice-President
Brother Stanislaus	Third Vice-President
Miss Margaret Lynch	Past President
1946	
Rev. B.W. Harrigan	President
Mr. R.J. Bergin	First Vice-President
Mrs. M. Weller	Second Vice-President
Sister St. Gabriel	Third Vice-President
Miss Mary Prunty	Treasurer
Rev. B.W. Harrigan	Past President
1947	
Mr. R.J. Bergin	President
Rev. Brother Thaddeus	First Vice-President
Sister Mary Rose	Second Vice-President
Mrs. E. O'Connell	Third Vice-President
Mr. T.J. Fitzmaurice	Treasurer
Rev. B.W. Harrigan	Past President
1948	
Mr. R.J. Bergin	President
Rev. Brother Thaddeus	First Vice-President
Sister Mary Rose	Second Vice-President
Mrs. J.J. O'Connell	Third Vice-President
Mr. T.J. Fitzmaurice	Treasurer
Rev. B.W. Harrigan	President
1949	
Rev. Brother Thaddeus	President
Miss Dorothea McDonnell	First Vice-President
Sister M. Alicia, C.S.J.	Second Vice-President
Miss Margaret Lynch	Third Vice-President
Mr. T.J. Fitzmaurice	Treasurer

Rev. Brother Thaddeus	Past President
1950	
Miss Dorothea McDonnell	President
Mr. Patrick Perdue	First Vice-President
Sister M. Alicia, C.S.J.	Second Vice-President
Miss Elizabeth MacDonald	Third Vice-President
Mr. T.J. Fitzmaurice	Treasurer
Miss Dorothea McDonell	Past President
1951	
Mr. Patrick Perdue	President
Sister Mary Lenore, S.P.	First Vice-President
Miss Anne Moser	Second Vice-President
Miss Margaret Drago	Third Vice-President
Mr. T.J. Fitzmaurice	Treasurer
Mr. Patrick Perdue	Past President
1952	
Sister Mary Lenore, S.P.	President
Miss Dorothea McDonell	First Vice-President
Miss Margaret Drago	Second Vice-President
Miss Hilda Brown	Third Vice-President
Mr. T.J. Fitzmaurice	Treasurer
Mr. Patrick Perdue	Past President
1953	
Sister Mary Lenore, S.P.	President
Miss Margaret Drago	First Vice-President
Rev. C.L. Siegfried, C.R.	Second Vice-President
Rev. Brother Maurice, F.S.C.	Third Vice-President
Mr. T.J. Fitzmaurice	Treasurer
Sister Mary Lenore, S.P.	Past President
1954	
Miss Margaret Drago	President
Rev. C.L. Siegfried, C.R.	First Vice-President
Rev. Brother Maurice, F.S.C.	Second Vice-President
Mr. Austin O'Leary	Third Vice-President
Mr. T.J. Fitzmaurice	Treasurer
Sister Mary Lenore, S.P.	Past President
1955	
Miss Margaret Drago	President
Rev. C.L. Siegfried, C.R.	First Vice-President
Miss Mary Flynn	Second Vice-President
Mr. Orlando Sicoly	Third Vice-President
Mr. T.J. Fitzmaurice	Treasurer
Miss Margaret Drago	Past President

1956	
Rev. C.L. Siegfried, C.R.	President
Miss Mary Flynn	First Vice-President
Sister M. Vincentia, C.S.J.	Second Vice-President
Mr. Joseph Stefani	Third Vice-President
Mr. T.J. Fitzmaurice	Treasurer
Miss Dorothea McDonell	Councillor
Rev. C.L. Siegried, C.R.	Past President
1957	
Miss Mary Flynn	President
Sister M. Vincentia, C.S.J.	First Vice-President
Mr. Joseph Stefani	Second Vice-President
Miss Virginia Mercurio	Third Vice-President
Mr. F.T. Fitzmaurice	Treasurer
Miss Mary Flynn, C.S.J.	Past President
1958	
Sister Mary Vincentia, C.S.J.	President
Rev. J.H. Conway, O.M.I.	First Vice-President
Mr. Blaise Healey	Second Vice-President
Miss Madeline Scissons	Third Vice-President
Miss Mary Flynn	Past President
1959	
Sister Mary Vincentia, C.S.J.	President
Rev. J.H. Conway, O.M.I.	First Vice-President
Mr. Blaise Healey	Second Vice-President
Miss Madeline Scissons	Third Vice-President
Miss Margaret Drago	Past President
1960	
Sister Mary Vincentia, C.S.J.	President
Rev. J.H. Conway, O.M.I.	First Vice-President
Mr. Patrick F. O'Leary	Second Vice-President
Sister Mary Aloysia, S.S.N.D.	Third Vice-President
Mr. T.J. Fitzmaurice	Treasurer
Sister Mary Vincentia, C.S.J.	Past President
1961	
Rev. J.H. Conway, O.M.I.	President
Mr. Patrick F. O'Leary	First Vice-President
Miss Veronica Houlahan	Second Vice-President
Sister Alice Marie C.S.J.	Third Vice-President
Miss Rose Cassin	Treasurer
Miss Margaret Drago	Councillor
Miss Margaret Lynch	Councillor
Sister M. Vincentia, C.S.J.	Past President

1962	
Rev. J.H. Conway, O.M.I.	President
Mr. Patrick O'Leary	First Vice-President
Miss Veronica Houlahan	Second Vice-President
Sister Alice Marie, C.S.J.	Third Vice-President
Miss Rose Cassin	Treasurer
Miss Margaret Drago	Councillor
Sister Mary Aloysia, S.S.N.D.	Councillor
Rev. J.H. Conway, O.M.I.	Past President
1963	
Mr. Patrick O'Leary	President
Miss Veronica Houlahan	First Vice-President
Miss Rose Cassin	Second Vice-President
Sister M. St. Boniface, C.S.J.	Third Vice-President
Mrs. Irene Pantaleo	Treasurer
Miss Margaret Drago	Councillor
Sister Mary Aloysia, S.S.N.D.	Councillor
Mr. Patrick O'Leary	Past President
1964	
Miss Veronica Houlahan	President
Sister St. John of Valencia, C.N.D.	First Vice-President
Miss Helen Sullivan	Second Vice-President
Mr. Karul Bohren	Third Vice-President
Mrs. Irene Pantaleo	Treasurer
Sister Mary Aloysia, S.S.N.D.	Councillor
Miss Veronica Houlahan	Past President
1965	
Sister St. John of Valencia, C.N.D.	President
Mr. Karl Bohren	First Vice-President
Sister Mary Aloysia, S.S.N.D.	Second Vice-President
Miss Ruth Willis	Third Vice-President
Miss Rose Cassin	Treasurer
Rev. J.H. Conway O.M.I.	Councillor
Mr. Patrick O'Leary	Councillor
Sister St. John of Valencia, C.N.D.	Past President
1966	
Mr. Karl Bohren	President
Sister Mary Aloysia, S.S.N.D.	First Vice-President
Miss Ruth Willis	Second Vice-President
Mrs. Marie Arthurs	Third Vice-PresidentMrs. Mary
Michell	Treasurer
Rev. J.H. Conway, O.M.I.	Councillor
Mr. Patrick O'Leary	Councillor
Mr. John Rodrigues	Councillor

Mr. Karl Bohren	Past President
1967	
Sister Mary Aloysia, S.S.N.D.	President
Miss Ruth Willis	First Vice-President
Mr. John Rodrigues	Second Vice-President
Mr. John Kuchinak	Third Vice-President
Mrs. Marie Kennedy	Treasurer
Rev. J.H. Conway, O.M.I.	Councillor
Mr. Patrick O'Leary	Councillor
Sister Mary Aloysia, S.S.N.D.	Past President
1968	
Miss Ruth Willis	President
Mr. John Rodrigues	First Vice-President
Mr. John Kuchinak	Second Vice-President
Rev. F.C. Malone, C.S.B.	Third Vice-President
Mrs. Marie Kennedy	Treasurer
Mr. Patrick O'Leary	Councillor
Mr. Karl Bohren	Councillor
Miss Ruth Willis	Past President
1969	
Mr. John Rodrigues	President
Mr. John Kuchinak	First Vice-President
Rev. F.C. Malone, C.S.B.	Second Vice-President
Mrs. Marie Kennedy	Third Vice-President
Mr. Patrick O'Neill	Treasurer
Mr. Karl Bohren	Councillor
Sister Mary Aloysia, S.S.N.D.	Councillor
Mr. John Rodrigues	Past President
1970	
Mr. John Kuchinak	President
Mrs. Marie Kennedy	First Vice-President
Rev. J.F. Kavanagh	Second Vice-President
Mr. James Carey	Third Vice-President
Mr. Peter Gazzola	Treasurer
Miss Ruth M. Willis	Councillor
Sister St. Boniface	Councillor
Mr. John Kuchinak	Past President
1971	
Mrs. Marie Kennedy	President
Rev. J.F. Kavanagh	First Vice-President
Mr. James Carey	Second Vice-President
Mr. John MacDonald	Third Vice-President
Mr. Peter Gazzola	Treasurer
Mrs. Marie Arthurs	Councillor

Mrs. Marie Kennedy	Past President
1972	
Rev. J.F. Kavanagh	President
Mr. James Carey	First Vice-President
Mr. John MacDonald	Second Vice-President
Mr. Robert Cooney	Third Vice-President
Mr. Peter Gazzola	Treasurer
Mrs. Marie Arthurs	Councillor
Mr. Leo Normandeau	Councillor
Rev. J.F. Kavanagh	Past President
1973	
Mr. James Carey	President
Mr. Robert Cooney	First Vice-President
Mr. Leo Normandeau	Second Vice-President
Mr. Brian Boucher	Third Vice-President
Mr. Peter Gazzola	Treasurer
Mrs. Marie Arthurs	Councillor
Mrs. Marie Kennedy	Councillor
Mr. James Carey	Past President
1974	
Mr. Robert Cooney	President
Mr. Leo Normandeau	First Vice-President
Mr. Derry Byrne	Second Vice-President
Mr. Peter Gazzola	Third Vice-President
Mr. George Saranchuk	Treasurer
Mrs. Marie Arthurs	Councillor
Mrs. Marie Kennedy	Councillor
Mr. Robert Cooney	Past President
1975	
Mr. Leo Normandeau	President
Mr. Derry Byrne	First Vice-President
Mr. John Brown	Second Vice-President
Mr. Bill Eckert	Third Vice-President
Mr. George Saranchuk	Treasurer
Mr. John MacDonald	Councillor
Mr. Tony Hunt	Councillor
Mr. Leo Normandeau	Past President
1976	
Mr. Derry Byrne	President
Mr. Peter Gazzola	First Vice-President
Mr. Anthony Hunt	Second Vice-President
Miss Doreen Brady	Third Vice-President
Mr. Paul Kelly	Treasurer
Mr. George Saranchuk	Councillor

Mr. Roland Laforet	Councillor
Mr. James Carey	Past President
1977	
Mr. Derry Byrne	President
Mr. Peter Gazzola	First Vice-President
Miss Doreen Brady	Second Vice-President
Mr. Roland Laforet	Third Vice-President
Mr. Paul Kelly	Treasurer
Mr. George Saranchuk	Councillor
Mr. Ron Smith	Councillor
Mr. Derry Byrne	Past President
1978	
Mr. Peter Gazzola	President
Miss Doreen Brady	First Vice-President
Mr. Roland Laforet	Second Vice-President
Mr. John Quinn	Third Vice-President
Mr. Don Soulliere	Treasurer
Mr. George Saranchuk	Counsellor
Mr. James Carey	OTF Executive Member
Mr. Peter Gazzola	Past President
1979	
Miss Doreen Brady	President
Mr. Roland Laforet	First Vice-President
Mr. George Saranchuk	Second Vice-President
Mr. Grant Webber	Third Vice-President
Mr. Don Soulliere	Treasurer
Mr. David MacDonald	Councillor
Mr. Mike McGinnis	Councillor
Mr. James Carey	OTF Executive Member
Mr. Peter Gazzola	Past President
1980	
Miss Doreen Brady	President
Mr. George Saranchuk	First Vice-President
Mr. Grant Webber	Second Vice-President
Ms. Beryl McNeil	Third Vice-President
Mr. Pascal LaRouche	Treasurer
Mr. Derry Byrne	Councillor
Mr. Mike McGinnis	Councillor
Mr. Fred Sweeney	OTF Executive Member
Miss Doreen Brady	Past President
1981	
Mr. George Saranchuk	President
Mr. Kevin Kennedy	First Vice-President
Ms. Vikki Hannah	Second Vice-President

Mr. Joe Ryan	Third Vice-President
Mr. Pascal LaRouche	Treasurer
Mr. Mike McGinnis	Councillor
Mr. John Fauteux	Councillor
Mr. Fred Sweeney	OTF Executive Member
Mr. George Saranchuk	Past President
1982	
Mr. Kevin Kennedy	First Vice-President
Mr. John Fauteux	Second Vice-President
Mr. Joe Rapai	Third Vice-President
Mr. Mike Donovan	Treasurer
Mr. Robert Boyle	Councillor
Mr. Colm Harty	Councillor
Mr. Fred Sweeney	OTF Executive Member
Mr. George Saranchuk	Past President
1983	
Mr. Kevin Kennedy	President
Mr. John Fauteux	First Vice-President
Mr. Joseph Rapai	Second Vice-President
Ms. Suzann Jones	Third Vice-President
Mr. Mike Donovan	Treasurer
Mr. Bob Boyle	Councillor
Mr. Dan Shea	Councillor
Mr. Fred Sweeney	OTF Executive Member
Mr. George Saranchuk	Past President
1984	
Mr. Kevin Kennedy	President
Mr. John Fauteux	First Vice-President
Mr. James Cooney	Second Vice-President
Ms. Suzann Jones	Third Vice-President
Mr. Mike Donovan	Treasurer
Mr. Bob Boyle	Councillor
Ms. Eileen Lennon	Councillor
Mr. Fred Sweeney	OTF Executive Member
Mr. Kevin Kennedy	Past President
1985	
Mr. John Fauteux	President
Mr. Michael Donovan	First Vice-President
Ms. Suzann Jones	Second Vice-President
Mr. Colm Harty	Third Vice-President
Ms. Noella Mulligan	Treasurer
Ms. Eileen Lennon	Councillor
Ms. Susan LaRosa	Councillor
Mr. Kevin Kennedy	OTF Executive Member

Mr. Kevin Kennedy	Past President
1986	
Mr. John Fauteux	President
Mr. James Cooney	First Vice-President
Mr. Colm Harty	Second Vice-President
Ms. Eileen Lennon	Third Vice-President
Ms. Noella Mulligan	Treasurer
Mr. Susan LaRosa	Councillor
Mr. Joseph Ravesi	Councillor
Mr. John Fauteux	Past President
1987	
Mr. James Cooney	President
Ms. Susan LaRosa	First Vice-President
Ms. Eileen Lennon	Second Vice-President
Mr. Michael Coté	Third Vice-President
Ms. Noella Mulligan	Treasurer
Mr. Joseph Ravesi	Councillor
Mr. Michael Haugh	Councillor
Mr. Jeff Heximer	OTF Executive Member
Mr. John Fauteux	Past President
1988	
Mr. James Cooney	President
Ms. Eileen Lennon	First Vice-President
Mr. Edward Chudak	Second Vice-President
Mr. Michael Haugh	Third Vice-President
Ms. Noella Mulligan	Treasurer
Mr. Michael Coté	Councillor
Sister Anna Clare	Councillor
Mr. Jeff Heximer	OTF Executive Member
Mr. James Cooney	Past President
1989	
Ms. Eileen Lennon	President
Mr. Michael Coté	First Vice-President
Mr. Michael Haugh	Second Vice-President
Sister Anna Clare	Third Vice-President
Ms. Claire Ross	Treasurer
Ms. Helen Biales	Councillor
Mr. Emile Timmermans	Councillor
Ms. Suzann Jones	OTF Executive Member
Mr. James Cooney	Past President
1990	
Ms. Eileen Lennon	President
Mr. Michael Coté	First Vice-President
Mr. Michael Haugh	Second Vice-President

Ms. Helen Biales	Third Vice President
Mr. Claire Ross	Treasurer
Ms. Karen Kirk	Councillor
Mr. Danny Shea	Councillor
Ms. Suzann Jones	OTF Executive Member
Ms. Eileen Lennon	Past President
1991	
Mr. Michael Coté	President
Mr. Michael Haugh	First Vice-President
Ms. Helen Biales	Second Vice-President
Mr. Danny Shea	Third Vice-President
Mr. Claire Ross	Treasurer
Ms. Karen Kirk	Councillor
Ms. Cathy Beaudette	Councillor
Mr. Horst Schweinbenz	OTF Executive Member
Ms. Eileen Lennon	Past President
1992	
Mr. Michael Coté	President
Ms. Helen Biales	First Vice-President
Ms. Claire Ross	Second Vice-President
Ms. Karen Kirk	Third Vice-President
Mr. James Smith	Treasurer
Ms. Cathy Beaudette	Councillor
Ms. Marilies Rettig	Councillor
Mr. Horst Schweinbenz	OTF Executive Member
Mr. Michael Coté	Past President
1993	
Ms. Helen Biales	President
Ms. Claire Ross	First Vice-President
Ms. Cathy Beaudette	Second Vice-President
Ms. Marilies Rettig	Third Vice-President
Mr. James Smith	Treasurer
Mr. Marshall Jarvis	Councillor
Ms. Kathy McVean	Councillor
Mr. Horst Schweinbenz	OTF Executive Member
Ms. Helen Biales	Past President
1994	
Mr. Claire Ross	President
Ms. Marilies Rettig	First Vice-President
Mr. Marshall Jarvis	Second Vice-President
Ms. Kathy McVean	Third Vice-President
Mr. James Smith	Treasurer
Mr. Brian Morrissey	Councillor
Mr. Pearse Shannon	Councillor
Mr. Horst Schweinbenz	OTF Executive Member

Life Memberships

1958 Very Reverend L.K. Poupore, O.M.I.*
Miss Cecilia Rowan*
1963 Miss Alicia Martin*
Mother Mary Lenore, S.P.*
1966 Mother Mary Lenore, S.P.*
Reverend E.C. Garvey, C.S.B.*
Very Reverend C.L. Siegfried, C.R.*
1967 Miss Marion Tyrrell *
1968 Miss Veronica Houlahan*
Miss Anne Moser *
1969 Miss Margaret Lynch*
1970 Miss Mary Lehane
1971 Mrs. Philomena Bulger*
Mr. Francis J. McElligott*
1973 Miss Margaret Drago
Miss Mary W. Flynn*
Mr. Patrick O'Leary*
Mrs. Irene Pantaleo*
1974 Mr. R.J. Bergin
1975 Miss Mary C. Babcock
Mrs. Mary Michell
Sister M. St. Maurice*
Sister M. Yvonne
1976 Miss Mary W. Flynn*
Mrs. May Lyons*
Mrs. Anne O'Brien
1977 Mr. John B. Connolly
Sister Nora Dolan*
Miss Patricia Seriani*
1978 Sister Frederica Boyle, I.B.V.M.
Reverend J.H. Conway, O.M.I.
1979 Mrs. Marie Arthurs
Mr. Francis Joseph Whelan
1981 Sister Helen Nolan
Miss Isabella O'Shea
1982 Mr. Frank Griffin*
1983 Mrs. Edna Gannon
Sister Noreen Hawley
1984 Miss Margaret Duggan*
1985 Sister Mary Hamilton, C.N.D.
1986 Mrs. Marie Kennedy
1987 Mr. Kevin Kennedy
1988 Mrs. Helen Dillon
Mr. Robert Scott
1990 Mr. Douglas Wm. Knott
Mr. Harry Polowy
1991 Rev. J.F. Kavanagh, O.M.I.
Mr. John Kuchinak
1992 Miss Margaret Durkin
Mr. Daniel J. Kelly
Mr. Richard "Dick" Marcella
Sister Sheila McAuliffe, C.N.D.
1993 Mr. Robert Cooney
Ms. Moyra O'Pallie
Mr. Sivanandy Peter

Honorary Memberships

1965 Dr. F.J. McDonald*
1966 Miss Hazel Guerin*
1967 Mrs. Blanch Leacy
1969 Miss Dorothy Beitz*
1970 Mr. Edgar Boland
1971 Miss Veronica Drohan*
Mr. Karl Bohren
Miss Mary C. Babcock
1972 Dr. John M. Bennett*
Miss Veronica Houlahan
Sister Aloysia, S.S.N.D.
1973 Miss Mary C. Babcock
Miss Ruth Willis
1974 Mr. M.J. Duggan*
Mr. John Rodrigues
Mrs. Marie Kennedy
1975 Mr. T.S. Melady
Mr. Patrick O'Leary*
Mr. James Carey

1976 Most Reverend Joseph F. Ryan, Hamilton*
Reverend J. Frank Kavanagh, O.M.I.
Mr. Robert Cooney
1977 Mr. Karl Bohren*
Sister M. Yvonne
Mr. Leo Normandeau
1978 Mr. Frederick Joseph Hodge
Mr. Derry Byrne
Mr. Peter Gazzola
1979 Mr. Francis Alexander McDonell
Sister Alice Marie
Mr. John Kuchinak
1980 Mr. Alexander Kuska
Mr. Tom Taylor
1981 Mr. Tim O'Grady
Miss Doreen Brady*
1982 Reverend T.V. Sobisch, C.R.*
Mr. Frank Griffin*
Miss Mary W. Flynn
1983 Mr. C.F. Gilhooly
Mr. Patrick Perdue*
Mr. Joseph Hugel
Mr. Raymond Bergin
1984 Mr. Edward Finan
Mr. Fred Sweeney
Sister Evva Melanson
Mr. George Saranchuk
1985 Mr. Edmund Nelligan
Mr. Kevin Kennedy
1986 Mr. James Page
Mr. T. John Fauteux
1987 Mr. Chris Asseff
Mr. Jim Cooney
Mr. Frank Kinlin
Mr. Colm Harty
1988 Mr. Paul Cavalluzzo
Mr. Douglas Wm. Knott
Mr. John Hourigan
Mrs. Suzann Jones
1989 Msgr. Ralph J. Egan
Mr. Patrick O'Neill
Sr. Catherine McCann, G.S.I.C.
Miss Eileen Lennon
Sister Sheila McAuliffe, C.N.D.
Mr. Frederick Scott (Ted) Johnstone
Mrs. Mary Ellen Carey
Miss Helen Biales
1990 Mrs. Rita Desjardins
Mr. Michael Coté
1991 Rev. Thomas McKillop
Ms. Vikki Hiebert-Hannah
1992 Mr. William Markle,Q.C.
Mrs. Claudette Foisy-Moon
Mr. Terry Mangan
1993 Ms. Beverly Saskoley
Mr. Horst Schweinbenz
Mrs. Kathy Soule

Marion Tyrell Award of Merit

1989 Mr. Randy Sasso
1990 Brother Anthony VandenHeuvel
1991 Mr.Ted Schmidt
1992 Mrs. Doreen Steele
1993 Mr. Lennox Farrell

Special Award

William Davis,
ex-Premier of Ontario

**deceased*

GLOSSARY

AAT	Archives of the Archdiocese of Toronto
ACEBO	Association des commissions des écoles bilingues
ACHSBO	Association of Catholic High School Boards of Ontario
AEFO	Association des enseignants franco-ontariens
AFCSO	Association française des conseils scolaires de l'Ontario
AGM	Annual General Meeting
AIB	Anti-Inflation Board
ALSBO	Association of Large School Boards of Ontario
ATA	Alberta Teachers' Alliance
CCDC	Catholic Curriculum Development Conference
CEFO	Catholic Education Foundation of Ontario
CNE	Canadian National Exhibition
COSS	Completion Office Separate Schools
CPTA	Catholic Parent-Teacher Association
CSF	Common School Fund
CTF	Canadian Teachers' Federation
DAL	Diocesan Archives of London
ECEAO	English Catholic Education Association of Ontario
ESL	English Second Language
ERC	Education Relations Commission
FCEAO	Federation of Catholic Education Associations of Ontario
FWTAO	Federation of Women Teachers' Association of Ontario
HSA	High School Assistant's Certificate
ICE	Institute of Catholic Education
LP	Letter of Permission
MSSB	Metropolitan Separate School Board
NDP	New Democratic Party
OAMR	Ontario Association for the Mentally Retarded
OCCB	Ontario Conference of Catholic Bishops
OCE	Ontario College of Education
OCOTA	Ontario Catholic Occasional Teachers' Association

OCSIA	Ontario Catholic Superintendents and Inspectors Association
OEA	Ontario Educational Association
OECTA	Ontario English Catholic Teachers' Association
OECTAA	Ontario English Catholic Teachers' Association Archives
OISE	Ontario Institute for Studies in Education
OPSMTF	Ontario Public School Men Teachers' Federation
OPSTF	Ontario Public School Teachers' Federation
OSIS	Ontario Schools: Intermediate Senior
OSSTA	Ontario Separate School Trustees' Association
OSSTAA	Ontario Separate School Trustees' Association Archives
OSSTF	Ontario Secondary School Teachers' Federation
OSTC	Ontario School Trustees' Council
OTC	Ontario Teachers' Council
OTF	Ontario Teachers' Federation
OTFA	Ontario Teachers' Federation Archives
PTR	Pupil-Teacher Ratio
QECO	Qualifications Evaluation Council of Ontario
RCSS	Roman Catholic Separate School
SERP	Secondary Education Review Project
STF	Saskatchewan Teachers' Federation
STO	Superannuated Teachers of Ontario
TMR	Trainable Mentally Retarded
UFW	United Farm Workers
WCOTP	World Conferation of the Organizations of the Teaching Profession
WUCT	World Union of Catholic Teachers

INDEX